DISCARD

Programming and Problem Solving
with Pascal

Introduction to Computer Science, Fourth Edition

Programming and Problem Solving
with Pascal

Neill Graham

West Publishing Company
St. Paul, New York, San Francisco, Los Angeles

Copyedited:	**Janet Hunter**
Interior design:	**David Corona Design**
Artwork:	**Carlisle Graphics**
Composition:	**Carlisle Graphics**
Cover art:	**Delor Erickson/Studio West, Inc.**

Copyright © 1979 by West Publishing Company
Copyright © 1982 by West Publishing Company
Copyright © 1985 by West Publishing Company
Copyright © 1988 by West Publishing Company
50 W. Kellogg Boulevard
P.O. Box 64526
St. Paul, MN 55164-1003

All rights reserved
Printed in the United States of America
Library of Congress Cataloging-in-Publication Data

Graham, Neill, 1941–
    Introduction to computer science.

    Includes index.
    1. Electronic digital computers.   2. Electronic data
processing.   3. PASCAL (Computer program language)
I. Title.
QA76.5.G658   1988   005.13′3   87-31712
ISBN 0-314-59994-0 (softcover)
        0-314-64968-9 (hardcover)

Contents

Chapter

Parameters, Functions, and Debugging   104

Chapter

Top-Down Development: A Case Study   129

Chapter **6**   Repetition and Arrays   162

Chapter **7**   Multiway Selection   204

Chapter **8** Programmer-Defined Types and Data Abstraction 234

Chapter **9** Arrays and Abstract Data Types 279

Chapter **10**   Files   315

Chapter **11**   Strings   350

Chapter **12**

More About Subprograms   396

Chapter **13**

Pointers and Linked Lists   428

Preface

his book is designed for a one-semester first course in computer science. More material is provided than is likely to be covered in one semester, thus allowing the instructor the flexibility to select the topics most appropriate for a particular course. This book is based on the 1984 revision of the ACM guidelines for a first course in computer science (CS1 '84).

The following are some noteworthy features of the fourth edition of *Introduction to Computer Science, Fourth Edition: Programming and Problem Solving with Pascal.*

■ **Emphasis on Problem Solving and Program Development.** The principles of problem solving are introduced early, with particular emphasis on decomposing a problem into subproblems, top-down development of programs, and outlining programs with pseudocode. Three forms of pseudocode are used: (1) structured English outlines of complete programs; (2) English descriptions intermixed with Pascal statements; and (3) pseudocode descriptions of abstract data types.

■ **Emphasis on Procedural Abstraction.** Functions and procedures are introduced early and used thereafter as basic units for program design, coding, and testing.

■ **Emphasis on Data Abstraction.** The concepts of data abstraction are used early to introduce the Pascal standard data types. Later, abstract data types are defined by pseudocode descriptions of operations and implemented with Pascal constant and type definitions and function and procedure declarations.

■ **Use of Standard Pascal.** This book uses American standard (ANSI/IEEE) Pascal, which is essentially the same as level 0 of international standard (ISO) Pascal. Conformant array parameters, which distinguish ISO level-1 from ISO level-0 and ANSI/IEEE, are introduced briefly but not used extensively. Appendices compare Turbo Pascal and UCSD Pascal with the standard Pascal used in the text.

■ **Syntax Described by Both Statement Formats and Syntax Diagrams.** In the main text, Pascal syntax is presented via general statement formats, which (because they look like Pascal statements) are readily understood by beginners. Appendix 2, however, presents syntax diagrams for ISO Pascal along with an extended discussion that provides not only an introduction to syntax diagrams but a review of Pascal syntax.

It may be of interest to contrast this book with the author's *Introduction to Pascal*, third edition, which differs from this book mainly in Chapters 2 through 5. This book focuses on program development, top-down design, and debugging; its treatment of language fundamentals, however, is not as systematic as *Introduction to Pascal*, which devotes somewhat more space to language fundamentals and somewhat less space to program development. This book may be better suited for students who already have been exposed to at least one programming language, whereas *Introduction to Pascal* may be better suited to students with little or no background in computing.

Chapter 1 is an overview of computers and computing. Students with previous background in computing can skim or skip much of this material. However, the attention of all students should be directed to the final section on computer science.

Chapter 2 introduces the elements of Pascal programming with emphasis on problem solving, pseudocode, and program structure. The elements of testing and debugging are introduced. Procedures and top-down design are also introduced in this chapter; variable parameters are used at this point since they allow data to be both passed to and returned from procedures. Value parameters are introduced in Chapter 4 in a section that can be easily taken up earlier if the instructor prefers.

Chapter 3 takes up the standard data types, operator precedence, and control structures. The **if** and **while** statements are introduced.

Chapter 4 discusses value parameters, standard functions, programmer-defined functions, testing, and debugging.

Chapter 5 illustrates the principles of top-down development by specifying, designing, coding, and testing a moderately complex program following the steps of the software development life cycle. The chapter concludes with a discussion of two alternatives to top-down development.

Chapter 6 continues the discussion of repetition by introducing the **for** and **repeat** statements. One-dimensional and multidimensional arrays are also introduced, and the use of the **for** statement in array processing is illustrated in several examples.

Chapter 7, which is devoted to multiway selection, introduces nested **if** statements and the **case** statement. The program examples review all forms of selection.

With Chapter 8, emphasis shifts from control structures to data structures. Type definitions and the Pascal enumerated, subrange, set, and record types are introduced. Type equivalence, compatibility, and assignment compatibility are discussed using the concepts and terminology of the ANSI/IEEE and ISO standards. Abstract data types, their pseudocode definition, and their implementation in Pascal are introduced and illustrated.

Chapter 9 continues the discussion of one-dimensional and multidimensional arrays by focusing on abstract data types implemented with arrays. Abstract data types discussed include multisets, directories, and grids (two-dimensional multisets).

Chapter 10 covers Pascal sequential files, the use of which are illustrated with programs for merging and updating files. Random (direct) files are described briefly but are not taken up in detail since they are not available in standard Pascal.

Chapter 11 is devoted to strings. Since standard Pascal provides only fixed-length strings, variable-length strings are implemented as an abstract data type. If the students are using an extended version of Pascal that supports variable-length strings, the variable-length-string types provided by the extended Pascal can be contrasted with the variable-length-string type defined and implemented in the text. String processing is illustrated with a program for replacing parameters in form letters.

Chapters 12 and 13 are included to complete the discussion of Pascal; however, some instructors may wish to defer all or part of the material covered to a second course in computer science. Chapter 12 takes up some of the more advanced aspects of functions and procedures, such as nested scopes, activation records and the run-time stack, functional and procedural parameters, implementation of parameter passing, recursion, and forward declarations. Chapter 13 covers pointer types and introduces linked structures, which are illustrated with linked lists. Chapter 13 ends with a review and summary of the Pascal type system.

Appendix 1 lists the Pascal reserved words, and Appendix 2 gives the syntax diagrams for ISO Pascal along with a fairly extended discussion. The diagrams are listed and discussed in roughly the same order that the corresponding constructions are taken up in the text, so instructors who wish to do so can begin using the syntax diagrams as early as Chapter 2. Appendix 3 gives the differences between Turbo and ISO Pascal, and Appendix 4 does the same for UCSD Pascal. Appendix 5 covers binary codes and the internal representation of values of the standard Pascal data types.

A For Further Reading section lists and briefly discusses works that students should find helpful and interesting.

I wish to thank the following reviewers for their comments and suggestions:

Jim Aman
St. Pius High School

George Beekman
Oregon State University

Lee Cornell
Mankato State University

George Crocker
Stamford University

Tim Dwight
University of Tulsa

Ron Elliott
Ohio State University

Rich Erwin
Westminster College

Patty Everett
University of Florida, Gainesville

Morris Firebaugh
University of Wisconsin, Parkside

John Forsyth
Michigan State University

John Fourlan
Harrisburg Community College

Ed Gallizi
Eckerd College

Bruce Gilland
University of Colorado

John Hammer
Russell Sage College

Joyce Harrio
DeAnza College

Ann Heard
Georgetown College

Sandra Hedetniemi
Clemson University

Larry Huff
University of Central Arkansas

Timothy Kearns
California Polytechnic, San Luis Obispo

David Martin
Jericko Public Schools

Michael Michaelson
San Diego State University

John Stone
Grinnell College

Ruth Unger
University of Connecticut

Louis Voit
McMurray College

Vicki Walker
Arizona State University

Laura White
University of Florida, Gainesville

Programming and Problem Solving
with Pascal

An Overview of Computers and Computing

1

This chapter surveys the history of computing, computer hardware and software, computer applications, and the basic concepts of computer science and software engineering. The background information provided here is essential for appreciating the more specialized details that we will take up in this book.

Development of Computers

A dominant theme in the history of civilization is our ever-increasing use of tools to shape and control the world around us. But most such tools were designed to extend the powers of our muscles rather than aid our minds. Until recently, only the simplest technical aids were available to extend the powers of our minds by storing, manipulating, and communicating information.

From the earliest times, the technologies of papermaking and writing (and later printing) preserved and distributed facts and ideas. Clockwork mechanisms kept track of times, dates, and the motions of celestial bodies. Simple mechanical devices helped diplomats and spies encode and decode secret messages. Simple reliable calculating devices and complex unreliable ones helped relieve the drudgery of arithmetical computation. Robots with clockwork mechanisms wrote letters and played musical instruments to amuse the courts of Europe. Automated looms wove complex patterns. The telegraph initiated an era of nearly instantaneous communication.

Although elements of all these innovations can be found in today's computer systems, it was the technology of arithmetical calculation that led most directly to the modern computer.

Early History

The Abacus.   The abacus, or counting frame, originated with the Babylonians about five thousand years ago and persisted into modern times in the Orient. Originally, it consisted of a board in which pebbles could slide; eventually the pebbles were replaced with beads that slide on wires mounted in a frame. Until the development of modern electronic calculators, an abacus—together with a trained operator—provided one of the most effective means for rapid, reliable arithmetical calculations.

Mechanical Calculators.   Mechanical calculators began to appear in the seventeenth century. The French mathematician and philosopher Blaise Pascal (after whom the programming language Pascal is named) invented a mechanical calculator for addition and subtraction. The German mathematician, philosopher and diplomat Gottfried Wilhelm Leibniz (best known as one of the inventors of calculus) designed a machine that would multiply and divide as well as add and subtract.

All early mechanical calculators were unreliable because the artisans of the day could not consistently make mechanical parts with the necessary precision. Reliable mechanical calculators were developed in the late 1800s and became commonplace in the early 1900s. They remained in widespread use until displaced by electronic calculators in the early 1970s.

The Slide Rule and Analog Computers.   The seventeenth century also saw the development of a simpler and more reliable calculating device, the slide rule, which allowed its user to perform multiplications and divisions by manipulating specially ruled scales.

A slide rule is an *analog* computing device; the answer is obtained by making a measurement—measuring a length with a ruled scale. The abacus and mechanical calculators, on the other hand, are *digital* computing devices, in that each digit of the data and result is represented by a particular configuration of the device's parts.

In the twentieth century, these two approaches to computing led to two kinds of computers: *analog computers* based on measurement and *digital computers* based on mechanically or electrically encoded representations of data. As with the slide rule and the mechanical calculator, early analog computers often proved simpler, less expensive, and more reliable than early digital computers. As the technology of computing advanced, however, the digital approach proved to be far more accurate, flexible, and powerful than the analog approach. Today analog computers are used only in very specialized applications. When the word *computer* is used without qualification, it always refers to a digital computer.

The Jacquard Loom.   Around the turn of the nineteenth century, the French inventor Joseph-Marie Jacquard devised an automated loom for weaving cloth containing decorative patterns. The loom was controlled by a set of punched cards that were fastened together to form a continuous tape. The holes punched in the cards determined what threads would be raised and lowered at each step of the weaving process and hence what pattern would be woven into the cloth.

The punched cards constitute what we would today call a *program*—a set of instructions governing the operation of a machine. The Jacquard loom was the first machine whose behavior could be changed by changing its program rather than by redesigning the machine. As such, it was the direct ancestor not only of modern automated machine tools but of the player piano as well.

Mechanical and Electromechanical Computers

The Analytical Engine.   Inspired by the Jacquard loom, the nineteenth-century English mathematician Charles Babbage set out to build a punch-card controlled mechanical calculator, which he called an *Analytical Engine*.

The Analytical Engine had many of the major components of modern computers. Data and results were stored until needed in a component that

Babbage called the *store*. The terms *store* and *storage* are still used for components that store information, although in America the term *memory* is more popular. The calculations were carried out by what Babbage called the *mill* and we call the *arithmetic/logic unit*. Operations were triggered in the proper sequence by a device Babbage called the *barrel* (because of its appearance) and we call the *control unit*. (Babbage's mill and barrel together are today known as the *central processing unit* and are often constructed on a single computer chip.) The calculations carried out by the Analytical Engine, like the patterns woven by a Jacquard loom, were governed by a set of punched cards—what we call a *computer program*.

Alas, Babbage's design proved too complex for the technology of the time and his computer was never completed. But even though the Analytical Engine was never built, a demonstration program for it was written by Augusta Ada Byron, later Countess of Lovelace, the only legitimate daughter of the poet Lord Byron. This demonstration program was the first computer program and Lady Lovelace was thus the first computer programmer. A programming language developed for the Department of Defense is named Ada in Lady Lovelace's honor.

Boolean Algebra.   Although he did not design or build any computing device, the English mathematician George Boole was another important nineteenth-century contributor to computer science. Boole invented an algebra of logical reasoning, now called *Boolean algebra* in his honor. In Boolean algebra, the truth or falsity of a statement is represented by 1 for true and 0 for false. In modern programming languages, the words *true* and *false* are often used in place of 1 and 0. The operations of Boolean algebra correspond to logical connectives such as *and, or,* and *not.* For example, if two statements are joined by *and,* the resulting statement is true only if both of the statements making it up are true. Thus the Boolean operator **and** is defined as follows:

> *true* **and** *true* = *true*
> *true* **and** *false* = *false*
> *false* **and** *true* = *false*
> *false* **and** *false* = *false*

In programming languages the adjective *Boolean* is often used to characterize logical data and operations.

Punched-card Tabulating Machines.   In the 1880s, the American engineer Herman Hollerith developed a series of electromechanical devices for sorting and tabulating data represented by holes punched in cards. Hollerith's machines were not computers; however, he pioneered the field of *automatic data processing (ADP)*—using machines to process large volumes of business, statistical, and scientific data. After the introduction of electronic computers, the name of the field was changed to *electronic data processing (EDP)*. Nowadays automatic and electronic are taken for granted and the field is just known as *data processing (DP)*.

Hollerith's Tabulating Machine Company eventually merged with other companies to form what ultimately became IBM (International Business Machines Corp.). IBM became the major supplier of punched-card data processing equipment. When it began to manufacture computers—a step it was initially reluctant to take—its experience and reputation with punched-card equipment stood it in good stead. IBM became and remains today the primary supplier of computers for business data processing.

Electromechanical Computers.   Babbage's ideas were independently rediscovered in the 1930s. Machines similar to the Analytical Engine were designed and, this time, actually built. Not only had mechanical technology improved in the intervening years, but electricity had been applied to automatic data processing and to automatic telephone switching (the dial system). Using electricity to carry data between components, rather than the complex mechanical linkages Babbage envisioned, went a long way toward making these latter-day analytical engines practical. Many components developed for automatic data processing and telephone switching could be used directly or with minor modifications.

The trouble with electromechanical computers was that they were too slow, because of the time required for their mechanical parts to move from one position to another. A computer breaks a complex calculation down into a large number of simple operations. If the complex calculation is to be completed in a reasonable time, the simple operations must be carried out at high speed. The further development of computers would be a quest for smaller size, lower power consumption, greater information storage capacity, and (perhaps most important of all) greater speed.

Electronic Computers and the Stored-Program Concept

What was needed was a machine whose computing, control, and memory components were completely electrical. The elements of such an *electronic computer* were demonstrated in the late 1930s by John V. Atanasoff of what is now Iowa State University. Although Atanasoff has been legally recognized as the inventor of the electronic computer, his work was not nearly as influential as that of John W. Mauchly and J. Presper Eckert who, in the 1940s, built ENIAC (Electronic Numerical Integrator and Computer), the first general purpose electronic computer. ENIAC was 500 times faster than the best electromechanical computers. A problem that ENIAC could solve in one minute would take eight to ten hours on an electromechanical computer.

For ENIAC and its predecessors, the controlling program was stored in a different form than the data to be manipulated. Babbage envisioned storing the program on punched cards; the electromechanical computers often used punched paper tape for this purpose. The program for ENIAC was stored on a plugboard (similar to an old-fashioned telephone switchboard), which had to be rewired for each problem the computer was to solve.

The mid-1940s saw the advent of the *stored-program concept,* according to which the program was stored in the computer's memory in the same form as the data being processed. Thus a program could be manipulated as if it were data. The original idea was to let a program modify* itself, but this concept was ultimately abandoned as too tricky and error prone. On the other hand, the ability of one program to manipulate another program is crucial to the operation of modern computer systems.

The Computer Generations

From the 1940s to the present, computer technology has gone through several major changes, and further changes are likely. People sometimes classify

---

*When we say that a program does something we always mean that a computer takes the specified action under the control of the program.

computers into *generations,* with each generation characterized by a particular technology. Although the idea of computer generations is useful for outlining the development of computer technology, its limitations should be noted. Different technologies overlap, so there is no sharp dividing line between one generation and the next. As a result, people sometimes differ as to the time span of each generation and which technologies should be associated with it.

The First Generation.   First-generation computers prevailed in the 1940s and for much of the 1950s. They used vacuum tubes for calculation, control, and sometimes for memory. A variety of other ingenious devices were also used for memory. One, for instance, stored data as sound waves circulating in a column of mercury. Another device stored data as patterns of electric charge on the face of a *cathode ray tube (CRT),* which is similar in construction to a television picture tube. This memory device became obsolete, but the cathode ray tube returned in the third generation as the primary device for displaying computer output.

The use of magnetism for data storage was pioneered in the first generation. Data was recorded on *magnetic tape* using the same principles that govern modern audio and video cassette recorders. *Magnetic drums* worked in a similar manner except that the data was recorded on the surface of a spinning drum rather than on tape. Magnetic tape and magnetic drums were important in both the first and second generations; both largely gave way to magnetic disks in the third generation.

Vacuum tubes (the radio tubes that were once familiar components of radio and television sets) are bulky (about the size of a salt shaker), unreliable (burn out frequently), heat producing (too hot to touch), and energy consuming (energy needed to keep tube hot). As long as computers were tied to vacuum tube technology, they could only be bulky, cumbersome, and expensive.

The Second Generation.   In the late 1950s, the transistor began to replace the vacuum tube. Transistors, which are only slightly larger than kernels of corn, generate little heat and enjoy long lives.

At about this time, *magnetic-core memory* was introduced. This consisted of a latticework of wires on which were strung tiny, doughnut-shaped beads called *cores.* Electric currents flowing in the wires stored data by magnetizing cores. Data could be stored in or retrieved from core memory in about a millionth of a second.

With the introduction of core memory, a clear distinction formed between *main memory* for short-term storage with fast access and *auxiliary memory* for longer-term storage with slower access. Main memory was core memory for the second and much of the third generations; even today oldtimers in the computing field often refer to main memory as core. Magnetic tape, introduced in the first generation, was the mainstay of auxiliary memory in the second generation.

Higher-level programming languages, which allow programs to be expressed in terms familiar to the programmer rather than in obscure codes, appeared during the second generation. In 1951, mathematician and naval officer Grace Murray Hopper conceived the first *compiler program* for translating from a higher-level language to the computer's native *machine language.* In 1957, John Backus at IBM completed a compiler for FORTRAN (FORmula TRANslator), the first higher-level language to receive widespread use.

The second generation saw the emergence of standard routines (parts of programs) for carrying out such frequent but complex operations as reading data into main memory and producing printed output. These routines could be kept in main memory and used by many programs. The routines for input and output were known collectively as the *input-output control system. Monitor programs* aided the user in loading other programs into main memory and controlling their execution. (A program is *executed* or *run* when the computer carries out the instructions in the program.) The monitor and the input-output control system ultimately evolved into the *operating system,* a master control program that manages the entire computer system under the direction of commands from users and requests made by programs.

The Third Generation.   *Integrated circuits* (computer chips), which incorporated hundreds of transistors on a single silicon chip, were introduced in the early 1960s. The chip itself was small enough to fit on the end of a finger; after being mounted in a protective package, it would still fit in the palm of the hand. With integrated circuits, computers could be made smaller, less expensive, and more reliable.

Integrated circuits made possible *minicomputers,* table-top computers small and inexpensive enough to find a place in the classroom and scientific laboratory. (The traditional large-scale computers began to be called *mainframes* to distinguish them from minicomputers.) In the late 1960s, integrated circuits began to be used for main memory. Except for some older machines still in use, integrated-circuit memory has now completely replaced magnetic-core memory.

Beginning in the 1960s, magnetic disks began to replace magnetic tape for auxiliary memory. Today, magnetic disks are the dominant technology for auxiliary memory, although optical discs* (similar to the videodiscs and compact discs used for movies and record albums) are expected to become increasingly important in the future.

The third generation saw the advent of *computer terminals* for communicating with a computer from remote locations. The first terminals were typewriter-like devices that produced printed output. During the course of the third generation, these evolved into *video display terminals* (*VDTs*) in which the computer's output is displayed on a video screen rather than printed.

The use of higher-level programming languages became widespread during the third generation. Compilers were written for well over 150 higher-level languages, although only about 10 to 20 languages received widespread use.

Operating systems came into their own in the third generation. The operating system was given complete control of the computer system; the computer operator, programmers, and users all obtained services by placing requests with the operating system via computer terminals. The computer's control console was used only for starting up the system and diagnosing malfunctions; eventually, elaborate control consoles disappeared.

Turning over control of the computer to the operating system made possible modes of operation that would have been impossible with manual control. In *multiprogramming,* for example, the computer is switched rapidly from program to program in round-robin fashion, giving the appearance that all the programs are being executed simultaneously. When one program must wait

---

*The word *disc* (with a *c*) is usually used for entertainment products, whereas the computer industry prefers the word *disk* (with a *k*). Optical discs originated in the entertainment industry, hence the spelling.

for a slow external device, such as a keyboard, it loses its turn at the central processing unit until the external operation is complete. Thus while one program is waiting, the central processing unit is kept busy working on other programs.

An important form of multiprogramming is *time-sharing,* in which many users communicate with a single computer from remote terminals. Although it appears to the users that each has sole control of the computer, in fact the central processing unit is being switched rapidly from one user's program to another. While one user is pausing to think, the computer is busy working on other users' programs.

The term *virtual* is used for any computing resource that appears to correspond to a hardware component but is actually simulated by a program. In *virtual memory,* for example, the operating system automatically transfers programs and data between main and auxiliary memory, thus making the system seem to have a much larger main memory than is in fact present in the hardware.

The Fourth Generation.   The 1970s saw the advent of *large-scale integration (LSI).* The first LSI chips contained thousands of transistors; later, it became possible to place first tens of thousands, then hundreds of thousands, and now millions of transistors on a single chip. LSI technology led to two innovations: *embedded computers,* which are incorporated into other appliances, such as cameras and television sets, and *microcomputers* or *personal computers,* which can be bought and used by individuals and organizations. The most important LSI chips are *microprocessors* (each a complete central processing unit) and *memory chips* (used in constructing main memory).

Despite the introduction of other technologies, the magnetic disk remained the preferred medium for auxiliary memory. Flexible plastic *diskettes* or *floppy disks* became popular for microcomputers.

In the late sixties and early seventies, the programming language Pascal was developed by Professor Niklaus Wirth of the Technical University of Zürich, Switzerland. Pascal was designed for teaching programming, for writing *systems software* such as compilers, and for promoting the then-new technique of *structured programming* (which emphasizes the correspondence between the structure of a program and the functions performed by its various parts). Pascal has enjoyed steadily increasing popularity in the seventies and eighties; its rapid acceptance stems in part from the widespread availability of Pascal language processors for popular microcomputers. Today, Pascal is the most widely used language for teaching computer science.

The Fifth Generation.   In 1982, Japan's Ministry of International Trade and Administration, together with eight leading Japanese computer companies, launched a project to develop the *fifth generation computers* that they anticipate will be used in the 1990s. Fifth generation computers are expected to be characterized by *parallel processing* (carrying out many operations at the same time) and by an emphasis on logical rather than numerical computation.

Hardware

A collection of machines and programs for providing computing services is known as a *computer system.* The machines are the *hardware* of the computer system; the programs are the *software*. The term *computer* refers to all the hardware of a computer system. This section summarizes and extends the hardware concepts introduced in the previous section on the development of computers.

Characterization of Computers

Because of wide variations in the technical details of computers and in the uses to which they are put, we will find it helpful to characterize them in the most general possible manner. This we can do with the following two statements:

- A computer is a machine for storing, communicating, and manipulating information.
- The behavior of a computer is controlled by a set of step-by-step instructions called a program.

Program control distinguishes computers from other information processing devices such as typewriters and tape recorders. Almost everything interesting or useful about a computer's behavior results from its program rather than from the hardware that carries out the instructions. Computers are often embedded in other machines largely to obtain the benefits of program control.

A *special purpose computer* is intended for a single task, often controlling or monitoring a machine such as an automobile, a video recorder, or a microwave oven. Its program is permanently installed and cannot be changed by the user. (By providing data such as when a microwave oven is to be turned on and off, the user can exert limited control over the machine.) In contrast, a *general purpose computer* is intended for a wide variety of tasks; its program can be and often is changed by the user. A major function of the computer's operating system is to make such changes as convenient and rapid as possible.

A special purpose computer is like a music box that always plays the same tune or (at best) allows the user to select one of a few built-in tunes. A general purpose computer is like a phonograph that will play any tune for which we have a record.

Classification of Computers

Computers are classified according to use, cost, speed of operation, and the technology used for main memory and the central processing unit. Without going into too much technical detail, we will look briefly at the major classifications.

- *Embedded computers.* Embedded computers are the special purpose computers incorporated into other devices such as consumer products. Embedded computers are usually microcomputers; however, some scientific instruments contain embedded minicomputers.
- *Microcomputers.* A microcomputer uses a microprocessor as its central processing unit. The microprocessor revolution has brought relatively low cost microcomputers into widespread use in offices, schools, and homes. A microcomputer is usually used by only one person at a time, leading to its alternative name of *personal computer*. Other names that refer to particular types of microcomputer are *desktop computer, workstation, laptop computer, portable computer,* and *home computer.*
- *Minicomputers.* Before the invention of the microprocessor, minicomputers were the lowest cost and most widely used computers;

now, minicomputers lie between microcomputers and mainframes in cost, speed, and computing power. To reflect this changed situation, minicomputers are now sometimes referred to as *midrange computers*.

■ *Mainframes*. Mainframes are the large-scale computers found in the computer rooms of most businesses, financial institutions, and universities. Most of the developed world's business and financial records are stored in mainframe computer systems.

■ *Supercomputers*. Supercomputers are the most powerful and expensive computers in existence. Applications that call for supercomputers include many scientific and engineering calculations, weather prediction, cryptography (trying to break the secret codes of foreign governments), and computer animation (computer generation of motion picture and television images).

Major Hardware Components

The hardware of a computer system consists of the following major components: the *central processing unit* (consisting of the *arithmetic/logic unit* and the *control unit*), *main memory, auxiliary memory,* and *input and output devices*. Devices for input, output, and auxiliary memory are often referred to as *peripherals*. Figure 1-1 illustrates the *logical* organization of these components—the paths along which data and control signals flow from component to component. Figure 1-2 illustrates the *physical organization*—the way in which they are often wired together inside the computer.

Figure 1-1.

Logical organization of a computer system. The arithmetic/logic unit and the control unit comprise the central processing unit. The control unit fetches program instructions from memory and carries out the instructions by sending appropriate control signals to other units. The results of tests carried out by the arithmetic/logic unit are sent to the control unit where they can be used to control program execution. The arithmetic/logic unit exchanges data with main memory and both data and device control codes with peripheral devices. Interrupt requests allow external devices to demand attention when they are ready to transfer data. Direct memory access allows some devices to transfer data directly to and from main memory without having to go through the central processing unit.

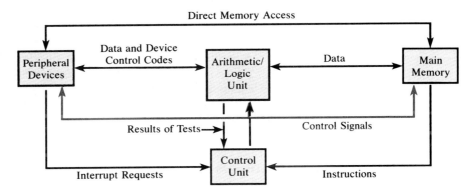

Figure 1-2. Physical organization of computer system. Components communicate over a bus—a group of 50 to 100 wires that carry data, addresses designating sources and destinations for data, and control signals. Computer circuits are constructed on fiberglass/resin printed circuit boards. For some systems, the central processing unit, main memory, and peripheral device controllers are on separate circuit boards that plug into a system board or mother board containing the bus. For other systems, however, the bus and all the circuits are on the same board. The peripherals, which are often external devices such as printers, are connected by cables to the corresponding device controllers.

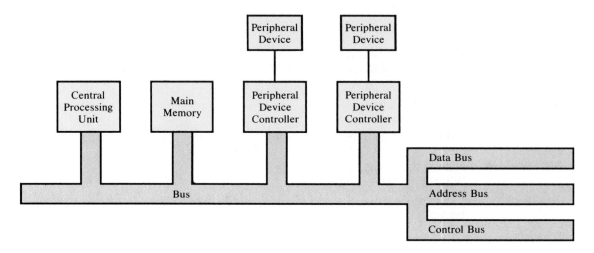

Main Memory

Main memory holds the programs that the computer is currently executing and the data that it is currently manipulating. As far as the data is concerned, main memory plays the role of a scratchpad or blackboard—it provides temporary storage for the data that is being processed.

Main memory is divided into individual *memory locations,* each of which can hold a fixed amount of data. We can visualize main memory as a set of post office boxes, each box corresponding to a memory location. Each memory location has a unique *address,* which corresponds to the number on a post office box, and which is used to designate a particular location for the purposes of storing data in it or retrieving data from it.

Information is represented inside a computer using only two symbols: 0 and 1. These two symbols are particularly easy to represent electrically because 1 can be represented by an electric circuit in which a current is flowing and 0 can be represented by a circuit in which no current is flowing. The symbols 0 and 1 are known as *binary digits* or *bits*. A scheme for representing data values by means of combinations of bits is known as a *binary code.* Techniques for coding familiar data values such as characters and numbers are discussed in Chapter 2.

Each memory location holds a fixed number of bits. For many computers, the smallest memory location holds eight bits, which are collectively referred to as one *byte*. The size of main memory is frequently given in bytes, *kilobytes,* or *megabytes*. A kilobyte is 2^{10} or 1024 bytes and is abbreviated K or KB. Thus a 64K or 64KB memory contains 64×1024 or 65,536 bytes. A megabyte is 1024×1024 or 2^{20} or 1,048,576 bytes and is abbreviated M or MB. Figure 1-3 illustrates the organization of a 64KB memory. Figure 1-4 illustrates how adjacent bytes can be combined to form two-byte and four-byte memory locations.

Main memory comes in two forms, known as ROM and RAM. ROM stands for *read only memory;* the information stored in ROM was placed there when the ROM was manufactured and can only be read (retrieved) by the computer. The computer cannot change the information stored in ROM. The most common use of ROM is for *firmware*—software permanently stored in the computer.

RAM, or *random access memory,* can be used for both storing and retrieving data. ROM is like a printed book whose contents are permanent. RAM is like a blackboard that can be erased and reused again and again. In fact, the computer doesn't even have to bother erasing RAM; any data stored in a RAM location automatically replaces whatever data was previously stored in that location.

The main drawback of RAM is that it is *volatile*—when the computer is turned off, the contents of RAM are lost unless battery power is supplied to the main memory when the rest of the computer is turned off. (This is often done for portable, laptop computers but not for desktop or larger computers.) With these exceptions, any information that is not to be lost when the computer is turned off must be permanently built into ROM or stored in auxiliary memory.

Figure 1-3.

Organization of a 64KB memory. Each memory location holds eight bits or one byte. Each location is designated by a unique numerical address. Because a 64KB memory contains 64×1024 or 65,536 bytes, the addresses range from 0 through 65,535. The addresses are shown in conventional decimal notation for clarity; inside a computer, however, the addresses would be represented by binary codes.

Addresses (decimal)	Memory Locations
0	10111000
1	10101111
2	10000001
3	00000000
4	00110111
65,532	00001111
65,533	10101111
65,534	11111111
65,535	10010111

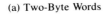

Figure 1-4. Adjacent bytes can be combined to form larger locations such as (a) two-byte words, and (b) four-byte double words. Unlike *byte,* the terms *word* and *double word* are not standardized; they may be defined differently for different computers. For example, on some machines, four bytes are called a word and two bytes are called a half word.

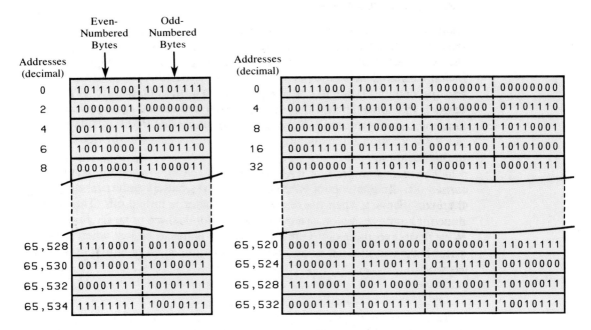

(a) Two-Byte Words

(b) Four-Byte Double Words

The term *random access* means that memory locations can be accessed in any order whatever. We do not need to first retrieve the contents of location 1, then the contents of location 2, then the contents of location 3, and so on. Both RAM and ROM allow random access, so RAM is a poor term for designating memory that allows data to be both read and written. *Read write memory* would be a better term for the latter; the reason it is not more widely used is that it abbreviates to the unpronounceable RWM.

The Central Processing Unit

The central processing unit (CPU) consists of the arithmetic/logic unit, which carries out all arithmetical and logical calculations, and the control unit, which controls the operation of the rest of the computer. The control unit operates in a *fetch-execute cycle* in which it repeatedly fetches a program instruction from main memory, generates the control signals to get that instruction carried out, fetches another instruction, and so on. No matter how complex or sophisticated the task that the computer is carrying out under the direction of its program, the control unit is just fetching and executing instructions one after another.

The arithmetic/logic unit can perform certain tests on the data; for example, it can test whether a number is positive or negative and whether two numbers are equal. The results of these tests are passed to the control unit, which can use them to govern program execution. For example, one sequence of program instructions may be carried out if a certain number is positive and another if the number is negative. The ability to execute different program instructions in different circumstances provides the computer with its famed decision-making capability. Of course, the program must dictate what tests are to be made and what actions are to be taken for each possible outcome.

Input and Output Devices

Input and output devices convert information between forms that are convenient for humans (such as printed text and drawings) and the binary codes that a computer requires. There are many types of input and output devices, including such diverse equipment as television cameras for the input of images and speech synthesizers for the output of spoken words. The input and output devices that programming students are most likely to encounter are *video displays, keyboards, mice, computer terminals,* and *printers*.

Video Displays. A video display is a device similar to a television set on which text and graphics (pictures and drawings) can be displayed. A *text display* can display only text; a *graphics display* can display both text and graphics. The display can be *monochrome* (black and white) or in color. For a monochrome display, ''white'' is often green or amber, both of which are more restful to the eyes than the bluish white of a monochrome television set. A television set or video monitor can be used as a video display, but a display specifically designed for computer use will usually give better performance.

When text is being entered, the screen usually shows a *cursor,* a line or block (often flashing) that indicates where the next typed character will appear on the screen. More generally, the cursor can be used to designate a particular point in the text, such as a point at which new text is to be inserted.

Keyboards. A computer keyboard is similar to an ordinary typewriter keyboard but with some additional keys to aid in using the computer. For versatility, some computer keyboards provide large numbers of special computer-oriented keys. For simplicity, others stay as close to the traditional typewriter keyboard as possible.

Mice. A mouse is a small boxlike device that is connected to the computer and can be rolled around on the top of a desk. Rolling the mouse on the desktop moves a pointer on the screen a corresponding distance in the corresponding direction; thus we can use the mouse to move the pointer quickly to any part of the screen. The mouse has one or more buttons that can be pressed to direct the computer's attention to the item indicated by the pointer. The mouse is used for such tasks as selecting commands from menus displayed on the screen, designating the data that will be affected by the next command, and moving objects about on the screen. Some recently developed microcomputers rely almost entirely on a mouse for conveying commands to programs, so that the keyboard is used only for entering data.

Computer Terminals. A computer terminal is a combination keyboard and display that is used for communicating with the computer. The terminal can be connected by a short cord to a nearby computer, or it can communicate over telephone lines or by other means with a distant computer. A microcomputer usually has its own keyboard and display, so that no terminal is required. Communication with minicomputers and mainframes, however, usually takes place via computer terminals. Microcomputers can be programmed to serve as computer terminals and are often used in this way for communicating with minicomputers and mainframes.

Printers.   Printers are used when a permanent copy of computer output (*hard copy*) is desired. Printers vary in cost, speed of operation, and quality of the printed output. A *dot matrix printer* forms printed images out of patterns of dots. It is inexpensive, fast, reliable, and can print both text and graphics, but many people are dissatisfied with the quality of the printed output. A *daisy wheel printer* can achieve the same quality as an office typewriter, but it can print only text (no graphics), and it is usually more expensive, slower, and less reliable than a dot matrix printer. An *ink jet printer* sprays ink onto the page in such a way as to form characters. One of its most desirable characteristics is that it operates quietly; dot matrix and daisy wheel printers are usually noisy enough to make it difficult to work when one is running nearby. A *laser printer* works much like (and often looks like) a copying machine. Laser printers can produce typeset-quality text and graphics. Although they do not have as great a resolution as the phototypesetting machines used for book publishing, they can serve well for many routine typesetting chores in business and advertising.

Auxiliary Memory

Auxiliary memory is used to store permanent data files and program libraries. Information can be stored in larger amounts and at lower cost than is possible in main memory. Data stored in auxiliary memory can be retained for long periods of time, whereas data stored in main memory is lost when the computer is turned off.

On the other hand, a much longer time is required to retrieve data stored in auxiliary memory than for data stored in main memory. For this reason, data is usually transferred between main memory and auxiliary memory in large blocks. A block of data is retained in main memory while it is being processed and transferred back to auxiliary memory when processing is complete. The most widely used forms of auxiliary memory are magnetic tape and magnetic disks.

The magnetic tape used by computers is similar to that used for sound and video recording, and it suffers from one of the same problems. If you have ever tried to locate a particular selection on an audio or video tape, you know how much time you waste "fast forwarding" and rewinding the tape until you find the part you want. To locate a particular data item on a computer tape would also require time-consuming winding and rewinding. Thus computer tapes are usually processed sequentially—we start at the beginning of the tape and process the items in the order in which they were recorded. For this reason, magnetic tape is known as a *sequential access medium*.

A magnetic disk (usually just referred to as a *disk*) looks something like a phonograph record but works on the same principal as magnetic tape—data is stored as magnetic patterns rather than in grooves. In use, the disk rotates like a phonograph record; data is written (recorded) and read (played back) by a *read/write head*. The data is recorded in circular *tracks*. The read/write head must be positioned over the track on which data is to be written or from which data is to be read. The actual data transfer takes place when the rotation of the disk carries the appropriate part of the track beneath the read/write head.

Disks vary in size, shape, and construction. Microcomputers often use *diskettes*, which include pocket-sized plastic disk cartridges and plastic film *floppy disks* or *flexible disks*. Diskettes can be removed from the computer and stored in a filing cabinet or file box. Microcomputers also use aluminum *fixed disks* (often called *hard disks*) which are permanently installed in the computer and cannot be removed. Access times are dramatically faster for fixed disks than for diskettes. Minicomputers and mainframes often use removable *disk packs*, each of which can contain up to 11 aluminum *platters* (individual disks).

Communications

Computers can communicate with one another by such means as telephone lines, coaxial cables (like the ones used in television cable systems), satellite links, and optical fibers. In the future, computers may be used as much for communicating information as for storing and manipulating it.

A set of computers capable of communicating with one another is called a *computer network*. In a *wide area network,* the computers may be widely separated—they may be in different cities, states, or even countries. Because of the expense of constructing communication links between widely separated computers, wide area networks usually rely on facilities (such as the telephone system) provided by communications companies. Connections via *dial-up* lines are made by dialing telephone numbers in the usual way. *Leased lines* or *private lines* are permanently installed lines connecting specific pieces of computer equipment.

Wide area communications frequently take place over the ordinary telephone system with the aid of a *modem* (modulator-demodulator), which serves as the computer's telephone set. The modem converts data from the computer into signals that can be sent over telephone lines (*modulation*) and converts signals received over the line into a form the computer can process (*demodulation*). The modem will dial numbers at the computer's request, inform the computer when ringing signals are received, and answer the phone when directed to do so by the computer.

A *local area network* (*LAN*) connects computers within a limited area such as an office building or factory. Computers in a local area network can communicate over twisted pairs (telephone wiring), coaxial cables, or optical fibers. Twisted pairs provide the lowest rate of data transmission but have the advantage that they are already installed in many office buildings. The *nodes* of a local area network (the pieces of equipment connected to it) may include *workstations* (microcomputers used by office workers), peripheral devices such as printers and fixed disks (which are shared by all the workstations), and perhaps a mainframe computer. *Gateway* nodes allow different local area networks to communicate with each other—via modems and the telephone system, for example.

Software

There are two kinds of software: *applications software* and *systems software*. Applications software consists of the programs that do the various jobs the computer was purchased to do in the first place. Programs that make up payrolls, play games, design electronic components, or compute the orbits of spacecraft are examples of applications software. Systems software, on the other hand, consists of programs that help people use the computer system— help them write and execute other programs. This section is devoted to systems software; applications programs are considered in the section on applications and in many of the other chapters of this book.

Programming Languages

We need some language in which to state the instructions we want a computer to follow. Unfortunately, natural languages such as English are insufficiently precise for giving instructions to computers. Instead, we must use special purpose languages called *programming languages*.

The central processing unit is designed to execute programs coded in *machine language* (also called *machine code* or *native code*). Machine language represents instructions and memory locations by binary codes that are convenient for the central processing unit but not for human beings. A program may consist of thousands, tens of thousands, hundreds of thousands, or even millions of such codes. A machine language programmer has to know the codes for the operations the computer can carry out as well as the coded addresses of the locations in main memory in which various data items are stored. Keeping track of all these codes is tedious and error prone, as you can well imagine, so programmers avoid machine language whenever possible.

The next step up from machine language is *assembly language*. Assembly language is similar to machine language except that easy-to-remember abbreviations are used in place of obscure codes. Assembly language is one step beyond machine language, but that step is not a very large one. The instructions still call for very simple operations, such as fetching a value from memory, so many thousands of instructions are still needed to do any job that isn't utterly trivial. And assembly language programs are still dominated by machine oriented concepts such as machine instructions and memory locations.

To avoid the difficulties of machine language and assembly language, programmers have devised a number of *higher-level languages*. A higher-level language allows a programmer to instruct the computer in much the same terms that might be used to tell a human being how to do the same job. The concepts and notations of the higher-level language are those appropriate for the kinds of problem being solved rather than those dictated by the internal workings of the computer. Pascal, the programming language studied in this book, is a popular higher-level language. Other well-known higher-level languages are Ada (named after Lady Lovelace), BASIC (Beginner's All-purpose Symbolic Instruction Code), COBOL (COmmon Business Oriented Language), and FORTRAN (FORmula TRANslator).

Language Processors

The only language that the central processing unit can accept directly is machine language. Under the control of an appropriate program, however, the computer will accept and carry out instructions written in other languages. A program that makes it possible for a computer to execute programs written in some language other than machine language is called a *language processor*. There are two kinds of language processors: *compilers* and *interpreters*.

A compiler translates a program from a higher-level language into a code that is easier to execute than the original program. In some cases the program in the higher-level language is translated into machine language, which can then be executed directly by the central processing unit. In other cases the higher-level-language program is translated into an intermediate code that must be further processed by an interpreter program.

An interpreter executes a program by fetching and executing the instructions one by one. The instructions in the interpreter program tell the computer how to fetch the higher-level-language instructions from main memory, analyze them, determine which operation each calls for, and how to carry out each requested operation. Unlike a compiler, an interpreter does not produce a machine language translation of the higher-level-language program; rather, the interpreter program itself carries out the instructions contained in the program it is executing. During interpretation, the only machine code present, and the only program executed directly by the central processing unit, is the interpreter program. An interpreter can be used to execute not only programs in higher-level languages but also intermediate code produced by a compiler.

Thus, there are three ways we can get a computer to execute a program written in a higher-level language.

1. We can use a compiler to translate the program into machine language, which is then executed by the central processing unit.
2. We can use an interpreter program to execute the higher-level-language program directly, without translating it.
3. We can use an interpreter to execute intermediate code produced by a compiler.

The compiler and interpreter can each be designed to simplify the job performed by the other. Many implementations of Pascal make use of both a compiler and an interpreter.

The Operating System

Early computers had complex control panels for monitoring and controlling the operation of the equipment. In modern computer systems these monitoring and control functions have been taken over by the operating system. Both users and programs operate the computer system by means of commands to the operating system. The operating system strongly influences the face that a computer system presents to the user; the same computer hardware can behave quite differently under the control of different operating systems. This holds for programs as well as for users: the same program can usually be executed by different computer systems provided that (1) the systems have the same central processing unit,* and (2) they have the same operating sys-

---

*In the past, each different model computer normally used a different kind of central processing unit. An important benefit of the microprocessor revolution has been to make central processing units (in the form of microprocessors) off-the-shelf components. As a result, it is now common for many different brands and models of microcomputers to use the same central processing unit.

tem. On the other hand, a program designed to run under one operating system usually cannot be run on even the same computer when it is under the control of another operating system.

A major responsibility of the operating system is keeping track of the programs and data files stored in auxiliary memory. On each disk, for example, the operating system maintains a directory of all the programs and data files stored on that disk. Each directory entry contains a name that was assigned to the program or data file by the user. When the user requests a program or data file by name, the operating system looks up the name in the disk directory, finds where the program or data file is stored on disk, and transfers the file to main memory. Because of the important role it plays in transferring programs and data to and from disk, an operating system is often referred to as a *disk operating system* or *DOS*.

An operating system may support *interactive processing, noninteractive processing,* or both. Interactive processing allows users to interact with (exchange information with) their programs while the programs are being executed. Interactive processing is essential for such modern applications as word processing, spreadsheet analysis, computer-assisted instruction, and game playing. Programming is much easier with interactive processing than with noninteractive processing.

Noninteractive processing does not allow the user to interact with a program while it is being executed. All data to be processed by a program must be provided before execution begins; the output produced by the program is usually not available until execution has been completed. Users of a noninteractive system submit *jobs,* each containing commands for the operating system and any needed programs or data that are not already stored in auxiliary memory. Noninteractive processing is often called *batch processing* because many jobs can be submitted at the same time and executed as the operating system gets around to them. Batch processing is not well suited to personal computing; it is best reserved for large production jobs such as printing paychecks for all workers or statements for all customers.

Applications

The kinds of information processing a computer can perform are so varied it's impossible to summarize them in a few words. Some examples, however, will give you a feeling for the computer's versatility.

Text Processing

A *text editor* program allows a computer to be used as an electronic typewriter. Text typed on the keyboard appears on the computer's display screen and is stored in the computer's memory. By giving appropriate commands to the computer, we can display any part of the stored text on the screen and make corrections, insertions, or deletions at any point. Blocks of text can be moved or copied from one part of the stored text to another. When we are satisfied with the stored text, we can print it out in whatever format we desire. The latter job is done by a *text formatter* program, which, in accordance with commands given by the user, might print the stored text in the proper format for a business letter, a legal contract, a student report, or a book manuscript.

A *word processor* is a text editor and a text formatter combined into the same program; word processors are among the most popular programs for personal computers.

There is growing interest in *desktop publishing,* in which microcomputer-based editing and formatting programs are used to typeset and lay out the pages of a printed document such as a report, newsletter, or book. A high-quality printer, such as a laser printer, is used to print one copy of the typeset pages. Material not generated by the computer, such as illustrations, is pasted in, and the resulting camera-ready copy is photographed. The photographic negatives are used to produce the printing plates required by a particular printing technology.

Text editors are also used for writing programs. A *program development system* includes a text editor, a language processor, and perhaps a *debugging program* to aid in finding errors in the program under development. Popular program development systems for Pascal programs are UCSD Pascal, Turbo Pascal, and Macintosh Pascal.

Simulation and Modeling

A computer can be programmed to simulate the behavior of such systems as a business, a spacecraft, or a telephone exchange. The computer, together with the simulation program, serves as a working model of the simulated system. Studying the model can yield valuable insight into the behavior of the real system. In engineering, computer models are used to predict the performance of such real systems as airplanes and spacecraft before they are actually constructed. Simulation is particularly valuable in education, since students can experiment freely with a computer model, something they could never do with such real systems as a large corporation or the economy of a country. Many computer games are simulations, although they may simulate imaginary systems, such as space battles or haunted castles.

A popular tool for modeling business operations is a *spreadsheet program,* which combines an accountant's spreadsheet with a powerful automatic calculator. Like a paper spreadsheet, the display screen is divided into rows and columns; the intersection of each row and column defines a *cell.* Numerical values are entered into some cells, and labels such as column headings are entered into others. Most important of all, some cells are assigned formulas specifying how the values in those cells are to be calculated from the values in other cells. The value that appears in such a cell is the one calculated by the formula. When a previously entered value is changed, the program automatically recalculates any values defined in terms of the one that was changed. This makes a spreadsheet very useful for "what-if" analysis in which data values are changed to reflect different assumptions about the operation of a business. For each set of assumptions the spreadsheet program will work out the quantities of interest, such as a prediction of future profits. The accuracy of the prediction depends, of course, on how well the formulas model the workings of the business.

Data Analysis

The raw data collected in a survey or a scientific experiment usually needs to be analyzed to extract its meaning. Frequently, one needs to *count* the number of data items satisfying a certain criterion. In processing data collected in a political poll, for example, we would want to count the number of people questioned favoring each candidate, the number belonging to each political party, the number who consider a particular issue important, and so on. *Measures of central tendency,* such as the mean (average), median, and mode; and *measures of dispersion,* such as the standard deviation, help us visualize the way data values are distributed. *Correlation coefficients* help us find relationships among the variables being studied. *Statistical tests* help us determine whether the data collected is meaningful or whether it can be explained by the workings of random chance. Having analyzed our data, we usually wish to display the results graphically—as line graphs, bar graphs, pie charts, and so on. *Statistical software packages* contain programs for analyzing data and displaying the results graphically.

Perhaps the best-known example of data analysis is that carried out on the data collected every 10 years during the United States Census. The data on millions of census forms must be tabulated and analyzed to determine facts of great social, political, and economic importance. For example, the population of a city affects the amount of federal aid the city will receive. Census figures are sometimes challenged in court by those who feel that their localities will be adversely affected. Hollerith's punched-card tabulating and sorting machines were originally developed for the census bureau.

Data Management

One of the most widely used applications of computers is for storing and maintaining large data files, such as the files containing data on a company's customers, employees, suppliers, and inventory. Such a collection of files is known as a *database* (the term *data bank* is also occasionally used). As we've seen, data management is important in business; however, its importance is not limited to that field. The data collected during a complex scientific experiment—say a rocket launch—may be stored in a database and manipulated with data management programs. Governments maintain many large databases, such as the one containing the records of all people who file income tax returns. Controversy frequently arises over the uses to which government databases are put, as when they are used to locate persons who are not paying child support, to detect persons cheating on welfare, and to ferret out young men who have not registered for the draft.

A database is maintained by a set of programs called a *database management system.* Users who access the data directly as well as programs that use it in their processing all work through the database management system. The database management system provides a simple, logical view of the data regardless of how it is actually stored on such media as tapes and disks. For one type of database, called a *relational database,* the data is viewed as if it were arranged in tables. By requesting the database management system to combine rows and columns selected from particular tables, the user can specify the data to be retrieved and processed. *Natural language interfaces,* which are still somewhat experimental, allow users to ask the system questions in English or some other natural language and receive answers based on the contents of the database.

Like spreadsheet programs and word processors, database management systems are popular with users of personal computers.

Integrated Software

Also popular with microcomputer users are *integrated programs* that combine into one program such popular applications as word processing, spreadsheet analysis, database management, business graphics, and data communications. Data is easily transferred from one application to another, something not always possible with separate programs. Thus data from a database can be inserted into reports with the word processor or used to construct a spreadsheet. Results calculated with spreadsheets can be inserted into reports with the word processor or used to produce charts (business graphics), which are then inserted into reports. Data communications allows any type of information handled by the program—text, spreadsheets, data records, or charts—to be transmitted or received over communications links such as the telephone system.

Games

One of the best-known computer applications is game playing. Computer games come in several forms: arcade games, video games to be attached to home television sets, hand-held video games with their own built-in displays, and game-playing programs for personal computers. Although computers are best known for video games, they can also play more traditional games, such as chess. The idea of a machine playing chess has fascinated people since the eighteenth century, when a (fraudulent) chess playing machine was widely exhibited. Chess tournaments in which computers play one another are now annual events, and computers sometimes also participate in human chess tournaments. The best chess programs play at the expert level, and one program was recently recognized as playing at the master level.

As mentioned earlier, many computer games simulate some real-world situation such as managing a business or flying an airplane. (The best-known simulation game is not a computer game at all but the board game Monopoly, which simulates real-estate investment.) If the game programs accurately reflect the systems they are supposed to simulate, then simulation games can be as educational as they are entertaining.

Computer Science

Computer science focuses not so much on the design of computer hardware but on the overall process of manipulating information under the control of step-by-step instructions. Some have suggested that the field be called *computing science* to emphasize its concern with the entire computing process. The word for computer science in many foreign languages translates into English as *information science* or *informatics*.

Two focal points of computer science are *data representation* (representing information in a form suitable for computer processing) and *algorithms* (sets of step-by-step instructions for solving a given problem).

Information and Data

We used the terms *information* and *data* in the preceding discussion. Although many people use these terms almost interchangeably, a careful distinction between them can shed some light on the computing process. *Information* is used with its customary meaning of facts, concepts, and knowledge. *Data* refers to the particular symbols, such as digits or letters of the alphabet or binary codes, that are used to represent information in a form suitable for storage, processing, and communication. A computer can only process data— that is, manipulate concrete symbols. The purpose of this data processing, however, is information processing—storing, modifying, and communicating the information represented by the symbols. It is up to us to make sure that the symbol manipulations carried out by a computer are appropriate and useful for the information that the symbols represent.

Another, more familiar, use of the term *data* is to refer to the input to a computation—for example, the numbers needed for an arithmetical calculation. We will often use the terms *input data* or just *input* to designate the data that serves as the starting point for a computation.

Finally, the term *data* is the subject of a grammatical dispute: people disagree over whether it is singular or plural. In Latin, *data* is plural, the singular form is *datum*. Most English dictionaries, however, authorize both the singular and plural usages. Those who, like the present author, prefer the singular usage, treat *data* as a collective noun, such as grass or sand or information. We say "the data has been processed" just as we say "the grass has been cut," "the sand has been shoveled," or "the information has been processed." Those who prefer the plural usage would say "the data have been processed."

Data Representation and Data Abstraction

Data representation often involves creating *data structures*—arrangements of data items—that reflect the real-world objects and situations with which a program is concerned. For example, suppose we wish to write a program to simulate the operation of an automobile, perhaps for the purpose of predicting the performance of a proposed new model. The corresponding data structure would contain, among many other things, numbers representing the speed at which the car is traveling, the amount of fuel in the tank, the amount of charge in the battery, and the amount by which the accelerator is depressed.

Each operation that can be carried out on an actual automobile must be reflected by a corresponding manipulation of the data structure. Thus there must be data manipulations corresponding to such operations as starting the car, putting it in reverse, and applying the brakes.

The term *abstraction* refers to focusing on significant details and ignoring those not relevant to the purpose at hand. For example, we learn how to use automobiles, television sets, and microwave ovens without having to understand the technical details of their internal construction and operation. From the many complex details of such devices, we *abstract* the few that are important for our purposes.

Data abstraction refers to defining data values and the operations that can be carried out on them independently of any particular computer representation. To this end we classify data values into *data types,* each of which consists of a set of data values and a set of operations that can be carried out on those values.

For example, we could define a data type whose values (which correspond to the data structures we have mentioned) represent various states of an automobile—parked, idling, traveling forward or backward at various speeds, and so on. To define the data values abstractly, we state what characteristics of an automobile must be represented but not how they would be coded inside a computer. Thus each value of the automobile data type must represent, among many other things, whether or not the engine is running and whether the transmission is in park, reverse, neutral, or drive.

The operations of a data type are defined in terms of their effects on the abstract characteristics of the data values. For example, the operation of starting the engine is valid only when applied to a value representing a car whose engine is not running and whose transmission is in park or neutral. And after the operation has been applied to a data value, the resulting value must represent a car whose engine is running.

Algorithms

An *algorithm* is a set of instructions for carrying out a particular task. Unlike a program, which must be expressed in a form suitable for processing by a computer, an algorithm can be expressed in whatever form is convenient— in English, in mathematical notation, with diagrams, or in a programming language. If a programming language is used, it may be chosen for its clarity of expression and may be different from the language into which the algorithm will eventually be translated for computer processing. Pascal is the programming language most frequently chosen for expressing algorithms.

The pair of terms *algorithm* and *program* are analogous to the pair *information* and *data*. In each case the first term of the pair refers to an abstract concept and the second to a concrete representation of the concept in a form suitable for computer processing. Like *information* and *data, algorithm* and *program* are frequently used almost interchangeably.

Every correct algorithm comes with a guarantee that, if we faithfully follow its instructions, we will solve a particular problem or accomplish a particular task. This guarantee is essential if we are to use the algorithm with confidence. We probably wouldn't bother learning the multiplication algorithm—the rules for multiplication we learned in grade school—if we weren't sure that it would give the right answer for any pair of numbers we chose to multiply. And we would be even more hesitant about incorporating an unreliable algorithm in our computers, where the results calculated under its direction might not be checked or even seen by human beings.

Frequently, we must place some restriction on the data an algorithm is to manipulate in order to guarantee correct results. For example, division by zero is not defined in arithmetic. Therefore, the guarantee for the division algorithm—the usual rules for long division—holds only if the divisor is not zero.

To assure that algorithms live up to their guarantees—that we can always carry out the instructions in an algorithm, and that doing so will always yield the desired results—every algorithm must have the following characteristics:

- *An algorithm must be precise.* Each step of the algorithm must state unambiguously what action is to be taken. It is for the sake of precision that algorithms are often expressed in precise notations such as mathematical notation and programming languages rather than in imprecise ones such as English.

- *An algorithm must be effective.* It must be possible to actually carry out every step of the algorithm. Thus certain mathematical operations that require an infinite number of steps cannot be called for in an algorithm, since such operations cannot be carried out in a finite amount of time by either people or computers.

■ *An algorithm must have a fixed, finite number of instructions.* Frequently the amount of data to be processed by an algorithm can vary. For example, the multiplication algorithm must work regardless of the number of digits in the numbers to be multiplied, and an algorithm for computing a payroll must work regardless of the number of employees on the payroll. The amount of data, and hence the number of processing steps, can vary, but the number of instructions in the algorithm must remain fixed. This is accomplished by specifying that some instructions are to be repeated as many times as needed.

■ *The execution of an algorithm must always terminate.* When we specify that one or more instructions are to be executed repeatedly, we must specify the conditions under which the repetitions are to terminate. If we specify these conditions incorrectly, the repetitions might never terminate, and the execution of the algorithm would continue indefinitely. An algorithm whose execution never terminates will never complete its calculations and hence is of no use to anybody.

We recall that data abstraction involves defining operations on data values independently of how the data is represented inside the computer. Likewise, *procedural abstraction* involves defining operations independently of the details of the algorithms that carry them out. Once an algorithm has been written, we can ignore its internal details and concern ourselves only with the task that it accomplishes. The ability to guarantee that an algorithm always accomplishes a particular task is essential to procedural abstraction.

Program Development and Software Engineering

Engineers apply the principles discovered by scientists to the design and production of practical commercial products. Software engineering seeks to apply the techniques of computer science together with those of such practical disciplines as project management to the production of reliable software with predictable development times and costs. This has proved to be no easy task. Software development projects tend to run far behind schedule and far over budget; worse yet, the resulting software is plagued with errors or *bugs*. The situation is so serious as to cause many people to speak of a *software crisis*. Although software engineers have found many ways to improve the software development process, no sure-fire solution to the problems of software development is in sight.

Development of a program can be broken down into six phases, which constitute the *software development life cycle*.

■ Requirements analysis.
■ Specification.
■ Design.
■ Implementation (coding).
■ Verification and testing.
■ Maintenance.

Requirements analysis studies the problem to be solved and determines what combination of hardware and software is needed to solve it. The specification phase determines precisely what the program to be written must do to meet the needs identified by the requirements analysis. In the design phase, the program is broken down into small parts, called *modules,* each of which performs an easily described and understood function. Procedural and data abstraction are the guiding principles of the design phase.

In the implementation phase, the program modules are written in a suitable programming language. Programming language statements are sometimes known as *code* and the implementation phase is often referred to as *coding.* The correctness of the modules is verified by a variety of means such as the programmer carefully examining the code (*desk checking*), explaining the code to colleagues (*structured walkthroughs*), and executing the program with test data (*testing*). After the modules have been tested individually, they are combined to test larger and larger parts of the complete program.

After being put into use, a program usually requires maintenance. This may seem strange since a program has no moving parts that wear out and must be replaced. Maintenance, however, is needed for two reasons: (1) bugs that were not found during testing will come to light after the program was put into service; and (2) the task that the program is to perform will change (often due to changes in business operations or government regulations), requiring that the program be modified.

Student programmers will usually not generate formal documents for these six phases, as would be done in a large software project. The specifications, for example, may be scribbled on the back of an envelope or held in the student's head. Nevertheless, the student must understand the problem to be solved (requirements analysis), determine what a program must accomplish to solve the problem (specification), and plan the solution (design). Only with this preliminary work out of the way is it reasonable to embark on coding. Desk checking (understand the program yourself) and structured walkthroughs (explain it to somebody else) will save much time during testing and catch many errors that would otherwise be overlooked. Students are mercifully spared maintenance unless the program is handed back with instructions to correct the errors found by the grader.

Review Questions

1. Describe some of the earliest techniques for storing, manipulating, and communicating information. Which of these led most directly to the modern computer?

2. In what century and by whom was the first computer designed? Who wrote a demonstration program for this computer?

3. What is a stored program computer?

4. Describe the technologies characteristic of each of the four computer generations and the proposed fifth generation.

5. Describe multiprogramming, time-sharing, and virtual memory.

6. Identify the two components of the central processing unit and give the function of each.

7. Describe the function and organization of main memory. What are bits and bytes? RAM and ROM? How many bytes are there in a 64KB memory? How many bits?

8. Contrast main and auxiliary memory. Contrast sequential and random access. Describe the two most widely used forms of auxiliary memory.

9. Describe the most commonly used input and output devices.

10. Contrast machine language, assembly language, and higher-level languages.

11. What is a language processor? Contrast compilers and interpreters.

12. What is the function of the operating system? Why is the operating system frequently referred to as a disk operating system or DOS?

13. Contrast interactive and noninteractive processing. Which would be most suitable for playing a game with the computer? For printing a monthly statement for each of a company's customers?

14. Describe three applications of text processing.

15. Give some applications of modeling and simulation. What type of popular microcomputer program is often used to model business operations?

16. Describe the applications commonly provided by an integrated program.

17. Contrast information and data.

18. Define data representation, data abstraction, and data type.

19. Contrast algorithms and programs. Describe four requirements that every correct algorithm must satisfy.

20. Describe the software development life cycle.

Programming in Pascal

2

This chapter introduces the structure of Pascal programs and the basic techniques of program design, coding, and testing. Only the most elementary features of Pascal are introduced in this chapter, thus allowing the reader to focus on the program development process rather than the technicalities of the language. Once mastered, the program development techniques introduced here can be readily applied to the many additional features of Pascal that will be introduced in succeeding chapters.

In this book we will follow the American (ANSI/IEEE) standard for Pascal, which differs only slightly from the international (ISO) standard. Appendix 2 provides syntax diagrams for ANSI/IEEE and ISO Pascal, together with an explanation of their use, and points out the major differences between the American and international standards. Unfortunately, the two most widely used Pascal implementations, Turbo Pascal and UCSD Pascal, are both nonstandard in some respects. Appendix 3 gives the differences between Turbo and standard Pascal, and Appendix 4 does the same for UCSD Pascal.

Basic Program Structure

Traditionally, the first program taken up in studying a programming language is one that prints a one-line message to the user. Figure 2-1 is our version of this traditional program.

A glance at Figure 2-1 reveals that the program contains two kinds of words: **reserved words**, which are printed in boldface; and *identifiers*, which are printed in italics. Reserved words introduce, partition, and terminate language constructs. For example, the reserved word **program** introduces

Figure 2-1.

The traditional first program in any programming text is a program that prints a greeting to the user.

---

program *PrintGreeting* (*output*);

{ Print greeting to user }

begin
   writeln ('Greetings from your friendly computer')
end.

a program; and the reserved words **begin** and **end** bracket the part of the program that tells the computer what actions to take. These words are reserved in the sense that they can be used only for their intended purposes and cannot be redefined by the programmer. The language processor uses the reserved words as a guide to processing the program; it would be confused if these words were used for some other purpose.

Identifiers are names of such things as subprograms (parts of a program that carry out specific tasks), data items, and memory locations. Some identifiers are predefined in the language, whereas others are defined by the programmer. Predefined identifiers can be redefined by the programmer, although this usually isn't recommended. Redefinition isn't forbidden, however, as it is for reserved words.

The first line of the program is the *program heading*:

> **program** *PrintGreeting* (*output*);

Following the reserved word **program** is the program name, *PrintGreeting*, which is a programmer-defined identifier. An identifier should describe as precisely as possible the construction that it names. Since the purpose of the program is to print a greeting to the user, we choose *PrintGreeting* for the program name. Other reasonable program names would be *PrintMessage*, *GreetUser*, or even *OurVeryFirstProgram*. Note how capital letters are used to combine several English words into a single identifier without sacrificing readability.

Every source from which data can be obtained and every destination to which data can be sent is known as a *file*. There is a standard input file (usually the user's keyboard) designated by the predefined identifier *input* and a standard output file (usually the user's display screen) designated by the predefined identifier *output*. The files used by a program must be listed in parentheses after the program name. Our program produces output only, so only the file *output* need be listed. The following is a heading for a program that both accepts input and produces output:

> **program** *Conversation* (*input, output*);

The program heading is terminated with a semicolon. Semicolons, which are used extensively to terminate or separate Pascal constructions, are the bane of a Pascal programmer's existence. They are easy to omit accidentally and their absence is easily overlooked when checking a program; yet missing semicolons can sometimes confuse a language processor, causing it to produce peculiar error messages.

The next line of the program

> { Print greeting to user }

is a *comment* describing what the program does; comments are intended for human readers and are ignored by the computer. Comments can be enclosed either with braces { and } or the two-character symbols (* and *). Braces are recommended if they are available on your computer.

The instructions that the computer is to follow are contained in the *statement part* of the program:

> **begin**
>   *writeln* ('Greetings from your friendly computer')
> **end**.

The instructions themselves are known as (imperative) *statements*; another term such as *instruction*, *order*, or *command* would probably be better than statement, but the term *statement* is traditional. The statement part opens with the reserved word **begin** and closes with the reserved word **end**. A series of statements bracketed by **begin** and **end** is known as a *compound statement*. We use a compound statement whenever we wish to group together a series of statements and treat them as a unit. The statement part of a program is a compound statement.

In our example program, the statement part contains only one statement:

writeln ('Greetings from your friendly computer')

This statement calls a *procedure*. A procedure is a part of a program that carries out a specific task; the procedure can be invoked, or called, whenever that task needs to be done. A procedure can be predefined—built into the Pascal language—or it can be written by the programmer. The predefined identifier *writeln* ("write line") names a predefined procedure for writing a line of text to a file; when no other file is specified, the line is written to the standard output file (usually the display or printer).

A procedure is called with a *procedure statement*, which consists of the name of the procedure followed by a parenthesized list of *parameters*. The parameters are used to pass input data to the procedure and to receive results computed by the procedure. For convenience, a procedure statement is sometimes referred to by the name of the procedure it calls; thus the procedure statement in the example could be referred to as a *writeln* statement.

The call to *writeln* in our example has a single parameter, which specifies the message to be printed for the user. The message is given by a *string constant*, a series of characters enclosed in single quotation marks (apostrophes).

'Greetings from your friendly computer'

We say that a program or a part of a program is *run* or *executed* when the instructions in it are carried out by the computer. When our example program is executed, the procedure statement (the only statement in the program) is executed, the procedure *writeln* is called with the parameter 'Greetings from your friendly computer', and the message

```
Greetings from your friendly computer
```

appears on the user's display or printout. Note that the enclosing single quotation marks are not printed; they are not part of the character string but merely serve to delimit (mark the beginning and end of) the string constant.

An apostrophe or single quotation mark within a string constant must be represented by two apostrophes in succession to prevent it from being confused with the single quotation marks that delimit the string constant. Thus the statement

writeln ('Don''t go near the water!')

causes the computer to print

```
Don't go near the water!
```

Don't confuse the two apostrophes in succession with the double quotation mark, which is a completely different character. Also, don't confuse the apostrophe with the grave accent (`), which slants or curves in the opposite direction.

The **end** that closes the statement part is followed by a period, which marks the end of the program.

Rules for Forming Identifiers

A striking difference between programming languages and natural languages is that in writing a program we must make up names for most of the objects to which we wish to refer. In everyday life, on the other hand, making up a name is a rare occurrence; normally, we refer to things by existing names (such as the names of people and cities) or by descriptive phrases such as "the chair by the window in the living room."

When making up names, or identifiers, the programmer must follow certain rules to assure that identifiers will not be confused with other elements of the langue, such as numbers or string constants. The following are the rules for forming identifiers in Pascal:

- Identifiers are made up of the letters of the alphabet and the numerals 0 through 9. Other characters, such as spaces, hyphens, and punctuation marks, are not allowed.
- An identifier must begin with a letter.
- An identifier must not have the same spelling as a reserved word. The reserved words in standard Pascal are as follows:

and	downto	if	or	then
array	else	in	packed	to
begin	end	label	procedure	type
case	file	mod	program	until
const	for	nil	record	var
div	function	not	repeat	while
do	goto	of	set	with

For your convenience, we've also listed the reserved words in Appendix 1.

Pascal does not distinguish between upper- and lowercase letters nor between boldface and italics; such type styles are used only to make the program clearer to a human reader. Thus the following words would be considered to be identical:

begin   BEGIN   *BEGIN*   *Begin*   *begin*

None of these can be used as an identifier, since all have the same spelling as the reserved word **begin**.

In standard Pascal, all the characters of an identifier are significant—all are taken into account in distinguishing between two identifiers. In some implementations of Pascal, however, only a fixed number of characters (normally the first eight) are significant. In such an implementation, two identifiers that are identical in their first eight characters are considered to be the same identifier even if they differ in other characters. Thus the identifiers *SubtractExpenses* and *SubtractReturns* are different in standard Pascal but would be regarded as the same by an implementation in which only the first eight characters are significant.

Program Style

Program style refers to those aspects of a program that are ignored by the computer but that render the program more comprehensible to human readers.

Such human comprehension is crucial to the success of a program. A program is written to make the computer carry out a specific task; no matter how cleverly the program is constructed, it is useless if people cannot understand what task the program does or convince themselves that the task will be accomplished reliably. Typical elements of program style are the arrangement of the program on the printed page, the use of comments, and the choice of programmer-defined identifiers.

Arrangements of the Program Text.   Pascal allows the programmer enormous flexibility in arranging the program on the display screen or printed page. Extra spaces and line breaks (transitions to new lines) can be inserted anywhere except within multicharacter symbols such as reserved words, identifiers, and string constants. Likewise, spaces and line breaks can be removed as long as adjacent words (identifiers or reserved words) are not run together. (Spaces in string constants are part of the string being defined and so cannot be inserted or removed arbitrarily.) The following are some guidelines for formatting the text of a program:

■ Begin each logically distinct construction on a new line. In Figure 2-1, for example, the program heading, the comment, the procedure statement, and the reserved words **begin** and **end** each begins on a new line. Normally, each statement of a program begins on a new line.

■ Use blank lines freely to separate distinct parts of a program and to make parts stand out. For example, the comment in Figure 2-1 is separated from the surrounding program text by blank lines.

■ Use indentation to show when one part of a program is subordinate to or enclosed within another part. In this book, for example, the statements of a compound statement will always be indented relative to the enclosing **begin** and **end**.

Comments.   Comments should be used freely to explain the functions of various parts of the program and to clarify anything (such as a tricky programming technique) that might not be immediately obvious to someone reading the program. A comment can be placed anywhere (except in a string constant) where a space or a line break is allowed. Usually, comments are positioned in one of two ways:

■ The comment is placed on a line by itself, as in Figure 2-1. This is usually done when the comment applies to the entire program or to a subsantial section of the program. To make the comment stand out, it is often separated from the surrounding program by blank lines.

■ The comment is placed on the same line as, and to the right of, a statement or other program construction.

  writeln ('Goodbye')   { Sign off }

This method is usually used when the comment applies to only one line of the program.

Note that a comment is often phrased as the command we might give to the computer if it could understand English.

Choosing Identifiers.   An identifier should be made up of English words or abbreviations that describe the program construction that the identifier names. Thus *FindNextMove* is a good name for a procedure that performs the indicated task, whereas *FNM* and *F0023* are not.

An identifier often incorporates several English words or abbreviations. In order for the identifier to be readable, we need some way to make the individual words stand out. Unfortunately, neither of the customary word separators, spaces and hyphens, are allowed in identifiers. The usual solution to this problem is to capitalize the first letter of each word (except possibly the first word). We have already seen several identifiers formed in this way; some additional examples are:

interestRate   highScore   GetNextRecord   userErrorCount

Some Pascal nonstandard implementations allow an identifier to contain the underscore character. In such an implementation we can use the underscore character as a word separator in identifiers as follows:

interest_rate   high_score   Find_next_move

Bear in mind, however, that programs using the underscore are not *portable*—they cannot be compiled by another Pascal implementation that does not allow the underscore in identifiers.

The programs in this book use the following capitalization conventions:

■ Reserved words and predefined identifiers are in all lowercase letters, since this is the form in which they usually appear in textbooks and reference manuals. The only exception is the predefined identifier *Boolean,* which is usually capitalized because it is derived from the name of a person, the mathematician George Boole.

■ Words making up a programmer-defined identifier are capitalized as described earlier. The first letter of an identifier is capitalized if the identifier names a major program unit, such as a program or procedure (examples: *GetListing, FindNextMove*). Otherwise, the first letter is lowercase (examples: *interestRate, highScore*).

The boldface and italics that we use to distinguish reserved words from identifiers are usually not available when programs are typed into a computer. In that case, a common convention is to type reserved words in all capital letters. Identifiers are still typed in a mixture of upper and lowercase letters, as just described.

Entering, Compiling, and Executing a Program

Entering, compiling, and executing a program involves the following steps:

■ *Editing.* With the aid of a text editor program, the programmer types in the Pascal program and corrects any immediately apparent errors, such as obvious typing errors. The Pascal program created with the text editor is called the *source program*.

■ *Compiling.* The source program is processed by the compiler program, which finds and reports *syntax* errors in the source program—errors in the use of the Pascal language. If errors are found, the programmer must return to the text editor and correct them; otherwise, the compiler translates the source program into the machine-coded *object program*.

- *Linking.* Before the object program can be executed, it must be linked to predefined subprograms such as *writeln*, which are stored in a disk file called a *library.* This task is accomplished by the linker program, which takes the object program as input and produces a ready-to-run *executable program.*

- *Execution.* We can now test our program by running the executable program, providing it with sample input data, and checking its output for correctness. Usually, testing will reveal additional errors, requiring the programmer to return to the text editor, correct the errors, and repeat the entire compile-link-execute process.

The editor, compiler, and linker can be separate programs, or they can be parts of an integrated *program development system.* With separate programs, each program must be provided with the names of the files that it needs. The editor must be given the name of the source file (the disk file containing the source program), the compiler must be given the names of the source and object files, and the linker must be given the names of the object and executable files. With an integrated program development system, the programmer may need only to strike a single key (such as R for run) to have the entire compile-link-execute process carried out.

Sequencing and Pseudocode

The statements of a program must be organized in such a way that, when the program is run, the proper statements will be executed, the statements will be executed in the proper order, and each statement will be executed the proper number of times. Methods of organizing statements to assure their proper execution are known as *control structures.* The discipline of *structured programming*, which we follow in this book, emphasizes the following three basic control structures:

- *Sequencing.* The statements are executed one after another in the order that they appear in the program.

- *Selection* (also called *alternation*). Certain statements are selected for execution and others are rejected; the selection depends on the data the program is manipulating. Thus if a program is run several times with different input data, different statements may be executed on each run.

- *Repetition* (also called *iteration*). A statement or series of statements is executed repeatedly. If a calculation needs to be done repeatedly, we can write the statements for the calculation once and let the computer execute them the required number of times.

Sequencing

Sequencing is realized in Pascal by means of the compound statement. A compound statement contains a list of statements, with the statements on the list separated by semicolons. When a compound statement is executed, the statements making it up are executed one after another in the order in which they appear in the program text.

For example, consider the following compound statement:

```
begin
    writeln ('A');
    writeln ('B');
    writeln ('C')
end
```

When this compound statement is executed, the three *writeln* statements are executed in the order in which they appear in the program. Thus, the computer prints

```
A
B
C
```

Note carefully that the semicolons separate (rather than terminate) the statements making up the compound statement; there is no semicolon before the first statement or after the last one. The role of the semicolons as statement separators becomes clearer if the entire compound statement is written on one line, like this:

begin *writeln* ('A'); *writeln* ('B'); *writeln* ('C') **end**

Pseudocode

The text of a program is often called *code* and the process of writing a program is called *coding*. These terms are not without justification. Like any other code, a program must be constructed with absolute precision. A single character omitted or out of place will cause the program to be rejected by the compiler or, worse, will yield a program that compiles without error but executes incorrectly. (For example, a multimillion-dollar space rocket once went astray and had to be destroyed because someone had left out a single minus sign in the large, complex program that controlled the rocket.) Another codelike aspect of program text is that it is often obscure to human readers; it is often difficult for a person to determine what a given piece of code causes the computer to do or what code must be written to cause the computer to take a particular action.

For these reasons, it is difficult to plan and code a program at the same time—to simultaneously focus both on what actions the computer should take to accomplish the given task and on how each action should be coded. It is thus a basic tenet of structured programming that planning and coding should be done separately. We should first analyze the task that a program is to accomplish and plan the actions that the computer must take. When this plan is complete, we can turn our attention to the detailed task of coding each action for the computer.

The plan for a program is often expressed in a notation called *pseudocode* (the prefix *pseudo* means *false* or *imitation*). Pseudocode is intended to be read by people rather than computers. It is usually less detailed than actual code, since people can be relied upon to understand things that must be spelled out in the tiniest detail for computers. Pseudocode is far more flexible than actual code, because the writer can use many forms of expression—English, mathematics, notation drawn from a particular problem domain such as chemistry—rather than being confined to the constructions of a single programming language. Pseudocode styles range from *structured English* (English written in an outline format that reflects the structure of a program) to code similar to that found in actual programming languages. The pseudocode used in this book is structured English.

As a simple example, let's plan and code a program that prints a particular address in the three-line format used to address an envelope. We know that Pascal provides a procedure for printing a single line of text. Our obvious plan, then, is to print the address one line at a time: to print the first line first, then the second line, and finally the third line. We express these three steps in pseudocode as follows:

1. Print the name of the addressee
2. Print the street address
3. Print the city, state, and zip code

The pseudocode describes clearly the steps the computer is to take. On the other hand, it omits such details as the Pascal procedure to be used and the actual address to be printed. Supplying these, we can easily translate the pseudocode into the corresponding Pascal statements:

> *writeln* ('West Publishing Company');
> *writeln* ('50 West Kellogg Boulevard');
> *writeln* ('St. Paul, MN 55164')

Figure 2-2 shows the complete program for printing a three-line address. When this program is run, it prints the address of the publisher of this book.

```
West Publishing Company
50 West Kellogg Boulevard
St. Paul, MN 55164
```

Types, Constants, Variables, and Blocks

In this section and the next we will look at some additional features of Pascal. We will then return to the main theme of this chapter, which is program design and coding.

Type *real*

Computer programs must manipulate many different kinds of data, such as numbers and character strings. Different kinds of data are represented dif-

Figure 2-2. Program to print a three-line address.

---

program *AddressLetter* (*output*);

{ Print three-line name and address }

begin
  writeln ('West Publishing Company');
  writeln ('50 West Kellogg Boulevard');
  writeln ('St. Paul, MN 55164')
end.

---

ferently inside the computer, are denoted differently in Pascal programs, and are manipulated with different operations. Operations appropriate for one kind of data are usually meaningless when applied to another. For example, arithmetical operations such as addition and subtraction are appropriate for manipulating numbers, but it would be absurd to try to add and subtract character strings such as people's names.

To prevent data values from being manipulated with the wrong operations and to prevent their internal representations from being misinterpreted, Pascal classifies data items into *data types*. Values belonging to the same type are subject to the same operations and are represented in the same way both inside the computer and in Pascal programs. Pascal language processors practice *strong type-checking*—the language processor keeps track of the types of all data values and indicates an error if the program attempts to manipulate a value in a manner that is inappropriate for its type. Data types and strong type-checking are central concepts in both Pascal and computer science.

Numbers containing decimal points, such as 3.14 and 99.95 are known in mathematics as *real numbers*. In Pascal, such numbers belong to the type *real* (which is designated in programs by the predefined identifier *real*). Values of a type are represented in Pascal programs by *constants*. Real constants (that is, constants representing values of type *real*) can be written in much the same way as we write real numbers in everyday life.

$$25.3 \quad -300.1 \quad 20.0 \quad 7.2985 \quad -0.00325$$

There are a few restrictions on the placement of the decimal point. First the decimal point must be present; otherwise, the constant does not represent a value of type *real*. Thus 25 is not a real constant (its value belongs to another Pascal type, type *integer*). To represent twenty-five as a value of type *real*, we must write 25.0 instead of 25. Second, the decimal point cannot be the first or last character of the constant. Thus 25. and .25 are both invalid; we must write 25.0 and 0.25 instead.

Addition, subtraction, multiplication, and division are defined for values of type *real*. Addition and subtraction are represented by the usual signs + and −. Because the usual signs for multiplication and division, × and ÷, are not found on many computer keyboards, multiplication is represented by an asterisk, *, and division by a slash, /.

Constant Definitions

Pascal allows the programmer to define *constant identifiers* to represent numbers, characters, and strings. In a Pascal program, constant identifiers are defined in a *constant definition part*, which is introduced by the reserved word **const**.

```
const
    taxRate = 0.0425;
    query   = 'What''s up, Doc?'
```

The reserved word **const** is followed by a series of *constant definitions*. Each definition consists of the identifier being defined followed by an equal sign and a constant representing the value to be given to the identifier. Each constant definition ends with a semicolon.

A constant identifier can be defined in terms of another, previously defined constant identifier. If the previously defined identifier represents a number, it can be preceded by a plus or a minus sign.

```
const
    upperLimit    = 100.0;
    largestValue = upperLimit;
    lowerLimit    = - upperLimit
```

When a constant identifier is used in a program, the effect is the same as if the constant identifier were replaced by its defined value. For example, if *query* is as just defined, then the statement

writeln (*query*)

is equivalent in every respect to the statement

writeln ('What''s up, Doc?')

Either statement causes the computer to print

What's up, Doc?

The use of constant identifiers is an important aspect of program style. If a program does computations involving a tax rate of 0.0425, and constant identifiers are not used, then the program will have 0.0425s sprinkled throughout it. A reader may have to analyze the program for some time to discover the significance of the 0.0425s. But if we define *taxRate* equal to 0.0425 and use *taxRate* throughout the rest of the program, the user will be able to see at a glance the significance of each use of the constant. What's more, if the tax rate changes, it will be far easier to change the definition of *taxRate* than to seek out and change each occurrence of 0.0425.

Variables

A computer's main memory is made up of individual *memory locations*, each of which holds a data value. Main memory is often visualized as a set of post office boxes or pigeonholes, with the individual boxes corresponding to memory locations. We need some ways of referring to particular memory locations for the purpose of storing values in them and retrieving values from them. The most common way of doing this is to use identifiers to name the memory locations that a program will use.

A *variable* is a named memory location. The name of the location (an identifier) is called the *variable name*; the value stored in the location is called the *value of the variable*. Variables are so called because the contents of the location, and hence the value of the variable, can change as program execution proceeds. Variables are thus in contrast to constants, which retain their values unchanged throughout the execution of a program.

We can visualize variables as boxes, each of which has a name and contains a value. Figure 2-3 depicts the variables *length*, *width,* and *height* in this way. Since the value of a variable is the value stored in the corresponding memory location, the value of *length* is 25.7, the value of *width* is 10.0, and the value of *height* is 2.9. It is often convenient to display the values of variables in a table, such as the following:

Variable	Value
length	25.7
width	10.0
height	2.9

Each variable that a program is to use must be declared in a *variable declaration part*. A variable declaration gives the identifier that will be used to name the variable and the type of values the variable can have; that is, the type of the data that will be stored in the corresponding memory location. The data type is required for two reasons. First, values of different types require different size memory locations; the language processor must know the type of data to be stored in order to determine how much memory to allocate to the variable. Second, the language processor can carry out strong type-checking only if it knows the data type of the value of every variable.

A variable declaration part consists of the reserved word **var** followed by a series of variable declarations. Each declaration consists of the variable name followed by a colon and the data type; each declaration ends with a semicolon. We often use the data type as an adjective in referring to variables; thus variables that can have real values are referred to as *real variables*. The following variable declaration part declares *length*, *width*, and *height* to be real variables:

```
var
    length : real;
    width  : real;
    height : real;
```

Pascal allows the declarations of variables with the same type to be combined. Thus *length*,*width*, and *height* can also be declared by

```
var
    length, width, height : real;
```

or by

```
var
    length,
    width,
    height : real;
```

Figure 2-3.

We can picture variables as boxes, each of which has a name and contains a value.

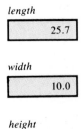

length

    25.7

width

    10.0

height

    2.9

Blocks

The constant definition and variable declaration parts of a program are placed between the program heading and the statement part. Pascal imposes an order on definition and declaration parts: if both a constant definition and a variable declaration part are present, the constant definition part must precede the variable declaration part.

It is convenient to define a structure called a *block*, which is part of several Pascal constructions. A block consists of a series of definition and declaration parts, in their proper order, followed by a statement part. Considering only the two definitions and declaration parts we have taken up so far, a block has the following structure:

> constant definition part
> variable declaration part
> statement part

Using the definition of a block, we can say that a program consists of a program heading followed by a block and a period. That is, a program has the following structure:

> program heading
> block
> period

Using Variables

Variables play a central role in most programs because most computations involve storing input data and intermediate results in memory until they are needed later in the computation. This section focuses on language constructions that use variables to store and retrieve data.

Expressions

An *expression* is a language construction that represents a value. Constants such as 3.5 and constant identifiers such as *taxRate* (which we defined to have the value of 0.0425) represent values and are thus clearly expressions. A variable represents a value, namely the value currently stored in the corresponding memory location. Thus a variable can serve as an expression by itself or can be part of a larger expression. Finally, a mathematical formula such as 2.0 + 3.0 represents a value (5.0) by describing how the value is to be computed; such formulas are thus also expressions.

We say that an expression is *evaluated* when the value that it represents is computed; we refer to the computed value as *the value of the expression*. In examples, we will often indicate the value of an expression with the arrow symbol $\Rightarrow$, which we can regard as an abbreviation for such phrases as "has the value," "evaluates to," or "yields." Thus, we read

$$2.0 + 3.0 \Rightarrow 5.0$$

as "the expression 2.0 + 3.0 evaluates to 5.0." Note that the symbol $\Rightarrow$ is *not* a part of the Pascal language but is part of our notation for discussing Pascal.

Now for some examples. Suppose that the following definitions and declarations apply

```
const
    taxRate = 0.0425;
var
    length, width : real;
```

and the variables *length* and *width* have the following values:

Variable	Value
length	25.7
width	10.0

The following are examples of expressions and their values. Note that we sometimes use the arrow notation to indicate intermediate steps in evaluating an expression as well as the final result.

$$3.14 \Rightarrow 3.14$$
$$taxRate \Rightarrow 0.0425$$
$$1000.0 * taxRate \Rightarrow 1000.0 * 0.0425 \Rightarrow 42.5$$
$$length \Rightarrow 25.7$$
$$2.0 * width \Rightarrow 2.0 * 10.0 \Rightarrow 20.0$$
$$length * width \Rightarrow 25.7 * 10.0 \Rightarrow 257.0$$

To summarize, a constant such as 3.14 evaluates to itself, a constant identifier evaluates to its defined value, and a variable evaluates to the value currently stored in the corresponding memory location. In expressions containing arithmetical operators such as *, constant identifiers and variables must be replaced by their values before arithmetical operations can be carried out.

The Assignment Statement

Assignment is the operation of storing a new value in a memory location and thus changing the value of the corresponding variable; we say that the new value is *assigned* to the variable. A variable retains its assigned value until its value is changed by another assignment.

The most common way of assigning values to variables is with the *assignment statement*, which has the following form:

variable : = expression

When an assignment statement is executed, the expression is evaluated and its value is assigned to the variable. The assignment operator : = is usually read as "becomes." As a result of the assignment, the value of the variable "becomes" equal to the value of the expression.

We have seen that an expression can be a constant, a variable, or an expression formed with operators. Figure 2-4 illustrates the assignment statement for each of these three cases. Assume that all variables in Figure 2-4 have been declared as real variables.

The assignment statement

creditLimit : = 1000.00

Figure 2-4. Execution of an assignment statement when the expression to the right of the assignment operator is (a) a constant, (b) a variable, and (c) an expression formed with operators.

(a)   *creditLimit* := 1000.0

(b)   *maxTotal* := *creditLimit*

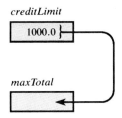

(c)   *volume* := *length* * *width* * *height*

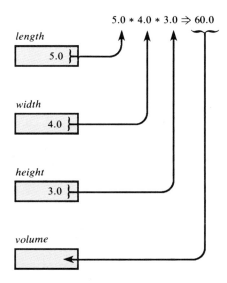

illustrates the case in which the expression is a constant. As shown in part (a) of this figure, the value 1000.0 is stored in the memory location named *creditLimit*.

The assignment statement

   maxTotal := *creditLimit*

illustrates the case in which the expression is a variable. As shown in part (b), the value in the memory location named *creditLimit* is copied into the location named *maxTotal*. The contents of the location *creditLimit* are unaffected.

The assignment statement

$$volume := length * width * height$$

illustrates the case in which the expression is formed with operators. As shown in part (c), the variables *length*, *width*, and *height* are replaced by their values, the three values are multiplied together, and the product is stored in the location named *volume*.

Beginners are sometimes confused by assignment statements such as

$$total := total + 23.7$$

in which the same variable appears on both sides of the assignment operator. But the interpretation of such statements is simple. The value that the variable has before the assignment statement is executed is used in evaluating the expression. The value of the expression then becomes the new value of the variable. Thus if *total* has the value 120.0 before the statement is executed, it will have the value 143.7 afterwards.

A variable is used differently depending on whether it appears on the right or left side of the assignment operator. When a variable appears on the right side of the assignment operator, its *value* is used to help evaluate an expression. When it appears on the left side of the assignment operator, its *name* is used to designate the memory location in which a new value is to be stored. This observation can be generalized. Whenever a variable appears in an expression or where an expression is expected, the value of the variable is used. When a variable appears where the name of a memory location is expected, the variable name is used to designate the corresponding memory location.

readln and More about *writeln*

readln.   The procedure *readln* reads data values from a file and assigns them to variables specified by the programmer. When no other file is specified, the data values are read from the standard input file *input*. The variables that are to receive new values are supplied as parameters when *readln* is called. For example, the procedure statement

$$readln\ (length,\ width,\ height)$$

reads three values from the standard input file and assigns the first value to *length*, the second to *width*, and the third to *height*.

Each data value must have the same type as the variable to which it is to be assigned; thus, if *length*, *width*, and *height* have been declared as real variables, the input must consist of three real values. Real data values are written in the same way as in Pascal programs, except that the decimal point can be omitted. Successive input values are separated by spaces or line breaks. For example, if the input file contains the line

```
32.9  17  2.8
```

the preceding *readln* statement will assign *length*, *width*, and *height* the following values:

Variable	Value
length	32.9
width	17.0
height	2.8

The data values can be separated by line breaks as well as spaces. Therefore, *length*, *width*, and *height* would receive the same values if the input was

```
32.9 17
2.8
```

or

```
32.9
17 2.8
```

or

```
32.9
17
2.8
```

After *readln* has assigned values to all its parameters, it discards all the text remaining on the current input line. For example, suppose that the statements

> *readln (length)*;
> *readln (width)*;
> *readln (height)*

are executed, and the input data is

```
38.2 29.1 18
30 28.5 3.8
2.9 4.5
```

Only the first value on each line is read; the remaining values are discarded. Thus values are assigned to the variables as follows:

Variable	Value
length	38.2
width	30.0
height	2.9

Since 4.5 is discarded, the next *readln* statement executed will have to begin reading from the next line of data in the input file. Thus, *readln* always reads to the end of a line, even though it may have to discard some of the values. It is this property that gives rise to the abbreviation *ln* (for "line") in the procedure name *readln*.

More about writeln. The procedure *writeln* allows the programmer to supply *field-width parameters* that control the appearance of the printed output.

To get real values printed in conventional (as opposed to scientific) notation, we must supply two field-width parameters. The first field-width parameter gives the number of character positions that will be reserved for the number in the printout; the second field-width parameter gives the number of decimal places that will be printed. A field-width parameter is separated from the preceding parameter by a colon, which distinguishes the field-width parameter from a parameter representing a value to be printed.

The area of the printout reserved for a printed value is called a *field*. The size of the field is governed by the first field-width parameter. A real number is positioned in its field as far to the right as possible, and any unused positions in the field are filled with spaces. For example, consider the *writeln* statement

> *writeln* (3.1416 :8:3)

The value 3.1416 is to be rounded off to three decimal places and printed in an eight-character field. To make it easy to count the unused positions in a field, we will place a dot in each unused position. The dots are not actually printed; in reality, a space is printed for each unused position. With this convention, the output produced by the preceding *writeln* statement can be represented as follows:

> ···3.142

The printed value is preceded by three spaces so that the printed value exactly fills an eight-character field. If the *writeln* statement had been

> *writeln* (3.1416 :8:2)

the printout would be

> ····3.14

Since only two decimal places are printed, four leading spaces are needed to fill the eight-character field.

If the size of the number to be printed exceeds the size of the field specified by the first field-width parameter, Pascal ignores the first field-width parameter and takes as many character positions as needed to print the number. If we use 1 for the first field-width parameter, Pascal will use only as many character positions as needed to print the number and will never supply any leading spaces. We usually use a field-width parameter of 1 when a number is to be inserted in running text (such as a sentence) where we do not want it preceded by any extraneous spaces.

We can supply *writeln* with any number of parameters. A parameter representing a value to be printed is separated from the preceding parameter (if any) by a comma; a field-width parameter is separated from the preceding parameter by a colon. For example, the statement

> *writeln* (3.5 :6:2, 1.23 :8:2, −6.54 :10:1)

causes the computer to print

> ··3.50····1.23······−6.5

Again, we have used centered dots to represent spaces.

A common use of a *writeln* statement is to print a number embedded in identifying text:

> *writeln* ('Total weight is ', 175.32 :1:2 ' pounds')

This statement causes the computer to print

```
Total weight is 175.32 pounds
```

Note that a space at the end of the first string constant and one at the beginning of the second string constant separate the text from the number. The use of 1 for the first field-width parameter prevents any extraneous spaces from being inserted between the number and the preceding text.

writeln can be called with no parameters, in which case the parentheses surrounding the parameter list are also omitted.

> *writeln*

When *writeln* is called without any parameters, it just causes the output device to go to the beginning of a new line. If the output device was already at the beginning of a new line, that line will be skipped. Thus *writeln* without any parameters is often used to skip a line in the printout.

read, write, and Prompts

readln and *writeln* always process to the end of a line; *readln* reads to the end of a line even if it has to discard some of the values read, and *writeln* always finishes up by sending the output device to a new line. The procedures *read* and *write* are similar to *readln* and *writeln* but do not insist on processing to the end of a line. *read* will stop reading within a line of input without losing the remaining values on the line, and *write* does not send the output device to a new line after it has finished printing.

For example, consider the following *read* statements:

> *read (length)*;
> *read (width)*;
> *read (height)*

Suppose that the input data is

```
35.7 12.3 4.9 3.1
```

The variables *length, width,* and *height* are assigned values as follows:

Variable	Value
length	35.7
width	12.3
height	4.9

What's more, the value 3.1 remains to be read by the next *read* or *readln* statement that is executed.

Now consider the following *write* statements;

> *writeln ('com')*;
> *writeln ('put')*;
> *writeln ('er')*

These statements produce the following printout:

```
computer
```

What's more, the output device is now positioned immediately after the *r* of "computer"; the next *write* or *writeln* statement to be executed will begin printing at that position.

A common application of *write* and *readln* is to prompt the user to enter some data and accept the user's response. Using *write* rather than *writeln* allows the prompt and response to appear on the same line. For example, consider the following statements:

> *write* ('Enter amount of purchase: ');
> *readln* (*amount*)

These statements print the prompt and wait for the user to type a number and hit the Return or Enter key. Note that the prompt ends with a space to separate the prompt from the value typed by the user. The value that the user enters is assigned to *amount*. The following is a typical exchange with the user:

```
Enter amount of purchase: 250.75
```

After this exchange, *amount* has the value 250.75.

Often a question mark is used to indicate that a value is being requested.

> *write* ('Amount of purchase? ');
> *readln* (*amount*)

After the exchange

```
Amount of purchase? 512.89
```

the value 512.89 is assigned to *amount*.

Some computer systems may not be able to display an incomplete line, with the result that *write* cannot be used for prompts. For such systems, use *writeln* for prompts; prompts and responses will then appear on separate lines.

Problem Solving and Stepwise Refinement

Programming is a problem-solving activity. The specification for a program poses a problem that the programmer solves by writing a program to accomplish the specified task. The following four steps, which outline a general approach to solving any problem, can serve as guidelines for developing a program:

- Understand the problem.
- Devise a plan to solve it.
- Carry out the plan.
- Check the results.

In programming terms, understanding the problem means knowing the input data for the program, the output the program must produce, and how the desired output is related to the given input. Devising a plan means planning the structure of the program and deciding what task will be accomplished by each part; one means of accomplishing this is to outline the program in pseudocode. Carrying out the plan means coding the program. Checking the results means testing the program to see that it accomplishes the specified task.

We will illustrate these techniques by applying them to a typical problem. We wish to write a program that, given the amount of a purchase and the sales tax rate, will compute the sales tax and the amount the customer must pay. Figure 2-5 shows the completed program.

Understanding the Problem

Given a programming problem, the first question to ask is what is the input data. The answer in this case is the amount of the purchase and the sales tax rate. The sales tax rate should be entered as a percentage—the user would enter 4.5 for a 4.5 percent rate—because this is the way in which sales tax rates are usually stated. Because the program is interactive, it will need to prompt the user for each item of input data.

The next question is what output the program should produce; in this case, it is the sales tax and the amount to be paid. Each item of output should be accompanied by an identifying label; there is nothing more annoying than

Figure 2-5. Program to compute the sales tax on a purchase.

```
program ComputeSalesTax (input, output);

{ Given the cost of a purchase and the sales tax rate, compute the sales tax
  and the total amount to be paid }

const
    convConst = 100.0;        { converts percent to decimal }
var
    amountOfPurchase,         { amount to be taxed }
    percentRate,              { sales tax rate as percent }
    decimalRate,              { sales tax rate as decimal }
    salesTax,                 { sales tax on purchase }
    totalAmount      : real; { amount to be paid }
begin

    { Obtain input from user }

    write ('Amount of purchase? ');
    readln (amountOfPurchase);
    write ('Sales tax rate (in percent)? ');
    readln (percentRate);

    { Calculate results }

    decimalRate := percentRate / convConst;
    salesTax := amountOfPurchase * decimalRate;
    totalAmount := amountOfPurchase + salesTax;

    { Print results }

    writeln ('The sales tax is $', salesTax :1:2);
    writeln ('Please pay $', totalAmount :1:2)
end.
```

a program that prints unlabeled numbers and leaves it up to the user to guess their meaning.

The final question concerns the relation between the input and the output. How is the desired output to be calculated from the given input? The best way to clarify this point is to work through a numerical example, preferably using numbers we can easily manipulate in our heads. Suppose the amount of the purchase is $1,000 and the sales tax rate is 4.5 percent. We recall from arithmetic that before a percentage can be used in an arithmetical calculation it must be converted to a decimal, which we do by moving the decimal point two places to the left. Moving the decimal point two places to the left is equivalent to dividing by 100. Thus our first step is to compute the decimal sales tax rate as follows:

$$4.5 / 100 = 0.045$$

The sales tax is just the amount of the purchase multiplied by the decimal sales tax rate.

$$1000 * 0.045 = 45$$

The total amount the customer must pay is the amount of the purchase ($1,000) plus the sales tax ($45).

$$1000 + 45 = 1045$$

With these figures, a typical dialogue between the user and the program we are to write would go like this.

```
Amount of purchase? 1000
Sales tax rate (in percent)? 4.5
The sales tax is $45.00
Please pay $1045.00
```

Devising a Plan

One of the most important techniques of program development is *stepwise refinement*. We begin with a rough outline of the major steps that a program must take; we then repeatedly refine this outline by showing how each step can be realized by a series of simpler actions. The refinement process continues until the steps are small enough and simple enough to be translated directly into Pascal statements.

Like many other programs, ours will obtain input data from the user, do calculations, and print its results. All such programs follow the same rough outline.

1. Obtain input from user
2. Calculate results
3. Print results

We can now refine this rough outline by filling in details for each step. Two items of input are required: the amount of the purchase and the sales tax rate. Thus our first refinement is

1. Obtain input from user
   1.1 Obtain amount of purchase from user
   1.2 Obtain sales tax rate from user

2. Calculate results
3. Print results

The user must be prompted for each input value and the value entered in response to each prompt must be read by the program. Thus our next refinement of the input process is as follows:

1. Obtain input from user
    1.1   Obtain amount of purchase from user
        1.1.1   Prompt user for amount of purchase
        1.1.2   Input amount of purchase
    1.2   Obtain sales tax rate from user
        1.2.1   Prompt user for sales tax rate in percent
        1.2.2   Input percentage sales tax rate
2. Calculate results
3. Print results

Step 1 has been refined to the point that it can be easily translated into Pascal *write* and *readln* statements. Let us, therefore, move on to step 2. From the numerical example that we worked out, we see that the calculation requires three steps:

    2.1   Convert the percentage sales tax rate to a decimal
    2.2   Compute the sales tax
    2.3   Compute the amount the customer must pay

There are two results to be printed: the sales tax and the amount that the customer must pay. Thus step 3 can be broken down into two steps, each corresponding to a Pascal *writeln* statement.

    3.1   Print sales tax
    3.2   Print amount that customer must pay

Inserting the refinements of steps 2 and 3 into the original outline gives us the complete pseudocode for our program.

1. Obtain input from user
    1.1   Obtain amount of purchase from user
        1.1.1   Prompt user for amount of purchase
        1.1.2   Input amount of purchase
    1.2.   Obtain sales tax rate from user
        1.2.1   Prompt user for sales tax rate in percent
        1.2.2   Input percentage sales tax rate
2. Calculate results
    2.1   Convert the percentage sales tax rate to a decimal
    2.2   Compute the sales tax
    2.3   Compute the amount the customer must pay

3. Print results
   3.1 Print sales tax
   3.2 Print amount that customer must pay

Carrying Out the Plan

Before starting to translate English descriptions into Pascal statements, we must define any constant identifiers and choose variables to hold the data values that the program will manipulate. We define a constant identifier *convConst* (conversion constant) for the constant 100.0 used to convert a percentage rate to a decimal rate.

We need a real variable to hold each of the input values obtained from the user; for these variables we choose the names *amountOfPurchase* and *percentRate*. We will also need a real variable for storing each of the calculated values; for this purpose we declare the variables *decimalRate*, *salesTax*, and *totalAmount*.

We can now write the definition and declaration parts of the sales tax program.

```
const
    convConst = 100.0;        { converts percent to decimal }
var
    amountOfPurchase,         { amount to be taxed }
    percentRate,              { sales tax ratc as percent }
    decimalRate,              { sales tax rate as decimal }
    salesTax,                 { sales tax on purchase }
    totalAmount      : real; { amount to be paid }
```

We now turn to the statement part of the program and the statements corresponding to step 1 of the pseudocode. Steps 1.1.1, 1.1.2, 1.2.1, and 1.2.2 each becomes a *write* or *readln* statement.

```
write ('Amount of purchase? ');
readln (amountOfPurchase);
write ('Sales tax rate (in percent)? ');
readln (percentRate)
```

Steps 2.1, 2.1, and 2.3 each becomes an assignment statement.

```
decimalRate := percentRate / convConst;
salesTax := amountOfPurchase * decimalRate;
totalAmount := amountOfPurchase + salesTax
```

Note that the Pascal statements carry out exactly the same arithmetical operations that we carried out in working the numerical example.

Steps 3.1 and 3.2 each becomes a *writeln* statement.

```
writeln ('The sales tax is $', salesTax :1:2);
writeln ('Please pay $', totalAmount :1:2)
```


Checking the Results: Testing and Debugging

Programming is an error-prone activity; most programs will have at least some errors, or *bugs*, that need to be corrected. Thus testing (determining if the program solves the given problem) and debugging (finding and correcting any errors revealed by testing) are major parts of the program development process. It is not unusual for more time to be spent on testing and debugging than on specification, design, and coding.

Programmers cope with three kinds of errors: *syntax errors*, *run-time errors*, and *logic errors*.

Syntax Errors. Syntax errors are errors in the use of the programming language. Beginners may commit syntax errors because of insufficient knowledge or experience—for example, because of forgetting the correct format of a programming-language construction. But even experienced programmers commit syntax errors because of slips of the finger while typing or careless mistakes in punctuation and spelling. The most common syntax errors in Pascal are omitted semicolons, misspelled reserved words, and inconsistently spelled identifiers.

Syntax errors are the easiest to find because they are detected and reported by the Pascal compiler. Compiler error messages can sometimes be misleading, however. The compiler processes the program from beginning to end and reports an error when it encounters a program construction that is inconsistent with the part of the program that has already been processed. The actual error, however, may occur earlier in the program. For example, if a semicolon or other required symbol is omitted, the compiler will often mark the next symbol in the program as erroneous. Another example: if an identifier is misspelled when it is declared but spelled correctly when it is used, the compiler will mark the uses as erroneous even though the actual error occurred in the declaration.

Some compilers will generate many error messages as a result of a single error. For example, if the definition or declaration of an identifier is omitted or incorrect, every use of the identifier will be marked as an error.

Students sometimes believe that when they have corrected all of their syntax errors, their programs must be correct. Nothing could be further from the truth. It is all too easy to write a program that obeys all the rules of Pascal but still does not give the computer the proper instructions for accomplishing the desired task. Finding syntax errors should be thought of as a preliminary exercise that must be gotten out of the way before real program testing can begin.

Run-time Errors. Even though a program is written in flawless Pascal, it may still instruct the computer to carry out an impossible operation, such as dividing by zero, or the program may exceed some limitation on the system, such as trying to use more memory than is available or trying to send data to a nonexistent output device. Such errors cannot be detected by the compiler; they can only be detected when the program is actually running: hence the name *run-time error*. Ideally, the computer system will report the error to the programmer, giving the nature of the error and stating the program line in which the error occurred. Less ideally, the system may give an obscure error code that will leave the programmer guessing as to what really happened. Still less ideally, the error may cause a system crash: the computer system will stop working until it is reinitialized or "rebooted" by reloading the operating system.

Many compilers have debugging options that cause the compiler to generate additional machine code to simplify the detection of run-time errors.

Some options cause data values to be tested for validity before certain operations are applied to them, therefore detecting erroneous values as soon as possible and preventing erroneous values from causing system crashes. Other options improve run-time error messages; one such option might have the error message give the line number of the program line in which the error occurred. Such debugging options should always be enabled when a program is being tested. These options are usually disabled when the final "production" version of the program is compiled, because the extra machine code that they generate takes up memory and slows down the execution of the program.

Logic Errors. Logic errors do not violate any rule of Pascal but just give the computer incorrect instructions for the task to be carried out. Sometimes logic errors cause run-time errors—cause the computer to attempt impossible operations—but they do not always do so. Sometimes they just cause the computer to do something other than what the programmer desired, such as arriving at an incorrect answer to a mathematical problem. Only thorough and systematic program testing can find run-time and logic errors, and there is no way to ever guarantee that all such errors have been found.

Elements of Program Testing.   There are two basic methods of program testing known as the *black box* and *glass box* techniques. In the former, the program is considered to be hidden away inside a black box so that its internal structure and operation cannot be observed. All we can do is feed input data into the black box and observe the results that come out. The glass box approach, on the other hand, allows us to monitor the internal operation of the program in addition to observing the output that it is intended to produce in normal operation.

Black box testing is analogous to testing an appliance by turning it on, operating its controls, and observing the extent to which it does or does not do what it is supposed to. Glass box testing corresponds to removing the appliance from its case and using test instruments, such as voltmeters and pressure gauges, to monitor its internal operation.

Because the program in Figure 2-5 is so simple, testing is misleadingly easy. Black box testing with a few simple sets of test data (such as $1000 for the amount of purchase and 4.5 percent for the sales tax rate) will quickly reveal whether or not the program is doing its calculations properly.

If black box testing reveals that the program is not performing properly, we will usually want to move on to glass box testing to determine which statement or statements are erroneous. The simplest form of glass box testing involves monitoring the values assigned to the variables during program execution. Some program development systems will automatically monitor the values of selected variables while the program is running. When such automatic monitoring is not available, the same effect can be had by temporarily inserting additional *writeln* statements into the program. These *writeln* statements display the values of selected variables at various points in the program's execution.

For example, suppose an imperfectly typed copy of the program in Figure 2-5 is producing incorrect results. The values of *salesTax* and *amountOfPurchase* are normally printed by the program, so we know what values are assigned to these variables. To further test the program's operation, however, we would like to know that the proper values are being read for *amountOfPurchase* and *percentRate*, and that the proper value is being computed for *decimalRate*. To determine the values assigned to these three variables, we can insert the following *writeln* statements immediately after the assignment statement that computes *decimalRate*:

```
writeln ('*** TEST OUTPUT ***');
writeln ('amountOfPurchase = ', amountOfPurchase :1:2);
writeln('percentRate  = ', percentRate :1:2);
writeln('decimalRate  =  ', decimalRate :1:4);
writeln ('*** END OF TEST OUTPUT ***')
```

Suppose, for example, that on a particular test run these statements produce the following output:

```
*** TEST OUTPUT ***
amountOfPurchase = 1000.00
percentRate = 4.50
decimalRate = 0.4500
*** END OF TEST OUTPUT ***
```

Inspection of the test output reveals that the value of *decimalRate* is too large by a factor of ten. (For a percent rate of 4.5, the decimal rate should be 0.045.) This observation immediately narrows the error down to the assingment statement that calculates *decimalRate* or (more likely) to the definition of *convConst*.

Procedures

A *module* is a part of a program that performs a well-defined function and can be designed, coded, and tested independently of the rest of the program. *Modularity* is the property enjoyed by programs that are constructed out of independent modules. Modularity is essential to the divide-and-conquer approach to programming (of which stepwise refinement is an example) in which a problem is broken down into simpler parts, which are then broken down into still simpler parts, and so on.

Different programming languages provide different constructions for implementing modules. In Pascal, modules are implemented as subprograms, which include procedures (introduced in this chapter) and functions (introduced in Chapter 4). We are already familiar with the standard procedures *read*, *write*, *readln*, and *writeln*; in this section we will see how programmers can write their own procedures. In the next section we will see how to apply procedures to program design and construction.

A procedure is declared by a *procedure declaration*. A procedure declaration has much the same structure as a program.

procedure heading
block
semicolon

Only the heading and the terminating punctuation mark differ from the corresponding parts of a program. The block, which comprises the body of the procedure, is the same as for a program.

Subprogram declarations must be placed with the other definitions and declarations that precede the statement part of a block. Subprogram declarations follow the variable declaration part and precede the statement part.

Thus the structure of a block must be revised as follows:

> constant definition part
> variable declaration part
> subprogram declarations
> statement part

The alert reader will have noticed that a procedure declaration contains a block and a block can contain procedure declarations. This means that procedure declarations can be nested; a procedure declaration can contain another procedure declaration, which can contain still another procedure declaration, and so on. Such nesting, however makes the program text hard to read and so is usually avoided in contemporary programming styles. Thus subprogram declarations are usually placed only in the block that defines the entire program rather than in the blocks associated with other subprogram declarations.

The *actual* parameters of a procedure are the parameters that are supplied when the procedure is called in a procedure statement. For example, in the procedure statement

> *readln* (*length*, *width*, *height*)

the variables *length*, *width*, and *height* are the actual parameters.

The actual parameters are not known when a procedure is written; indeed, one procedure can be called with many different sets of actual parameters. To provide a means of referring to the actual parameters from within a procedure declaration, identifiers called *formal parameters* are declared in the procedure heading, which has the following form:

> **procedure** procedure-name (formal-parameter-declarations);

The formal parameters correspond to the actual parameters one-to-one. The first formal parameter declared in the procedure heading refers to the first actual parameter in the procedure statement; the second formal parameter declared in the procedure heading refers to the second actual parameter in the procedure statement, and so on. The formal parameter declarations often occupy more than one line, so that the closing parenthesis in the procedure heading may be on a different line than the opening parenthesis.

Pascal allows several kinds of subprogram parameters; the most important of these are *value parameters*, which allow values to be passed to subprograms, and *variable parameters*, which give the subprogram access to variables declared in the calling program. For our present purposes, variable parameters are the most useful because they allow values to be passed in both directions between a calling program and a subprogram. Value parameters, on the other hand, are "one-way streets" that only allow values to be passed from the calling program to the subprogram.

Formal parameter declarations are similar to variable declarations; each consists of the identifier being declared followed by a colon and a type identifier. The declaration of a variable parameter is preceded by the reserved word **var**; adjacent declarations are separated by semicolons.

For example, the following procedure heading declares four variable parameters:

> **procedure** *Compute Volume* (**var** *length* : *real*;
> **var** *width* : *real*;
> **var** *height* : *real*;
> **var** *volume* : *real*);

Each occurrence of **var** declares the corresponding parameter to be a variable parameter. Each occurrence of *real* declares the corresponding parameter to be a real parameter—the corresponding actual parameter must be a real variable.

As with variable declarations, formal parameter declarations can sometimes be combined so that the word **var** and the type identifier do not have to be repeated. For example, the preceding example can be rewritten as follows:

> **procedure** *ComputeVolume* (**var** *length,*
> width,
> height,
> volume : real*);

Beware of omitting the word **var** for variable parameters; this hard-to-find error will often not be detected by the compiler, but will have the effect that no results will be returned from the subprogram to the calling program. (The error changes the parameters to value parameters, which cannot be used to return results.)

Formal variable parameters stand in place of the variables that will be provided as actual parameters when the procedure is called. Thus the formal parameters can be used just like variables; we can use them in expressions and we can assign values to them. The following is a complete procedure using the preceding procedure heading:

> **procedure** *ComputeVolume* (**var** *length,*
> width,
> height,
> volume : real);
> **begin**
>   volume : = length * width * height
> **end**;

When this procedure is executed, each formal parameter will refer to the corresponding actual parameter (which must be a variable). The effect is the same as if the actual parameters were substituted for the formal parameters in the statement part of the procedure. For example, suppose that *lnth, wdth, hght,* and *vlm* are real variables, and the following statements are executed:

> lnth   : = 30.0;
> wdth : = 20.0;
> hght : = 10.0;
> *ComputeVolume* (lnth, wdth, hght, vlm)

When the procedure is called, the statement part of the procedure is executed with the formal parameters replaced by the corresponding actual parameters. Thus the effect of the procedure call is the same as if the statement

> vlm : = lnth * wdth * hght

has been executed. When the procedure returns control to the calling program, the values of *lnth, wdth,* and *hght* will remain unchanged, and the value of *vlm* will be 6000.0, the product of the values of *lnth, wdth,* and *hght*.

Identifiers defined or declared in a subprogram (including the formal parameters but not the name of the subprogram) are said to be *local* to the declaration. The definitions and declarations for local identifiers are valid only within the subprogram declaration in which the identifier definitions and declarations appear. Local identifiers cannot be referred to, and indeed do not even exist, outside the subprogram in which they are defined or declared. Different subprograms can have local identifiers with the same spelling; identically spelled local identifiers defined or declared in different subprograms have nothing to do with one another. Likewise, local identifiers can have the same spelling as identifiers declared in the main program (the program with all subprogram declarations excluded); again, the identically spelled identifiers have nothing to do with each other.

More generally, every identifier has a *scope*, which is the part of a program in which the identifier is defined and can be referred to. The scope of an identifier extends from its point of declaration to the end of the program or subprogram in which the declaration appears. When identically spelled identifiers are declared in the main program and in a subprogram, the scope of the identifier declared in the main program has a hole in it that coincides with the scope of the identically spelled identifier in the subprogram. Thus, each use of the identifier in the subprogram refers to the declaration in the subprogram and not to the declaration of the identically spelled identifier in the main program. A more general discussion of identifier scopes is given in Chapter 12.

In particular, for variable parameters, we often use the same names for the actual parameters in a procedure statement and the corresponding formal parameters in the procedure declaration. This naming convention can clarify the program by making it obvious at a glance which formal parameter corresponds to which actual parameter. On the other hand, there is a danger that the reader might actually confuse the actual and formal parameters. The actual parameters are declared in the calling program; the formal parameters are declared in the subprogram. Thus the identifiers that name the actual parameters have nothing to do with the identifiers that name the formal parameters, even if the names of some actual parameters are spelled in the same way as the names of some formal parameters.

Top-Down Development with Procedures

In stepwise refinement, we start with a rough outline of a program, then refine the outline by showing how each step in the rough outline can be realized by a sequence of smaller and simpler steps. Those simpler steps can be refined still further, and so on, until we arrive at steps simple enough to be translated directly into Pascal statements.

With procedures, we can apply this divide-and-conquer strategy directly to the program code rather than to an outline. We convert our original rough outline into a main program by translating each outline step into a call to an (as yet unwritten) procedure. We then refine not the outline but the program code itself by writing the procedures called by the main program. When we write the procedures called by the main program, we can include calls to other not-yet-written procedures. We then refine the program further by writing the procedures called by the procedures called by the main program, and so on. The refinement process stops when the procedures become simple enough that they can accomplish their tasks without calling any other procedures (except predefined ones such as *writeln*).

This program-development technique is called *top-down development* because we start at the top level with the main program and work down to the second-level procedures called by the main program, the third-level procedures called by the second-level procedures, and so on.

Let's apply top-down development to the sales tax program that we previously constructed by stepwise refinement. Our analysis of the problem will proceed in the same way and lead us to the same rough outline.

1. Obtain amount of purchase and percentage tax rate
2. Calculate sales tax and total amount to be paid
3. Print sales tax and total amount to be paid

Instead of refining this outline directly, however, we want to convert it into a main program by translating each outline step into a procedure call.

Before we can translate the outline into a main program, however, we must choose variables to store the data passed to and returned by the procedures. We will use somewhat shorter variable names in this version of the program than in the previous one to prevent some of our declarations and diagrams from being too cumbersome. Thus we will use *amount* for the amount of purchase, *rate* for the percentage tax rate, *tax* for the computed sales tax, and *total* for the total amount to be paid.

Figure 2-6 shows the main program. The variables just mentioned are declared as follows:

```
var
    amount,        { amount to be taxed }
    rate,          { sales tax rate as percent }
    tax,           { sales tax on purchase }
    total    : real; { amount to be paid }
```

Figure 2-6.   Main program for the version of the sales tax program constructed with procedures.

---

program *ComputeSalesTax* (*input, output*);

{ Given the cost of a purchase and the sales tax rate, compute the sales tax and the total amount to be paid }

```
var
    amount,        { amount to be taxed }
    rate,          { sales tax rate as percent }
    tax,           { sales tax on purchase }
    total    : real; { amount to be paid }
```

{ *** Procedure declarations not yet written *** }

```
begin
    GetData (amount, rate);
    ComputeTax (amount, rate, tax, total);
    PrintResults (tax, total)
end.
```

The statement part of the main program contains a procedure call for each step of the pseudocode outline.

> GetData (*amount, rate*);
> Compute Tax (*amount, rate, tax, total*);
> PrintResults (*tax, total*)

The procedure *GetData* (which, of course, has not yet been written) must accomplish step 1 by obtaining the amount of purchase and the tax rate from the user and assigning these to *amount* and *rate*. The procedure *ComputeTax* must accomplish step 2 by calculating the sales tax and the total amount to be paid; *amount* and *rate* provide the data for the calculation; *tax* and *total* receive the results. The procedure *PrintResults* must accomplish step 3 by printing the sales tax and the total amount to be paid; *tax* and *total* supply the data values to be printed.

With the main program complete, we now turn our attention to writing the procedure declaration for *GetData*. This procedure must obtain the amount of the purchase and the sales tax rate. We can thus outline the procedure in pseudocode as follows:

1. Obtain amount of purchase from user
2. Obtain sales tax rate from user

From our previous experience we know that each of these steps can be accomplished by a call to two standard procedures, *write* and *readln*. Thus *GetData* will not have to call any not-yet-written procedures to accomplish its purpose.

Figure 2-7 shows the complete procedure declaration for *GetData*. We have given the formal parameters the same names as the corresponding actual parameters. As already mentioned, however, we must not confuse the formal parameters with the corresponding main program variables in spite of the fact that they have the same names. Each formal parameter is accompanied by a comment indicating whether it provides the procedure with input data or (as is the case for both of the parameters of this procedure) receives output produced by the procedure. With the formal parameters decided upon, we can easily translate the preceding pseudocode into the statement part of the procedure.

Figure 2-7.   Procedure for reading input data for sales tax calculation.

```
procedure GetData (var amount,          { output }
                        rate     : real); { output }

{ Get amount of purchase and sales tax rate }

begin
   write ('Amount of Purchase? ');
   readln (amount);
   write ('Sales tax rate (in percent)? ');
   readln (rate)
end; { GetData }
```

```
write ('Amount of purchase? ');
readln (amount);
write ('Sales tax rate (in percent)? ');
readln (rate)
```

Note that the formal parameters *amount* and *rate* can, in turn, be passed as actual parameters to the procedure *readln*.

We proceed in the same way with the procedure *ComputeTax*. This procedure must accomplish the second step of the main program outline, which is to compute the sales tax and the amount the customer must pay. The pseudocode for this procedure is as follows:

1. Convert the percentage sales tax rate to a decimal
2. Compute the sales tax
3. Compute the amount the customer must pay

Figure 2-8 shows the complete procedure. Again, we give the formal parameters the same names as the corresponding actual parameters. Parameters *amount* and *rate* provide input data to the procedure; *tax* and *total* receive the procedure's results. We also need to define a constant *convConst* (for converting the tax rate from a percentage to a decimal) and a variable *decimalRate* (to store the converted rate).

```
const
    convConst = 100.0; { converts percent to decimal }
var
    decimalRate : real;  { sales tax rate as decimal }
```

Figure 2-8.

Procedure for computing sales tax on a purchase and total amount that customer must pay.

```
procedure ComputeTax (var amount,        { input }
                          rate,           { input }
                          tax,            { output }
                          total    : real); { output }

{ Compute sales tax and total amount to be paid from amount of purchase
    and sales tax rate }

const
    convConst = 100.0; { converts percent to decimal }
var
    decimalRate : real;  { sales tax rate as decimal }
begin
    decimalRate := rate / convConst;
    tax := amount * decimalRate;
    total := amount + tax
end; { ComputeTax }
```

With the definitions and declarations out of the way, we can easily translate the pseudocode into Pascal statements.

decimalRate := *rate* / *convConst*;
tax := *amount* * *decimalRate*;
total := *amount* + *tax*

Finally, we must write the procedure *PrintResults*, which prints the values of *tax* and *total*. The pseudocode for the procedure is as follows:

1. Print sales tax
2. Print amount that customer must pay

Figure 2-9 shows the complete procedure declaration. Again, we give the formal parameters the same names as the corresponding actual parameters; both parameters supply input to the procedure. The pseudocode steps translate into Pascal code as follows:

writeln ('The sales tax is $', *tax* :1:2);
writeln ('Please pay $', *total* :1:2)

Figure 2-10 shows the entire sales tax program, with all the procedure declarations in place. To make the individual procedure declarations stand out, each is preceded by a comment consisting of a horizontal line and the procedure name, such as

{ ---------------------------- Procedure *GetData* ---------------------------- }

The statement part of the main program is preceded by the comment

{ -------------------------------- Main Program -------------------------------- }

Note that the procedure declarations separate the definitions and declarations of the main program from its statement part; for large programs, the two parts of the main program will be on different pages. This is an annoying characteristic of Pascal.

We can display the structure of our program with the *structure chart* shown in Figure 2-11. The topmost box represents the main program; the remaining boxes represent procedures. Lines connect the box for the main program to the boxes for each of the procedures that the main program calls.

Figure 2-9.   Procedure for printing results of sales tax calculation.

---

procedure *PrintResults* (**var** *tax*,   { input }
                                    total : *real*); { input }

{ Print sales tax and total amount to be paid }

begin
    writeln ('The sales tax is $', *tax* :1:2);
    writeln ('Please pay $', *total* :1:2)
end; { *PrintResults* }

Figure 2-10.

Complete code for the version of the sales tax program constructed with procedures.

```
program ComputeSalesTax (input, output);

{ Given the cost of a purchase and the sales tax rate, compute the sales tax
  and the total amount to be paid }

var
    amount,         { amount to be taxed }
    rate,           { sales tax rate as percent }
    tax,            { sales tax on purchase }
    total    : real; { amount to be paid }

{ -------------------------------- Procedure GetData  ------------------------------- }

procedure GetData (var amount,          { output }
                       rate     : real); { output }

{ Get amount of purchase and sales tax rate }

begin
    write ('Amount of purchase? ');
    readln (amount);
    write ('Sales tax rate (in percent)? ');
    readln (rate)
end; { GetData }

{ ----------------------------- Procedure ComputeTax ----------------------------- }

procedure ComputeTax (var amount,          { input }
                          rate,            { input }
                          tax,             { output }
                          total    : real; { output }

{ Compute sales tax and total amount to be paid from amount of purchase
  and sales tax rate }

const
    convConst = 100.0; { converts percent to decimal }
var
    decimalRate : real;  { sales tax rate as decimal }
begin
    decimalRate := rate / convConst;
    tax := amount * decimalRate;
    total := amount + tax
end; { ComputeTax }
```

Figure 2-10. *Continued.*

{ ------------------------------ Procedure *PrintResults* ----------------------------- }

procedure *PrintResults* (**var** *tax*,   { input }
                   total : *real*); { input }

{ Print sales tax and total amount to be paid }

begin
   writeln ('The sales tax is $', *tax* :1:2);
   writeln ('Please pay $', *total* :1:2)
end; { *PrintResults* }

{ ------------------------------------- Main Program ----------------------------------- }

begin
   GetData (*amount*, *rate*);
   ComputeTax (*amount*, *rate*, *tax*, *total*);
   PrintResults (*tax*, *total*)
end.

Figure 2-11. Structure chart for the version of the sales tax program constructed with procedures.

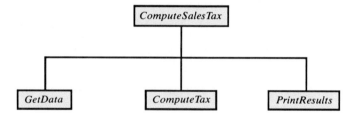

Note that the structure chart has the same form as the organization chart of a corporation. The main program corresponds to the president of the corporation; the procedures called by the main program correspond to the president's immediate subordinates.

The method of top-down development described in this section alternates design and coding; we design the main program and code it, then design and code each procedure called by the main program, and so on. But if we wish to complete the design before we begin coding, we could do so by building the structure chart from the top down and by writing the pseudocode for the main program and for each procedure as we add it to the structure chart. The structure chart and the pseudocode would then constitute our design; from it, we can code the main program and the procedures in any order that is convenient. The main program and the different procedures could even be coded by different people, a common practice for very large programs that are written by teams rather than individuals.

1. Describe the structure of the program heading.

2. Give the significance of the program parameters *input* and *output*.

3. What part of a program is bracketed by the reserved words **begin** and **end**? What is a compound statement?

4. What is a string constant? How is it written in Pascal? How is an apostrophe represented within a string constant?

5. What are identifiers? Give the rules according to which identifiers are formed. In what typeface are identifiers often printed?

6. What are reserved words? In what typeface are reserved words often printed?

7. What is a statement? Why might some other term be better than *statement*?

8. What is a procedure? A procedure statement? Procedure parameters?

9. Describe the structure of a block. What two Pascal constructions discussed in this chapter contain blocks?

10. What part of a block is introduced by the reserved word **const**?

11. What is a constant identifier? In what part of a program is a constant identifier defined?

12. What is a variable? Why is the term *variable* used?

13. What is a variable name? What is the value of a variable?

14. What do we mean when we say that *length* is a real variable?

15. What is the role of the variable declaration part of a block?

16. What is assignment? Give the general form of an assignment statement. What is the assignment operator in Pascal?

17. What is an expression? Give examples of three kinds of expressions considered in this chapter, and illustrate how each example is evaluated.

18. Consider an assignment statement in which variables appear in the expression to the right of the assignment operator. Which variable in this statement represents a memory location? Which variables represent values?

19. Contrast the *read* and *readln* statements.

20. Describe the use of field-width parameters.

21. Contrast the *write* and *writeln* statements.

22. When a variable appears in the list of items to be printed by a *write* or *writeln* statement, does the variable represent a value or a memory location? Why?

23. Do the variables whose values are to be read by a *read* or *readln* statement represent values or memory locations? Why?

24. What is the purpose of a prompt? What Pascal code is used to display a prompt and receive the user's response?

25. Summarize the reasoning process by which we arrive at a program for solving a given problem.

26. What is pseudocode? Describe stepwise refinement using pseudocode.

27. Describe the structure of a procedure declaration.

28. Describe the structure of a procedure heading.

29. Contrast actual and formal parameters. What is the distinguishing characteristic of variable parameters? If the formal parameters are variable parameters, what must the actual parameters be?

30. Contrast stepwise refinement using pseudocode with top-down development using procedures.

31. What is a structure chart? Describe how structure charts and pseudocode can be used to document a program design.

Exercises

1. Explain why each of the following identifiers is invalid.
   (a) *final score*
   (b) *R2-D2*
   (c) *4thDivision*
   (d) *begin*
   (e) *employee#*

2. Write a program to input a length expressed in feet and inches and output the same length expressed in centimeters. *Hint*: There are 2.54 centimeters in an inch.

3. Write a program to obtain five numbers from the user and print their average.

4. Salespeople at a certain company get an 8 percent commission on their sales. Write a program to input the amount that a person sold and output both the salesperson's commission and the amount the company receives after the salesperson's commission has been deducted. Use a constant identifier to represent the commission rate expressed as a decimal.

5. Items in a store are often sold at a discount from the list price, and the customer must pay sales tax on the total amount of the purchase. Write a program to input the list price of an item, the percentage discount, the number of items ordered, and the sales tax rate. The program should print the cost of the order before the discount is applied, the amount of the discount, the discounted cost, the amount of the sales tax, and the total amount that the customer must pay.

6. A video store sells tapes at five different prices and offers a discount that depends on the price of the tape. The following table shows the prices and discounts:

Price	Discount
19.95	0.75
29.95	1.50
39.95	3.25
59.95	8.00
79.97	12.70

Write a Pascal program to print this table. The prices and discounts should be represented in the program by real numbers, not by string constants. *Hints*: Specify the same field width for each entry in a particular column; a string constant can be followed in a *writeln* statement by a single field-width parameter that specifies the width of the field in which the string will be printed.

7. The batting average of a baseball player is calculated by subtracting the number of times the player walked from the number of times at bat and dividing the difference into the number of hits the player made. The result is traditionally expressed with three decimal places, as in 0.297. Write a program to obtain the necessary data from the user and compute the batting average. Why will this program fail if the player was walked every time he came to bat?

8. We can check an automobile speedometer for accuracy by noting the time required to travel a measured mile while maintaining a certain indicated speed. Write a program that will input the time in minutes and seconds required to travel between two milestones and output the speed the car was traveling.

9. Write a program that obtains from the user the length, width, and average depth of a pool and computes the number of gallons of water needed to fill the pool. The volume of water is the product of the length, width, and average depth. If the dimensions are in feet, the volume will be in cubic feet. *Hint*: Each cubic foot holds 7.48 gallons.

10. Write a program to convert temperatures from the Fahrenheit to the Celsius scale. The two scales are related as indicated by the following formula:

$$C = \frac{5}{9} (F - 32)$$

where F is the Fahrenheit temperature and C is the Celsius temperature. Some students may know how to translate this entire formula into a single Pascal assignment statement. However, it is also a useful exercise to carry out the calculation with a series of assignment statements, none of which uses more than one arithmetical operator.

11. A well-known trick for finding the height of a tree is to measure the length of the tree's shadow as well as the length of the shadow cast by some object of known height, such as yardstick. The height of the tree is then computed by dividing the height of the known object by the length of its shadow and multiplying the quotient by the length of the tree's shadow. Write a program to compute the height of a tree by this method after having obtained the necessary data from the user.

12. Write a program to compute the surface area of a box, given its length, width, and height.

13. Suppose that water flows into a container at a given rate (say in gallons per minute) and leaks out at a slower rate. Write a program that, given the two rates and the volume of the container, computes the time required for the container to fill up. Note that this program will not give a meaningful answer if the water is leaking out as fast as or faster than it is flowing in; often we must place restrictions on the input data to assure that a program will give a meaningful answer.

14. Write a program to print the following pattern of two diamonds:

```
        *
      * * *
    * * * * *
      * * *
        *
        *
      * * *
    * * * * *
      * * *
        *
```

Hint: Let the main program call twice in succession a procedure that prints one diamond.

15. As an exercise in top-down development, write a program to print the following pattern:

```
* * * # # # - - - O O O
- - - O O O * * * # # #
* * * # # # - - - O O O
- - - O O O * * * # # #
```

Note that the top half of the pattern is the same as the bottom half; both halves can be printed by calls to the same procedure. Within each half, each line is made up of the same two subpatterns: ***### and - - -OOO. Recall that a *write* statement leaves the output device on the same line after printing, whereas a *writeln* statement with no parameters will take the output device to a new line.

Types, Operators, and Control Structures

3

This chapter introduces additional features of the Pascal language, including the standard data types, the operators associated with each data type, more about the use of operators in expressions, and two control structures.

Standard Data Types

Pascal provides five standard predefined data types. All other types have to be defined by the programmer. The following table lists the five standard types and describes the values that belong to each:

Type	Description of Values
Boolean	The truth values *true* and *false*.
char	Characters such as the letters of the alphabet.
integer	Positive and negative whole numbers.
real	Positive and negative numbers containing decimal points.
text	Textfiles—files containing text such as English words, sentences, and paragraphs. The standard files *input* and *output* are textfiles.

Types *Boolean*, *char*, *integer*, and *real* are said to be *simple* because their values are not composed of values of other types. In contrast, type *text* is said to be *structured* because its values are composed of values of another type: a textfile contains values of type *char*. Detailed study of type *text* is deferred to Chapter 10, which is devoted to files. In this chapter we will focus on the simple standard types *Boolean*, *char*, *integer*, and *real*.

String constants do not belong to a standard (that is, predefined) data type. They belong to programmer-defined data types that are discussed in Chapter 11.

Type *Boolean*

Values of type *Boolean* are used to specify whether statements are true or false. For example, the answers to a true-false test could be represented entirely with values of type *Boolean*. Accordingly, type *Boolean* has two values, which are represented by the constants *true* and *false*.

There are three *Boolean operators*, **and**, **or**, and **not**, which take Boolean values as operands and return Boolean values as results. The Boolean operators correspond to the English conjunctions *and*, *or*, and *not*. If two English sentences are joined by *and*, the resulting compound sentence is true only if both of the sentences that were joined are true. Accordingly, the Boolean operator **and** returns the value *true* only if both of its operands have the value *true*. The following table completely defines the operator **and**:

Expression	Value
true **and** *true*	*true*
true **and** *false*	*false*
false **and** *true*	*false*
false **and** *false*	*false*

In English the word *or* can be used *exclusively* or *inclusively*. The exclusive use is more common. When you say, "I will have steak or chicken for lunch," we presume that you mean one or the other and are not considering having both. On the other hand, suppose you say, "I will come home this weekend if I finish studying for the test or if the test is postponed." This is an inclusive use of *or*, since presumably you would go home if both those situations came to pass. Because the exclusive use is the most common in English, we often use *and/or* when the inclusive use is intended. In computing, however, the inclusive use is the most common. Thus the Boolean operator **or** returns *true* if the values of either or both of its operands are *true*.

Expression	Value
true **or** *true*	*true*
true **or** *false*	*true*
false **or** *true*	*true*
false **or** *false*	*false*

The negation of a statement is true only if the original statement was false, and vice versa. Thus the Boolean operator **not** changes *true* to *false* and *false* to *true*.

Expression	Value
not *true*	*false*
not *false*	*true*

An ordering is defined for the values of each simple data type; given any two distinct values belonging to the same simple type, we can say whether one value precedes or follows the other in the order defined for the type. The order for values of type *Boolean* is not much used but, for the record, *false* precedes *true*.

Figure 3-1 summarizes the properties of type *Boolean*. Note that six *relational operators* are also defined for values of type *Boolean*. These operators, which are defined for all the simple (and some structured) types, will

Figure 3-1.

Type	*Boolean*
Values	*true*, *false*
Operators	
Boolean	**and**, **or**, **not**
Relational	$=, <, >, <=, >=, <>$
Order	*false* precedes *true*

be considered once and for all later in the chapter rather than being discussed in connection with each type.

Type *char*

Values of type *char* are the characters that can be typed on a computer keyboard. They include the letters of the alphabet (lowercase and uppercase), the numerals 0 through 9, punctuation marks such as :, ;, and ?, and special symbols such as $+$, $-$, &, and $. Also included may be nonprinting *control characters* that computers can employ to send commands to peripheral devices and users can employ to convey commands to programs.

A character constant consists of a single character enclosed by single quotation marks (apostrophes).

'a'   'A'   '0'   '9'   '&'   '$'

Thus a character constant differs from a string constant only in that the former represents one character whereas the latter represents more than one character. As in string constants, an apostrophe in a character constant is represented by two apostrophes in succession. Thus the character constant that represents one apostrophe consists of two apostrophes (representing the apostrophe character) enclosed in apostrophes (serving as single quotation marks), which gives four apostrophes altogether.

''''

One of the most important properties of type *char* is the order of the values, since this order defines *lexicographical order*—an extension of alphabetical order that includes all values of type *char* and not just the letters of the alphabet. Sorting operations, which occur very frequently, are governed by lexicographical order.

Unfortunately, lexicographical order is representation dependent: different methods of representing characters yield different orders. There are a few basic requirements, however, that any reasonable representation must satisfy: both the lowercase and the uppercase letters must be in normal alphabetical order, and the numerals 0 through 9 must be in numerical order. On the other hand, representations may differ on such questions as whether the numerals precede or follow the letters and whether the lowercase letters precede or follow the uppercase letters.

The order imposed by a particular representation is given by a *collating sequence*, which lists all the printing characters in order. Figure 3-2, which

Figure 3-2. Summary of type *char*. The square box represents the blank space, which is a value of type *char*.

Type	*char*
Values	Uppercase and lowercase letters, numerals, punctuation marks, special signs, and possibly graphics characters.
Operators	
Relational	$=$, $<$, $>$, $<=$, $>=$, $<>$
Order	Representation dependent and given by a collating sequence. The collating sequences for the two most popular representations, ASCII and EBCDIC, are shown here.
ASCII	▢ ! " # $ % & ' ( ) * + , - . / 0 1 2 3 4 5 6 7 8 9 : ; < = > ? @ A B C D E F G H I J K L M N O P Q R S T U V W X Y Z [\ ] ^ _ ` a b c d e f g h i j k l m n o p q r s t u v w x y z { ¦ } ~
EBCDIC	▢ ¢ . < (+ ¦ & ! $ *) ; ¬ - / ^ , % _ > ? : # @ ' = " a b c d e f g h i j k l m n o p q r s t u v w x y z \ { } [ ] A B C D E F G H I J K L M N O P Q R S T U V W X Y Z 0 1 2 3 4 5 6 7 8 9

summarizes the properties of type *char*, gives the collating sequences for the two most widely used representations. ASCII (American Standard Code for Information Interchange, pronounced "AS key") is almost universally used for microcomputers and minicomputers; EBCDIC (Extended Binary Coded Decimal Interchange Code, pronounced "EBB see dick") is mainly used for IBM and IBM-compatible mainframes.

Type *integer*

The values of type *integer* are the positive and negative whole numbers; Figure 3-3 summarizes the properties of type *integer*. Integer constants are written as in everyday arithmetic except that commas are not allowed. Thus

$$-100 \quad -25 \quad 0 \quad 50 \quad 30000$$

are examples of integer constants. On the other hand, the following integer constants are invalid:

$$-3,729 \quad -1,425 \quad 7,684 \quad 25,973$$

To be correct, they must be written

$$-3729 \quad -1425 \quad 7684 \quad 25973$$

The order for values of type *integer* is ordinary numerical order for signed numbers—numerical order with the signs of the numbers taken into account. Thus -100 precedes -50, -50 precedes 0, 0 precedes 50, and 50 precedes 100.

Only a limited range of integer values can be represented with a given number of bits. Since the number of bits used to represent an integer value will vary from one Pascal implementation to another, so will the range of values that can be represented. To help programmers cope with these differ-

Figure 3-3. Summary of type *integer*.

Type	*integer*
Values	Positive and negative whole numbers in the range $-maxint$ through *maxint*. The value of *maxint* is representation dependent.
Operators	
Integer	$+$, $-$, $*$, **div**, **mod** The definition of **mod** is implementation dependent. See the summary of type *real* (Figure 2-4) for more information on $+$, $-$, and $*$.
Real	$/$ See the summary of type *real* (Figure 2-4) for more information.
Relational	$=$, $<$, $>$, $<=$, $>=$, $<>$
Order	Numerical order for signed numbers: $-maxint, \ldots, -1, 0, 1, \ldots, maxint.$
Error Conditions	
Overflow	The result of an operation is outside the range $-maxint$ through *maxint*.
Division by Zero	The second operand of $/$, **div**, or **mod** is zero.
Invalid Operand	For the standard definition of **mod**, it is an error if the second operand is negative.

ences, Pascal provides a predefined integer constant *maxint* that represents the largest value of type *integer*. Values of type *integer* range from $-maxint$ through *maxint*. For example, if 16 bits are used to represent an integer, then the value of *maxint* is 32767, and integer values range from -32767 through 32767.

The following are the arithmetical operators defined for values of type *integer*:

Operator	Operation
$+$	Addition
$-$	Subtraction
$*$	Multiplication
$/$	Real division: returns real quotient
div	Integer division: returns integer quotient
mod	Integer division: returns integer remainder

Because there are no generally accepted symbols for integer division, Pascal uses **div** and **mod** for the operations that return the integer quotient and the integer remainder, respectively. **mod** comes from *modulus* or *modulo*, words mathematicians sometimes use for the operation of taking a remainder.

In general, dividing one integer by another yields a real number; for example, 3 / 2 equals 1.5. Thus / represents real division; integer operands are converted to real numbers before the division is carried out, and the result is a real number. The operators $+$, $-$, and $*$ are defined for both real and integer operands. They yield an integer result only if both operands are integers; if either operand is a real number, the result is also real. The operators $+$, $-$, $*$, and $/$ are discussed further in the subsection on type *real*.

The operators **div** and **mod** require integer operands and yield integer results. Integer division is the quotient-remainder division that schoolchildren often study before taking up fractions and decimals.

$$
\begin{array}{r}
7 \quad \text{integer quotient} \\
13\overline{)100} \\
\underline{91} \\
9 \quad \text{integer remainder}
\end{array}
$$

For positive arguments, **div** returns the integer quotient and **mod** returns the integer remainder.

Expression	Value
100 **div** 13	7
100 **mod** 13	9

When one or both of the operands is negative, **div** follows the usual rules for determining the sign of a quotient. If both operands have the same sign, the quotient is positive; if the operands have opposite signs, the quotient is negative.

Expression	Value
100 **div** 13	7
(-100) **div** 13	-7
100 **div** (-13)	-7
(-100) **div** (-13)	7

Unfortunately, there is disagreement over the definition of **mod** for negative operands; the Pascal implementation you are using may not follow the standard definition given here. Because of this variation in the definition of **mod**, it is probably unwise to use **mod** with negative operands.

In the standard definition, the second operand of **mod** must be positive; negative divisors are not allowed. When the dividend is negative, the positive remainder obtained when working out the division is subtracted from the divisor. The standard definition always yields a positive result ranging from 0 through one less than the divisor.

Expression	Value
100 **mod** 13	9
(-100) **mod** 13	4 (Positive remainder was 9.)
100 **mod** (-13)	Invalid
(-100) **mod** (-13)	Invalid

The result for (-100) **mod** 13 was computed by subtracting the positive remainder from the divisor $(13 - 9 = 4)$.

It is an error if any integer operation yields a result outside the range of values allowed for type *integer*. Division by zero is mathematically undefined, so it is an error if the second operand of /, **div**, or **mod** is zero. For the standard definition of **mod**, it is an error if the second operand is negative.

Type *real*

Figure 3-4 summarizes the properties of type *real*. Note that the operators $+$, $-$, $*$, and / can be applied to integers, real numbers, or a combination of the two. Operators that can be applied to values of more than one type are said to be *overloaded*; overloading is fairly common because of the limited number of symbols available for representing operators. If both operands of $+$, $-$, $*$ are integers, integer arithmetic is used and the result is an integer. If either or both operands are real numbers, integer operands are converted to real numbers, the operation is carried out with real-number arithmetic, and the result is a real number. For /, integer operands are always converted to

Figure 3-4.   Summary of type *real*.

Type	*real*
Values	Positive and negative floating-point numbers. Range of available values and accuracy with which an arbitrary value can be represented are implementation dependent and difficult to state precisely.
Operators	
Real	$+$, $-$, $*$, / Operators are defined for integer and real operands; *mixed-mode expressions* with one real and one integer operand are allowed. The operator / always returns a real result; the operators $+$, $-$, and $*$ return an integer result if both operands are integers and a real result for mixed-mode expressions and when both operands are real.
Relational	$=$, $<$, $>$, $<=$, $>=$, $<>$ The operators $=$ and $<>$ must be used with care because the inaccuracies inherent in real-number arithmetic may cause two values that should be equal to actually differ slightly.
Order	Numerical order for signed real numbers.
Error Conditions	
Overflow	The result of an operation is outside the range of values allowed for type *real*.
Underflow	Because a nonzero value is too small to be represented, it must be set to zero, causing all significant digits to be lost. Not all implementations consider this error; those that do usually consider it *nonfatal,* meaning that program execution is allowed to continue after the error message.
Division by Zero	The second operand of / is zero.

real numbers, the operation is always carried out with real-number arithmetic, and the result is always real.

The significant digits of a number are the digits exclusive of leading and trailing zeros that serve only as placeholders. Thus 1250000000.0 and 0.000000175 both have three significant digits. On the other hand, 1.0005 has five significant digits, since zeros embedded within a number are significant. To keep from having to write large numbers of leading or trailing zeros, we can express real constants in *floating-point notation* (also called *exponential* or *scientific* notation), in which only the significant digits have to be written out.

Floating-point notation is most easily explained by means of examples. Consider the following number in floating-point notation:

$$1.25E+9$$

The letter E stands for ''exponent'' and the number to the right of the E (9 in this case) is called the exponent. The exponent specifies the number of places the decimal point is to be moved to the left or right. If the exponent is positive, the decimal point is moved to the right; if the exponent is negative, the decimal point is moved to the left.

To express $1.25E+9$ in conventional notation, we start with 1.25 and move the decimal point nine places to the right. We immediately see a problem: there are only two digits to the right of the decimal point. How can we move the decimal point nine places to the right? The answer is that we add as many zeros to the right as necessary to move the decimal point the number of places specified by the exponent. If we write seven zeros after the 5 in 1.25, we can then move the decimal point nine places to the right, getting 1250000000.0. (The zero to the right of the decimal point is there just to satisfy the rule that a real constant cannot end with a decimal point.) Therefore, a $1.25E+9$ represents the same real number as 1250000000.0. Plus signs in front of exponents can be omitted, so the same value can also be written as 1.25E9.

When the exponent is negative, the decimal point is moved to the left. Taking $1.75E-7$ as an example, we start with 1.75 and move the decimal point seven places to the left, writing down additional zeros as needed. The result is 0.000000175; the 0 to the left of the decimal point is there only to satisfy the Pascal rule that a real constant cannot begin with a decimal point. Thus, $1.75E-7$ represents the same real number as 0.000000175. The following are a few more examples of numbers in floating-point notation:

Floating-Point Notation	Conventional Notation
1.5E3	1500.0
3.1416E2	314.16
2.79E−2	0.0279
475.0E−1	47.5

Floating-point constants always represent real numbers, even if the decimal point is omitted. When the decimal point is omitted, it is assumed to occur immediately to the left of the E. Thus in the following examples, the three constants on each line represent the same value:

475E−1	475.0E−1	47.5
1E3	1.0E3	1000.0
1E−4	1.0E−4	0.0001

As with type *integer*, the possible values of type *real* are limited by the number of alternatives that can be represented with a given number of bits. Unfortunately, there is no single constant, analogous to *maxint*, that characterizes the limitations on values of type *real*. Indeed, such limitations are difficult to state precisely. For practical purposes, what we usually need to know is the number of significant digits that can be represented accurately and the range of exponent values allowed in floating-point notation.

The order for type *real* is ordinary numerical order for real numbers. It is an error if the second operand of / is zero or if the absolute value of a result (the value with the sign disregarded) is larger than the largest positive number that can be represented.

Assignment Compatibility

We have seen that the operators $+$, $-$, $*$, and / are overloaded in that both real numbers and integers are allowed as operands; when one operand is a real number and the other an integer, Pascal automatically converts the integer to the corresponding real number. As an additional convenience, Pascal allows an integer to be assigned to a real variable; again, the integer is automatically converted to the corresponding real number. For example, if *length* is a real variable, the following assignment is valid:

> *length* := 25

The value assigned to *length* is 25.0, the real number corresponding to the integer 25.

When we later take up programmer-defined types, we will encounter other cases in which a value of one type can be assigned to a variable of another type. To handle such cases uniformly, the Pascal standard employs the concept of *assignment compatibility*. A value of type T1 is *assignment compatible* with type T2 if the value can be assigned to a variable of type T2. For types *Boolean*, *char*, *integer*, and *real*, the rules for assignment compatibility are as follows. A value of type T1 is assignment compatible with type T2 if one of the following holds:

1. T1 and T2 are the same type.
2. Type T1 is *integer* and type T2 is *real*.

These rules will be extended as additional types are taken up.

Relational Operators

From Figures 3-1 through 3-4 we see that the six *relational operators*

> = < > <= >= <>

are defined for each of the types *Boolean*, *char*, *integer*, and *real*. The relational operators are thus overloaded, since each is defined for operands of more than one type (including some types we have not yet considered). With one exception, both operands must have the same type. The exception is that one operand may be an integer and the óther a real number. As with $+$, $-$, and $*$, the integer is converted to the corresponding real number and the operation for real numbers is carried out.

Each relational operator corresponds to a relation of equality or order that can exist between two values. Relational operators return Boolean values;

the result of a relational operation is *true* if the corresponding relation holds for the operands and *false* otherwise. In deciding questions of order, the order defined for the values of each type is used. Remember that the order for values of type *char* is representation dependent, so the result obtained by applying a relational operator to two character values may be different for different implementations of Pascal. The following table gives the correspondence between relational operators and relations:

Relational Operator	Relation
=	Equals
<	Precedes
>	Follows
<=	Precedes or equals
>=	Follows or equals
<>	Does not equal

Thus the value of $3 < 5$ is *true* because the value of 3 precedes the value of 5. Likewise, the value of $'0' > '9'$ is *false*, because (for all reasonably designed character codes) it is false that $'0'$ follows $'9'$. The following are some additional relational expressions and their values:

Expression	Value
true > false	*true*
true = false	*false*
$'A' > 'Z'$	*false*
$'a' < 'A'$	*false* for ASCII
	true for EBCDIC
$100 >= 100$	*true*
$-10 > -5$	*false*
$-100 <= 0$	*true*
$3.14 < 3.15$	*true*
$-2.5 <> 2.5$	*true*

Beware of confusing the relational operator = with the algebraic equal sign. The relational operator instructs the computer to test whether two values are equal; the algebraic equal sign states that they are equal, as in $2 + 2 = 4$. In Pascal, = represents only the relational operator, not the algebraic equal sign. The equal sign may occur in explanations, however, both in the text and in the explanatory comments often inserted in Pascal programs.

Ordinal Types

Types *Boolean*, *char*, and *integer* are *ordinal* types, whereas type *real* is not. What is the distinction? An ordinal type must have two properties.

- The values of the type are ordered.

- The values are *discrete*. That is, any value except the first has a unique *predecessor* that immediately precedes it without any other values intervening. Likewise, any value except the last has a unique *successor* that immediately follows it without any other values intervening.

The values of types *Boolean*, *char*, and *integer* are both ordered and discrete. Values of type *real* are ordered, but they are not discrete: between any two values of type *real* other values intervene. Thus 1.4 cannot be the predecessor of 1.5 because 1.49 (and many other values) intervene; 1.49 cannot be the predecessor of 1.5 because 1.499 intervenes; 1.499 cannot be the predecessor of 1.5 because 1.4999 intervenes; and so on.

Because of its lack of discreteness, type *real* is rather an outcast among the simple types. Values of ordinal types can be used for a variety of purposes other than the ones for which they were originally defined, such as counting executions of program statements and locating entries in tables. Values of type *real*, excluded from all these additional applications, can be used only for real-number arithmetic.

Using Field-Width Parameters

In Chapter 2 we saw how to use field-width parameters to control the printing of real values; we now consider how to print values of the other standard types and we extend our previous discussion of type *real*.

When no field-width parameter is supplied, a default field width is used. For string and character values, the default field width is simply the number of characters making up the value to be printed. Thus

writeln ('abc')

prints three characters

```
abc
```

without any additional blanks. Likewise,

writeln ('abc', 'def', 'ghi')

prints each value in a three-character field.

```
abcdefghi
```

Note that a field width equal to the number of characters to be printed is often exactly what we want for strings, so frequently we do not need to use field-width parameters when printing strings.

Character values are printed in much the same way as strings. The default field width for a character is 1; a larger field width can be specified with a field-width parameter. The printed character is right-justified within its field. The space character is often printed with a field-width parameter to print a given number of spaces; that is, to move the printing mechanism a given number of positions to the right. For example,

write (' ' :20)

moves the printing mechanism right by 20 columns.* This kind of *write* statement is the Pascal version of the space or tab function found in some other languages.

---

*Character positions on a printed line are often referred to as *columns* because on a printed page all the characters in a given position line up to form a vertical column.

The Boolean values *true* and *false* are printed in the same way as the character strings 'true' and 'false', except that the default field width is implementation defined. Because the values are printed as if they were strings, they can be truncated to *t* or *f*, which may be convenient when many Boolean values are to be printed. For example,

$\quad\quad$ *writeln* (*true* :1, *false* :1, *true* :1, *true* :1)

prints

```
tftt
```

Some implementations may print

```
TFTT
```

The default field widths for integer and real values also vary from one implementation to another. Thus

$\quad\quad$ *writeln* (10, 200, 3000)

prints

```
· · · · · ·10· · · · ·200· · · ·3000
```

if the default field width is eight characters and prints

```
102003000
```

if the default field width is the number of digits to be printed. Because we cannot rely on all implementations to have the same default field width, and because the default field widths for a particular implementation may not be convenient for our purposes, we usually use field-width parameters when printing integer and real values.

Like strings, integers are printed right-justified in their fields, with any unused positions filled with blanks. Thus,

$\quad\quad$ *writeln* (10 :6, −200 :6, 300 :6)

would print

```
· · · ·10· · −200· ·3000
```

As usual, the dots represent the blanks that would appear in the actual printout.

```
10   -200   3000
```

For real values, if we specify only the field widths, the values are printed in floating-point notation. Thus

$\quad\quad$ *writeln* (105.25 :15, −73.5 :15, 1000.0 :15)

prints each value in floating-point notation in a field that is 15 characters wide.

```
· · · ·1.05250E+02· · · ·−7.35000E+01· · · ·1.00000E+03
```

Some details of the floating-point representation, such as the number of decimal places and the number of digits in the exponent, are implementation dependent.

To get real numbers printed in conventional fixed-point notation, we must follow the field-width parameter with another parameter giving the number of decimal places to be printed. For example

$\quad\quad$ *writeln* (105.25 :15:2, −73.5 :15:2, 1000.0 :15:2)

also prints each value in a 15-character value. But this time each value is printed in fixed-point notation with two decimal places.

```
·········105.25··········-73.50········1000.00
```

For integers and real numbers, if the specified field width makes the field too small to hold the value to be printed, the field-width parameter is ignored and the field is made as large as needed to hold the printed value. Integer and real values are *not* truncated as string values are.

Example 3-1. *A Program for Making Change*

Type *integer* is one of the most important Pascal types. However, its division operations, particularly **mod**, may be unfamiliar to many students. To gain more familiarity with reading, writing, and manipulating integers, we will look at a program for making change. The techniques used in this program can be applied to other problems of expressing a quantity in arbitrary units, such as expressing a length in feet and inches; expressing an angle in degrees, minutes, and seconds; or expressing a time in hours, minutes, and seconds.

Specifically, our problem is to write a program that, given an amount of change less than a dollar, will determine the number of half dollars, quarters, dimes, nickels, and pennies that should be returned to the customer.

The input to the program is the amount of change to be handed back. Since the amount of change is less than one dollar, it is most conveniently expressed in cents rather than as a decimal. Expressing the change in cents will also turn out to be convenient for doing the calculations, since it will allow us to use the integer-arithmetic operators, which provide the simplest method of solving this kind of problem.

The output is the number of half dollars, quarters, dimes, nickels, and pennies needed to make up the given amount of change. The problem statement leaves the exact form of the output up to the programmer. We could make the problem moderately complex by requiring, for example, that the program print an English sentence stating, in words, how many of each kind of coin should be handed back. We will take a simpler approach and have the program print a table of two columns, one column containing the names of the denominations and the other column containing the number of coins to be handed back for each denomination. Thus an exchange between the user and the program might go like this:

```
Amount of change (in cents)? 97
Halves     1
Quarters   1
Dimes      2
Nickels    0
Pennies    2
```

The simplest solution would be, of course, to hand back the entire amount in pennies; most customers, however, would find this solution unsatisfactory and would cease to patronize any establishment that used it. Accepted practice in making change, then, imposes the following constraint on the solution: The number of coins of each denomination must be chosen in such a way as to minimize the total number of coins to be handed back. Indeed, so firmly entrenched is this principle that clerks often apologize when the lack of a particular denomination of coin prevents them from observing it.

The constraint is easily met by starting with the largest denomination and handing back as much of the change as possible with coins of a given denomination before going on to the next smaller denomination. That is, we begin by handing back as many half dollars as possible (without exceeding the total amount to be returned), then as many quarters as possible, and so on. If we started with some smaller denomination, say nickels, we would be in danger of handing back 10 nickels instead of a half dollar or 5 nickels instead of a quarter or 2 nickels instead of a dime.

For each denomination we must determine

1. How many coins of that denomination are to be handed back.
2. How many cents remain to be handed back using coins of smaller denominations.

The simplest approach to carrying out this calculation uses the **div** and **mod** operators. Suppose we have 80 cents to hand back and want to know how many half dollars to return. Since there are 50 cents in a half dollar, we need to know how many times 50 will go into 80. We are interested only in the whole-number part of the result because, unlike the legendary pieces of eight, a half dollar cannot be divided into fractional parts. The **div** operator yields the desired integer quotient.

80 **div** 50 = 1

Thus, we should hand back one half dollar. To continue, we will need to know how much change remains to be returned after the half dollar was handed back. But this number is just the remainder that results when 80 is divided by 50.

80 **mod** 50 = 30

Thus after handing back one half dollar, 30 cents remain to be handed back in quarters, dimes, and nickels. (In fact, the 30 cents can be handed back as one quarter and one nickel. Why is this preferable to three dimes?)

Let's try choosing identifiers before we begin outlining the program. The calculations will certainly involve the number of cents in each of the given coins. Rather than having mysterious 50s, 25s, 10s, and 5s cropping up in the program, let's define a constant identifier for the number of cents in each denomination of coin (except the penny). Acting on this intention gives us the constant definition section of the change-making program that appears in Figure 3-5.

```
const
    centsPerHalf    = 50; { values of coins }
    centsPerQuarter = 25;
    centsPerDime    = 10;
    centsPerNickel  =  5;
```

For each denomination, we must compute two things: the number of coins of that denomination to be handed back and the amount of change

Figure 3-5.

A program for making change is a traditional example in introductory computer science courses. The program is easiest to write in languages that, like Pascal, have **div** and **mod** operators.

```pascal
program MakeChange (input, output);

{ Given an amount of change less than one dollar, compute the number of
  half dollars, quarters, dimes, nickels, and pennies to be returned }

const
    centsPerHalf    = 50;        { values of coins }
    centsPerQuarter = 25;
    centsPerDime    = 10;
    centsPerNickel  =  5;
var
    numberOfCoins,              { number of coins of a
                                  particular denomination }
    amountRemaining : integer;  { number of cents not yet
                                  handed back }
begin
    write ('Amount of change (in cents)? ');
    readln (amountRemaining);

    { Half dollars }

    numberOfCoins := amountRemaining div centsPerHalf;
    amountRemaining := amountRemaining mod centsPerHalf;
    writeln ('Halves   ', numberOfCoins :3);

    { Quarters }

    numberOfCoins := amountRemaining div centsPerQuarter;
    amountRemaining := amountRemaining mod centsPerQuarter;
    writeln ('Quarters', numberOfCoins :3);

    { Dimes }

    numberOfCoins := amountRemaining div centsPerDime;
    amountRemaining := amountRemaining mod centsPerDime;
    writeln ('Dimes   ', numberOfCoins :3);

    { Nickels }

    numberOfCoins := amountRemaining div centsPerNickel;
    amountRemaining := amountRemaining mod centsPerNickel;
    writeln ('Nickels ', numberOfCoins :3);

    { Pennies }

    writeln ('Pennies ', amountRemaining :3)
end.
```

remaining after the number of coins in question have been returned. We declare an integer variable to hold the result of each of these calculations.

var
> *NumberOfCoins,*   { number of coins of a
>   particular denomination
>   to be handed back }
> *amountRemaining* : *integer*; { number of cents not yet
>   handed back }

In outlining the program, we will use a variation of the usual read-calculate-write scenario. The program will indeed begin by obtaining from the user the amount of change to be returned. But after calculating the number of coins to be returned for a particular denomination, the program will output this result before going on to the next denomination. This allows us to group together all the statements that handle a particular denomination. It also reduces the number of variables that we must declare, since we do not have to declare a separate number-of-coins variable for each denomination, as we would if we had to calculate and store the number of coins for all the denominations before printing any of them. These considerations give us the following outline:

1. Obtain amount of change from user
2. Calculate and print number of half dollars
3. Calculate and print number of quarters
4. Calculate and print number of dimes
5. Calculate and print number of nickels
6. Print number of pennies

Throughout the program, the value of *amountRemaining* will be the amount of change that has not yet been handed back. We start out, then, by assigning to *amountRemaining* the total amount of change to be handed back, the amount entered by the user:

1.1 Prompt user to enter amount of change to be handed back
1.2 Assign amount entered to *amountRemaining*

These steps translate into Pascal as follows:

> *write* ('Amount of change (in cents)? ');
> *readln* (*amountRemaining*)

Each of the remaining steps except the last is the same. If we let *n* represent 2, 3, 4, or 5, we can write the refinements of steps 2 through 5 as follows:

n.1 Calculate number of coins (of the denomination handled in step *n*) to be handed back
n.2 Calculate amount of change still remaining to be returned after handing back the number of coins calculated in step *n*.1
n.3 Print number of coins to be handed back

Consider the calculations for half dollars. At the start of the calculation, the value of *amountRemaining* is the amount of change to be returned. To determine how many half dollars to return, we divide the value of *amountRemaining* by *centsPerHalf* (the number of cents in a half dollar) and assign the quotient to *numberOfCoins*.

numberOfCoins : = *amountRemaining* **div** *centsPerHalf*

To compute the amount of change remaining after half dollars have been handed back, we divide the value of *amountRemaining* by *centsPerHalf* and assign the remainder back to *amountRemaining*.

amountRemaining : = *amountRemaining* **mod** *centsPerHalf*

After this assignment, the value of *amountRemaining* once again represents the amount of change yet to be handed back. Finally, we print the value of *numberOfCoins* as the number of half dollars to be handed back.

writeln ('Halves ', *numberOfCoins* :3)

The calculations for quarters, dimes, and nickels proceed in the same way. When halves, quarters, dimes, and nickels have all been handed back, then the value of *amountRemaining* is the number of pennies to be returned. The final step in our outline, then, can be implemented with a single *writeln* statement.

writeln ('Pennies ', *amountRemaining* :3)

To make the names of the coins line up in one column and the numbers in another, we do two things. First, we make the strings representing the names all the same length. The longest such string, 'Quarters', contains eight characters. Each of the other names is followed by a sufficient number of blank spaces to make the string eight characters long. Thus the first column, the name column, is eight characters wide.* Second, each number is printed in a three-character-wide field (field-width parameter equal to 3). Thus the numbers of coins are printed right-justified in a column that is three characters wide.

More Complex Expressions

An expression such as

2 + 3 + 4

can hardly be misinterpreted. It's obvious that the values of the three variables are to be added, and we will get the same result regardless of which of the two additions is carried out first. On the other hand, we must be more careful with an expression such as

---

*Another possible approach would be to let the lengths of the strings vary but print each with a field-width parameter of 8. This would indeed print all the names in an eight-character-wide column. Unfortunately, the names would be right-justified—aligned on the right. In general, text (as opposed to numbers) looks much better aligned on the left than on the right. Although right-aligned text is sometimes used for design purposes in titles, company logos, and the like, it is almost never used for such down-to-earth purposes as entries in data tables.

$$2 + 3 * 4$$

This expression can evaluate to either 20 or 14 depending on whether the addition or the multiplication is done first. Clearly, if expressions are to have well-defined values, we need rules for determining the order in which operations will be carried out.

Operator Precedence: Arithmetical Operators

The proper order for applying operators (hence, for carrying out the corresponding operations) is referred to as *operator precedence*. The following table gives the precedence of the arithmetical operators:

*, /, **div**, **mod**,	Applied first
+, −	Applied last

Operators listed on the same line of the table are applied in left-to-right order as they occur in the expression. Thus multiplications and divisions are carried out in left-to-right order, as are additions and subtractions. But operators on the first line are applied before those on the second. Thus multiplications and divisions are carried out before additions and subtractions. This means that in our previous example $(2 + 3 * 4)$, the correct result is 14, not 20.

Let's look at an example of operator precedence.

Example 3-2.

---

5 + 7 * 4	Multiplication first,
5 + 28	then addition.
33	

We often write the successive steps of an evaluation below one another instead of using the arrow symbol introduced in the previous chapter. That is, we write

$$5 + 7 * 4$$
$$5 + 28$$
$$33$$

instead of

$$5 + 7 * 4 \Rightarrow 5 + 28 \Rightarrow 33$$

Now, on to more examples.

Example 3-3.

---

9 * 8 − 4 * 3	Multiplication first,
72 − 12	then subtraction.
60	

Example 3-4.

$$9 * 5 + 7 \textbf{ div } 3$$
$$45 + 2$$
$$47$$

Multiplication and division first, then addition.

Example 3-5.

$$1.5 * 1.1 + 4.5 / 9.0 - 0.1$$
$$1.65 + 0.5 - 0.1$$
$$2.05$$

Multiplication and division first, then addition and subtraction.

Example 3-6.

$$3.6 / 1.2 * 3.0$$
$$3.0 * 3.0$$
$$9.0$$

Operators are applied in left-to-right order.

Expressions like the one in Example 3-6 are sometimes confused with built-up fractions, for which the numerator and denominator would be evaluated before carrying out the division.

$$\frac{3.6}{1.2 \times 3.0} \Rightarrow \frac{3.6}{3.6} \Rightarrow 1.0$$

But the expression in Example 3-6 is not a built-up fraction and is not evaluated like one. Instead, the multiplication and division operators are applied in left-to-right order, as usual. Since the division operator is to the left of the multiplication operator, the division is done before the multiplication.

Using Parentheses

Suppose we want to write an expression that *is* equivalent to the built-up fraction, one in which the multiplication will be done before the division. The expression

$$3.6 / (1.2 * 3.0)$$

will do the job. The parentheses override operator precedence, causing the multiplication to be done before the division. We use parentheses whenever we want an expression evaluated in some way other than the one dictated by operator precedence.

The rule for parentheses is simply this: Any part of an expression enclosed in parentheses must be evaluated before the adjacent operators outside the parentheses can be applied. For example, in the expression

$$3 * (4 + 5) * 6$$

the addition must be carried out before either of the multiplications can be done. The following examples illustrate the use of parentheses:

Example 3-7.

3.6 / (1.2 * 3.0)	Parenthesized part first,
3.6 / 3.6	then division.
1.0	

Example 3-8.

3 * (4 + 5) * 6	Parenthesized part first,
3 * 9 * 6	then multiplication.
162	

Example 3-9.

3 * (5 * 3 − 9) + 7	Multiplication inside parentheses,
3 * (15 − 9) + 7	then subtraction inside parentheses.
3 * 6 + 7	Multiplication next,
18 + 7	then addition.
25	

Sets of parentheses can be nested one inside the other. In such cases, we begin with the innermost set of parentheses and work outward, as shown in Example 3-10.

Example 3-10.

3 * (5 + 2 * (6 − 2))	Innermost parenthesized part first,
3 * (5 + 2 * 4)	then multiplication inside parentheses.
3 * (5 + 8)	Addition inside parentheses next,
3 * 13	then multiplication.
39	

There is no penalty for using unnecessary parentheses, and sometimes their use will make an expression easier to understand. For example, a beginning programmer might be unsure as to how the computer will evaluate the expression

$$i * j + 5 * k$$

Enclosing the multiplications in parentheses

$$(i * j) + (5 * k)$$

assures the programmer that the multiplications will be done before the addition. Although the parentheses do not change the order in which the operators are applied, they make that order clearer to both the programmer and someone reading the program. A rule of thumb for programmers is "when in doubt, parenthesize."

Operator Precedence: Relational Operators

The relational operators are applied before any arithmetical operators. Thus in any expression involving both arithmetical and relational operators, the arithmetic will be carried out before the relational operators are applied. The following table gives the precedence of the arithmetical and relational operators; for completeness we include a relational operator, **in**, that we haven't yet taken up:

*, /, **div**, **mod**	Applied first
+, −	Applied second
=, <, >, <=, >=, <>, **in**	Applied last

The following examples illustrate the evaluation of expressions containing both arithmetical and relational operators:

Example 3-11.

$3 + 5 < 4 * 2 - 1$	Multiplication first.
$3 + 5 < 8 - 1$	Addition and subtraction next.
$8 < 7$	Relational operator last.
false	

Example 3-12.

---

13 **div** $3 = 3 + 1$	Division first,
$4 = 3 + 1$	addition next,
$4 = 4$	relational operator last.
true	

Operator Precedence: Boolean Operators

The Boolean operator **not** takes precedence over all other operators. The operator **and** has the same precedence as *, and **or** has the same precedence as +. The following precedence table includes all Pascal operators:

not	Applied first
*, /, **div**, **mod**, **and**	Applied second
+, −, **or**	Applied third
=, <, >, <=, >=, <>, **in**	Applied last

The Boolean operators are most frequently used in expressions such as the following:

$$(i = j) \textbf{ or } (i < j + k)$$

Such expressions correspond to conditions stated in English using the words *not*, *and*, and *or*. For example, the expression just given corresponds to the following condition:

> The value of i is equal to the value of j, or the value of i is less than the value of $j + k$.

The parentheses in the expression are mandatory. This is because the Boolean operators are applied before the relational operators. If the parentheses were not present, the computer would attempt* to apply **or** before applying the relational operators. That is, it would attempt to apply **or** to the values of i and j, which does not make sense because the Boolean operators can only be applied to Boolean values, not to the integer values of i and j. The parentheses assure that the relational operators will be applied before the Boolean operators. The parentheses also contribute to the readability of the expression, so in this respect Pascal may be ahead of some other languages whose operator precedence schemes allow the parentheses to be omitted.

Now let's look at a Boolean expression that involves all the rules we have discussed. This expression is much more complicated than those usually encountered in practice.

$$(11 < 3 * 2 + 5) \textbf{ or } (6 * 2 = 4 * 3) \textbf{ and not } (2 + 2 = 4)$$

We begin by working out the arithmetical expressions inside the parentheses—multiplications first and then additions.

$$(11 < 6 + 5) \textbf{ or } (12 = 12) \textbf{ and not } (2 + 2 = 4)$$
$$(11 < 11) \textbf{ or } (12 = 12) \textbf{ and not } (4 = 4)$$

Continuing to work out the parts of the expression that are in parentheses, we apply the relational operators next.

> *false* **or** *true* **and not** *true*

Of the Boolean operators, **not** is applied first.

> *false* **or** *true* **and** *false*

The operator **and** is applied before **or**.

> *false* **or** *false*

Applying **or** gives us *false* as the value of the original Boolean expression.

Control Structures

In Chapter 2 we considered sequencing, the most basic of all control structures. Now we turn to the two remaining control structures: selection, which determines which statements will be executed; and repetition, which determines how many times a statement will be executed.

---

*Actually, the Pascal language processor would reject the erroneous expression with an error message, thus preventing the meaningless calculation from ever being attempted. The ability of language processors to detect errors such as this is the main advantage of strong type-checking.

Selection: The *if* Statement

Control structures are implemented in programming languages by means of *control statements*. There may be several different control statements for each control structure. The most important use of Boolean expressions is in control statements.

The **if** statement is a control statement that implements selection. It has the following general form:

> **if** Boolean-expression **then**
>   controlled-statement-1
> **else**
>   controlled-statement-2

The controlled statements are the statements whose execution is controlled by the **if** statement. Only one of the two controlled statements will be executed, and the value of the Boolean expression determines which one. When the **if** statement is executed, the Boolean expression is evaluated. If the value of the Boolean expression is *true*, then controlled-statement-1 is executed. If the value of the Boolean expression is *false*, controlled-statement-2 is executed.

For example, suppose that the value of *quantityOnHand* is the quantity of a certain item currently in inventory. We want the computer to print "Time to reorder" if there are fewer than 10 items in inventory and "Sufficient stock on hand" if there are 10 or more items. We can program this with the following **if** statement:

> **if** *quantityOnHand* < 10 **then**
>   *writeln* ('Time to reorder')
> **else**
>   *writeln* ('Sufficient stock on hand')

If the value of *quantityOnHand* is less than 10, the Boolean expression will evaluate to *true* and the message "Time to reorder" will be printed. If the value of *quantityOnHand* is greater than or equal to 10, the Boolean expression evaluates to *false* and the message "Sufficient stock on hand." is printed.

The controlled statements are embedded in and are a part of the **if** statement. The semicolon that separates the **if** statement from the statement that follows comes at the end of the entire **if** statement; that is, after the second controlled statement. Note particularly that there is no semicolon between the first controlled statement and the word **else**. The following sequence of statements illustrates these points:

> *writeln* ('Checking stock level');   { semicolon }
> **if** *quantityOnHand* < 10 **then**
>   *writeln* ('Time to reorder')   { no semicolon }
> **else**
>   *writeln* ('Sufficient stock on hand'); { semicolon }
> *writeln* ('Stock-level check complete')

It often happens that we wish to execute a statement when a Boolean expression evaluates to *true* but take no action if the expression evaluates to *false*. For example, we might want to print "Time to reorder" when the value of *quantityOnHand* is less than 10 but not bother printing "Sufficient stock is on hand" when there are 10 or more items in stock. We could program this as follows:

```
    writeln ('Checking stock level');
    if quantityOnHand < 10 then
        writeln ('Time to reorder')
    else
        ;                                    { empty statement }
    writeln ('Stock-level check complete')
```

The semicolon on a line by itself follows the *empty statement*—the statement that contains no text and takes no action. When the Boolean expression evaluates to *true*, the message "Time to reorder" is printed. When the Boolean expression evaluates to *false*, the empty statement is executed; that is, no action is taken.

Because the use of empty statements can be cumbersome and confusing, Pascal provides a second form of the **if** statement in which the entire **else**-part is omitted.

```
    if Boolean-expression then
        controlled-statement
```

If the Boolean expression evaluates to *true*, the controlled statement is executed. Otherwise, no action is taken, and the computer goes on to the next statement in the program. This form of the **if** statement can be considered as an abbreviation for

```
    if Boolean-expression then
        controlled-statement
    else
        { empty statement }
```

Our previous example can now be written more concisely as follows:

```
    writeln ('Checking stock level');
    if quantityOnHand < 10 then
        writeln ('Time to reorder');          { note semicolon }
    writeln ('Stock-level check complete')
```

Note that the semicolon separating the **if** statement from the following statement comes after the (one and only) controlled statement.

The **if** statement might seem limited in that only a single controlled statement can occur in the **then** or **else** part. This limitation can be removed with the aid of the compound statement, which allows a sequence of statements to be treated as a single statement. For example, the compound statement

```
    begin
        writeln ('Time to reorder');
        writeln ('Fewer than 10 items on hand')
    end
```

allows the two *writeln* statements to be treated as a single statement. If the compound statement is selected for execution, then the statements contained in it will be executed in the order in which they occur in the compound statement. If the compound statement is not selected for execution, then, of course, none of the statements contained in it will be executed. The following version of our stock-level example uses compound statements in the **then** and **else** parts of the **if** statement:

```
      writeln ('Checking stock level');
      if quantityOnHand < 10 then
        begin
          writeln ('Time to reorder');
          writeln ('Fewer than 10 items on hand')
        end                                  { no semicolon }
      else
        begin
          writeln ('Sufficient stock on hand');
          writeln ('Do not reorder this item')
        end;                                 { semicolon }
      writeln ('Stock-level check complete')
```

Note that the semicolon that separates the **if** statement from the following statement comes after the **end** of the second compound statement. We can also use a compound statement in the abbreviated form of the **if** statement that has only one controlled statement.

```
      writeln ('Checking stock level');
      if quantityOnHand < 10 then
        begin
          writeln ('Time to reorder');
          writeln ('Fewer than 10 items on hand')
        end;                                       { note semicolon }
      writeln ('Stock-level check complete')
```

Again, the semicolon that separates the **if** statement from the following statement comes after the **end** of a compound statement.

Repetition: The *while* Statement

Repetition is the control structure that provides for the repeated execution of some statements during a single execution of the entire program. The usefulness of computers often hinges on repetition. If calculations are to be carried out only once, it will probably be as easy to do them by hand (perhaps with the aid of a calculator) as to write a program telling a computer how to do them. But when the same calculation must be carried out repeatedly, a computer allows us to write out the instructions for the calculation once and have them executed as many times as needed.

Repetition imposes an obligation on the programmer. We must assure ourselves that every repetition will eventually terminate, lest our programs "hang up" the computer by causing it to repeat some statements indefinitely. Such nonterminating repetitions, or *infinite loops*,* are among the most common program bugs. Few people who have used a computer for any length of time have been spared the experience of having the machine hang up in an infinite loop.

---

*A repetition construction is often referred to as a *loop*. The term is suggested by *flowcharts*, diagrams that show how control of the computer passes (or "flows") from statement to statement as a program is executed. In a flowchart, a repetition construction appears as a circular path, or loop.

The **while** statement has the following general form:

> **while** Boolean-expression **do**
> controlled-statement

The controlled statement is executed repeatedly as long as the Boolean expression evaluates to *true*. The Boolean expression is evaluated just prior to each execution of the controlled statement. If the value of the Boolean expression is *true*, the controlled statement is executed, after which the Boolean expression is evaluated again, and so on. If the value of the Boolean expression is *false*, the controlled statement is not executed, and the computer goes on to the next statement in the program, thus terminating the repetition. If the value of the Boolean expression is *false* the first time the expression is evaluated, the controlled statement will not be executed at all.

Consider the following example in which *count* is an integer variable:

```
count := 0;
while count <= 20 do
   count := count + 5
```

These statements cause

```
count := count + 5
```

to be executed repeatedly. Since each execution adds 5 to the value of *count*, *count* takes on the values 0, 5, 10, 15, 20, and 25. Before each execution, the value of *count* is compared with 20. When the value of *count* is 0, 5, 10, 15, and 20, the value of *count* is less than or equal to 20, the value of the Boolean expression *count* <= 20 is *true*, and the controlled statement is executed. When the value of *count* is 25, however, the value of the Boolean expression *count* <= 20 is *false*, the controlled statement is not executed, and the computer goes on to whatever statement follows the **while** statement in the program.

Every time we use a **while** statement, we need to convince ourselves that execution of the statement will eventually terminate. Specifically, we need to convince ourselves that repeated execution of the controlled statement will eventually cause the Boolean expression to evaluate to *false*, thus terminating the repeated executions. In the present case, each execution of the controlled statement increases the value of *count* by 5. Repeated executions must eventually increase the value of *count* beyond 20, at which time the Boolean expression *count* <= 20 will evaluate to *false*, terminating the execution of the **while** statement.

As with the **if** statement, the controlled statement can be a compound statement. By using a compound statement, we can get the computer to print the successive values of *count*.

```
count := 0;
while count <= 20 do
   begin
      write (count :3);
      count := count + 5
   end
```

When these statements are executed, the computer prints

```
0   5 10 15 20
```

The final value of *count*, 25, isn't printed. Why?

The semicolon that separates a **while** statement from the following statement in the program comes after the controlled statement. If the controlled statement is a compound statement, the semicolon follows the **end** of the compound statement.

```
count := 0;
while count <= 20 do
   begin
     write (count :3);
     count := count + 5
   end;                        { note semicolon }
writeln ('That''s all, folks')
```

If the initial value given to *count* makes the Boolean expression evaluate to *false*, then the controlled statement will not be executed at all. For example, consider

```
count := 21;
while count <= 20 do
   begin
     write (count :3);
     count := count + 5
   end
```

No values are printed. The first time the Boolean expression is evaluated, the value of *count* is 21 and the value of the Boolean expression is *false*. Thus the computer goes on to the next statement in the program without executing either the *write* statement or the assignment statement.

Because the Boolean expression is evaluated before the first execution of the controlled statements, the variables appearing in the Boolean expression must all be given initial values before the **while** statement is executed.

As illustrations of the **while** statement, we will look at two programs for reading and processing a series of data items.

Example 3-13. *Counting and Summing Integers*

The program in Figure 3-6 accepts a series of integers from the user and prints the number of values that were entered along with their sum. Our interest is not so much in the simple tasks of counting the values and computing their sum as in using a **while** statement to read and process a series of data values.

To let the program know when all the data values have been entered, the user enters a special *sentinel* value after entering the final data value. When the program recognizes the sentinel value, it prints the number of values previously entered along with their sum. For a sentinel we can use any value that cannot be mistaken for a valid data value. For example, if the data values must be positive numbers, then we can use a negative number as a sentinel.

The program in Figure 3-6 can be outlined as follows:

1. Initialize variables
2. Input first value

Figure 3-6.   This program uses a negative number as a sentinel to
determine when the last input value has been entered.

---

program *ComputeTotal* (*input*, *output*);

{ Compute sum of integers entered by user }

var
    count, *number*, *total* : *integer*;
begin
    count := 0;
    total := 0;
    write ('Enter a number: ');
    readln (*number*);
    while *number* >= 0 **do**
        begin
            count := *count* + 1;
            total := *total* + *number*;
            write ('Enter a number: ');
            readln (*number*)
        end;
    writeln ('Number of values added: ', *count* :1);
    writeln ('Total: ', *total*:1)
end.

---

3. While the most recent input value is not the sentinel value, repeat the
    following:
    3.1   Process the most recent input value
    3.2   Input another value
4. Print results

Step 3 of the outline corresponds to a **while** statement; steps 3.1 and 3.2
correspond to statements whose execution is controlled by the **while** statement. The tricky point here is that the first value to be processed must be
read before the **while** statement corresponding to step 3 is executed. Thus,
the statements for inputting a value occur in two places: before the **while**
statement and after the statements that process one value. The reason for this
arrangement is that each input value must be tested to see if it is the sentinel
before it is processed, since we don't want to process the sentinel as if it were
a data value. (Specifically, we don't want to include the sentinel in the count
and total.) With the arrangement shown, each value is tested for sentinelhood
immediately after it is read and before it is processed. Thus when the sentinel
value is read, it will cause the repetition to terminate before the sentinel value
is erroneously processed.

Figure 3-6 counts and adds a series of nonnegative numbers. Since the
numbers to be added are nonnegative, any negative number will be considered
a sentinel value. When the sentinel is entered, the program prints both the
number of values that were entered and their sum.

```
Enter a number: 10
Enter a number: 15
Enter a number: 20
Enter a number: -1
Number of values added: 3
Total: 45
```

Note that the sentinel value, -1, is not included in either the count or the total.

The details of the program are straightforward. The variables *count* and *total* hold a running count and total; the program initializes both to zero before beginning to input data values. Processing a data value consists of adding one to the value of *count* and adding the data value to the value of *total*. The following statements read and process values until a sentinel value is entered.

```
write ('Enter a number: ');
readln (number);
while number >= 0 do
  begin
    count := count + 1;
    total := total + number;
    write ('Enter a number: ');
    readln ( number)
  end
```

As usual with the **while** statement, we must convince ourselves that the repetition will eventually terminate. We must show that each execution of the controlled statements makes progress toward a situation in which the Boolean expression will evaluate to *false*. We assume that the input data consists of a finite number of nonnegative data values followed by a negative sentinel value. Each execution of the controlled statements reads one data value and hence makes progress toward the situation in which the sentinel value will be read. When the negative sentinel value is finally read into *number*, the Boolean expression *number* $>= 0$ has the value *false* and so the repetition terminates. The assumption that the data values are followed by a sentinel value is essential for proving termination. If the user never enters a sentinel value, the program will process data values forever or (more likely) wait forever for the next data value to be entered.

Example 3-14. *Printing a Sales Report*

The program in Figure 3-6 is *interactive*—it prompts the user to enter each item of input data. Now let's see how to use a sentinel with a *noninteractive* or *batch-processing* program—one that reads all its input from a disk file and processes it without further user intervention.

The details of creating and accessing disk files will vary from system to system. Generally, a disk file to be processed as a textfile can be created with the same text editor that you use to create your Pascal programs. The data is typed exactly as if it were being read directly from the keyboard. The data items are arranged in lines, with one or more spaces separating adjacent items on the same line.

Many systems allow the standard files *input* and *output* to be *redirected* to disk files. File redirection (also called I/O redirection) allows us to read disk files from the standard file *input* and thus avoid for now some additional technicalities associated with programmer-defined files. If the system you are using does not allow file redirection, your instructor will provide you with the necessary information for accessing or simulating disk files.

Our example program is to compute salespeople's commissions. A typical input file is shown in Figure 3-7. Each line of data gives the salesperson's employee number, amount sold, and percentage commission rate. Thus, employee 1259 sold $5,734.25 worth of goods and earns an 8 percent commission; employee 2976 sold $8,364.00 worth and earns a 9.5 percent commission. The file is terminated with a sentinel consisting of an employee number of 9999. An employee who sells $200 worth or more is paid a commission on the amount sold at the rate given for that employee. An employee who sells less than $200 worth receives no commission.

In data processing, a *report* is a printout of data in tabular form. Our program is to print a report showing each employee's identification number, amount sold, percent commission, and commission paid to the employee. The data is to be printed in four columns, with each column 15 characters wide. Figure 3-8 shows the report produced from the sample data file in Figure 3-7.

Figure 3-7.

Sample input data for the sales-report program. Note the sentinel value on the last line.

```
1259 5734.25 8
2976 8364.00 9.5
3712 6945.50 10
3805 150.00 7
3996 9275.75 11
5213 2765.00 6.5
9999
```

Figure 3-8.

Printout produced by the sales-report program when given the input data in Figure 3-7.

Employee Number	Amount Sold	Percent Commission	Commission Paid
1259	5734.25	8.0	458.74
2976	8364.00	9.5	794.58
3712	6945.50	10.0	694.55
3805	150.00	7.0	0.00
3996	9275.75	11.0	1020.33
5213	2765.00	6.5	179.73

The employee number must be read and tested (to see if it is the sentinel) before the remaining data for the employee can be read. If the employee number were not tested before reading the amount sold and percent commission, the last line of the file, which contains only the sentinel, would be processed incorrectly: the program would attempt to read a nonexistent amount sold and percent commission following the sentinel. These considerations lead to the following outline for our program:

1. Print column headings and blank line
2. Read employee number for first employee
3. While the most recently read employee number is not equal to the sentinel value, repeat the following:
   3.1 Read remaining data for current employee
   3.2 Compute commission
   3.3 Print one *detail line*—one line of data and results
   3.4 Read employee number for next employee

Looking at the program listing in Figure 3-9, we see that the pseudocode translates straightforwardly into the statement part of the main program. We use a *read* statement to read the employee number and a *readln* statement to read the remaining data for each employee. Using the technique of top-down design, pseudocode steps 1 and 3.2 are translated into procedure calls.

The procedure *PrintColumnHeadings* prints two lines of column headings followed by a blank line. The only point to be noted about this procedure is the following: each word in a column heading is followed by spaces, if necessary, so that the two string constants representing the heading for a given column have the same length.

```
'Employee' 'Amount' 'Percent    ' 'Commission'
'Number  ' 'Sold  ' 'Commission' 'Paid      '
```

The extra spaces cause the words making up a column heading to be aligned with one another on the left. If the extra spaces had not been included, Pascal would have aligned the words on the right. As mentioned earlier, left alignment generally looks better for text items such as column headings.

Figure 3-9.   Program to print a sales report.

---

program *SalesReport* (*input, output*);

{ Print report showing sales amounts and commissions }

const
    sentinel = 9999;   { signals end of data }
var
    employeeNo   : *integer*; { employee ID number }
    amountSold,   { amount of employee's sales }
    percentRate,   { commission rate as percent }
    commission   : *real*;   { commission paid to salesperson }

Figure 3-9. *Continued.*

```pascal
{ ----------------------- Procedure PrintColumnHeadings ---------------------- }

procedure PrintColumnHeadings;

{ Print two lines of column headings and one blank line }

begin
  writeln ('Employee' :15, 'Amount' :15, 'Percent      ' :15, 'Commission' :15);
  writeln ('Number  ' :15, 'Sold    ' :15, 'Commission' :15, 'Paid        ' :15);
  writeln
end; { PrintColumnHeadings }

{ ------------------------- Procedure ComputeCommission ---------------------- }

procedure ComputeCommission (var amountSold,          { input }
                                 percentRate,          { input }
                                 commission  : real); { output }

{ Compute salesperson's commission }

const
  limit      = 200.0  { amount below which no commission is paid }
  convFactor = 100.0; { converts percentage to decimal }
var
  decimalRate: real;   { commission rate as decimal }
begin
  if amountSold < limit then
    commission := 0.0
  else
    begin
      decimalRate := percentRate / convFactor;
      commission := amountSold * decimalRate
    end
end; { ComputeCommission }

{ ---------------------------------- Main Program ---------------------------------- }

begin
  PrintColumnHeadings;
  read (employeeNo);
  while employeeNo <> sentinel do
    begin
      readln (amountSold, percentRate);
      ComputeCommission (amountSold, percentRate, commission);
      writeln (employeeNo :15, amountSold :15:2, percentRate :15:1,
               commission :15:2);
      read (employeeNo)
    end
end.
```

The procedure *ComputeCommission* computes the commission to be paid. If the amount sold is less than $200, the commission is zero. Otherwise, the commission is computed from the amount sold and the percentage rate. Before being used in the commission calculation, the percentage rate must be converted to a decimal rate. These considerations lead to the following pseudocode:

1. Depending on the amount sold, do one of the following:
    1.1 *Amount sold less than $200*: Set the commission to zero
    1.2 *Amount sold is $200 or more*: Compute the commission as follows:
        1.2.1 Convert percentage rate to decimal rate
        1.2.2 Compute commission as product of amount sold and decimal rate

Review Questions

1. Name and describe briefly the five Pascal standard data types.

2. What is a simple data type? Which of the five standard types are simple? Why is the remaining one not?

3. Describe briefly the type *Boolean*; your description should include all the information summarized in Figure 3-1.

4. Describe briefly the type *char*, including all the information summarized in Figure 3-2. What is a collating sequence? What does it mean to say that the collating sequence is representation dependent?

5. Describe briefly the type *integer*, including all the information summarized in Figure 3-3. What is the role of *maxint*? Define the **div** and **mod** operators.

6. Describe briefly the type *real*, including all the information summarized in Figure 3-4.

7. What does it mean to say that an operator is overloaded? Discuss the overloading of the operators $+$, $-$, $*$, and $/$. Is there a one-to-one correspondence between operator symbols and the operations they call for?

8. Define assignment compatibility. What two rules govern assignment compatibility for simple standard data types?

9. Define the six relational operators. What purpose do they serve? To what types of operands can they be applied? What type of results do they produce? Are the relational operators overloaded?

10. What are the two defining characteristics of an ordinal type? Which of the simple data types is not ordinal? Why?

11. In the absence of rules governing the order in which the operators are to be applied, what two possible values can we arrive at for the expression

    $7 * 5 - 4$

12. What is operator precedence? For what purpose is it used?

13. Give the precedence for the arithmetical operators in Pascal.

14. Give the rule governing the order in which operators with the same precedence are applied.

15. What is the effect of parentheses on the order in which operators are applied?

16. What is a condition? How is a condition represented in Pascal?

17. In an expression involving relational and arithmetical operators, which is applied first?

18. How are the Boolean operators **not**, **and**, and **or** related to the corresponding English words?

19. Give a table showing the precedence of the arithmetical, relational, and Boolean operators.

20. Why must expressions containing relational operators be enclosed in parentheses before being joined by Boolean operators?

21. What is the relation between control structures and control statements? What control structure does the **if** statement implement?

22. Give the two forms of the **if** statement that were introduced in this chapter and describe how each is executed.

23. For each of the two forms of the **if** statement, give the location of the following:
    a. the semicolon that separates the **if** statement from the statement that precedes it.
    b. the semicolon that separates the **if** statement from the statement that follows it.

24. How are compound statements used in connection with the **if** statement? In what way would Pascal **if** statements be limited if compound statements were not available?

25. Describe how a **while** statement is executed.

26. What is a sentinel? For what purpose is it used?

Exercises ——————————————————————————————————————

1. Write a program to convert a time in seconds into hours, minutes, and seconds. For example, 4,000 seconds would be converted to 1 hour, 6 minutes, and 40 seconds.

2. Modify the program in Figure 3-9 so that it prints the following information at the bottom of the report:
   a. the number of salespeople listed in the report.
   b. the total amount sold.
   c. the total commission paid.

3. Write a program to compute the sum of all the integers from 1 through 100.*

4. The nth power of a number can be computed by starting with one and multiplying by the number in question n times. For example, the 3rd power of 5 equals
   $$1 \times 5 \times 5 \times 5$$

————————————————
*Although Exercises 3 through 5 can be solved a bit more simply with the aid of the **for** statement introduced in Chapter 6, solving them with the **while** statement is good practice.

which equals

$$5 \times 5 \times 5$$

or 125. Write a program that raises a given real number to the power of a given positive integer.

5. You are offered work for one month under the following terms. You will be paid one cent for the first day you work, two cents for the second day, four cents for the third day, and so on, doubling the amount for every day of the month. Write a program to determine how much you would earn for the month. The program should accept from the user the number of days in a month so that you can see how much more you could make by working in July rather than February or June.

6. Write a program to determine how many days it would take you to become a millionaire working under the terms given Exercise 5.

7. Each line of a textfile contains a student's ID number and the student's final number grade (both integers). Write a program to read this file and print a three-column report. The first column contains the ID numbers and the second contains the number grades. The third column contains the word *passed* for each student whose number grade is 70 or more and the word *failed* for each student whose number grade is less than 70.

8. Salespeople at a certain company earn a 10 percent commission on the first $5,000 of monthly sales and a 15 percent commission all sales after the first $5,000. The sales data is stored in a textfile, each line of which contains the department number, the salesperson number (both integers) and the amount sold (real). Write a program to read this file and print a report showing, for each salesperson, the department number, the salesperson number, the amount sold, the commission earned at the 10 percent rate, the commission earned at the 15 percent rate, the total commission earned, and the amount received by the company after the salesperson's commission has been deducted.

9. A machine part is in the shape of a block, whose length, width, and height are required to lie within specified limits. Write a program to determine which blocks meet the requirements. The first line of data for the program should give the lower and upper limits allowed for each of the three dimensions. Each remaining line of data consists of the identification number of a block followed by its dimensions. For each block, the program will print its identification number, its dimensions, and the word REJECTED if any of its dimensions are outside the specified limits. *Hint*: The **and** operator will be useful.

10. A company makes storage tanks in the shape of cylinders and spheres. Write a program that employees can use to compute the volumes of tanks of either shape. When the program is started, it displays the following prompt:

    `Cylinder, Sphere, or Quit (C/S/Q)?`

    If the user enters C or c, the program prompts for and accepts the necessary data, then computes the volume of a cylindrical tank. If the user enters S or s, the same is done for a spherical tank. An entry of Q or q terminates the program. When a computation is complete, the program again displays the prompt. The formula for the volume of a cylinder is

    $$V = \frac{\pi d^2 h}{4}$$

where V is the volume of the cylinder, d is its diameter, h is its height, and π is the constant pi (approximately equal to 3.1416). The formula for the volume of a sphere is

$$V = \frac{\pi d^3}{6}$$

where V is the volume and d is the diameter of the sphere.

11. Write a procedure *Sort* to sort three integer values into ascending order. Specifically, the procedure call

    Sort (first, second, third)

    should rearrange the values of the integer variables *first*, *second*, and *third* such that *first* receives the smallest of the three values and *second* receives the largest. The following algorithm can be used to sort three numbers into ascending order:

    1. Compare the first and second numbers; if they are out of order, exchange them
    2. Compare the second and third numbers; if they are out of order, exchange them
    3. Again compare the first and second numbers (the second number may have been changed by step 2); if they are out of order, exchange them

    Write a program to test this procedure.

12. Write a program to find the highest and lowest temperatures recorded during a given period. The input file consists of integer temperatures, each on a separate line. The file is terminated by a sentinel value of 9999. The program should read the file and print the highest and lowest temperatures read. *Hint*: As the program reads the temperatures, it should keep track of the highest and lowest temperatures read so far. Each newly read temperature is compared with the record high and low maintained by the program; if the new temperature breaks one of the records, it becomes the new record high or low.

13. Modify the program for Exercise 12 as follows. Each line of the input file now consists of a temperature followed by the time at which it was recorded. The program is to report not only the high and low but the time at which each was recorded. If a high or low occurs more than once, the time that occurs first in the input file is the one reported.

14. An integer greater than one is a *prime number* if it is not evenly divisible by any integer greater than 1 and less than itself. Write a program to test whether a given integer greater than 1 is prime by attempting to divide it by every integer from 2 up to (but not including) the integer in question. *Hints*: One positive integer divides another evenly if

    dividend **mod** *divisor* $\Rightarrow$ 0

    The repetition that tests the different trial divisors will terminate if a divisor was found or if all divisors have been tested. After the repetition terminates, the program can examine the values of appropriate variables to determine which condition caused the termination.

15. We know the volume of a container, the amount of water initially in it, the rate at which water is flowing in, and the rate at which water is leaking out. Write a program to determine if the container fills up, if it empties out, or if the water level remains steady. In the first two cases, the program should compute the time required for the container to fill or empty. The program will have the following structure:

1. Depending on whether the rate of flow into the container is less than the rate of flow out of the container, do one of the following:

    1.1 *Rate in is less than rate out*: Compute time required for container to empty

    1.2 *Rate in is not less than rate out*: Depending on the flow rates, do one of the following:

        1.2.1 *Rate in equals rate out*: Inform user that level is steady

        1.2.2 *Rate in does not equal (and hence is greater than) rate out*: Compute time required for container to fill

Hint: **if** statements can be nested. The statement in the **then** or **else** part of an **if** statement can itself be another **if** statement.

4

Parameters, Functions, and Debugging

In this chapter, we extend our knowledge of Pascal by considering another kind of subprogram (the function) and another kind of subprogram parameter (the value parameter). In the area of programming technique, we look at the problems of testing and debugging programs that use selection and repetition.

Value Parameters

Value parameters are so-called because the actual parameters, which may be arbitrary expressions, are evaluated and their *values* are passed to the subprogram. Because the actual parameters are not necessarily variables, they are not able to receive values returned by the subprogram. Thus value parameters can only be used to transmit data to a subprogram; variable parameters must be used to return data to the calling program. The following summarizes the properties of value parameters:

■ The actual parameters are expressions, which may be constants, variables, or expressions formed with operators and functions.

■ Before the statements in the subprogram declaration are executed, the actual-parameter expressions are evaluated, and their values are assigned to the corresponding formal parameters. Each actual-parameter value need only be assignment compatible with the corresponding formal parameter. Thus an integer value can be passed to a real formal parameter, because a value of type *integer* can be assigned to a variable of type *real*.

■ During the execution of the statement part of the subprogram, the formal parameters behave like variables. Initially, the values of the formal parameters are the values of the corresponding actual parameters. As long as the values of the formal parameters are not changed, the formal parameters can be used in expressions to refer to the values of the corresponding actual parameters.

■ An assignment to a formal parameter during the execution of a function or procedure changes the value of the formal parameter but has no effect whatever on the corresponding actual parameter.

■ A value parameter is declared in the same way as a variable parameter *except* that the reserved word **var** is omitted. For example, the procedure heading

```
procedure Sample (var oldCount,
                      newCount : integer;
                  length,
                  width        : real);
```

declares *oldCount* and *newCount* as variable parameters and *length* and *width* as value parameters.

Standard Functions

Like a procedure, a function is a subprogram that can be called whenever the calculation that it carries out is needed. Functions differ from procedures, however, in how they are called and how they return their results. A function call is not a statement but an expression, which can stand alone or be part of a larger expression. When called, the function returns a value that becomes the value of the function-call expression and can be used in evaluating any larger expression of which the function call may be a part.

Pascal provides a number of predefined standard functions that the programmer can use without having to write function declarations for them. In this section, we will explore the standard functions; in the next section, we will see how to write our own function declarations.

To use a function, we write an expression called a *function designator*, which consists of the name of the function followed by a parenthesized list of actual parameters; the actual parameters for a function are often called *arguments*. The actual parameters provide the input data for the function's calculations. For example, the function designator

   sqr(5)

indicates that the function *sqr* is to be applied to the value 5.

In an expression, the function designator represents the value that results when the function is applied to its actual parameters. We sometimes refer to this value as the *value returned by the function*. For example, the function *sqr* computes the square of its parameter—the result of multiplying the parameter value by itself. Thus for a parameter value of 5, the function *sqr* returns 25, the result of multiplying 5 by itself. The expression *sqr*(5) represents 25 in the same way as does 5 * 5 or 12 + 13. The following table shows the values of some other function designators constructed with the function *sqr*:

Expression	Value
sqr(1)	1
sqr(2)	4
sqr(3)	9
sqr(4)	16

Function designators can be used as parts of larger expressions. The values of the function designators are worked out before any of the other operators are applied.

Expression	Value
sqr(2) + 3	7
2 * *sqr*(3)	18
2 * *sqr*(4) + 3	35

The last example is evaluated as follows:

2 * *sqr*(4) + 3	Apply function,
2 * 16 + 3	multiplication next,
32 + 3	then addition.
35	

The actual parameters of a standard function can themselves be expressions.* The expressions serving as parameters are always evaluated before applying the function.

Expression	Value
sqr(3 + 5)	64
sqr(2 * 3 − 2)	16
2 * *sqr*(4 * 3 − 7) + 1	51

The last example is evaluated as follows:

2 * *sqr*(4 * 3 − 7) + 1	Evaluate parameter: multiplication.
2 * *sqr*(12 − 7) + 1	Evaluate parameter: subtraction.
2 * *sqr*(5) + 1	Apply function next,
2 * 25 + 1	then multiplication,
50 + 1	then addition.
51	

We will now look briefly at all the predefined functions provided by standard Pascal.

Arithmetical Functions: General Purpose

The functions defined in this section are useful in many kinds of arithmetical calculations.

Function	Definition
abs	Returns the absolute value of its parameter. If the parameter is negative, the corresponding positive value is returned; if the parameter is positive, its value is returned unchanged. Thus the value of both *abs*(−5) and *abs*(5) is 5.
sqr	Returns the square of its parameter. Thus the value of *sqr*(3) is 9 and the value of *sqr*(1.5) is 2.25.

*For programmer-defined functions, the programmer has the choice of using value parameters, which allow expressions as actual parameters, or of using variable parameters, which allow only variables.

Function	Definition
sqrt	Returns the square root of its parameter—the value that, when multiplied by itself, is equal to the parameter value. Thus, the value of *sqrt*(9) is 3.0 and the value of *sqrt*(2.25) is 1.5. *Sqrt* is not defined for negative parameter values.

The parameters of *sqr* and *abs* can be either integers or real numbers; the value returned has the same type as the parameter. The parameter of *sqrt* can be either an integer or a real number; the value returned is always real.

Arithmetical Functions: Scientific

The functions defined in this section are mainly used in scientific calculations. The functions are only identified here; their definitions are left to mathematics courses. We will look at an application of *exp* and *ln* later in this chapter.

Function	Definition
sin	Returns the sine of its parameter; the parameter must be in radians.
cos	Returns the cosine of its parameter; the parameter must be in radians.
arctan	Returns the arctangent of its parameter; the value returned is in radians.
exp	Returns e^x where x is the parameter value; *exp* is the *inverse* of the *ln* function: if $y = ln(x)$ then $x = exp(y)$
ln	Returns the natural logarithm of the parameter value. It is an error if the parameter value is zero or negative.

The parameters of the scientific functions are real numbers, and these functions return real results.

Transfer Functions

In most circumstances, Pascal will automatically convert an integer to a real number if necessary. However, Pascal does not automatically perform the reverse conversion of a real number to an integer. The functions *trunc* and *round* allow the programmer to specify the latter conversion when it is needed.

Function	Definition
trunc	Converts a real number to an integer by discarding all digits to the right of the decimal point. Thus the values of both *trunc*(3.25) and *trunc*(3.75) are 3.
round	Converts a real number to an integer by rounding the real value to the nearest integer. Thus the value of *round*(3.25) is 3 and the value of *round*(3.75) is 4.

The parameters of *trunc* and *round* are always real numbers, and the values returned are always integers.

There are two standard ways of converting a real number to an integer. One, known as *truncation*, simply discards all digits to the right of the decimal point; for instance, 6.72 becomes 6. The other, known as *rounding*, converts the real value to the nearest integer; for instance, 6.72 becomes 7. The functions *trunc* and *round* carry out the operations of truncation and rounding.

If we wish to assign a real value to an integer variable, we must first use either *trunc* or *round* to convert the real value to an integer. Thus if *stingy* and *generous* are integer variables, the following statements are both valid:

```
stingy := trunc(6.72);
generous := round(6.72)
```

The value of *stingy* becomes 6 and the value of *generous* becomes 7.

Ordinal Functions

We recall that the values of an ordinal type can be put in a standard order, so that each value (except the first) has an immediate predecessor and each value (except the last) has an immediate successor. The values of each ordinal type are numbered; the numbers are called the *ordinal numbers* of the values. The ordinal number of the immediate predecessor of a value is one less than the ordinal number of the value; the ordinal number of the immediate successor of a value is one greater than the ordinal number of the value.

The ordinal numbers of Boolean values are 0 for *false* and 1 for *true*. Integers are their own ordinal numbers: the ordinal number of 20 is 20, the ordinal number of −5 is −5, and so on. The ordinal numbers for characters are representation dependent; ordinal numbers for the ASCII and EBCDIC representations can be found in Appendix 5. Figure A5-1 gives the ordinal numbers for ASCII and Figure A5-2 gives the ordinal numbers for EBCDIC.

Function	Definition
ord	Returns the ordinal number of its parameter value. Thus the value of *ord(false)* is 0 and the value of *ord(true)* is 1.
chr	Returns the character having a given ordinal number; thus the value returned by *chr* is representation dependent. For the ASCII code, the value of *chr*(97) is 'a' and the value of *chr*(122) is 'z'.
succ	Returns the immediate successor of the parameter value; it is an error if the parameter value has no successor. Thus the value of *succ(false)* is *true* and attempting to evaluate *succ(true)* will cause an error.
pred	Returns the immediate predecessor of the parameter value; it is an error if the parameter value has no predecessor. Thus the value of *pred(true)* is *false* and attempting to evaluate *pred(false)* will cause an error.

The functions *ord* (ordinal number), *succ* (immediate successor), and *pred* (immediate predecessor) are defined for parameters of all ordinal types. The function *chr* is more specialized; it converts ordinal numbers of characters to the corresponding values of type *char*. There is no predefined function corresponding to *chr* for any ordinal type other than *char*.

Boolean Functions

A Boolean function provides information about a parameter value by returning *true* if the parameter value satisfies a certain condition and *false* otherwise. The function *odd*, which distinguishes between odd and even numbers, is useful in mathematical calculations. The functions *eof* (end-of-file) and *eoln* (end-of-line) are useful for processing data read from files.

Function	Definition
odd	Returns *true* if its parameter is an odd integer and *false* otherwise. Thus the value of *odd*(3) is *true* and that of *odd*(4) is *false*.
eof	*eof*(*f*) has the value *true* if the end-of-file *f* has been reached: all the data has been read from the file. If the file parameter is omitted, the standard input file is assumed. Thus *eof* by itself is equivalent to *eof*(*input*).
eoln	*eoln*(*f*) has the value *true* if the end of the line of text currently being read from *f* has been reached. File *f* must be a textfile (type *text*), the only kind of file for which lines are defined. If the file parameter is omitted, the standard input file is assumed. Thus *eoln* by itself is equivalent to *eoln*(*input*).

Example 4-1. *Reading Data Using the eof Function*

We have seen how a sentinel can be used to let a program detect the end of a file from which it is reading input data. The use of a sentinel does complicate the program slightly, though. In each input record, the data item that may be the sentinel must be read separately and tested before any other data items can be read or processed. In the sales-report program in Figure 3-9, for example, the employee number (which may be the sentinel) must be read and tested before *amountSold* and *percentRate* are read and before any processing is done.

```
read (employeeNo);
while employeeNo <> sentinel do
  begin
    readln (amountSold, percentRate);
    ComputeCommission (amountSold, percentRate, commission);
    writeln (employeeNo :15, amountSold :15:2, percentRate :15:1,
          commission :15:2);
    read (employeeNo)
  end
```

We must use two *read* statements for *employeeNo* to assure that a new employee number is always read just before the test for the sentinel is performed.

The *eof* function uses information maintained by the operating system to detect the end of a file, thus freeing us from having to provide a sentinel value in the file and having to test for it in the program. When *eof* is used, none of the values in an input record have to be treated specially, so all can be read with a single *readln* statement. Figure 4-1 shows a version of the sales-report program that uses *eof* rather than a sentinel to detect the end of the input data. The statements that read and process records are simpler and more straightforward than in the previous version.

```
while not eof(input) do
    begin
        readln (employeeNo, amountSold, percentRate);
        ComputeCommission (amountSold, percentRate, commission);
        writeln (employeeNo :15, amountSold :15:2, percentRate :15:1,
                commission :15:2)
    end
```

Note that an entire input record—all the data for one employee—is now read with a single *readln* statement.

The *eof* function is used mainly when reading from disk files. To be sure, some Pascal systems do designate a special key that can be pressed to signal end-of-file when the program is reading from the keyboard; *eof* returns *false* before the special key is presented and *true* afterwards. However, the exact point in the data entry process at which the special key is pressed may be critical. If the special key is inadvertently preceded by a space or a carriage return, the program may malfunction. Special keys that must be used in tricky ways are not characteristics of user-friendly programs. Thus sentinels (or other techniques, such as the program asking the user whether or not more data is to be entered) are recommended for interactive programs.

Figure 4-1.

This version of the sales-report program uses the *eof* function rather than a sentinel to detect the end of the input file.

program *SalesReport* (*input*, *output*);

{ Print report showing sales amounts and commissions }

var
    employeeNo : *integer*; { employee ID number }
    amountSold,   { amount of employee's sales }
    percentRate,   { commission rate as percent }
    commission : *real*; { commission paid to salesperson }

Figure 4-1.   *Continued.*

```
{ ------------------------ Procedure PrintColumnHeadings ----------------------- }

procedure PrintColumnHeadings;

{ Print two lines of column headings and one blank line }

begin
  writeln ('Employee' :15, 'Amount' :15, 'Percent      ' :15, 'Commission' :15);
  writeln ('Number   ' :15, 'Sold      ' :15, 'Commission' :15, 'Paid        ' :15);
  writeln
end; { PrintColumnHeadings }

{ ------------------------ Procedure ComputeCommission ----------------------- }

procedure ComputeCommission (var amountSold,          { input }
                                 percentRate,          { input }
                                 commission : real); { output }

{ Compute salesperson's commission }

const
  limit       = 200.0  { amount below which no commission is paid }
  convFactor  = 100.0; { converts percentage to decimal }
var
  decimalRate : real;     { commission rate as decimal }
begin
  if amountSold < limit then
    commission := 0.0
  else
    begin
      decimalRate :=  percentRate / convFactor;
      commission := amountSold * decimalRate
    end
end; { ComputeCommission }

{ ------------------------------- Main Program -------------------------------- }

begin
  PrintColumnHeadings;
  while not eof (input) do
    begin
      readln (employeeNo, amountSold, percentRate);
      ComputeCommission (amountSold, percentRate, commission);
      writeln (employeeNo :15, amountSold :15:2, percentRate :15:1,
               commission :15:2)
    end
end.
```

Function Declarations

In addition to using the standard functions, programmers can define their own functions in function declarations. A function declaration has the following structure:

> function heading
> block
> semicolon

A function heading has the following form:

> **function** function-name (formal-param-decls) : return-type

The formal parameters are declared in the same way as for a procedure. Either value or variable parameters can be declared; value parameters are preferred, however, because they allow the actual parameters to be expressions, thus making it possible to express complex calculations compactly. The return type gives the type of values that the function can return. Thus a function with a return type of *real* can only return real values; a function with a return type of *integer* can only return integer values, and so on.

For example, a function that computes the volume of a box from its length, width, and height might have the following heading:

> **function** *Volume* (*length*, *width*, *height* : *real*) : *real*;

The name of the function is *Volume*, which describes the computation that the function carries out and the value it returns. The formal parameters are *length*, *width*, and *height*, which are declared as value parameters of type *real*. The return type, *real*, specifies that the function *Volume* returns real values. Note that a function heading, like a procedure or program heading, is terminated by a semicolon.

The statement part of a function declaration must contain a statement specifying the value that the function is to return. The return value is specified by assigning it to the function name. That is, there must be an assignment statement with the following form:

> function-name := expression

When this statement is executed, the expression is evaluated, and its value is designated as the value that the function will return. If more than one such assignment statement is present, the last one that is executed determines the value that will be returned.

A complete function declaration for *Volume* is as follows:

> **function** *Volume* (*length*, *width*, *height* : *real*) : *real*;
> **begin**
>   *Volume* := *length* * *width* * *height*
> **end**;

When the function is called, the values of the actual parameters are assigned to the corresponding formal parameters. For example, when the statement

> *V* := *Volume*(5.0, 4.0, 3.0)

is executed, *Volume* is called with the actual parameters 5.0, 4.0, and 3.0.

When the function is called, the following assignments automatically take place:

    length := 5.0;
    width := 4.0;
    height := 3.0

Since the formal parameters are value parameters of type *real*, the actual parameter values must be assignment compatible with type *real*—they must be values that can be assigned to real variables. Thus the statement

    V := *Volume*(5, 4, 3)

is valid because integer values can be assigned to real variables—the following assignment statements are valid:

    length := 5;
    width := 4;
    height := 3

On the other hand, the statement

    V := *Volume* ('5', '4', '3')

is invalid because character values cannot be assigned to real variables.

Because of the simplicity of the calculation performed, the function declaration for *Volume* does not contain any definitions or declarations. The statement part contains only a single statement.

    Volume := *length* ∗ *width* ∗ *height*

The expression to the right of the assignment operator computes the product of the values of the three formal parameters. Since the values of the actual parameters have been assigned to the corresponding formal parameters, the actual-parameter values are used in evaluating the expression. The value of the expression is assigned to the function name; this designates the value of the expression as the value the function is to return.

Thus *Volume* returns the product of the values of its actual parameters. For example, in the statement

    V := *Volume*(5.0, 4.0, 3.0)

Volume returns the value 60.0, and the value 60.0 is assigned to the variable *V*.

Example 4-2. *The Function* **Power**

A serious deficiency of Pascal for scientific and engineering applications is its lack of an exponentiation operator (such as ^ in BASIC and ∗∗ in FORTRAN) for raising numbers to powers. All is not lost, however, for we can still raise numbers to powers using the method of logarithms, which was widely used with logarithm tables and slide rules back in the days before pocket calculators. The calculation with logarithms proceeds in three steps.

1. Find the logarithm of the *base*—the number that is to be raised to a power.

2. Multiply the logarithm of the base by the *exponent*—the power to which the base is to be raised.

3. Find the antilogarithm of the product—that is, find the number whose logarithm is equal to the product of the exponent and the logarithm of the base. This number is the desired result, the result of raising the base to the power given by the exponent.

In Pascal, the standard function *ln* computes logarithms and the standard function *exp* computes antilogarithms. Thus we can use the following expression to raise a number to a power:

$$exp(ln(base) * exponent)$$

The *ln* function computes the logarithm of the base and the function *exp* computes the antilogarithm of the product of the logarithm of the base and the exponent. The only restriction on the use of this expression is that the value of *base* must be greater than zero, because the function *ln* is not defined for zero and negative arguments.

We can use this expression to define a function *Power* that returns the result of raising a number to a given power. The first argument of *Power* (which must be greater than zero) is the number that is to be raised to a power; the second argument is the power to which the first argument is to be raised.

function *Power* (*base, exponent* : *real*) : *real*;
begin
    Power := *exp(ln(base) * exponent)*
end;

The value of *Power*(2.0, 3.0), for example, is 8.0 and the value of *Power*(3.0, 2.0) is 9.0.

An important advantage of functions and procedures is that they can be written and tested independently of the program in which they will eventually be incorporated. We will frequently write a short program to test or exercise a just-completed function or procedure, and you will be expected to do likewise when working end-of-chapter exercises that call for a function or procedure. Figure 4-2 shows the program *ExercisePower* (no pun intended!), which obtains a base and exponent from the user and displays the result returned by *Power*. The program requests the user to enter a number and the power to which it is to be raised; the number is read into *number* and the power to which it is to be raised is read into *pwr*. The statement

result := *Power(number, pwr)*

calls *Power* with actual parameters *number* and *pwr*. The values of the actual parameters *number* and *pwr* are assigned to the formal parameters *base* and *exponent*, after which the statement part of the function is executed. Thus the expression

$$exp(ln(base) * exponent)$$

is evaluated with the value of *base* set to that of *number* and the value of *exponent* set to that of *pwr*. The value of the expression is returned as the

Figure 4-2.

The function *Power* embedded in a program to test or exercise the function. Such a program is often called a test driver or a test harness.

---

program *ExercisePower* (*input*, *output*);

{ Use the function *Power* to raise a number to a power }

var
   number,   { number to be raised to a power }
   pwr,   { power to which it is to be raised }
   result : *real*; { result of raising number to power }

{ ------------------------------- Function *Power* ------------------------------- }

function *Power* (*base*, *exponent* : *real*) : *real*;

{ Compute result of raising base to the power *exponent*. The value of base
  must be greater than zero }

begin
   Power := *exp*(*ln*(*base*) * *exponent*)
end; { *Power* }

{ ---------------------------------- Main Program ---------------------------------- }
begin
   write ('Enter number (must be greater than 0) and power: ');
   readln (*number*, *pwr*);
   result := *Power*(*number*, *pwr*);
   writeln ('Result: ', *result* :1:3)
end.

---

value of *Power* and so is assigned to *result*. The value of *result* is then printed for the user's inspection.

    If the first argument of *Power* is not greater than zero, a run-time error will result when the function attempts to apply the *ln* function to a zero or negative value. Run-time error messages are often cryptic; with the aid of an **if** statement we can arrange for *Power* to print a more meaningful error message when it is invoked with an invalid argument.

begin
  if *base* <= 0 **then**
     writeln ('ERROR: Power called with zero or negative base');
  Power := *exp*(*ln*(*base*) * *exponent*)
end;

If the value of *base* is less than or equal to zero, the Boolean expression

    base <= 0

evaluates to *true* and the error message is printed. If the value of *base* is greater than zero, the Boolean expression evaluates to *false* and the **if** statement takes no action. Note that even when an erroneous value for *base* is detected, the evaluation of *ln(base)* is still attempted so that the execution of the program will be terminated.

Example 4-3. *The Function* **Max**

We sometimes need to determine which of two numbers is the larger. This can be done with a function *Max*, which returns the larger of its two argument values.

```
function Max (numberA, numberB : integer) : integer;
begin
  if numberA > numberB then
    Max := numberA
  else
    Max := numberB
end;
```

When the function is invoked, the values of its actual parameters are assigned to the formal parameters *numberA* and *numberB*. The statement part of the function contains a single **if** statement, which controls the execution of two assignment statements. When the **if** statement is executed, the Boolean expression

numberA > numberB

is evaluated. If the value of *numberA* is greater than that of *numberB*, the Boolean expression will evaluate to *true* and the statement

Max := numberA

will be executed. Thus the value of *numberA* will be returned as the value of *Max*. If the value of *numberA* is less than or equal to the value of *numberB*, the Boolean expression will evaluate to *false* and the statement

Max := numberB

will be executed. In this case, the value of *numberB* will be returned as the value of *Max*. Thus the value of *Max*(7, 4) is 7 and the value of *Max*(8, 10) is 10.

Figure 4-3 shows a program to exercise *Max*. Two integers are requested from the user and read into the variables *number1* and *number2*. The statement

larger := Max(number1, number2)

invokes *Max* to find the larger of the two numbers. The result returned by *Max* is assigned to *larger*, after which it is printed for the user's inspection.

Figure 4-3.

The function *Max* and a program to exercise it.

```
program ExerciseMax (input, output);

{ Use function Max to find the larger of two integers }

var
   number1, number2,        { numbers to be compared }
   larger              : integer; { larger of two numbers }

{ ---------------------------------- Function Max ---------------------------------- }

function Max (numberA, numberB : integer) : integer;

{ Return the larger of the values of the two parameters }

begin
   if numberA > numberB then
      Max := numberA
   else
      Max := numberB
end; { Max }

{ ---------------------------------- Main Program ---------------------------------- }

begin
   write ('Enter two numbers: ');
   readln (number1, number2);
   larger := Max(number1, number2);
   writeln ('Larger number: ', larger :1)
end.
```

Example 4-4.   *The Function* Commission

Our final example has been deliberately made a bit convoluted so as to illustrate a slightly more complex function declaration. We wish to write a function *Commission* that will compute the commission earned by a salesperson. Figure 4-4 shows the function declaration and a program for exercising it.

We assume the salesperson both works in the store and goes out on the road. Sales made on the road count for 1.25 as much as sales made in the store; that is, a dollar's worth sold on the road is the equivalent, in terms of commission earned, to a dollar and a quarter's worth sold in the store. If someone sold $3,000 worth in the store and $2,000 on the road, an effective total sale of

$$\$3000 + 1.25 \times \$2000 = \$3000 + \$2500 = \$5500$$

would be used in computing that person's commission.

Figure 4-4.

The function *Commission* and a program to exercise it.

```
program ExerciseCommission (input, output);

{ Test function Commission }

var
    storeSales, roadSales,          { sales in and out of store }
    break,                          { sales at which rate changes }
    standardRate, bonusRate,        { low and high rates in percent }
    commOnSales              : real; { commission earned }

{ ----------------------------- Function Commission ----------------------------- }

function Commission(inSales,        { amount of sales inside store }
                    outSales,       { amount of sales outside store }
                    breakPoint,     { sales amount at which commission
                                      changes from loRate to hiRate }
                    loRate,         { decimal rate for sales amounts
                                      not exceeding breakPoint }
                    hiRate    : real { decimal rate for sales amounts
                                      in excess of breakPoint }
                    ) : real;

{ Compute commission according to total amount sold }

var
    totalSales : real; { effective total sales }
begin
    totalSales := inSales + 1.25 * outSales;
    if totalSales <= breakPoint then
        Commission := loRate * totalSales
    else
        Commission := loRate * breakPoint +
                      hiRate * (totalSales − breakPoint)
end; { Commission }

{ ----------------------------- Main Program ----------------------------- }

begin
    write ('Enter sales in store and on road: ');
    readln (storeSales, roadSales);
    write ('Enter sales amount at which commission increases: ');
    readln (break);
    write ('Enter low and high commission rates; ');
    readln (standardRate, bonusRate);
    commOnSales := Commission(storeSales, roadSales, break,
                              standardRate / 100.0, bonusRate / 100.0);
    writeln ('Commission earned: ', commOnSales :1:2)
end.
```

There are two commission rates; the lower rate applies to total sales amounts up to a certain break-point amount, and the higher rate applies to total sales amounts greater than the break-point amount. For example, suppose that the break-point amount is $5,000 and the two rates are 0.10 (10 percent) and 0.15 (15 percent). A salesperson whose total sales were $7,000 would be paid

$5000 × 0.10 = $500

for the first $5,000 of sales and

$2000 × 0.15 = $300

for the $2,000 of sales in excess of $5,000. Thus the salesperson's total earnings would be

$500 + $300 = $800

Referring to Figure 4-4, we see that the formal parameters for commission are *inSales* and *outSales* (the amounts sold inside and outside the store), *breakPoint* (the total sales amount at which the commission rate changes), and *loRate* and *hiRate* (the two commission rates, expressed as decimals; for example, 0.15 instead of 15 percent). All the formal parameters are of type *real*. Note that each formal parameter is declared on a separate line so that its use can be described in a comment. Spreading a function heading over a number of lines is common when there are a large number of formal parameters or the individual parameter declarations need to have comments.

We declare a variable *totalSales* to hold the effective total of the sales made inside and outside the store. The variable *totalSales* is known as a *local variable* since it can be referred to only from within the declaration for *Commission*. The identifier *totalSales* declared in *Commission* has nothing whatever to do with any other identifier *totalSales* that might be declared in the main program or in any other procedure or function declaration.

Because sales made outside the store count for 1.25 as much sales made in the store, we multiply the value of *outSales* by 1.25 and add the product to the value of *inSales* to get the effective total sales.

   totalSales := *inSales* + 1.25 * *outSales*;

We have two possible expressions for calculating the salesperson's commission. If the value of *totalSales* does not exceed that of *breakPoint*, then only one commission rate, the value of *loRate* applies. We compute the commission by multiplying the values of *loRate* and *totalSales*

   loRate * *totalSales*

If the value of *totalSales* exceeds that of *breakPoint*, the commission calculation is more complex. A sales amount equal to the value of *breakPoint* earns commission at the value of *loRate*. The amount by which the value of *totalSales* exceeds that of *breakPoint*, which is equal to the value of *totalSales* − *breakPoint*, earns commission at the value of *hiRate*. The total commission, which is the sum of commissions earned at the two different rates, is computed by the following expression:

   loRate * *breakPoint* +
   hiRate * (*totalSales* − *breakPoint*)

The program contains two statements for calculating the value to be returned, each statement using one of the two possible expressions for calculating commission. An **if** statement selects the proper statement for execution depending on whether or not the value of *totalSales* is less than or equal to the value of *breakPoint*.

The program *ExerciseCommission* accepts sales and commission figures from the user and prints the commission calculated by *Commission*. The program accepts the commission rates as percentages; for example, 15 should be entered for a 15 percent commission rate. The function *Commission*, however, requires that the commission rates be supplied as decimals: 0.15 for a 15 percent commission rate. A percentage must be divided by 100 to convert it to a decimal. This conversion is performed in the function designator that invokes *Commission*. The expressions

> *standardRate* / 100.0

and

> *bonusRate* / 100.0

are evaluated before the function is invoked and their values are passed as the last two actual parameters of the function. Thus if the values of *standardRate* and *bonusRate* are 12 and 17, the function will receive 0.12 and 0.17 as the values of its fourth and fifth actual parameters.

Testing and Debugging Selections and Repetitions

Selection and repetition constructions, which are crucial to all nontrivial programs, greatly complicate testing and debugging. Because of selection, the statements actually executed during a run of the program depend upon the input data. Different sets of input data cause different sequences of statements to be executed. To test the program thoroughly, we would like to test every possible execution sequence. But doing so often turns out to be totally impractical.

Let's call each such execution sequence a *path* through the program; different sets of input data, then, cause the computer to take different paths through the program. Each execution of an **if** statement potentially doubles the number of paths through the program, because the path that the computer is on when it encounters the **if** statement splits into two paths: one that goes through the **then**-part of the **if** statement and one that goes through the **else**-part.

Thus if a program contains n **if** statements, there may be as many as 2^n paths through the program. For example, 10 **if** statements give us 2^{10} or 1,024 paths; 20 **if** statements give us 2^{20} or 1,048,576 paths, and 30 **if** statements give us 2^{30} or 1,073,741,824 paths. One hundred **if** statements—by no means an unusual number for a program of modest size—gives us 2^{100} or approximately 1.26×10^{30} (126 followed by 28 zeros) paths.

Repetition makes matters worse because each *execution* of an **if** statement—not just each occurrence of an **if** statement in the program—can double the number of paths. Thus, a single **if** statement executed 100 times could still give 1.26×10^{30} paths through the code. Also, repetition constructions introduce a new kind of error: the repeated executions may fail to terminate, causing the program to *hang* (stop functioning)—often before it has produced any output that might help diagnose the error.

We regretfully conclude that exhaustive testing of a complex program is totally impractical. Even with years of testing on a fast computer, we could not run the program with enough sets of test data to test every possible path. Thus although testing can find errors, it can never guarantee the correctness of a program, because there will always be many paths that remain untested. We may hope that the future will see the development of some more effective method of program validation, such as a computerized logical analysis of the program. But at the present state of software technology, testing is often the only validation technique at our disposal, and we must make the best of it.

The following two techniques will help us get the most out of testing:

■ Break the program down into small modules—subprograms in Pascal— and test each module separately. Because of the small size of the modules, there will be fewer paths through each module, allowing it to be tested more effectively. This is one reason that modularity is emphasized so strongly in modern software engineering. (The other reason is that the simple structure of small modules helps us avoid making errors in the first place.)

■ Choose test data carefully to make testing as effective as possible. Each path tested should be (1) representative of many similar paths, or (2) a path along which an error is likely to occur.

Choosing Test Data

We recall (from our discussion in Chapter 2) that there are two basic approaches to choosing input data for testing. In black box, or functional testing, the selection of test data is based entirely on the program specifications. The internal operation and construction of the program are ignored. In glass box, or structural testing, on the other hand, the structure and operation of the program serve as a guide to test data selection. For example, test data items may be chosen to cause a specific sequence of statements to be executed or to cause a repetition construction to execute the repeated statements a specific number of times.

Black Box Testing. In black box testing, we divide the input data into *input classes*—classes of data items that, according to the specifications, are to be processed differently by the program. For example, the action taken by a billing program might depend on how long the bill is overdue.

Months Overdue	Action
2 months or less	Send normal bill.
3 to 6 months	Send special reminder.
7 to 9 months	Send threatening letter.
10 months	Transfer bill to collection agency.

Time intervals for which different actions are to be taken belong to different input classes.

The largest and smallest values in each input class are called *boundary values*; in the example, 2, 3, 6, 7, 9, and 10 months are boundary values. Program errors frequently occur for boundary values. For example, a very simple error, such as using $<=$ when $<$ is called for, might cause the billing program to send a special reminder instead of a threatening letter for a bill that is seven months overdue. It is thus fruitful to test a program for the largest and smallest value in each input class; such testing is called *boundary-value testing*.

We will also test the program for typical values—values that are not boundary values—in each input class. We can think of each typical value as representing all the other values in the class. Since values in the same input class are processed in similar ways by the program, we hope that if the typical values are processed correctly, then the remaining values will be also.

There may also be special values that should be tested because of the likelihood that they may cause errors. Zero is often a special value. Division by zero is prohibited, making zero likely to cause errors in arithmetical calculations. Also likely to cause trouble are sets of data for which the program should omit an action that it would normally take one or more times. Such input data includes input files containing zero records, requests that the program process zero input values, requests that it produce zero output values, or requests that it set up a table containing zero entries.

Black box testing should be applied to individual modules as well as to the entire program. The specifications for each module are used to determine input classes and choose the values to be tested. This approach is sometimes referred to as design-based functional testing, since it works from the design, which specifies the individual modules, rather than from the specification, which describes the behavior of the overall program.

Glass Box Testing. In glass box testing, we use the details of the program to suggest useful test data. For example, we would want to make sure that for each **if** statement in the program, some of the test data caused the **then** part of the statement to be executed and some data caused the **else** part to be executed. For each **while** statement, we might choose test cases that cause the controlled statements to be executed zero times, one time, and some large number of times.

The relational operators are frequent sources of error. For example, suppose that the first line of an **if** statement reads as follows (where *grade* is an integer variable):

   if *grade* < 60 **then**

A properly skeptical tester might wonder whether the operator should be $\leq$ instead of <. Or, perhaps the programmer got the direction of the sign wrong, so the operator should be > or $\geq$. Thus, we would certainly want to check that the program produces the correct results for values of *grade* less than 60, equal to 60, and greater than 60.

Likewise, consider the following **while** statement, which prints a number of asterisks equal to the initial value of *count*:

```
while count > 0 do
  begin
    write ('*');
    count := count − 1
  end
```

We might test this code with −1, 0, 1, and (say) 5 as values of *count*. No asterisks should be printed for the first two values and the appropriate number should be printed for the last two values. What would this test reveal if the Boolean expression had been written as

$$count <> 0$$

With exhaustive testing usually out of the question, we need to find some way to judge the adequacy of what testing we have been able to do. One approach is to count how many times each program statement has been executed during testing. This will assure us that at least no segment of the code has been slighted or (worse) neglected entirely during testing.

One way to make sure that no code segment is neglected during testing is to declare a counter variable for each branch of the code: each alternative path that the computer could take as a result of a selection or repetition. At the beginning of each branch, we insert a statement that increments the corresponding counter. The counters are initialized to zero at the beginning of program execution; their final values, which give the number of times each statement was executed, are printed just before the program terminates.

For example, we can insert counting statements in an **if** statement as follows:

```
if grade < 60 then
   begin                          { branch A }
      countA := countA + 1;
      writeln ('You fail');
      writeln ('Too bad!')
   end
else
   begin                          { branch B}
      countB := countB + 1;
      writeln ('You pass');
      writeln ('Congratulations!')
   end
```

When program execution is complete, the value of *countA* will indicate how many times the statements in branch A have been executed, and the value of *countB* will indicate how many times the statements in branch B have been executed. In the same way, we can user a counter to determine how many times the statements controlled by a **while** statement have been executed.

```
while not eof(input) do
   begin
      countC := countC + 1;    { branch C }
      readln (value);
      writeln (value)
   end
```

Another approach to judging the adequacy of testing is to deliberately introduce errors into a program and then see if the tests catch them. For example, we might run all our test problems with a < operator changed to >; if all the tests give the same results as before the change, then those tests are not adequate to determine whether the operator in question should be < or >. We may then try to remedy this situation by devising an additional test that will give different results for the two operators.

Debugging

Once testing has revealed that a program is not functioning properly, we must track down and correct the errors. Sometimes the test that revealed an error will also pinpoint its location in the program (because only one program statement could produce the incorrect results that were observed). More frequently, however, the programmer will have to probe the program's internal operation in order to find out what's wrong. The programmer's situation is similar to that of a service technician, who usually cannot diagnose the problem with a piece of equipment purely from the customer's complaint, but must use test instruments to probe the device's internal operation in order to locate the malfunction.

We recall that among the programmer's best test instruments are statements that print out the values of variables, thus allowing the values of the variables to be monitored as the program executes. Such variable monitoring is even more important in the presence of selection and repetition, because the values of variables can affect which statements are executed and how many times a statement is executed.

For example, suppose that the **if** statement discussed earlier is printing the wrong message. There are two possible problems:

1. *grade* has the wrong value when the **if** statement is executed.
2. *grade* has the correct value, but the **if** statement is incorrect.

To find out which is the case, we can insert a *writeln* statement to print the value of *grade* just before the **if** statement is executed.

```
writeln ('*** Test Point A: grade = ', grade :1);
if grade < 60 then
   begin
      writeln ('You fail');
      writeln ('Too bad!')
   end
else
   begin
      writeln ('You pass');
      writeln ('Congratulations!')
   end
```

Likewise, suppose that the following code is printing the wrong number of asterisks:

```
while count > 0 do
   begin
      write ('*');
      count := count − 1
   end
```

We can monitor the execution of this code by inserting a *writeln* statement as follows:

```
while count > 0 do
   begin
      writeln ('*** Test Point B: count = ', count :1);
      write ('*');
      count := count − 1
   end
```

The values printed by the *writeln* statement will allow us to determine both whether *count* has the correct value when the controlled statements are executed for the first time and whether the controlled statements are properly decrementing the value of *count*.

Sometimes it can be difficult to determine which statements are being executed or how many times a statement is being executed; this is particularly true when the program hangs up in an infinite loop without producing any output. Determining which statements are being executed is known as *tracing*. We can accomplish tracing by inserting *writeln* statements that simply announce that execution has reached a certain point. For example, the statement

writeln ('*** At Test Point C ***')

prints a message indicating that the computer has arrived at the point in the program designated as Test Point C.

Some program development systems have excellent facilities for variable monitoring and tracing, thus relieving us of the need to insert additional statements in the program. During execution, several windows appear on the screen. One window shows the user's input and the output produced by the program. Another window shows the part of the program currently being executed; the statement being executed is highlighted. The remaining window shows the values of the variables the program is currently manipulating. Program execution can be slowed down to the point where it can be conveniently followed by the programmer; execution can be temporarily halted any time the programmer needs more time to examine the values of the variables.

Review Questions

1. Distinguish between value parameters and variable parameters. What is the main advantage of value parameters? What is their main disadvantage?

2. How must the type of an actual value parameter be related to the type of the corresponding formal value parameter?

3. How must the type of an actual variable parameter be related to the type of the corresponding formal variable parameter?

4. Contrast functions and procedures.

5. How is a function invoked? What is a function designator and how is it used?

6. Describe the general-purpose arithmetical functions *abs*, *sqr*, and *sqrt*. Give examples of the use of each.

7. Name the scientific functions available in standard Pascal.

8. Describe the use of the transfer functions *trunc* and *round*.

9. Describe briefly the ordinal functions. Define *pred*, *succ*, and *ord* for each of the ordinal types we have take up so far.

10. Which of the ordinal functions is unique to type *char*? Why is the value of this function representation dependent?

11. Describe briefly the Boolean functions *odd*, *eof*, and *eoln*? Which two of these functions are important for file processing? Of those, which applies only to textfiles?

12. Give the general form of a function heading.

13. Describe two ways in which a function declaration differs from a procedure declaration.

14. What does the return type of a function specify?

15. Why are functions usually declared with value parameters, even though variable parameters are also allowed?

16. Why do selection and repetition constructions greatly complicate testing and debugging? Why is exhaustive testing impossible?

17. Distinguish between black box and glass box testing.

18. What are input classes and how are they used? What are boundary values? Special values?

19. How can counters be used to assure that no part of the program code is neglected during testing?

20. Describe how variable monitoring and tracing are used in debugging.

Exercises

When one of the following exercises calls for a function declaration, you should also write a program to exercise the function. In describing a function, we will often give an abbreviated function heading such as

    Max (numberA, numberB)

The abbreviated heading includes the name of the function and its formal parameters, but does not declare the types of the formal parameters or the return type of the function.

1. A company sponsors a contest to guess how many beans are in a jar in the company's showroom. A file of contest data is prepared as follows. The first line of the file consists of the actual number of beans in the jar. Each remaining line consists of a contestant number followed by a guess. Write a program to read this file and print the number and guess of the contestant whose guess is closest to the actual number of beans in the jar. In the case of ties, the contestant whose data comes first in the contest file wins. *Hint*: The value of *abs(m − n)* is a measure of how close the value of *m* is to that of *n* and is independent of which of the two values is larger.

2. The length of the diagonal of a rectangular solid is computed by squaring each of the three dimensions of the solid, adding the squares, and taking the square root of the result. Write a function
    Diagonal (length, width, height)
that returns the length of the diagonal of a rectangular solid with the given dimensions. The parameters and value returned should all have type *real*.

3. (For students familiar with trigonometry.) Write a procedure
    Triangle (base, angle1, height, hypotenuse, angle2)
to solve a right triangle. The input parameters *base* and *angle1* give the base and the angle it forms with the hypotenuse. The output parameters *height*, *hypotenuse*, and *angle2* are used to return the height of the triangle, the length of its hypotenuse, and the other non-right angle. All angles should be in degrees; since the Pascal scientific functions are defined for angles in radians, appropriate conversions must be performed.

4. (For students familiar with logarithms.) The logarithm of a number can be computed to a given base by dividing the natural logarithm of the number by the natural logarithm of the desired base. Write a function
    Log (*number*, *base*)
that returns the logarithm of a given number to a given base. Both the number and the base are real numbers. The value of *base* must be greater than one.

5. In financial calculations, it is frequently necessary to round an intermediate result to two decimal places before continuing with the calculation. Write a function
    Round2 (*amount*)
that returns the value of *amount* rounded to two decimal places.

6. Write a program for exploring a computer's character set. The program accepts two characters from the user, then prints all characters from the first input character through the second. *Hint*: Students familiar with the **for** statement should avoid it; use the **while** statement and the *succ* function instead.

7. Write two functions
    DigitChar (*val*)
and
    DigitVal (*ch*)
to convert between the digit characters '0' through '9' and the numerical values they represent. Given an integer value in the range 0 through 9, *DigitChar* returns the corresponding character in the range '0' through '9'. Given a character in that range, *DigitVal* returns the corresponding integer value.
Hint: In both the ASCII and EBCDIC character sets, the ordinal number of a digit character minus the ordinal number of '0' is equal to the numerical value represented by the digit character. (Why?)

8. The hexadecimal number system, widely used in computer programming, uses 16 digits. Digits '0' through '9' represent the same numerical values as in the decimal system; digits 'A' through 'F' represent the numerical values 11 through 15. Write functions analogous to *DigitChar* and *DigitVal* (Exercise 7) for the hexadecimal system.

9. Write a program to read a textfile and print the number of characters and lines in the file. Read the file character-by-character and use the function *eoln* to determine when the end of a line is reached.

10. A class of students must be split into two classes, which we refer to as Class A and Class B. To assure the division is performed fairly, all students with even student numbers will be put in Class A and those with odd student numbers will be put in Class B. Write a program to read a file of student numbers (each number on a separate line) and print a list showing the class to which each student is assigned.

11. Write a function
    Min (*m*, *n*)
that returns the smaller of the values of *m* and *n*.

12. Write a function
    Sqn (*n*)
that returns −1 if the value of *n* is negative; 0 if the value of *n* is zero; and 1

that returns -1 if the value of n is negative; 0 if the value of n is zero; and 1 if the value of n is nonzero and positive. The value of n and the value returned by the function are both integers. *Hint:* If the value of n is not zero, dividing the value of n by its absolute value yields the desired result. (Why?)

13. Write a function

    FractionalPart (x)

that returns the fractional part—the part to the right of the decimal point—of the value of x.

14. Many workers receive time-and-a-half for overtime work: each overtime hour is counted as an hour and a half. Write a function

    AdjustedHours (hoursWorked, overtimeLimit)

that returns *hoursWorked* adjusted so that each hour in excess of *overtimeLimit* is counted as a hour and a half. Thus the value of *AdjustedHours*(35.0, 40.0) is 35.0, since non-overtime hours are not changed. But the value of *AdjustedHours* (50.0, 40.0) is 55.0, since each of the 10 overtime hours was counted as an hour and a half.

15. The amount of an investment at compound interest is given by the formula

    $A = P(1 + R)^N$

where P is the *principal* (the amount initially invested), R is the interest rate expressed as a decimal (for example, 0.07 for a 7 percent rate), and A is the amount of the investment after interest has been compounded N times. Write a function

    Amount (principal, rate, numberOfPeriods)

to compute the amount of an investment at compound interest. *Amount* should call the function *Power* (discussed in Example 4-2) to raise $1 + rate$ to the power *numberOfPeriods*. In the program that exercises *Amount*, the declaration for *Power* must precede the declaration for *Amount*. (Why?)

Top-Down Development: A Case Study

To further our understanding of top-down development, we will now work through the specification, design, coding, and testing of a program to print a payroll report from a file of payroll data. Although this program is not large by professional standards, it is more elaborate than any we have considered so far, and it is complex enough that some planning is needed to arrive at a suitable structure for it. Our discussion is organized around the six steps of the software development life cycle, which was introduced in Chapter 1. These steps are requirements analysis, specification, design, coding, testing, and maintenance.

Requirements Analysis

Requirements analysis determines what criteria a program must satisfy to be acceptable to its intended users. The results of the requirements analysis are expressed in a *requirements definition*. The requirements definition can be considered as a preliminary specification, one that specifies only what is required for the program to perform its intended function. Additional details that need to be pinned down but are not crucial to the usefulness of the program are saved for the specification.

In an organization, such as a business, a program is usually requested by a particular department to meet some need in their operations. It is the job of the systems analyst to determine what is actually required of the proposed program. Unfortunately, the prospective users of the program are often not very helpful. They may have only the vaguest ideas of such crucial details as how the program should interact with users or what kinds of printouts it should produce.

When the completed program is put into service, and some aspects of its operation turn out to be less convenient than expected, the users are quite likely to claim that the program that was written is not the one that they asked for or were led to believe that they would receive. The problem of clients providing vague specifications and being dissatisfied with the results is one that plagues not only programmers but other professionals as well, particularly architects.

One approach to helping users formulate requirements is to use simulation to give hands-on experience with a proposed program before it is actually written. There are two approaches to simulating a program. In the first, the simulation program responds to selected user inputs with the same screen displays and printouts that the proposed program would produce. However, the simulation program does not actually carry out any of the calculations of the proposed program; all the displays and printouts have been created manually and stored on disk; the simulation program merely produces them on demand.

More interesting is a simulation program that actually carries out all the computations demanded of the program being simulated. The simulation need not achieve the same level of performance as the completed program will; it may not be able to handle as much data and it may not be able to operate as fast. Within these limits, however, the simulation can show prospective users exactly how the proposed program will operate.

Researchers are working on languages for stating specifications in a form that can be processed by a computer, and on simulation programs that will accept such specifications and simulate the specified program. Because many details of a program must be pinned down to make a simulation possible, simulation approaches tend to combine requirements analysis, specification, and at least premilinary design into a single step.

Texts on software engineering often assume that a program is always written to meet the needs of a specific client. But nowadays, programs are often designed to be marketed as commercial products. Requirements analysis then becomes a matter of market research—of trying to determine who the prospective purchasers of a program are and what features will make the proposed program more attractive than competing products. Usually, all the features offered by major competing products must be included. Also, once a program is on the market, new features must be devised so that existing users can be encouraged to purchase upgraded versions at regular intervals. These commercial pressures can result in "creeping featurism," in which programs become overloaded with features of doubtful utility.

Programming students are often given a brief assignment, from which they are expected to devise a reasonable set of requirements for the program to be written. For example, the program that we will develop in this chapter might be assigned as follows:

> Write a program to read employee payroll data and print a payroll report. The program's input should give the hours worked and hourly rate for each employee. Hours in excess of 40 are overtime, and employees are paid time-and-a-half for overtime. The program should compute the regular wages (earned during non-overtime hours), overtime wages (earned during overtime hours), and gross wages (total of regular and overtime wages) of each employee. The pages of the report should be numbered, and a footer line showing the number of employees processed and the total gross wages should be printed at the bottom of the final page.

Now let's see how this problem assignment leads to the requirements definition in Figure 5-1. From the assignment, we know that the input must include the hours worked and the hourly rate for each employee. Clearly, we also need some way of identifying each employee. Since the assignment does not state how this is done, we will choose the simplest method, which is an integer employee number. These considerations yield item 1 of the requirements definition, which describes the input to be processed.

Item 2 of the requirements definition describes the calculations to be carried out. All the information in item 2 comes from the assignment.

Item 3 of the requirements definition describes the report to be produced and, in doing so, expands considerably on the assignment. First, the detail line printed for each employee should include the employee's identifying number (employee number), should give the input data for that employee

Figure 5-1.   Requirements definition for the payroll-report program.

1. The input to the program consists of employee records, each of which contains an employee number, the hours that the employee worked, and the hourly rate at which the employee is paid.

2. The program is to compute the regular wages, overtime wages, and gross wages for each employee. Hours in excess of 40 are overtime, and employees are paid time-and-a-half for overtime.

3. The program is to print a report giving the employee number, hours worked, hourly rate, regular wages, overtime wages, and gross wages for each employee. The headings for each page of the report will give the title of the report, the page number, the name of the company for which the report was prepared, and the column headings for the columns of data. The final page of the report will also have a footer giving the number of employees listed in the report and the total of their gross wages.

(hours worked and hourly rate), and should show the results computed by the program for that employee (regular wages, overtime wages, and gross wages). Thus the report will have six columns of data.

The assignment implies a multiple-page report. Each page needs suitable headings, which include the page number called for in the assignment. A reasonable set of page headings is the report title, the page number, the company name, and headings for each of the six data columns. Finally, as called for in the assignment, the last page of the report must also contain a footer giving the number of employees processed and the total gross wages.

Specification

The specification for a program describes as precisely as possible the behavior that the program is expected to exhibit. The specification states what kinds of input a program must accept, what kinds of output it must produce, and how the output is related to the input. On the other hand, the specification says nothing about the internal operation of a program—about how the program is to achieve the required behavior. A specification states *what* a program must do but not *how* the program is to do it.

We can consider the specification to be an elaboration of the requirements definition. The requirements definition focuses on what is needed to solve the given problem in a manner satisfactory to the user; the requirements definition is often stated in broad terms, avoiding any unnecessary detail. The specification fills in the details needed to describe the behavior of one particular program (perhaps one of many) that meets the criteria set forth in the requirements definition.

Figure 5-2 shows the specification for our payroll-report program. (Figures 5-3, 5-4, and 5-5 are referred to by and considered to be part of the specification.) The specification elaborates on the requirements definition by describing the formats of the input and output data in greater detail and by

Figure 5-2.

Specification for the payroll-report program. Figures 5-3
through 5-5 are also part of the specification.

---

1. The input data consists of a textfile with one employee record per line.
    The three data items on each line are, from left to right, as follows:
    a. a four-digit employee number.
    b. the hours worked, which may have up to one decimal place.
    c. the hourly rate, which many have up to two decimal places.

    Each data item can be preceded by any number of spaces; adjacent
    items must be separated by at least one space. Figure 5-3 shows a
    sample data file.

2. The program is to compute regular wages, overtime wages, and gross
    wages for each employee. Regular and overtime wages are computed
    as in specification items 3 and 4. Gross wages are the sum of regular
    wages and overtime wages.

3. If an employee worked 40 hours or fewer, regular and overtime wages
    are computed as follows:

    regular-wages = hours-worked × hourly-rate
    overtime-wages = 0

4. If an employee worked more than 40 hours, regular and overtime
    wages are computed by

    regular-wages = 40 × hourly-rate
    overtime-wages = 1.5 × overtime-hours × hourly-rate

    where overtime-hours are the hours worked in excess of 40.

5. After processing all the input data, the program will output the
    employee count and the total gross wages. The employee count is the
    number of employee records in the input file, which is also equal to the
    number of detail lines in the payroll report. The total gross wages is
    the total of the gross wages computed for each of the employees.

6. The format of the printed report is illustrated by the sample printout in
    Figure 5-4 and the printer layout form in Figure 5-5. Each page of the
    report except the last will have 58 lines. The last page can have up to
    60 lines; this allows for a one-line footer (separated from the last detail
    line by one blank line) to be printed at the bottom of an otherwise full
    page. Each data column is 10 characters wide. Employee numbers and
    the employee count are printed as integers, and hours worked are
    printed with one decimal place. All other numeric items are printed
    with two decimal places.

---

providing a more detailed description of the calculation that the program is
to perform.

   Item 1 of the specification states that the program is to read its input
from a Pascal textfile. The specification describes the format of the input data
in detail, describing what items will be found on each line of the textfile, how
they will be separated, whether or not they will contain decimal points, and
(when relevant) how many digits or decimal places an item has. Data formats
are often more easily illustrated than described; for this reason, Item 1 refers
to Figure 5-3, which illustrates a typical input file.

   Items 2, 3, and 4 describe the results that are to be computed for each
employee. Items 3 and 4 describe how regular and overtime wages are to be

Figure 5-3.   Sample data for the payroll-report program.

1276	31.9	17.38
1643	45.2	21.25
2479	20.1	18.75
2935	50.2	25.40
3163	43.7	9.65
4721	30.4	10.45
5657	48.5	19.95
5723	25.0	35.84
6654	28.5	39.99
7128	37.2	18.45

Figure 5-4.   Sample printout for the payroll-report program.

```
Payroll Report                                              Page   1
CloneMaster Computer Corp.

    Employee      Hours      Hourly     Regular   Overtime        Gross
    Number        Worked     Rate       Wages     Wages           Wages

        1276        31.9       17.38      554.42       0.00       554.42
        1643        45.2       21.25      850.00     165.75      1015.75
        2479        20.1       18.75      376.87       0.00       376.87
        2935        50.2       25.40     1016.00     388.62      1404.62


Payroll Report                                              Page   2
CloneMaster Computer Corp.

    Employee      Hours      Hourly     Regular   Overtime        Gross
    Number        Worked     Rate       Wages     Wages           Wages

        3163        43.7        9.65      386.00      53.56       439.56
        4721        30.4       10.45      317.68       0.00       317.68
        5657        48.5       19.95      798.00     254.36      1052.36
        5723        25.0       35.84      896.00       0.00       896.00


Payroll Report                                              Page   3
CloneMaster Computer Corp.

    Employee      Hours      Hourly     Regular   Overtime        Gross
    Number        Worked     Rate       Wages     Wages           Wages

        6654        28.5       39.99     1139.71       0.00      1139.71
        7128        37.2       18.45      686.34       0.00       686.34

Employee Count   10                       Total Gross Wages      7883.31
```

computed from hours worked and hourly rate. The purpose here is not to describe the detailed program steps but rather to state how two output values (regular and overtime wages) are related to two input values (hours worked and hourly rate). Any realization of this calculation by program statements is satisfactory as long as the program statements produce the same results as the formulas given in the specification.

The relationship between the output value gross wages and the input data is given indirectly in item 2, which states that gross wages are the sum of regular wages and overtime wages. Since items 3 and 4 relate regular and overtime wages to the input data, the relationship for gross wages can be inferred.

Item 5 defines the output values employee count and total gross wages. The employee count is not computed from any input values but rather is obtained by counting the number of input records. The total gross wages is the sum of the gross wages computed for each employee. As with gross wages, the value of total gross wages is defined indirectly in terms of other computed values rather than directly in terms of input values.

Item 6 describes the format of the printed report the program must produce. Report formats are also better illustrated than described; thus item 6 describes the report format only very briefly and refers to illustrations for details. Two ways to illustrate a report format are

1. a sample printout.
2. a printer layout form.

Although normally only one of these methods would be used, we used both here for the sake of illustration.

Sample printouts are often available because a program may be intended to duplicate the format of a report currently available from some other source. For example, a microcomputer program may be expected to produce a report that was formerly produced by a mainframe or minicomputer. Or an in-house computer system may be expected to produce a report that was formerly produced by an outside service bureau. A special *forms ruler* can be used to measure the horizontal and vertical spacings between the printed items in the sample. Figure 5-4 shows a sample printout for the report to be produced by the payroll program; the report was produced from the sample data in Figure 5-3. The sample printout differs from the actual printout only in that the number of lines per page has been reduced to 11, thus allowing a small test file to produce a printout of several pages.

If no sample printout is available, the output format can be illustrated with a *printer layout form*, a gridded form whose numbered rows correspond to lines on the printout and whose numbered columns correspond to character positions. The items that will appear on the actual report are written in their proper positions on the printer layout form. When the actual printed items are not known, as is the case for values in a detail line, their positions and sizes are indicated by using Xs to represent arbitrary characters and 9s to represent arbitrary digits. Thus a number with up to four digits before the decimal point and two digits after would be written 9999.99. Given a printer layout form, the horizontal and vertical spacings between items are easily obtained by counting boxes or by using the row and column numbers at the left and top of the form. Figure 5-5 shows a printer layout form for the payroll report; the layout form shows only one detail line.

Figure 5-5. Printer layout form for the payroll-report program.

```
         1         2         3         4         5         6        7
1234567890123456789012345678901234567890123456789012345678901234567890
 1
 2
 3
 4 Payroll Report                                              Page 99
 5 CloneMaster Computer Corp.
 6
 7
 8     Employee      Hours      Hourly    Regular   Overtime      Gross
 9      Number       Worked      Rate      Wages      Wages       Wages
10
11        9999        99.9      99.99    9999.99    9999.99     9999.99
12
13 Employee Count 999                    Total Gross Wages 999999.99
14
15
16
17
18
```

Often items must be positioned so that they will appear in the proper places on a preprinted business form, such as an invoice. Manufacturers of such preprinted forms will often provide a special printer layout form consisting of the business form printed on a gridded sheet.

Design

The specification describes the external behavior that a program must exhibit but says nothing about the internal structure of the program. In the design phase, we outline this structure in detail while avoiding the still finer details of coding in a particular programming language. Some of the topics addressed in the design phase are as follows:

- The decomposition of the program into modules.
- The function each module is to perform.
- The input and output data for each module.
- The algorithms and data structures to be employed by each module.
- The computations to be carried out by each module; these computations are usually described in pseudocode.

In this chapter we will use structure charts to describe the decomposition of the program into modules. For each module, we will provide a detail description that gives the purpose of the module, its relation to other modules, its input and output data, and pseudocode for the operations that it carries out.

The Main Program

As usual, our top-level module will be the main program. The task that the main program must perform—read and process the input data and print the report—can be broken down into four major subtasks as follows:

1. Assign initial values to the running counts and totals.
2. Print the headings for the first page of the report. (It will be up to a subordinate module that prints detail lines to print the headings of succeeding pages.)
3. Process one input record. This task must be carried out once for every record in the input file.
4. Print the footer line at the end of the report.

To perform each of these four tasks, the main program will call one of the following procedures: *Initialize*, *PrintHeadings*, *ProcessOneRecord*, and *Print Footer*. This modular decomposition of the main program is illustrated by the structure chart in Figure 5-6, which shows the main program and the four procedures that it calls.

We complete the design of the main program by providing pseudocode for the program together with some additional descriptive information. There are many ways of presenting the design for a module; the one we will use is illustrated in Figure 5-7, which gives our design for the main program.

The Heading section of the design gives the program or subprogram heading of the module. Since the heading gives the name of the module as well as the parameters to be used for input and output, it serves as a good starting point for the design. From the Heading section in Figure 5-7, we see that our main program is named *PayrollReport*, and that it communicates with the rest of the computer system via two parameters, the predefined identifiers *input* and *output*.

The Purpose section contains a brief statement of the task the module is to perform. The purpose of the payroll program is to produce a payroll report from a file of payroll data.

Each of the parameters listed in the module heading is described separately. The parameters are classified as input, output, and input/output parameters, and a separate section is provided for each classification. The main program has one input parameter, *input*, and one output parameter, *output*. Every parameter and variable name is followed by its type, if that has not been previously given. (The types of subprogram parameters are given in the

Figure 5-6.

Structure chart showing the main program and the subprograms that it calls. The subprogram boxes are drawn with broken lines to indicate that these subprograms have not yet been designed.

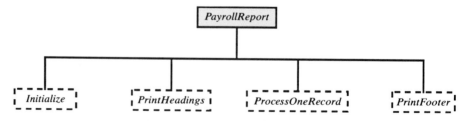

Figure 5-7. The design for the main program.

HEADING
  program *PayrollReport* (*input*, *output*);

PURPOSE
  To produce a payroll report from a file of payroll data.

INPUT PARAMETERS
  input text Payroll data file. Each line of text contains an employee number (integer), hours employee worked (real), and hourly pay rate (real).

OUTPUT PARAMETERS
  output text File for payroll report. Each detail line of the report gives the employee number, hours worked, hourly rate, regular wages, overtime wages, and gross wages for one employee. A footer on the last page gives the number of employees processed and the total gross wages.

VARIABLES
  employeeNo   integer Employee's ID number
  hoursWorked   real   Hours employee worked
  hourlyRate   real   Employee's hourly pay rate
  employeeCount   integer Number of employees processed so far
  totalGrossWages   real   Total gross wages of employees processed so far
  nextPageNumber   integer Number of next page to be printed
  linesPrinted   integer Number of lines printed on current page

SUBPROGRAMS CALLED
  Initialize, *PrintHeadings*, *ProcessOneRecord*, *PrintFooter*

PSEUDOCODE
  1. Call *Initialize* to assign initial values to *employeeCount*, *nextPageNumber*, and *totalGrossWages*

  2. Call *PrintHeadings* to print a set of page headings at the top of a new page, increment *nextPageNumber*, and set *linesPrinted* to the number of heading lines printed

  3. While the end of file *input* has not been reached, repeat the following:

     3.1 Read data for one employee into *employeeNo*, *hoursWorked*, and *hourlyRate*

     3.2 Call *ProcessOneRecord* to carry out the wage computations for one employee and print one detail line of the report; *ProcessOneRecord* updates the values of *employeeCount*, *totalGrossWages*, *nextPageNumber*, and *linesPrinted*

  4. Call *PrintFooter* to print the final values of *employeeCount* and *totalGrossWages*

---

subprogram heading and so do not have to be repeated in the parameter sections of the design.) Both *input* and *output* have the type *text*, which is the type of a Pascal textfile. The parameter *input* represents the payroll file from which the program is to read its data; the parameter *output* represents the output file to which the payroll report is to be sent. By using the standard files *input* and *output*, we assume that file redirection is available, so that *input* can be assigned to the appropriate disk file and *output* can be assigned to a printer.

The Variables section names and describes the variables that the program will use. It could be argued that choosing variables is a low-level task that could be deferred to the coding phase. The advantage of including the variables in the design, however, is that they provide a concise way of referring to the quantities that the module must manipulate; hence they simplify the pseudocode. The variables *employeeNo*, *hoursWorked*, and *hourlyRate* hold the values read from an input record; *employeeCount* and *totalGrossWages* hold the running count and total that the program must compute; *nextPageNumber* and *linesPrinted* are used to keep track of the number to be printed on the next page and the number of lines already printed on the current page.

The Subprograms Called section lists the programmer-defined subprograms that this module calls. (Predefined subprograms, such as *eof* and *readln*, are considered to be part of the Pascal language and are not listed in the design.) As previously discussed, the main program calls the four subprograms *Initialize*, *PrintHeadings*, *ProcessOneRecord*, and *PrintFooter*. The use to which each of these subprograms is put is described in the pseudocode.

The Pseudocode section describes the actions that the module will take when it is executed. The pseudocode for our main program consists of the following four steps:

1. Call *Initialize* to assign initial values to *employeeCount*, *nextPageNumber*, and *totalGrossWages*

2. Call *PrintHeadings* to print a set of page headings at the top of a new page, increment *nextPageNumber*, and set *linesPrinted* to the number of heading lines printed

3. While the end of file *input* has not been reached, repeat the following:

    3.1   Read data for one employee into *employeeNo*, *hoursWorked*, and *hourlyRate*

    3.2   Call *ProcessOneRecord* to carry out the wage computations for one employee and print one detail line of the report. *ProcessOneRecord* updates the values of *employeeCount*, *totalGrossWages*, *nextPageNumber*, and *linesPrinted*

4. Call *PrintFooter* to print the final values of *employeeCount* and *totalGrossWages*

The Procedure *Initialize*

Figure 5-8 shows the design for the procedure *Initialize*, which assigns initial values to its parameters. *Initialize* has two integer parameters (*employeeCount* and *nextPageNumber*) and one real parameter (*totalGrossWages*). Since the purpose of the procedure is to assign values to these parameters, all three must be output parameters; hence all three must be declared as variable parameters in the procedure heading. This procedure does not have any local

Figure 5-8.

The design for the procedure *Initialize*.

HEADING
　　procedure *Initialize* (**var** *employeeCount*,
　　　　　　　　　　　　nextPageNumber : *integer*;
　　　　　　　　var *totalGrossWages* : *real*);

PURPOSE
　　To set output parameters to their initial values.

OUTPUT PARAMETERS
　　employeeCount　　Number of employees processed so far
　　nextPageNumber　Number of next page to be printed
　　totalGrossWages　Total gross wages of all employees processed so far

PSEUDOCODE
　　1.　Set *employeeCount* to 0

　　2.　Set *nextPageNumber* to 1

　　3.　Set *totalGrossWages* to 0.0

---

variables and does not call any other subprograms. Its pseudocode is as follows:

1.　Set *employeeCount* to 0

2.　Set *nextPageNumber* to 1

3.　Set *totalGrossWages* to 0.0

The Procedure *PrintHeadings*

Figure 5-9 shows the design for the procedure *PrintHeadings*, which prints a set of headings at the top of a new page. *PrintHeadings* has two integer variable parameters: *nextPageNumber* and *linesPrinted*. When the procedure is called, the value of the input/output parameter *nextPageNumber* is the page number to be included in the headings. Before returning, the procedure increments the value of *nextPageNumber* by one, so that the pages will be numbered consecutively. The output parameter *linesPrinted*, which represents the number of lines already printed on the current page, is set to the number of lines of headings (including blank lines) that the procedure printed.

　　PrintHeadings does not have any local variables and does not call any other programmer-defined subprograms. The pseudocode for *PrintHeadings* is straightforward:

1.　Go to a new page

2.　Print report title and page number

3.　Print company name

4.　Skip two lines

5.　Print first line of column headings

6.　Print second line of column headings

7.　Skip one line

8.　Increment the value of *nextPageNumber*

9.　Set *linesPrinted* to 7, the number of heading lines (including blank lines)

Figure 5-9.

The design for the procedure *PrintHeadings*.

HEADING
   procedure *PrintHeadings* (**var** *nextPageNumber*,
                              linesPrinted   : *integer*);

PURPOSE   To go to a new page and print page and column headings. The
          procedure increments the value of *nextPageNumber* and
          assigns *linesPrinted* its initial value.

OUTPUT PARAMETERS
   linesPrinted   Number of lines printed on current page

INPUT/OUTPUT PARAMETERS
   nextPageNumber   Page number of the next page to be printed

PSEUDOCODE
   1. Go to a new page
   2. Print report title and page number
   3. Print company name
   4. Skip two lines
   5. Print first line of column headings
   6. Print second line of column headings
   7. Skip one line
   8. Increment the value of *nextPageNumber*
   9. Set *linesPrinted* to 7, the number of heading lines (including blank
       lines)

Steps 2 through 7 were obtained by examining either the sample printout or
the printer layout form and determining what lines (including blank lines) need
to be printed.

The Procedure *ProcessOneRecord*

Figure 5-10 shows the design for the procedure *ProcessOneRecord*, which is
responsible for carrying out the computations for one data record and printing
the corresponding detail line. It must update the running count *employeeCount*
and total *totalGrossWages* as well as the counts *nextPageNumber* and
linesPrinted used for page numbering and paging control.

   ProcessOneRecord has three input parameters—*employeeNo*,
hoursWorked, and *hourlyRate*—whose values are just the data items read
from an employee record. The input/output parameters *employeeCount*,
totalGrossWages, *nextPageNumber*, and *linesPrinted* represent the one total
and three counts that must be updated.

   ProcessOneRecord declares three real variables: *regularWages*,
overtimeWages, and *grossWages*. Each variable holds one of the three results
that is computed for each employee.

   The task assigned to *ProcessOneRecord* can be broken down into three
subtasks: calculating wages, updating the running count and total, and printing
the detail line. To accomplish these subtasks, *ProcessOneRecord* calls three
procedures: *CalculateWages*, *UpdateCountAndTotal*, and *PrintDetailLine*.

Figure 5-10.

The design for the procedure *ProcessOneRecord*.

HEADING

   procedure *ProcessOneRecord* (*employeeNo*   : *integer*;
                                  hoursWorked,
                                  hourlyRate   : *real*;
                                  var *employeeCount*   : *integer*;
                                  var *totalGrossWages* : *real*;
                                  var *nextPageNumber*,
                                  linesPrinted   : *integer*);

PURPOSE

   To compute regular, overtime, and gross wages for one employee and print one detail line. Procedure also updates *employeeCount*, *totalGrossWages*, *nextPageNumber* (if detail line is first on a new page), and *linesPrinted*.

INPUT PARAMETERS

   employeeNo   Employee's ID number
   hoursWorked   Hours employee worked
   hourlyRate   Employee's hourly pay rate

INPUT/OUTPUT PARAMETERS

   employeeCount   Number of employees processed so far
   totalGrossWages Total gross wages of employees processed so far
   nextPageNumber Number of next page to be printed
   linesPrinted   Number of lines printed on current page

VARIABLES

   regularWages   real   Wages earned during first 40 hours
   overtimeWages   real   Wages earned after first 40 hours
   grossWages   real   Total wages earned

SUBPROGRAMS CALLED

   CalculateWages, *UpdateCountAndTotal*, *PrintDetailLine*

PSEUDOCODE

1. Call *CalculateWages* to compute values for *regularWages*, *overtimeWages*, and *grossWages*

2. Call *UpdateCountAndTotal* to update values of *employeeCount* and *totalGrossWages*

3. Call *PrintDetailLine* to print one detail line and update values of *nextPageNumber* and *linesPrinted*

    Because most of the actual work of *ProcessOneRecord* is done by the called subprograms, the pseudocode has only three steps:

1. Call *CalculateWages* to compute values for *regularWages* *overtimeWages*, and *grossWages*

2. Call *UpdateCountAndTotal* to update values of *employeeCount* and *totalGrossWages*

3. Call *PrintDetailLine* to print one detail line and update values of *nextPageNumber* and *linesPrinted*

Figure 5-11.   The design for the procedure *PrintFooter*.

HEADING
   procedure *PrintFooter* (*employeeCount*   : *integer*;
                      totalGrossWages : *real*);

PURPOSE
   To print a footer line showing the number of employees processed and
   the total of their gross wages.

INPUT PARAMETERS
   employeeCount   Number of employees processed
   totalGrossWages   Total of employees' gross wages

PSEUDOCODE
   1.   Skip a line
   2.   Print footer line containing values of *employeeCount* and
        totalGrossWages

The Procedure *PrintFooter*

Figure 5-11 shows the design for the procedure *PrintFooter*, which prints the
footer line giving the employee count and the total gross wages. *PrintFooter*
has two input parameters, *employeeCount* and *totalGrossWages*, which represent the values to be printed. Noting that the footer line is to be separated
from the last detail line by one blank line, we get the following pseudocode:

1.   Skip a line
2.   Print footer line containing values of *employeeCount* and
     totalGrossWages

   At this point, we have designed all the second-level procedures: the
procedures called directly by the main program. The structure chart in Figure
5-12 summarizes our progress by showing the first- and second-level modules
that we have designed as well as the third-level modules that have been
mentioned but not yet designed.

The Procedure *CalculateWages*

Figure 5-11 shows the design for the procedure *CalculateWages*, which does
the actual wage calculation. Its input parameters are *hoursWorked* and
hourlyRate, which represent the input data for the calculation. Its output
parameters are *regularWages*, *overtimeWages*, and *grossWages*, which represent the results to be calculated.

   The computation for *regularWages* and *overtimeWages* has two cases,
depending on whether the value of *hoursWorked* exceeds 40. (These two
cases correspond to items 3 and 4 of the specification.) Regardless of which
case occurs, the gross wages are computed as the sum of the regular and
overtime wages:

1.   Depending on the value of *hoursWorked*, do one of the following:

    1.1 *Hours worked do not exceed 40*: Compute regular and overtime wages for employee who worked no overtime

    1.2 *Hours worked exceed 40*: Compute regular and overtime wages for employee who worked some overtime

2. Compute gross wages as sum of regular and overtime wages

Figure 5-12.

Structure chart showing the first- and second-level modules along with the third-level modules that they call. The boxes for the third-level modules are drawn with broken lines to indicate that these modules have not yet been designed.

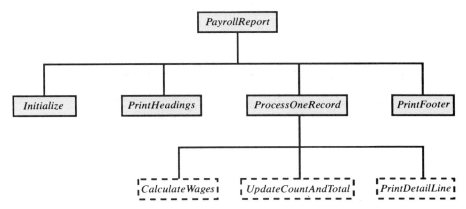

Figure 5-13.

Design for the procedure *CalculateWages*.

HEADING
    procedure *CalculateWages* (*hoursWorked*,
                            hourlyRate   : *real*;
                            var *regularWages*,
                                overtimeWages,
                                grossWages   : *real*);

PURPOSE
    To calculate regular, overtime, and gross wages from hours worked and hourly rate.

INPUT PARAMETERS
    hoursWorked   Hours employee worked
    hourlyRate   Employee's hourly pay rate

OUTPUT PARAMETERS
    regularWges   Wages earned during first 40 hours
    overtimeWages   Wages earned after first 40 hours
    grossWages   Total wages earned

PSEUDOCODE
    1. Depending on the value of *hoursWorked*, do one of the following:

        1.1 *Hours worked do not exceed 40*: Compute regular and overtime wages for employee who worked no overtime

        1.2 *Hours worked exceed 40*: Compute regular and overtime wages for employee who worked some overtime

    2. Compute gross wages as sum of regular and overtime wages

The Procedure *UpdateCountAndTotal*

Figure 5-14 shows the design for the procedure *UpdateCountAndTotal*, which updates the employee count and the total gross wages. The procedure has one input parameter, *grossWages*, whose value is needed to update the total gross wages. The procedure has two input/output parameters, *employeeCount* and *totalGrossWages*, which represent the values to be updated. The procedure increments the employee count by one and adds the gross wages of the current employee to the total gross wages:

1. Increment value of *employeeCount*
2. Add the value of *grossWages* to that of *totalGrossWages*

The Procedure *PrintDetailLine*

Figure 5-15 shows the design for the procedure *PrintDetailLine*, the primary responsibility of which is to print a line showing the input data and computed results for one employee. Before printing the detail line, the procedure must check whether the current page is full; if it is, *PrintDetailLine* must call *PrintHeadings* to go to a new page and print a new set of page headings. Finally, *PrintDetailLine* must update *nextPageNumber* and *linesPrinted*, whose values are used for page numbering and control of paging.

The input parameters for *PrintDetailLine* are those representing the values to be printed: *employeeNo*, *hoursWorked*, *hourlyRate*, *regularWages*, *overtimeWages*, and *grossWages*. The input/output parameters, *nextPageNumber* and *linesPrinted*, represent the quantities to be updated.

PrintDetailLine calls one other programmer-defined procedure, *PrintHeadings*, which we have already designed. Note that *PrintHeadings* is called the first time by the main program. Thereafter, it is up to *PrintDetailLine* to call *PrintHeadings* when needed, that is, when the current page is full.

Figure 5-14.   Design for the procedure *UpdateCountAndTotal*.

HEADING
    procedure *UpdateCountAndTotal* (*grossWages*   : *real*;
                                      var *employeeCount*   : *integer*;
                                      var *totalGrossWages* : *real*);

PURPOSE
    To update the employee count and the total gross wages.

INPUT PARAMETERS
    grossWages   Total wages earned
    employeeCount   Number of employees processed so far
    totalGrossWages Total gross wages of employees processed so far

PSEUDOCODE
    1. Increment value of *employeeCount*
    2. Add the value of *grossWages* to that of *totalGrossWages*

HEADING
   procedure *PrintDetailLine* (*employeeNo*   : *integer*;
                           hoursWorked,
                           hourlyRate,
                           regularWages,
                           overtimeWages,
                           grossWages   : *real*;
                           var *nextPageNumber,*
                             linesPrinted   : *integer*);

PURPOSE
   To print one detail line of the report and update the values
   nextPageNumber and *linesPrinted.*

INPUT PARAMETERS

employeeNo	Employee's ID number
hoursWorked	Hours employee worked
hourlyRate	Employee's hourly pay rate
regularWages	Wages earned during first 40 hours
overtimeWages	Wages earned after first 40 hours
grossWages	Total wages earned

INPUT/OUTPUT PARAMETERS

nextPageNumber	Number of next page to be printed
linesPrinted	Number of lines printed on current page

SUBPROGRAMS CALLED
   PrintHeadings

PSEUDOCODE
1. If the value of *linesPrinted* equals the maximum number of lines per page, do the following:
   1.1 Call *PrintHeadings* to go to a new page, print page and column headings, and update the values of *nextPageNumber* and *linesPrinted*
2. Print detail line containing the values of *employeeNo, hoursWorked, hourlyRate, regularWages, overtimeWages,* and *grossWages*
3. Increment the value of *linesPrinted*

These considerations yield the following pseudocode:

1. If the value of *linesPrinted* equals the maximum number of lines per page, do the following:
   1.1 Call *PrintHeadings* to go to a new page, print page and column headings, and update the values of *nextPageNumber* and *linesPrinted*
2. Print detail line containing the values of *employeeNo, hoursWorked, hourlyRate, regularWages, overtimeWages,* and *grossWages*
3. Increment the value of *linesPrinted*

The structure chart in Figure 5-16 illustrates the complete design of the payroll program.

Figure 5-16.　　　Complete structure chart for the payroll-report program.

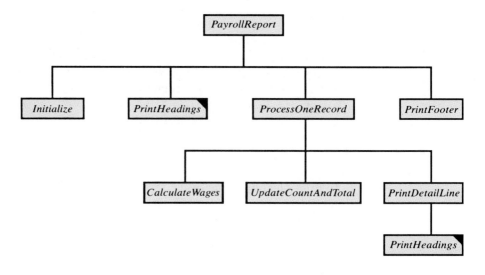

Coding

With a detailed design in hand, coding is relatively straightforward. The coder can concentrate on expressing each pseudocode step in the programming language, without having to worry about the overall structure of the program. The modules could be coded in any order; indeed, several people could be coding different modules at the same time. As we will see in the section on testing, however, coding in top-down order allows us to combine coding and testing in such a way that the partially coded program serves as a test driver for each newly coded procedure.

Figure 5-17 shows the code for the entire program. The coding of several of the procedures is obvious and requires little comment. *Initialize* has three assignment statements, each of which assigns an initial value to one of the variables passed to the procedure. *UpdateCountAndTotal* uses two assignment statements to update the running count and total. The pseudocode for *ProcessOneRecord* translates into three procedure calls, one for each step of the pseudocode. *PrintFooter* uses one *writeln* statement to skip a line and a second *writeln* statement to print the required footer.

The main program begins by calling *Initialize* to initialize variables and *PrintHeadings* to print the headings for the first page. A **while** statement reads and processes input records until the end of the input file is reached. Each input record is read with a *readln* statement and processed with a call to *ProcessOneRecord*. When the **while** statement terminates, *PrintFooter* is called to print the footer line.

Figure 5-17.   The complete code for the payroll-report program.

---

program *PayrollReport* (*input*, *output*);

{ Produce payroll report from payroll data file. Each line of input file contains an employee number (integer), hours employee worked (real), and hourly pay rate (real). Each detail line of report gives employee number, hours worked, hourly rate, regular wages, overtime wages, and gross wages. A footer line gives number of employees processed and total gross wages }

var
```
    employeeNo        : integer; { input data for one employee }
    hoursWorked,
    hourlyRate        : real;
    employeeCount     : integer; { running count and total }
    totalGrossWages   : real;
    nextPageNumber,              { page number of next page }
    linesPrinted      : integer; { lines printed on current page }
```

{ ------------------------------- Procedure *Initialize* ------------------------------- }

procedure *Initialize* (**var** *employeeCount*,
                          nextPageNumber : *integer*;
                  var *totalGrossWages* : *real*);

{ Assign initial values to *employeeCount*, *nextPageNumber*, and *totalGrossWages*. }

begin
```
    employeeCount := 0;
    nextPageNumber := 1;
    totalGrossWages := 0.0
```
end; { *Initialize* }

{ ---------------------------- Procedure *PrintHeadings* ---------------------------- }

procedure *PrintHeadings* (**var** *nextPageNumber*,
                          linesPrinted   : *integer*);

{ Go to top of new page and print page and column headings. Increment *nextPageNumber* and assign initial value to *linesPrinted*. }
begin
```
    page;
    writeln ('Payroll Report', 'Page' : 43, nextPageNumber :3);
    writeln ('CloneMaster Computer Corp.');
    writeln;
    writeln;
    writeln ('Employee' :10, 'Hours  ' :10, 'Hourly' :10,
             'Regular' :10, 'Overtime' :10, 'Gross ' :10);
    writeln ('Number  ' :10, 'Worked' :10, 'Rate  ' :10,
             'Wages ' :10, 'Wages  ' :10, 'Wages ' :10);
```

Figure 5-17. *Continued.*

```
        writeln;
        nextPageNumber := nextPageNumber + 1;
        linesPrinted := 7
    end; { PrintHeadings }
```

{ ----------------------------- Procedure *CalculateWages* ---------------------------- }

```
procedure CalculateWages (hoursWorked,
                          hourlyRate        : real;
                      var regularWages,
                          overtimeWages,
                          grossWages        : real);
```

{ Compute values of *regularWages*, *overtimeWages*, and *grossWages* from
  values of *hoursWorked* and *hourlyRate*. }

```
begin
    if hoursWorked <= 40.0 then
      begin
        regularWages :=  hoursWorked * hourlyRate;
        overtimeWages := 0.0
      end
    else
      begin
        regularWages := 40.0 * hourlyRate;
        overtimeWages := 1.5 * (hoursWorked − 40.0) * hourlyRate
      end;
    grossWages := regularWages + overtimeWages
end; { CalculateWages }
```

{ ------------------------ Procedure *UpdateCountAndTotal* ----------------------- }

```
procedure UpdateCountAndTotal (grossWages          : real;
                           var employeeCount   : integer;
                           var totalGrossWages : real);
```

{ Increment value of *employeeCount* and add value of *grossWages* to value
  of *totalGrossWages*. }

```
begin
    employeeCount := employeeCount + 1;
    totalGrossWages := totalGrossWages + grossWages
end { UpdateCountAndTotal }
```

{ ----------------------------- Procedure *PrintDetailLine* ---------------------------- }

```
procedure PrintDetailLine (employeeNo         : integer;
                           hoursWorked,
                           hourlyRate,
                           regularWages,
```

Figure 5-17.   *Continued.*

```
                              overtimeWages,
                              grossWages            : real;
                           var nextPageNumber,
                              linesPrinted          : integer);
```
{ Print one detail line, going to new page first if there is no room on
  current page. Update values of *nextPageNumber* (if new page started)
  and *linesPrinted.* }

```
const
   linesPerPage  = 58;
begin
   if linesPrinted = linesPerPage then
      PrintHeadings (nextPageNumber, linesPrinted);
   writeln (employeeNo :10, hoursWorked :10:1, hourlyRate :10:2,
            regularWages :10:2, overtimeWages :10:2, grossWages :10:2);
   linesPrinted := linesPrinted + 1
end; { PrintDetailLine }
```

{ -------------------------- Procedure *ProcessOneRecord* -------------------------- }

```
procedure ProcessOneRecord (employeeNo          : integer;
                            hoursWorked,
                            hourlyRate          : real;
                         var employeeCount      : integer;
                         var totalGrossWages    : real;
                         var nextPageNumber,
                            linesPrinted         : integer);
```

{ Process and print results for one input record. Data from input record is
  passed as values of *employeeNo*, *hoursWorked*, and *hourlyRate*. Update
  values of *employeeCount*, *totalGrossWages*, *nextPageNumber* (if new
  page is started), and *linesPrinted*. }

```
var
    regularWages,        { wages earned during first 40 hours }
    overtimeWages,       { wages earned after first 40 hours }
    grossWages    : real; { total wages earned }
begin
    CalculateWages (hoursWorked, hourlyRate, regularWages,
                    overtimeWages, grossWages);
    UpdateCountAndTotal (grossWages, employeeCount, totalGrossWages);
    PrintDetailLine (employeeNo, hoursWorked, hourlyRate,
                     regularWages, overtimeWages, grossWages,
                     nextPageNumber, linesPrinted)
end; { ProcessOneRecord }
```

Figure 5-17. *Continued.*

```
{ ----------------------------- Procedure PrintFooter ----------------------------- }

procedure PrintFooter (employeeCount   : integer;
                       totalGrossWages : real);

{ Print footer line giving values of employeeCount and totalGrossWages. }

begin
  writeln;
  writeln ('Employee Count', employeeCount :4,
          'Total Gross Wages' :32, totalGrossWages :10:2)
end; { PrintFooter }

{ ----------------------------------- Main Program ----------------------------------- }

begin
  Initialize (employeeCount, nextPageNumber, totalGrossWages);
  PrintHeadings (nextPageNumber, linesPrinted);
  while not eof(input) do
    begin
      readln (employeeNo, hoursWorked, hourlyRate);
      ProcessOneRecord (employeeNo, hoursWorked, hourlyRate,
                        employeeCount, totalGrossWages,
                        nextPageNumber, linesPrinted)
    end;
  PrintFooter (employeeCount, totalGrossWages)
end.
```

The only difficulty in writing *PrintHeadings* is in positioning the printed items as set forth in the sample printout and the printer layout form. For example, consider the first line of the headings. The report title is flush left—printed as far to the left as possible—so the string 'Payroll Report' can be printed without any field-width parameter. The string 'Page' is to be printed in a field that begins immediately after the t of Payroll Report and extends through the e of Page. From Figure 5-5, we see that this field occupies 43 squares on the printer layout form. Therefore, 'Page' is printed with a field-width parameter of 43. The page number is printed in a field that begins immediately after the e of Page and extends through the rightmost digit of the page number. This field occupies three squares on the printer layout form, so the page number is printed with a field-width parameter of 3.

The data columns are each 10 characters wide, so each of the column headings can be printed with a field-width parameter of 10. As usual, we want the two words making up each column heading to align on the left; therefore, we follow the shorter of the two words by enough spaces to make its string constant the same length as the one for the longer word. The following are the string constants for the words in the column headings:

```
'Employee'   'Hours '   'Hourly'   'Regular'   'Overtime'   'Gross'
'Number '    'Worked'   'Rate '    'Wages '    'Wages '     'Wages'
```

In *CalculateWages*, the statements for calculating regular and overtime wages follow the formulas given in the specification. The calculation for employees who worked overtime differs from the one for those who worked no overtime; an **if** statement checks whether or not the value of *hoursWorked* is less than or equal to 40 and selects the statements to be executed accordingly. The value of *grossWages* is computed as the sum of the values of *regularWages* and *overtimeWages*.

In *PrintDetailLine*, the constant identifier *linesPerPage* is defined equal to 58, the maximum number of heading and detail lines on a page. For testing purposes, it is often useful to give this constant a smaller value so that a small test file will produce a multipage report; a value of 11 will give the page size shown in Figure 5-4.

Before a new detail line is printed, an **if** statement checks whether the value of *linesPrinted* is equal to *linesPerPage*; if so, *PrintHeadings* is called to start a new page. Since the data columns are 10 characters wide, each item on the detail line is printed with a field width of 10. After the detail line has been printed, the value of *linesPrinted* is incremented by 1.

Top-Down Testing

Testing can be divided into module testing, in which the modules are tested individually, and integration testing, in which the entire program is tested.

To test a module apart from the rest of the program, we must write a *test driver*: a program that invokes the module under test, provides it with data, and prints the results that the module produces. Some of our example programs illustrating functions used a test driver to test, or exercise, the subprogram under consideration.

An alternative approach is top-down testing, in which modules are coded and tested in the same top-down order that was followed in the design phase. As each module is completed, it is inserted into the partially coded program and tested in place. The partially coded program serves as a test driver; no separate test drivers need be written. On the other hand, we must write dummy modules called *stubs* to take the place of those that have not yet been coded.

Writing stubs is about as much work as writing test drivers, so with respect to the amount of extra programming that must be done for testing purposes, there is little to distinguish the two methods. The advantage of top-down testing is that testing can be more realistic because a module is tested by the program in which it will actually be used rather than by an artificial test driver. What's more, even the first tests of a module involve elements of integration testing, of assuring that the different modules interact properly. As more and more modules are completed, the integration of the modules is tested more and more rigorously. Also, every test run tests all the modules that have been completed; a test aimed at one module may uncover errors in another.

A disadvantage of top-down testing is that higher-level modules often place restrictions on the data that can be passed to lower-level modules. For example, a higher-level module might consider certain values to be erroneous and print an error message rather than passing the values on to lower-level modules. As a result, it may be difficult to test lower-level modules with as wide a variety of input values as would be possible when test driver is used. When this problem arises, it may be advisable to test a lower-level module with a test driver in addition to testing it in place in the partially coded program.

To illustrate top-down testing, we will see how to test the top-level module (the main program) of our payroll-report program. When we test the main program, the situation is as shown in the structure chart in Figure 5-6. The main program has been coded, and we know the four subprograms that it calls; however, none of the subprograms have been coded. Before we can test the main program, we must code stubs to take the place of the four unwritten subprograms: *Initialize*, *PrintHeadings*, *ProcessOneRecord*, and *PrintFooter*.

A stub could be a dummy routine that does absolutely nothing, such as the following:

```
procedure Initialize (var employeeCount,
                             nextPageNumber : integer;
                       var totalGrossWages : real);
   begin
   end;
```

Usually, however, we want a stub to generate printed output and data values that will aid us in testing the program. To these ends, a stub should do the following:

- Announce (on the output device) that it has been called.
- Print the data passed to the stub—the values of its input and input/output parameters.
- Generate output by assigning values to its output and input/output parameters. This output can be used for testing other modules, or at least for seeing that the output produced by this module reaches the other modules that are supposed to receive it.

Figure 5-18 shows a test version of the payroll-report program. The main program has been completely coded, but the procedures that it calls—*Initialize*, *PrintHeadings*, *ProcessOneRecord*, and *PrintFooter*—are stubs.

The stub for *Initialize* prints its name (to announce that it has been called) and assigns values to its output parameters.

```
writeln ('*** Initialize ***');
writeln;
employeeCount := 0;
nextPageNumber := 0;
totalGrossWages := 0.0
```

In this case, the values assigned by the stub are the same as those assigned by the actual procedure, since they are the obvious values to assign. This situation is exceptional; the data generated by a stub is usually not the same as that generated by the actual procedure. The data generated by the stub, however, must be realistic enough that it will be accepted as valid by other modules.

After the stub for *PrintHeadings* announces itself, it prints the value of the input/output parameter *nextPageNumber*. The value of *nextPageNumber* is then incremented by 1; in this program we will follow the convention of having a stub add 1 to any value that is supposed to modify. The output parameter *linesPrinted* is assigned the value 10, which is a reasonable guess as to the value, 7, that the actual procedure will assign.

The stub for *ProcessOneRecord* follows the same pattern: it prints the value of its input and input/output parameters, and increments the value of each of its input/output parameters by 1. The stub for *PrintFooter* prints the values of its input parameters.

The program in Figure 5-18 was run with an input file containing three records:—the first three records of the data file shown in Figure 5-3. Figure 5-19 shows the output produces. Although the output may seem confusing at first glance, careful examination of its reveals the following:

- The procedures *Initialize* and *PrintHeadings* were called, after which *ProcessOneRecord* was called once for each input record. After all input records were processed, *PrintFooter* was called.

- The output values produced by *Initialize* were transmitted to *PrintHeadings* and the first call of *ProcessOneRecord*; the output values produced by *PrintHeadings* were transmitted to the first call of *ProcessOneRecord*.

- The output values produced by *ProcessOneRecord* (that is, the modifications to the values of its input/output parameters) were transmitted to successive invocations of the same procedure. The values for *employeeCount* and *totalGrossWages* returned by the final call to *ProcessOneRecord* were transmitted to *PrintFooter*.

- The three data values on each record were read and passed to *ProcessOneRecord*.

Figure 5-18.

A preliminary version of the payroll-report program used to test the main program during coding. Only the main program is in final form; the four subprograms that the main program calls are represented by stubs.

---

program *PayrollReport* (*input*, *output*);

{ Produce payroll report from payroll data file. Each line of input file contains an employee number (integer), hours employee worked (real), and hourly pay rate (real). Each detail line of report gives employee number, hours worked, hourly rate, regular wages, overtime wages, and gross wages. A footer line gives number of employees processed and total gross wages }

var
```
    employeeNo        : integer; { input data for one employee }
    hoursWorked,
    hourlyRate        : real;

    employeeCount     : integer; { running count and total }
    totalGrossWages   : real;

    nextPageNumber,              { page number of next page }
    linesPrinted      : integer; { lines printed on current page }
```

Figure 5-18.   *Continued.*

```
{ -------------------------------- Procedure Initialize -------------------------------- }

procedure Initialize (var employeeCount,
                          nextPageNumber : integer;
                      var totalGrossWages   : real);

{ Assign initial values to employeeCount, nextPageNumber, and
  totalGrossWages. }

begin
  writeln ('*** Initialize ***');
  writeln;
  employeeCount := 0;
  nextPageNumber := 0;
  totalGrossWages := 0.0
end; { Initialize }

{ --------------------------- Procedure PrintHeadings --------------------------- }

procedure PrintHeadings (var nextPageNumber,
                             linesPrinted        : integer);

{ Go to top of new page and print page and column headings. Increment
  nextPageNumber and assign initial value to linesPrinted. }

begin
  writeln ('*** PrintHeadings ***');
  writeln ('nextPageNumber = ', nextPageNumber :1);
  writeln,
  nextPageNumber := nextPageNumber + 1;
  linesPrinted := 10
end; { PrintHeadings }

{ --------------------------- Procedure ProcessOneRecord --------------------------- }

procedure ProcessOneRecord (employeeNo          : integer;
                            hoursWorked,
                            hourlyRate          : real;
                        var employeeCount    : integer;
                        var totalGrossWages  : real;
                        var nextPageNumber,
                            linesPrinted        : integer);
```

{ Process and print results for one input record. Data from input record is
  passed as values of *employeeNo*, *hoursWorked*, and *hourlyRate*. Update
  values of *employeeCount*, *totalGrossWages*, *nextPageNumber* (if new
  page is started), and *linesPrinted*. }

Figure 5-18.   *Continued.*

```
begin
   writeln ('*** ProcessOneRecord ***');
   writeln ('employeeNo = ', employeeNo :1,
            '    hoursWorked = ', hoursWorked :1:2);
   writeln ('hourlyRate = ', hourlyRate :1:2,
            '    employeeCount = ', employeeCount :1);
   writeln ('totalGrossWages = ', totalGrossWages :1:2,
            '    nextPageNumber = ', nextPageNumber :1);
   writeln ('linesPrinted = ', linesPrinted :1);
   writeln;
   employeeCount := employeeCount + 1;
   totalGrossWages := totalGrossWages + 1.0;
   nextPageNumber := linesPrinted + 1;
end; { ProcessOneRecord }


{ ------------------------------ Procedure PrintFooter ------------------------------ }


procedure PrintFooter (employeeCount   : integer;
                       totalGrossWages : real);


{ Print footer line giving values of employeeCount and totalGrossWages. }


begin
   writeln ('*** PrintFooter ***');
   writeln ('employeeCount = ', employeeCount :1,
            '    totalGrossWages = ', totalGrossWages :1:2);
   writeln
end; { PrintFooter }


{ ------------------------------------ Main Program ------------------------------------ }


begin
   Initialize (employeeCount, nextPageNumber, totalGrossWages);
   PrintHeadings (nextPageNumber, linesPrinted);
   while not eof(input) do
      begin
         readln (employeeNo, hoursWorked, hourlyRate);
         ProcessOneRecord (employeeNo, hoursWorked, hourlyRate,
                           employeeCount, totalGrossWages,
                           nextPageNumber, linesPrinted);

      end;
   PrintFooter (employeeCount, totalGrossWages)
end.
```

Figure 5-19.

Printout produced by the preliminary test version of the payroll-report program.

```
*** Initialize ***

*** PrintHeadings ***
nextPageNumber = 0

*** ProcessOneRecord ***
employeeNo = 1276        hoursWorked = 31.90
hourlyRate = 17.38   .   employeeCount = 0
totalGrossWages = 0.00       nextPageNumber = 1
linesPrinted = 10

*** ProcessOneRecord ***
employeeNo = 1643        hoursWorked = 45.20
hourlyRate = 21.25        employeeCount = 1
totalGrossWages = 1.00       nextPageNumber = 2
linesPrinted = 11

*** ProcessOneRecord ***
employeeNo = 2479        hoursWorked = 20.10
hourlyRate = 18.75       employeeCount = 2
totalGrossWages = 2.00       nextPageNumber = 3
linesPrinted = 12

*** PrintFooter ***
employeeCount = 3        totalGrossWages = 3.00
```

Taken together, these observations give us a high degree of confidence in the correctness of the main program.

The main program that has been coded and tested can serve as a test driver for testing *Initialize*, *PrintHeadings*, *ProcessOneRecord*, and *PrintFooter* when they are coded. Since *Initialize*, *PrintHeadings*, and *PrintFooter* do not call any subprogram, no stubs need be written to them; they can be tested completely using only the main program as a test driver. To test *ProcessOneRecord*, however, we will have to write stubs for the three subprograms it calls: *CalculateWages*, *UpdateCountAndTotal*, and *PrintDetailLine*. When the corresponding actual subprograms are coded, each can be tested using the first- and second-level modules (and any third-level modules that have been completed) as test drivers.

Maintenance

It is normal for changes to be made to a program after the program has been put into service; making these changes is referred to as *maintenance*. Maintenance activities can be classified according to the reasons they are carried out:

- *Corrective Maintenance.* The program is modified to correct errors that have come to light since the program was put into service.

- *Adaptive Maintenance.* The program is modified to adapt it to changing requirements. For example, changes in the structure of a business, such as caused by a merger or an acquisition, are likely to change the requirements for many data processing programs. Changes in the law, particularly tax law, can also change the requirements for data processing programs.

- *Perfective Maintenance.* The program is modified to improve the manner in which it carries out the task for which it is designed. Perfective maintenance may be needed when users, after working with a program for a while, realize the need for features that were not thought of when the original requirements definition was written.

The primary difficulty of maintenance is that the maintenance programmers (who are almost never the same as those who originally wrote the program) must understand a complex program before they can modify it. If the program is poorly documented, this understanding may be very hard to come by. If the program is not modular, so that its different parts interact in hard-to-understand ways, modifying one part of the program may cause other parts to malfunction. Compounding this problem is the fact that maintenance programmers are usually the least experienced programmers in an organization; the more experienced programmers are assigned to developing new programs. Programmers who have a choice of assignments usually choose anything but maintenance.

The keys to writing maintainable programs are documentation and modularity. Documentation consists of comments in the program together with *external documentation* (such as a program logic manual) that describe the internal operation of a program. The explanations of programs in this text are examples of external documentation; the structure charts and designs in Figures 5-6 through 5-16 could serve well as external documentation for the payroll-report program. The need for good documentation is obvious, since the maintenance programmer must understand the program to modify it.

Modularity allows the maintenance programmer to focus on the parts of the program that need to be modified and avoid having to study the entire program in detail. Modularity also avoids the kinds of subtle interactions between parts of a program that can cause a change in one part of a program to produce an error in the operation of some other part.

Several of the exercises at the end of this chapter ask you to carry out maintenance operations on the payroll-report program.

Alternative Approaches

Top-down design, coding, and testing are among the most powerful techniques at the programmer's command, techniques that every programming student should thoroughly master. But they are not panaceas capable of automatically solving every programming program. Other approaches to program development do exist and may in some circumstances be preferable to the top-down approach. In this section we will look at two such alternatives: bottom-up development and stepwise improvement.

Bottom-Up Development

Bottom-up development proceeds in exactly the opposite direction from top-down development. In bottom-up development, we first write the lowest-level subprograms, those that do not call any other subprograms. We then write the subprograms on the next highest level, the ones that call the lowest-level subprograms. We continue to work our way upwards, writing higher- and higher-level subprograms, until eventually we are able to complete the main program. The following are two *disadvantages* of bottom-up development:

- We are working in opposition to the "natural" direction of problem solving, which is to start with the given problem and successively break it down into simpler and simpler subproblems. Thus as development proceeds, we may find that the lower-level modules we have already written are not the best ones for constructing the higher-level modules on which we are now working.

- A subprogram cannot be tested by substituting it for a stub in an existing partially completed program. Thus, if we wish to test subprograms as they are written, we must write a separate test driver or test harness program to exercise each subprogram.

Why, then, might we ever be tempted to use bottom-up development? One reason is that, in top-down development, we might have trouble predicting the performance of the as-yet-unwritten lower-level modules (how fast they run, how much memory they need); yet that performance might be crucial to choosing a strategy for the higher-level modules. For example, suppose we are writing an animation program that will display moving images on the computer screen. The module that actually sends the images to the display device will be a fairly low-level one. Yet the speed with which objects can be drawn on the screen will determine the entire approach to animation used by the higher-level modules.

Another situation that may call for bottom-up development is when no meaningful testing of higher-level modules can take place in the absence of some lower-level modules (usually input and output modules). For example, it would be difficult to do any testing of the aforementioned animation program without the low-level module that sends images to the screen, since that module is the program's primary channel of communication with the outside world.

Still another situation arises when we wish to use an existing *subprogram library*—a set of previously written subprograms for handling some specific task such as displaying images or maintaining a database. In this situation we do not have the option of designing the lower-level subprograms that are best suited to solving our problem; rather, we must tailor our higher-level subprograms to make the best use of the lower-level subprograms available in the existing library.

Rarely will a program be completely designed, coded, and tested in a bottom-up fashion. But when circumstances similar to those just mentioned exist, it may be necessary to write and test some low-level modules before beginning work on higher-level modules. Often the best approach in such situations is to do a preliminary top-down design (structure chart and module descriptions) and then code and test the modules bottom-up. If some of the lower-level modules do not perform as expected, the design can be revised accordingly before proceeding.

Stepwise Improvement

Many programs, particularly interactive ones, provide the user with a wide range of capabilities or *features*. Such programs focus not on solving a specific problem but on providing the user with a wide range of capabilities for manipulating a particular kind of data. A word processor, for example, provides many features for manipulating text; a spreadsheet program provides many features for manipulating tables of numbers; and a database program provides many features for manipulating files of records.

A common approach to developing such a program is to design, code, and test an initial version providing only a minimal set of features. This version is then gradually improved by the addition of new features. We can refer to this approach as "stepwise improvement," although that is not standard terminology.

As in top-down development, the existing version of the program provides an environment in which each new feature can be tested. Normally, each new feature will be implemented by one or more modules, so modularity is maintained. One pitfall of stepwise improvement is possibly making design decisions early in the development process that preclude or make difficult the later addition of certain desirable (but perhaps originally unanticipated) features. Another pitfall is the "creeping featurism" mentioned earlier in this chapter, in which the performance of the program is eventually degraded and the complexity of its use increased by the addition of too many features, most of which will not be employed by the average user.

Review Questions

1. What is the purpose of requirements analysis? What is the requirements definition?

2. Why is it that users often have trouble specifying the program that they want and are consequently often dissatisfied with the program that they get?

3. How can simulation help users formulate requirements?

4. How does requirements analysis differ when a program is to be marketed as a commercial product rather than being written for a particular client?

5. Describe some ways in which a problem assignment may have to be elaborated to produce a reasonable requirements definition for the problem.

6. Contrast the specification and the requirements definition for a program.

7. What does the specification tell us about a program? What does it deliberately not tell us?

8. Describe two ways of specifying the format of printed output.

9. What does the design tell us about a program? What details does the design deliberately avoid?

10. List five topics addressed by a program design.

11. How did the design we wrote in this chapter illustrate the decomposition of a program into modules?

12. What information did our design give about each module?

13. What are some advantages of designing a program in considerable detail before beginning coding?

14. With a complete design at hand, the modules can be coded in any order. What is one advantage of coding in top-down order?

15. Describe the process of top-down testing. What is a stub?

16. Give some advantages of top-down testing. What is a possible disadvantage? Is there any labor saved in writing stubs instead of test drivers?

17. List three things that a stub should do when called.

18. Give three reasons why program maintenance is required. What are some of the difficulties of maintenance? What two characteristics of a program are most important for simplifying maintenance?

19. What are some disadvantages of bottom-up development? What are some circumstances in which it may, nevertheless, be called for?

20. Describe the technique referred to here as stepwise improvement.

Exercises

1. Write stubs for *CalculateWages*, *UpdateCountAndTotal*, and *PrintDetailLine*.

    Exercises 2-4, which request modifications to the payroll-report program, are intended to illustrate program maintenance. They are unrealistic only in that the payroll-report program is small and well documented, whereas programs that have to be maintained in practice are usually large and poorly documented.

2. Modify the payroll-report program so that it also prints for each employee the number of overtime hours that the employee worked.

3. Modify the payroll-report program so that it also prints at the end of the report the number of employees who worked overtime.

4. Suppose that the first digit of an employee number designates the department in which the employee works: employee 1879 works in Department 1 and employee 5239 works in Department 5. Suppose that the records in the input file for the payroll-report program are sorted according to department; the records for Department 1 precede those for Department 2, which precede those for Department 3, and so on. Modify the payroll-report program so that, after printing the last detail line for a particular department, it prints a summary line giving the number of employees in that department and the total gross wages earned by the employees in that department. The summary line is separated by one blank line from the detail lines that precede and follow it. *Hints*: The department number can be extracted from the employee number with the expression:

    employeeNo **div** 1000

    The program must remember the number of the department whose employee records are currently being processed. When a record with a different department number is read, the program must print a summary line before processing the record just read—the first record for a new department.

    Exercises 5-10 are based on carrying a project of moderate complexity through all six stages of the software development life cycle. The exercises will be more realistic if a number of students work on the same project. One team of students, representing the prospective users of the software, will define the requirements for the project. Other teams will be responsible for specification, design, implementation, testing, and maintenance. The teams should avoid looking over one another's shoulders throughout the project, but should communicate through formal meetings and documents.

No specific project is described here, since defining the requirements for the program to be written is the responsibility of the user team. If hard up for ideas, note that programs to play casino games such as roulette and blackjack are at the desired level of complexity. (An example of such a program can be found in Chapter 7, Example 7-3). If the project is postponed until elementary data structures such as records, files, arrays, and strings have been taken up, then a simple information retrieval system, text editor, or text formatter would also provide a suitable project.

5. The user team should decide on the task to be accomplished, set reasonable levels for performance, convenience, reliability, and development time, and write the requirements definition. It will help if the user team investigates and, if possible, experiments with existing programs carrying out the same or similar tasks before defining the requirements for the program they want written. Software reviews in computer magazines are good sources of critical descriptions of existing programs.

6. Working mainly from the requirements definition, but consulting with the user team when questions arise, the specification team should write the specification for the program. The completed specification should be submitted to the user team for approval.

7. Working from the specification, the design team should divide the program into modules and write the specifications for the individual modules. Difficulties encountered during design may require changes in the requirements or specifications, in which case the project must backtrack to the appropriate earlier phase.

8. The implementation team should code the various modules from the design and perform enough testing to catch gross errors. When each module seems to be working properly, it can be passed to the testing team for more rigorous testing. The implementation and testing teams should agree on the order in which modules are to be implemented and tested. As in the design phase, problems arising in the implementation phase may force a return to earlier phases. Since users often request changes when they actually see the implementation, it may be well to demonstrate a working implementation to the user team as soon as possible, even if the program has not yet been fully debugged.

9. The testing team is responsible for thoroughly testing the individual modules and the complete program. They should devise a testing strategy, select test data, and carry out the tests. When errors are discovered, the module or program should be returned to the implementation team for debugging.

10. The user team should request and the maintenance team should implement an enhancement to the completed program. The maintenance team should have no knowledge of the program other than that provided by the documents created during the development process (including, of course, the program listing).

6 Repetition and Arrays

Pascal provides three statements for controlling repetition: the **while** statement (which has already been introduced), the **for** statement, and the **repeat** statement. In this chapter we will look at the **for** and **repeat** statements as well as at some general principles that govern all repetition constructions. We will also look at *arrays*—lists and tables of values. Processing arrays is one of the most important applications of repetition.

The *for* Statement

The **for** statement is the safest of the three repetition statements in that its execution always terminates. We can never accidentally write a nonterminating repetition using the **for** statement. On the other hand, the **for** statement requires that we know in advance the number of times the controlled statement is to be executed—that is, the number of executions of the controlled statement must be known before the **for** statement is executed. If we want the controlled statement to be executed until some desired situation occurs, and there is no way of knowing in advance how many executions will be needed to bring that situation about, then we must use the **while** or **repeat** statement instead of the **for** statement.

The **for** statement is best introduced with an example.

```
for count := 1 to 5 do
    writeln (count)
```

The integer variable *count* is the *control variable*; it is assigned the values 1, 2, 3, 4, and 5 in succession. The statement *writeln (count)* is the controlled statement; it is executed once for each value of the control variable. Thus *writeln (count)* is executed once with the value of *count* equal to 1, once with the value of *count* equal to 2, and so on. When the **for** statement is executed, the computer prints the following:

```
1
2
3
4
5
```

As in the **while** statement, the controlled statement is indented relative to the **for** statement. The controlled statement is considered part of the **for** statement, so the semicolon separating the **for** statement from the following statement comes after the controlled statement.

```
for count := 1 to 5 do
    writeln (count);
writeln ('That''s all, folks')
```

The **for** statement extends from the word **for** to (but not including) the semicolon; the semicolon separates the **for** statement from the *writeln* statement that prints "That's all, folks".

As with the **while** statement, the **for** statement can control the execution of only a single Pascal statement, but we can get around this limitation by letting the controlled statement be a compound statement.

```
for count := 1 to 5 do
    begin
        write ('aa');
        write ('BB')
    end
```

On each repetition, the statements making up the compound statement are executed, causing the computer to print

```
aaBBaaBBaaBBaaBBaaBB
```

By using **downto** instead of **to**, we can make the computer count backward.

```
for count := 5 downto 1 do
    writeln (count)
```

When this statement is executed, the computer prints

```
5
4
3
2
1
```

The **to** form of the **for** statement will only step through a series of increasing values. If the final value for the control variable is less than the initial value, the controlled statement is not executed. Thus the following statement produces no output:

```
for count := 5 to 1 do
    writeln (count)
```

Likewise, the **downto** form will only step through a series of decreasing values. If the final value for the control variable is greater than the initial value, the controlled statement is not executed. Thus the following statement also produces no output:

```
for count := 1 downto 5 do
    writeln (count)
```

The initial and final values of the control variable can be given by expressions as well as by constants. For example, the statements

```
j := 3;
k := 5;
for i := k - j to k + j do
    write (i :3)
```

cause the computer to print

```
2   3   4   5   6   7   8
```

When the **for** statement is executed, the computer begins by evaluating the expressions $k - j$ and $k + j$. Since the values of these expressions are, respectively, 2 and 8, the **for** statement is executed as if it had been written

> **for** $i := 2$ **to** 8 **do**
>   *write* (i :3)

The control variable can be of any ordinal type; integer, Boolean, and character variables can serve as control variables. In contrast to some other programming languages, however, Pascal does not allow real variables as control variables. The following **for** statement uses a character variable, *letter*, as a control variable:

> **for** *letter* := 'a' **to** 'z' **do**
>   *write* (*letter*)

When the statement is executed, the computer prints the following*:

```
abcdefghijklmnopqrstuvwxyz
```

We could use the **downto** form of the **for** statement to step through the alphabet backward.

> **for** *letter* := 'z' **downto** 'a' **do**
>   *write* (*letter*)

This statement causes the computer to print

```
zyxwvutsrqponmlkjihgfedcba
```

To summarize, the **for** statement has the following two general forms:

> **for** control-variable := expr-1 **to** expr-2 **do**
>   controlled-statement

and

> **for** control-variable := expr-1 **downto** expr-2 **do**
>   controlled-statement

expr-1 and expr-2 are expressions whose values give the initial and final values of the control variable. The control variable can have any ordinal type. The two expressions must have (that is, must yield values of) the same type as the control variable. (This statement is true for the standard types; it will have to be generalized slightly for the programmer-defined types taken up in Chapter 8.) In the **to** form, the controlled statement is not executed if the initial value follows the final value; in the **downto** form, the controlled statement is not executed if the initial value precedes the final value.

Another way to express the meaning, or *semantics*, of the **for** statement is to express each form in terms of assignment, **if**, and **while** statements. The **to** form is equivalent to the following statements:

---

*This printout and the one that follows assume that the letters are contiguous, as they are in the ASCII code. In other codes, non-letter characters may come between adjacent letters of the alphabet.

```
temp1 := expr-1;
temp2 := expr-2;
if temp1 <= temp2 then
   begin
      control-variable := temp1;
      controlled-statement;
      while control-variable <> temp2 do
         begin
            control-variable := succ(control-variable);
            controlled-statement
         end
   end
```

First, note that control-variable, expr-1, expr-2, and controlled-statement are part of our notation for talking about Pascal; they must be replaced by actual variables, expressions, and statements in order for our equivalent statements to be valid Pascal.

The assignments to *temp1* and *temp2* tell us that expr-1 and expr-2 are evaluated only once, before any executions of the controlled statement, and these initial values (the values of *temp1* and *temp2*) govern the execution of the **for** statement. Thus if the controlled statement should assign a new value to some variable that appears in expr-1 or expr-2, this will have no effect on the execution of the **for** statement. (Why?)

The **if** statement tells us that no assignments to the control variable or executions of the controlled statement take place unless the initial value of expr-1 (the value of *temp1*) is less than or equal to the initial value of expr-2 (the value of *temp2*). If the value of *temp1* is less than or equal to that of *temp2*, the value of *temp1* is assigned to the control variable and the controlled statement is executed. Before each succeeding execution of the controlled statement, the statement

$$\text{control-variable} := succ(\text{control-variable})$$

updates the control variable to the immediate successor of its current value. The **while** statement causes execution of the controlled statement to be repeated with successively larger values of the control variable until the value of the control variable becomes equal to the value of *temp2*.

The equivalent statements for the **downto** form differ only in that the <= in the **if** statement is replaced by >=, and *succ* is replaced by *pred* (the function that returns the immediate predecessor of an ordinal value).

```
temp1 := expr-1;
temp2 := expr-2;
if temp1 >= temp2 then
   begin
      control-variable := temp1;
      controlled-statement;
      while control-variable <> temp2 do
         begin
            control-variable := pred(control-variable);
            controlled-statement
         end
   end
```

Programs Using the *for* Statement

The programs in this section illustrate the **for** statement as well as the fundamental techniques for using repetition in programs.

Example 6-1. *Personal Investment*

Suppose that interest for a savings account is compounded monthly. If we start with a given amount in the account and deposit the same amount at the beginning of each month, how much will we have after a given number of months have elapsed? Figure 6-1 shows a program for computing this amount. A typical exchange with the program goes like this:

```
Amount in your account now? 1000
Monthly deposit? 100
Yearly interest rate in percent? 6
Number of months? 36
New amount is $5149.96
```

Proceeding in top-down fashion, we begin with the main program of Figure 6-1. The variable *amount* holds the amount in the account at the beginning of each month (before the deposit is made). The value of *amount* is updated month-by-month as deposits are made and interest accumulates; the initial value of *amount* is the amount already in the account when the deposits are started; the final value of *amount* is the answer we are seeking. Additional input data values needed for the calculation are the amount of the monthly deposit (*deposit*), the annual percentage interest

Figure 6-1.

Program to compute the amount in a bank account after a given number of months. We focus our attention mainly on the procedure *ComputeAmount,* which uses a **for** statement to carry out the desired computation

---

program *Investment* (*input, output*);

{ Compute amount resulting from monthly deposits in a savings account. Assume that interest is compounded monthly }

var
    amount, deposit, yearlyRate : *real*;
    months   : *integer*;

{ -------------------------------- Procedure *GetData* -------------------------------- }

procedure *GetData* (**var** *amount, deposit, yearlyRate* : *real*;
                                  var *months*   : *integer*);

{ Obtain input data from user }

Figure 6-1. *Continued.*

```pascal
begin
  write ('Amount in your account now? ');
  readln (amount);
  write ('Monthly deposit? ');
  readln (deposit);
  write ('Yearly interest rate in percent? ');
  readln (yearlyRate);
  write ('Number of months? ');
  readln (months)
end; { GetData }

{ ---------------------------- Procedure ComputeAmount ---------------------------- }

procedure ComputeAmount (var amount         : real;
                             deposit, yearlyRate : real;
                             months              : integer);

{ Compute amount in account after given number of months }

var
  monthNo              : integer;
  monthlyRate, interest : real;
begin
  monthlyRate := yearlyRate / 1200.0;
  for monthNo := 1 to months do
    begin
      amount := amount + deposit;
      interest := amount * monthlyRate;
      amount := amount + interest
    end
end; { ComputeAmount }

{ ---------------------------- Procedure DisplayAmount ---------------------------- }

procedure DisplayAmount (amount : real);

{ Display calculated amount for the user }

begin
  writeln ('New amount is $', amount :1:2)
end; { DisplayAmount }

{ ---------------------------- Main Program ---------------------------- }

begin
  GetData (amount, deposit, yearlyRate, months);
  ComputeAmount (amount, deposit, yearlyRate, months);
  DisplayAmount (amount)
end.
```

rate (*yearlyRate*), and the number of months for which the calculation is to be done (*months*).

The program must obtain the initial value of *amount* and the values of *deposit*, *yearlyRate*, and *months* from the user, calculate the value of *amount* after the given number of months have elapsed, and display the final value of *amount* to the user. Thus we can code the statement part of the main program as follows:

```
GetData (amount, deposit, yearlyRate, months);
ComputeAmount (amount, deposit, yearlyRate, months);
DisplayAmount (amount)
```

The parameters of *GetData* are all variable parameters, since this procedure must obtain data from the user and return it to the main program. For *ComputeAmount*, only *amount*, whose value is to be updated as a result of the calculation, is passed as a variable parameter; the remaining three parameters of *ComputeAmount* are value parameters. *DisplayAmount* has one value parameter.

GetData and *DisplayAmount* are straightforward, so we will focus our attention on *ComputeAmount*, which uses a **for** statement to compute the final amount in the account. Since the elapsed time is given in months rather than years, *ComputeAmount* must begin by converting the annual percentage rate to a monthly decimal rate (*monthlyRate*); this is accomplished by dividing the annual percentage rate by 1200 (equivalent to dividing by 12 to convert to a monthly rate and by 100 to convert the percentage to a decimal).

```
monthlyRate := yearlyRate / 1200.0
```

We say that a program *simulates* some real-world activity when each step of the program's calculations corresponds to a step of the activity. *ComputeAmount* simulates the process by which the amount in a bank account grows as a result of monthly deposits and interest. At the beginning of each step of the calculation, the value of *amount* is the amount currently in the account. The procedure simulates the monthly deposit by adding the amount of the deposit to the value of *amount*. It then simulates the accumulation of one month's interest by calculating the interest for the current month and adding the result to the value of *amount*. The resulting value of *amount* is the amount in the account at the beginning of the next month (before next month's deposit is made). The variable *amount* both provides input data for each month's calculation and holds the result that the calculation produces.

```
for monthNo := 1 to months do
  begin
    amount := amount + deposit;
    interest := amount * monthlyRate;
    amount := amount + interest
  end
```

This **for** statement illustrates some general characteristics of repetition constructions.

- One or more variables (*amount* in this case) are assigned initial values before the first execution of the controlled statement, and their values are updated by each succeeding execution of the controlled statement. The values assigned to these variables by one execution of the controlled statement provide data for the calculations done during the next execution.

■ When the repetitions terminate, one or more of these variables (again *amount* in the present case) contain the results that were to be computed by the repetition construction.

■ The repetition construction can be characterized by an *invariant assertion*, an assertion that is true before the first execution of the controlled statement (that is, it is true of the initial values assigned to the variables) and whose truth is not affected by executing the controlled statement. Thus the invariant assertion will still be true when the repetitions terminate, and from the truth of the invariant assertion we will be able to conclude that the repetition construction carried out the proper computation.

A suitable invariant assertion for the repetition construction in *ComputeAmount* is

The value of *amount* is the amount in the account at the beginning of each month (before the deposit is made).

This assertion is certainly true just before the calculations for the first month are done because the initial value assigned to *amount* is the initial amount supplied by the user. And because the purpose of the calculations done by the controlled statements is to update the value of *amount* to reflect the amount at the beginning of the following month, the assertion will be true at the beginning of the calculations for each succeeding month and after all the calculations are done. But from the invariant assertion we easily conclude that when all the calculations have been done, the value of *amount* is the amount in the account after the number of months specified by the user.

Example 6-2. *Fibonacci's Rabbit Problem*

A mathematician named Leonardo Fibonacci proposed the following problem. Suppose that a pair of rabbits has one pair of offspring each month and each new pair becomes fertile at the age of one month. If we start with one fertile pair and none of the rabbits die, how many pairs will we have after a year's time?

The program in Figure 6-2 solves the problem by simulating the reproduction of the rabbits according to Fibonacci's rather unrealistic rules. The program keeps track of the number of pairs (*pairs*) and the number of fertile pairs (*fertilePairs*) alive at the beginning of each month. For each month the program computes the number of pairs and fertile pairs alive at the beginning of the next month from the number of each alive at the beginning of the current month.

The program in Figure 6-2 generalizes Fibonacci's problem slightly by allowing the user to enter the initial number of pairs and fertile pairs (both are 1 in the original problem). The user can also specify the value for *months*, the number of months that the rabbits are to reproduce (12 in the original problem). We outline the program as follows:

Figure 6-2.

Program to solve a slightly generalized version of Fibonacci's
rabbit problem.

---

program *Fibonacci* (*input*, *output*):

{ Solve Fibonacci's rabbit problem }

var
  pairs, *fertilePairs*, *months*,
  pairsNextMonth, *monthNo* : *integer*;
begin
  write ('Starting number of pairs? ');
  readln (*pairs*);
  write ('Starting number of fertile pairs? ');
  readln (*fertilePairs*);
  write ('Number of months? ');
  readln (*months*);
  for *monthNo* := 1 **to** *months* **do**
    begin
      pairsNextMonth := *pairs* + *fertilePairs*;
      fertilePairs := *pairs*;
      pairs := *pairsNextMonth*
    end
  writeln ('After ', *months* :1, ' months you will have ', *pairs* :1, ' pairs')
end.

---

1. Obtain initial values for *pairs, fertilePairs,* and *months* from the user
2. For each month do the following:
   2.1 Update the values of *pairs* and *fertilePairs* to reflect the number of pairs that were born and the number that became fertile during the current month
3. Print the value of *pairs* as the number of pairs after the specified number of months have elapsed

Our only remaining problem is to refine the controlled statement; that is, to determine how to update the values of *pairs* and *fertilePairs* in accordance with Finonacci's rules for rabbit reproduction. Each fertile pair produces exactly one pair of offspring each month; thus the number of pairs born during the month is equal to the value of *fertilePairs*. The number of pairs at the beginning of next month is the sum of the number at the beginning of this month (the value of *pairs*) and the number born this month (the value of *fertilePairs*). Because we don't want to change the value of *pairs* just yet, we temporarily assign this sum to another variable, *pairsNextMonth*.

    pairsNextMonth := *pairs* + *fertilePairs*

A pair becomes fertile after one month. All pairs alive at the beginning of the current month (the value of *pairs*) will be fertile at the beginning of the next month regardless of whether they are fertile now or not. Thus the value of *fertilePairs* at the beginning of next month is equal to the value of *pairs* at the beginning of this month.

> *fertilePairs* := *pairs*

We delayed assigning *pairs* its new value because we still needed its current value to compute the new value for *fertilePairs*. With that chore out of the way, we can assign *pairs* its previously computed new value.

> *pairs* := *pairsNextMonth*

If we use our program to solve Fibonacci's original problem, the following dialogue ensues:

```
Starting number of pairs? 1
Starting number of fertile pairs? 1
Number of months? 12
After 12 months you will have 377 pairs
```

A suitable invariant assertion for the repetition construction is as follows:

> The values of *pairs* and *fertilePairs* are, respectively, the total number of pairs and the number of fertile pairs alive at the beginning of the current month.

Verify that this assertion is true for the initial values of *pairs* and *fertilePairs*, and that its truth is not affected by executing the controlled statement. How does this invariant assertion allow us to conclude that the **for** statement in Figure 6-2 carries out the desired computation?

Example 6-3. *The Inventor's Request*

Once upon a time, the inventor of chess was called before the king and told to name his own reward. The inventor responded, "All I ask is one grain of wheat for the first square of my chessboard, two grains for the second square, four grains for the third square, and so on for all 64 squares, doubling the number of grains for each square." Would the king be wise to agree to this request?

We can answer this question without having to order any wheat by using the program in Figure 6-3 to simulate the accumulation of wheat according to the inventor's instructions. The program steps through the 64 squares of the chessboard, computes the number of grains on each square (*grains*) and keeps a running total (*total*) of the grains on all the squares considered *prior* to the current one.

Suspecting that the wiley inventor may have devised a tricky way to ask for a lot of wheat, we will use real variables for *grains* and *total* so that large numbers can be stored. The values of these variables will not be accurate to the last grain, but only to the number of significant figures with which real numbers are stored by a particular implementation of Pascal.

Just before doing the calculations for the first square, the value of *grains* is the number of grains to be placed on the first square, which is 1.0. The value of *total* is the number of grains placed on previous squares,

Figure 6-3.

Program to compute the number of grains of wheat requested
by the inventor of chess.

---

program *Wheat* (*input*, *output*);

{ Compute number of grains of wheat requested by inventor of chess }

var
  grains, *total* : *real*;   { Values may be very large }
  squareNo   : *integer*;
begin
  grains := 1.0;
  total := 0.0;
  for *squareNo* := 1 **to** 64 **do**
    begin
      total := *total* + *grains*;
      grains := 2.0 * *grains*
    end;
  writeln ('Inventor requested ', *grains* :1, ' grains')
end.

---

which is 0.0 since at this point there are no previous squares. Thus *grains*
and *total* are given initial values as follows:

  grains := 1.0;
  total := 0.0

The calculations for each square must update the running total by
adding to it the number of grains placed on the current square.

  total := *total* + *grains*

The value of grains must be updated to reflect the number of grains to be
placed on the next square. According to the inventor's instructions, the
number of grains is doubled for each square.

  grains := 2.0 * *grains*

Why must *total* be updated before *grains*?
  When the program is executed, it prints the following:

  Inventor requested 1.8E+19 grains

The inventor requested about 18 billion billion grains of wheat. (The
answer printed by your computer may take a slightly different form since
Pascal implementations vary as to the number of decimal places printed
when a field-width parameter of 1 is specified for a floating-point number.
The number of decimal places can be increased by increasing the value of
the field-width parameter.)
  Formulate a suitable invariant assertion and use it to show that the **for**
statement carries out the desired calculation.

Nested *for* Statements

The term *nested* is often applied to a set of containers whose sizes are such that each fits snugly into the next larger one. Programming language statements are said to be nested when one statement contains another of the same kind. **for** statements can be nested because a **for** statement contains a controlled statement, which can itself be a **for** statement or a compound statement that includes a **for** statement. What's more, a **for** statement contained in another **for** statement can itself contain a **for** statement, which in turn can contain still another **for** statement, and so on. In fact, all statements that control repetition can be nested, and nested repetition constructions are an extremely common programming device.

For example, consider the program in Figure 6-4, which prints the pattern

```
*
* *
* * *
* * * *
* * * * *
```

Printing this pattern involves repetition on two levels. First, the five lines have to be printed, so the statements for printing one line have to be executed five times. Second, the proper number of asterisks have to be printed on each line, so the statement for printing one asterisk has to be executed the proper number of times for each line.

Nested repetition statements are often best constructed and understood inside out, starting with the innermost controlled statement (which performs the most basic task) and working outward through the controlling statements. Thus we start with the statement

write ('*')

Figure 6-4.

This program for printing a triangular pattern illustrates nested **for** statements.

```
program Pattern (output);

{ Print triangular pattern }

var
  row, col : integer;
begin
  for row := 1 to 5 do
    begin
      for col := 1 to row do
        write ('*');
      writeln
    end
end.
```

which prints one asterisk. Because *write* is used instead of *writeln,* the output device remains on the same line after printing the asterisk.

The number of asterisks to be printed on a particular row of the pattern is equal to the row number—one asterisk on the first row, two on the second, and so on. To print the row whose row number is the value of *row,* we must execute the *write* statement *row* times and then execute a *writeln* statement to send the output device to the next line.

```
for col := 1 to row do
  write ('*');
writeln
```

These two statements need to be executed five times, one for each row of the pattern. What's more, the value of *row* needs to be set to 1 before printing the first row, 2 before printing the second, and so on, so that the proper number of asterisks will be printed on each row. We can accomplish both these goals by bracketing the two statements with **begin** and **end** and embedding them in a **for** statement that steps *row* from 1 through 5.

```
for row := 1 to 5 do
  begin
    for col := 1 to row do
      write ('*');
    writeln
  end
```

The outermost **for** statement causes the compound statement to be executed five times, with the value of *row* stepping from 1 to 5. For each value of *row,* the innermost **for** statement—the one inside the compound statement—prints *row* asterisks, after which the *writeln* statement sends the output device to a new line.

Devise invariant assertions for both the inner and outer **for** statements. The assertions should state, in terms of the current values of *row* and *col,* what progress has been made so far in printing the current row (for the inner **for** statement) and the entire pattern (for the outer **for** statement).

Example 6-4. *The Rabbit Problem and the while Statement*

To further contrast the **while** and **for** statements, we will look at a variation of Fibonacci's rabbit problem that requires the **while** statement for its solution.

In the original version of the problem (Example 6-2) we were asked how many pairs there will be after the rabbits have reproduced for a given number of months. Since the number of months was given, we used a **for** statement to repeat the calculations for one month the required number of times. But suppose we turn the problem around and ask how many months the rabbits must reproduce for the number of pairs to equal or exceed a given value. Now, the number of times the controlled statement must be executed is not only not known in advance but is the result we are trying to find. Instead of a **for** statement, for which the number of executions must be specified in advance, we use a **while** statement so the controlled statement can be executed as many times as required to obtain the desired number of pairs.

The program in Figure 6-5 solves this version of Fibonacci's rabbit problem. As before, *pairs* and *fertilePairs* are the total number of pairs and the number of fertile pairs. *pairsDesired* is the number of pairs that must be reached or exceeded, and the variable *months* is used to count the number of months that the rabbits reproduce. After *pairs* and *fertilePairs* have received their initial values, we initialize *months* to zero and repeat the monthly update of *pairs* and *fertilePairs* until the value of *pairs* equals or exceeds that of *pairsDesired*. Each time the monthly update is performed, the value of *months* is increased by 1.

```
months := 0;
while pairs < pairsDesired do
  begin
    pairsNextMonth := pairs + fertilePairs;
    fertilePairs := pairs;
    pairs := pairsNextMonth;
    months := months + 1
  end;
```

Figure 6-5.   Program for a variation of Fibonacci's rabbit problem in which the unknown is the number of months the rabbits reproduce. This version of the problem uses a **while** statement rather than a **for** statement.

```
program Fibonacci (input, output);

{ Find number of months needed to produce a given number of pairs }

var
  pairs, fertilePairs, months,
  pairsNextMonth, pairsDesired : integer;
begin
  write ('Starting number of pairs? ');
  readln (pairs);
  write ('Starting number of fertile pairs? ');
  readln (fertilePairs);
  write ('Number of pairs desired? ');
  readln (pairsDesired);
  months := 0;
  while pairs < pairsDesired do
    begin
      pairsNextMonth := pairs + fertilePairs;
      fertilePairs := pairs;
      pairs := pairsNextMonth;
      months := months + 1
    end;
  writeln ('After ', months :1, ' months you will have ', pairs :1, ' pairs')
end.
```

A typical exchange with the program goes like this:

```
Starting number of pairs? 1
Starting number of fertile pairs? 1
Number of pairs desired? 500
After 13 months you will have 610 pairs
```

The end of the 13th month (the beginning of the 14th month) is the first time the number of pairs equals or exceeds 500; the actual number of pairs present at that time is 610.

As usual, we must convince ourselves that the repetitions will terminate. The repetitions continue as long as the value of *pairs* is less than some limit set by the user. We thus need to show that, as the calculation proceeds, the value of *pairs* will steadily increase and thus eventually exceed whatever limit the user has imposed. By increasing the value of *pairs,* each execution of the controlled statement will make progress towards taking the value of *pairs* over the limit and hence terminating the repetitions.

On each execution of the controlled statement, the new values of *pairs* is the sum of the old value of *pairs* and the old value of *fertilePairs.* If the old value of *fertilePairs* is a positive number (not zero or negative), then the new value of *pairs* must be greater than the old—the value of *pairs* will increase, as desired.

The new value of *fertilePairs* is equal to the old value of *pairs.* If the old value of *pairs* is a positive number, so will be the new value of *fertilePairs.* Since the new value of *pairs* is greater than the old value, and the old value was a positive number, so also will be the new value.

We conclude that if the old values of *pairs* and *fertilePairs* are positive numbers, the new values will be also, and the new value of *pairs* will be greater than the old. Thus if the initial values of *pairs* and *fertilePairs* are positive, the values of those variables will remain positive no matter how many times the controlled statement is executed, and the value of *pairs* will increase steadily from one execution of the controlled statement to the next. So, if the initial values of *pairs* and *fertilePairs* are positive, termination is guaranteed.

Let's look a bit more closely at the conditions on the initial values of *pairs* and *fertilePairs.* We can discard negative values at once. Since there is no such thing as a negative number of pairs, negative values do not represent valid data for our problem. Also we can easily see that negative values can lead to nontermination. For example, if both initial values are negative then our preceding argument can be adapted to show that the value of *pairs* will get smaller—more negative—with each repetition.

But what about the cases in which one or both of the initial values is zero? If the value *fertilePairs* is zero, but that of *pairs* is not, then at the beginning of the next month both *pairs* and *fertilePairs* will have positive values (the original nonfertile pairs will have become fertile) and the calculation will proceed as already discussed. Termination is guaranteed in this case. Termination is likewise guaranteed if the initial value of *pairs* is zero but that of *fertilePairs* is not.* After one month, the number of pairs

---

*It may seem unrealistic for *fertilePairs* to have a greater initial value than *pairs,* but we can interpret this situation as representing the introduction of newly born pairs from an outside source. The excess fertile pairs contribute offspring during the first month but do not themselves join the group under consideration. At the end of the first month the value of *fertilePairs* is set to the initial value of *pairs,* so after the first month the excess fertile pairs play no further role.

will be positive and the number of fertile pairs will be zero, a situation for which we have just seen that termination is guaranteed. On the other hand, if both values are initially zero, they will remain so no matter how many times the controlled statement is executed.

Thus we see that termination is guaranteed if the initial values of *pairs* and *fertilePairs* are both greater than or equal to zero and at least one of the values is not equal to zero.

The *repeat* Statement

The **repeat** statement has the following form:
> **repeat**
>> controlled-statements
>
> **until** Boolean-expression

The **repeat** statement differs from the **while** statement in three ways:

1. The reserved words **repeat** and **until** form a natural pair of brackets between which any number of controlled statements can be placed. Thus with **repeat** we do not have to use **begin** and **end** to package a sequence of controlled statements as a single compound statement.

2. The controlled statements are executed repeatedly until the Boolean expression evaluates to *true*; that is, execution continues as long as evaluating the expression yields *false*. We can think of the Boolean expression in the **repeat** statement as a *termination condition*; the repetitions *terminate* when the expression evaluates to *true*. In contrast, the Boolean expression in a **while** statement is a *continuation condition*: the repetitions *continue* as long as the expression evaluates to *true*.

3. The Boolean expression is evaluated *after* each execution of the repeated statements, rather than before each execution as with the **while** statement. This means that the controlled statements are always executed at least once, since the termination condition is not checked until after the first execution. In contrast, the statements controlled by a **while** statement will not be executed at all if the continuation condition is already false when the computer reaches the **while** statement.

The **repeat** statement comes in handy when the termination condition cannot be meaningfully checked until after the controlled statements have been executed. For example, when an interactive program has finished processing one set of data entered by the user, it should usually give the user the option of entering another set of data for processing. This saves the user trouble of having to load and execute the program for each set of data. After processing one set of data, the program asks:

> `Enter another set of data (y/n)?`

If the user enters y or Y, the statements for processing a set of data are repeated; if the user enters n or N, the program terminates. Since it makes no sense to check whether the user wants to process another set of data until at least one set has been processed, the repetition is most simply controlled by a **repeat** statement.

Figure 6-6 shows our personal investment program (from Figure 6-1) modified to provide the option just described. A new procedure, *CheckIfMoreData,* is given the task of determining whether the user wishes to process another set of data. The Boolean variable *terminate* is passed as a variable parameter to *CheckIfMoreData,* which sets the variable to *true* if the program is to terminate and to *false* if the user wishes to repeat the calculations with another set of data. We modify Figure 6-1 so that the statements in the main program will be executed repeatedly until *CheckIfMoreData* sets *terminate* to *true:*

> **repeat**
>   *GetData* (*amount, deposit, yearlyRate, months*);
>   *ComputeAmount* (*amount, deposit, yearlyRate, months*);
>   *DisplayAmount* (*amount*);
>   *CheckIfMoreData* (*terminate*)
> **until** *terminate*

Thanks to modularity, *GetData, ComputeAmount,* and *DisplayAmount* are unaffected by the modification. Our only remaining task is to write the new procedure, *CheckIfMoreData,* to determine the user's wishes and set *terminate* accordingly.

The procedure heading for *CheckIfMoreData* declares *terminate* as a Boolean variable-parameter:

> **procedure** *CheckIfMoreData* (**var** *terminate : Boolean*);

As usual, the formal parameter *terminate* is not the same as the main-program variable *terminate,* even though we have given both the same name. The local character variable *response* is declared to hold the user's response to the procedure's query.

We want the question "Enter another set of data (y/n)?" to be repeated until the user enters one of the four valid responses: y, n, Y, or N. We could assure a valid response as follows:

> **repeat**
>   *write* ('Enter another set of data (y/n)? ');
>   *readln* (*response*)
> **until** (*response* = 'y') **or** (*response* = 'n') **or**
>   (*response* = 'Y') **or** (*response* = 'N')

This works, but the termination condition is rather cumbersome. We can simplify it by using the Pascal *set* data type. A set is a collection of values, such as 1, 3, and 5, which are called the elements of the set. We represent a set in a Pascal program by listing its elements between square brackets. Thus

> [1, 3, 5]

represents the set whose elements are 1, 3, and 5. The relational operator **in** determines whether a value is an element of a set. Thus the Boolean expression

> 3 **in** [1, 3, 5]

evaluates to *true,* since 3 is an element of [1, 3, 5]. Likewise, the Boolean expression

> 2 **in** [1, 3, 5]

evaluates to *false,* since 2 is not an element of [1, 3, 5].

Figure 6-6.

A modified version of the personal investment program in
Figure 6-1. After each computation, this program gives the
user the option of doing another computation or terminating
the program. Note the **repeat** statements in the main program
and in *CheckIfMoreData*.

```
program Investment (input, output);

{ Compute amount resulting from monthly deposits in a savings account.
  Assume that interest is compounded monthly }

var
   amount, deposit, yearlyRate : real;
   months                      : integer;
   terminate                   : Boolean;

{ -------------------------------- Procedure GetData -------------------------------- }

procedure GetData (var amount, deposit, yearlyRate : real;
                   var months                      : integer);

{ Obtain input data from user }

begin
   write ('Amount in your account now? ');
   readln (amount);
   write ('Monthly deposit? ');
   readln (deposit);
   write ('Yearly interest rate in percent? ');
   readln (yearlyRate);
   write ('Number of months? ');
   readln (months)
end; { GetData }

{ --------------------------- Procedure ComputeAmount --------------------------- }

procedure ComputeAmount (var amount           : real;
                         deposit, yearlyRate : real;
                         months              : integer);

{ Compute amount in account after given number of months }

var
   monthNo               : integer;
   monthlyRate, interest : real;
begin
   monthlyRate := yearlyRate / 1200.0;
   for monthNo := 1 to months do
      begin
         amount := amount + deposit;
```

Figure 6-6.

Continued.

```
            interest := amount * monthlyRate;
            amount := amount + interest
        end
    end; { ComputeAmount }


{ ----------------------------Procedure DisplayAmount ---------------------------- }

procedure DisplayAmount (amount : real);

{ Display calculated amount for the user }

begin
    writeln ('New amount is $', amount :1:2)
end; { DisplayAmount }


{ ----------------------------Procedure CheckIfMoreData---------------------------- }

procedure CheckIfMoreData (var terminate : Boolean);

{ Determine if user wishes to repeat calculations for another set of data }

var
    response : char;
begin
    repeat
        write ('Enter another set of data (y/n)? ');
        readln (response)
    until response in ['y', 'n', 'Y', 'N'];
    terminate := response in ['n', 'N'];
    writeln
end; { CheckIfMoreData }


{ ----------------------------------- Main Program ----------------------------------- }

begin
    repeat
        GetData (amount, deposit, yearlyRate, months);
        ComputeAmount (amount, deposit, yearlyRate, months);
        DisplayAmount (amount);
        CheckIfMoreData (terminate)
    until terminate
end.
```

With the aid of a set, we can simplify the termination condition of the **repeat** statement as follows:

```
    repeat
        write ('Enter another set of data (y/n)? ');
        readln (response)
    until response in ['y', 'n', 'Y', 'N']
```

When the **repeat** statement terminates, the value of *response* will be y, n, Y, or N. We want to set *terminate* to *true* if the response was n or N and to *false* otherwise. Again, a set comes in handy.

terminate : = *response* **in** ['n', 'N']

One-Dimensional Arrays

Arrays, which serve to represent lists and tables in main memory, are one of the most widely used data structures. Almost all general-purpose programming languages offer arrays, and in some languages arrays are the only available means of structuring data. Array processing is one of the most important applications of the **for** statement.

Array Types and Values

We can think of a *one-dimensional* or *linear* array as a correspondence between *index values* and *component values*:

index	component
1	3.5
2	6.9
3	7.2
4	9.5
5	4.2

All the components have the same type, which is the *component type* of the array. In the example, the component type is *real,* and the components of the array are 3.5, 6.9, 7.2, 9.5, and 4.2.

The components of the array are labeled by values of an *index type,* which must be an ordinal type. The most common index type is a *subrange type,* which contains a range of values selected from some other ordinal type. A subrange type is designated by giving the first and last values of the subrange, separated by two periods. The following are examples of subrange types:

1..100	The integers 1 through 100
−10..+10	The integers −10 through +10
'a'..'i'	The characters 'a' through 'i'
'J'..'R'	The characters 'J' through 'R'

Each value of the index type labels a component of the array; the number of components in the array is thus the same as the number of values in the index type. In our example, the array components are labeled with the index values 1, 2, 3, 4, and 5; the index type for the array is thus 1..5.

Only the component values are stored in main memory. The computer can find the component corresponding to any index value by using the index value to calculate the memory address at which the component is stored. Thus the components stored in main memory do not need to be labeled with their index values, and so the index values do not have to be stored. Figure 6-7 illustrates how the example array might be stored in main memory.

Figure 6-7.

An array of five real numbers stored in main memory. Each component value occupies a separate memory location. Only component values are stored; index values need not be stored because the computer can calculate which memory location corresponds to any given index value.

3.5
6.9
7.2
9.5
4.2

Pascal does not provide predefined array types but instead provides us with the means to define our own. An array type is defined by a *type definition* with the following structure:

array-type = **array** [index-type] **of** component-type;

For example, the type definition

list = **array** [1..5] **of** *real*;

defines type *list* to be type of all arrays with index type 1..5 and component type *real*; our example array belongs to this array type.

Types are defined in a *type definition part,* which is introduced by the reserved word **type.** The type definition part follows the constant definition part (if any) and precedes the variable declaration part. The following shows how the definition for type *list* would appear in the type definition part.

type
    list = **array** [1..5] **of** *real*;

Array Variables

The variable *listA* declared by

var
    listA : *list*;

is an *array variable* whose possible values are arrays of type *list*. Such a variable is called an *entire variable* because it holds a complete array. We can think of an array variable such as *listA* as composed of *component variables,* each of which holds one component of the value of *listA*. Each component variable is designated by a unique index value, which is written in brackets following the name of the array variable. Thus the component variables of *listA* are written *listA*[1], *listA*[2], *listA*[3], *listA*[4], and *listA*[5]. Figure 6-8 illustrates the component variables of *listA*.

Component variables can be assigned values and used in expressions just like any other variables. For example, after the assignments

listA[1] := 0.5;
listA[2] := 0.7;
listA[3] := 0.2;

Figure 6-8.

The array *listA* with each of its component variables labeled.

listA

listA[1]	3.5
listA[2]	6.9
listA[3]	7.2
listA[4]	9.5
listA[5]	4.2

$$listA[4] := 0.9;$$
$$listA[5] := 0.3$$

the value of *listA* is given by the following table:

index	component
1	0.5
2	0.7
3	0.2
4	0.9
5	0.3

and the value of the expression

$$3.0 * listA[1] + 4.0 * listA[2]$$

is 4.3.

Elements of Array Processing

In this section we will look at some basic techniques for processing data stored in arrays. All of these techniques involve using a **for** statement to step through the components of an array.

Arrays and the *for* Statement

A **for** statement is frequently used to carry out similar or identical operations on each component of an array. For example, let *data* be an array variable of type *list* and assume that we want to set all the component variables of *data* to zero. Since *data* has only five component variables, we could do the job with the five assignments

$$data[1] := 0.0;$$
$$data[2] := 0.0;$$
$$data[3] := 0.0;$$
$$data[4] := 0.0;$$
$$data[5] := 0.0$$

But for larger arrays with hundreds or thousands of components, a separate assignment statement for each component is out of the question. A better approach is to use a **for** statement to step through the components of *data*, setting each component to zero in turn.

> **for** *index* := 1 **to** 5 **do**
>   *data*[*index*] := 0.0

The value of *index* is stepped from 1 to 5, and the controlled statement

> *data*[*index*] := 0.0

is executed once for each value of *index*. When the value of *index* is 1, the controlled statement is equivalent to

> *data*[1] := 0.0

When the value of *index* is 2, the controlled statement is equivalent to

> *data*[2] := 0.0

and so on. When the repetition terminates, each of the component variables of *data* will have been assigned the value 0.0.

Averaging the Components of an Array

Let's compute the average of the components of the array *data*. The first step is to compute the sum of the component values. We will use the real variable *total* to hold a running total of all the values added so far. We begin by clearing the value of *total* to zero.

> *total* := 0.0

We then step through the components of *data* adding the value of each component in turn to the value of *total*.

> **for** *index* := 1 **to** 5 **do**
>   *total* := *total* + *data*[*index*]

Finally, the value of *total* is divided by 5, the number of components of *data*, to get the average. The complete set of statements for computing the average follows:

> *total* := 0.0;
> **for** *index* := 1 **to** 5 **do**
>   *total* := *total* + *data*[*index*];
> *average* := *total* / 5.0

Finding the Largest and Smallest Components of an Array

Suppose that the temperature is recorded each hour and the 24 temperatures recorded on a given day are stored as the components of a 24-component array. We wish to find the high and low temperature for the day. We define the type *tempArray* and declare the array variable *temp* as follows:

> **type**
>   *tempArray* = **array** [1..24] **of** *real*;
> **var**
>   *temp* : *tempArray*;

As we step through the components of *temp*, we will use the real variable *low* to keep track of the lowest temperature encountered so far. Likewise, we will use the real variable *high* to keep track of the highest temperature encountered so far. When a temperature lower than the value of *low* is encountered, that temperature becomes the new value of *low*. When a temperature higher than the value of *high* is encountered, that temperature becomes the new value of *high*. *high* and *low* are set initially to the value of *temp*[1], the first temperature in the array. After the entire array *temp* has been scanned, the values of *high* and *low* are the largest and smallest components of the value of *temp*.

```
low := temp[1];
high := temp[1];
for hour := 2 to 24 do
   begin
      if temp[hour] < low then
         low := temp[hour];
      if temp[hour] > high then
         high := temp[hour]
   end
```

Now suppose that the value of *temp*[1] is the temperature recorded at 1:00 A.M., *temp*[2] is the temperature recorded at 2:00 A.M., and so on. We want to know not only the high and low temperatures but the times at which the high and low first occurred. That is, we want to know the index of the first occurrence of the largest component value of *temp* and the index of the first occurrence of the smallest component of *temp*.

We proceed by stepping through the array, using the variables *lowHour* and *highHour* to keep track of the index values of the first occurrences in *temp* of the values of *low* and *high*. Each time the value of a component of *temp* is assigned to *low*, the index of that component must be assigned to *lowHour*. Likewise, each time the value of a component of *temp* is assigned to *high*, the index of that component must be assigned to *highHour*.

```
low := temp[1];
lowHour := 1;
high := temp[1];
highHour := 1;
for hour := 2 to 24 do
   begin
      if temp[hour] < low then
         begin
            low := temp[hour];
            lowHour := hour
         end;
      if temp[hour] > high then
         begin
            high := temp[hour];
            highHour := hour
         end
   end
```

When the repetition terminates, the value of *low* is the smallest component of the value of *temp,* and the value of *lowHour* is the smallest index value for which the condition

$$low = temp[lowHour]$$

is true. Likewise, the value of *high* is the largest component of the value of *temp,* and the value of *highHour* is the smallest index value for which the condition

$$high = temp[highHour]$$

is true.

Input and Output of Arrays

To input the value of an array variable from a textfile, we use a **for** statement to step through the component variables of an array variable and read a value for each. For example, the following **for** statement inputs the value of the array variable *data* from the standard input file:

```
for index := 1 to 5 do
    readln (data[index])
```

Because the *readln* statement discards any unread data on a line, this statement requires that each array component appear on a separate line of the textfile. If more than one input value appears on a line, we should use *read* rather than *readln.*

```
for index := 1 to 5 do
    read (data[index])
```

Likewise, we can write the components of the value of *data* to the standard output file with the following statements:

```
for index := 1 to 5 do
    writeln (data[index])
```

Each component, however, is written on a separate line. To write all five components on the same line, we can use

```
for index := 1 to 5 do
    write (data[index] :6)
```

More elaborate formatting is easily programmed. For example, suppose we want to print the 24 components of the array *temp* on four lines with six values on each line. The six values on each line are to be arranged in columns 10 characters wide. This printout can be produced by using the following statements:

```
column := 0;
for hour := 1 to 24 do
    begin
        write (temp[hour] :10);
        if column = 5 then
            writeln;
        column := (column + 1) mod 6
    end
```

The field-width parameter 10 causes the values to be arranged in columns that are 10 characters wide. The statement

$$column := (column + 1) \bmod 6$$

causes the value of *column* to cycle repeatedly from 0 to 5 and then back to 0 again. Each time the value of *column* reaches 5, the **if** statement executes a *writeln* statement, which causes the output device to go to a new line. The following is an alternate version of the code that does not use the **mod** operator; in this version the value of *column* goes from 1 to 6:

```
column := 1;
for hour := 1 to 24 do
  begin
    write (temp[hour] :10);
    if column = 6 then
      begin
        column := 1;
        writeln
      end
    else
      column := column + 1
  end
```

Example 6-5. *Grade Report*

We conclude our discussion of one-dimensional arrays by looking at a complete program that uses arrays. The input data for the program will be grade records, each consisting of a student indentification number and a numerical grade. The program is to print a report showing the ID number and grade of each student. The average grade is to be printed at the bottom of the report, and each grade that is more than ten points below the average is to be flagged (marked) with an asterisk. The following is a typical printout:

```
ID Number          Grade

     1234           71.0
     2694           62.0*
     3721           87.0
     5923           60.0*
     6683           99.5

Average Grade: 75.9
```

Grades are represented by real numbers so that fractions of a point can be awarded. Note that we do not know which grades should be marked with asterisks until the average has been computed, and the average cannot be computed until all the grades have been read. Therefore, the input records must be read and stored in arrays until all the data has been read and the average has been computed. The stored data is then used to print the output, with the computed average being used to determine which grades will be flagged.

Our input data consists of records, each containing two fields (data values). There are two methods of storing records in arrays. The one we will use here is to use a separate array for each field. Thus we will store all the ID numbers in an array *idNum* and all the grades in an array *grade*. For each value of *index*, the values of *idNum*[*index*] and *grade*[*index*] will be the fields of a particular grade record. Arrays used in this way are called *parallel arrays*, because we can think of them as representing parallel columns in a table. (The other method of storing records, which we will discuss in Chapter 9, uses record data types—which we have not yet taken up—to store all the fields of a record in a single array component. That way, only one array is needed no matter how many fields the records have.)

Looking at the program in Figure 6-9, we find the following definitions and declarations:

```
const
    maxRecords    = 50;      { maximum number of records program can
                               handle }
    maxPointsLow  = 10.0;    { maximum number of points a grade can be
                               below average and not be flagged }
type
    idList    = array [1..maxRecords] of integer;
    gradeList = array [1..maxRecords] of real;
var
    idNum   : idList;        { ID numbers }
    grade   : gradeList;     { grades }
    count   : integer;       { number of records }
    average : real;          { average grade }
```

In the constant definition part we define two constants: *maxRecords*, which is the largest number of records that can be stored; and *maxPointsLow*, which is the largest number of points that a grade can be below average and not be flagged in the printout.

Figure 6-9.   Program for printing a grade report. The input data consists of grade records, each containing a student ID number and a numerical grade. The output is a report listing the ID numbers and grades. The average grade is printed at the bottom of the report, and each grade that is more than 10 points below the average grade is flagged (marked) with an asterisk.

```
program LowGrades (input, output);

{ Print student ID numbers and grades; print an asterisk after each grade
  that is more than 10 points below average }

const
    maxRecords    = 50;    { maximum number of records
                             program can handle }
```

Figure 6-9.   *Continued.*

```pascal
          maxPointsLow = 10.0; { maximum number of points
                                 a grade can be below average
                                 and not be flagged }
   type
     idList    = array [1..maxRecords] of integer; { array types }
     gradeList = array [1..maxRecords] of real;
   var
     idNum   : idList;         { ID numbers }
     grade   : gradeList;      { grades }
     count   : integer;        { number of records }
     average : real;           { average grade }


{ ------------------------------- Procedure ReadData ------------------------------- }


   procedure ReadData (var idNum : idList;
                       var grade   : gradeList;
                       var count   : integer);

   { Read and store input data; count number of input records }

   begin
     count := 0;
     while (not eof) and (count < maxRecords) do
       begin
         count := count + 1;
         readln (idNum[count], grade[count])
       end;
     if (not eof) and (count = maxRecords) then
       writeln ('*** More than ', maxRecords :1,
                ' input records--excess ignored ***')

   end; { ReadData }

{ --------------------------- Procedure ComputeAverage --------------------------- }


   procedure ComputeAverage (var grade   : gradeList;
                             var average : real;
                             count        : integer);

   { Compute average grade }

   var
     index : integer;
     total : real;
   begin
     total := 0.0;
     for index := 1 to count do
       total := total + grade[index];
     average := total / count
   end; { ComputeAverage }
```

Figure 6-9. *Continued.*

{ ------------------------------ Procedure *PrintReport* ------------------------------ }

```
procedure PrintReport (var idNum : idList;
                       var grade  : gradeList;
                       average    : real;
                       count      : integer);
```

{ Prints ID numbers and grades with an asterisk following each grade that
  is more than *maxPointsLow* below average }

```
var
    index    : integer;
    lowLimit : real;
begin
    lowLimit : = average − maxPointsLow;
    writeln ('ID Number' :15, 'Grade' :15);
    writeln;
    for index : = 1 to count do
        begin
            write (idNum[index] :15, grade[index] :15:1);
            if grade[index] < lowLimit then
                writeln ('*')
            else
                writeln
        end;
    writeln;
    writeln ('Average Grade: ', average :1:1)
end; { PrintReport }
```

{ ------------------------------ Main Program ------------------------------ }

```
begin
    ReadData (idNum, grade, count);
    if count > 0 then
        begin
            ComputeAverage (grade, average, count);
            PrintReport (idNum, grade, average, count)
        end
    else
        writeln ('*** No data in input file ***')
end.
```

In the type definition part we define the array types *idList* and *grade-List* for the arrays that will hold the ID numbers and grades. Because ID numbers are integers and grades are real numbers, the component type of *idList* is *integer* and that of *gradeList* is *real*. The index type for both *idList* and *gradeList* is the subrange type 1..*maxRecords*. Note that definitions of index types often make use of constant identifiers (such as *maxRecords*) that were defined in the constant definition part; this is why the constant definition part comes before the type definition part.

The main program uses four variables: *idNum* is the array of ID numbers; *grade* is the array of grades. *count* stores the number of records actually read; this number will usually be less than *maxRecords*—the maximum number of records the arrays can hold. *average* stores the average grade that is computed after all the input records have been read.

The remainder of our discussion can be brief, because the basic array-processing techniques that our program uses have already been discussed. The pseudocode for the program will be included in the discussion; the corresponding actual code is in Figure 6-9.

The main program must read the input data. If any records were read, then the program should compute the average grade and print the grade report. If no records were read, however, the program should print a message to that effect rather than attempting to compute the average and print a report. (Attempting to compute an average of zero values causes a division-by-zero error. Why?) The following is the pseudocode for the main program:

1. Read and count input records
2. Depending on the number of records read, do one of the following:
   2.1 *One or more records read*: Process the data that was read.
       2.1.1 Compute the average grade
       2.1.2 Print the grade report
   2.2 *No records read*: Print an error message

Pseudocode steps 1, 2.1.1, and 2.1.2 are implemented by the following procedure calls:

Step 1:   *ReadData (idNum, grade, count)*
Step 2.1.1: *ComputeAverage (grade, average, count)*
Step 2.1.2: *PrintReport (idNum, grade, average, count)*

The arrays *idNum* and *grade* are passed to *ReadData* and *PrintReport,* and *grade* is passed to *ComputeAverage.* Arrays are normally passed via variable parameters, regardless of whether the value of the array variable is to be modified by the subprogram. The reason is that when an array is passed as a value parameter, a copy of the array must be made for the subprogram. Since arrays are often large, the copy can take up a substantial amount of memory, and the time required to make the copy can be significant.

The procedure *ReadData* must read the input records into *idNum* and *grade,* and it must set *count* to the number of records read. If the number of records exceeds the maximum number that can be stored, the excess records must be ignored and the user must be informed that this has been done:

1. Initialize the record count to zero.
2. While the end of the input file has not been reached and the arrays are not full, repeat the following:
   2.1 Increase the record count by 1.
   2.2 Read each field of the input record into the next available component of the corresponding array. (The index of the array component will be equal to the current record count.)

3. If the end of the file has not been reached and the arrays are full, do the following:

   3.1 Print a message warning the user that some input records could not be processed.

The total of the grades, which is needed to compute the average, could have been computed by *ReadData* as the records were read. (How?) For the sake of modularity, however, and to emphasize array processing, we use a separate procedure, *ComputeAverage* to compute the total and average. The technique for averaging the components of an array has already been discussed. The pseudocode for *ComputeAverages* is as follows:

1. Clear the running total to zero.
2. For each value of *index* from 1 to the record count, do the following:

   2.1 Add the value of *grade[index]* to the running total.
3. Compute the average by dividing the running total by the record count.

How can we be sure the step 3 will not cause a division-by-zero error?

The procedure *PrintReport* uses the computed average and the data in the arrays to print the final report. The pseudocode is as follows:

1. Set the lower limit for unflagged grades ten points below the average grade.
2. Print the column headings.
3. For each value of *index* from 1 to the record count, do the following:

   3.1 Print the values of *idNum[index]* and *grade[index]*. Do not go to a new line.

   3.2 Depending on the current grade (the value of *grade[index]*), do one of the following:

      3.2.1 *The current grade is less than the lower limit*: Print an asterisk and go to a new line.

      3.2.2 *The current grade is greater than or equal to the lower limit*: Go to a new line without printing an asterisk.

Multidimensional Arrays

Consider a table with numbered rows and columns, such as the table shown in Figure 6-10. We would like to store this table as one or more arrays. One way to do this is to store each row of the table as a one-dimensional array. For example, if we define the type *row* by

> **type**
> $row = $ **array** $[1..3]$ **of** *integer*;

then each row of the table shown in Figure 6-10 is a value of type *row*.

Now let's represent the entire table as one array. Define the array type *table* by

Figure 6-10.

A table that can be stored as a two-dimensional array. The first array index designates the row of the table and ranges from 1 through 4; the second array index designates the column of the table and ranges from 1 through 3.

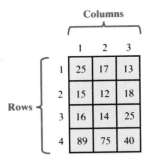

```
type
     table = array [1..4] of row;
```

Since the component type of *table* is *row,* each component of a value of type *table* is an array of three integers—one row of the table we are trying to represent. If we did not wish to define the type *row* separately, we could just define *table* by

```
type
     table = array [1..4] of array [1..3] of integer;
```

Suppose we declare the variable *tab* by

```
var
     tab : table;
```

and assign to *tab* the table shown in Figure 6-10. Then, as shown in Figure 6-11, *tab*[1] corresponds to row 1 of the table and has the value

    25   17   13

tab[2] corresponds to row 2 of the table and has the value

    15   12   18

and so on.

Since *tab*[1], *tab*[2], *tab*[3], and *tab*[4] are themselves array variables, they have component variables that refer to the individual components of each row. Thus *tab*[1][3], which designates the component at the intersection of row 1 and column 3, has the value 13 (for the array shown in Figure 6-10). Likewise, *tab*[3][2], which designates the component at the intersection of row 3 and column 2, has the value 14.

Although the notation just given is valid Pascal, it is rarely used because Pascal also offers an abbreviated notation similar to that used for the same purpose in other programming languages. Type definitions such as

```
type
     table = array [1..4] of array [1..3] of integer;
```

can be abbreviated to

Figure 6-11.

Each of the component variables of *tab* stores one row of the table in Figure 6-10.

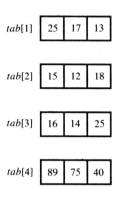

type
    table = **array** [1..4, 1..3] **of** *integer*;

This definition says that two index values are required to designate a component of a value of type *table*. The first index must have the index type 1..4 and the second index must have the index type 1..3.

Likewise, subscripted variables such as *tab*[1][3] can be abbreviated to *tab*[1, 3]. Thus, for the table in Figure 6-10, *tab*[2, 1] has the value 15; *tab*[4, 3] has the value 40; and *tab*[3, 3] has the value 25.

The number of *dimensions* of an array is the number of index values necessary to designate a component value. Pascal allows us to define array types with any number of dimensions; all the index types are listed within the square brackets of the type constructor. For example, the type definition

type
    fourD = **array** [1..4, 1..3, 0..7, −1..2] **of** *integer*;

defines *fourD* as a type whose values are four-dimensional arrays. If *fD* is an entire variable of type *fourD,* then typical component variables would be *fD*[3, 1, 0, −1] and *fD*[4, 2, 3, 1].

The number of components in an array value is the product of the number of values in each index type. Thus the number of components in a value of type *table* is 4 (the number of values in 1..4) times 3 (the number of values in 1..3), which equals 12. Likewise, the number of components in a value of type *fourD* is $4 \times 3 \times 8 \times 4$, which equals 384.

We have seen that a one-dimensional array can be pictured as a horizontal or vertical list, and a two-dimensional array can be pictured as a table with numbered rows and columns. One way to picture a three-dimensional array is as a book of tables, each page of which contains a table with numbered rows and columns. The first index of the three-dimensional array designates a particular page in the book; the remaining two indexes designate a row and a column in the table on the designated page. Likewise, we can think of a four-dimensional array as a multivolume work, each volume of which is a book of tables. The first index of the four-dimensional array gives a volume number, the second index gives a page number in the designated volume, and the third and fourth indexes give row and column numbers in the table on the designated page in the designated volume.

One of the most important applications of nested **for** statements is processing the components of a multidimensional array. The number of **for** statements needed is the same as the number of dimensions of the array—we use two nested **for** statements to process the components of a two-dimensional array, three nested **for** statements to process the components of a three-dimensional array, and so on.

For example, suppose we wish to clear *tab* by setting all its component variables to zero. The following statement sets one component variable to zero:

$$tab[row, col] := 0$$

The values of the index variables *row* and *col* determine which component variable is set to zero.

We can store zeros in a given row of the array by keeping the value of *row* fixed and executing the preceding statement with the value of *col* equal to 1, 2, and 3. The following code accomplishes this:

```
for col := 1 to 3 do
  tab[row, col] := 0
```

This **for** statement zeros one row of the array—the row determined by the value of *row*. To zero all the rows of the array, we must execute this **for** statement with *row* equal to 1, 2, 3, and 4. We bring about this repeated execution with another **for** statement:

```
for row := 1 to 4 do
  for col := 1 to 3 do
    tab[row, col] := 0
```

Because of the two **for** statements, the statement

$$tab[row, col] := 0$$

is executed for every valid combination of values of *row* and *col,* with the result that every component variable of *tab* is set to zero.

Example 6-6. *Magic Squares*

A *magic square* is a square array of numbers such that the numbers in each row, column, and diagonal have the same sum. The number of rows, which is the same as the number of columns, is the *order* of the square. For example, the following is a magic square of order 3:

```
4 9 2
3 5 7
8 1 6
```

The numbers in each row, column, and diagonal add up to 15.

We will use a well-known algorithm for generating magic squares as an example of processing two-dimensional arrays. The algorithm we will use generates squares of odd order—of order 3, 5, 7, 9, and so on. Each square will contain all the integers from 1 through $order^2$, *where the value of order* is the order of the square. Thus a square of order 3 contains the integers 1 through 9, a square of order 5 contains the integers 1 through 25, and so on. The algorithm must state how the integers are to be placed in the square in order to make it a magic square.

The rules for placing the integers tell us how to move from the position in which the previous integer was placed to the position in which the next integer will be placed. In making such moves, we must use the idea of *wraparound*. We treat the square as if it had been rolled into a cylinder and its top and bottom edges pasted together. Moving up from the top row puts us on the bottom row, and moving down from the bottom row puts us on the top row. Likewise, we treat the square as if the left and right edges were pasted together. Moving left from the leftmost column puts us in the rightmost column, and moving right from the rightmost column puts us in the leftmost column.

Given the idea of wraparound, we use the following rules to place the integers 1 through $order^2$ in the magic square:

1. The integer 1 goes in the middle of the bottom row.

2. Let the *current position* be the one in which we have just placed an integer. To determine the position of the next integer, we move diagonally down and to the right by one position. (This move may require wraparound.) If the new position does not already contain an integer, the next integer is placed in this position.

3. If the position diagonally down and to the right from the current position is already occupied, we move up one position from the current position and place the next integer there. This move will never require wraparound.

Figure 6-12 shows the program *MagicSquare*. The value of *maxOrder* is order of the largest square that the algorithm can generate; *maxOrder* is set to 19, the order of the largest square that can be conveniently shown on most computer displays. As the magic square is constructed, it is stored in the array variable *square,* whose value is a two-dimensional array with *maxOrder* rows and *maxOrder* columns.

```
const
    maxOrder = 19;
type
    sq = array [1..maxOrder, 1..maxOrder] of integer;
var
    row, col, nextRow,
    nextCol, number, order : integer;
    square                 : sq;
```

Figure 6-12. Program for generating magic squares.

---

program *MagicSquare* (*input, output*);

{ Generate a magic square of odd order }

const
    maxOrder = 19; { order of largest magic square that can be conveniently displayed }

Figure 6-12.   *Continued.*

```
type
  sq = array [1..maxOrder, 1..maxOrder] of integer;
var
  row, col,                          { current position in magic square }
  nextRow, nextCol,                  { trial next position in magic square }
  number,                            { number to be placed in magic square }
  order           : integer;         { order of magic square }
  square          : sq;              { array to hold magic square }
begin
  writeln ('Order of square must be odd');
  writeln ('integer in range 1 to ', maxOrder :1);
  write ('Enter order: ');
  readln (order);

{ Clear square by zeroing all positions }

  for row := 1 to order do
    for col := 1 to order do
      square[row, col] := 0;

{ Go to starting position }

  row := order;
  col := (1 + order) div 2;

{ Insert numbers }

  for number := 1 to sqr(order) do
    begin
      square[row, col] := number;
      nextRow := row mod order + 1;
      nextCol := col mod order + 1;
      if square[nextRow, nextCol] = 0 then
        begin
          row := nextRow;
          col := nextCol
        end
      else
        row := row - 1
    end;

{ Print square }

  for row := 1 to order do
    begin
      for col := 1 to order do
        write (square[row, col] :4);
      writeln
    end
end.
```

The values of *row* and *col* are the indexes of the current position, the component of *square* in which the last integer was stored. The values of *nextRow* and *nextCol* are the indexes of the next position, the position diagonally down and to the right from the current position. The value of *number* is the integer placed in the current square, and the value of *order* is the order of the square being generated.

The program begins by asking the user to enter the order of the magic square to be printed. The user is asked to enter an odd number in the range 1 through *maxOrder,* but the user's response is not checked for validity. The algorithm will not work properly if an even number or a number outside the specified range is entered.

We use a zero value to indicate an empty component of *square*—a component in which no number has yet been placed. Before beginning to place numbers, therefore, we must set to zero all the components of *square* that will be used—all those with row and column indexes in the range 1 through *order*. This we do with a pair of nested **for** statements.

for *row* := 1 **to** *order* **do**
  for *col* := 1 **to** *order* **do**
    square [*row*, *col*] := 0

Throughout the process of placing the numbers in the square, *row* and *col* are the indexes of the component in which the next number is to be placed. We begin by setting *row* and *col* to the indexes of the component in the middle of the bottom row, the component in which the first number is to be placed.

row := *order*;
col := (1 + *order*) **div** 2

The statements for placing the numbers can be outlined as follows:

1. For each value of *number* from 1 through *order*^{2}, do the following:
  1.1 Place the current number (the value of *number*) in the component *square*[*row*, *col*] designated by the current values of *row* and *col*.
  1.2 Compute the indexes *row* and *col* of the array component in which the next number will be placed.

To detemine the component in which the next number is to be placed, we must compute the indexes *nextRow* and *nextCol* of the component that is one position diagonally down and to the right from the current position. If it were not for wraparound, we could use the following statements:

nextRow := *row* + 1;
nextCol := *col* + 1

Because of wraparound, however, we must use

nextRow := *row* **mod** *order* + 1;
nextCol := *col* **mod** *order* + 1

If the value of *row* is in the range 1 to *order* − 1, the value of *row* **mod** *order* is the same as the value of *row*, and *nextRow* will be set to the value of *row* + 1, the index of the next row down. If the value of *row* is equal to the value of *order*, the index of the bottom row, the value of *row* **mod** *order* is 0, and *nextRow* will be set to 1, the index of the top row. Likewise, *nextCol* will be set to the index of the next row to the right unless the value of *col* is the index of the rightmost row, in which case *nextCol* will be set to the index of the leftmost row.

If the value of *square[nextRow, nextCol]* is zero, no number has been placed in this component, so the next number should be placed there. Thus *row* and *col* are set to *nextRow* and *nextCol*. If a number has already been placed in *square[nextRow, nextCol]*, the next number is to be placed one position up from the current position. In this case, therefore, the value of *row* is decreased by 1. The following **if** statement sets *row* and *col* to the indexes of the component in which the next number is to be placed:

```
if square[nextRow, nextCol] = 0 then
   begin
      row := nextRow;
      col := nextCol
   end
else
      row := row – 1
```

To print the magic square that has been generated, we again use nested **for** statements. The statements

```
for col := 1 to order do
   write (square [row, col] :4);
writeln
```

print one row of the magic square. The values on each row are printed in four-character fields, thus assuring that values on different rows will line up in columns. The *writeln* statement following the **for** statement causes the output device to go to a new line. To print the entire magic square, the statements just given must be executed for all values of *row* in the range 1 through *order*.

```
for row := 1 to order do
   begin
      for col := 1 to order do
         write (square[row, col] :4);
      writeln
   end
```

Review Questions

1. Which three control statements are used for repetition in Pascal?

2. For which repetition statement is execution guaranteed to terminate?

3. Which repetition statement requires that the number of repetitions be known in advance—that is, before the first execution of the controlled statement?

4. What is a control variable?

5. What do we mean when we say that two statements are nested? Give an example of nested **for** statements.

6. Describe a characteristic way in which variables are used in repetition constructions.

7. Give and explain two examples of repetition constructions that simulate some real or imaginary activity.

8. What is an invariant assertion? How can we use an invariant assertion to convince ourselves that a repetition construction carries out the task for which it was designed?

9. Describe the process by which the statements controlled by a **repeat** statement are executed.

10. If the Boolean expression in a **repeat** statement yields *true* the first time it is evaluated, how many times are the controlled statements executed?

11. Distinguish between a continuation condition and a termination condition.

12. Give three differences between the **repeat** statement and the **while** statement.

13. Under what circumstances is the use of a **repeat** statement rather than a **while** statement indicated?

14. What is a set? How are sets represented in Pascal programs?

15. How is the **in** operator used?

16. Describe the relationship between the indexes and components of a one-dimensional array.

17. Give the general form of the type definition for a one-dimensional-array type. What are the index type and the component type?

18. Why is the **for** statement so important for processing arrays?

19. Describe how to find the average of the components of a one-dimensional array.

20. Describe how to find the largest and smallest components of a one-dimensional array. How can this algorithm be modified to locate the first occurrence in the array of the smallest component and the largest component?

21. Describe multidimensional arrays. Give one way of visualizing one-, two-, three-, and four-dimensional arrays.

22. Describe the (abbreviated form of) type definitions and component variables for multidimensional arrays.

23. Describe the use of nested **for** statements for processing multidimensional arrays.

24. Give the principles behind the program for generating magic squares. What is wraparound?

Exercises _____

1. Formulate an invariant assertion for the repetition construction in Figure 6-3.

2. Formulate invariant assertions for both the inner and outer **for** statements in Figure 6-4. Note that since the purpose of these **for** statements is to produce

printed output, the invariant assertions must refer to the output being produced as well as to the values of the variables *row* and *col*.

3. Modify the program in Figure 6-5 so that it only accepts initial values of *pairs* and *fertilePairs* for which the **while** statement is guaranteed to terminate. If invalid values are entered for *pairs* and *fertilePairs,* the program informs the user of the error and requests a new set of values. This process is repeated until a valid set of values is entered.

4. Write a program to print the pattern

```
*****
****
***
**
*
```

Each line of asterisks in Exercises 5 and 6 must be preceded by an appropriate number of spaces. A straightforward way to obtain the spacing is the execute *write* (' ') the necessary number of times. A less-obvious approach uses the fact that a field-width parameter can be a variable; if the value of *n* is positive, the statement *write* (' ' :*n*) will print *n* spaces.

5. Write a program to print the pattern

```
    *
   ***
  *****
 *******
*********
```

6. Modify the program in Exercise 5 to print the pattern

```
    *
   ***
  *****
 *******
*********
 *******
  *****
   ***
    *
```

7. The king has just been told how many grains of wheat would be required to satisfy the request made by the inventor of chess. Before ordering the inventor beheaded for daring to request so much wheat, the king decides, for amusement, to see how far the kingdom's grain surplus will go toward satisfying the inventor's request. Write a program to input the number of grains of wheat available and calculate how many squares of the chessboard the available wheat would take care of if used to partially satisfy the inventor's request.

Exercises 8-12 refer to the following definitions and declarations:

```
const
    size = 100; {could be any value greater than zero}
type
    list   = array [1..size] of integer;
    table = array [1..size, 1..size] of integer;
var
    count  : integer;
    aList   : list;
    aTable : table;
```

Assume that the procedure required by each exercise is declared in a main program that also contains the constant, type, and variable declarations just given. The procedures can access *size, list,* and *table* as global identifiers; the array variables *aList* and *aTable* are passed to procedures as variable parameters. The value of *count* gives the number of components of *aList* that are in use; that is, components *aList*[1] through *aList*[*count*] contain valid data and components *aList*[*count* + 1] through *aList*[*size*] contain meaningless values (garbage).

8. Write a procedure *Initialize* such that after the call

    Initialize (aList, count)

    each of the components *aList*[1] through *aList*[*count*] will be set to its own index value; that is, the value of *aList*[1] will be 1, the value of *aList*[2] will be 2, and so on.

9. Write a procedure *Reverse* such that after the call

    Reverse (aList, count)

    the values of *aList*[1] through *aList*[*count*] are in reverse of their previous order: The new value of *aList*[1] will equal the previous value of *aList*[*count*], the new value of *aList*[2] will equal the previous value of *aList*[*count* − 1], and so on.

10. Write a procedure *Insert* such that the call

    Insert (aList, count, index, data)

    inserts the value of *data* in the array at the position given by the value of *index*. To make room for the new value, the values that will follow the inserted value—the values of *aList*[*index*] through *aList*[*count*] must be moved down one position in the array, so that they now occupy components *aList*[*index* + 1] through *aList*[*count* + 1]. After the values have been moved, the value of *data* can be assigned to *aList*[*index*]. The value of *count* is increased by one to reflect that a new value has been inserted.

11. Write a procedure *Delete* such that the call

    Delete (aList, count, index)

    deletes the value at position *index*. The deletion is accomplished by moving the values that follow the value to be deleted—the values of *aList*[*index* + 1] through *aList*[*count*]—up one position in the array, so that they now occupy components *aList*[*index*] through *aList*[*count* − 1]. The value of *count* is decreased by one to reflect that one value has been deleted.

12. Write a procedure *Transpose* such that the call

   Transpose (aTable)

   interchanges the rows and columns of *aTable*. After the call, the values that were in the first row will be in the first column, the values that were in the second row will be in the second column, and so on. In general, the value of *aTable*[*row*, *col*] after the call will equal the value that *aTable*[*col*, *row*] had before the call.

13. Write a program to test whether a given square array of integers is a magic square. The input data for the program consists of the order of the square followed by the numbers in the first row, the numbers in the second row, and so on. The program should compute and print the sum of the numbers in each row of the square, the sum of the numbers in each column, and the sum of the numbers in each of the two diagonals. It should then state whether or not the square is magic.

14. A company has four salespeople and five products. Let the salespeople be denoted by numbers 1 through 4 and the products by numbers 1 through 5. Suppose we are given as data the monthly sales of each product by each salesperson. For example, the external data record (line of textfile)

   3   5   750.00

   indicates that salesperson number 3 sold $750 worth of product number 5. Write a program to read a file of such records and print the following: (1) the total amount sold by each person, (2) the total amount sold of each product, (3) the people who sold the largest and smallest amount of each product, and (4) the products for which each person sold the largest and smallest amount.

15. We wish to compute the average grades of college students having particular classifications and major fields. There are four classifications, coded as follows: freshman, 1; sophomore, 2; junior, 3; and senior, 4. There are three major fields, coded as follows: English, 1; History, 2; and Mathematics, 3. Each external data record (line of textfile) gives the classification code, major field code, and grade for a student. Thus

   3   1   85

   represents a grade of 85 earned by a junior English major. Your program should read a file of such records and then print a table showing the average grade for each combination of classification and major field. If there were no data entries for a particular combination of classification and major field, leave the corresponding entry in the printed table blank.

7

Multiway Selection

Selection (also called *alternation*) was introduced through the two forms of the **if** statement:

> **if** Boolean-expression **then**
> > controlled-statement-1
>
> **else**
> > controlled-statement-2

and

> **if** Boolean-expression **then**
> > controlled-statement

We can think of each form as implementing *two-way selection,* since each selects one of two alternatives. In the first form, the alternatives are to execute either controlled-statement-1 or controlled-statement-2. In the second form, the alternatives are either to execute the controlled statement or to do nothing.

The logical extension of two-way selection is *multiway selection,* in which the statement to be executed is selected from an arbitrary number of alternatives (including, possibly, the alternative of doing nothing). In this chapter we will look at multiway selection and at some example programs that illustrate all forms of selection as well as other programming techniques.

Constructions for Multiway Selection

In Pascal, we can accomplish multiway selection with either nested **if** statements or the **case** statement. The **case** statement is especially designed for multiway selection.

Nested *if* Statements

For displaying complex nested **if** statements, we find it convenient to abbreviate our notation slightly. We use "expression-1," "expression-2," "expression-3," and so on to represent Boolean expressions. Likewise, we will use "statement-1," "statement-2," "statement-3," and so on to represent controlled statements. As usual, each controlled statement can be a compound statement made up of an arbitrary sequence of statements bracketed by **begin** and **end.** With these conventions, the two forms of the **if** statement can be displayed as

```
if expression-1 then
    statement-1
else
    statement-2
```

and

```
if expression-1 then
    statement-1
```

Because statement-1 and statement-2 can be any Pascal statements, they can also be **if** statements; if that is the case, we have **if** statements within **if** statements, or nested **if** statements. For example, suppose that statement-1 is the following **if** statement:

```
if expression-2 then
    statement-3
else
    statement-4
```

If we substitute this for statement-1 in the general form for an **if** statement with **else** part, we get the following nested **if** statements:

```
if expression-1 then
    if expression-2 then
        statement-3
    else
        statement-4
else
    statement-2
```

When the computer executes this statement, it starts by evaluating expression-1. If expression-1 evaluates to *false,* statement-2 is executed. If expression-1 evaluates to *true,* however, the computer executes the indented **if** statement. To execute the indented **if** statement, the computer begins by evaluating expression-2. If expression-2 evaluates to *true,* statement-3 is executed; if expression-2 evaluates to *false,* statement-4 is executed. We can summarize this discussion in a table that shows which statement will be executed for each combination of values of expression-1 and expression-2.

Expression-1	Expression-2	Statement
true	*true*	statement-3
true	*false*	statement-4
false	*true*	statement-2
false	*false*	statement-2

We see that for each possible set of values for expression-1 and expression-2, one of the three statements is selected for execution. Two sets of values select statement-2, whereas statement-3 and statement-4 are each selected by only one set of values.

For another example, let's go back to the general form of the **if** statement with **else** part and replace statement-2 with another **if** statement.

```
if expression-1 then
    statement-1
else
    if expression-2 then
        statement-3
    else
        statement-4
```

If expression-1 evaluates to *true*, then statement-1 is executed. If expression-1 evaluates to *false*, then the value of expression-2 determines whether statement-3 or statement-4 will be executed. Again, we can use a table to show which statement will be executed for each possible set of values of the two Boolean expressions.

Expression-1	Expression-2	Statement
true	*true*	statement-1
true	*false*	statement-1
false	*true*	statement-3
false	*false*	statement-4

We see that there are two sets of values that select statement-1, whereas statement-3 and statement-4 are each selected by only one set of values.

If some of the **if** statements in a set of nested **if** statements do not have **else** parts, an additional complication occurs. Consider the following pair of nested **if** statements (in which we abbreviate ''expression'' to ''expr'' and ''statement'' to ''stm''):

if expr-1 **then if** expr-2 **then** stm-3 **else** stm-4

This way of writing an **if** statement is perfectly valid. (Remember: All line breaks and indentation are for the convenience of human readers and are ignored by the language processor.) But the example points up a problem: To which **if** statement does the **else** part belong—the outer one controlled by expr-1 or the inner one controlled by expr-2? Put another way, if this **if** statement is written in the more usual indented form, which of the following two indentations reflects the way in which the statement will be executed?

```
if expr-1 then
    if expr-2 then
        stm-3
    else
        stm-4
```

or

```
if expr-1 then
    if expr-2 then
        stm-3
else
    stm-4
```

A special rule is required to resolve this ambiguity. The rule is this: An **else** *part always goes with the nearest preceding* **if** *that does not already have an* **else** *part.* Therefore, the **else** part in the example goes with the second (inner) **if** statement, not with the first (outer) one. Our first indented form is correct and our second indented form is incorrect. Note that if we indent incorrectly we are only fooling ourselves, because the language processor ignores the indentation and follows the special rule. Incorrect indentation can produce hard-to-find errors, since the incorrectly indented statements will not be executed in the way that the indentation seems to imply.

The special rule can be overridden by the statement brackets **begin** and **end** in the same way that operator precedence can be overridden by parentheses. Thus if we need the behavior implied by the second (incorrect) indented form, we can achieve it with

```
if expr-1 then
   begin
      if expr-2 then
         stm-3
   end
else
   stm-4
```

Because a compound statement is always treated as an indivisible unit, the special rule does not consider an **if** statement that is enclosed in a compound statement. Thus the **else** part now goes with the outer **if** statement, the one controlled by expr-1.

Multiway Selection Using *if* Statements

We have seen several ways in which **if** statements can be nested, and there are many other possibilities we have not considered. For each different nesting scheme, the circumstances under which each statement will be executed are different. Tricky aspects of nesting, such as the problem of matching **if**s and **else**s, can make complex nested **if** statements hard to write correctly and even harder to understand.

Matters would be simplified if we settled on one particular nesting scheme, memorized its properties, and used it for all our needs. This nesting scheme would constitute a multiway-selection version of the **if** statement. The following nesting scheme is often used for this purpose:

```
if expression-1 then
   statement-1
else
   if expression-2 then
      statement-2
   else
      if expression-3 then
         statement-3
      else
         statement-4
```

Each **if** statement is nested in the **else** part of the preceding one. The construction can be extended to any number of **if** statements. For example, statement-4 could be an **if** statement, whose **else** part could contain still another **if** statement, and so on.

In what circumstances will each statement be executed? The Boolean expressions are evaluated in top-to-bottom order. If expression-1 evaluates to *true,* statement-1 is executed. If expression-1 evaluates to *false,* then expression-2 is evaluated. If expression-2 evaluates to *true,* statement-2 is executed. If expression-2 also evaluates to *false,* then expression-3 is evaluated. If expression-3 evaluates to *true,* statement-3 is executed. If expression-3 also evaluates to *false* (so that all three expressions evaluate to *false*), statement-4 is executed. The final **else** part—the one containing statement-4— is optional. If it is omitted, no statement is executed when all the expressions evaluate to *false.*

As before, we can use a table to show which statement is selected by each set of values for the Boolean expressions.

Expression-1	Expression-2	Expression-3	Statement
true	*true*	*true*	statement-1
true	*true*	*false*	statement-1
true	*false*	*true*	statement-1
true	*false*	*false*	statement-1
false	*true*	*true*	statement-2
false	*true*	*false*	statement-2
false	*false*	*true*	statement-3
false	*false*	*false*	statement-4

Note that the first (leftmost) *true* entry in each row determines which statement will be executed. If the first *true* on a row is in the first column, statement-1 will be executed; if the first *true* is in the second column, statement-2 will be executed; and so on.

We can think of this kind of multiway selection as representing a list of Boolean expressions and another list of statements to be executed, like this:

```
expression-1   statement-1
expression-2   statement-2
expression-3   statement-3
               statement-4
```

To find out which statement will be executed, we go down the list of Boolean expressions, evaluating each as we come to it. When an expression evaluates to *false,* we move on to the next expression on the list. The first time an expression evaluates to *true,* however, we stop working our way down the list and execute the corresponding statement. Only that one statement is executed; after it has been executed the computer goes on to the next statement in the program, the one following the entire set of nested **if** statements. Thus the first Boolean expression that evaluates to *true* determines which statement will be executed. If none of the expressions evaluate to *true,* the statement in the final **else** part, statement-4, is executed. (If the final **else** part is omitted, then no statement is executed when all the expressions evaluate to *false.*)

Previously, we indented these nested **if** statements so as to emphasize the nesting of each **if** statement inside the **else** part of the preceding one. It is often clearer, however, to indent these statements so as to emphasize the list of Boolean expressions and the corresponding list of statements.

```
if expression-1 then
    statement-1
else if expression-2 then
    statement-2
else if expression-3 then
    statement-3
else
    statement-4
```

It is this easily understood form of nested **if** statements that we will use for multiway selection.

Calculator Simulation with Nested *if* Statements

One of the most common applications of multiway selection is command driven programs—interactive programs that carry out a series of commands entered by the user. A multiway selection construction is used to select the program statements that carry out each command. This application of multiway selection is illustrated by the program in Figure 7-1, which simulates a simple four-function calculator.

Although the program simulates the internal operation of the calculator, input and output are still in the prompt-response style typical of computer programs. Thus to have the simulated calculator perform an addition, the user responds to the prompt "Operator:" by typing + and pressing the Enter or Return key. With a real calculator, of course, there would be no prompt—just punching the + key would be sufficient to trigger the addition.

As with many kinds of real calculators, numbers and operators are entered in the order number-operator-number. For example, to have the calculator compute the sum 2 + 3, we enter the number 2 followed by the operator + followed by the number 3. Each time the program carries out an operation, it prints an updated value for the calculator display—the number that would appear on the display of an actual calculator. The program prompts for each number and operator. For example, when we calculate the sum 2 + 3 the exchange with the user goes like this:

```
Number: 2
Operator: +
Number: 3
Display: 5.00
```

Figure 7-1. Program to simulate a four-function calculator. Nested **if** statements are used for multiway selection.

---

program *Calculator* (*input*, *output*):

{ Simulate calculator }

var
   display,   { simulated display }
   entry   : *real*; { number most recently entered }
   operator : *char*; { operator most recently entered }

Figure 7-1. *Continued.*

```
begin
  operator := 'E';
  while operator <> 'Q' do
    begin
      if operator = '+' then
        begin
          write ('Number: ');
          readln (entry);
          display := display + entry
        end
      else if operator = '−' then
        begin
          write ('Number: ');
          readln (entry);
          display := display − entry
        end
      else if operator = '*' then
        begin
          write ('Number: ');
          readln (entry);
          display := display * entry
        end
      else if operator = '/' then
      begin
          write ('Number: ');
          readln (entry);
          display := display / entry
        end
      else if operator = 'C' then
        display := 0.0
      else if operator = 'E' then
        begin
          write ('Number: ');
          readln (display)
        end
      else if operator = 'S' then
        display := −display;
      writeln ('Display: ', display :1:2);
      write ('Operator: ');
      readln (operator)
    end
end.
```

The user entered 2, +, and 3 in response to the prompts. The program printed the value of the display after doing the addition.

The program permits *chained calculations,* in which the current result serves as the first operand of the next operation. For example, to compute the sum

$$7 + 5 + 4 + 3$$

we just enter the numbers and operators 7, +, 5, +, 4, +, and 3 in that order.

```
Number: 7
Operator: +
Number: 5
Display: 12.00
Operator: +
Number: 4
Display: 16.00
Operator: +
Number: 3
Display: 19.00
```

The operator E (which stands for "enter") allows us to terminate a chained calculation by discarding the current display value and entering a new one. In the following example, we first compute $7 + 5$ and then compute $4 + 3$. The E operator allows us to discard the result of the first computation and enter 4, the first number of the second computation.

```
Number: 7
Operator: +
Number: 5
Display: 12.00
Operator: E
Number: 4
Display: 4.00
Operator: +
Number: 3
Display: 7.00
```

The simulation program accepts the following operators:

Operator	Name	Description
+	Add	Accept number and add to contents of display.
−	Subtract	Accept number and subtract from contents display.
*	Multiply	Accept number and multiply by contents of display.
/	Divide	Accept number and divide into contents of display.
C	Clear	Set display to zero.
E	Enter	Accept number and enter into display.
S	Sign change	Change sign of contents of display.
Q	Quit	Terminate program.

We can think of the operators as commands from the user to the program. A program, or a part of one, that carries out commands from the user is called a *command interpreter*. Command interpreters are quite common; for example, many programs display a *menu* of acceptable commands and ask the user to press a key or enter a number or letter corresponding to the desired command. A command interpreter then carries out the operation requested by the user. All command interpreters use some form of multiway selection to execute the proper set of statements to carry out each command entered by the user.

Let the current operator be the operator most recently entered by the user. Our program will start out by setting the current operator to E, so that the program will begin by allowing the user to enter a number. After that, each new operator entered by the user will become the current operator. The program accepts operators and carries out the corresponding operations as long as the current operator is not Q. We can outline this process as follows:

1. Set the current operator to E
2. While the current operator is not Q, repeat the following:
   2.1 Carry out the operation corresponding to the current operator
   2.2 Print the value of the display
   2.3 Obtain a new operator from the user and make it the current operator

The continuation condition ("the current operator is not Q") is checked before each execution of the controlled statements. Therefore, each new operator obtained in Step 2.3 is checked to see if it is Q *before* the corresponding operation is carried out in Step 2.1. If the new operator is Q, the repetition construction terminates, and hence so does the program.

It is often convenient to translate some steps of an outline into Pascal while leaving others in pseudocode. We indicate a pseudocode step by enclosing it in double quotation marks; since double quotation marks have no significance in Pascal, no confusion can arise when we use them to enclose pseudocode.

Let us translate all of our outline—except Step 2.1—into Pascal. The current operator is the value of the character variable *operator*.

```
operator: = 'E';
while operator<> 'Q' do
  begin
    "Carry out the operation corresponding to the
      current operator"
    writeln ('Display: ', display :1:2);
    write ('Operator: ');
    readln (operator)
  end
```

Mixing Pascal and pseudocode in this way is an alternative approach to outlining. Some people prefer this method to the numbered paragraph approach that we have been using so far.

Now let's refine Step 2.1, which carries out the operation corresponding to the current operator. If the user accidentally enters an invalid operator, it is to be ignored. Thus Step 2.1 takes no action for any operator other than the ones for which operations are defined.

2.1 Depending on the current operator, do one of the following:
   2.1.1 *Current operator is* +: accept number and add it to display
   2.1.2 *Current operator is* −: accept number and subtract it from display
   2.1.3 *Current operator is* ∗: accept number and multiply it by display
   2.1.4 *Current operator is* /: accept number and divide it into display
   2.1.5 *Current operator is* C: clear display

2.1.6 *Current operator is E*: accept number and enter it into display

2.1.7 *Current operator is S*: change sign of display

2.1.8 *None of the above*: do nothing

Note that no operation is provided for a current operator of Q. Because Q causes Step 2 to terminate, Step 2.1 is never carried out with a current operator of Q. To see how this selection can be implemented with nested **if** statements, we partially translate the refinement of Step 2.1 into Pascal.

> **if** *operator* = '+' **then**
> "accept number and add it to display"
> **else if** *operator* = '−' **then**
> "accept number and subtract it from display"
> **else if** *operator* = '*' **then**
> "accept number and multiply it by display"
> **else if** *operator* = '/' **then**
> "accept number and divide it into display"
> **else if** *operator* = 'C' **then**
> "clear display"
> **else if** *operator* = 'E' **then**
> "accept number and enter it into display"
> **else if** *operator* = 'S' **then**
> "change sign of display"

Since there is no final **else** part, no action is taken if the value of *operator* is other than '+', '−', '*', '/', 'C', 'E', or 'S'.

Refining the remaining pseudocode steps gives us the program in Figure 7-1. Note the use of compound statements in the multiway-selection construction.

The *case* Statement

A Boolean expression can have only two values and so can be used to select from among at most two alternatives; we must use more than one Boolean expression to select from among more than two alternatives. But by allowing selection to be controlled by non-Boolean values, such as integers and characters, the **case** statement can select from among any number of alternatives. The following is the general form of the **case** statement:

> **case** expression **of**
> case-list-1: controlled-statement-1;
> case-list-2: controlled-statement-2;
> case-list-3: controlled-statement-3;
> .
> .
> .
> case-list-n: controlled-statement-n
> **end**

The expression is sometimes called the *selector* because its value selects which controlled statement will be executed. The type of the selector expression (the data type to which the value of the expression belongs) must be an ordinal type. Each case list is a list of constants separated by commas; the type of each constant must be the same as the type of the expression.* The case lists must be *disjoint*; that is, no constant can appear on more than one case list. When the **case** statement is executed, the computer evaluates the expression and then executes the controlled statement whose case list contains the value of the expression. It is an error if none of the case lists contain the value of the expression. As usual, the controlled statements can be compound statements.

The following is an outline of a **case** statement for carrying out a user command:

```
case command of
    'e', 'E': "edit file";
    'l', 'L': "load file";
    's', 'S': "save file"
end
```

The value of the character variable *command* is a command letter entered by the user. If the user enters e or E, the statement corresponding to "edit file" is executed; if the user enters l or L, the statement corresponding to "load file" is executed; and if the user enters s or S, the statement corresponding to "save file" is executed.

Standard Pascal imposes an inconvenient and artificial restriction on **case** statements: An error occurs if the value of the expression is not on any of the case lists. Thus, in our example, if the user enters an invalid command, the program "crashes" or "bombs"—it is terminated with a system error message that will almost surely be meaningless to the user. Many Pascal implementations improve the **case** statement by having it ignore invalid values of the selector expression or (better) by providing the **case** statement with an **else** part that can contain statements to be executed when the value of the selector expression does not occur on any of the case lists. If we are confined to standard Pascal, however, we must devise some way of intercepting invalid values before they get to the **case** statement and cause the program to crash.

The simplest solution is to use an **if** statement to "protect" the **case** statement—to execute the **case** statement only if the selector expression has a valid value. Thus, in our example, we could protect the **case** statement from invalid values of *command* by "wrapping an **if** statement around it" as follows:

```
if command in ['e', 'E', 'l', 'L', 's', 'S'] then
    case command of
        'e', 'E': "edit file";
        'l', 'L': "load file";
        's', 'S': "save file"
    end
else
    writeln ('Invalid command--please try again')
```

The **case** statement is executed only if the value of *command* belongs to the set of valid command characters. The **else** part of the **if** statement contains the statement to be executed for an invalid command; if the **else** part is omitted, invalid commands are ignored.

---

*This restriction holds for the standard ordinal types *Boolean*, *char*, and *integer*; it will need to be modified for the programmer-defined ordinal types discussed in Chapter 8.

Calculator Simulation with *case* Statement

The program in Figure 7-2 is a version of the calculator simulation using a **case** statement instead of nested **if** statements. As just described, an **if** statement is used to protect the **case** statement from invalid values of *operator.*

> **if** *operator* **in** [' + ', ' − ', '*', '/', 'C', 'E', 'S'] **then**
>   "**case** statement"

Since the **if** statement has no **else** part, the calculator simulation just ignores invalid operators. No action is taken if the operator is invalid.

In the **case** statement, each case list contains the character for one operator and the corresponding statement carries out the action called for by that operator.

> **case** *operator* **of**
>   ' + ': "accept number and add it to display"
>   ' − ': "accept number and subtract it from display"
>   '*': "accept number and multiply it by display"
>   '/':   "accept number and divide it into display"
>   'C':   "clear display"
>   'E':   "accept number and enter it into display"
>   'S':   "change sign of display"
> **end**

Figure 7-2 shows the complete calculator simulation program using the **case** statement. Note the indentation style. If a controlled statement is not compound, it is written on the same line as the case list. A compound statement, however, begins on a new line and is indented relative to the beginning of the case list.

Procedures and Multiway Selection

In the preceding examples, the statements to be executed for each case were made into a compound statement and embedded in the multiway-selection statement. This approach was followed for two reasons: (1) there were only a few statements for each case, and (2) we wished to illustrate the use of compound statements in multiway-selection statements. In a command in-

---

Figure 7-2.

This version of the calculator-simulation program uses **case** statements for multiway selection. Note how an **if** statement is used to protect the **case** statement from invalid values of *operator.*

---

program *Calculator* (*input, output*);

{ Simulate calculator }

var
    display,   { simulated display }
    entry   : *real*; { number most recently entered }
    operator : *char*; { operator most recently entered }

Figure 7-2.   *Continued.*

```pascal
begin
  operator := 'E';
  while operator <> 'Q' do
    begin
      if operator in ['+', '-', '*', '/', 'C', 'E', 'S'] then
        case operator of
          '+':
            begin
              write ('Number: ');
              readln (entry);
              display := display + entry
            end;
          '-':
            begin
              write ('Number: ');
              readln (entry);
              display := display - entry
            end;
          '*':
            begin
              write ('Number: ');
              readln (entry);
              display := display * entry
            end;
          '/':
            begin
              write ('Number: ');
              readln (entry);
              display := display / entry
            end;
          'C': display := 0.0;
          'E':
            begin
              write ('Number: ');
              readln (display)
            end;
          'S': display := -display
        end; { case }
      writeln ('Display: ', display :1:2);
      write ('Operator: ');
      readln (operator)
    end
end.
```

terpreter, however, the statements for each case often constitute a substantial part of a large program. In that situation, the statements for each case are placed in a procedure and the procedures are called from the multiway-selection statement. If we organize the **case**-statement version of our calculator simulation in this way, the **case** statement will look like this:

```
case operator of
    '+': DoAddition (display);
    '-': DoSubtraction (display);
    '*': DoMultiplication (display);
    '/':  DoDivision (display);
    'C': DoClearDisplay (display);
    'E': DoEnterNumber (display);
    'S': DoChangeSign (display)
end
```

The variable *display* is passed as a variable parameter to each procedure, which modifies it as appropriate. The procedure *DoAddition,* for example, could be written as follows:

```
procedure DoAddition (var display : real);
var
    entry : real;
begin
    write ('Number: ');
    readln (entry);
    display := display + entry
end;
```

Many programs, such as word processors and spreadsheet programs, provide the user with a large number of commands. A common approach to outlining such a program is to write the command interpreter along with a stub for each procedure that carries out a command. This outline is then refined by writing the procedures for the various commands. Often the program will be usable and useful before all the commands have been implemented, allowing a preliminary version of the program to be released. Later versions can be released as additional commands are implemented. If new commands are thought of during the development process, the command interpreter can be easily expanded to include them.

Example Programs

The programs in this section illustrate several aspects of selection including the use of Boolean operators, the order in which tests are to be made, and the use of flags.

Example 7-1. *Classifying Triangles*

The program in Figure 7-3 inputs the lengths of the three sides of a triangle and classifies the triangle as *equilateral, isosceles,* or *scalene.* A triangle is equilateral if all three sides have the same length, isosceles if any two sides have the same length, and scalene if no two sides have the same length.

Let the values of a, b, and c be the lengths of the three sides of the triangle. The triangle is equilateral if a, b, and c have the same value, which they will if the following expression evaluates to *true:*

$$(a = b) \text{ and } (b = c) \text{ and } (a = c)$$

Figure 7-3.

Given the lengths of the three sides of a triangle, this program classifies the triangle as equilateral, isosceles, or scalene. The order in which we test for different kinds of triangles is important; the program would not work as desired if a triangle was tested for being isosceles before it was tested for being scalene.

```pascal
program Triangles (input, output);

{ Classify triangles as equilateral, isosceles, or scalene }

var
   a, b, c   : real; { sides of triangle }
   response : char; { Does user wish to continue? }
begin
   repeat
      write ('Enter three sides of triangle: ');
      readln (a, b, c);
      if (a = b) and (b = c) then
         writeln ('Equilateral')
      else if (a = b) or (b = c) or (a = c) then
         writeln ('Isosceles')
      else
         writeln ('Scalene');
      writeln;
      repeat
         write ('Classify another triangle (y/n)? ');
         readln (response)
      until response in ['y', 'n', 'Y', 'N']
   until response in ['n', 'N']
end.
```

This expression can be simplified. If a has the same value as b and b has the same value as c, then a and c must also have the same value, since both have the same value as b. Thus the subexpression $a = c$ is redundant and can be omitted.

$$(a = b) \textbf{ and } (b = c)$$

This is the Boolean expression we will use to test for equilateral triangles.

A triangle is isosceles if any two of the values a, b, and c are equal. The test for isosceles triangles must check all three of the possible ways in which two sides can be equal.

$$(a = b) \textbf{ or } (b = c) \textbf{ or } (a = c)$$

This expression cannot be simplified. (Why?)

A triangle that is not equilateral or isosceles must be scalene. Therefore, we can use our two expressions to test for equilateral and isosceles triangles; triangles that fail both tests must be scalene. We must be careful of the order in which the two tests are performed, however, since equilateral triangles will also pass the test for isosceles triangles. Thus we must test first for equilateral triangles and then for isosceles triangles; if we tested for isosceles triangles first, both isosceles and equilateral triangles would be selected, and further testing would be needed to separate the two.

In Figure 7-3, the following multiway-selection construction tests a triangle and prints its classification:

if $(a = b)$ **and** $(b = c)$ **then**
    writeln ('Equilateral')
else if $(a = b)$ **or** $(b = c)$ **or** $(a = c)$ **then**
    writeln ('Isosceles')
else
    writeln ('Scalene')

From the preceding discussion, we see how important it is that the Boolean expressions are evaluated in the order in which they appear in the selection construction. When the triangle is equilateral, both expressions evaluate to *true;* in that case it is the first controlled statement, and not the second, that must be executed.

A program that classifies geometrical figures or other objects according to some useful criterion is said to perform *pattern recognition*. Advanced applications of pattern recognition include recognizing typed and handwritten characters, identifying objects in a picture, and locating abnormalities in an electrocardiogram.

Example 7-2. *Dealing Blackjack*

The program in Figure 7-4 simulates the actions of a blackjack dealer. On each turn, a blackjack player has the option to *hit* (take another card) or to *stay* (elect to take no more cards). The player's hand consists of all the cards the player has taken, and the value, or *count* of the hand, is the sum of the values of all the cards in the hand. The player with the highest count not exceeding 21 wins; any player whose count goes over 21 *busts* or loses. A player hits to increase the count of his or her hand and stays in fear of busting.

The cards 2 through 10 are counted at their face values. The face cards (jack, queen, and king) are each counted as 10. The ace can be counted as 1 or 11; it is counted as 11 unless doing so would put the count over 21, in which case it is counted as 1. An ace initially counted as 11 may have to be later counted as 1 to prevent the count from going over 21 after additional cards have been taken. A count that includes an ace counted as 11 is said to be *soft* since the value of the ace may be changed later. Note that two aces counted as 11 would always put the count over 21; therefore a count can be soft only by virtue of one ace being counted as 11.

The dealer plays a hand just like the other players, but the dealer has no options. If the dealer's count is 16 or less, the dealer must hit—take another card. If the dealer's count is greater than 16, the dealer must stay. And the dealer, like the players, will bust if his or her count goes over 21.

Our program simulates the behavior of the blackjack dealer. The program hits by prompting the user to enter the value of a card. Cards are represented by their values—integers in the range 1 through 10. An ace is represented by the value 1; it is up to the program to determine when an

Figure 7-4.

This program simulates the actions of a blackjack dealer.

```
program Dealer (input, output);

{ Simulate blackjack dealer }

var
    count,                    { current count of dealer's hand }
    card       : integer;  { card just drawn }
    softCount  : Boolean;  { Is ace being counted as 11? }
begin
    count := 0;
    softCount := false;
    repeat
      write ('Card? ');
      readln (card);
      count := count + card;
      if (card = 1) and not softCount then
        begin
          count := count + 10;
          softCount := true
        end;
      if (count > 21) and softCount then
        begin
          count := count - 10;
          softCount := false
        end
    until count > 16;
    if count <= 21 then
      writeln ('Dealer stays')
    else
      writeln ('Dealer busts');
    writeln ('Dealer''s count is ', count :1)
end.
```

ace should be counted as 11. The program inputs card values until the dealer stays or busts, at which time the program prints the action taken by the dealer and the dealer's final count.

```
Card? 4
Card? 10
Card? 3
Dealer stays
Dealer's count is 17
```

The following exchange illustrates an ace counted as 11:

```
Card? 1
Card? 9
Dealer stays
Dealer's count is 20
```

In the following exchange, the dealer busts:

```
Card? 9
Card? 6
Card? 10
Dealer busts
Dealer's count is 25
```

In Figure 7-4, *count* holds the current count of the hand and *card* holds the most recent card value entered by the user. The Boolean variable *softCount* has the value *true* when the hand is soft and *false* otherwise. If it were not for *softCount*, the program would have to remember the cards in each hand so it could determine if the count reflected an ace being counted as 11. With *softCount*, the program has only to remember the total count and whether or not the count is soft. Whenever the program changes the status of the count, it must also change the value of *softCount*. *Count* and *softCount* are assigned initial values as follows:

> *count* := 0;
> *softCount* := *false*

A variable used to remember whether or not a certain situation exists or has occurred is called a *flag*. Flags are usually Boolean variables, although other types of variables can also be used for this purpose. We can use flags to remember whether certain events have occurred and, as in the present case, to remember facts about data that is no longer available. Even when the data to which a condition applies remains available, a flag can save the program from having to evaluate a possibly complex Boolean expression each time it must check whether the condition is satisfied.

The **repeat** statement inputs card values until the count is greater than 16, at which time the dealer has either busted (count over 21) or is required to stay (count in range 17 through 21). The first three controlled statements obtain a card value and add it to the value of count.

> *write* ('Card? ');
> *readln* (*card*);
> *count* := *count* + *card*

If the card was an ace, it has been counted as 1. But if the count is not already soft, then the ace should be counted as 11. This is done by adding 10 to the value of *count* (since the ace has already been counted as 1) and setting *softCount* to *true* to record that the count is now soft.

> **if** (*card* = 1) **and not** *softCount* **then**
>   **begin**
>   *count* := *count* + 10;
>   *softCount* := *true*
>   **end**

Counting a newly drawn ace as 11, or drawing some other card when an ace is already being counted as 11, can cause the count to go over 21. If the count is soft and greater than 21, the program tries to save itself from busting by counting the ace as 1 instead of 11. This it does by subtracting 10 from the count and setting *softCount* to *false*.

```
if (count > 21) and softCount then
    begin
        count := count − 10;
        softCount := false
    end
```

The two **if** statements just discussed are *not* nested into a multiway-selection construction for two reasons. First, if both Boolean expressions yield *true,* then both of the controlled statements may need to be executed. In a multiway-selection construction, no more than one controlled statement is ever executed. Second, executing the statement controlled by the first **if** statement can affect whether or not the second **if** statement should be executed. Again, this effect is impossible if both belong to the same multiway-selection construction.

Note that the order in which the two **if** statements appear is important. If the order were reversed, the program would ignore the possibility that the most recently drawn card might be an ace that (by being counted as 11) would take the count over 21.

When the repetition terminates, the dealer either must stay or has busted. An **if** statement determines which situation prevails and prints the appropriate message. A *writeln* statement prints the final count.

Example 7-3. *Playing Craps*

Figure 7-5 shows a program for playing craps with the user. This program illustrates several forms of selection and provides another example of top-down development. Figure 7-6 shows a structure chart for the program.

A craps player rolls a pair of dice, each of which is marked with numbers in the range 1 through 6. When the dice come to rest, the sum of the numbers on their tops, which ranges from 2 through 12, determines the outcome of the roll as follows:

- 7 or 11 rolled. The player wins.
- 2, 3, or 12 rolled. The player loses.
- 4, 5, 6, 8, 9, or 10 rolled. The number rolled becomes the player's "point." The dice are then rolled repeatedly until the player wins by "making the point" (rolling the same number as on the first roll) or loses by "crapping out" (rolling a 7).

In accordance with the top-down approach, we begin work with the main program, which declares variables for the amount the user has to play with (*bankroll*) and the amount the user bets on the current round (*bet*). The real variable *seed* is used by the random number generator, the procedure that generates apparently random numbers to simulate the rolling of dice. Flags indicate whether the player has won the current round (*won*) and whether the player wishes to play another round (*playing*).

We can now write the statement part of the main program, which also serves as an outline for the remainder of the program.

Figure 7-5.

This program, which plays craps with the user, illustrates
several forms of selection. It also provides a good example of
top-down development.

```
program Craps (input, output);

{ Play craps with user }

var
   bankroll,              { amount available to player for betting }
   bet,                   { amount bet on this round }
   seed        : real;    { value used by random number generator }
   won,                   { true if player has won current round }
   playing    : Boolean;  { true if game is to continue }

{ ------------------------- Procedure GetStartingBankroll ------------------------ }

procedure GetStartingBankroll (var bankroll : real);

{ Find out how much money player has }

begin
   write ('How much money do you have to play with? ');
   readln (bankroll);
   while bankroll <= 0.0 do
      begin
         write ('Please enter an amount greater than zero: ');
         readln (bankroll)
      end
end; { GetStartingBankroll }

{ ----------------------------- Procedure GetPlayersBet ---------------------------- }

procedure GetPlayersBet (bankroll : real; var bet : real);

{ Get amount player wishes to bet on current round }

begin
   write ('How much do you want to bet? ');
   readln (bet);
   while (bet < 0.0) or (bet > bankroll) do
      begin
         write ('Invalid bet--please try again: ');
         readln (bet)
      end
end; { GetPlayersBet }
```

Figure 7-5. *Continued.*

```
{ ------------------------------ Procedure Random ------------------------------ }

procedure Random (largestRandomInteger  : integer;
                  var randomInteger      : integer;
                  var seed               : real );

{ Generate random integer in range 1 through largestRandomInteger }

begin
   seed := sqr(seed + 3.1415927);
   seed := seed − trunc(seed);
   randomInteger := trunc(largestRandomInteger * seed) + 1
end; { Random }


{ ------------------------------ Procedure RollDice ------------------------------ }

procedure RollDice (var dice : integer; var seed : real );

{ Simulate roll of dice; print value rolled on each die and return their sum
  as value of dice }

var
   die1, die2 : integer; { number rolled on each die }
begin
   Random (6, die1, seed );
   Random (6, die2, seed );
   writeln ('You rolled a ', die1 :1, ' and a ', die2 :1);
   dice := die1 + die2
end; { RollDice }


{ -------------------------- Procedure PlayRemainingRolls -------------------------- }

procedure PlayRemainingRolls ( point     : integer;
                               var won : Boolean;
                               var seed : real );

{ Roll dice until user makes point or craps out }

var
   dice : integer; { value rolled }
begin
   repeat
      RollDice (dice, seed )
   until (dice = point) or (dice = 7);
   won := (dice = point)
end; { PlayRemainingRolls }


{ ----------------------------- Procedure PlayOneRound ----------------------------- }

procedure PlayOneRound (var won : Boolean; var seed : real );

{ Play one round; determine whether player wins or loses }
```

Figure 7-5.   *Continued.*

```
var
   dice : integer; { value rolled }
begin
   RollDice (dice, seed);
   case dice of
      7, 11              : won := true;
      2, 3, 12           : won := false;
      4, 5, 6, 8, 9, 10 : PlayRemainingRolls (dice, won, seed )
   end
end; { PlayOneRound }
```

{ ------------------------ Procedure *UpdatePlayersBankroll* ------------------------ }

```
procedure UpdatePlayersBankroll (var bankroll : real;
                                     bet       : real;
                                     won       : Boolean;
                                 var playing  : Boolean);
```

{ Update *bankroll* and report results of play. If player is broke, set *playing* to *false*. Otherwise, determine if user wishes to play another round and set value of *playing* to *true* or *false* accordingly }

```
var
   response : char;
begin
   if won then
      begin
         writeln ('You win');
         bankroll := bankroll + bet
      end
    else
      begin
         writeln ('You lose');
         bankroll := bankroll − bet
      end;
   if bankroll < 0.01 then
      begin
         writeln ('You''re broke');
         playing := false
      end
   else
      begin
         writeln ('You have $', bankroll :1:2);
         repeat
            write ('Do you want to play again (y/n)? ');
            readln (response)
         until response in ['y', 'n', 'Y', 'N'];
         playing := response in ['y', 'Y']
      end
end; { UpdatePlayersBankroll }
```

Figure 7-5.   *Continued.*

{----------------------------------- Main Program ----------------------------------- }

```
begin
   write ('Enter number between 0 and 1: ');
   readln (seed);
   GetStartingBankroll (bankroll);
   repeat
      writeln;
      GetPlayersBet (bankroll, bet);
      PlayOneRound (won, seed);
      UpdatePlayersBankroll (bankroll, bet, won, playing)
   until not playing
end.
```

Figure 7-6.   Structure chart for the craps program of Figure 7-5. Note that
the procedure called by *RollDice* is shown for only one of the
two occurrences of *RollDice* in the structure chart.

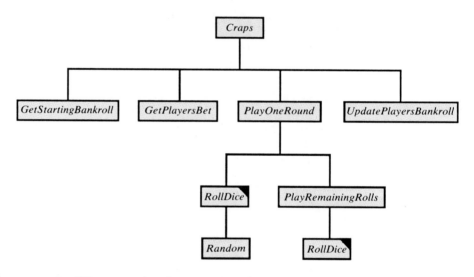

```
   write ('Enter number between 0 and 1: ');
   readln (seed);
   GetStartingBankroll (bankroll);
   repeat
      writeln;
      GetPlayersBet (bankroll, bet);
      PlayOneRound (won, seed);
      UpdatePlayersBankroll (bankroll, bet, won, playing)
   until not playing
```

The first two statements obtain a starting value for *seed*, which will be
used by the random number generator. Obviously, the author must have in
mind an algorithm for the random number generator to know that *seed* is
needed and what kind of an initial value it should be given. This is an
example of how one sometimes needs to think ahead during top-down
development.

The procedure *GetStartingBankroll* is called to determine how much money the user has to play with and assign that amount to the variable parameter *bankroll*. The statements that play a round are repeated until the flag *playing* becomes false. The procedure *GetPlayersBet* determines how much the player wishes to bet on the current round and assigns that amount to the variable parameter *bet*. *bankroll* is passed to *GetPlayersBet* as a value parameter so that the procedure can reject bets that exceed the player's bankroll. The procedure *PlayOneRound* plays one round of the game; the variable parameter *won* is set to *true* or *false* according to whether the player won or lost the game. *seed* must be passed down through several procedures to reach the low-level random number generator; we begin by passing it to *PlayOneRound*. Since *seed* is assigned new values by the random number generator, it is always passed as a variable parameter.

UpdatePlayerBankroll adds the bet to the bankroll if the player won and subtracts the bet from the bankroll if the player lost. The player is informed of the win or loss and given the amount he or she has left. *playing* is set to *true* or *false* according to whether or not another round is to be played. If the player goes broke, *playing* is set to *false*; otherwise, the player is asked whether he or she wishes to play another round, and the value of *playing* is set accordingly. Only *bankroll* and *playing* are passed as variable parameters. *bet* and *won*, whose values are not changed by the procedure, are passed as value parameters.

Note that our main program could be used for any game program in which bets are placed on chance events. All the rules of craps are incorporated in the procedure *PlayOneRound*. If we wish to modify the finished program to play another game, only this procedure and those that it calls need be modified. If our finished program fails to observe the rules of the game, we can focus our debugging efforts on *PlayOneRound* and the procedures it calls.

We now turn our attention to the second-level procedures, the ones called by the main program. *GetStartingBankroll* and *GetPlayersBet* both obtain the designated information from the user. The user's entries are checked for validity; if invalid data is entered the user is (repeatedly, if necessary) informed of the error and prompted to try again.

Note that the checking is done with **while** statements rather than **if** statements as we might at first expect. When repetition is involved, **while** statements can sometimes take the place of **if** statements. The reason we can use the **while** statement for selection is that the controlled statement is not executed at all if the Boolean expression yields *false* the first time it is evaluated. We can think of the **while** statement as a generalization of the **else**-less **if** statement, a generalization that provides for repeated execution of the controlled statement.

PlayOneRound plays one round of the game. The variable parameter *won* is set to *true* or *false* according to whether the player won or lost the round. The procedure *RollDice* is called to simulate the roll of a pair of dice and set the variable parameter *dice* to the number rolled. If a 7 or 11 was rolled, the player wins and *won* is set to *true*. If a 2, 3, or 12 was rolled, the player loses and *won* is set to *false*. If any other number was rolled, *PlayRemainingRolls* is called to play the additional rolls required and set *won* to *true* or *false* depending on the outcome. Note the use of a **case** statement to select the proper action depending on the value rolled.

PlayRemainingRolls must be passed the value of *dice*—the value that came up on the first roll—because this will become the player's point for the remaining rolls. *seed*, which was passed to *PlayOneRound* by the main program, is passed on to *RollDice* and *PlayRemainingRolls*.

RollDice simulates the roll of two dice by calling the random number generator *Random* twice to assign random numbers in the range 1 through 6 to the variables *die1* and *die2*. A *writeln* statement displays for the user the numbers that were rolled, and their sum is returned via the variable parameter *dice*. *RollDice* passes *seed* on to its ultimate destination, *Random*.

Pseudorandom numbers are numbers that appear to have been chosen at random, such as by rolling dice or spinning a roulette wheel, but were actually computed by an algorithm. Applications for pseudorandom numbers include game playing, simulation, and cryptography (secret messages). We often take the "pseudo" for granted and speak of *random numbers* and *random number generators* for short. The procedure *Random* is the (pseudo) random number generator for our craps program.

Random generates random integers. The value parameter *largestRandomInteger* gives the upper limit to the range in which the generated integer is to lie. The lower limit is 1, so each call to *Random* generates a random integer in the range 1 through *largestRandomNumber*. The generated integer is returned to the caller via the variable parameter *randomInteger*. For example, the procedure call

   Random(100, *secretNumber*, *seed*)

sets the integer variable *secretNumber* to a randomly chosen integer in the range 1 through 100. In effect, we have asked the procedure to pick a number from 1 to 100.

Random numbers are often generated from a value called a *seed*. Each time the generating procedure is called, a new value of the seed is computed from the old value; the computation is chosen to make successive values of the seed as unpredictable as possible. The random number to be returned is either the new value of the seed or is obtained from the new value of the seed by a simple computation.

Because the new value of the seed is computed from the old value, the value of the seed must be preserved between procedure activations. This can be done by assigning the seed to a variable in the main program that is either accessed directly as a global variable or is passed to the random number generator as a variable parameter. Because we have chosen to avoid direct access to global variables, the variable *seed* is declared in the main program and passed to *Random* as a variable parameter.

There are many methods of generating pseudorandom numbers, none of which is suitable for every purpose. We will use a "quick and dirty" method that is suitable for uncritical applications such as game playing but may not yield random numbers with the statistical properties required for advanced applications such as simulation and cryptography.

In the method we will use, the value of *seed* is a real number in the range 0 to (but not including) 1. To compute a new value of the seed, we add a constant to the old value (the mathematical constant *pi* was chosen for this purpose), square the sum, and take the fractional part of the result (the part of the result to the right of the decimal point). This fractional part, which is again a number in the range 0 to (but not including) 1, becomes the new seed.

$$seed := sqr(seed + 3.1415927);$$
$$seed := seed - trunc(seed)$$

If we needed random real numbers in the range 0 to 1, we could return the new value of *seed* as the next random number. But since we need random integers in the range 1 through *largestRandomInteger*, an additional computation is needed. Since the value of *seed* ranges from 0 to slightly less than 1, the value of the expression

$$largestRandomInteger * seed$$

is a real number ranging from 0.0 to slightly less than the value of *largestRandomInteger*. Thus the value of

$$trunc(largestRandomInteger * seed)$$

is an integer ranging from 0 through *largestRandomInteger* − 1. Finally, the value of

$$trunc(largestRandomInteger * seed) + 1$$

is an integer in the desired range of 1 through *largestRandomInteger*. The statement

$$randomInteger := trunc(largestRandomInteger * seed) + 1$$

assigns the newly generated random integer to the variable parameter *randomInteger*.

We recall that Pascal requires that a function or procedure be declared before it is called. Thus the declaration for *Random* must precede that of *RollDice*, and the declaration of *RollDice* must precede those of *PlayOneRound* and *PlayRemainingRolls*, both of which call *RollDice*.

PlayRemainingRolls plays the additional rolls needed if the player did not win or lose on the first roll. The player's point—the value that came up on the first roll—is passed to the procedure as the value of *point*. The procedure repeatedly calls *RollDice* until the player makes the point (the value of *dice* = *point* is *true*) or craps out (the value of *dice* = 7 is *true*). *won* is then set to *true* if the player made the point and to *false* otherwise.

$$won := (dice = point)$$

Note that

$$(dice = point)$$

is a Boolean expression; the parentheses are not required but are included to emphasize the expression whose value is being assigned.

The declaration of *PlayRemainingRolls* must precede that of *PlayOneRound*, the procedure that calls *PlayRemainingRolls*.

UpdatePlayersBankroll informs the player of a win or loss and updates the value of *bankroll* accordingly. If the player is broke, the player is informed and *playing* is set to *false*. Because of the possibility of slight errors in floating-point arithmetic, we check whether the value of *bankroll* is less than 0.01—less than one cent—rather than whether it is exactly equal to zero. If the player is not broke, the value of *bankroll* is printed and the player is asked whether he or she wishes to play another game. The value of *playing* is set according to the player's desires.

Review Questions

1. Define multiway selection.

2. Give several examples of nested **if** statements.

3. Give the rule that determines to which **if** statement each **else** part belongs. Explain how indentation that contradicts this rule can be highly misleading.

4. How can we use compound statements to achieve a nesting that would otherwise violate the rule for **else** parts?

5. Why is it better to use a standard form of nesting rather than to devise a different nesting scheme for each multiway selection?

6. Describe the standard nesting scheme used for multiway selection and give the rules that determine which controlled statement will be executed.

7. What is a command interpreter? For what purpose do command interpreters use multiway selection?

8. Give the general form of a **case** statement and describe how the statement is executed.

9. What is a selector expression? A case list? A case constant?

10. What kind of types are allowed for the selector expression and the case constants?

11. For the standard types we have studied so far, how must the type of the case constants be related to the type of the selector expression?

12. Describe how an **if** statement can be used to protect a **case** statement against invalid values of the selector expression. Why is such protection often necessary?

13. Describe how sets can be used in constructing the protective **if** statements referred to in Question 12.

14. What is a flag? For what purpose is it used?

15. In a multiway-selection construction using nested **if** statements, why is the order in which the conditions are tested often crucial?

16. Why are the first two **if** statements in the program shown in Figure 7-4 not nested?

17. What are pseudorandom numbers? Name some applications areas in which pseudorandom numbers are often used. How are pseudorandom numbers used in game-playing programs?

Exercises

1. Write a program that reads sets of data consisting of the length, width, and height of a box and the diameter and height of a cylindrical jar. For each set of data the program should print whether or not the jar will fit inside the box.

The jar can sit upright in the box or it can lie on its side with its top parallel to one of the sides of the box.

2. The following table shows how the cost of an item depends on the quantity ordered:

Quantity Ordered	Cost per Item
0–99	$5.95
100–199	$5.75
200–299	$5.40
300 or more	$5.15

Write a program that reads quantities ordered and prints for each the cost per item and the total cost of the order.

3. Write a program to convert numeric scores to letter grades according to the following scale:

Score	Letter Grade
0–59	F
60–69	D
70–79	C
80–89	B
90–100	A

4. Write a program that will, at the user's request, print one of the following figures:

```
******          *              *
******         ***            ***
******        *****          *****
******       *******          ***
******      *********          *
```

The program presents the user with the following menu and prompt:

```
R. Rectangle
T. Triangle
D. Diamond
Enter letter for figure desired:
```

The program will print the figure corresponding to the letter entered by the user. The letters can be entered in uppercase or lowercase. If the user enters some letter other than R, T, or D, the message "Invalid request" will be printed. After printing a figure (or an error message), the program will determine if the user wishes another figure printed; if so, the menu and prompt will be displayed again.

5. Suppose a financial institution offers investments with the following initial amounts, lifetimes, and annual percentage interest rates:

$500, 5 years, 6 percent
$1,000, 5 years, 6.5 percent

$1,000, 10 years, 7 percent
$5,000, 10 years, 7.5 percent
$10,000, 15 years, 7.9 percent
$20,000, 30 years, 8.2 percent

Write a program that allows the user to choose one of these alternatives, then computes the value of the investment at maturity (at the end of its lifetime). Assume that the interest is compounded monthly. The calculations are similar to those of the personal investment program in Chapter 6 (Figure 6-6) except that there are no additional deposits after the initial investment.

6. Each salesperson employed by a certain company works in one of three territories, numbered 1, 2, and 3. At the end of each month, each salesperson turns in the following data: ID number, territory number, and amount sold. The data record

        1134 2 375.24

means that the salesperson with ID number 1134 sold $375.24 worth in territory 2. Write a program to process a file of such records. The printout should consist of four columns. The first column should contain the ID numbers, and the remaining three columns should correspond to territories 1, 2, and 3. The amount sold should be printed in the column of the territory in which the sales were made. At the foot of each territory column, the program should print the total sales for that territory.

7. Write a program to input three characters and print them in alphabetical order. Thus if the user enters XQA, the program will print AQX. Read the three input characters into three character variables: *first, second,* and *third.* Use a separate *writeln* statement for each of the six possible orders in which the values of *first, second,* and *third* can be printed, and use nested **if** statements to select the proper *writeln* statement for execution.

8. Suppose we are given a sequence of numbers such as

        1 3 8 9 4 12 25 24 17 19 19 35 28 40

Those segments of the sequence that are in nondecreasing order are called *runs;* the runs for the given sequence are

        1 3 8 9
        4 12 25
        24
        17 19 19 35
        28 40

The runs of a sequence are important in sorting. Write a program to read a sequence of integers and print each run on a separate line. Note that the end of each run (except the last) is signaled by a *step down*—a larger value followed by a smaller one.

9. Write a program to read a textfile and print the number of commas, semicolons, colons, periods, and exclamation points in the file.

10. Rewrite both versions of the calculator simulation (Figure 7-1 and Figure 7-2) so that a separate procedure is called for each operation the calculator is to perform.

11. Modify the calculator simulation in Exercise 10 to provide the calculator with additional features, such operations for computing squares and square roots.

12. Modify the craps program (Figure 7-5) to allow the user to choose whether to bet for or against the dice; if the user chooses to bet against the dice, the usual rules for winning and losing will be reversed. Needless to say, the user must make the choice before the dice are rolled.

13. Modify the craps program to play some other game of chance, such as matching pennies (for a simple example) or roulette (for a more complex one). Note how the modular construction of the program makes it easy to determine which parts must be modified for playing a different game.

14. An integer greater than zero is *perfect* if it is equal to the sum of all its factors except itself; 28 is a perfect number because $28 = 1 + 2 + 4 + 7 + 14$. A number is *deficient* if it is less than the sum of the factors and *abundant* if it is greater than the sum. Write a program to print for each integer from 1 through 100 whether it is deficient, perfect, or abundant. *Hint:* Integer m is a factor of integer n if and only if the value of n **mod** m is zero.

15. The number and nature of the solutions to the quadratic equation

$$ax^2 + bx + c = 0$$

depend on the *discriminant*

$$D = b^2 - 4ac$$

If D is greater than zero, there are two real solutions given by

$$\frac{-b \pm \sqrt{D}}{2a}$$

If D equals zero, there is one real solution given by

$$-\frac{b}{2a}$$

If D is less than zero, there are two complex solutions given by

$$-\frac{b}{2a} \pm \frac{\sqrt{-D}}{2a} i$$

where i is the imaginary unit, the square root of -1. Write a program to accept values for the coefficients a, b, and c of the quadratic equation and print the solution or solutions, with complex solutions printed in the form

$$x + yi$$

where x and y are real numbers.

Programmer-Defined Types and Data Abstraction

There are two aspects to computer programming: (1) organizing the data to be processed, and (2) describing the processing to be carried out. So far, we have concentrated on describing the processing. In this chapter we shift our attention to organizing the data to be processed.

In describing the processing to be carried out, our guiding principle was *procedural abstraction*—understanding the effect of a processing operation without having to know how that effect was achieved. In organizing the data, our guiding principle will be *data abstraction*—understanding the operations that can be carried out on a particular kind of data without having to know how the data items are represented inside the computer. Data abstraction is often referred to as *information hiding* because the intricacies of the data representation are deliberately concealed.

In Pascal, data organization and data abstraction are achieved with the help of data types, which are classified as *simple*, *structured*, and *pointer* types. A simple type determines an *ordered* set of values. The simple types are type *real*, which is in a class by itself, and the *ordinal* types, of which we have so far encountered *Boolean, char, integer*, and the subrange types. The structured types are those whose values are constructed from values of other types. The only structured types we have studied in detail so far are the array types; an array value is constructed from values of the component type. Other structured values we have encountered are string constants and textfiles, both of which are constructed from characters; and sets, which are constructed from ordinal values. The pointer types are those whose values designate memory locations. One of the most important applications of pointers is establishing cross references between structured values.

Just as we learned to create our own functions and procedures out of the standard functions, procedures, and statements provided by Pascal, so we will now learn many ways to define our own data types using the predefined types as raw material. In this chapter we will review type definitions and investigate several programmer-defined ordinal and structured types. We will also look at *type equivalence and compatibility*, which determine under what circumstances types defined by different definitions can be treated as if they were the same type. Finally, we will investigate *abstract data types*—data types defined by pseudocode and implemented in Pascal via constant and type definitions and function and procedure declarations.

Type Definitions

We begin with a review of type definitions, which appear in the *type definition part* of a Pascal program, function, or procedure. Type definitions must follow constant definitions but precede variable declarations. The following list shows the required order for the definitions and declarations that precede the statement part of a program, function, or procedure:

1. Constant definitions
2. Type definitions
3. Variable declarations
4. Procedure and function declarations

Any definition or declaration parts that are not needed can be omitted, but those that are present must be in the order shown.

A type definition part has the following form:

type
    type definitions

Each type definition has the following form:

    type-identifier = type-denoter;

A "type-denoter" is either a type identifier—the name of a standard type or of a type defined earlier in the program—or a *type constructor*—a construction that defines a new type in terms of standard types and previously defined types. Like other definitions and declarations, a type definition is terminated by a semicolon.

For example, the type definition part

type
    floatingPoint = *real*;
    logical   = *Boolean*;

defines type *floatingPoint* as equivalent to type *real* and type *logical* as equivalent to type *Boolean*. Any operations that are valid for real values are valid for values of type *floatingPoint*, and likewise for Boolean values and values of type *logical*. Thus if we declare variables $x, y, p,$ and q by

var
    x, y : *floatingPoint*;
    p, q : *logical*;

then the following statements are valid:

$x := 3.0 * y + 5.4$;
if p **or** q **then**
    $y := 2.0 * y$

Definitions of array types provide examples of type constructors. For example, in the definitions

type
    list = **array** [1..5] **of** *integer*;
    table = **array** [1..4, 1..3] **of** *integer*;

the type constructors are

array [1..5] **of** *integer*

and

array [1..4, 1..3] **of** *integer*

Type constructor is not standard Pascal terminology; the term is sometimes used in computer science, however, and we will use it to name those Pascal constructions that define a new type in terms of existing types. The Pascal standard uses the term *new type* for what we call a type constructor.

Enumerated and Subrange Types

Pascal provides two kinds of programmer-defined ordinal types: (1) *enumerated types*, in which each value is represented by a programmer-defined identifier, and (2) *subrange types*, each of which is a range of values taken from some other ordinal type.

Enumerated Types

Pascal allows programmers to define new ordinal types by listing, or enumerating, the values of each new type. The programmer chooses identifiers to represent the values; the type constructor for an enumerated type consists of a parenthesized list of all the identifiers that are to represent values of the type. Definitions of some enumerated types follow:

type
    day   = (*sun, mon, tue, wed, thurs, fri, sat*);
    chessman = (*pawn, knight, bishop, rook, queen, king*);
    grade   = (*f, d, c, b, a*);

Type *day*, for example, consists of seven values denoted by the identifiers *sun, mon, tue, wed, thurs, fri,* and *sat*. The order in which the identifiers are listed is important, since it allows us to define the relations "precedes" and "follows," which must be defined for every ordinal type. Thus *sun* precedes *mon* and *tue* precedes *fri*. Similarly, *sat* follows *fri* and *fri* follows *mon*.

The same identifier cannot be used for values of more than one enumerated type. If we define

    rank = (*private, corporal, sergeant, lieutenant,*
           captain, major, colonel, general);

then we cannot also define

    officer = (*lieutenant, captain, major, colonel,*
         general);

since doing so would define *lieutenant, captain, major, colonel,* and *general* as values of more than one enumerated type. We will see shortly how *officer* can be defined as a subrange type.

We use an enumerated type whenever we need a type with a relatively small number of named values. For example, suppose a program must deal with the three primary colors red, yellow, and blue. We can define an enumerated type

    primary = (*red, yellow, blue*);

whose values represent the three colors. We can define variables of type *primary*

var
    color, hue : *primary*;

and assign them values of type primary with statements such as

    color : = *red*;
    hue := *blue*

We could have represented the primary colors by values of existing types such as integers (0 for red, 1 for yellow, 2 for blue) or characters ('r' for red, 'y' for yellow, and 'b' for blue). But there are two advantages to using an enumerated type. First, the program is clearer because the colors are represented by meaningful identifiers rather than the meaningless 0, 1, and 2 or the nondescriptive 'r', 'y', and 'b'.* Second, whereas integers can be assigned to any integer or real variable and characters can be assigned to any character variable, the values *red*, *yellow*, and *blue* can only be assigned to variables of type *primary*. We are thus assured that values intended to represent colors will not be mistakenly used for some other purpose.

Type constructors can be incorporated directly in variable declarations. For example, instead of defining type *primary* by

type
    primary = (*red, yellow, blue*);

and using *primary* to declare *color* and *hue*

var
    color, hue : *primary*;

we could have used the type constructor for the enumerated type in the variable declarations.

var
    color, hue : (*red, yellow, blue*);

A type constructor used in this way is said to define an *anonymous type*, because the type has not been given a name in a type definition. Variables *color* and *hue* both have the same anonymous type, which is an enumerated type with values *red*, *yellow*, and *blue*. Since the type has no name, there is no way to refer to it outside the variable declaration. Therefore, we cannot give any other variable or formal parameter the same type as *color* and *hue*.

Anonymous types are not allowed for declaring formal parameters or for specifying the return type of a function: only type identifiers can be used in a function or procedure heading. Thus in the function declaration

function *Rotate* (*tint* : *primary*) : *primary*;
begin
  case *tint* **of**
    red   : *Rotate* := *yellow*;
    yellow : *Rotate* := *blue*;
    blue   : *Rotate* := *red*
  end
end.

---

*We could overcome this difficulty by defining constant identifiers *red, yellow,* and *blue* equal to 0, 1, and 2 or 'r', 'y', and 'b'. But defining a series of constant identifiers is more cumbersome than defining an enumerated type.

the type identifier *primary* must be used; we could not replace either occurrence of *primary* with the type constructor (*red*, *yellow*, *blue*).

Because of the limitations just discussed, programmers often avoid anonymous types. Another reason for avoiding anonymous types is that carefully chosen type names can greatly aid anyone struggling to understand a program.

Subrange Types

One type is a *subtype** of another if all values of the first type belong to the second, or *parent*, type. The values in the subtype are values from the parent type that satisfy some restriction or *constraint* that defines the subtype. The subtype *inherits* operations from the parent type, so that any operation on values of the parent type is also defined for values of the subtype. Although there are many possibilities for defining subtypes in programming languages, Pascal recognizes only two kinds of subtypes, one of which is the subrange types.

For every ordinal type, we can define a new type whose values are some subrange of the original type. For example,

```
type
    oneDigitNumber = 0..9;
```

defines a subrange of type *integer* whose values are 0 through 9. Likewise, the type definition

```
type
    workday = mon..fri;
```

defines a subrange of type *day* whose values are *mon* through *fri*, and

```
type
    officer = lieutenant..general;
```

defines a subrange of type *rank* whose values are *lieutenant* through *general*.

The parent of a subrange type, the type from which the subrange was taken, is called the *host* type. All operations that can be performed on values of the host type can also be performed on values of the subrange type. The only difference between the subrange type and the host type is that values of the subrange type are required to lie in the specified subrange.

For example, suppose that *big* and *little* are declared as follows:

```
var
    big   : integer;
    little : oneDigitNumber;
```

The assignment

```
big := little
```

is always valid, since a value of type *oneDigitNumber* is also a value of type *integer*. On the other hand,

```
little := big
```

---

*Note that *subtype* is a computer-science term and not part of the terminology associated with Pascal. Thus the term *subtype* will not be found in Pascal standards and reference manuals nor in most Pascal textbooks.

is valid only if the value of *big* lies in the range of 0 through 9. A value of type *integer* is also a value of type *oneDigitNumber* only if it lies in the range 0 through 9.

All the operations that can be carried out on integers are allowed for one digit numbers as well. For example, the statements

> *little* : = 5;
> *little* : = *little* − 3;
> *little* : = 2 ∗ *little*

are valid (when executed in the order shown). In each statement the value assigned to *little* lies in the range 0 through 9. On the other hand, consider the statements

> *little* : = 7;
> *little* : = *little* + 3

After 7 is assigned to *little*, the value of *little* + 3 is 10. Attempting to assign 10 to *little* will cause a runtime error.

We say that a subrange type and its host type are *compatible*, meaning that (1) values of the two types are subject to the same operations, and (2) values of one of the two types can generally be used where values of the other type are expected. A value of a subrange type is always *assignment compatible* with the host type, meaning that a value of the subrange type can always be assigned to a variable of the host type. A value of the host type, however, is assignment compatible with the subrange type only if the value lies in the specified subrange. Compatibility and assignment compatibility will be discussed in more detail later in this chapter.

Use of a subrange type rather than its host type serves two purposes. First, it notifies someone reading the program that only a small range of values of the host type are meaningful as values for a certain variable. Second, it allows the computer to check that the values assigned to a variable lie in the expected subrange and to warn of an error if they do not.

Set Types

We have already seen how convenient sets can be for expressing conditions in control statements. We now look at the types to which set values belong. Set types are structured types because each set value is built out of other values, the elements of the set.

A set is a collection of values, all of which must belong to the same ordinal type. For example, the set that contains the integers 1, 3, 5, and 9 can be expressed in Pascal as

> [1, 3, 5, 9]

The set that contains the characters 'a', 'e', 'i', 'o', and 'u' can be expressed as

> ['a', 'e', 'i', 'o', 'u']

The values that belong to a set are called its *elements*. The elements of [1, 3, 5, 9] are 1, 3, 5, and 9.

The type constructor for a set type has the following form:

> **set of** base-type

The base type is the type of the elements of the sets and must be an ordinal type. Also, each Pascal implementation imposes limits on the range of ordinal numbers allowed for the base type; one implementation may allow a base type only if the ordinal numbers of its values range from 0 through 127; another implementation may allow a range of 0 through 255; another may allow a range of 0 through 4095; and so on. Thus some implementations allow *char* (whose ordinal numbers usually range from 0 through 127 or 0 through 255) as a base type while others do not.

The type definition

$$letterSet = \textbf{set of } 'a'..'z'$$

defines *letterSet* as a type whose values are all possible sets of lowercase letters. Some possible values of type *letterSet* are

$$['a'], ['a', 'c'], ['a', 'e', 'i', 'o', 'u'], []$$

Note [], which denotes the empty set, the set that has no elements. Every set type includes the empty set as a value, regardless of the base type.

Now consider the following type definitions:

$$primary \quad = (red, yellow, blue);$$
$$primarySet = \textbf{set of } primary;$$

Type *primarySet* has the following values:

$$[], [red], [yellow], [blue], [red, yellow],$$
$$[red, blue], [yellow, blue], [red, yellow, blue]$$

A variable of type *primarySet* must have one of these eight values.

Suppose we define *twoColor* and *twoSet* as follows:

$$twoColor = red..yellow;$$
$$twoSet \quad = \textbf{set of } twoColor;$$

Because *twoColor* is a subrange of *primary*, the sets of type *twoSet*

$$[], [red], [yellow], [red, yellow]$$

are also sets of type *primary*. Thus *twoSet* is a subtype of type *primary*; this is the other case of subtyping in Pascal that we referred to earlier. As in the corresponding situation for subrange types, we say that type *twoColor* is compatible with type *primary*.

Set values are created by means of *set constructors*. We have been using set constructors all along to display set values.

$$[1, 3, 5, 9], ['a', 'b', 'c', 'd'], [red, yellow]$$

A set constructor is an expression that is evaluated as the program executes. This means it can contain variables as well as constants. For example, suppose the variables i and j have the values 5 and 3. The set constructor

$$[i, j, i + j, i - j, i * j, i \textbf{ div } j]$$

has the value

$$[5, 3, 8, 2, 15, 1]$$

(The order in which the elements are listed is immaterial.) On the other hand, if the values of i and j were 7 and 2, the same set constructor would have the value

[7, 2, 9, 5, 14, 3]

The list of elements in a set constructor can contain subranges as well as the values of individual elements. Thus the set constructor

[1..5]

is equivalent to

[1, 2, 3, 4, 5]

and

[1..3, 7, 12..15]

is equivalent to

[1, 2, 3, 7, 12, 13, 14, 15]

The order in which values or expressions are listed in a set constructor is immaterial. Thus

[1, 2, 3], [1, 3, 2], [3, 2, 1]

all represent the same set. Also, duplicate values have no effect. Thus

[1, 2, 3, 1], [1, 2, 2, 3, 3], [2, 1, 2, 3]

all represent the same set as [1, 2, 3].

There are three operations that can be carried out on sets to yield other sets. These are *union*, *intersection*, and *difference*, which in Pascal are denoted by $+$, $*$, and $-$. They are defined as follows, where s and t represent values of compatible* set types:

$s + t$ Yields the union of s and t, which contains those elements that belong to s, to t, or to both s and t.

$s * t$ Yields the intersection of s and t, which contains those elements belonging to both s and t.

$s - t$ Yields the difference of s and t, which contains those elements that belong to s but do not belong to t.

Union, intersection, and difference are illustrated in the following table:

Expression	Value
[1, 2, 3, 4] $+$ [3, 4, 5, 6]	[1, 2, 3, 4, 5, 6]
[1, 2, 3, 4] $*$ [3, 4, 5, 6]	[3, 4]
[1, 2, 3, 4] $-$ [3, 4, 5, 6]	[1, 2]

The following relational operators are used with sets:

$=$, $<>$, $<=$, $>=$, **in**

These operators can be defined as follows, where s and t represent values of compatible set types, and the type of e is compatible with the base type of s:

---

*A type is always compatible with itself, so pending further discussion of type compatibility, we can just think of s and t as having the same type.

$s = t$	Yields *true* if s equals t; that is, if s and t contain the same elements.
$s <> t$	Yields *true* if s is not equal to t; that is, if s and t do not have the same elements.
$s <= t$	Yields *true* if s is a *subset* of t; that is, if every element of s is also an element of t.
$s >= t$	Yields *true* if s is a *superset* of t; that is, if every element of t is also an element of s.
e **in** s	Yields *true* if e is an element of s.

Relational operators for sets are shown in the following table:

Expression	Value
[1, 2, 3] = [1, 2, 4]	*false*
[1, 2, 3] <> [1, 2, 4]	*true*
[2, 3] <= [1, 2, 3]	*true*
[1, 2, 3] >= [1, 2, 3, 4]	*false*
2 **in** [1, 2, 3]	*true*
4 **in** [1, 2, 3]	*false*

Example 8-1. *Using Sets: The Sieve of Eratosthenes*

Our next program computes prime numbers using the classic Sieve of Eratosthenes. An integer greater than one is said to be *prime* if it is not exactly divisible by any numbers other than 1 and itself. Thus 2, 3, 5, 7, and 11 are prime numbers, but 4, 6, 8, 9, 10, and 12 are not. Any number that is not prime is a multiple of some smaller prime number. For example, 4, 6, 8, and 12 are multiples of 2, and 9 is a multiple of 3.

The Sieve of Eratosthenes is an algorithm for finding all the prime numbers less than a certain limit. We start by writing down all the integers from 2 through the limit. If the limit is 15, for example, we start by writing

2   3   4   5   6   7   8   9   10   11   12   13   14   15

The first number in the sequence, 2, is a prime number. We now strike out 2 and all multiples of 2 in our sequence of integers.

2̸   3   4̸   5   6̸   7   8̸   9   1̸0̸   11   1̸2̸   13   1̸4̸   15

The smallest number that has not been struck out, 3, is also a prime. We add 3 to our list of primes and strike out all multiples of 3.

2̸   3̸   4̸   5   6̸   7   8̸   9̸   1̸0̸   11   1̸2̸   13   1̸4̸   1̸5̸

It will always be true that the smallest number not struck out is a prime. The reason? If the number were not a prime, it would have to be a multiple of some smaller prime. But all multiples of smaller primes have already been struck out. Thus 5 is also a prime; we add 5 to our list of primes and strike out all multiples of 5. (Actually, all multiples of 5 other than 5 itself

Figure 8-1.

Program for computing prime numbers using the Sieve of Eratosthenes.

```
program Primes (output);

{ Find all prime numbers in range 2 through 255 }

const
  rangeLimit = 255;
type
  range    = 2..rangeLimit;
  rangeSet = set of range;
var
  sieve    : rangeSet; { set from which nonprime numbers
                         are to be removed }
  prime    : range;    { current prime number }
  multiple : integer;  { multiple of current prime number }
begin
  sieve := [2..rangeLimit];
  prime := 2;
  repeat
    while not (prime in sieve) do
      prime := prime + 1;
    write (prime :8);
    multiple := prime;
    while multiple <= rangeLimit do
      begin
        sieve := sieve − [multiple];
        multiple := multiple + prime
      end
  until sieve = []
end.
```

have already been struck out, but the algorithm doesn't know this and will strike them out again.)

2̶ 3̶ 4̶ 5̶ 6̶ 7 8̶ 9̶ 1̶0̶ 11 1̶2̶ 13 1̶4̶ 1̶5̶

Proceeding in this way, we find that 7, 11, and 13 are also primes, so that the primes less than 15 are

2   3   5   7   11   13

The program in Figure 8-1 uses the Sieve of Eratosthenes to find all the prime numbers in the range 2 through 255. We begin by putting all integers in this range in a set and then using the set difference operation to remove the integers one by one as they are struck out. (In fact, 255 was chosen as the upper limit because it is the largest ordinal number allowed for a base type in the version of Pascal in which the program was written.) The program uses the following definitions and declarations:

```
const
    rangeLimit = 255;
type
    range    = 2..rangeLimit;
    rangeSet = set of range;
var
    sieve    : rangeSet;
    prime    : range;
    multiple : integer;
```

Range is the subrange type corresponding to the range of integers we are considering, and *rangeSet* is the type of all sets whose elements lie in *range*. The value of *sieve* is the particular set with which we will be working. The value of *prime* will be stepped through all the values of *range*, with a pause for additional processing whenever the value of *prime* is a prime number. The value of *multiple* will be set to the value of *prime* and to its multiples, which are to be struck out of *sieve*.

We begin by setting *sieve* to the set of all numbers in *range*, and setting *prime* to 2, the first prime number in *range*.

```
sieve := [2..rangeLimit];
prime := 2
```

We can outline the remainder of the processing as follows:

```
repeat
    "Increment prime, if necessary, until its value
    equals an element of sieve. Print the value of
    prime as the next prime number, and remove the
    value of prime and all its multiples from
    sieve."
until sieve = []
```

We use a **while** statement to increment the value of *prime* until it is equal to an element of *sieve*. This element of *sieve* will be the first one that has not been struck out, and hence will be a prime number.

```
while not (prime in sieve) do
    prime := prime + 1;
write (prime :8)
```

Next, we generate all multiples of the value of *prime* and remove them from the value of *sieve*. To generate the multiples, we initialize *multiple* to the value of *prime* and then repeatedly add the value of *prime* to that of *multiple*. To remove a multiple, we use the set constructor [*multiple*] to create a set containing only the value of multiple, and use the set difference operation to remove the contents of that set from the value of *sieve*.

```
multiple := prime;
while multiple <= rangeLimit do
    begin
        sieve := sieve − [multiple];
        multiple := multiple + prime
    end
```

Note that when the **while** statement terminates, the value of *multiple* will be greater than *rangeLimit*. That is why *multiple* had to be declared with type *integer*, whereas *prime*, whose value always remains within the range of interest, could be declared with type *range*.

Record Types

A *record* is a collection of data values, each of which occupies a designated position called a *field*. This use of the term *record* coincides with its everyday use in referring to medical records, school records, tax records, and the like. We have previously represented a record by a series of values typed on the same line of a textfile. Now we will see how to represent records as values of Pascal *record types*, structured types specifically designed for representing records.

Record Types and Values

A record type is a type whose values are records having a given structure. We define a record type by giving the structure of the corresponding records. We give the structure of a record by defining its fields—by naming each field with a *field identifier* and giving the type of data to be stored in the field. The type constructor for a record type has the following form:

> **record**
>   list of field definitions
> **end**

A field definition has the same form as a variable declaration:

> field-identifier : type-denoter

The field identifier is used to designate the field; the type denoter gives the type of values to be stored in the field. The field definitions are separated by semicolons, so there is no semicolon after the last field definition in a record.

For example, consider the following type definition section:

> **type**
>   *skyCondition* = (*cloudy, partlyCloudy, clear*);
>   *precipitation* = (*rain, snow, sleet, hail, none*);
>   *weather*   = **record**
>   *sky*   : *skyCondition*;
>   *precip* : *precipitation*;
>   *low*,
>   *high*   : *integer*
>   **end**;

skyCondition and *precipitation* are both enumerated types. A value of type *weather* is a record with four fields: *sky*, which holds a value of type *sky-Condition*; *precip*, which holds a value of type *precipitation*; and *low* and *high* which hold values of type *integer*. Note that each field definition except the last ends with a semicolon. Also note that the last definition is a combined one that defines both *low* and *high* as integer fields.

The values that make up a structured value are called *component values*, or just *components*, of the structured value.* The structured value itself is called an *entire value*. The components of a record value are the values of its fields. Thus a value of a type *weather* is an entire value having four component values, one for each its four fields: *sky*, *precip*, *low*, and *high*.

Likewise, a variable that holds a structured value is called an *entire variable*; it can be broken down into *component variables*, each of which holds one of the components of the structured value. For record types, the component variables are *field designators*, each consisting of an entire variable followed by a period and a field identifier.

entire-variable.field-identifier

For example, suppose *v* and *w* are declared as entire variables of type *weather*.

var
    v, w : *weather*;

The four component variables of *w* are designated as follows:

w.sky
w.precip
w.low
w.high

The following assignment of an entire value:

w := *v*

is equivalent to the following four assignments of component values:

w.sky := *v.sky*;
w.precip := *v.precip*;
w.low := *v.low*;
w.high := *v.high*

Unlike some other languages, Pascal does not provide any kind of record constructor that would create a record value in the same way that a set constructor creates a set value. The only way to create a record value is to assign appropriate component values to the component variables (field designators) of a record variable. Thus, after the assignments

w.sky := *cloudy*;
w.precip := *rain*;
w.low := 50;
w.high := 75

w contains a value of type *weather* whose *sky* field has the value *cloudy*, whose *precip* field has the value *rain*, and so on.

The only relational operator that applies to record values is =. Two records are equal if and only if the values of their corresponding fields are equal. Thus after the assignment

---

*The information on component and entire values and variables does not apply to set types, which are organized somewhat differently than other structured types. It does, however, apply to array types.

$$w := v$$

or

$$v := w$$

the Boolean expression

$$w = v$$

evaluates to *true*.

Nested Records

A component value of a record can itself be a record value, so that record values can be nested one inside the other. Consider, for example, the following type definitions:

```
date    = record
              month : 1..12;
              day    : 1..31;
              year   : integer
          end;
report = record
              curDate : date;
              curWx    : weather
          end;
```

Each report record contains a date record and a weather record. If *rpt* is declared by

```
var
    rpt : report;
```

the component variables of *rpt* are *rpt.curDate* and *rpt.curWx*. Since each of these contains a record value, however, each is an entire variable with component variables of its own. The component variables of *rpt.curDate* are

```
rpt.curDate.month
rpt.curDate.day
rpt.curDate.year
```

and the component variables of *rpt.curWx* are

```
rpt.curWx.sky
rpt.curWx.precip
rpt.curWx.low
rpt.curWx.high
```

Record values can be nested as deeply as needed, though in practice using more than three or four levels of nesting is rare. Likewise, a record variable can be followed by as many field identifiers (each preceded by a period) as needed to designate a particular component variable.

Scopes of Field Identifiers

The *scope* of an identifier is the part of the program in which it is defined and accessible; for example, the scope of a local variable begins at its point of declaration and extends to the end of the function or procedure containing the declaration. With one exception, the scope of a field identifier is the record description in which it is defined; the field identifiers of a record type are not accessible from outside the record description. The one exception is that field identifiers can be used in field designators. We can think of the period that precedes a field identifier in a field designator as an operator that opens up the record description and makes the field identifiers accessible.

Because of the limited scope of field identifiers, no confusion results if records of different types have the same field identifiers. And since field identifiers can never be confused with variables (why?), variables and field identifiers can have the same names.

For example, consider the following definitions and declarations:

```
type
    realInt     = record
                      first    : real;
                      second : integer
                  end;
    BoolChar = record
                      first     : Boolean;
                      second : char
                  end;


var
    first, second : set of char;
    rlIntRec      : realInt
    BlChRec       : BoolChar
```

No confusion can arise between the field identifiers of type *realInt*, and the field identifiers of type *BoolChar* nor between the field identifiers and the variables *first* and *second*. For example, *rlIntRec* is a variable of type *realInt* and *BlChRec* is a variable of type *BoolChar*. Hence *rlIntRec.first* refers to the *first* field of a record of type *realInt*, and *BlChRec.first* refers to the *first* field of a record of type *BoolChar*. Just plain *first* refers to a variable whose value is a set of characters. Thus, the following assignments are valid:

```
    rlIntRec.first := 3.5;
    BlChRec.first := true;
    first := ['x', 'y', 'z']
```

The *with* Statement

The **with** statement allows us to abbreviate field designators. For example, if *wthr* is a variable of type *weather*, then instead of writing

```
    wthr.sky = cloudy;
    wthr.precip := rain;
    wthr.low := 50;
    wthr.high := 75
```

we can write

```
with wthr do
  begin
    sky := cloudy;
    precip := rain;
    low := 50;
    high := 75
  end
```

The assignments to the field identifiers are interpreted as assignments to component variables of *wthr*. Put another way, the **with** statement causes *wthr*. to be prefixed to each of the field identifiers *sky, precip, low,* and *high*.

Any number of record variables can be listed between **with** and **do**. The record variables must have different types; otherwise, the Pascal system will not know which record variable to prefix to which field identifier. For example, the following **with** statement assigns a value to the record variable *rpt*, which is of type *report*:

```
with rpt, curDate, curWx do
  begin
    month := 5;
    day := 24;
    year := 1992;
    sky := cloudy;
    precip := rain;
    low := 55;
    high := 75
  end
```

Once the Pascal language processor encounters *rpt* in the **with** list, it will prefix *rpt.* to *curDate* and *curWx*. In the remainder of the **with** list, therefore, we can write *curDate* and *curWx* instead of *rpt.curDate* and *rpt.curWx*.

The type of a record variable determines to which field identifiers it will be prefixed. Since *rpt* is of type *report*, *rpt.* will be prefixed to *curDate* and *curWx*; since *rpt.curDate* is of type *date*, *rpt.curDate.* will be prefixed to *month, day,* and *year*; since *rpt.curWx* is of type *weather*, *rpt.curWx.* will be prefixed to *sky, precip, low,* and *high*.

A **with** statement that lists more than one record variable is an abbreviation for a group of nested **with** statements, with one level of nesting for each record variable. Thus the **with** statement we just saw is an abbreviation for the following nested **with** statements:

```
with rpt do
  with curDate do
    with curWx do
      begin
        month := 5;
        day := 24;
        year := 1992;
        sky := cloudy;
        precip := rain;
        low := 55;
        high := 75
      end
```

It is now clear why *rpt.* is prefixed to *curDate* and *curWx*: the **with** statements for *curDate* and *curWx* are nested within the **with** statement for *rpt*; hence *rpt.* will be prefixed to every occurrence of a field identifier of *report*.

Record Variants

It is sometimes convenient to allow records belonging to the same type to have different structures. To accommodate this situation, Pascal allows a record to have a *fixed part* followed by a *variant part*. The fixed part is the same for all records of a given type. The variant part, however, can differ for records belonging to the same type.

For example, suppose that student records can refer to both undergraduate and graduate students. An undergraduate has a class (freshman, sophomore, junior, or senior) and a grade point average. A graduate student does not have a class and has a standing rather than a grade point average. Consider the following definitions:

```
statusType    = (undergrad, grad);
classType     = (freshman, sophomore, junior, senior);
standingType = (satisfactory, unsatisfactory);
student       = record
                   id : integer;
                   case status : statusType of
                      undergrad:
                         (class : classType;
                          gpa   : real);
                      grad:
                         (standing : standingType)
                end;
```

The fields *id* and *status* belong to the fixed part; they are present in every record of type *student*. The status field is the *tag field* for the record; its value determines the structure of the variant part. If the value of the status field is *undergrad*, the variant part contains the fields *class* and *gpa*. If the value of the status field is *grad*, the variant part contains the single field *standing*. Note that each possible variant part is enclosed in parentheses and labeled with the corresponding value of the tag field.

Thus a value of type student having the value *undergrad* for the status field has the same structure as if were described by

```
record
   id     : integer;
   status : statusType;
   class  : classType;
   gpa    : real
end
```

Likewise, a value of type student having the value *grad* for the status field has the same structure as if it were described by

```
record
   id       : integer;
   status   : statusType;
   standing : standingType
end
```

If *stdnt* is a variable of type *student*, the assignments

    stdnt.id := 3794;
    stdnt.status := *undergrad*;
    stdnt.class := *junior*;
    stdnt.gpa := 2.9

are valid, as are the statements

    stdnt.id := 7196;
    stdnt.status := *grad*;
    stdnt.standing := *satisfactory*

The fields of a given record must be designated by distinct field identifiers even if they belong to different variants. For example, the following type definition is invalid:

    realOrInt = **record**
            case *kind* : *Boolean* **of**
              true:
                (*value* : *real*);
              false:
                (*value* : *integer*)
        end;

We must use different field identifiers for the real and integer fields, even though they belong to different variants.

    realOrInt = **record**
            case *kind* : *Boolean* **of**
              true:
                (*realValue* : *real*);
              false:
                (*intValue* : *integer*)
        end;

With the correct declaration, the Pascal compiler knows that if *number* is a variable of type *realOrInt*, then *number.realValue* is a real variable and that *number.intValue* is an integer variable. If the incorrect definition were allowed, the compiler would not be able to determine whether *number.value* were a real variable or an integer variable and so could not do the strong type-checking required in Pascal.

Variant parts can be nested. Each possible variant part can contain both a fixed part and another variant part. Those variant parts can contain still other variant parts, and so on.

Functions, Procedures, and Structured Types

Structured values can be passed to functions and procedures via either value or variable parameters. When a value is passed a value parameter, a new copy of the value is made and assigned to the formal parameter. When a variable is passed as a variable parameter, however, the subprogram is just given access to the value of the variable that was passed—no copy of the value is made. Because structured values can be large, copying them can be time-consuming, and significant amounts of memory may be required to hold the copies. For this reason, it is more efficient to pass structured values (particularly large ones) via variable parameters rather than value parameters.

The return type of a Pascal function must be a simple type or a pointer type; functions cannot return structured values. Thus the only way for a subprogram to return a structured value is by assigning it to a variable passed as a variable parameter. Note that when an entire variable is passed as a variable parameter, the subprogram gains access not only to the entire variable but to its component variables as well. The most usual way of returning a record value is by assigning values to the component variables of a variable parameter.

A type constructor for a set, array, or record type can be preceded by the word **packed**, which indicates that values of the type are to be stored as compactly as possible, even if this means storing more than one component value in each memory location. The following illustrates definitions of packed types:

type
   smallSet = **packed set of** $0..15$;
   flagList = **packed array** $[1..10]$ **of** *Boolean*;
   flagRec = **packed record**
                    terminate,
                    waitForInput,
                    signalUser   : *Boolean*
           end;

Packing saves space by storing several values in each memory location. The time required to store and retrieve values is increased, however, because of the extra time needed to insert a value in or extract it from its position within a larger location. How values of a given type are packed and even whether they will be packed at all is implementation dependent. As a rule, you should define a type as packed only if you know that packing values of that type will save significant space on your Pascal system. There is one exception to this rule: Pascal string types are required to be packed types even if no space saving results (as it usually does not on byte-oriented computers).

The mechanism for passing variables via variable parameters assumes that each variable names a complete memory location. When values are packed, however, component values are stored in parts of memory locations, and it is to these partial memory locations that component variables refer. Thus, component variables of variables having packed types cannot be passed via variable parameters. For example, if the variable *flags* is declared by

var
   flags : *flagRec*;

then the component variables *flags.terminate*, *flags.waitForInput*, and *flags.signalUser* cannot be passed via variable parameters.

In standard Pascal, the *read* and *readln* procedures are exceptions to this rule: component variables of variables with packed types can be used as parameters for *read* and *readln*. This exception was introduced only recently, however, so some existing Pascal implementations forbid such component variables as parameters to *read* and *readln*.

Type Equivalence and Compatibility

As long as we were concerned with only a few standard types designated by predefined identifiers, there was no question as to when two types were the same—they were the same only if they were designated by the same identifier. With programmer-defined types, however, things are not so simple. Suppose two identical type constructors occur in different parts of a program. Do they define the same type? Or suppose that the two type constructors are different but nevertheless describe the same set of values. Should we consider the types so defined to be the same?

Even though two types are different, we may sometimes wish to treat them as if they were the same. One reason for doing this is subtyping. A subtype is different from the parent type, yet all the values of the subtype also belong to the parent type. It seems reasonable, then, to allow values of the subtype wherever values of the parent type are allowed. Another reason for treating different types as if they were the same is *coercion*—automatic conversion of a value from one type to another. For example, Pascal automatically converts integers to real values in many situations. In those situations, then, we are able to ignore the distinction between integers and reals. The concepts of *compatibility* and *assignment compatibility* cover those situations in which values belonging to different types can be treated as if they belonged to the same type.

Type Equivalence

We say that two types are equivalent, identical, or the same if no distinction whatever can be made between them—each can be used wherever the other can be used, and all operations defined for one type are also defined for the other. There exist two approaches to deciding when two types are equivalent.

■ *Name Equivalence*. Two types are equivalent if one is defined equal to the other in a type definition or if they are both defined by the same occurrence of a type constructor. The "name" in name equivalence refers not to the type identifiers appearing in the program but to a unique internal name that the compiler assigns to each occurrence of a type constructor (including those that define anonymous types).

■ *Structural Equivalence*. Two types are structurally equivalent if their values have the same structure; that is, if they are built from or related to values of other types in the same way. For example, we might consider two subrange types to be structurally equivalent if both contain only the integers 0 through 9. Likewise, we might consider two record types to be structurally equivalent if each contains records consisting of two fields; for example, an integer field with field identifier *idNumber* and a real field with field identifier *balance*.

In many ways structural equivalence is the more natural concept, yet in programming languages it has certain drawbacks.

■ If the type system is sufficiently complex, structural equivalence may be *undecidable*. That is, there may not be any algorithm that can, from analysis of the type constructors, determine in every case whether two types are structurally equivalent.

- Even if structural equivalence is decidable, detecting it may be complex. The part of the compiler responsible for detecting structural equivalence may be as complex as all the rest of the compiler put together. Indeed, the algorithm used for detecting structural equivalence, the *unification algorithm*, is the same algorithm on which logic programming languages such as Prolog are based.

- Finally, even though two types contain the same values, we may still wish to distinguish between them if their values are to be used for different purposes. The Pascal compiler can then warn us if a value created for one purpose is inadvertently used for a different one.

For these reasons, Pascal uses name equivalence rather than structural equivalence. Thus, two Pascal types are the same only if one is defined equal to the other in a type definition or if they are both defined by the same occurrence of a type constructor.

Now let's look at some examples. Consider the following type definitions:

```
type
   accountRec = record
                   idNumber : integer;
                   balance   : real
                end;
   floatingPt  = real;
   billingRec  = accountRec;
```

Type *floatingPt* is equivalent to type *real* because it is defined equal to type *real* in a type definition. For the same reason, type *billingRec* is equivalent to type *accountRec*. Also, because of the equality, *billingRec* is defined by the same type constructor that defines *accountRec*; hence, the equivalence of the *billingRec* and *accountRec* can also be justified by saying that both are defined by the same occurrence of a type constructor.

Now consider the following declarations:

```
var
   aRec1, aRec2 : accountRec;
   bRec1, bRec2 : billingRec
```

Since *accountRec* and *billingRec* are equivalent, the variables *aRec1*, *aRec2*, *bRec1*, and *bRec2* all have the same type. Thus the following assignments are all valid:

```
aRec1 := aRec2;
aRec2 := aRec1;
bRec1 := bRec2;
bRec2 := bRec1;
aRec1 := bRec2;
bRec1 := aRec2;
```

Now consider the following type definitions:

```
type
   accountRec = record
                   idNumber : integer;
                   balance   : real
                end;
```

```
billingRec =    record
                    idNumber : integer;
                    balance   : real
                end;
```

In this case, *accountRec* and *billingRec* are *not* the same type, since they are not defined by the same *occurrence* of a type constructor. It doesn't matter that the two type constructors have identical structures, because we are using name equivalence and not structural equivalence. Suppose we again declare *aRec1*, *aRec2*, *bRec1*, and *bRec2* by

```
var
    aRec1, aRec2 : accountRec;
    bRec1, bRec2 : billingRec
```

As before, both *aRec1* and *aRec2* have the same type and both *bRec1* and *bRec2* have the same type. But the type of *aRec1* and *aRec2* is not the same as that of *bRec1* and *bRec2*, because now *accountRec* and *billingRec* do not designate the same type. Thus in this case the assignments

```
aRec1 := bRec2;
bRec1 := aRec2;
```

are not allowed.

A similar situation holds for anonymous types. Consider the following declarations:

```
var
    aRec1, aRec2 : record
                        idNumber : integer;
                        balance   : real
                    end;
    bRec1, bRec2 : record
                        idNumber : integer;
                        balance   : real
                    end;
```

Variables *aRec1* and *aRec2* have the same anonymous type, since their types are defined by the same occurrence of a type constructor. Likewise, *bRec1* and *bRec2* have the same anonymous type. But the type of *aRec1* and *aRec2* is not the same as the type of *bRec1* and *bRec2*, because the two types are defined by different occurrences of a type constructor.

Note that no other variable, record field, or formal parameter can have the same type as *aRec1* and *aRec2*. Thus the value of *aRec1* or *aRec2* cannot be assigned to a variable (other than *aRec1* and *aRec2*), assigned to a record field, or passed to a function or procedure. These restrictions are one of the main reasons that Pascal programmers often avoid anonymous types.

Although type equivalence has been illustrated with record types, the same concepts also apply to array types. For example, the types *list1* and *list2* defined by

```
type
    list1 = array [1..100] of Boolean;
    list2 = array [1..100] of Boolean;
```

are not equivalent, because they are not defined by the same occurrence of a type constructor. Likewise, if variables *aList1* and *aList2* are declared by

var
    aList1, *aList2* : **array** [1..100] **of** *Boolean*;

then they have the same type, and the assignments

    aList2 := *aList1*

and

    aList1 := *aList2*

are valid. On the other hand, if *aList1* and *aList2* are declared by

var
    aList1 : **array** [1..100] **of** *Boolean*;
    aList2 : **array** [1..100] **of** *Boolean*;

then their types are not equivalent and the preceding assignment statements are invalid.

Type Compatibility

Types defined by different occurrences of type constructors normally have nothing whatever to do with one another, even though it may be clear to a person reading the program that the two types contain the same values. There are two specific situations, however, in which Pascal recognizes (via the concept of compatible types) that different types can contain the same or similar values.

One of these situations involves subtyping: two types are compatible if one is a subtype of the other or if both are subtypes of the same parent type. The other situation involves string types, the types to which string constants such as 'dog' and 'wolf' belong. When we take up string types (in Chapter 11), we will see that a given string value, such as 'dog', can belong to many distinct string types—string types defined by different occurrences of type constructors. Pascal recognizes that different string types can contain the same values by declaring two string types compatible if their strings contain the same number of characters. Thus 'dog' and 'cat' can belong to compatible string types, since they contain the same number of characters. But 'dog' and 'wolf' cannot belong to compatible string types, because 'dog' and 'wolf' contain different numbers of characters.

With these general considerations understood, we can give the formal definition of type compatibility in Pascal. Two types, which we denote T1 and T2, are compatible if any of the following statements are true:

1. T1 and T2 are the same type (that is, they are name equivalent).
2. T1 is a subrange of T2 or T2 is a subrange of T1, or both T1 and T2 are subranges of the same host type (subtyping for subrange types).
3. T1 and T2 are set types with compatible base types. T1 and T2 must be both packed or both unpacked (subtyping for set types).
4. T1 and T2 are string types whose strings contain the same number of characters.

One of the most important uses of type compatibility is in defining the related concept of assignment compatibility.

Assignment Compatibility

Assignment compatibility governs whether a given value can be assigned to a given variable. A value of type T2 is assignment compatible with type T1 if the value of type T2 can be assigned to a variable of type T1. Note that assignment compatibility is a relation between a value and a type, not between two types. Whether a value of one type can be assigned to a variable of another type may depend on the particular value in question.

The rules for assignment compatibility are similar to those for compatibility. Assignment compatibility, however, allows one more liberty and imposes one more restriction than assignment compatibility. The liberty involves the coercion of integers to real values: an integer value can be assigned to a real variable. The restriction involves file values, which cannot be assigned. Assignment involves copying a value from one part of main memory to another. Files are not normally stored in main memory, and may not even exist in their entireties at any one time. For example, a keyboard-input file is created character-by-character as the user types it, and characters sent to a printer-output file are lost to the computer as they are printed on paper. Thus assignment is not allowed for files or for structured values containing files as components.

The following are the formal rules for assignment compatibility. A value of type T2 is assignment compatible with a type T1 if any of the following statements are true:

1. T1 and T2 are the same type (they are name equivalent) and neither is a file type nor a structured type having component values (however deeply nested) that are files.
2. T1 is type *real* and T2 is type *integer*.
3. T1 and T2 are compatible ordinal types and the value of type T2 belongs to type T1. (This refers to subrange types; note that the value to be assigned must belong to the subrange declared for the variable.)
4. T1 and T2 are compatible set types and all members of the value of type T2 belong to the base type of type T1. (Again the validity of the assignment depends on the particular value being assigned.)
5. T1 and T2 are compatible string types.

Applications of Compatibility and Assignment Compatibility

In this section we will look at the restrictions imposed on Pascal statements by the requirements of compatibility and assignment compatibility. Note that some of the rules given here generalize more restricted rules given earlier in the book.

Assignment. A value can be assigned to a variable only if the value is assignment compatible with the type of the variable.

Input. Values read from a textfile must be assignment compatible with the types of the corresponding variables in the *read* or *readln* statement.

Actual and Formal Parameters. We recall that for value parameters, the value of an actual parameter is assigned to the corresponding formal parameter. For variable parameters, however, an actual parameter is (in effect, at least) substituted for the formal parameter. For value parameters, then, the value of an actual parameter must be assignment compatible with the type of the corresponding formal parameter. For variable parameters, however, the types of the actual and formal parameters must be the same (name equivalent).

The case Statement.   In a **case** statement, the type of each case constant must be compatible with the type of the selector expression.

The for Statement.   We recall that the **for** statement has the following general forms:

> **for** control-variable : = expression-1 **to** expression-2
> controlled-statement

and

> **for** control-variable : = expression-1 **downto** expression-2
> controlled-statement

The control variable must have an ordinal type, and the types of expression-1 and expression-2 must be compatible with the type of the control variable. If any executions of the controlled statement actually take place, the values of expression-1 and expression-2 must also be assignment compatible with the type of the control variable.

We recall that if the initial values of expression-1 and expression-2 are such that no executions of the controlled statements take place, then no assignment is made to the control variable. Thus assignment compatibility is required only if at least one execution of the controlled statement takes place. For example, suppose that *count* has the type *oneDigitNumber* defined as the subrange 0..9. Both of the following statements are valid:

> **for** *count* : = 100 **to** 50 **do**
> *writeln* (*count*);
> **for** *count* : = 10 **downto** 15 **do**
> *writeln* (*count*);

In each case no assignments to the control variable and no executions of the controlled statement take place. Therefore, it doesn't matter that 100, 50, 10, and 15 are not assignment compatible with the type of *count*. Note, however, that 100, 50, 10, and 15 are all of type *integer*, which is compatible with type *oneDigitNumber*.

Data Abstraction

We recall that a data type is defined not only by the values it contains but by the operations that can be carried out on the values. An *abstract data type* (*ADT*) is one whose values and operations are defined independently of any programming-language implementation. There are several methods of defining an abstract data type, including pseudocode, algebraic equations, and formulas in mathematical logic. We will use pseudocode, which is more intuitive and less technically complex than the other methods, and which has served us well for defining algorithms.

We implement an abstract data type with type definitions (which define the values of the type) and procedure and function declarations (which define the operations). Many programming languages provide a construction for wrapping up, or *encapsulating*, the definitions and declarations that implement an abstract data type. Identifiers that are intended for use only within the implementation can be declared *private*; private identifiers are accessible only from within the encapsulation construction; they cannot be accessed inadvertently from elsewhere in the program.

Encapsulation constructions are known variously as *modules, packages, units, envelopes,* and *capsules*. Some extensions to standard Pascal, such as UCSD Pascal and Microsoft Pascal, do provide such constructions (which are called *units*). Encapsulation constructions are present in many recently developed languages, such as Ada and Modula-2, and are planned for a standard extended Pascal that is now under development.

Other extended versions of Pascal, such as Turbo Pascal, do not provide an encapsulation construction, but they do allow definitions and declarations to occur in the program in any order, and they allow multiple occurrences of the various definition and declaration parts. These liberties allow the programmer to group together all the definitions and declarations that implement an abstract data type. On the other hand, there is no provision for private identifiers, so it is up to the programmer to assure that identifiers intended only for use within the implementation are not inadvertently accessed from elsewhere in the program.

Standard Pascal, however, neither provides an encapsulation construction nor allows logically related definitions and declarations to be grouped together. The definitions and declarations that implement an abstract data type must be sprinkled throughout a Pascal program, with the constant definitions going in the constant definition part, the type definitions going in the type definition part, and the procedure and function declarations being grouped with all other procedure and function declarations in the program.

In order to group together the definitions and declarations of an abstract-data-type implementation yet remain consistent with standard Pascal, we will display each implementation as a separate figure rather than as part of a Pascal program. To use the implementation in a Pascal program, the definitions and declarations in the figure will have to be inserted in the appropriate parts of the program. If the version of Pascal you are using provides any support for implementing abstract data types, such as encapsulation constructions or arbitrary order for definitions and declarations, you should take advantage of these features to group together the definitions and declarations that implement each abstract data type.

Example 8-2. *Simulating a Counter*

We know that a computer program sometimes simulates some real-world process, such as the accumulation of interest. Likewise, an abstract data type often simulates a real or imaginary machine; in fact, an abstract data type is sometimes called an *abstract machine*. The values of the data type correspond to possible *states* of the machine; that is, to configurations of its internal parts. The operations of the data type correspond to the controls and instrument readings by which we communicate with the machine. The two examples of abstract data types discussed in this chapter can best be thought of as abstract machines.

As our first example, we will define and implement an abstract data type that simulates a simple three-digit hand counter, such as those used in taking inventory. The counter reading can range from 0 through 999. If the count exceeds 999, only the rightmost three digits of the count are retained. Thus a count of 1000 gives a reading of 000, a count of 1001 gives a reading of 001, a count of 1002 gives a reading of 002, and so on. When the count exceeds 999, we say that the counter has *overflowed*; this is an error condition because after an overflow the counter reading is no longer accurate. We assume that the counter has an indicator showing whether or not it has overflowed.

Each value of the abstract data type *Counter* must correspond to a possible state of the mechanical counter. Thus each value of *Counter* must be able to represent a reading in the range 0 through 999 and indicate whether overflow has occurred. Exactly how the reading and overflow indication are represented are not important for the abstract data type—these are matters for an implementation to resolve, and different implementations may well resolve them differently.

There are four operations that can be carried out on a value of type *Counter*. *ResetCounter* resets the counter reading to zero and clears the overflow indicator; *Increment* increases the counter reading by one and sets the overflow indicator if necessary; *Count* returns the current counter reading; and *OverflowQ* returns *true* if the counter has overflowed and *false* otherwise. (The Q represents a question mark and indicates that *OverflowQ* asks and gets the answer to a question about the state of the counter.)

We define an abstract data type by describing its values (as has just been done) and by providing a pseudocode description for each operation. In the following descriptions, *aCounter* refers to a value of type *Counter* (we can think of *aCounter* as a variable whose value has type *Counter*; operations may change the value of *aCounter*). The word *returns* indicates that a value is to be returned as the value of a function.

ResetCounter (aCounter)	Resets the reading and overflow indicator of *aCounter*. The reading is set to 000 and the overflow indicator is set to the ''no overflow'' position.
Increment (aCounter)	If the reading of *aCounter* is less than or equal to 999, one is added to the counter reading and the overflow indicator remains unchanged. If the reading of the counter is 999, the reading is set to zero and the overflow indicator is set to the ''overflow has occurred'' position.
Count (aCounter)	Returns the reading of *aCounter*. The state of *aCounter* is not changed.
OverflowQ (aCounter)	Returns *true* if the overflow indicator of *aCounter* is in the ''overflow has occurred'' position and returns *false* otherwise. The state of *aCounter* is not changed.

We now turn to implementing the abstract data type *Counter* in Pascal. We must define a Pascal type, *counter*, whose values represent the values of the abstract data type *Counter*. (To help distinguish between the abstract type and the Pascal type, we will begin the name of the abstract type with a capital letter and that of the Pascal type with a lowercase letter. Note that the abstract type includes the operations but the Pascal type does not.) We must then define Pascal procedures and functions that act on values of the Pascal type *counter* in the same way that the abstract operations just defined act on values of the abstract data type *Counter*.

Figure 8-2 shows our Pascal implementation of the abstract data type *Counter*. The constant *maxCount* is defined as 999, the maximum possible counter reading. The type *counterReading* is defined as the subrange 0..999, the range of integer values allowed for counter readings. The identifiers *maxCount* and *counterReading* are private in that they are for use only within the implementation of *Counter*—they are not intended for use by any program statements outside of the implementation.

The type *counter* is the Pascal type whose values represent those of the abstract data type *Counter*. The type *counter* is public; it is available outside of the implementation, where it can be used to declare variables, record fields, and formal parameters of type *counter*. Making the type *counter* available is one of the main objectives of the implementation. The remaining objective is to declare functions and procedures that will manipulate values of type *counter* in the manner specified for the operations of the abstract data type *Counter*.

For our discussion of the abstract type, we know that a value of type *counter* must represent a counter reading and an indication of whether or not the counter has overflowed. We thus define *counter* as a record type with two fields.

```
const
    maxCount = 999;
type
    counterReading = 0..maxCount;
    counter        = record
                         overflowFlag : Boolean;
                         curCount     : counterReading
                     end;
```

Figure 8-2.

A Pascal implementation of the abstract data type *Counter*. The definitions and declarations shown here must be inserted in the appropriate definition and declaration parts of a Pascal program that is to use the implementation.

{ ***************** Implementation of *Counter* ******************* }

```
const
    maxCount = 999; { largest possible counter reading }
type
    counterReading = 0..maxCount;
    counter        = record
                         overflowFlag : Boolean;
                         curCount     : counterReading
                     end;
```

Figure 8-2.   *Continued.*

{---------------------------------- Procedure *Reset* ---------------------------------- }

procedure *ResetCounter* (**var** *aCounter* : *counter*);

{ Clear count to zero and reset overflow indicator }

begin
  aCounter.overflowFlag := *false*;
  aCounter.curCount := 0
end; { *ResetCounter* }

{---------------------------------- Procedure *Increment* ---------------------------------- }

procedure *Increment* (**var** *aCounter* : *counter*);

{ Increase count by one. If overflow, set count to zero and overflow flag to
  false }

begin
  if *aCounter.curCount* = *maxCount* **then**
    begin
      aCounter.overflowFlag := *true*;
      aCounter.curCount := 0
    end
  else
      aCounter.curCount := *aCounter.curCount* + 1
end; { *Increment* }

{---------------------------------- Function *Count* ---------------------------------- }

function *Count* (*aCounter* : *counter*) : *integer*;

{ Return current count }

begin
  Count := *aCounter.curCount*
end; { *Count* }

{---------------------------------- Function *Overflow* ---------------------------------- }

function *OverflowQ* (*aCounter* : *counter*) : *Boolean*;

{ Return *true* if overflow has occurred and *false* otherwise }

begin
  OverflowQ := *aCounter.overflowFlag*
end; { *OverflowQ* }

The Boolean field *overflowFlag* has the value *true* if the counter has overflowed and the value *false* otherwise. The value of the field *curCount* is the counter reading, an integer value in the range 0 through 999 (since type *counterReading* is defined as the subrange of *integer* type 0..999).

The operations of the abstract data type will be implemented by Pascal procedures and functions. The parameters of the operations, such as *aCounter*, correspond to formal parameters of the Pascal procedures and functions. The questions that remain are (1) when should we use procedures, (2) when should we use functions, and (3) should the formal parameters be value or variable parameters?

The circumstance that most strongly influences the answers to these questions is that abstract data types are almost always implemented as record types. Record values cannot be represented by constants, nor can they be returned by expressions or functions. Hence every record value must be the value of a variable (or something that behaves like a variable, such as a formal parameter or a field designator). Since record values cannot be returned by functions, any record value created by an operation must be returned via a variable parameter.

Thus any operation that creates or modifies values of the abstract data type will be represented by a procedure with at least one variable parameter. Any operation that does not create or change values of the abstract data type, and which returns only nonstructured values, can be represented by a function.

In the case of *Counter*, *ResetCounter* creates a new value of the abstract type and *Increment* modifies an existing value. Thus each will be represented in Pascal as a procedure with a single variable parameter. *Count* and *OverflowQ*, on the other hand, do not modify values of the abstract data type, and both return nonstructured values of types *integer* and *Boolean* respectively. Therefore, *Count* and *OverflowQ* will be represented in Pascal by functions with value parameters.

Now let us turn to Figure 8-2 and the procedure *Reset*, which implements the abstract operation of the same name. By means of assignment to the component variables of the variable parameter *aCounter*, *ResetCounter* creates and returns a value of type *counter* with *overflowFlag* set to *false* and *curCount* set to zero.

```
procedure ResetCounter (var aCounter : counter);
begin
  aCounter.overflowFlag := false;
  aCounter.curCount := 0
end;
```

The procedure *Increment* is passed (via the variable parameter *aCounter*) a variable whose value is of type *counter*. By means of assignments to the component variables of *aCounter*, the procedure *Increment* modifies the value of the variable as called for by the *Increment* operation. Thus if the value of *aCounter.curCount* is equal to *maxCount*, *aCount.overflowFlag* is set to *true* and *aCount.curCounter* is set to zero. On the other hand, if the value of *aCounter.curCount* is not equal to *maxCount*, the value of *aCounter.curCount* is incremented by one.

```
procedure Increment (var aCounter : counter);
begin
  if aCounter.curCount = maxCount then
    begin
      aCounter.overflowFlag := true;
      aCounter.curCount := 0
    end
  else
    aCounter.curCount := aCounter.curCount + 1
end;
```

The function *Count* returns the value of the *curCount* field of its argument. Since *Count* does not change the value of *aCounter*, *aCounter* can be a value parameter.

```
function Count (aCounter : counter) : integer;
begin
  Count := aCounter.curCount
end;
```

Likewise, the function *OverflowQ* returns the value of the *overflowFlag* field of its argument. Since the function does not change the value of its argument, *aCounter* can be a value parameter.

```
function OverflowQ (aCounter : counter) : Boolean;
begin
  OverflowQ := aCounter.overflowFlag
end;
```

Example 8-3. *Counting Consonants and Vowels*

As an example of a program that uses an implementation of an abstract data type, we will write a program that uses counters to count the number of consonants and vowels in a textfile. Our first version of the program, shown in Figure 8-3, is written in standard Pascal, so that the standard order for definitions and declarations must be followed. This means that the type definition for the main program must be grouped with the type definitions of the implementation, and the variable declarations for the main program must be inserted between the type definitions and the procedure and function declarations of the implementation.

Figure 8-4 shows a version of the same program written in a nonstandard version of Pascal (Turbo Pascal) that does not enforce the standard order and allows multiple occurrences of the various definition and declaration parts. In this version, the definitions and declarations that implement the abstract type *Counter* are grouped together and bracketed by comments. The type definition and variable declarations for the main program are placed outside the area reserved for the implementation of *Counter*. If the program implemented more than one abstract data type, each implementation could be given its own area of the program, eliminating any possibility of confusing the definitions and declarations of one implementation with those of another implementation or with those of the main program.

Figure 8-3.

This program, which counts the consonants and vowels in a textfile, uses our implementation of the abstract data type *Counter* (Figure 8-2). This program is written in standard Pascal, so that the standard order for definitions and declarations must be followed. This means that the definitions and declarations of the implementation must be intermixed with those of the main program.

```pascal
program TextStatistics (input, output);

{ Count consonants and vowels in textfile }

const
    maxCount = 999;                                    { implementation }
type
    counterReading = 0..maxCount;                      { implementation }
    counter        = record                            { implementation }
                        overflowFlag : Boolean;
                        curCount     : counterReading
                     end;
    charSet        = set of char;                      { main program }
var
    vowels, consonants              : charSet;         { main program }
    vowelCounter, consonantCounter : counter;          { main program }
    inChar                          : char;            { main program }

{ --------------------------------- Procedure Reset --------------------------------- }

procedure ResetCounter (var aCounter : counter);       { implementation }

{ Clear count to zero and reset overflow indicator }

begin
    aCounter.overflowFlag := false;
    aCounter.curCount := 0
end; { ResetCounter }

{ ----------------------------- Procedure Increment ----------------------------- }

procedure Increment (var aCounter : counter);          { implementation }

{ Increase count by one. If overflow, set count to zero and overflow flag to false }

begin
    if aCounter.curCount = maxCount then
       begin
          aCounter.overflowFlag := true;
          aCounter.curCount := 0
       end
    else
          aCounter.curCount := aCounter.curCount + 1
end; { Increment }
```

Figure 8-3.   *Continued.*

```
{ ---------------------------------- Function Count ----------------------------------- }

function Count (aCounter : counter) : integer;                    { implementation }

{ Return current count }

begin
  Count := aCounter.curCount
end; { Count }


{ ---------------------------------- Function OverflowQ ---------------------------------- }

function OverflowQ (aCounter : counter) : Boolean;       { implementation }

{ Return true if overflow has occurred and false otherwise }

begin
  OverflowQ := aCounter.overflowFlag
end; { OverflowQ }


{ ----------------------------------- Main Program ----------------------------------- }

begin
  vowels := ['A', 'E', 'I', 'O', 'U', 'a', 'e', 'i', 'o', 'u'];
  consonants := ['A'..'Z', 'a'..'z'] − vowels;
  ResetCounter (vowelCounter);
  ResetCounter (consonantCounter);
  while not eof(input) do
    begin
      read (inChar);
      if inChar in vowels then
        Increment (vowelCounter)
      else if inChar in consonants then
        Increment (consonantCounter)
    end;
  if OverflowQ(vowelCounter) then
    writeln ('Vowel counter overflowed')
  else
    writeln ('Vowels:        ', Count(vowelCounter) :1);
  if OverflowQ(consonantCounter) then
    writeln ('Consonant counter overflowed')
  else
    writeln ('Consonants: ', Count(consonantCounter) :1)
end.
```

Figure 8-4.

This version of the program in Figure 8-3 is written in a nonstandard version of Pascal that does not enforce the standard order of definitions and declarations. This freedom allows us to group the definitions and declarations of the abstract-data-type implementation separately from those of the main program.

---

program *TextStatistics* (*input*, *output*);

{ Count consonants and vowels in textfile }

{ ****************** Implementation of *Counter* ****************** }

const
  maxCount = 999;
type
  counterReading = 0..*maxCount*;
  counter   = **record**
                overflowFlag : *Boolean*;
                curCount   : *counterReading*
             end;

{ --------------------------------- Procedure *Reset* --------------------------------- }

procedure *ResetCounter* (**var** *aCounter* : *counter*);

{ Clear count to zero and reset overflow indicator }

begin
  aCounter.overflowFlag := *false*;
  aCounter.curCount := 0
end; { *ResetCounter* }

{ ------------------------------- Procedure *Increment* ------------------------------- }

procedure *Increment* (**var** *aCounter* : *counter*);

{ Increase count by one. If overflow, set count to zero and overflow flag to
  false }

begin
  if *aCounter.curCount* = *maxCount* **then**
    begin
      aCounter.overflowFlag := *true*;
      aCounter.curCount := 0
    end
  else
      aCounter.curCount := *aCounter.curCount* + 1
end; { *Increment* }

Figure 8-4.   *Continued.*

```
{----------------------------------- Function Count ----------------------------------- }

function Count (aCounter : counter) : integer;

{ Return current count }

begin
   Count := aCounter.curCount
end; { Count }

{----------------------------------- Function OverflowQ ----------------------------------- }

function OverflowQ (aCounter : counter) : Boolean;

{ Return true if overflow has occurred and false otherwise }

begin
   OverflowQ := aCounter.overflowFlag
end; { OverflowQ }

{ *************** End of Implementation of Counter *************** }

{----------------------------------- Main Program ----------------------------------- }

type
   charSet = set of char;
var
   vowels, consonants                  : charSet;
   vowelCounter, consonantCounter : counter;
   inChar                          : char;

begin
   vowels := ['A', 'E', 'I', 'O', 'U', 'a', 'e', 'i', 'o', 'u'];
   consonants := ['A'..'Z', 'a'..'z'] − vowels;
   ResetCounter (vowelCounter);
   ResetCounter (consonantCounter);
   while not eof(input) do
      begin
         read (inChar);
         if inChar in vowels then
            Increment (vowelCounter)
         else if inChar in consonants then
            Increment (consonantCounter)
      end;
   if OverflowQ(vowelCounter) then
      writeln ('Vowel counter overflowed')
   else
      writeln ('Vowels;      ', Count(vowelCounter) :1);
   if OverflowQ(consonantCounter) then
      writeln ('Consonant counter overflowed')
   else
      writeln ('Consonants: ', Count(consonantCounter) :1)
end.
```

Now let's see how the example program actually uses the implementation for counting vowels and consonants. The program declares two variables of type *counter*.

> *vowelCounter, consonantCounter : counter*;

Each of these variables corresponds to a physical counter that we might use if we were doing the job manually. Before beginning to count, we use the procedure *Reset* to clear each of the counters to zero.

> *ResetCounter (vowelCounter)*;
> *ResetCounter (consonantCounter)*

The procedure *Increment* is used to increment the reading of a counter whenever a letter of the appropriate kind is encountered. Thus

> *Increment (vowelCounter)*

counts a vowel and

> *Increment (consonantCounter)*

counts a consonant. After the textfile has been processed, we use *OverflowQ* to determine if each counter overflowed and *Count* to get the reading of each counter. The following statements print for both vowels and consonants either the number counted or a statement that a particular counter overflowed:

> **if** *OverflowQ(vowelCounter)* **then**
>   *writeln* ('Vowel counter overflowed')
> **else**
>   *writeln* ('Vowels: ', *Count(vowelCounter)* :1);
> **if** *OverflowQ(consonantCounter)* **then**
>   *writeln* ('Consonant counter overflowed')
> **else**
>   *writeln* ('Consonants: ', *Count(consonantCounter)* :1)

Example 8-4. *Simulating a Blackjack Dealer*

A straightforward approach to simulating a real or imaginary system is to design an abstract machine that reflects those properties of the actual system that we wish to include in our simulation. Indeed, the first programming language to provide an encapsulation construction for implementing abstract data types was Simula, a language designed for simulation. Those parts of our previous programs that simulate real or imaginary systems can be reformulated as implementations of abstract data types. As an example of this, we will design and implement an abstract data type *Dealer* that serves as a blackjack dealer according to the rules given in Chapter 7.

Each value of the abstract type *Dealer* must represent a possible internal state of a blackjack-dealing machine. From our work in Chapter 7, we know that two things must be represented: the value of the dealer's hand and whether the hand is soft—that is, whether the hand contains an ace that is being counted as 11. We define the following operations on values of the abstract type *Dealer*:

NewGame (aDealer)	Initializes *aDealer* to play a new game. The value of the hand is set to zero and the soft count indicator is set to indicate "not soft."
Hit (aDealer, card)	Causes the dealer to hit by taking a card of the given value. This operation has no effect if the dealer has stayed or busted. If the new card is an ace, it will be counted as 11 if this can be done without busting. If the hand already contains an ace counted as 11, and the new card would cause the dealer to bust, the existing ace will be counted as 1 in an attempt to avoid busting.
StayQ (aDealer)	Returns *true* if the dealer has stayed but not busted and returns *false* otherwise.
BustQ (aDealer)	Returns *true* if the dealer has busted and returns *false* otherwise.

Figure 8-5 shows the implementation of the abstract data type *Dealer*. The implementation contains the following constant and type definitions:

```
const
    ace           = 1;
    aceDifference = 10;
    stayLimit     = 16;
    bustLimit     = 21;
type
    dealer = record
                soft     : Boolean;
                curCount : integer
             end;
```

The constant *ace* represents the lower of the two possible values for an ace; *aceDifference* represents the difference between the higher and lower values; *stayLimit* represents the count beyond which the dealer must stay; and *bustLimit* represents the value beyond which the dealer busts. Values of the Pascal type *dealer* represent values of the abstract type *Dealer*. Each value of type *dealer* has two fields: a Boolean field *soft*, which indicates whether the count is soft, and an integer field *curCount*, which contains the value of the dealer's hand.

NewGame and *Hit*, which modify the value of *aDealer*, are implemented as procedures with *aDealer* as a variable parameter. The operations *StayQ*, *BustQ*, and *Count*, which do not modify or create a value of the abstract type, are implemented as functions with *aDealer* as a value parameter.

The procedure *NewGame* initializes the value of *aDealer* for a new game by setting the field *soft* to *false* and the field *curCount* to zero.

Figure 8-5.

Implementation of the abstract data type *Dealer*.

{ ******************** Implementation of *Dealer* ******************** }

```
const
  ace           = 1;  { low value for ace }
  aceDifference = 10; { difference between two values for ace }
  stayLimit     = 16; { count beyond which dealer must stay }
  bustLimit     = 21; { count beyond which dealer busts }
type
  dealer = record
             soft     : Boolean; { Is an ace being counted as 11? }
             curCount : integer   { current value of hand }
           end;
```

{------------------------------ Procedure *NewGame* ------------------------------ }

```
procedure NewGame (var aDealer : dealer);
```

{ Initialize dealer for new game }

```
begin
  aDealer.soft := false;
  aDealer.curCount := 0;
end; { NewGame }
```

{------------------------------------ Procedure *Hit* ------------------------------------ }

```
procedure Hit (var aDealer : dealer; card : integer);
```

{ Accept value of next card. Take no action if dealer cannot hit or has
  busted. }

```
begin
  with aDealer do
    begin
      if curCount <= stayLimit then
        begin
          curCount := curCount + card;
          if (card = ace) and not soft then
            begin
              curCount := curCount + aceDifference;
              soft := true
            end;
          if (curCount > bustLimit) and soft then
            begin
              curCount := curCount − aceDifference;
              soft := false
            end
        end
    end
end; { Hit }
```

Figure 8-5.   *Continued.*

```
{ ------------------------------- Function StayQ ------------------------------ }

function StayQ (aDealer : dealer) : Boolean;

{ Return true if dealer has stayed and false otherwise }

begin
  with aDealer do
    begin
      StayQ := (curCount > stayLimit) and (curCount <= bustLimit)
    end
end; { StayQ }

{ ------------------------------- Function BustQ ------------------------------ }

function BustQ (aDealer : dealer) : Boolean;

{ Return true if dealer has busted and false otherwise }

begin
  BustQ := (aDealer.curCount > bustLimit)
end; { BustQ }

{ ------------------------------- Function Count ------------------------------ }

function Count (aDealer : dealer) : integer;

{ Return current count }

begin
  Count := aDealer.curCount
end; { Count }
```

```
procedure NewGame (var aDealer : dealer);
begin
  aDealer.soft := false;
  aDealer.curCount := 0;
end;
```

The procedure *Hit* does most of the actual work of implementing the blackjack machine. Because of the greater complexity of the procedure, a **with** statement is used to simplify the code by allowing the prefix "*aDealer.*" to be omitted before the field identifiers. Since the procedure has no effect if the dealer has stayed or busted, the statements that change the value of *aDealer* are executed only if the value of *curCount* is less than or equal to *stayLimit*.

The statements that change the value of *aDealer* are very similar to the corresponding statements in the program in Chapter 7. The value of the card is added to the current count. If the card is an ace and the count is not soft, then the ace is counted as 11. If the count is greater than *bustLimit* and the hand is soft, the ace that makes the hand soft is counted as 1 in an attempt to avoid busting.

```
curCount := curCount + card;
if (card = ace) and not soft then
   begin
      curCount := curCount + aceDifference;
      soft := true
   end;
if (curCount > bustLimit) and soft then
   begin
      curCount := curCount - aceDifference;
      soft := false
   end
```

The Boolean function *StayQ* returns *true* if *aDealer.curCount* is greater than *stayLimit* but less than or equal to *bustLimit*. A **with** statement is used to simplify the Boolean expression.

```
function StayQ (aDealer : dealer) : Boolean;
begin
   with aDealer do
      begin
         StayQ := (curCount > stayLimit) and
                  (curCount <= bustLimit)
      end
end;
```

The Boolean function *BustQ* returns *true* if the value of *aDealer.curCount* exceeds *bustLimit*.

```
function BustQ (aDealer : dealer) : Boolean;
begin
   BustQ := (aDealer.curCount > bustLimit)
end;
```

The integer function *Count* returns the value of *aDealer.curCount*.

```
function Count (aDealer : dealer) : integer;
begin
   Count := aDealer.curCount
end;
```

Review Questions

1. Characterize the simple, structured, and pointer data types.

2. Describe how types are defined in Pascal.

3. Give the order in which the various definition and declaration parts must appear in a program written in standard Pascal. Why is this order often inconvenient?

4. Describe the enumerated types.

5. Why is defining an enumerated type superior to using values of some existing type (such as integers or characters) for representing a small number of discrete values?

6. Describe the computer-science concept of a subtype. Give two instances of subtyping in Pascal. Does Pascal recognize subtyping in every instance in which it may seem to be intuitively reasonable?

7. Describe the subrange types. What determines the order of the values of a subrange type?

8. Describe the set types. Characterize the values that can belong to sets. What implementation-dependent restriction applies to values of set types?

9. Describe the record types. What is a field? A field identifier? A field designator?

10. Contrast entire values and variables with component values and variables.

11. Distinguish between packed and unpacked data types.

12. What are anonymous data types? In what Pascal contexts are anonymous data types forbidden?

13. Give the rule for determining when two programmer-defined Pascal data types are equivalent (identical, the same). Contrast name equivalence and structural equivalence. Which is used in Pascal? Why?

14. Give the rules determining when two Pascal data types are compatible.

15. What is assignment compatibility? Give the rules for determining when a value of one Pascal data type is assignment compatible with another type.

16. Give examples of how the concepts of name equivalence, compatibility, and assignment compatibility are used to state the restrictions that apply to Pascal program constructions.

17. Define data abstraction. Why is it sometimes referred to as information hiding?

18. What is an abstract data type? Give three ways in which abstract data types can be defined. Which way is used in this book?

19. What is an encapsulation construction? How do such constructions aid the implementation of abstract data types? Why are some extended versions of Pascal better suited than standard Pascal for implementing abstract data types?

20. Why can an abstract data type often be thought of as defining an abstract machine?

Exercises

1. Modify the Sieve of Eratosthenes program (Figure 8-1) so that instead of printing each prime number as it is generated, the program constructs a set of all prime numbers in the given range. When prime-number generation is complete, the program should print all the numbers belonging to the set of prime numbers it has created.

2. It is clear that, aside from 2, all prime numbers are odd integers. Since only a limited range of integer values can be stored in *sieve*, we can generate primes in a larger range if every element of *sieve* represents an odd integer. We can represent an odd integer greater than 2 by an (odd or even) integer n as follows. The expression $2n + 3$ yields an odd integer greater than 2 if n is an (odd or even) integer greater than or equal to 0. For example, if n is any integer in the range $0..255$, then the value of $2n + 3$ will be an odd integer in the range $3..513$. Using these ideas, modify the program shown in Figure 8-1 to increase the range over which prime numbers can be found. *Hint:* Suppose *prime* $= 2n + 3$ for some n. What value should be repeatedly added to n to step the value of $2n + 3$ through the odd multiples of *prime*?

3. Define and implement an abstract data type *WordCounter* that counts the words in a piece of text. Words are sequences of nonspace characters separated by spaces (or carriage returns, which Pascal reads in as spaces). Type *WordCounter* provides the following operations:

> *Reset (aWordCounter)*
> *EnterChar (aWordCounter, character)*
> *Count (aWordCounter)*

Reset creates a new word counter with reading zero. *EnterChar* transmits a character of the text to the word counter. *Count* returns the number of words counted so far. A value of type *WordCounter* must include the current word count and an indication of whether the most recently entered character was a space.

4. An essential component of all language processors is a *scanner*, which breaks a program down into its smallest meaningful constituents (called *tokens*) such as identifiers, numbers, and operators. Write a scanner for a simple programming language that contains identifiers, integer constants, and operators. Identifiers and integers should be defined as in Pascal. Operators should be sequences of special symbols such as $+$, $;$, $<=$, and $:=$. A program must end with a period, which may not occur in an identifier, integer, or operator. The scanner should print each token on a separate line and identify it as an identifier, integer, or operator. Spaces and carriage returns (which Pascal reads in as spaces) should be ignored. Thus the one-statement program

```
cost := base + rate * quantity.
```

will be printed as

```
cost            identifier
:=              operator
base            identifier
+               operator
rate            identifier
*               operator
quantity        identifier
                end of program
```

Hints: A scanner classifies a token by its first character. For each token, the scanner reads and ignores any spaces until a nonspace character is read. A **case** statement examines this character, which is the first character of a token, and selects the code for reading in the rest of the token. The code for reading a token reads characters as long as they belong to a particular set. A character not belonging to the set signals the end of the token. Our program will print each character it reads and, at the end of each token, print the kind of token and go to a new line. After each token has been read, the program will again skip spaces until a nonspace character is read, then use the **case** statement to select the code for reading the next token.

5. The scanner described in Exercise 4 is deficient in that any sequence of special symbols will be run together into a single operator. Thus in

```
result := (2+3)*(7-5)
```

)*(will be printed as a single operator. Modify the scanner to distinguish between symbols such as (,), and ∗, which never combine with other symbols, and symbols such as : and <, which can combine with other symbols as in :=, <=, and <>.

6. Specify and implement an abstract data type *Scanner* with the following operations:

> *NewScanner (aScanner)*
> *Enter (aScanner, character)*
> *CurrentToken (aScanner)*
> *NewTokenQ (aScanner)*

NewScanner initializes a new scanner. *Enter* enters the current input character into a scanner. *CurrentToken* returns a value of the enumerated type (*identifier*, *int*, *operator*, *space*, *endOfProgram*) indicating the token or other classification to which the last character entered belongs. *NewTokenQ* returns *true* after the first character of an identifier, integer, or operator is entered and returns *false* otherwise. *CurrentToken* returns *endOfProgram* when a period is entered and continues to return *endOfProgram* for any subsequent characters (the scanner must be reset with *NewScanner* before it can be used to scan another program). *Hint*: A value of type *Scanner* must specify the values to be returned by *CurrentToken* and *NewTokenQ*.

7. Modify the abstract data type *Scanner* (Exercise 6) to recognize comments and strings. A comment is any sequence of characters, other than a brace, enclosed by { and }. A string is any sequence of characters (other than an apostrophe; embedded apostrophes are not allowed) enclosed by apostrophes. The delimiting braces, { and }, are considered part of a comment and (for the purposes of this exercise) the delimiting apostrophes are considered part of a string. Comments and strings will present a problem because the end of a comment or string is signaled by the last character of the token rather than the first character that does not belong to the token. One solution to this problem is for a value of type *Scanner* to contain a flag that is set to *true* only when the previous character processed was the terminating character of a comment or string.

8. Specify and implement an abstract data type *Calculator* with the following operations:

> *ReadDisplay (aCalculator)*
> *Clear (aCalculator)*
> *Enter (aCalculator, entry)*
> *Add (aCalculator, entry)*

Subtract (aCalculator, entry)
Multiply (aCalculator, entry)
Divide (aCalculator, entry)
ChangeSign (aCalculator)
Save (aCalculator)
Recall (aCalculator)

A calculator has a display and an internal memory register; *ReadDisplay* returns the value of the display. *Clear* clears both the display and the memory register. *Enter* enters a number into the display. *Add, Subtract, Multiply,* and *Divide* carry out the corresponding arithmetic operation on the value of the display and the number entered; the result is stored in the display. *ChangeSign* changes the sign of the value of the display. *Save* copies the value of the display to the internal memory register, and *Recall* copies the value of the internal memory register to the display.

9. Define and implement an abstract type *ComplexNumber*. Complex numbers are pairs of real numbers denoted as (x, y); x and y are, respectively, the *real* and *imaginary* parts of the complex number. Two complex numbers are equal if and only if their respective real and imaginary parts are equal. Arithmetic for complex numbers is defined by the following equations:

$$(x, y) + (u, v) = (x + y, u + v)$$
$$(x, y) - (u, v) = (x - y, u - v)$$
$$(x, y) * (u, v) = (xu - yv, xv + yu)$$
$$(x, y) / (u, v) = ((xu + yv)/d, (yu - xv)/d)$$
$$\text{where } d = u^2 + v^2$$

It is an error if the value of d is zero.

10. Define and implement an abstract data type *RndNumbGen* that generates pseudorandom integers in a given range. *RndNumbGen* has the following operations:

Initialize (aRndNumbGen, seed, lower, upper)
NextRndNumb (aRndNumbGen, rndNumb)

Initialize provides the random number generator with a seed value and sets the lower and upper limits of the range in which the random integers are to lie. *NextRndNumb* sets *rndNumb* to the next random integer produced by *aRndNumbGen*.

11. Design and implement an abstract data type *Craps* for playing craps. There should be operations to (a) initialize a craps-playing machine giving it the size of the player's bankroll and a seed for its random number generator, (b) place a bet, (c) roll the dice one time and return the values rolled and whether the player won, lost, or must continue trying to make a point, and (d) return the current size of the player's bankroll. Where appropriate, an operation should provide an error parameter that is set to *true* if an erroneous operation is attempted and to *false* otherwise. It is erroneous to begin rolling the dice before a bet is placed for the current game or to place a bet before the current game has been completed. *Craps* should use an implementation of *RndNumbGen* (Exercise 10) to generate random numbers.

12. In *circular arithmetic* (also known as *clockface arithmetic* and *modulo arithmetic*), integers ranging from zero up to some limit behave as if they are arranged around a circle. If we start at zero and move around the circle in the

direction of increasing integers, we will eventually come back to zero. Examples are the minutes and seconds on the face of a clock, which go from 0 to 59 and then back to zero; the degrees in an angle, which go from 0 to 359 and then back to zero; and the reading of any counter that goes back to zero after reaching its maximum possible reading. If the integers range from 0 through *limit*, then an integer greater than *limit* can be reduced to the proper range by dividing by *limit* + 1 and taking the remainder; that is, by evaluating

> *number* **mod** (*limit* + 1)

Design and implement an abstract data type *CircNum* whose values range from 0 to *limit*, where *limit* can be defined as a Pascal constant. The following operations should be provided:

> *MakeCircNum (aCircNum, aNonnegativeInteger, error)*
> *Add (op1, op2)*
> *Multiply (op1, op2)*
> *ValueOf (aCircNum)*

MakeCircNum makes a circular number by reducing a nonnegative integer to the proper range; it is an error if the integer supplied is negative. *Add* and *Multiply* return the sums and products of circular numbers, which are computed by finding the integer sums and products and reducing them to the proper range. *ValueOf* returns the integer value of a circular number; this function need not be implemented if *CircNum* is implemented as a type that is assignment compatible with type *integer*.

13. A police department has a number of gangster hideouts under surveillance and wants to use a computer program to keep track of the occupants of each hideout. Each hideout will be represented by a value of the abstract type *Hideout*. The gangsters will be represented by an enumerated type with values such as *mugsy, lefty, bugsy, knuckles*, and *scarface*. The type *Hideout* provides the following operations:

> *NewHideout (aHideout)*
> *Enter (aHideout, aGangster)*
> *Leave (aHideout, aGangster)*
> *InsideQ (aHideout, aGangster)*
> *ErrorQ (aHideout, aGangster)*

NewHideout creates an empty hideout containing no gangsters and having no error conditions. *Enter* and *Leave* are invoked when a particular gangster is seen to enter or leave a particular hideout. *InsideQ* returns *true* if a particular gangster is inside a particular hideout, and *false* otherwise. *ErrorQ* returns *true* if an error has been made in tracking a particular gangster; for instance, if Lefty has been seen to enter a hideout in which he was thought to be already or was seen leaving a hideout in which he was not thought to be present.

Arrays and Abstract Data Types

In this chapter, we continue our study of both arrays and abstract data types by considering the array implementations of four abstract types: *Multiset*, *Directory*, *Grid*, and *Matrix*. *Multiset* and *Directory* are implemented with one-dimensional arrays; *Grid* and *Matrix* are implemented with two-dimensional arrays.

An essential feature of abstract data types is that the method of implementation is independent of the abstract definition of the type. Thus *Multiset*, *Directory*, *Grid*, and *Matrix* can also be implemented using structures other than arrays; the most common alternative structures for these types are the linked lists introduced in Chapter 13. Chapter 13 presents a linked-list implementation of *Directory*, and an exercise in Chapter 13 invites the reader to construct a linked-list implementation of *Multiset*.

Multisets

In both mathematics and Pascal, a set does not distinguish repeated occurrences of an element. Inserting an element in a set to which the element already belongs has no effect on the set. As a consequence, there is no way to determine how many times an element of a set has been inserted in that set. A set that does distinguish repeated occurrences of an element is called a *multiset*. Given a multiset, we can determine how many times each element occurs in the set. Multisets are frequently used in collecting statistics, where we wish to keep a running count of the occurrences of each kind of item or event in which we are interested.

The Abstract Data Type *Multiset*

As with ordinary sets, we assume that there is a base type containing all the values that can belong to a multiset. A multiset is characterized by the number of times each value of the base type occurs in the multiset; thus two multisets are equal if each value of the base type occurs the same number of times in each multiset. If a value of the base type does not belong to a multiset, the number of occurrences of that value is zero. The following operations are defined for the abstract data type *Multiset*:

Clear (aMultiset)	Sets *aMultiset* to the null multiset that contains zero occurrences of every value of the base type.

Insert (aMultiset, element)	Inserts the value of *element* into *aMultiset*. The number of occurrences of the value of *element* is increased by one.
Remove (aMultiset, element)	Removes the value of *element* from *aMultiset*. The number of occurrences of the value of *element* is decreased by one. If the number of occurrences of *element* is already zero, the remove operation has no effect.
Count (aMultiset, element)	Returns the number of occurrences of the value of *element* in *aMultiset*.
TotalCount (aMultiset)	Returns the total number of elements in *aMultiset*.
Union (op1, op2, result)	Sets *result* to the result of combining the contents of multisets *op1* and *op2*. Repeated occurrences of identical values are distinguished regardless of the operand set in which each value originated. The number of occurrences of an element in *result* is the sum of the number of occurrences of that element in *op1* and *op2*.

Note that two multisets *multi1* and *multi2* are equal if

$$Count(multi1, element) = Count(multi2, element)$$

is true for every value *element* of the base type.

Implementing Multisets

Since a multiset is characterized by the number of occurrences of each value of the base type, an obvious implementation is an array of nonnegative integers indexed by the base type. For each index value belonging to the base type, the corresponding array component gives the number of occurrences of that value in the multiset. This implementation is preferable when the number of values in the base type is small, as for an enumerated type or a small subrange of a larger type. An implementation that is more suitable for large base types, such as *integer*, is described in Exercise 2 at the end of this chapter.

To make our implementations as general as possible, we will often leave some definitions and declarations to be supplied by the program in which the implementation is to be used. By supplying the omitted definitions and declarations, we can customize our implementation for use with a particular program. Thus we will leave it to the program that uses our multiset implementation to define the ordinal type *baseType*, which is the base type of the multisets. Our implementation will work regardless of the definition supplied. The program using the implementation must also supply identifiers *firstElement* and *lastElement* representing the smallest and largest values of *baseType*.

These identifiers can be constant identifiers, identifiers representing values of enumerated types, or variables to which the appropriate values are assigned in the main program.

Figure 9-1 shows an implementation of the abstract data type *Multiset*. Assuming *baseType* to be already defined, we define the type *multiset* as follows:

type
    multiset = **array** [*baseType*] **of** 0..*maxint*;

If *multi* is a variable of type *multiset* and the value of *element* belongs to the base type, then the value of *multi[element]* is the number of occurrences of the value of *element* in the multiset *multi*.

Figure 9-1.   Implementation of the abstract data type *Multiset*.

{ ****************** Implementation of *Multiset* ****************** }

{ Type *baseType* and constants or initialized variables *firstElement*
    (smallest value of *baseType*) and *lastElement* (largest value of
    baseType) are supplied by program using *Multiset* }

type
    multiset = **array** [*baseType*] **of** 0..*maxint*;

{--------------------------------- Procedure *Clear* --------------------------------- }

procedure *Clear* (**var** *aMultiset* : *multiset*);

{ Initialize multiset to contain no elements }

var
    element : *baseType*;
begin
    for *element* := *firstElement* **to** *lastElement* **do**
        aMultiset[element] := 0
end; { *Clear* }

{--------------------------------- Procedure *Insert* --------------------------------- }

procedure *Insert* (**var** *aMultiset* : *multiset*;
                    element   : *baseType*);

{ Insert a given element into a multiset }

begin
    aMultiset[element] := *aMultiset[element]* + 1
end; { *Insert* }

Figure 9-1. *Continued.*

```
{ -------------------------------- Procedure Remove -------------------------------- }

procedure Remove (var aMultiset : multiset;
                      element        : baseType);

{ Remove a given element from a multiset. No action is taken if given
  element does not belong to the multiset. }

begin
  if aMultiset[element] > 0 then
    aMultiset[element] := aMultiset[element] − 1
end; { Remove }

{ -------------------------------- Function Count -------------------------------- }

function Count (var aMultiset : multiset;
                    element        : baseType) : integer;

{ Return number of occurrences of element in multiset }

begin
  Count := aMultiset[element]
end; { Count }

{ -------------------------------- Function TotalCount -------------------------------- }

function TotalCount (var aMultiset : multiset) : integer;

{ Return total number of elements in multiset }

var
  element : baseType;
  total      : integer;
begin
  total := 0;
  for element := firstElement to lastElement do
    total := total + aMultiset[element];
  TotalCount := total
end; { TotalCount }

{ -------------------------------- Procedure Union -------------------------------- }

procedure Union (var op1, op2, result : multiset);

{ Compute the union of two multisets }

var
  element : baseType;
begin
  for element := firstElement to lastElement do
    result[element] := op1[element] + op2[element]
end; { Union }
```

The procedure *Clear* creates a multiset in which the number of occurrences of each element is zero.

```
procedure Clear (var aMultiset : multiset);
var
   element : baseType;
begin
   for element := firstElement to lastElement do
      aMultiset[element] := 0
end;
```

The procedure *Insert* inserts an element into a multiset by adding one to the corresponding component of the multiset array.

```
procedure Insert (var aMultiset : aMultiset;
                      element       : baseType);
begin
   aMultiset[element] := aMultiset[element] + 1
end;
```

The procedure *Remove* removes an element from a multiset by subtracting one from the corresponding component of the multiset array. The subtraction is done only if at least one instance of the element already belongs to the multiset; that is, if the corresponding array component is greater than zero.

```
procedure Remove (var aMultiset : multiset;
                      element       : baseType);
begin
   if aMultiset[element] > 0 then
      aMultiset[element] := aMultiset[element] − 1
end;
```

The function *Count* returns the number of occurrences of an element in a multiset, which is just the value of the corresponding component of the multiset array.

```
function Count (var aMultiset : multiset;
                    element       : baseType) : integer;
begin
   Count := aMultiset[element]
end;
```

The function *TotalCount* returns the total number of elements in the multiset, which is the sum of all the components of the multiset array.

```
function TotalCount (var aMultiset : multiset) : integer;
var
   element : baseType;
   total    : integer;
begin
   total := 0;
   for element := firstElement to lastElement do
      total := total + aMultiset[element];
   TotalCount := total
end;
```

The procedure *Union* combines two multisets by adding the corresponding components of the multiset arrays.

```
procedure Union (var op1, op2, result : multiset);
var
    element : baseType;
begin
    for element := firstElement to lastElement do
        result[element] := op1[element] + op2[element]
end;
```

Note that arrays have been passed as variable parameters even when it would have been possible to pass them as value parameters. When arrays are passed as value parameters, they are copied into the activation record of each function or procedure activation; since arrays are often large, this copying is often excessively time-consuming.

Example 9-1. *A Program Using a Multiset*

Figure 9-4 shows a program that uses a multiset to count the number of A's, B's, C's, D's, and F's made by the students in a class. The program displays the grade counts as a bar graph; a bar graph display of such counts (or *frequencies*, as they are called in statistics) is called a *histogram*. A histogram can be thought of as a graphical representation of a multiset.

Since our grade-counting program is to use our implementation of multisets, all the declarations and definitions of Figure 9-1 need to be included in Figure 9-2. For clarity and simplicity, however, we will not actually copy the text of the implementation into the program, but merely indicate with the following comment that the multiset implementation is to be included:

{ *** Include *Multiset* *** }

Figure 9-2.

This program for counting grades and printing a histogram uses our implementation of the abstract data type *Multiset*.

---

program *GradeStatistics* (*input*, *output*);

{ Compute grade distribution and display as histogram }

{*** Include *Multiset* *** }

```
type
    baseType = (gradeF, gradeD, gradeC,
                gradeB, gradeA);              { used by Multiset }
var
    firstElement   : baseType;              { used by Multiset }
    lastElement    : baseType;              { used by Multiset }
```

Figure 9-2.   *Continued.*

```
    grade           : baseType;                        { internal representation
                                                          of letter grade }
    score           : 0..100;                          { numerical score }
    index           : integer;                         { array index and
                                                          control variable }
    scoreToGrade : array [0..100] of baseType; { translation table }
    gradeToLetter : array [baseType] of char;   { translation table }
    gradeSet        : multiset;                        { multiset of grades }
begin

{ Initialize firstElement, lastElement, translation tables, and gradeSet }

    firstElement := gradeF; lastElement := gradeA;

    for index := 0 to 59 do scoreToGrade[index] := gradeF;
    for index := 60 to 69 do scoreToGrade[index] := gradeD;
    for index := 70 to 79 do scoreToGrade[index] := gradeC;
    for index := 80 to 89 do scoreToGrade[index] := gradeB;
    for index := 90 to 100 do scoreToGrade[index] := gradeA;

    gradeToLetter[gradeF] := 'F';
    gradeToLetter[gradeD] := 'D';
    gradeToLetter[gradeC] := 'C';
    gradeToLetter[gradeB] := 'B';
    gradeToLetter[gradeA] := 'A';

    Clear (gradeSet);

{ Read and count grades }

    while not eof(input) do
      begin
        read (score);
        Insert (gradeSet, scoreToGrade[score])
      end;

{ Print histogram }

    writeln ('Grade Histogram: ');
    writeln;
    for grade := gradeA downto gradeF do
      begin
        write (gradeToLetter[grade], ' ' :3);
        for index := 1 to Count(gradeSet, grade) do
          write ('*');
        writeln
      end;
    writeln;
    writeln ('Student Count: ', TotalCount(gradeSet) :1)
end.
```

Remember that—for standard Pascal, at least—all the definition and declaration parts from both the implementation and the main program must be arranged in the proper order; the constant definition part must be first, the type definition part must be second, and so on. If a particular kind of declaration or definition part (such as a type definition part) occurs in both the implementation and the main program, then the two corresponding parts must be combined so that the final program contains only one constant definition part, one type definition part, and so on. In each definition or declaration part, main-program definitions or declarations that *are used by* the implementation must *precede* the definitions or declarations brought in from the implementation. Main program definitions or declarations that *make use of* the implementation must *follow* the definitions and declarations brought in from the implementation.

The type definition and variable declaration parts for the main program follow:

```
type
    baseType = (gradeF, gradeD, gradeC, gradeB, gradeA);
var
    firstElement  : baseType;
    lastElement   : baseType;
    grade         : baseType;
    score         : 0..100;
    index         : integer;
    scoreToGrade  : array [0..100] of baseType;
    gradeToLetter : array [baseType] of char;
    gradeSet      : multiset;
```

The program defines *baseType* as an enumerated type whose five values represent each of the five possible letter grades. We would like (if it were possible) to define *firstElement* as a constant equal to *gradeF* and *lastElement* as a constant equal to *gradeA*. This is not possible, however, because the constant definition part must precede the type definition part in which *gradeF* and *gradeA* are defined, and the identifiers *gradeF* and *gradeA* cannot be used to define constants before they themselves are defined. Therefore, we declare *firstElement* and *lastElement* as variables; the first line of the main program assigns these variables the desired values, which they retain throughout the program.

    firstElement := *gradeF*; *lastElement* := *gradeA*

Thus *firstElement* and *lastElement* are used like constants even though they are actually variables.

Another important application of arrays is illustrated by *scoreToGrade* and *gradeToLetter*. An array can be used as a *translation table* to translate or map one set of values to another. The index type for the array is the set of values to be translated; the component type is the type of the translated values. Each value of the index type is translated into the value of the corresponding component of the array. The array *scoreToGrade* translates from numeric scores in the range 0–100 to *gradeF*, *gradeD*, and so on, according to the usual scale (0–59 translate to *gradeF*, 60–69 translate to *gradeD*, and so on). The index type of *scoreToGrade* is 0..100 and the component type is *baseType*.

Likewise, the array *gradeToLetter* translates *gradeF*, *gradeD*, and so on into the actual letter grades 'F', 'D', and so on. The index type of *gradeToLetter* is *baseType* and the component type is *char*.

Translation tables must be initialized before they can be used. Characteristically, Pascal provides no array constructor that would allow an array to be initialized merely by listing the values of its components. Each component variable must be initialized individually with an assignment statement. If many components have the same value, however, or if the component values can be computed, then **for** statements can be used to simplify the initialization process. *scoreToGrade* is initialized with the following statements:

```
for index := 0 to 59 do scoreToGrade[index] := gradeF;
for index := 60 to 69 do scoreToGrade[index] := gradeD;
for index := 70 to 79 do scoreToGrade[index] := gradeC;
for index := 80 to 89 do scoreToGrade[index] := gradeB;
for index := 90 to 100 do scoreToGrade[index] := gradeA
```

gradeToLetter is initialized with the following statements:

```
gradeToLetter[gradeF] := 'F';
gradeToLetter[gradeD] := 'D';
gradeToLetter[gradeC] := 'C';
gradeToLetter[gradeB] := 'B';
gradeToLetter[gradeA] := 'A'
```

The data collected by the program will be stored in the multiset variable *gradeSet*. The program clears *gradeSet* with *Clear*, then reads the numerical scores from the input file. Each score is converted to a grade with *scoreToGrade* and inserted into the multiset with *Insert*.

```
Clear (gradeSet);
while not eof(input) do
  begin
    read (score);
    Insert (gradeSet, scoreToGrade[score])
  end;
```

To print the results as a histogram, a **for** statement steps through all the values of *baseType*; *Count* is used to obtain the number of occurrences of each value in *gradeSet*. For each value of *baseType*, the program prints the corresponding letter grade and then (using another **for** statement) prints one asterisk for each occurrence of the value in *gradeSet*. Note the use of *gradeToLetter* to translate values of *baseType* to letter grades. Finally, *TotalCount* is used to obtain the total number of elements of *gradeSet*, which is printed for the user. The code looks like this:

```
for grade := gradeA downto gradeF do
  begin
    write (gradeToLetter[grade], ' ' :3);
    for index := 1 to Count(gradeSet, grade) do
      write ('*');
    writeln
  end;
writeln;
writeln ('Student Count: ', TotalCount(gradeSet) :1)
```

A typical printout looks like this:

```
A      * * * * *
B      * * * *
C      * * * * * *
D      * *
F      *

Student Count: 18
```

Directories

One of the most common methods of accessing data is to look up a value in a table or directory. We look up a name in the telephone directory to obtain the person's phone number or address; we look up a word in the dictionary to find its definition and related information; we look up a number in one column of a mathematical table to obtain the related values in other columns. Such directories and tables go under various names; the term we will use here is *directory*. In this section we will specify and implement the abstract data type *Directory*.

The Abstract Data Type *Directory*

A directory is made up of *entries*, each of which consists of a *key* (the item that we look up) and a *value* (the information that we are trying to find). Since each key must identify a unique entry, no two entries can have the same key. The value part of an entry can be a record or array and hence can contain as much related information as we wish. For example, the key of an entry in a telephone directory is the name, and the value can be thought of as a record with two fields: the address and the telephone number.

We define the following operations for values of the abstract data type *Directory*:

Clear (aDirectory)	Sets *aDirectory* to the empty directory, which contains no entries.
Insert (aDirectory, insertKey, insertValue, error)	Inserts in *aDirectory* a new entry with key *insertKey* and value *insertValue*. If an error occurs, *error* is set to *true* and *aDirectory* is not changed; otherwise, *error* is set to *false*. An error occurs if an entry with key *insertKey* is already present or if there is no room in the directory for another entry.
Lookup (aDirectory, searchKey, valueFound, error)	Searches *aDirectory* for the entry with key *searchKey*; if such an entry is found,

	valueFound is set to the value part of the entry and *error* is set to *false*. If no entry with key *searchkey* is found, *error* is set to *true*.
Delete (aDirectory, deleteKey, error)	Searches *aDirectory* for an entry with key *deleteKey*; if such an entry is found, that entry is removed from *aDirectory* and *error* is set to *false*; if no such entry is found, *error* is set to *true*.

Implementing Directories

There are many approaches to implementing directories; in this chapter we take the most obvious approach of implementing a directory as an array of entries. Each entry will be a record having a key field and a value field. The complete implementation appears in Figure 9-3.

Figure 9-3.

Implementation of the abstract data type *Directory*.

{ ****************** Implementation of *Directory* ****************** }

{ Constant *maxEntries* and types *keyType* and *valueType* are defined in the program using *Directory* }

```
type
  indexType = 0..maxEntries;
  entry     = record
                key   : keyType;   { key of directory entry }
                value : valueType  { data stored in directory entry }
              end;
  directory = record
                free  : indexType;                { index of first unused
                                                    component of table }
                table : array [indexType] of entry { array of entries }
              end;
```

{--------------------------------- *Procedure Search* --------------------------------- }

```
procedure Search (var aDirectory : directory;
                  searchKey      : keyType;
                  var found      : Boolean;
                  var index      : indexType);
```

{ Locate entry, if any, with given key; set *found* to reflect outcome of search; if search successful, set *index* to the index in *aDirectory.table* of the entry found }

Figure 9-3. *Continued.*

```
var
   ndx : indexType;
begin
   with aDirectory do
     begin
       table[free].key := searchKey;
       ndx := 0;
       while table[ndx].key <> searchKey do
         ndx := ndx + 1;
       if ndx < free then
         begin
           index := ndx;
           found := true
         end
       else
         found := false
     end
end; { Search }
```

{ ---------------------------------- Procedure *Clear* ---------------------------------- }

```
procedure Clear (var aDirectory : directory);
```

{ Remove all entries from a directory }

```
begin
   aDirectory.free := 0
end; { Clear }
```

{ ---------------------------------- Procedure *Insert* ---------------------------------- }

```
procedure Insert (var aDirectory : directory;
                      insertKey      : keyType;
                      insertValue    : valueType;
                      var error      : Boolean);
```

{ Insert a new entry into a directory }

```
var
   found : Boolean;
   index : indexType;
begin
   Search (aDirectory, insertKey, found, index);
   with aDirectory do
     if found or (free = maxEntries) then
       error := true
```

Figure 9-3.　　*Continued.*

```
     else
       begin
         error := false;
         table[free].key := insertKey;
         table[free].value := insertValue;
         free := free + 1
       end
 end; { Insert }
```

{ ------------------------------- Procedure *Lookup* ------------------------------- }

```
procedure Lookup (var aDirectory  : directory;
                      searchKey    : keyType;
                      var valueFound : valueType;
                      var error      : Boolean);
```

{ Look up value corresponding to given key and return value found }

```
var
  found : Boolean;
  index : indexType;
begin
  Search (aDirectory, searchKey, found, index);
  error := not found;
  if found then
    valueFound := aDirectory.table[index].value
end; { Lookup }
```

{ ------------------------------- Procedure *Delete* ------------------------------- }

```
procedure Delete (var aDirectory : directory;
                      deleteKey    : keyType;
                      var error      : Boolean);
```

{ Delete entry with given key }

```
var
  found     : Boolean;
  index, ndx : indexType;
begin
  Search (aDirectory, deleteKey, found, index);
  error := not found;
  if found then
    with aDirectory do
      begin
        for ndx := index to free - 2 do
          table[ndx] := table[ndx + 1];
        free := free - 1
      end
end; { Delete }
```

As we did with multisets, we will allow a program that uses the implementation to provide some basic definitions, thereby customizing the implementation to the needs of that particular program. Any program using the implementation must define an integer constant *maxEntries* (the maximum number of entries a directory can hold) and types *keyType* (the type of keys) and *valueType* (the type of values). The only restriction on the key type is that we be able to compare keys with <>. Typical key types are ordinal types and string types, the latter consisting of packed arrays of characters. If a key has several components, such as a first, middle, and last name, the key type can also be a record type.

In the implementation itself we have the following type definitions:

```
type
    indexType = 0..maxEntries;
    entry     = record
                    key   : keyType;
                    value : valueType
                end;
    directory = record
                    free  : indexType;
                    table : array [indexType] of entry
                end;
```

The type *indexType* is the index type for the directory array. This array must always have at least one unused component in which a sentinel entry can be stored; therefore it must have one more component than the maximum number of entries specified in the program using the implementation. Thus the *indexType* is defined as the subrange 0..*maxEntries*; this subrange contains *maxEntries* + 1 values, so the directory array will contain *maxEntries* + 1 components. A value of type *entry* is a record having a field *key* of type *keyType* and a field *value* of type *valueType*. A value of type *directory* is a record having a field *free* of type *indexType* and an array-of-*entry* field *table*; *table* is the directory array.

The size of the array is determined by the *maximum* number of entries that we can store in the directory; usually, the number of entries actually stored will be less than the maximum, and part of the array will go unused. To specify which part of *table* actually contains entries, *free* is set to the index of the first unused component of *table*. Thus components 0 through *free* − 1 of *table* contain valid entries and components *free* through *maxEntries* are unused. (See Figure 9-4.) When *free* is equal to zero, the directory is empty; when *free* is equal to *maxEntries*, the directory is full.

We need a private procedure, *Search*, to find the entry having a given key. The reason that *Search* is a private procedure is that it returns the index of the entry it finds; other procedures need this index to access or modify the entry. Indexes, however, are only for internal use within the implementation; a program using the implementation has no need to know where an entry is stored in the array (or even whether entries are stored as an array or in some other way). Thus a program using the implementation is required to search the table with the public procedure *Lookup*, which returns only the value part of an entry, not the index at which the entry is stored.

Search uses the simplest (and slowest) search algorithm, which is known as *sequential search* or *linear search*. In sequential search, we start at the beginning of a table and go through it entry by entry, comparing the key of

Figure 9-4.

The value of *free* designates the first component of *table* that is not currently in use. We say that *free* points to the first unused component, and we indicate this relationship graphically by drawing an arrow from the location *free* to the location designated by the value of *free*.

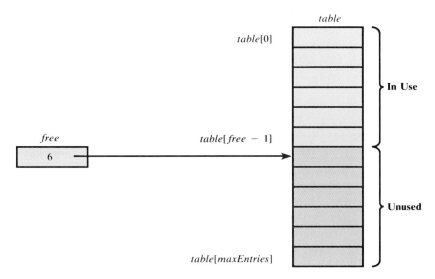

each entry with the key for which we are searching. We stop when we find an entry with the desired key or when we reach the end of the table. In the latter case, the table does not contain an entry with the key for which we are searching.

Sequential search is suitable only for small tables; for example, it would be absurd to look up a name in the telephone directory with sequential search, starting at the beginning of the directory and examining each name in turn. Sequential search does have one advantage besides simplicity: it places minimal requirements on the key values. For sequential search we only have to be able to compare key values with $=$ and $<>$. More advanced search techniques usually take advantage of the order of the keys (just as we use alphabetical order to look up names efficiently in a telephone directory). But these methods require that we be able to compare keys with $<$, $<=$, $>$, and $>=$, as well as $=$ and $<>$.

Referring to the procedure *Search* in Figure 9-3, we see that it uses a **with** statement to allow the omission of the prefix "*aDirectory.*" before the field identifiers *free* and *table*. Our first problem in designing a sequential search is making sure the search stops when it reaches the end of the table (actually, the end of the part of *table* that is in use). The simplest solution is to place a sentinel entry after the last valid entry in the table. What should we use for the sentinel entry? A sequential search is designed to stop when it finds an entry whose key is equal to *searchKey*, the key for which we are looking. Therefore, we can use an entry with key *searchKey* as the sentinel. Thus *Search* begins by storing the value of *searchKey* in the key field of *table*[*free*], the first unused component of *table*.

$$table[free].key := searchKey$$

We require that there always be at least one unused component of *table* available for this sentinel. That is why *table* was given one more component than the maximum number of entries specified by the user program.

We have seen, and will continue to see, how useful the **for** statement is for processing arrays. But the **for** statement is not the best choice for a search, because there is no clean way to terminate the **for** statement when the desired entry is found. With a **while** statement, however, sequential search is straightforward. The index variable *ndx* is initialized to zero so that it designates the first entry of *table*. By incrementing *ndx*, the **while** statement advances from entry to entry until an entry with the desired key is found.

$ndx := 0;$
while *table[ndx].key* <> *searchKey* **do**
$ndx := ndx + 1$

Because we installed a sentinel with the same key as the one for which we are searching, our search will always find an entry with the desired key and the search will always terminate.

When the search terminates, the value of *ndx* will be the index of the entry that was found. We must now determine whether that entry is a valid data entry or whether it is the sentinel we created. The indexes for valid data entries range from 0 through *free* − 1; the index of the sentinel value is *free*. Thus if the value of *ndx* is less than that of *free*, a valid data entry was found; the parameter *index* is set to the index of the entry that was found and the parameter *found* is set to *true*. On the other hand, if the value of *ndx* equals that of *free*, the sentinel entry was found, indicating that there was no valid data entry with the desired key; in this case, the parameter *found* is set to *false*.

if *ndx* < *free* **then**
  begin
    index := *ndx*;
    found := *true*
  end
else
  found := *false*

The public procedures *Clear*, *Insert*, *Lookup*, and *Delete* are straightforward. The simplest of these is *Clear*, which creates an empty directory by setting *free* to zero.

aDirectory.free := 0

Insert begins by calling *Search* to find an entry with *insertKey*, the key of the entry to be inserted. If *Insert* sets *found* to *true*, indicating that the search was successful, then the directory already contains an entry with key *insertKey* and another entry with the same key cannot be inserted. Also, if the value of *free* is equal to that of *maxEntries*, the directory is full and no new entry can be inserted. Thus if *found* or the Boolean expression *free* = *maxEntries* has the value *true*, *error* is set to *true*. Otherwise, *error* is set to *false* and the new entry is stored in *table[free]*, the first unused component of *table*. The value of *free* is then incremented by one so that it is again the index of the first unused component, the one immediately following the newly inserted entry.

```
if found or (free = maxEntries) then
    error := true
else
    begin
        error := false;
        table[free].key := insertKey;
        table[free].value := insertValue;
        free := free + 1
    end
```

Lookup begins by calling *Search* to find the index of the entry whose key is equal to *SearchKey*. An error occurs if *Search* was unable to find such an entry; thus *error* is set to the value of **not** *found*. If an entry with the requested key was found, the parameter *valueFound* is set to the value part of the entry. Note that the value of *index* is used to access the entry that was found by *Search*.

```
Search (aDirectory, searchKey, found, index);
error := not found;
if found then
    valueFound := aDirectory.table[index].value
```

Delete begins by calling *Search* to find the entry to be deleted, the entry whose key is equal to *deleteKey*. It is an error if no such entry is found, so *error* is set to **not** *found*. If an entry with the given key was found, then we must delete that entry.

Deletion from a data structure is often a troublesome operation, because we cannot get rid of the deleted component without changing other parts of the data structure. Either we must mark the deleted component as unused but leave it in place, where it will take up space and possibly make other operations more complicated, or we must rearrange a substantial portion of the data structure to get rid of the deleted component.

In the case at hand, a deleted entry leaves a gap in the array *table*. We follow the second course mentioned and rearrange the components of *table* to get rid of the gap. Specifically, every entry following the one to be deleted must be moved up (that is, toward the beginning of *table*) by one position. Thus the entry following the deleted entry will move up to the position occupied by the deleted entry; the entry following the one that was just moved will be moved up to fill the position just vacated, and so on for all the remaining valid data entries.

Let the value of *index* be the index of the entry to be deleted. We want the value of *ndx* to be stepped through the indexes of all components that are to receive entries moved up from below them. The initial value of *ndx* is, then, the value of *index*, since the component occupied by the entry to be deleted is the first to receive an entry moved up from below. The final value of *ndx* is *free* $-$ 2, since *table*[*free* $-$ 2] receives the value moved up from the former last component in use, *table*[*free* $-$ 1]. After the moves have been made, the value of *free* is decremented by one because there is now one less valid data entry.

```
for ndx := index to free − 2 do
    table[ndx] := table[ndx + 1];
free := free − 1
```

Example 9-2.   *A Program Using a Directory*

Figure 9-5 shows a program for maintaining a price list in main memory. Each entry consists of the catalog number and price of an item of merchandise. The user can insert new entries, delete existing ones, and find the price corresponding to any catalog number. The main limitation of the program is that there is no provision for loading a price list from disk or saving an updated price list to disk. Even in its present form, however, the program can provide a scratchpad for storing temporary prices, such as special prices that are in effect for a short period or recent price changes that have not yet been incorporated into the main price list.

The implementation of *Directory* is to be included in the program *PriceList* in the manner described earlier. Because the type definitions in the implementation depend on the types *keyType* and *valueType*, the type definitions brought in from the implementation must follow the definitions of *keyType* and *valueType* in the type definition part. Several of the procedures in the program call procedures defined in the implementation; therefore, the procedures brought in from the implementation must precede the procedures declared in the program.

As with all programs of any complexity at all, we wish to follow a top-down approach to designing and implementing *PriceList*. How are we to handle abstract data types and their implementations in a top-down design and implementation? One approach is to design and implement the abstract data type in the course of top-down development, just as we do with procedures and functions. If at some point in the top-down design process, we realize that some of the operations needed by the previously designed, higher-level modules can be supplied by an abstract data type, we design the entire abstract data type (rather than designing each procedure and function separately) and implement it in due course.

Another approach is to consider abstract data types and their implementations as off-the-shelf parts that are available for us to use as

Figure 9-5.   This program uses our implementation of the abstract data type *Directory* to maintain a price list in main memory.

---

program *PriceList* (*input*, *output*);

{ Maintain a price list in main memory }

{*** Include *Directory* *** }

const
   maxEntries = 100;   { used by *Directory* }
type
   keyType   = *integer*; { used by *Directory* }
   valueType = *real*;   { used by *Directory* }
var
   priceList   : *directory*; { the price list }
   command : *char*;   { command letter entered by user }

Figure 9-5.   *Continued.*

```
{ ----------------------------- Procedure GetCommand ----------------------------- }

procedure GetCommand (var cmnd : char);

{ Obtain command letter from user and check for validity }

begin
    writeln;
    write ('Insert, Lookup, Delete, or Quit (I/L/D/Q)? ');
    readln (cmnd);
    if not (cmnd in ['i', 'I', 'l', 'L', 'd', 'D', 'q', 'Q']) then
        cmnd := 'E'
end; { GetCommand }


{ -------------------------------- Procedure DoInsert -------------------------------- }

procedure DoInsert (var priceList : directory);

{ Insert new entry into price list }

var
    catalogNum : keyType;
    price       : valueType;
    error       : Boolean;
begin
    write ('Enter catalog number and price: ');
    readln (catalogNum, price);
    Insert (priceList, catalogNum, price, error);
    if error then
        writeln ('Catalog number already present or price list full')
end; { DoInsert }


{ ------------------------------- Procedure DoLookup ------------------------------- }

procedure DoLookup (var priceList : directory);

{ Find price corresponding to given catalog number }

var
    catalogNum : keyType;
    price       : valueType;
    error       : Boolean;
begin
    write ('Enter catalog number: ');
    readln (catalogNum);
    Lookup (priceList, catalogNum, price, error);
    if error then
        writeln ('Catalog number not found')
    else
        writeln ('Price: $', price :1:2)
end; { DoLookup }
```

Figure 9-5.

Continued.

```
{ ------------------------------ Procedure DoDelete ------------------------------ }

procedure DoDelete (var priceList : directory);

{ Remove from price list entry with given catalog number }

var
   catalogNum : keyType;
   error      : Boolean;
begin
   write ('Enter catalog number: ');
   readln (catalogNum);
   Delete (priceList, catalogNum, error);
   if error then
      writeln ('Catalog number not found')
end; { DoDelete }

{ ---------------------------- Procedure DoBadCommand ---------------------------- }

procedure DoBadCommand;

{ Prompt user to retry erroneous command }

begin
   writeln ('Command error--please enter I, L, D, or Q')
end; { DoBadCommand }

{ ------------------------------------ Main Program ------------------------------------ }

begin
   Clear (priceList);
   GetCommand (command);
   while not (command in ['q', 'Q']) do
      begin
         case command of
            'i', 'I'  : DoInsert (priceList);
            'l', 'L'  : DoLookup (priceList);
            'd', 'D'  : DoDelete (priceList);
            'E'       : DoBadCommand
         end;
         GetCommand (command)
      end
end.
```

fundamental building blocks for our programs. The nature of the program tells us which such off-the-shelf parts will be needed. Just as an automobile designer knows from the start that such fundamental parts as an engine, a battery, and a radiator will be needed, so we can conclude that a program for collecting statistics will need a multiset and a program for maintaining a price list will need a directory. Having decided to use a particular abstract data type, we will treat the operations it provides as basic building blocks, just as we do the statements and predefined procedures and functions of Pascal. Thus the lowest level functions and procedures in our design will be those that can be expressed entirely in terms of (1) the statements and predefined functions and procedures of Pascal, and (2) the functions and procedures provided by the abstract data types used by the program. This approach will often be the most natural one for us, since we will often write programs to illustrate applications of abstract data types that we have previously designed and implemented.

Turning to Figure 9-5, the main program declares the price list as a variable *priceList* of type *directory*. The procedure *Clear* (provided by the implementation of *Directory*) is called to initialize *priceList* to the empty directory. The procedure *GetCommand* (which in our top-down development has yet to be written) is called to obtain a single-letter command from the user and assign it to the character variable *command*. The characters returned by *GetCommand* are to be interpreted as follows:

Character	Command	Description
i, I	Insert	Inserts a new entry.
l, L	Look up	Looks up a price.
d, D	Delete	Deletes an entry.
q, Q	Quit	Terminates the program.
E	Error	Indicates that command was none of the above.

Command interpretation is controlled by a **while** statement and a **case** statement. The case statement calls one of the procedures *DoInsert*, *DoLookup*, *DoDelete*, and *DoBadCommand* depending on the command character returned by *GetCommand*. All the procedures except *DoBadCommand* take *priceList* as a variable parameter. *GetCommand* is called to get a new command character before the execution of the **while** statement and after each execution of the **case** statement. The **while** statement executes the **case** statement and *GetCommand* repeatedly until *GetCommand* returns q or Q. Since command letters q and Q are intercepted by the **while** statement, they need not be handled by the **case** statement.

Continuing with the top-down development, we must write the procedures called by the main program but not provided by the implementation of *Directory*. These procedures are *GetCommand*, *DoInsert*, *DoLookup*, *DoDelete*, and *DoBadCommand*.

The procedure *GetCommand* prompts the user to enter one of the command letters I (for Insert), L (for Lookup), D (for Delete), or Q (for Quit). Although only uppercase letters are listed in the prompt, lowercase letters are acceptable also. The character entered by the user is read by a *readln* statement and assigned to variable parameter *cmnd* for return to the main program. Before returning, however, *GetCommand* checks whether the value that was assigned to *cmnd* belongs to the set of valid command letters. If it does not, the value of *cmnd* is changed to E, to indicate to the main program that an erroneous command was entered.

The procedures *DoInsert*, *DoLookup*, and *DoDelete* interface between the user and the procedures *Insert*, *Lookup*, and *Delete* provided by the implementation of *Directory*. Each interface procedure does the following:

1. It obtains from the user the input data needed by the implementation procedure.

2. It calls the implementation procedure and passes it the data obtained from the user.

3. It prints an error message if the implementation procedure returns with its error parameter set to *true*.

4. If no error occurred, it prints for the user the results (if any) returned by the implementation procedure.

The procedure *DoBadCommand* informs the user that the previous command was erroneous and admonishes the user to enter one of the valid command letters I, L, D, or Q.

The Abstract Data Type *Grid*

In this section we will see how to generalize multisets to two dimensions; we call the resulting abstract data type *Grid*. The concepts behind type *Grid* can be easily applied to generalize multisets to any number of dimensions.

Type *Grid* is useful when we wish to count events that can be classified in two ways. For example, consider an election with three candidates (Jones, Roberts, and Smith) and with voters having three possible political affiliations (Democrat, Republican, and Independent). A political pollster questions selected voters, asking each for his or her candidate preference and political affiliation. Each person questioned can thus be classified as to candidate preference and political affiliation. The data collected by the pollster could be summarized in a table as follows:

	Democrat	Republican	Independent
Jones	100	75	24
Roberts	95	183	58
Smith	150	200	10

This table tells us that, of the people questioned, 100 Democrats were for Jones, 183 Republicans were for Roberts, 10 Independents were for Smith, and so on.

We wish to represent such tables as values of type *Grid*. As with multisets, we want to be able to read out each table entry—the number of Democrats for Jones, and so on. Also as with multisets, we are interested in the total of all the table entries—the total number of people questioned. With *Grid*, we are also interested in the row and column totals. In our example, the row totals give the number of respondents who favor each candidate, which are the results for which the poll was taken. The column totals give the number of respondents with each political affiliation; if these numbers are not proportional to the number of Democrats, Republicans, and Independents in the total electorate, the validity of the poll will be in question.

When the operations of an abstract data type are reasonably self-explanatory, we will often just list them and comment briefly on them rather than giving a separate pseudocode definition for each operation. The operations for type *Grid* are as follows:

Clear (*aGrid*)
Insert (*aGrid, row, col*)
Remove (*aGrid, row, col*)
Count (*aGrid, row, col*)
RowCount (*aGrid, row*)
ColCount (*aGrid, col*)
TotalCount (*aGrid*)
Union (*op1, op2, result*)

Clear sets *aGrid* to the empty grid in which all counts are zero. *Insert* records an event in *aGrid* by incrementing the count at the intersection of the given row and column; *row* and *col* are row and column labels, which will usually be either integers or values of enumerated types. *Remove* removes an event by decrementing the corresponding table entry. *Count* returns the entry at the intersection of the given row and column; *RowCount* returns the sum of the entries in the given row; *ColCount* returns the sum of the entries in the given column; and *TotalCount* returns the sum of all the entries in the table. *Union* sets *result* to the grid obtained by adding the corresponding entries in *op1* and *op2*.

Figure 9-6 shows an implementation of the abstract data type *Grid*. The program that uses the implementation must provide definitions for types *rowType* and *colType* (the types of the row and column labels) and for constants or variables *rowFirst*, *rowLast*, *colFirst*, and *colLast* (which give the first and last row label and the first and last column label). Type *grid* is defined in the obvious way as the type of two-dimensional arrays of nonnegative integers indexed by values of *rowType* and *colType*.

type
  grid = **array** [*rowType, colType*] **of** 0..*maxint*;

Clear sets all the components of *aGrid* to zero. Setting all the components of *aGrid* to zero requires two nested **for** statements, which can best be understood if examined from inside out. The innermost controlled statement

  aGrid[*row, col*] := 0

sets a given component of *aGrid* (the one determined by the values of *row* and *col*) to zero. To set all the components in a given row to zero, we must step the value of *col* from *colFirst* through *colLast* while the value of *row* remains fixed.

  for col := colFirst **to** colLast **do**
    aGrid[*row, col*] := 0

Finally, to set all the rows of *aGrid* to zero, we must step the value of *row* from *rowFirst* through *rowLast*.

  for row := rowFirst **to** rowLast **do**
    for col := colFirst **to** colLast **do**
      aGrid[*row, col*] := 0

Figure 9-6.

Implementation of the abstract data type *Grid*.

{ ******************** Implementation of *Grid* ******************** }

{ Index types *rowType* and *colType* and constants or initialized variables
rowFirst and *rowLast* (first and last values of *rowType*) and *colFirst* and
colLast (first and last values of *colType*) are supplied by the program
using *Grid* }

type
  grid = **array** [*rowType*, *colType*] **of** 0..*maxint*;

{----------------------------------- Procedure *Clear* ----------------------------------- }

procedure *Clear* (**var** *aGrid* : *grid*);

{ Initialize a grid to contain no elements }

var
  row : *rowType*;
  col : *colType*;
begin
  for *row* := *rowFirst* **to** *rowLast* **do**
    for *col* := *colFirst* **to** *colLast* **do**
      aGrid[*row*, *col*] := 0
end: { *Clear* }

{----------------------------------- Procedure *Insert* ----------------------------------- }

procedure *Insert* (**var** *aGrid* : *grid*;
                row   : *rowType*;
                col   : *colType*);

{ Insert a given element into a grid }

begin
  aGrid[*row*, *col*] := *aGrid*[*row*, *col*] + 1
end; { *Insert* }

{----------------------------------- Procedure *Remove* ----------------------------------- }

procedure *Remove* (**var** *aGrid* : *grid*;
                row   : *rowType*;
                col   : *colType*);

{ Remove a given element from a grid. No action is taken if the given
element does not belong to the grid }

begin
  if *aGrid*[*row*, *col*] > 0 **then**
    aGrid[*row*, *col*] := *aGrid*[*row*, *col*] − 1
end; { *Remove* }

Figure 9-6. *Continued.*

```
{ ----------------------------------- Function Count ----------------------------------- }

function Count (var aGrid : grid;
                    row      : rowType;
                    col      : colType) : integer;

{ Return number of occurrences of element in grid }

begin
   Count := aGrid[row, col]
end; { Count }

{ ----------------------------- Function RowCount -------------------------------- }

function RowCount (var aGrid : grid;
                        row      : rowType) : integer;

{ Return number of elements in given row of grid }

var
   col   : colType;
   total : integer;
begin
   total := 0;
   for col := colFirst to colLast do
      total := total + aGrid[row, col];
   RowCount := total
end; { RowCount }

{ ----------------------------- Function ColCount -------------------------------- }

function ColCount (var aGrid : grid;
                       col      : colType) : integer;

{ Return number of elements in given column of grid }

var
   row   : rowType;
   total : integer;
begin
   total := 0;
   for row := rowFirst to rowLast do
      total := total + aGrid[row, col];
   ColCount := total
end; { ColCount }

{ ----------------------------- Function TotalCount -------------------------------- }

function TotalCount (var aGrid : grid) : integer;

{ Return total number of elements in grid }
```

Figure 9-6.   *Continued.*

```
var
  row  : rowType;
  col   : colType;
  total : integer;
begin
  total := 0;
  for row := rowFirst to rowLast do
    for col := colFirst to colLast do
      total := total + aGrid[row, col];
  TotalCount := total
end; { TotalCount }
```

{ -------------------------------- Procedure *Union* ---------------------------------- }

procedure *Union* (**var** *op1*, *op2*, *result* : *grid*);

{ Compute union of two grids }

```
var
  row : rowType;
  col  : colType;
begin
  for row := rowFirst to rowLast do
    for col := colFirst to colLast do
      result[row, col] := op1[row, col] + op2[row, col]
end; { Union }
```

Insert increments the specified component of *aGrid*.

$$aGrid[row, col] := aGrid[row, col] + 1$$

Remove decrements the specified component provided its value is greater than zero.

if *aGrid*[*row*, *col*] > 0 **then**
  aGrid[*row*, *col*] := *aGrid*[*row*, *col*] $- 1$

Count returns the specified component of *aGrid*.

Count := *aGrid*[*row*, *col*]

RowCount totals all the components in the specified *row* of *aGrid*; note that the value of *row* remains fixed while the value of *col* is stepped from *colFirst* through *colLast*.

```
total := 0;
for col := colFirst to colLast do
  total := total + aGrid[row, col];
RowCount := total
```

Likewise, *ColCount* totals all the components in the specified column. The value of *col* remains fixed while the value of *row* is stepped from *rowFirst* to *rowLast*.

```
      total := 0;
      for row := rowFirst to rowLast do
         total := total + aGrid[row, col];
      ColCount := total
```

TotalCount computes the sum of all the components of *aGrid*

```
      total := 0;
      for row := rowFirst to rowLast do
         for col := colFirst to colLast do
            total := total + aGrid[row, col];
      TotalCount := total
```

Union sets each component of *result* to the sum of the corresponding components of *op1* and *op2*.

```
      for row := rowFirst to rowLast do
         for col := colFirst to colLast do
            result[row, col] := op1[row, col] + op2[row, col]
```

In each case note the use of nested **for** statements to process all of the components of a two-dimensional array.

The Abstract Data Type *Matrix*

One of the most common and useful mathematical relationships is that of *proportionality*, in which one quantity is equal to another quantity multiplied by a constant. For example, if the value of y is always five times the value of x, then x and y are related by the following equation:

$$y = 5x$$

This is called a *linear equation*, because if we plot a graph of y against x, we get a straight line that rises five units vertically for every unit that it covers horizontally. We also say that y and x are *linearly related*.

Linear equations occur in many application areas, ranging from science and technology to business and economics. The following are a few examples of linear relationships (some of which hold only under restrictive assumptions not given here): the voltage across an electrical circuit element is proportional to the current flowing through it; the stress (force attempting to stretch a solid object) is proportional to the strain (the amount the body is stretched); simple interest is proportional to the amount on which it is computed; tax is often proportional to the amount subject to taxation; and the production rate of an industry is proportional to the rate at which it consumes raw material.

But what if we have several "output" quantities that are linearly related to several other "input" quantities? We might have several voltages that are linearly related to several currents; several stresses that are linearly related to several strains; or production rates for several products may be linearly related to consumption rates for several raw materials. In such cases the linear relationship is more complicated. Such a linear relationship is illustrated by the following example in which there are two input quantities (x_1 and x_2) and two output quantities (y_1 and y_2):

$$y_1 = 5x_1 + 3x_2$$
$$y_2 = 7x_1 + 2x_2$$

Here we now have four constants, each giving the dependence of one of the output quantities on one of the input quantities. Each output quantity is computed by multiplying each input quantity by a constant and adding the results. The operations of adding and multiplying by constants define a general linear relationship. The branch of mathematics that studies linearly related quantities is called *linear algebra*.

The linear relationship just given is often written as follows:

$$\begin{bmatrix} y_1 \\ y_2 \end{bmatrix} = \begin{bmatrix} 5 & 3 \\ 7 & 2 \end{bmatrix} \begin{bmatrix} x_1 \\ x_2 \end{bmatrix}$$

The square array of numbers

$$\begin{bmatrix} 5 & 3 \\ 7 & 2 \end{bmatrix}$$

is called a *matrix*. Although in general a matrix can have any number of rows and any number of columns, we will focus on *square matrices*, which have the same number of rows as columns. The number of rows (alternately, the number of columns) is called the *order* of the matrix; thus the matrix in the example is of order two. Clearly, matrices can be represented as two-dimensional arrays, and indeed it was to represent matrices that such arrays were originally put in programming languages.

We will define an abstract data type matrix to provide some of the common operations that can be carried out on matrices. Again, we list all the operations first and then discuss them briefly (only the matrix product will require extended discussion).

> *Transpose (op, result)*
> *Add (op1, op2, result)*
> *ScalarMultiply (op1, op2, result)*
> *MatrixMultiply (op1, op2, result)*

Each operation sets *result* to the result computed from the operand or operands. *Transpose* interchanges the rows and columns of a matrix, so that the first row of the original matrix becomes the first column of the transposed matrix, the second row of the original matrix becomes the second column of the transposed matrix, and so on. *Add* adds two matrices by adding their corresponding components. In linear algebra an ordinary number is called a *scalar*; *ScalarMultiply* multiplies a matrix by a scalar, which it does by multiplying every component of the matrix by the scalar; the first parameter (*op1*) of *ScalarMultiply* is the scalar and the second parameter (*op2*) is the matrix.

The most complex of the operations is *MatrixMultiply*; let's see how this operation arises in linear algebra. Continuing our previous example, suppose we introduce a third set of variables z_1 and z_2, which are related to y_1 and y_2 as follows:

$$\begin{bmatrix} z_1 \\ z_2 \end{bmatrix} = \begin{bmatrix} 7 & 8 \\ 4 & 5 \end{bmatrix} \begin{bmatrix} y_1 \\ y_2 \end{bmatrix}$$

The question is, how are the *z*s related to the *x*s? If we replace the *y*s in the equation by the equation that defines them, we get

$$\begin{bmatrix} z_1 \\ z_2 \end{bmatrix} = \begin{bmatrix} 7 & 8 \\ 4 & 5 \end{bmatrix} \begin{bmatrix} 5 & 3 \\ 7 & 2 \end{bmatrix} \begin{bmatrix} x_1 \\ x_2 \end{bmatrix}$$

This equation defines the matrix product. The product of the matrices

$$\begin{bmatrix} 7 & 8 \\ 4 & 5 \end{bmatrix}$$

and

$$\begin{bmatrix} 5 & 3 \\ 7 & 2 \end{bmatrix}$$

is the single matrix that transforms the xs into the zs.

The following is the rule for computing the matrix product. Consider any component of the product matrix; this component lies at the intersection of a particular row and column. Select the corresponding row from the first matrix to be multiplied and the corresponding column from the second. Multiply the corresponding values in the selected row and column, and add the products. The sum is the product component that we set out to compute.

For example, to compute the component in the second row and second column of the product of the two example matrices, we select the second row of the first matrix to be multiplied and the second column of the second matrix. The second row of the first matrix is

4 5

and the second column of the second matrix is

3
2

Multiplying the corresponding components and adding gives us $4 \times 3 + 5 \times 2$ or 22 for the component in the second row and second column of the product matrix. The following shows how each component of the product matrix is calculated:

$$7 \times 5 + 8 \times 7 = 91 \qquad 7 \times 3 + 8 \times 2 = 37$$
$$4 \times 5 + 5 \times 7 = 55 \qquad 4 \times 3 + 5 \times 2 = 22$$

Thus

$$\begin{bmatrix} 7 & 8 \\ 4 & 5 \end{bmatrix}\begin{bmatrix} 5 & 3 \\ 7 & 2 \end{bmatrix} = \begin{bmatrix} 91 & 37 \\ 55 & 22 \end{bmatrix}$$

and the zs are related to the xs by

$$\begin{bmatrix} z_1 \\ z_2 \end{bmatrix} = \begin{bmatrix} 91 & 37 \\ 55 & 22 \end{bmatrix}\begin{bmatrix} x_1 \\ x_2 \end{bmatrix}$$

Figure 9-7 shows an implementation of the abstract data type *Matrix*. The implementation follows familiar patterns and only a few points need to be noted. The program that uses the implementation defines the constant *order*, whose value is the order of the matrices, and *cmpntType*, which is the component type of the matrices. (The component type must be *real*, *integer*, or a subrange of *integer*.) The implementation contains the following type definitions:

type
  indexType = 1..*order*;
  matrix = **array** [*indexType*, *indexType*] **of** *cmpntType*;

Figure 9-7.

Implementation of the abstract data type *Matrix*.

{ ****************** Implementation of *Matrix* ******************* }

{ Constant *order* and type *cmpntType* are defined by the program using *Matrix* }

type
   indexType = 1..*order*;
   matrix = **array** [*indextype*, *indexType*] **of** *cmpntType*;

{ ------------------------------- Procedure *Transpose* ------------------------------- }

procedure *Transpose* (**var** *op*, *result* : *matrix*);

{ Compute the transpose of a matrix }

var
  row, *col* : *indexType*;
begin
  for *row* := 1 **to** *order* **do**
    for *col* := 1 **to** *order* **do**
      result[*row*, *col*] := *op*[*col*, *row*]
end; { *Transpose* }

{ ----------------------------------- Procedure *Add* ----------------------------------- }

procedure *Add* (**var** *op1*, *op2*, *result* : *matrix*);

{ Compute the sum of two matrices }

var
  row, *col* : *indexType*;
begin
  for *row* := 1 **to** *order* **do**
    for *col* := 1 **to** *order* **do**
      result[*row*, *col*] := *op1*[*row*, *col*] + *op2*[*row*, *col*]
end; { *Add* }

{ ----------------------------- Procedure *ScalarMultiply* ----------------------------- }

procedure *ScalarMultiply* (*op1*   : *cmpntType*;
                      var *op2*, *result* : *matrix*);

{ Compute the result of multiplying a matrix by a scalar }

Figure 9-7.   *Continued.*

```
var
   row, col : indexType;
begin
   for row := 1 to order do
      for col := 1 to order do
         result[row, col] := op1 * op2[row, col]
end; { ScalarMultiply }
```

{ ---------------------------- Procedure *MatrixMultiply* ----------------------------- }

procedure *MatrixMultiply* (**var** *op1*, *op2*, *result* : *matrix*);

{ Compute the product of two matrices }

```
var
   row, col, index : indexType;
   total           : cmpntType;
begin
   for row := 1 to order do
      for col := 1 to order do
         begin
            total := op1[row, 1] * op2[1, col];
            for index := 2 to order do
               total := total + op1[row, index] * op2[index, col];
            result[row, col] := total
         end
end; { MatrixMultiply }
```

Transpose interchanges the rows and columns of a matrix by assigning to *result*[*row*, *col*] the component *op*[*col*, *row*] of the operand (note the reversal of the indexes). Two nested **for** statements are used to step through the rows and columns of the two matrices.

```
for row := 1 to order do
   for col := 1 to order do
      result[row, col] := op[col, row]
```

MatrixMultiply uses the following code to compute the product of two matrices:

```
for row := 1 to order do
   for col := 1 to order do
      begin
         total := op1[row, 1] * op2[1, col];
         for index := 2 to order do
            total := total + op1[row, index] * op2[index, col];
         result[row, col] := total
      end
```

The statements bracketed by **begin** and **end** compute the sum of the products of the components of the selected row of the first operand and the selected column of the second operand. Normally, we would initialize *total* to zero before beginning to compute the sum. However, the type of *total* must be the same as the component type of the array, and we allow the component type to be a subrange-of-*integer* type, which might not contain zero. Thus we initialize *total* to the first product to be added, then use a **for** statement to add in turn all the remaining products to the value of *total*.

Review Questions

1. What is a multiset?

2. Describe six operations on multisets.

3. Describe the array representation of multisets that is discussed in the text.

4. Describe briefly how each of the six operations on multisets is implemented in the array representation discussed in the text.

5. We often present programs in an abbreviated form in which a comment indicates that an implementation of an abstract data type is to be included. Describe the procedure for including an abstract-data-type implementation in a program in response to such a comment.

6. What is a directory?

7. Define the terms *key* and *value* as used in connection with directories.

8. Describe four operations on directories.

9. Describe the array representation of directories that is discussed in the text.

10. Define *sequential search*.

11. Describe the operation of the procedure *Search* used in the implementation of *Directory*. What do we mean when we say the *Search* is a private procedure? Why did we make this procedure private?

12. The abstract data type *Grid* is a generalization of what other abstract data type discussed in this chapter?

13. Describe an application of *Grid* to processing the results of political polls.

14. Describe the eight operations defined for *Grid*.

15. Describe the implementation of *Grid* that is discussed in the text.

16. What is a linear equation? What do we mean when we say that two variables are linearly related?

17. Describe how a linear relationship can be represented by means of a matrix.

18. What data type was originally put in many programming languages for the purpose of representing matrices?

19. Describe the four operations that the text defines for the abstract data type *Matrix*.

20. Give the role of each of the three nested **for** statements in the implementation of *MatrixMultiply*.

1. For the programs in Figures 9-2 and 9-5, show by outlining the definition and declaration parts how the abstract-data-type implementation would be included in the main program. For each definition and declaration part, list the defined or declared identifiers in the order in which their definitions or declarations would occur. Remember that in each definition or declaration part, main-program definitions or declarations that the implementation uses must precede the definitions and declarations imported from the implementation, whereas main-program definitions or declarations that use the implementation must follow the definitions and declarations imported from the implementation.

2. If the number of values in the base type of a multiset exceeds the maximum number of elements we expect to store in the multiset, it will be more efficient to store each element in a separate array component rather than provide an array component for each value of the base type. Thus a multiset will be stored as a sequence of element values rather than as an array of counters. Implement the abstract data type *Multiset* in this way. *Hint:* Some of the techniques used to implement *Directory* may prove helpful here.

3. The implementation of *Directory* (Figure 9-3) uses a single data array *table*, each component of which contains a key and its corresponding value. An alternate approach is to use two arrays: *key*, which contains all the keys; and *value*, which contains all the values. For any value of *index* less than the value of *free*, the values of *key[index]* and *value[index]* are a key and the corresponding value. Arrays whose components correspond in this way are called *parallel arrays*; we can think of them as representing parallel columns in a table. Implement *Directory* using parallel arrays.

4. Often each value entry in a table corresponds to a range of keys rather than to a single key; common examples are tables giving price breaks and tax brackets. For instance, an item of merchandise may be priced as follows:

Quantity Ordered	Price Each
1–12	$27.95
13–47	$26.49
48–95	$23.99
96 or more	$21.79

Since the ranges are contiguous, we need only store the largest value in each range. Thus the table we store in the computer would be

Quantity	Price
12	27.95
47	26.49
95	23.99
sentinel	21.79

The sentinel can be either the value we are looking up or the largest possible key value. The table entries must be stored in the order shown; with the possible exception of the sentinel value, the key values will be in ascending order. Modify the procedures *Search* and *Lookup* in the implementation of *Directory* to handle this kind of table. Note that no error parameters are needed, because a value will be found for every possible key.

5. Write a program that uses an implementation of the abstract data type *Grid* to analyze the results of a political poll. The input data for the program should give the candidate preference and political affiliation of each person questioned. The program should output the number of people questioned, the percentage that were for each candidate, and the percentage that professed each political affiliation.

6. Design and implement a three-dimensional version of *Grid*. In accordance with the suggested method of visualizing three-dimensional arrays, the three indexes of the grid array will be designated *page*, *row*, and *col*. Giving values for any combination of these indexes designates a particular part of the grid array; for example, giving values for *page* and *row* designates a particular row on a particular page. In addition to a total count for the entire array, the abstract data type must be able to return a total count for the part of the array specified by each of the following combinations of index values:

    page, row, col
    page, row
    page, col
    row, col
    page
    row
    col

   Describe in words the portion of the array specified by each combination of index values.

7. It is often desirable to keep the entries in a directory in ascending order according to their keys; this allows entries to be read out in order of increasing keys (as we will see in Exercise 9) and permits faster search algorithms (as we will see in Exercise 10). Modify Procedure *Insert* shown in Figure 9-3 so that each new entry is inserted in the proper position to keep the keys in ascending order. The modified *Insert* should begin by inserting the new entry as the last entry in the directory, as in the existing version of *Insert*. The new entry must now be moved up in the table until it is in the proper position. Compare the key of the new entry with the key of the immediately preceding entry. If the key of the new entry is less than that of the preceding entry, the new entry is out of order, and should change places with the immediately preceding entry. Repeat this process of comparing keys and changing places until the new entry is in the proper position, as evidenced by the fact that its key is greater than or equal to the key of the immediately preceding entry. *Problem:* If the new entry moves all the way to the beginning of the directory, we may try to compare its key with that of the (nonexistent!) entry preceding the first entry of the directory. *Solution:* Extend the index type to include −1 and set *table*[−1].*key* to the key of the new entry. Since a key cannot be less than itself, *table*[−1].*key* will serve as a sentinel to terminate the compare-and-change-places process when the new entry is in *table*[0].

8. Rather than maintain a directory in key order as new entries are inserted (as in Exercise 7), it may sometimes be best to insert entries in arbitrary order and then sort them all into key order in a single operation. Provide the implementation of *Directory* with an operation *Sort (aDirectory)* that sorts the entries of *aDirectory* into ascending order according to their keys. A simple sorting algorithm, called an *insertion sort,* can be derived from the insertion procedure described in Exercise 7. At each step of the sorting process, the directory will be divided into two contiguous parts, the first part of which is sorted and the second part of which is not. The first entry in the unsorted part is then transferred to the sorted part by inserting it in its proper position with the algorithm described in Exercise 7. Starting with a sorted part consisting of only the first directory entry (a one-entry table is always sorted), the remaining entries are transferred to the sorted part one by one until the entire directory is sorted.

9. Suppose the entries in a directory are in ascending order according to their keys either because that order was maintained by *Insert* (Exercise 7) or because the directory was sorted with a *Sort* operator (Exercise 8). We now wish to read out the directory entries in key order, perhaps to produce a printout of the directory. Extend the implementation of *Directory* to provide the following operations:

   ResetDir (aDirectory)
   ReadDir (aDirectory, aKey, aValue)
   EndOfDirQ (aDirectory)

   ResetDir sets *aDirectory* so that the next call to *ReadDir* will return the first entry—the entry with the smallest key. Each call to *ReadDir* returns the next succeeding entry—the entry with the next largest key. *EndOfDirQ* returns *true* if all the entries have been read from the directory and *false* otherwise. If *ReadDir* is called after the last entry has been read, it will return the last entry again.

10. Maintaining or sorting a directory in ascending key order (Exercises 7 and 8) allows search algorithms that are enormously faster than sequential search. A simple yet highly efficient search algorithm is *binary search*, which repeatedly divides the part of the directory remaining to be searched in half, determines which half must contain (if either one does) the entry with the search key, and confines further search to that half. Let the part of the directory yet to be searched be *table*[*low*] through *table*[*high*]. Set *mid* to (*low* + *high*) **div** 2, an index approximately midway between *low* and *high*. If *searchKey* is equal to *table*[*mid*].*key*, we have found the entry for which we are looking. If *searchKey* is less than *table*[*mid*].*key*, the desired entry (if present at all) must be in the first half of the part of *table* under consideration; set *high* to *mid* − 1 to confine further searching to the first half. If *searchKey* is greater than *table*[*mid*].*key*, the desired entry (if present at all) must be in the second half of the part of *table* under consideration; set *low* to *mid* + 1 to confine further searching to the second half. Repeat until the desired entry is found or until *low* becomes greater than *high*, indicating that the desired entry could not be found. Rewrite the procedure *Search* in the implementation of *Directory* to use binary search.

11. Implement an abstract data type to deal cards at random from a 52-card deck. The abstract data type *Deck* provides the following two operations:

Initialize (aDeck, seed)
DealCard (aDeck, value, suit, error)

Initialize creates a new 52-card deck; *seed* provides a seed for the pseudorandom number generator that will be used to draw the cards at random. *DealCard* draws a card at random and returns its *value* and *suit* (which can be values of enumerated types). If the deck is empty—all 52 cards have been drawn—*DealCard* returns with the error parameter *error* set to *true*. *Implementation Hints*: Initialize an array to contain all 52 cards; each card can be represented by a record with a value field and a suit field. Since the number of cards will decrease as cards are drawn, you must keep track of the number of cards currently in the deck. To draw a card, make a (pseudo) random selection from the cards currently in the deck; then exchange the selected card with the last card currently in the deck. This will allow us to always deal from the bottom of the deck and thus keep the cards remaining in the deck in a contiguous block at the beginning of the array.

12. Modify the abstract data type *Deck* (Exercise 11) so that *Initialize* randomly shuffles the entire card array. *DealCard* can then just read out the cards in the order they are stored in the shuffled array. At each step of the shuffle algorithm, the array will be divided into two contiguous parts, the first part unshuffled and the second part shuffled. Transfer a card from the unshuffled part to the shuffled part by selecting it at random and exchanging it with the last card in the unshuffled part, thus allowing it to become the first card of the shuffled part. Note that this shuffle algorithm is almost exactly the reverse of an insertion sort.

Files

10

Like a one-dimensional array, a file consists of a series of component values, all belonging to the same type. In contrast to arrays, however, the number of components in a file can vary. Also, whereas arrays are stored in main memory, files are normally stored in auxiliary memory, read from input devices, or written to output devices. The entire file may not even be in existence at one time; a keyboard-input file is created as the user types it, and data sent to a display is lost to the system as it is displayed and the user reads it. These characteristics of files impose limitations on our ability to access the data stored in files.

There are two methods for accessing data stored in files: *sequential access* and *random* or *direct access*. Files for which only sequential access is possible are called *sequential files*, whereas those for which *random access* is possible are called *random* or *direct files*.

In sequential access, data items must be read in the order in which they are stored in the file and therefore must be stored in the order in which they are to be eventually read. A file can be read only by starting at the beginning and reading the values one after another until the end is reached; a value can be written to a file only by appending the value to the end of a file.

In random or direct access, the components of a file can be accessed in any order. Each component is designated by a record number, which is used like an array index to designate the component that we wish to access. Even with random access, however, we cannot access file components as freely as we would components of an array. A program that jumps around a lot in a file may run very slowly, due to the time required for the accessing mechanism of the storage device to move from one position to another. A storage device that permits random access is called a *direct access storage device* (abbreviated DASD, and pronounced "DAZZ dee"). By far the most common DASDs are disk drives.

In this chapter we will confine our attention to sequential files, which are the only kind provided by standard Pascal. Note, however, that many Pascal implementations provide random files as an extension to the standard. As with all extensions, however, the details of random files vary from one implementation to another.

Files and File Processing

We begin our study of files by looking at Pascal file types and the basic processing operations that can be carried out on file values.

Type Definitions

The type constructor for a file type has the following form:

> **file of** component-type

The component type is the type of the values stored in the file. The only restriction on the component type is that the components of a file may not themselves be files or contain files as components. Thus the component type may not be a file type nor a structured type whose values contain file components at any level of nesting.

Pascal provides one predefined file type, *text*, whose values are the textfiles we have been working with all along. Files of type *text* are similar to files of type **file of** *char*. The contents of a textfile, however, are divided into lines and perhaps also into pages. On input from a textfile, sequences of characters representing integers, real numbers, and Boolean values are automatically converted into the binary representations for those values. On output to a textfile, the binary representations of integer, real, and Boolean values are automatically converted to the corresponding sequences of characters. The standard files *input* and *output* are of type *text*.

File Variables

File variables are used to name files within a program. We say that file variables serve as *internal* names for files, *internal* meaning "within the program." Internal names are in contrast to the *external* names by which files are known to the operating system; examples of external names are the names of hardware devices (such as LPT1 for line printer 1) and the names by which files are listed in disk directories (such as A:EXAMPLE for the file listed as EXAMPLE in the directory of the disk in drive A).

The following definition and declarations illustrate how file variables are declared in Pascal:

```
type
    student = record
                  id    : integer;
                  grade : char
              end;
    studentFile = file of student
var
    roll   : studentFile;
    data   : file of real;
    report : text;
```

roll is declared as a file of student records, *data* as a file of real numbers, and *report* as a textfile.

input and *output* are predeclared as file variables of type *text*. These file variables must not be redeclared by the programmer.

Standard Pascal does not provide any statement for associating internal and external file names. Instead, file variables that represent external files must be listed as parameters in the program heading. It is left up to the operating system to obtain from the user the external names of these files. The correspondence between internal and external file names is set up before program execution begins and cannot be changed while the program is being executed.

For example, if the program *FileProcessing* uses files *roll, data,* and *report* as well as the standard files *input* and *output*, it might have the following program heading:

program *FileProcessing* (*input*, *output*, *roll*, *data*, *report*);

Unless the user requests otherwise, files *input* and *output* will be associated with standard input and output devices such as the user's keyboard and display. The user must supply the names of the remaining files when requesting the operating system to execute the program. This is often done in a cryptic command line such as the following:

FILEPROC CLASSLST STAT3.DAT LPT1

In this command line, FILEPROC is the name of the disk file containing the program *FileProcessing*, the program to be executed; CLASSLST is the external name of the file corresponding to *roll*; STAT3.DAT is the external name of the file corresponding to *data*; and LPT1 is the external name of the file corresponding to *report*. CLASSLST and STAT3.DAT are the names of disk files; they refer to directory entries on the disk in the *default* disk drive—the one assumed when no particular disk drive is named. LPT1 refers, as before, to line printer 1.

This method of associating internal and external file names is unsatisfactory for many purposes. For example, user-friendly programs usually prompt the user to enter the names of the files to be processed, instead of requiring that the file names be included in a cryptic command line. Some programs even allow the user to select the files to be processed from a menu of relevant file names by means of a pointing device such as a mouse. To allow user-friendly programs to be written, many versions of Pascal provide, as a nonstandard extension, means by which internal and external file names can be associated within a Pascal program.

Whatever methods may be used for associating internal and external file names, these will be the only ways in which file values can be associated with file variables. As we recall from our discussion of assignment compatibility, assignment is not allowed for files or for structured values containing files as components (however deeply nested the file components may be). File variables (and structured variables containing file variables) can be passed to functions and procedures via variable parameters. But files and structured values containing files cannot be passed via value parameters, because this would involve an implicit assignment of the file values to the corresponding formal parameters.

Reset and *Rewrite*

Standard Pascal provides two modes for file access: *inspection* and *generation*. In inspection mode, the file is read sequentially, starting with the first component and proceeding through the file component by component until the end of the file is reached. The Pascal system keeps track of its current position in the file so that it always knows which is the next component to be read. In generation mode, the file is written sequentially, starting with the empty file and appending each newly written component to the end of the file.

Before a Pascal program can read from or write to a file, it must request the operating system to establish a link between the program and the file; this process is known as *opening* the file. When a file is open in inspection mode, we say that it has been *opened for input*; when a file is opened in generation mode, we say that it has been *opened for output*. When the program has finished accessing the file, it breaks this link by *closing* the file. Closing a file assures that all the data written to a file has actually been sent to the output or storage device (data is frequently stored temporarily in main memory before being sent to the output or storage device).

In standard Pascal, opening files is handled by the predefined procedures *reset* and *rewrite*. Files are closed automatically when execution of a program terminates. Since data can be lost if a program failure occurs before files are closed, some implementations of Pascal provide a *close* procedure as a nonstandard extension. If *reset* or *rewrite* is executed for a file that is already open, standard Pascal will automatically close the file, then reopen it with the specified procedure. However, nonstandard versions of Pascal may require that a *close* procedure be executed for an open file before it can be reopened with *reset* or *rewrite*.

If *f* is a file variable, file *f* is opened for input with the following procedure call:

> *reset* (*f*)

This call accomplishes three things: (1) the current position of *f* is set to the beginning of the file, (2) inspection mode is established, and (3) the first value in the file is transferred to main memory.

File *f* is opened for output with the following procedure call:

> *rewrite* (*f*)

This call accomplishes two things: (1) the current contents of file *f* are deleted, so that the value of *f* becomes the empty file, and (2) generation mode is established. We invoke *reset* before beginning to read from a file and *rewrite* before beginning to write to a file.

Before execution of a program begins, the standard file *input* is automatically opened with *reset* and the standard file *output* is automatically opened with *rewrite*. Thus the user's program does not have to open the standard input and output files; every other file, however, must be opened with either *reset* or *rewrite* before any other file processing operation can be applied to it.

Buffer Variables, *get*, *put*, and *eof*

A *buffer* is an area of main memory for holding values read from a file or values to be written to a file. Normally, the operating system maintains at least one buffer for each file that a program accesses. To read a value from a file, the program requests the operating system to transfer the value from the file to the buffer area. To write a value to a file, the program places the value in the buffer area and requests the operating system to transfer the contents of the buffer area to the file.

Pascal allows programmers to access the buffer area directly. Associated with each file variable is a *buffer variable* that refers to the buffer area. The buffer variable is denoted by the file variable followed by an upward arrow (which will appear as a caret or circumflex on most computer terminals). Thus *f*↑ denotes the buffer variable corresponding to the file variable *f*. A buffer variable can be used just like any other variable: the program can refer to the value of the buffer variable, and the buffer variable can be assigned new values.

For example, suppose that the file variable f is declared by

f : **file of** *integer*;

and the current contents of the file are as follows:

10 30 15 99 75

Executing

reset (f)

resets the current position to the beginning of the file, establishes inspection mode, and assigns the first value in the file to the buffer variable. After executing *reset*, we can represent the state of the file and the buffer variable as follows:

10 30 15 99 75 $f\uparrow$ = 10
↑

The arrow beneath 10 represents the current position of the file. Thus executing *reset* has set the current position to 10, the first component of the file, and has assigned 10 to the buffer variable. The value of the buffer variable can be accessed just like the value of any other variable. For example, the statement

$x := f\uparrow$

assigns the value 10 to x.

To access the next value in the file, we use the procedure *get*, which can be called only in inspection mode. The procedure call

get (f)

moves the current position to the next value and assigns that value to the buffer variable. The new state of the file and buffer variable is as follows:

10 30 15 99 75 $f\uparrow$ = 30
    ↑

Each time *get* is called, the current position is moved to the next file position and the value at that position is assigned to the buffer variable. Thus after *get* has been called three more times, the state of the file and buffer variable is as follows:

10 30 15 99 75 $f\uparrow$ = 75
                ↑

Now suppose that *get* is called yet another time. The current position is advanced one position beyond the last component in the file; we refer to this position as the *end position*. Since no component value is stored at the end position, none can be transferred to the buffer variable, and the value of the buffer variable is undefined. This situation can be represented as follows:

10 30 15 99 75 $f\uparrow$ = ?
                  ↑

The program must be alerted to this situation so that it will not attempt to refer to the value of the buffer variable when the buffer variable has no valid value. This is done with the predefined predicate *eof*. The function call *eof(f)* returns *true* if the current position of the file is at the end position and *false* otherwise. The value of the buffer variable is defined when *eof* returns *false* and undefined when *eof* returns *true*. If we include the value returned by *eof* in the state of the file, we can represent the state just before the end position is reached as follows:

$$10 \quad 30 \quad 15 \quad 99 \quad 75 \qquad\qquad f\uparrow = 75$$
$$\uparrow \qquad\qquad\qquad eof(f) = false$$

The state after the end position has been reached is represented as follows:

$$10 \quad 30 \quad 15 \quad 99 \quad 75 \qquad\qquad f\uparrow = ?$$
$$\uparrow \qquad\qquad\qquad eof(f) = true$$

The procedure call

> *rewrite (f)*

deletes the current contents of file *f* and establishes generation mode. After the call, the value of file *f* is the empty file and the value of *f↑* is undefined. We can represent the state of file *f* as follows:

$$f\uparrow = ?$$
$$\uparrow$$

In generation mode, the current position is always the end position, the position at which the next value will be written. To store a value in the file, we first assign the value to the buffer variable.

> $f\uparrow := 64$

The state of the file and the buffer variable is now as follows:

$$f\uparrow = 64$$
$$\uparrow$$

The predefined procedure *put*, which can only be called in generation mode, transfers the value of the buffer variable to the file and moves the current position forward to the new end position. After the procedure call

> *put (f)*

the state of the file and buffer variable is as follows:

$$64 \qquad\qquad\qquad\qquad f\uparrow = ?$$
$$\uparrow$$

Note that after the call to *put*, the value of the buffer variable is once again undefined.

Succeeding values are stored in the file in the same way. For example, the statements

> $f\uparrow := 50;$
> *put (f)*

store 50 in the file; the statements

> $f\uparrow := 13;$
> *put (f)*

store 13 in the file; and the statements

$$f\uparrow := 88;$$
$$put\ (f)$$

store 88 in the file. After these three sets of statements have been executed, the state of the file and the buffer variable is as follows:

64   50   13   88 $f\uparrow = ?$

            ↑

In generation mode, *eof* always returns the value *true*, since the current position is always at the end position.

Sequential File Processing with *get* and *put*

Let us define an account record by

    type
        accountRecord = **record**
                      accountNumber : *integer*;
                      balance   : *real*
             end;

and declare *oldFile* and *newFile* as files of account records.

    var
        oldFile, *newFile* : **file of** *accountRecord*;

Suppose that we want to read account records from *oldFile*, increase the balance of each record by $10 to reflect a service charge, and write the updated records to *newFile*. The following statements accomplish this task:

    reset (*oldFile*);
    rewrite (*newFile*);
    while not *eof*(*oldFile*) **do**
      begin
        newFile↑.*accountNumber* := *oldFile*↑.*accountNumber*;
        newFile↑.*balance* := *oldFile*↑.*balance* + 10.00;
        put (*newFile*);
        get (*oldFile*)
      end

Reset assigns the first value in *oldFile* to the buffer variable *oldFile*↑. Since *oldFile*↑ and *newFile*↑ are record variables, we can use them to construct field designators. The value of *oldFile*↑.*accountNumber* is assigned to *newFile*↑.*accountNumber*; $10 is added to the value of *oldFile*↑.*balance*; and the sum is assigned to *newFile*↑.*balance*. *Put* is called to write the value of *newFile*↑ to *newFile*, and *get* is called to read the next value in *oldFile* into *oldFile*↑. Processing continues until *eof*(*oldFile*) returns the value *true*, indicating that all the records in *oldFile* have been processed.

Sequential File Processing with *read* and *write*

As alternatives to *get* and *put*, Pascal also provides *read* and *write*, which transfer data between the file and program variables, so that the programmer does not have to access the buffer variable. In standard Pascal, we can use either *get* and *put* or *read* and *write* to process a file. Unfortunately, some popular Pascal implementations provide only one of these two pairs of procedures, forcing use of either *get* and *put* or *read* and *write*, whichever is available in the implementation at hand. Programs written for an implementation that offers only one of the two pairs of procedures must obviously be rewritten for use with an implementation that offers only the other pair.

The procedure call *read* (*f*, *x*) is defined as equivalent to the following statements:

$$x := f\uparrow;$$
$$get\ (f)$$

The value of the buffer variable is assigned to *x*, and *get* is called to obtain a new value from the file.

Likewise, the procedure call *write* (*f*, *x*) is defined as equivalent to

$$f\uparrow := x;$$
$$put\ (f)$$

The value of *x* is assigned to the buffer variable and *put* is called to write the value to the file.

The definitions of *read* and *write* can be extended so that more than one value is read or written during a single invocation. The procedure statement

$$read\ (f,\ x1,\ x2,\ \ldots,\ xn)$$

is defined as equivalent to the following sequence of statements:

$$read\ (f,\ x1);\ read(f,\ x2);\ \ldots;\ read(f,\ xn)$$

Likewise, the procedure statement

$$write\ (f,\ x1,\ x2,\ \ldots,\ xn)$$

is defined as equivalent to the following sequence of statements:

$$write\ (f,\ x1);\ write(f,\ x2);\ \ldots;\ write(f,\ xn)$$

If the file parameter *f* is omitted, *read* is assumed to read from the standard file *input* and *write* is assumed to write to the standard file *output*. Note that the file variable can never be omitted from a *reset, rewrite, get* or *put* statement.

Taken literally, the definition of *read* presents problems for interactive programming. Suppose file *f* is the user's keyboard. The call *read* (*f*, *x*) assigns the character just typed by the user to *x* and then calls *get* to obtain the next character that the user types. *The user must type another character before the previously typed character will be returned to the program for processing.* This rules out the common situation in which the user gives commands to a program by striking a key for each command. The user would have to strike the key for the next command before the previous command could be obeyed.

One solution to this problem uses *lazy evaluation*, which puts off operations as long as possible rather than carrying them out as soon as they are requested by the program. With lazy evaluation, a new value is not obtained from the file when *get* is called; the system merely notes that a new value has been requested. When the program actually refers to the value of *f*↑, the system gets busy and obtains the new value that was previously requested by *get*.

Now suppose *read* (*f*, *x*) is used to read a character from the user's keyboard. The following statements are executed:

$$x := f\uparrow;$$
$$get(f)$$

Because of lazy evaluation, the reference to the value of $f\uparrow$ causes the system to obtain a new character from the user's keyboard, a character that was requested by an earlier call to *get*. The call to *get* requests another character from the keyboard, but this request will be put off until the value of $f\uparrow$ is referred to again. Thus *read* does not have to wait for another character to be typed before returning the character that was assigned to x.

Let's rewrite our example of sequential file processing to use *read* and *write* instead of *get* and *put*. Since we will not refer to the buffer variables, we will need a variable *accnt* to hold the account record currently being updated. *Accnt* is declared as follows:

accnt : *accountRecord*;

The following statements read records from *oldFile* and write updated records to *newFile*:

```
reset (oldFile);
rewrite (newFile);
while not eof(oldFile) do
   begin
      read (oldFile, accnt);
      accnt.balance := accnt.balance + 10.00;
      write (newFile, accnt)
   end
```

Note that *reset*, *rewrite*, and *eof* are used in the same way in both versions of the example.

Textfiles

Textfiles, files of type *text*, have two properties. First, the characters in a textfile are divided into lines and possibly into pages. (Usually, only files that are to be sent to a printer are divided into pages.) Second, values of types *integer*, *real*, *char*, and *Boolean* can be read from and written to textfiles. The procedures *read* and *write* perform data conversion for integer, real, and Boolean values. *Read* converts from the sequences of characters (such as 3.14) that represent values in a textfile to the binary codes that represent values in main memory. *Write* performs the reverse conversion from binary codes to sequences of character. Field-width parameters can be used to control the exact format in which values are written to textfiles.

The *read* and *write* statements that we have been using all along read from the textfile *input* and write to the textfile *output*. Thus we are already familiar with many details of input from and output to textfiles. For example, we know the formats in which values must be stored in a textfile so that they can be read by a *read* statement, and we know how to use field-width parameters to control the formats in which values will be stored in a textfile by a *write* statement.

Different computer systems may use different methods for dividing a textfile into lines. Some use a special end-of-line character to terminate each line; the code for the end-of-line character can vary from system to system. Some systems use two special characters to terminate each line; this method is a concession to printers, most of which require two control characters, *carriage return* and *line feed*, to move the printing mechanism to the beginning of a new line. Still another method is to extend each line with enough blank spaces so that all lines contain the same number of characters. Since the number of characters in a line is known, no special character is required to signal the end of a line.

The Pascal procedures for processing textfiles are designed to be independent of the method actually used to divide the file into lines. Pascal processes a textfile as if each line is terminated by a single end-of-line character. The end-of-line character is read as a blank space; this allows the Pascal program to be independent of whatever code or codes are used to represent the end of a line in the textfile. To distinguish the end-of-line character from an ordinary blank space, Pascal provides the predicate *eoln* (end of line). The value of *eoln(f)* is *true* when the current position of *f* is at an end-of-line character and *false* otherwise.

For example, consider the textfile that would be printed as follows:

```
Line one
Line two
Line three
```

If we use the symbol | to represent the end-of-line character, we can represent this textfile as follows:

```
Line one|Line two|Line three|
```

Suppose that the file is being read and the current file position is at some character other than the end-of-line character. We can represent the state of the file, the buffer variable, and *eoln* as follows:

```
Line one|Line two|Line three|
  ↑
```

$f\uparrow = \text{'n'}$
$eoln(f) = false$

Now suppose the current file position is at an end-of-line character. The value of $f\uparrow$ is a blank space (since the end-of-line character is read as a blank space) and *eoln* returns *true*.

```
Line one|Line two|Line three|
            ↑
```

$f\uparrow = \text{' '}$
$eoln(f) = true$

The procedure *readln* moves the current file position to the beginning of the next line. The procedure call *readln (f)* has the same effect as the statements

> **while not** *eoln(f)* **do**
>   *get (f)*;
> *get (f)*

readln can be extended to read values from the file before moving to the beginning of a new line. The procedure statement

> *readln (f, x1, x2, ..., xn)*

is defined as equivalent to the following two-statement sequence:

read (*f*, *x1*, *x2*, ..., *xn*); *readln* (*f*)

The procedure call *writeln* (*f*) terminates the line currently being written to file *f*. *Writeln* can be extended to write a series of values before terminating the line. The procedure statement

writeln (*f*, *x1*, *x2*, ..., *xn*)

is defined to be equivalent to the following two-statement sequence:

write (*f*, *x1*, *x2*, ..., *xn*); *writeln* (*f*)

The procedure *page* (*f*) terminates the page currently being written to file *f*. If the last line on the page to be terminated does not end with an end-of-line character, the system executes *writeln* (*f*) before terminating the page. The method of dividing a textfile into pages varies from system to system. One method is to end each page with the control character *form feed*. When a printer receives a form feed character, it advances to the top of a new page.

If the file parameter *f* is omitted for *read*, *readln*, *eof*, or *eoln*, the standard file *input* is assumed. If the file parameter is omitted for *write*, *writeln*, or *page*, the standard file *output* is assumed. Thus we can write *eof* instead of *eof*(*input*), *eoln* instead of *eoln*(*input*), and *page* instead of *page* (*output*). We are already familiar with using *read*, *readln*, *write*, and *writeln* with the file parameter omitted.

Example Programs

Our ultimate goal in this section will be a program for the classic file-update problem, in which a master file (such as a file of customer accounts) is updated from a transaction file (such as a file of purchases and payments). Along the way to this goal we will look at programs for creating the master file and the transaction files, for printing out or *listing* the created files, and for merging two files.

Example 10-1. *Creating a Master File*

Figure 10-1 shows a program to obtain data from the user and store it in a master file. For the sake of illustration, we will make the records in our master file as simple as possible. Each record will have a key, which uniquely identifies the individual to whom the record refers, a transaction code, which distinguishes master records and the different kinds of transaction records, and an amount, which for a master record represents the balance in the individual's account. Records in an actual master file would, of course, contain much more information, such as an individual's name, address, telephone number, and credit rating.

The structure of master and transaction records is determined by the following definitions, which will appear in all our programs:

Figure 10-1.

Program for creating a master file.

```pascal
program CreateMaster (input, output, mastFile);

{ Create a master file from user input }

const
    sentinel = 9999;
type
    transCdType = (add, update, delete, master);
    recType     = record
                    key      : 0..sentinel;
                    transCd  : transCdType;
                    amount   : real
                  end;
var
    mastFile : file of recType; { master file to be created }
    acctNo   : integer;          { account number }
    acctBal  : real;             { account balance }
begin
    rewrite (mastFile);
    write ('Account number (9999 to stop)? ');
    readln (acctNo);
    while acctNo <> sentinel do
      begin
        write ('Account balance? ');
        readln (acctBal);
        mastFile↑.key := acctNo;
        mastFile↑.transCd := master;
        mastFile↑.amount := acctBal;
        put (mastFile);
        writeln;
        write ('Account number (9999 to stop)? ');
        readln (acctNo)
      end;
    mastFile↑.key := sentinel;
    mastFile↑.transCd := master;
    mastFile↑.amount := 0.0;
    put (mastFile)
end.
```

```
const
    sentinel = 9999;
type
    transCdType = (add, update, delete, master);
    recType = record
                    key     : 0..sentinel;
                    transCd : transCdType;
                    amount  : real
              end;
```

The records in each file must be in ascending order according to their key values. Each file is terminated by a sentinel record whose key, which is the sentinel value 9999, is larger than the key of any data record. We use a sentinel record only because it simplifies the merging of files. If it were not for merging, we could rely on *eof* to indicate the end of a file and would not need a sentinel record.

Values of *transCdType* distinguish four kinds of records: master records and records for Add, Update, and Delete transactions. Values of type *recType* represent master and transaction records. The value of the key field is an integer in the range 0 through 9999; the value of *transCd* field belongs to the enumerated type *transCdType*, and the value of the *amount* field is real.

It is crucial that the type definitions describing the contents of a file be the same for every program that processes the file. The Pascal system has no way of determining the type of values stored in a file; it merely assumes that they have the type specified in the program that reads the file. Thus if values are written with one type and read with another, the system will be unable to detect the error and the data read from the file will be processed incorrectly. It is a good policy to write the definitions that describe the contents of a file only once, then use the text editor to copy them into every program that processes the file.

The master file will be represented by the file variable *mastFile*, which is declared with type **file of** *recType*. Note that *mastFile* is listed along with *input* and *output* in the program heading. The variables *acctNo* and *acctBal* hold the account number and balance obtained from the user.

```
var
    mastFile : file of recType;
    acctNo   : integer;
    acctBal  : real;
```

The program reads data from the textfile *input* and stores it in the binary file *mastFile*.* We are already familiar with reading from a textfile, so we will focus our attention on the statements for writing the master file. The program begins by using *rewrite* to open *mastFile* in generation mode; that is, to create a new, empty master file that can be written to.

rewrite (*mastFile*)

---

*Files other than textfiles are sometimes called *binary files*, because values are represented in the file by the same binary codes that are used to represent the values in main memory. This is in contrast to textfiles, in which all values are represented by sequences of characters such as '3.14' and '−25'.

Each record is created by assigning the values to be stored to the appropriate fields of the buffer variable *mastFile*. The values of *acctNo* and *acctBal*, which were obtained from the user, are assigned to the *key* and *amount* fields of *mastRec↑*; since we are writing only master records, the *transCd* field is always assigned the value *master*. When values have been assigned to all the fields of *mastRec↑*, the new record is written to the file with *put*.

```
mastFile↑.key := acctNo;
mastFile↑.transCd := master;
mastFile↑.amount := acctBal;
put (mastFile)
```

After all the data records have been written, the program must write a sentinel record as the last record of the file. Only the key of the sentinel record is important; however, for the sake of writing a well-defined record, the program also assigns dummy values to the other fields of the sentinel record.

```
mastFile↑.key := sentinel;
mastFile↑.transCd := master;
mastFile↑.amount := 0.0;
put (mastFile)
```

We could have used a **with** statement to keep from having to repeatedly write "*mastFile↑.*". Thus the code segments just given could have been written as

```
with mastFile↑ do
  begin
    key := acctNo;
    transCd := master;
    amount := acctBal
  end;
put (mastFile)
```

and as

```
with mastFile↑ do
  begin
    key := sentinel;
    transCd := master;
    amount := 0.0
  end;
put (mastFile)
```

A variable listed in a **with** statement must not be changed by any of the statements governed by the **with** statement. Since the *get* and *put* statements change the value of the buffer variable, they cannot be governed by any **with** statement that lists the buffer variable. Thus we cannot use one **with** statement for the entire program; each sequence of assignments to the fields of the buffer variable must be governed by its own **with** statement. Because of this restriction, it's often a toss-up as to which is more concise—to use a separate **with** statement for each series of assignments to fields of the buffer variable, or to just write out all the field designators in full.

Example 10-2.   *Creating a Transaction File*

The program shown in Figure 10-2 creates a transaction file. Its overall structure is similar to the program for creating a master file, so only a few additional points need to be noted.

All the records in the master file have their *transCd* fields set to *master*. For a transaction record, however, we must set the *transCd* field to *add*, *update*, or *delete* depending on the kind of transaction represented. Values of enumerated types cannot be read from textfiles; thus the user cannot enter *add*, *update*, and *delete* directly; instead, the user must enter some integer or character code, which the program then converts to a value of *transCdType*. For this program a character code was chosen: the user enters A for add, U for update, and D for delete. Either uppercase or lowercase letters can be used.

The next question is how to convert the letters to the corresponding values of *transCdType*. The most elegant approach would be to use an array as a translation table. However, because the prompt for the value of the *amount* field also varies with the kind of transaction record, we will use a **case** statement to handle each kind of transaction separately. The statements for each case will include an assignment statement to assign the appropriate value of *transCdType* to *transCd*.

After obtaining the account number, the program prompts for the transaction code; if an invalid code is entered, the prompt is repeated.

```
repeat
    write ('Transaction Code (A/U/D)? ');
    readln (trCode)
until trCode in ['a', 'A', 'u', 'U', 'd', 'D']
```

A **case** statement uses the character entered to choose the proper statements to create each kind of transaction record.

Figure 10-2.   Program for creating a transaction file.

```
program CreateTrans (input, output, transFile);

{ Create a transaction file from user input }

const
    sentinel = 9999;
type
    transCdType = (add, update, delete, master);
    recType     = record
                      key     : 0..sentinel;
                      transCd : transCdType;
                      amount  : real
                  end;
```

Figure 10-2. *Continued.*

```pascal
var
    transFile : file of recType; { transaction file to be created }
    acctNo    : integer;         { account number }
    trCode    : char;            { external transaction code }
    amt       : real;            { amount of transaction }
begin
    rewrite (transFile);
    write ('Account number (9999 to stop)? ');
    readln (acctNo);
    while acctNo <> sentinel do
       begin
          transFile↑.key := acctNo;
          repeat
             write ('Transaction Code (A/U/D)? ');
             readln (trCode)
          until trCode in ['a', 'A', 'u', 'U', 'd', 'D'];
          case trCode of
             'a', 'A':
                begin
                   transFile↑.transCd := add;
                   write ('Account balance? ');
                   readln (amt);
                   transFile↑.amount := amt
                end;
             'u', 'U':
                begin
                   transFile↑.transCd := update;
                   write ('Debit (+) or credit (−) amount? ');
                   readln (amt);
                   transFile↑.amount := amt
                end;
             'd', 'D':
                begin
                   transFile↑.transCd := delete;
                   transFile↑.amount := 0.0
                end
          end;
          put (transFile);
          writeln;
          write ('Account number (9999 to stop)? ');
          readln (acctNo)
       end;
    transFile↑.key := sentinel;
    transFile↑.transCd := add;
    transFile↑.amount := 0.0;
    put (transFile)
end.
```

```
case trCode of
    'a', 'A': "create record for Add transaction"
    'u', 'U': "create record for Update transaction"
    'd', 'D': "create record for Delete transaction"
end
```

An Add transaction adds a new master record to the master file—that is, it creates a new account. The *transCd* field of the transaction record is set to *add*, and the *amount* field is set to the account balance of the new account.

transFile↑.transCd := *add*;
write ('Account balance? ');
readln (*amt*);
transFile↑.amount := *amt*

An Update transaction increases or decreases the balance of an account; an increase might represent a new purchase and a decrease might represent a payment or a return. The *amount* field of the transaction record will contain a value to be added to the account balance. Since the balance represents the amount owed by the customer, an additional amount owed (debit) will be represented by a positive number, and a payment or return (credit) will be represented by a negative number. The user is prompted to enter the amount of the debit or credit with the appropriate sign.

transFile↑.transCd := *update*;
write ('Debit (+) or credit (−) amount? ');
readln (*amt*);
transFile↑.amount := *amt*

A Delete transaction closes an account by deleting the corresponding master record from the master file. For a Delete transaction, only the key of the record to be deleted and the transaction code are needed; the *amount* field of the transaction record is not used. The program sets the unused *amount* field to the dummy value 0.0

transFile↑.transCd := *delete*;
transFile↑.amount := 0.0

The **case** statement is followed by a *put* statement that writes the record created by the **case** statement to the transaction file.

Example 10-3.   *Listing a File*

A *listing* of a file is just a printout of all the records in the file. When developing programs that create files, we will generally need a listing program to check that the file creation programs are working properly. Figure 10-3 shows a program for listing a file.

Since values of enumerated types cannot be written to textfiles, the listing program must convert the value of the *transCd* field into a form that can be printed. This is done with a translation table, *trChar*, which is declared as

trChar : **array** [*transCdType*] **of** *char*;

Figure 10-3.

Program for listing (printing the contents of) a master or a
transaction file.

```
program ListFile (output, inFile);

{ Print contents of master or transaction file }

const
   sentinel = 9999;
type
   transCdType = (add, update, delete, master);
   recType     = record
                    key     : 0..sentinel;
                    transCd : transCdType;
                    amount  : real
                 end;
var
   inFile  : file of recType;        { file to be listed }
   acctNo  : integer;                { account number }
   trCd    : transCdType;            { external transaction code }
   amt     : real;                   { balance or transaction amount }
   trChar  : array [transCdType] of char; { translation table for
                                            converting transaction
                                            codes from internal
                                            to external form}
begin
   trChar[add]    := 'A'; trChar[update] := 'U';
   trChar[delete] := 'D'; trChar[master] := 'M';
   writeln ('Account' :15);
   writeln ('Number ' :15, 'Code' :15, 'Balance' :15);
   writeln;
   reset (inFile);
   while not eof(inFile) do
      begin
         acctNo := inFile↑.key;
         trCd := inFile↑.transCd;
         amt := inFile↑.amount;
         if acctNo <> sentinel then
            writeln (acctNo :15, trChar[trCd] :15, amt :15:2);
         get (inFile)
      end
end.
```

and initialized at the beginning of the program as follows:

   $trChar[add]$:= 'A'; $trChar[update]$:= 'U';
   $trChar[delete]$:= 'D'; $trChar[master]$:= 'M'

After initializing *trChar*, the program prints the column headings for the
three-column table (one for each record field) in which the records will be
listed.

The statements for reading and listing the records of *inFile* follow the general form for processing a sequential file.

```
reset (inFile);
while not eof(inFile) do
    begin
        "list inFile↑ if it is not the sentinel record"
        get (inFile)
    end
```

Note that even though the file ends with a sentinel record, we use *eof* to detect the end of the file, because this gives the most straightforward code. We must take care, however, that the statements for listing a record ignore the sentinel record. (Alternatively, with program testing in mind, we might choose to print the sentinel record to make sure that it was written by the file creation program.)

The statements for listing a record are straightforward.

```
acctNo := inFile↑.key;
trCd := inFile↑.transCd;
amt := inFile↑.amount;
if acctNo <> sentinel then
    writeln (acctNo :15, trChar[trCd] :15, amt :15:2)
```

Two points need to be noted: (1) the value assigned to *trCd* is of type *transCdType*; it must be converted to a character via the translation table *trChar* before being printed; and (2) the **if** statement is needed to prevent the sentinel record from being printed.

Example 10-4. *Merging Files*

Merging is an operation that combines two ordered sequential files to produce a third ordered sequential file—the merged file. In the most straightforward case, the merged file contains all the records that were in the two original files. But several variations on merging are possible. For example, a record with a given key might occur in the merged file only if records with that key occur in *both* the original files. (In other words, a record in one of the original files will go into the merged file only if it can be matched with a record having the same key in the other original file.) Or, a record with a given key might occur in the merged file only if a record with that key occurs in one of the original files but not the other. Also, records with matching keys are often combined into a single record before being sent to the merged file.

Merging can be thought of as a means of bringing together records having the same key but residing in different files. For example, in the file-update problem, transaction records with a given key must be brought together with the master record having the same key, so that the master record can be updated by the corresponding transaction records. Another application of merging is *record matching*, a sometimes controversial technique of comparing or combining records referring to the same individual but stored in different files. For example, if people are not supposed to receive payments simultaneously from two particular sources, the records in the payment files for the two sources can be matched to identify people who are violating the regulations. Or records of people who have applied for their driver's licenses can be matched with those of people who have registered for the draft to ferret out young men who have applied for their driver's licenses but have not registered for the draft.

For now, we will consider the straightforward merge that merely combines the two original files. Our only problem, then, is to make sure that the merged file is ordered—that records will be written to the merged file in ascending order according to their keys. The solution is as follows. We consider the next record to be read from each of the two original files. We now compare the keys of the two next records to be read, and select the record with the smaller key; the selected record is read from its file and written to the merged file.

This procedure for selecting the next record to be written to the merged file assures that the merged file will be ordered. Since the original files are ordered, the next record to be read from each file has the smallest key of all the records remaining in the file. More precisely, the key of the next record to be read is less than or equal to the keys of all the records remaining to be read from the file. Since the key of the selected record is the smaller of the keys of the two next records to be read, the key of the selected record is less than or equal to the keys of all the records remaining in the two original files. Thus our selection process will cause the record with the smallest key to be written first to the merged file, the record with the next smallest key to be written next, and so on. The merged file will be ordered, as desired.

If the two next records to be read have the same key, we can select either record to be transferred to the merged file. Sometimes there are reasons for selecting one record over the other in this case. For example, if we are merging a master file and a transaction file, we would want a master record to precede a transaction record with the same key, so that a master record will come before all the transaction records that are to be used to update it.

When the end of one of the original files is reached, all the remaining records in the other file are just copied to the merged file. The easiest way to cause this copying to take place is to end each file with a sentinel record whose key is larger than that of any valid data record. When the end of one of the files is reached, then the next record to be read from that file will be the sentinel record. If the next record to be read from the other file is a valid data record, then it will have a smaller key than the sentinel record; it will therefore be selected for transfer to the merged file. This will be true for all the valid data records in the other file, so all such records will just be copied to the merged file, as desired.

Figure 10-4 shows a program for merging original files *inFile1* and *inFile2* to produce a merged file *outFile*. The records in all three files are of type *recType*, the same record type that we used in our previous examples. We assume that *inFile1* and *inFile2* are both ordered, and each ends with a sentinel record having a key of 9999, the value of the constant *sentinel*. The merged file *outFile* must also be ordered and must also end with a sentinel record.

The program begins by opening *inFile1* and *inFile2* for input and the *outFile* for output.

Figure 10-4.

Program for merging two files.

```
program Merge (inFile1, inFile2, outFile);

{ Merge contents of two input files and store result in output file }

const
    sentinel = 9999;
type
    transCdType = (add, update, delete, master);
    recType     = record
                       key     : 0..sentinel;
                       transCd : transCdType;
                       amount  : real
                  end;
var
    inFile1, inFile2,                    { input files }
    outFile          : file of recType; { output file }
begin
    reset (inFile1);
    reset (inFile2);
    rewrite (outFile);
    while (inFile1↑.key <> sentinel) and
          (inFile2↑.key <> sentinel)        do
       if inFile1↑.key <= inFile2↑.key then
          begin
             outFile↑ := inFile1↑;
             put (outFile);
             get (inFile1)
          end
       else
          begin
             outFile↑ := inFile2↑;
             put (outFile);
             get (inFile2)
          end;
    outFile↑ := inFile1↑; { sentinel record }
    put (outFile)
end.
```

```
    reset (inFile1);
    reset (inFile2);
    rewrite (outFile)
```

The statements for transferring a record from an input file to the output file are repeated until the sentinel record has been reached in *both* input files. When the sentinel record has been reached in only one input file, then the records in the other input file are copied to the output file.

```
         while (inFile1↑.key <> sentinel) and
             (inFile2↑.key <> sentinel)    do
           "Select the next record to be transferred
           to the merged file; read the selected record
           from inFile1 or inFile2 and write it to
           outFile."
```

If *inFile1↑.key* is less than or equal to *inFile2↑.key,* the next record in *inFile1* is copied to *outFile*; otherwise, the next record in *inFile2* is copied to *outFile*. A record is copied by assigning the value of *inFile1↑* or *inFile2↑* to *outFile↑*, calling *put* to write the contents of *outFile↑*, and calling *get* to read a new record into *inFile1↑* or *inFile2↑*.

```
      if inFile1↑.key <= inFile2↑.key then
        begin
          outFile↑ := inFile1↑;
          put (outFile);
          get (inFile1)
        end
      else
        begin
          outFile↑ := inFile2↑;
          put (outFile);
          get (inFile2)
        end
```

Note that if the two keys are equal, the next record in *inFile1* is selected for transfer to *outFile*. Thus if we were using this program to merge a master file and a transaction file, we would want the master file to be *inFile1*.

When all the valid data records have been written to *outFile*, we need to write a final sentinel record to terminate *outFile*. At this point, the next record to be read from each of the input files is the sentinel record, so the sentinel record of either input file can be copied to *outFile*. We use the sentinel record from *inFile1*.

```
      outFile↑ := inFile1↑; { sentinel record }
      put (outFile)
```

Example 10-5. *The File Update Program*

We now turn to the file update problem, in which records in a transaction file are used to update records in a master file. Record keys serve to establish a correspondence between transaction records and master records. A transaction record with a given key is used to update the master record having the same key. The problem is that records in a sequential file must be processed in the order in which they are stored in the file; there is no way to magically extract the records having a particular key. Given that the master and transaction files are both sequential files, we need some way to bring together the master and transaction records having a common key value, thus allowing the master record to be updated with information contained in the transaction records. This can be accomplished efficiently provided the records in both the master and transaction files are in order according to their key values. The keys could be in either ascending or descending order, but ascending order is almost invariably chosen.

We can use merging to bring together corresponding master and transaction records. Suppose the master and transaction files were merged using the program in Figure 10-4, with the master file as *inFile1* and the transaction file as *inFile2*. Because the records in *outFile* are in ascending order according to key values, records with the same key will be grouped together in *outFile*. Because the current record of *inFile1* is transferred to *outFile* when the current records of *inFile1* and *inFile2* both have the same key, each master record in *outFile* will precede the corresponding transaction records. Thus *outFile* consists of groups of records, each group consisting of a master record followed by zero or more transaction records having the same key as the master record. (The first record of a group can also be a transaction record for an Add transaction, which creates a new master record.) The records in each group have the same key, and the different groups are arranged so that their keys are in ascending order.

We could complete the file update problem by writing another program to read *outFile* and process each group of records as follows: (1) read and temporarily store each master record; (2) read the transaction records and apply the specified updates to the master record; and (3) write the updated master record to the new master file. (If the first record of a group is a transaction record for an Add transaction, it will create the master record to be updated by the remaining transaction records; a Delete transaction deletes a master record by causing it *not* to be written to the new master file.)

For the sake of speed and convenience, we would like to combine the merging and updating into a single program, which does not have to create and then read an intermediate file such as *outFile*. A good approach to organizing a program that carries out several distinct processing steps is to realize each step by an implementation of an abstract data type. The main program can then use the operations defined for the abstract data types to move the data through the various processing steps. We will follow this course by defining two abstract data types: *Merge*, which merges records from the master and transaction files; and *Apply*, which applies transactions to master records.

The abstract data type *Merge* reads the old master file and the transaction file, merges the records, and delivers the merged records one at a time to the program. Thus the main program has only to deal with the stream of merged records created by *Merge*; the management of the actual old master and transaction files is the responsibility of *Merge*. The operations of *Merge* are similar to the file-processing operations that would be used to read an actual merged file.

InputInitialize	Prepares for input by opening the old master and transaction files.
GetRecord (*inRec*)	Sets *inRec* to the next record in the stream of merged records.
EndOfInputQ	Returns *true* if all records have been read from the stream of merged records and returns *false* if there are still more records to be read.

Figure 10-5.

Program for updating a master file from a transaction file. The old master file (the file to be updated) and the transaction file provide the program's input; the output is the updated new master file together with error messages indicating any transactions that could not be carried out.

```pascal
program FileUpdate (output, oldMast, trans, newMast);

{ Update old master file from transaction file and store result
  in new master file. Old master file is not changed }

const                                    { used by both Merge and Apply }
   sentinel = 9999;
type                                     { used by both Merge and Apply }
   transCdType = (add, update, delete, master);
   recType     = record
                    key     : 0..sentinel;
                    transCd : transCdType;
                    amount  : real
                 end;
var
   inBuffer          : recType;          { used by main program }
   oldMast, trans : file of recType;     { used by Merge }
   newMast           : file of recType;  { used by Apply }
   curKey            : integer;          { used by Apply }
   validMastRec   : Boolean;             { used by Apply }

{ ******************** Procedures for Merge  ********************}

{----------------------------- Procedure InputInitialize ----------------------------- }

procedure InputInitialize;

{ Open old master and transaction files }

begin
   reset (oldMast);
   reset (trans)
end; { InputInitialize }

{--------------------------------- Procedure GetRecord --------------------------------- }

procedure GetRecord (var inRec : recType);

{ Get next record from merged input files. This is
  the procedure that actually does the merging }

begin
   if oldMast↑.key <= trans↑.key then
      begin
         inRec := oldMast↑;
         get (oldMast)
      end
```

Figure 10-5.   *Continued.*

```
      else
        begin
          inRec := trans↑;
          get (trans)
        end
end; { GetRecord }
```

{ ----------------------------- Function *EndOfInputQ* ----------------------------- }

function *EndOfInputQ* : *Boolean*;

{ Return *true* only if the ends of both input files have been reached }

```
begin
   EndOfInputQ := (oldMast↑.key = sentinel) and
                  (trans↑.key = sentinel)
end; { EndOfInputQ }
```

{ ********************* Procedures for *Apply* ********************* }

{ ----------------------------- Procedure *OutputInitialize* ----------------------------- }

procedure *OutputInitialize*;

{ Open output file and initialize state of "*Apply* machine" }

```
begin
   rewrite (newMast);
   curKey := -1;
   validMastRec := false
end; { OutputInitialize }
```

{ ----------------------------- Procedure *DoAdd* ----------------------------- }

procedure *DoAdd* (**var** *inRec* : *recType*);

{ Process Add transaction }

```
begin
   if validMastRec then
     writeln ('Attempt to add existing record for key ',
              inRec.key :1)
   else
     begin
       inRec.transCd := master;
       newMast↑ := inRec;
       validMastRec := true
     end
end; { DoAdd }
```

Figure 10-5.   *Continued.*

```
{ ------------------------------- Procedure DoUpdate ------------------------------- }

procedure DoUpdate (var inRec : recType);

{ Process Update transaction }

begin
  if validMastRec then
    newMast↑.amount := newMast↑.amount + inRec.amount
  else
    writeln ('Attempt to update nonexistent record for key ',
           inRec.key :1)
end; { DoUpdate }

{ ------------------------------- Procedure DoDelete ------------------------------- }

procedure DoDelete (var inRec : recType);

{ Process Delete transaction }

begin
  if validMastRec then
    validMastRec := false
  else
    writeln ('Attempt to delete nonexistent record for key ',
           inRec.key :1)
end; { DoDelete }

{ ------------------------------- Procedure DoMaster ------------------------------- }

procedure DoMaster (var inRec : recType);

{ Process master record }

begin
  if validMastRec then
    writeln ('Duplicate master record for key ',
           inRec.key :1)
  else
    begin
      newMast↑ := inRec;
      validMastRec := true
    end
end; { DoMaster }
```

Figure 10-5. *Continued.*

{------------------------------- Procedure *PutRecord* ------------------------------- }

procedure *PutRecord* (**var** *inRec* : *recType*);

{ Process master or transaction record }

begin
  if *inRec.key* <> *curKey* **then**
    begin
      if *validMastRec* **then**
        put (*newMast*);
      curKey : = *inRec.key*;
      validMastRec : = *false*
    end;
  case *inRec.transCd* **of**
    add: *DoAdd* (*inRec*);
    update: *DoUpdate* (*inRec*);
    delete: *DoDelete* (*inRec*);
    master: *DoMaster* (*inRec*)
  end
end; { *PutRecord* }

{----------------------------- Procedure *OutputFinalize* ----------------------------- }

procedure *OutputFinalize*;

{ Write remaining master record (if any) and
  sentinel record to new master file }

begin
  if *validMastRec* **then**
    put (*newMast*);
  newMast↑.*key* : = *sentinel*;
  newMast↑.*transCd* : = *master*;
  newMast↑.*amount* : = 0.0;
  put (*newMast*)
end; { *OutputFinalize* }

{ *********************** Main Program *********************** }

begin
  InputInitialize;
  OutputInitialize;
  while not *EndOfInputQ* **do**
    begin
      GetRecord (*inBuffer*);
      PutRecord (*inBuffer*)
    end;
  OutputFinalize
end.

The main program transfers records one by one from *Merge* to *Apply*. *Apply* has the responsibility of applying the transactions—of adding, updating, and deleting master records in accordance with the instructions contained in the transaction records—and of writing updated and newly added master records (but not deleted ones) to the new master file. All master record processing is hidden within *Apply*; as far as the main program is concerned, *Apply* is simply a destination to which records can be sent. The operations for *Apply* are similar to those used to write records to a file.

OutputInitialize	Prepares for output by opening the new master file and initializing variables used by *Apply*.
PutRecord (inRec)	Delivers the master or transaction record *inRec* to *Apply* for further processing.
OutputFinalize	Assures that the last master record that was processed is written to the new master file, then writes a sentinel record to terminate the new master file.

Figure 10-5 shows the complete file-update program. The main program is very simple, consisting almost entirely of calls to the procedures of *Merge* and *Apply*.

```
InputInitialize;
OutputInitialize;
while not EndOfInputQ do
   begin
      GetRecord (inBuffer);
      PutRecord (inBuffer)
   end;
OutputFinalize
```

InputInitialize prepares *Merge* for input and *OutputInitialize* prepares *Apply* for output. The program then transfers records from *Merge* to *Apply*, using *GetRecord* to read a record from *Merge* and *PutRecord* to send a record to *Apply*. The record variable *inBuffer* provides temporary storage for the record currently being processed. Both *GetRecord* and *PutRecord* access *inBuffer* via variable parameters, so that a record is not unnecessarily copied when it is transferred from *Merge* to *Apply*. Transfer of records continues until *EndOfInputQ* indicates that there are no more old master or transaction records to process. *OutputFinalize* is then called to assure that all added and updated master records have been properly written to the new master file.

Since our main program merely calls procedures from the abstract data types *Merge* and *Apply*, the rest of our discussion will focus on the implementation of those types.

Global Variables and Implicit Parameters

You may have already noticed a difference between the pseudocode defining *Merge* and *Apply* and that defining other abstract data types. In our previous definitions, each operation had a parameter (such as *aDictionary*) representing the value of the abstract data type on which operations are to be performed. In the implementation, each function or procedure had a corresponding parameter whose type represented the abstract type being implemented; thus, in an implementation of the abstract type *Dictionary*, each procedure contains a parameter *aDictionary* of type *dictionary*. But no such parameters are to be found in the pseudocode defining *Merge* and *Apply*.

The reason for the difference is this. A value of type *Merge* is a source of merged records; a value of type *Apply* is a destination for records to be further processed. But our program does not need the ability to declare any number of sources and destinations. Only one source and destination are needed. Therefore, the source and destination can be implicit; all the operations of type *Merge* will implicitly refer to the program's one source of merged records, and all the operations of *Apply* will refer implicitly to the program's one destination for records to be processed. Since there is only one source and one destination, the operations do not require a parameter to specify a source or a destination.

How can we represent such implicit parameters in an implementation? We recall that there are two ways in which a subprogram can access a variable declared in the main program: (1) the variable can be passed to the subprogram as a variable parameter, and (2) the subprogram can access the variable directly as a *global variable*. We can use the second method for implicit data structures that we do not wish to pass explicitly as parameters. If we represent such a structure as the value of one or more global variables, then the structure can be accessed implicitly by the operations that manipulate it without its having to be passed as an explicit parameter to each operation.

This usage is not without drawbacks. In standard Pascal, a global variable is accessible to every function and procedure in the program. Thus, someone reading the program may have difficulty in determining which subprograms access which global variables, and the programmer runs the risk of accidentally accessing a global variable from the wrong subprogram.

Fortunately, this situation improves considerably in languages that allow implementations of abstract data types to be *encapsulated*. Because of encapsulation, a global variable within an implementation can be accessed only by the functions and procedures of the implementation. Someone reading the program can immediately see which functions and procedures have access to a global variable, and encapsulation prevents the programmer from accidentally accessing a global variable from outside the implementation. Of course, the standard Pascal we are using in this book does not provide the desired encapsulation. But, because many languages that the student will eventually encounter do provide encapsulation, we will occasionally illustrate the use of global variables in implementing abstract data types.

Definitions and Declarations

The program *FileUpdate* uses the following definitions and declarations:

```
const
    sentinel = 9999;
```

```
type
   transCdType = (add, update, delete, master);
   recType     = record
                    key     : 0..sentinel;
                    transCd : transCdType;
                    amount  : real
                 end;
var
   inBuffer          : recType;
   oldMast, trans    : file of recType;
   newMast           : file of recType;
   curKey            : integer;
   validMastRec      : Boolean;
```

The definitions of *sentinel*, *transCdType*, and *recType* are already familiar from previous examples; these definitions are shared by the implementations of both *Merge* and *Apply*. The variable *inBuffer* is used by the main program to store the master or transaction record currently being processed. The remaining variables are global variables used by the implementations of *Merge* and *Apply*. *Merge* uses *oldMast* and *trans*, which are the file variables for the old master and the transaction file. *Apply* uses *newMast*, *curKey*, and *validMastRec*. *newMast* is the file variable for the new master file that is being created; *curKey* holds the key of the master record that is currently being processed; and the value of *validMastRec* is *true* or *false* according to whether or not the buffer variable *newMast*↑ contains valid data—whether a master record has been assigned to *newMast*↑ but not yet written to the new master file.

We can think of *Merge* as an abstract machine whose internal state is given by the values of *oldMast* and *trans* (that is, by the contents of the old master file and the transaction file). Likewise, we can think of *Apply* as an abstract machine whose internal state is given by the value of *newMast* (the contents of the new master file) and the values of the variables *curKey* and *validMastRec*. The operations defined for these abstract machines send values to them, obtain values from them, and change their internal states.

Implementing the Operations of *Merge*

We now turn to the subprograms that implement the operations of *Merge*. The procedure *InputInitialize* opens both the old master file and the transaction file for input.

```
reset (oldMast);
reset (trans)
```

The procedure *GetRecord* obtains the next input record and, in doing so, accomplishes the merging operation that *Merge* is designed to perform. The procedure compares the keys of the current old master and transaction records, and it returns the record with the smaller key via the variable parameter *inRec*.

```
if oldMast↑.key <= trans↑.key then
   begin
     inRec := oldMast↑;
     get (oldMast)
   end
```

else
  begin
    inRec := *trans*↑;
    get (*trans*)
  end

Note that if the current old master and transaction records have the same key, the master record is returned. This is important, because in the stream of records going from *Merge* to *Apply*, a master record must precede any transaction records that are to be applied to it.

The Boolean function *EndOfInputQ* returns *true* if both the old master and transaction files have been exhausted.

$$EndOfInputQ := (oldMast\uparrow.key = sentinel) \textbf{ and}$$
$$(trans\uparrow.key = sentinel)$$

Implementing the Operations of *Apply*

The procedure *OutputInitialize* initializes the state variables of *Apply*. The new master file *newMast* is opened for output with *rewrite*. *curKey* is set to −1, a dummy value that is not equal to any valid record key; and *validMastRec* is set to *false*, indicating that no master record has yet been assigned to *newMast*↑.

  rewrite (*newMast*);
  curKey := −1;
  validMastRec := *false*

The main program uses the procedure *PutRecord* to transfer the next old master or transaction record to *Apply* via the variable parameter *inRec*. *PutRecord* begins by comparing the key of the new record with *curKey*, the key of the master record currently being processed. If the two keys are the same, the input record is a transaction record applying to the current master record, and the appropriate procedure can be called to apply the transaction. If the two keys differ, however, then the current input record *does not apply* to the current master record. In that case, the current master record (if any) must be written to the new master file, and *Apply* must be set up to process a new master record, one having the same key as the input record. Thus, if the value of *validMastRec* is *true* (*newMast*↑ contains a valid master record), the value of *newMast*↑ is written to the new master file. Then *curKey* is set to the key of the current input record (which is the key of the next master record to be processed), and *validMastRec* is set to *false*, since the next master record has not yet been assigned to *newMast*↑.

  if *validMastRec* **then**
    put (*newMast*);
  curKey := *inRec.key*;
  validMastRec := *false*

A different procedure is called to handle each kind of input record. A **case** statement calls *DoAdd*, *DoUpdate*, *DoDelete*, or *DoMaster* depending on the value of *inRec.transCd*. The procedure called is passed *inRec* via a variable parameter.

```
        case inRec.transCd of
          add     : DoAdd (inRec);
          update : DoUpdate (inRec);
          delete  : DoDelete (inRec);
          master : DoMaster (inRec)
        end
```

The procedure *DoAdd* adds a new master record to the file. It is an error if the value of *validMastRec* is *true*, since in that case there already exists a master record with the same key as the master record we are trying to add. If the value of *validMastRec* is *false*, the transaction record is converted to a master record by changing the value of *transCd* to *master*. This master record is assigned to *newMast↑*, and *validMastRec* is set to *true*.

```
        if validMastRec then
          writeln ('Attempt to add existing record for key ',
                   inRec.key :1)
        else
          begin
            inRec.transCd : = master;
            newMast↑ : = inRec;
            validMastRec : = true
          end
```

The procedure *DoUpdate* updates the current master record by adding the amount contained in the transaction record to the amount contained in the current master record. An error occurs if the value of *validMastRec* is *false*, since in that case there is no master record having the same key as the transaction record (that is, there is no master record to update). If the value of *validMastRec* is *true*, the addition is performed and the result is stored in *newMast↑.amount*.

```
        if validMastRec then
          newMast↑.amount : = newMast↑.amount + inRec.amount
        else
          writeln ('Attempt to update nonexistent record for key ',
                   inRec.key :1)
```

The procedure *DoDelete* deletes the current master record by setting *validMastRec* to *false*, thereby preventing the current master record from being written to the new master file. It is an error, however, if the value of *validMastRec* is already *false*, because this means there is no master record with the same key as the transaction record—there is no master record to delete.

```
        if validMastRec then
          validMastRec : = false
        else
          writeln ('Attempt to delete nonexistent record for key ',
                   inRec.key :1)
```

The procedure *DoMaster* installs the input record as the current master record. It is an error if the value of *validMastRec* is *true*, because this means that there is already a master record with the same key as the input record, and duplicate master records are not allowed. If the value of *validMastRec* is *false*, the value of *inRec* is assigned to *newMast↑* and *validMastRec* is set to *true*.

```
if validMastRec then
    writeln ('Duplicate master record for key ',
            inRec.key :1)
else
   begin
     newMast↑ := inRec;
     validMastRec := true
   end
```

The procedure *OutputFinalize* has two tasks. First, if the value of *validMastRec* is *true*, the final master record must be written to the new master file. Second, a final sentinel record must be written to the new master file.

```
if validMastRec then
    put (newMast);
newMast↑.key := sentinel;
newMast↑.transCd := master;
newMast↑.amount := 0.0;
put (newMast)
```

Review Questions

1. Describe files and contrast them with arrays.

2. Define and contrast sequential and random (or direct) files.

3. Describe how file types are declared. Characterize the types that are not allowed as component types of file types.

4. Define and contrast the internal and external names for a file.

5. Describe how the correspondence between the internal and external names for files is established in standard Pascal.

6. Describe the restrictions on assignment and parameter passing that are imposed on files and structured values containing files as components.

7. Describe the operations of opening and closing a file.

8. Define inspection mode and generation mode.

9. What is a buffer variable? How is the buffer variable associated with a particular file designated?

10. Describe the operations *reset* and *rewrite*.

11. Describe the operations *get* and *put*; illustrate their use in sequential file processing.

12. Describe the use of the *eof* function in sequential file processing.

13. Describe the operations *read* and *write*; illustrate their use in sequential processing.

14. What is lazy evaluation? What problem of standard Pascal is it sometimes used to solve?

15. Contrast textfiles and nontext or binary files. What is the type of a textfile?

16. Define the function *eoln*.

17. Define *readln, writeln,* and *page*.

18. Which file-processing procedures and functions allow the name of the file to be omitted, and what default file name does each subprogram use? To which files are *reset* and *rewrite* automatically applied before program execution begins?

19. Describe the process of merging two files.

20. Describe the operation of the file-update program.

21. What approach to program organization is exemplified by the file-update program?

Exercises

1. Write a program to list the file *input* on *output*. That is, each line read from *input* should be written to *output*. The program should work regardless of the number of characters on a line or the number of lines in *input*.

2. Modify the program of Exercise 1 so that each line written to *output* begins with a line number. The line number is right-justified in a four-character field and is separated from the remainder of the line by one blank space.

3. Modify the program of Exercise 2 to print the listing with 60 lines to a page and with a page number in the upper-right hand corner of each page.

4. Write a program to count the number of lines in a textfile.

5. Write a program to count the number of words in a textfile. For the purpose of this exercise, a word is a contiguous sequence of nonblank characters. Words are separated by blanks and by line breaks (a line break is a transition to a new line).

6. Files are sometimes used for temporary storage when a program must manipulate more data than will fit into main memory at one time. To demonstrate this, write a program to generate and then find the sum of 200,000 random numbers between 0 and 1. The catch is that you must first generate—and then store—the numbers and only then start adding. Reading and writing each of the 200,000 numbers individually would be excessively time-consuming because of the time required for the 400,000 file accesses; therefore, transfer the numbers to and from the file in blocks of 2,000. *Hint*: The component type of a file type can be an array; an array of 2,000 real numbers would be appropriate here.

7. Suppose that students may take either of two courses but are not allowed to take both, since the courses are considered to cover essentially the same material. Suppose that the ID numbers of the students who have taken each course are stored in ascending order in a file of integers. Write a program to read the two files of ID numbers and print the ID numbers of all students who have violated the regulations by taking both courses.

8. Suppose that students who register for course A must also register for course B (for example, course B might be the laboratory for course A).

Suppose that the ID numbers of the students registered for each course are stored in ascending order in a file of integers. Write a program to read two files of ID numbers and print the ID numbers of all students who have registered for course A but not for course B.

9. *CreateTrans* is supposed to create a file whose records are in ascending order according to their record keys, but it will not do so if the operator enters the records in the wrong order.

    a. Modify *CreateTrans* to reject as invalid any record key that is less than the key of a record that has already been written to the file.

    b. Write a program to read an existing transaction file and report the keys of any records that are out of order. (Note that different records with the same key are allowed in a transaction file but not in a master file.)

10. In this and the next two exercises we will develop a program to sort a transaction file. We will rearrange the file's records so that their keys are in ascending order. The main difficulty facing us is that we can only process files sequentially; that is, we can only read records in the order they are stored in the file and write them in the order that they are to be stored. Our approach will be to break the original file down into runs. As we learned in Chapter 7, runs are segments that happen to already be in order. We will merge these runs into larger and larger runs, all of which will be ordered because merging produces an ordered sequence when the sequences to be merged are ordered. Eventually we will end up with a file containing only one run; this file will be the ordered file that we desire.

    To begin, write a program to read *inFile* and *distribute* the runs to two temporary files, *tempFile1* and *tempFile2*. The first run in *inFile* will be written to *tempFile1*; the second run, to *tempFile2*; the third run, to *tempFile1* again; and so on. Thus the program switches output files whenever it detects the end of a run in the input file. The end of a run is signaled by the end of the input file or by a *step down*—a record whose key is larger than the key of the following record. The bulk of this program should be in the form of a procedure that can be incorporated in the sorting program to be written in Exercise 12.

11. Write a program to read files *tempFile1* and *tempFile2*, merge corresponding runs, and write the result to *inFile*. This program differs from one that just merges *tempFile1* and *tempFile2* in that this program merges corresponding runs rather than the entire files. What this means in practice is that when the end of the current run is reached in one temporary file, all the records remaining in the current run in the other file are copied to *inFile*. The program then goes on to the next run in each file. When the end of one of the two files is reached, the remaining runs in the other file are copied to *inFile*. The program should count the number of runs written to *inFile*, since this number will determine whether further processing of *inFile* is necessary. As in Exercise 10, the bulk of the program should be in the form of a procedure that can be incorporated in the program of Exercise 12.

12. Using the results of Exercises 10 and 11, write a program to sort *inFile*. The program begins by *distributing* the runs in *inFile* to *tempFile1* and *tempFile2*, then merging the runs in these two files and writing the result back to *inFile*. Each time this process is repeated, the size of the runs in *inFile* will grow larger and their number will grow smaller, since adjacent runs are being merged. Thus the program should repeat the distribute-and-merge process until *inFile* contains only one run.

11 Strings

A *string* is a sequence of characters. Such a sequence can be stored in an array or a file. What distinguishes strings from arrays and files, however, is the operations that are performed on strings. These operations often involve segments of a string called *substrings*. The following are common operations with substrings:

1. Locate each occurrence of one string as a substring of another string. For example, we may wish to find every occurrence of the string 'the' in

    'the quick brown fox jumps over the lazy dog'

2. Delete a substring. For example, deleting the string 'quick ' from the previous string gives

    'the brown fox jumps over the lazy dog'

3. Create a substring by inserting one string at a given point within another. For example, inserting the string 'very ' before 'lazy' in the last string gives

    'the brown fox jumps over the very lazy dog'

4. Replace a substring by a given string. The replacement can be accomplished by locating the substring to be replaced, deleting it, and inserting its replacement. For example, replacing each occurrence of the string 'the' by 'a' in the last string gives

    'a brown fox jumps over a very lazy dog'

Each of the last three operations changes the length of the string—the number of characters that it contains. The length of an array cannot be changed, and the length of a file can be changed only by extending it, by appending values to its end. The need to make insertions, deletions, and replacements within a string assures us that string data types are distinct from array types and file types.

The *length* of a string is the number of characters it contains. String types can be classified as *fixed-length-string types* and *variable-length-string types*. All strings belonging to a given fixed-length-string type have the same length; strings belonging to a variable-length-string type can have different lengths. We refer to strings belonging to a fixed-length-string type as *fixed-length-strings* and to those belonging to a variable-length-string type as *variable-length strings*.

Standard Pascal provides only fixed-length strings, although variable-length strings are among the most common extensions to the standard. We will begin by looking at fixed-length strings as they are implemented in standard Pascal. Then, rather than turning to an extended Pascal for variable-length strings, we will define variable-length strings as values of an abstract data type and see how to implement that type in standard Pascal.

Fixed-Length Strings

When all the strings belonging to a string type have the same length, the distinction between string types and array types vanishes, thus allowing fixed-length strings to be represented as arrays of characters. In standard Pascal, a *string type* is any array type of the form

> **packed array** [1..*length*] **of** *char*

where *length* is the number of characters in each string belonging to the type. For example, the type of all strings of length 10 can be defined as

> **type**
>   *fixedString10* = **packed array** [1..10] **of** *char*;

and the type of all 80-character strings can be defined as

> **type**
>   *fixedString80* = **packed array** [1..80] **of** *char*;

Thus a Pascal array type must satisfy three requirements to be regarded as a string type.

1. The array type must be declared as **packed** (even though packing of character arrays serves no useful purpose for many computer systems).

2. The index type must be a subrange of type *integer* having a lower limit of 1. The upper limit of the index type is the common length of all the strings belonging to the string type. Index values are used to designate particular characters in a string. Thus, index 1 designates the leftmost character, index 2 designates the next-to-leftmost character, and so on.

3. The component type must be type *char*.

Two string types are *compatible* if their strings have the same length; also, strings of one such type are *assignment compatible* with the other type. For example, suppose types *fixedString10* and *fString10* are defined by

> **type**
>   *fixedString10* = **packed array** [1..10] **of** *char*;
>   *fString10*   = **packed array** [1..10] **of** *char*;

Then *fixedString10* and *fString10* are compatible string types, and values of either type are assignment compatible with the other. If we declare variables *s* and *t* by

> **var**
>   *s* : *fixedString10*
>   *t* : *fString10*

then the assignments

> *s* := *t*

and

> *t* := *s*

are allowed. The same principle also holds for anonymous types. If variables *u* and *v* are declared by

var
  u : **packed array** [1..10] **of** *char*;
  v : **packed array** [1..10] **of** *char*;

then the types of *s*, *t*, *u*, and *v* are all compatible, and values of any one of the four types are assignment compatible with each of the other three. Thus assignments such as the following are valid:

  s := *u*;
  v := *t*;
  u := *v*

String constants such as 'computer' are defined in such a way that they will be values of Pascal string types. A sequence of two or more characters enclosed in single quotation marks is defined to represent a value of type

  packed array [1..*length*]

where *length* is the number of characters in the sequence. Thus

  'computer'

represents a value of type

  packed array [1..8] **of** *char*

and

  'This is a string constant'

represents a value of type

  packed array [1..25] **of** *char*

The type of a string constant is compatible with (and the constant itself is assignment compatible with) any string type whose strings have the same length as the constant.

Constants such as 'a', '0', and '$' represent values of type *char* rather than values of type

  packed array [1..1] **of** *char*

For fixed-length strings, this makes good sense. We would never bother to define an array type whose values are single characters; we would just use type *char* instead. When one attempts to implement variable-length strings, however, this convention becomes an annoyance, because a variable-length string containing a single character is perfectly reasonable.

Fixed-length strings can be compared with the relational operators =, <, >, <=, >=, and <>. The two strings being compared must belong to compatible string types, which means that they must have the same length. Two strings are equal if they contain the same characters in the same order. One string precedes another if it comes before the other in lexicographical order (alphabetical order extended to include characters other than letters). Lexicographical order is defined by the collating sequence for values of type *char*. For example, suppose *s* and *t* are declared by

  s : **packed array** [1..8] **of** *char*;
  t : **packed array** [1..8] **of** *char*;

Then the assignments

$s := $ 'hardware';
$t := $ 'software'

are valid, as are the following Boolean expressions:

$s < t$
$s = $ 'computer'
'operator' $>$ 'computer'

Assuming that the indicated assignments have been carried out, the value of the first Boolean expression is *true*, because 'hardware' precedes 'software' in alphabetical order. The value of the second expression is *false*, because 'hardware' and 'computer' are not equal. The value of the third expression is *true*, because 'operator' follows 'computer' in alphabetical order.

String values can be written by *write* and *writeln* statements but cannot be read by *read* and *readln* statements. Strings must be read character by character. Thus if s is declared by

var
    $s : $ **packed array** $[1..10]$ **of** *char*

then

write (s)

is allowed and will write 10 characters. However, to read 10 characters and store them in the components of s, we must use

for $i := 1$ **to** 10 **do**
    read $(s[i])$

For versions of Pascal that do not allow components of packed variables in *read* and *readln* statements, we must use

for $i := 1$ **to** 10 **do**
    begin
        read (c);
        $s[i] := c$
    end

where c is a character variable.

Variable-Length Strings

Some languages, including many extended versions of Pascal, provide a variable-length-string type *string*, whose values include all one-character strings, all two-character strings, all three-character strings, and so on. Also included is the *null string*, which contains zero characters. Note that (in Pascal, at least) there is no such thing as a fixed-length null string. Such a string could only be represented as an array with zero components, and Pascal does not allow definition of an array type whose values have no components.

Suppose we declare s to be a string variable:

$s : $ *string*;

If *s* corresponds to a fixed area of memory, then that memory area must be large enough to hold the longest string that can be assigned to *s*. In order for the language processor to know how much memory to allocate for *s*, we must impose some upper limit on the length of strings that can be assigned to *s*. An upper limit of 80 is often used; we will assume that limit here. Thus type *string* consists of all strings having from 0 to 80 characters.

If the strings with which we are dealing are shorter than 80 characters, we may wish to reserve less memory than would be required to hold an 80-character string. This is particularly true if a large number of strings must be stored, as in an array or file. On the other hand, we may want to allocate more than 80 characters worth of memory to store a particularly long string. To accommodate such requirements, we may specify the maximum length of the strings belonging to a variable-length-string type. Type *string*[10] consists of all strings up to 10 characters long, type *string*[20] consists of all strings up to 20 characters long, and so on.

The integer constant in brackets is a *parameter value*. When some aspect of a type is specified by a parameter value, we refer to the type as a *parametric type*. If the parameter value is omitted, a default value of 80 is assumed. Thus *string* and *string*[80] refer to the same type.

The types *string*[1], *string*[2], *string*[3], and so on are equivalent in every respect save the maximum length of the strings. Thus all values of *string*[10] also belong to *string*[20], but the reverse is not true. If we declare *s* and *t* by

> *s* : *string*[10];
> *t* : *string*[20];

then the assignment

> *t* := *s*

is always allowed, since every value of *string*[10] also belongs to *string*[20]. But the assignment

> *s* := *t*

is allowed only if the value of *t* belongs to *string*[10]—if it has no more than 10 characters. If the value of *t* has more than 10 characters, the attempted assignment causes an error.

To provide a uniform notation for strings, character constants and fixed-length-string constants are also used to denote variable-length strings. A constant is converted from type *char* or a fixed-length-string type to a variable-length-string type as required. For example, if *s* is a variable of type *string*, then the assignments

> *s* := 'c'

and

> *s* := 'computer'

are both valid. In the first example, the value of 'c' is converted from type *char* to type *string* before being assigned to *s*. In the second example, the value of 'computer' is converted from type **packed array** [1..8] **of** *char* to type *string* before being assigned to *s*. The null string, which contains zero characters, is denoted by

> ''

This is *not* a fixed-length-string constant since, as mentioned earlier, there is no such thing as a fixed-length null string.

Operations on Variable-Length Strings

In this section we will look at some typical operations on variable-length strings. The descriptions of the operations serve two purposes: (1) to describe some operations usually available in languages that provide variable-length strings, and (2) to specify the operations of the abstract string data type that we will implement later in the chapter.

Comparisons

Variable-length strings can be compared with relational operators $=$, $<$, $>$, $<=$, $>=$, and $<>$. If the two strings being compared are the same length, the comparison is the same as for characters or for fixed-length strings. If the strings are of different lengths, they cannot be equal. Lexicographical order determines which of two strings precedes the other. Thus the value of

> 'correspondent' < 'corridor'

is *true* since 'correspondent' precedes 'corridor' in lexicographical order. If one string is equal to the initial part of another, the shorter string precedes the larger. Thus

> 'compute' < 'computer'

and

> 'program' < 'programmer'

both have the value *true*.

Append

We can append, or join, one string to the end of another, a process sometimes called *concatenation* (literally, "chaining together"). The procedure call

> *Append* (*s1*, *s2*)

sets *s1* to the result of appending the value of *s2* to the value of *s1*. *s1* must be a variable, since its value is changed by the append operation. *s2* can be either a variable or a constant, since its value is not changed.

For example, after the statements

> *s* := 'program';
> *Append* (*s*, 'mer')

the value of *s* is 'programmer'. Likewise, after the statements

> *s* := '';
> *Append* (*s*, 'to');
> *Append* (*s*, 'get');
> *Append* (*s*, 'her');
> *Append* (*s*, 'ness')

the value of *s* is 'togetherness'.

Substring

A substring is a segment of a larger string. We can specify a substring by giving the position of its first character together with the number of characters in the substring. For example, in the string

'programmer'

the substring

'ram'

begins at character 5 of the larger string and is 3 characters long. An alternate method of specifying a substring is to give the positions of its first and last characters. Using this method we could say that the substring 'ram' consists of characters 5 through 7 of 'programmer'.

The procedure

Substring (s1, s2, i, n)

extracts a designated substring from string *s2* and assigns the extracted substring to *s1*. The value of *i* is the position of the first character of the substring, and the value of *n* is the number of characters in the substring. Thus after the procedure call

Substring (s, 'programmer', 5, 3)

the value of *s* is 'ram'. Likewise, after the procedure call

Substring (s, 'concatenate', 4, 3)

the value of *s* is 'cat', and after

Substring (s, 'concatenate', 8, 4)

the value of *s* is 'nate'. After the sequence

Substring (s, 'concatenate', 8, 4);
Substring (s, s, 2, 3)

the value of *s* is 'ate'. Note that in the final call, the variable *s* both supplies the string from which a substring is to be extracted and receives the result of the extraction.

Insert

The insert procedure creates a new string by inserting a given string within another string. Specifically, the procedure call

Insert (s1, s2, i)

inserts string *s1* before the *i*th character of string *s2*. *s2* must be a variable, the value of which will be changed by the procedure. The other two parameters supply values only. For example, after the statements

s := 'the lazy dog';
Insert ('very ', s, 5)

the value of *s* is

'the very lazy dog'

If the value of *i* is one greater than the number of characters in the value of *s2*, the value of *s1* is appended to the end of the value of *s2*. For example, the statements

> *s* := 'program';
> *Insert* ('mer', *s*, 8)

have the same effect as the statements

> *s* := 'program';
> *Append* (*s*, 'mer')

In either case, the final value of *s* is 'programmer'.

Delete

The procedure

> *Delete* (*s*, *i*, *n*)

deletes from the value of the string variable *s* the *n*-character substring beginning at position *i*. For example, after the statements

> *s* := 'the quick brown fox';
> *Delete* (*s*, 11, 6)

the value of *s* is

> 'the quick fox'

Note that the blank following 'brown' is part of the substring to be deleted.

Delete and Insert can be used together for the common string-processing operation of replacing a substring by another string. *Delete* is used to delete the existing substring, and *Insert* is used to insert its replacement. For example, if the preceding two statements are followed by

> *Insert* ('red ', *s*, 11)

the value of *s* will be

> 'the quick red fox'

The overall effect of the deletion followed by the insertion is to replace 'brown ' with 'red '.

Index and Length

The function

> *Index*(*s1*, *s2*, *i*)

searches the string *s1* for the first occurrence of a substring equal to string *s2*. The search begins at position *i* in *s1*. If the given substring is found, *Index* returns the position of its first character. If the given substring is not found, *Index* returns the value zero.

Expression	Value
Index('computer', 'ter', 1)	6
Index('computer', 'tor', 1)	0
Index('concatenate', 'ate', 1)	5
Index('concatenate', 'ate', 6)	9
Index('concatenate', 'ate', 10)	0

The function

Length(s)

returns the number of characters in the string s.

Expression	Value
Length('concatenate')	11
Length('computer')	8
Length('')	0

Index can be used to locate a substring that is to be deleted with *Delete* or to be replaced with *Delete* followed by *Insert*.

Skip

In processing a string, we may wish to skip over occurrences of a certain character. Blank spaces are the characters most commonly skipped, since blanks usually have no significance in themselves, but serve only to separate significant items such as words and numbers. In the procedure call

Skip (s, i, c)

the value of the integer variable i designates a position in the string s. The procedure call increases the value of i until the character at position i is not equal to c, thus skipping any occurrences of character c. For example, after the execution of the statements

$i := 4$;
Skip ('xxxyyyyyzzzyyy', i, 'y')

the value i is 9, the position of the first occurrence of 'z'. If we think of the value of i as a pointer into the string, then the pointer was moved forward in the string until a character other than 'y' was encountered.

Data Conversion

Suppose that the value of s is the string

'Quantity ordered: 2500'

We may wish to extract the number 2500 and carry out numerical processing on it; for example, we may multiply it by a unit price to get the total cost of the quantity ordered. The substring operation

Substring (t, s, 19, 4)

extracts the string '2500' and assigns it to *t*. But as far as the computer is concerned, '2500' is a string, not a number, and no numerical operations can be carried out on it. To perform numerical computations with numbers embedded in strings, we need to convert strings representing numbers into the corresponding values of type *integer* or *real*.

The function *StringToInteger* takes as its argument a string representing an integer value and returns the corresponding integer. Any leading blanks—blanks preceding the first character of the integer—are ignored. It is an error if the string does not represent a value of type *integer*. The following table illustrates the function *StringToInteger*:

Expression	Value
StringToInteger('2500')	2500
StringToInteger(' +2500')	2500
StringToInteger(' −2500')	−2500
StringToInteger(' 2500')	2500
StringToInteger('2y500')	Error

Likewise, we may need to convert a numerical result to a string, perhaps so that the value can be inserted in the proper position in a line of a report. The procedure

IntegerToString (*s*, *n*)

assigns to string variable *s* the string corresponding to integer *n*. For example, the procedure call

IntegerToString (*s*, −1000)

assigns the string '−1000' to *s*.

Similar procedures can be devised for real numbers. If the value of *s* is a string representing a real number, then the value of *StringToReal*(*s*) is the corresponding value of type *real*. If the value of *x* is a real number, the procedure call

RealToString (*s*, *x*)

assigns the corresponding string to *s*.

The Pascal system uses data conversion procedures to implement the statements for reading from and writing to a textfile. For example, when a string representing an integer is read from a textfile with *readln*, the system must call *StringToInteger* to convert the string to the corresponding integer. When a real number is to be written to a textfile with *writeln*, *RealToString* must be called to convert the real number to a sequence of characters that can be stored in the file.

Implementation Considerations

In this section we will look at three common approaches to implementing variable-length strings. In the following section we will employ one of these approaches to implement an abstract data type for variable-length strings.

The memory area allocated for a variable-length string will usually be larger than the actual length of the string stored there. We need, then, some way of determining the length of the string, of determining which memory locations hold characters of the string and which are unused. The most obvious way to do this is to store both the length of the string as well as the characters making it up. For example, a value of type *string*[10] might be stored as a record with the following form:

> **record**
>   *length* : 0..10;
>   *data*   : **packed array** [1..10] **of** *char*
> **end**

In all our implementations, the word **packed** can be omitted if its use does not save any space for a particular Pascal implementation.

The value of the *length* field gives the length of the string. If the value of the *length* field is 10, then the string is 10 characters long, and all the components of the *data* field are in use. If the value of the *length* field is 5, then the string is contained in the first five characters of the data field; the remaining five characters are unused and contain garbage. If the value of the *length* field is 0, the record represents the null string, which contains no characters; in that case, all the components of the *data* field are unused. Figure 11-1 illustrates this method of representing variable-length strings.

Instead of storing the length of the string as an integer, we can terminate the string with a sentinel character. The ASCII null character, the character with ordinal number zero, is usually used as the sentinel. (Don't confuse the null *character*, which has ordinal number zero, with the null *string*, which has length zero.) With this method, values of type *string*[10] can be stored in an 11-character array of type

> **packed array** [1..11] **of** *char*

Figure 11-1.

Representing a variable-length string by a record with an integer field and an array-of-character field. The integer field holds the length of the string, and the array-of-character field holds the characters comprising the string. The shaded positions of the character array are unused.

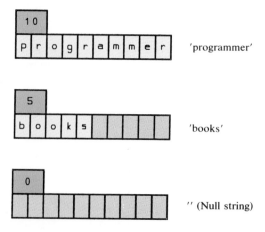

Figure 11-2.

Representing a variable-length string by an array of characters. The end of the string is marked by a sentinel character, represented here by ϕ. The shaded positions following the sentinel character are unused.

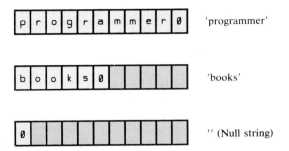

Up to 10 components of the array can be used for string characters and one component is used for the sentinel. When the string 'computer' is stored, for example, components 1 through 8 of the array contain the characters of the string, component 9 contains the sentinel character, and components 10 and 11 are unused. Figure 11-2 illustrates this method of representing variable-length strings.

This method has the advantage of using a simpler data structure, since only an array is required rather than a record with an integer field and an array field. A disadvantage is that string-processing operations must scan the string for the sentinel character in order to locate the end of the string. When the length is stored as a separate field, no such scan is necessary.

Figure 11-3 illustrates a variation on this method, in which the array has only enough components to store the maximum number of characters in the string. That is, values of type *string*[10] would be stored in a 10-character array of type

packed array [1..10] **of** *char*

If the string has the maximum length, then all the components of the array will be used for string characters, and no sentinel will be present. If the string

Figure 11-3.

In this variation on the representation of Figure 11-2, a variable-length string that is shorter than the character array in which it is stored is terminated by a sentinel character. If the string takes up all the positions in the array, however, no sentinel character is present.

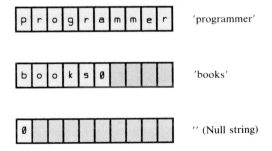

has less than the maximum length, then it will be followed by a sentinel character.

The advantage of this method, aside from saving one array component, is that it unifies fixed-length and variable-length strings. When all the array components are in use, as is always the case for fixed-length strings, then fixed-length and variable-length strings are stored in exactly the same way. When the string being stored has fewer characters than the number of array components, then (and only then) is the last character of the string followed by a sentinel character. The disadvantage of this method is that the statements for locating the end of the string become even more complex, since not only must they scan for the sentinel character, they must make sure that they do not run off the end of the array if the sentinel character is not present.

Each of the implementation techniques discussed so far requires that enough memory be allocated for the largest possible string that can belong to a given type. In some circumstances, this can result in large amounts of memory being wasted. For example, consider an array of strings, most of which are short but a few of which are much longer than the average. Since all the components of the array must be of the same string type, the longest string will determine how much memory must be allocated to each component. Since most of the strings are short, most of this memory will be wasted.

We can avoid this waste of memory by storing all the strings used by a program in a single array of characters known as *string space*. By allowing all strings to share the same memory area, we do not have to allocate a fixed number of memory locations to each string variable. The value of a string variable is represented not by the characters of the string itself but by a *descriptor* that gives the length of the string and the index of the first character of the string. The string itself is stored in string space. Thus the value of a string variable is a record of the form

> **record**
>   *length* : *integer*;
>   *index* : *integer*
> **end**

If *s* is a string variable, and *stringSpace* is the character array in which all strings are stored, then the string corresponding to *s* is stored in components

> *stringSpace*[*s.index*]

through

> *stringSpace*[*s.index* + *s.length* − 1]

of the character array. Figure 11-4 illustrates this method of implementing variable-length strings.

When a string is assigned to a string variable, the string is stored in the unused area at the end of string space, and the *length* and *index* components of the string variable are modified to refer to the new string. The area of string space occupied by the previous value of the string variable becomes unused. After many assignments have taken place, string space becomes *fragmented*, with used and unused areas intermixed with one another. Although the total size of all the unused areas may be large, no one area may be large enough to hold a particular string that needs to be stored.

Figure 11-4.

In this representation of variable-length strings, all the strings used by a program are stored in a single character array called *stringSpace*. The value of a string variable is not the characters comprising the string but rather a descriptor giving the length of the string and a pointer to the location containing the string's first character.

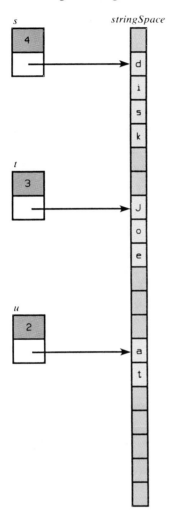

When string space becomes fragmented, a procedure called the *garbage collector* is invoked. The garbage collector eliminates the fragmentation by collecting all the strings into a block at the beginning of the array and all the unused areas (the garbage) into another block at the end of the array. Memory for new strings can now be allocated from the block of unused locations at the end of the array. Figure 11-5 illustrates the fragmentation of string space and the effect of garbage collection.

When the garbage collector moves a string, it must appropriately modify the index component of the string variable that refers to that string. In general, the garbage collector has three tasks.

Figure 11-5.

Before garbage collection, string space is fragmented. Here, for example, there is no single block of unused space in which a 10-character string can be stored even though there are more than 10 unused locations. Garbage collection collects all the strings into one block and all the unused locations into another, thus making the unused locations available for storing new strings. Note that the pointer components of the string descriptors must be adjusted to reflect the new positions of the strings.

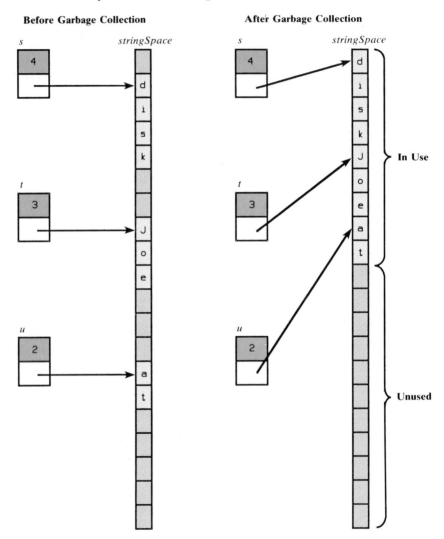

1. Determine which areas of string space are in use; that is, which areas are referred to by string variables.

2. Move each string as far as possible toward the beginning of the array, so that all the strings are collected into a single block.

3. Update the index components of the string variables to refer to the new locations of the strings that were moved.

Garbage collection can be time-consuming, particularly if it is poorly imple-mented, as it is in some microcomputer versions of BASIC.

This method of representing strings is one of the best for strings stored in main memory. It is not useful, however, for storing strings in records that are to be written to files. The fields of the records must contain the actual characters of the string, rather than references to a string space in main memory, the contents of which will be lost when the computer is turned off. Other than this, the main disadvantage of the method is the need to occasionally interrupt processing to perform a garbage collection.

An Abstract Data Type for Variable-Length Strings

In this section we will see how to obtain variable-length strings in standard Pascal by implementing an abstract data type *VariableLengthString* (see Figure 11-6). This type has been largely defined by the preceding discussions of variable-length strings, so we can turn at once to the implementation.

Our implementation contains the following definitions and declarations:

```
type
    ndxRange = 1..maxLength;
    vString = record
                    length : 0..maxLength;
                    data   : packed array [ndxRange] of char
                 end;

    var
    errorFlag : Boolean;
```

The program that uses the implementation must define the constant *maxLength*, which is the maximum length that a string can have. The actual length of a string, however, can vary from 0 through *maxLength*. Type *ndxRange*, which is the subrange 1..*maxLength*, is the index type of the array used to hold the characters of a string.

Figure 11-6.

Implementation of an abstract data type for variable-length strings. The program using the implementation specifies the maximum length of the strings by defining the constant *maxLength*.

{ ************ Implementation of *VariableLengthString* ************* }

{ Constant *maxLength* defined by program using *VariableLengthString* }

```
type
    ndxRange = 1..maxLength;
```

{ Values of type *vString* are variable-length strings with maximum length *maxLength* }

```
vString = record
                length : 0..maxLength;
                data   : packed array [ndxRange] of char
             end;
    var
    errorFlag : Boolean; { Global variable set by each subprogram }
```

Figure 11-6   *Continued.*

{ ----------------------------------- Function *Error* ----------------------------------- }

function *Error* : *Boolean*;

{ Return value of and clear error indicator }

```
begin
  Error := errorFlag;
  errorFlag := false
end; { Error }
```

{ ----------------------------------- Procedure *Skip* ----------------------------------- }

procedure *Skip* (**var** *s* : *vString*; **var** *i* : *integer*; *c* : *char*);

{ Increment *i* while the character at position *i* in *s* equals *c* }

```
var
  skipping : Boolean;
begin
  if (i < 1) or (i > s.length) then
    errorFlag := true
  else
    begin
      errorFlag := false;
      skipping := true;
      while (i <= s.length) and skipping do
        if s.data[i] = c then
          i := i + 1
        else
          skipping := false
    end
end; { Skip }
```

{ ----------------------------- Function *StringToInteger* ----------------------------- }

function *StringToInteger* (**var** *s* : *vString*) : *integer*;

{ Convert the string *s* to the corresponding integer }

```
var
  value, limit : real;
  j, sign      : integer;
  c            : char;
```

Figure 11-6 *Continued.*

```
begin
  limit := maxint;
  value := 0.0;
  sign := 1;
  j := 1;
  Skip (s, j, ' ');
  if j <= s.length then
    begin
      c := s.data[j];
      if c = '+' then
        j := j + 1
      else if c = '−' then
        begin
          sign := −1;
          j := j + 1;
        end
    end;
  errorFlag := false;
  while (j <= s.length) and (not errorFlag) do
    begin
      c := s.data[j];
      if not (c in ['0'..'9']) then
        errorFlag := true
      else
        begin
          value := 10.0 * value + ord(c) − ord('0');
          if value > limit then
            begin
              value := limit;
              errorFlag := true;
            end;
          j := j + 1;
        end;
    end;
  StringToInteger := sign * round(value)
end; { StringToInteger }


{------------------------------ Function Length ------------------------------ }

function Length (var s : vString) : integer;

{ Return the length of string s }

begin
  errorFlag := false;
  Length := s.length
end; { Length }
```

Figure 11-6   *Continued.*

```
{ ------------------------------- Function EqualTo ------------------------------- }

function EqualTo (var s1, s2 : vString) : Boolean;

{ Return true if the values of s1 and s2 are equal }

var
  j       : integer;
  equal : Boolean;
begin
  errorFlag := false;
  if s1.length <> s2.length then
    equal := false
  else
    begin
      equal := true;
      j := 1;
      while (j <= s1.length) and equal do
        begin
          if s1.data[j] <> s2.data[j] then
            equal := false;
          j := j + 1
        end;
    end;
  EqualTo := equal
end; { EqualTo }


{ ------------------------------- Function Index ------------------------------- }

function Index (var s1, s2 : vString; i : integer) : integer;

{ Return the position of the first occurrence of s2 in the part of s1
  beginning at position i. Return zero if no such occurrence is found }

var
  j, k, m : integer;
  found  : Boolean;
begin
  j := i;
  k := s1.length - s2.length + 1;
  if (j < 1) or (j > k) then
    begin
      errorFlag := true;
      Index := 0
    end
  else
    begin
      errorFlag := false;
      repeat
        found := true;
        m := 1;
```

Figure 11-6   *Continued.*

```
            while (m <= s2.length) and found do
              begin
                if s1.data[j + m - 1] <> s2.data[m] then
                  found := false;
                m := m + 1
              end;
            j := j + 1
          until (j > k) or found;
          if found then
            Index := j - 1
          else
            Index := 0
        end
end; { Index}
```

{ ------------------------------- Procedure *ReadLine* ------------------------------- }

procedure *ReadLine* (**var** *f* : *text*; **var** *s* : *vString*);

{ Read a line from textfile *f* and assign line read to *s* }

```
var
  j : integer;
  c : char;
begin
  errorFlag := false;
  j := 1;
  while (j <= maxLength) and (not eoln(f)) do
    begin
      read (f, c);
      s.data[j] := c;
      j := j + 1
    end;
  s.length := j - 1;
  readln (f)
end; { ReadLine }
```

{ ------------------------------- Procedure *WriteString* ------------------------------- }

procedure *WriteString* (**var** *f* : *text*; **var** *s* : *vString*);

{ Write string *s* to textfile *f*; do not terminate line }

```
var
  j : integer;
begin
  errorFlag := false;
  for j := 1 to s.length do
    write(f, s.data[j])
end; { WriteString }
```

Figure 11-6   *Continued.*

```
{ --------------------------------- Procedure WriteLine --------------------------------- }

procedure WriteLine (var f : text; var s : vString);

{ Write string s to textfile f; terminate line }

begin
  WriteString (f, s);
  writeln (f)
end; { WriteLine }

{ --------------------------------- Procedure Append --------------------------------- }

procedure Append (var s1, s2 : vString);

{ Append string s2 to the end of string s1 }

var
  j, k : integer;
begin
  if s1.length + s2.length > maxLength then
    errorFlag := true
  else
    begin
      errorFlag := false;
      j := s1.length + 1;
      for k := 1 to s2.length do
        begin
          s1.data[j] := s2.data[k];
          j := j + 1
        end;
      s1.length := s1.length + s2.length
    end
end; { Append }

{ --------------------------------- Procedure Insert --------------------------------- }

procedure Insert (s1 : vString; var s2 : vString; i : integer);

{ Insert string s1 into string s2 before position i. If i equals Length(s2) + 1,
  append s1 to s2 }

var
  j, k : integer;
begin
  if (i < 1) or (i > s2.length + 1) or
     (s1.length + s2.length > maxLength) then
    errorFlag := true
```

Figure 11-6 *Continued.*

```
    else
      begin
        errorFlag := false;
        j := s2.length;
        k := s1.length + s2.length;
        while j >= i do
          begin
            s2.data[k] := s2.data[j];
            j := j − 1;
            k := k − 1
          end;
        j := i;
        for k := 1 to s1.length do
          begin
            s2.data[j] := s1.data[k];
            j := j + 1
          end;
        s2.length := s1.length + s2.length
      end
end; { Insert }

{---------------------------------- Procedure Delete ---------------------------------- }

procedure Delete (var s : vString; i, n : integer);

{ Delete n characters from string s starting at position i }

var
  j, k : integer;
begin
  if (i < 1) or (i + n − 1 > s.length) then
    errorFlag := true
  else
    begin
      errorFlag := false;
      j := i;
      k := i + n;
      while k <= s.length do
        begin
          s.data[j] := s.data[k];
          j := j + 1;
          k := k + 1
        end;
      s.length := s.length − n
    end
end; { Delete }
```

Figure 11-6   *Continued.*

```
{-------------------------------- Procedure Substring --------------------------------}

procedure Substring (var s1 : vString; s2 : vString; i, n : integer);

{ Assign to s1 the substring of length n beginning at position i in string s2 }

var
  j, k : integer;
begin
  if (i < 1) or (i + n − 1 > s2.length) or (n < 0) then
    errorFlag := true
  else
    begin
      errorFlag := false;
      s1.length := n;
      j := i;
      for k := 1 to n do
        begin
          s1.data[k] := s2.data[j];
          j := j + 1
        end
    end
end; { Substring }


{-------------------------------- Procedure Assign --------------------------------}

procedure Assign (var s1 : vString;
                  s2      : packed array [lo..hi : integer] of char);

{ Convert fixed-length string s2 to variable-length string s1; s2 is a
  conformant array parameter }

var
  j, k : integer;
begin
  if hi − lo + 1 > maxLength then
    errorFlag := true
  else
    begin
      errorFlag := false;
      s1.length := hi − lo + 1;
      k := 1;
      for j := lo to hi do
        begin
          s1.data[k] := s2[j];
          k := k + 1
        end
    end
end; { Assign }
```

Type *vString* is the type of a variable-length string. A string is represented as a record with two fields: the *length* field, which holds the length of the string; and the *data* field, which holds the characters making up the string.

The global variable *errorFlag* is set to *true* or *false* depending on whether or not the immediately preceding string operation caused an error. The variable *errorFlag* is considered private to the implementation; users access its value via a Boolean function *Error*. The value returned by *Error* is *true* or *false* depending on whether or not the immediately preceding string operation caused an error.

As we have seen, the wisdom of using global variables is debatable. As an alternative to *errorFlag* and *Error*, we could provide each function and procedure with an error parameter for returning *true* or *false* depending on whether the function or procedure caused an error. But functions and procedures will be frequently invoked in circumstances in which no error can occur; such invocations would have to contain an error parameter even though it would serve no useful purpose. The function *Error*, however, need only be called when there is the possibility that an error actually occurred.

The following are the full headings for the functions and procedures that our implementation provides:

```
function Error : Boolean;
procedure Skip (var s : vString; var i : integer; c : char);
function StringToInteger (var s : vString) : integer;
function Length (var s : vString) : integer;
function EqualTo (var s1, s2 : vString) : Boolean;
function Index (var s1, s2 : vString; i : integer) : integer;
procedure ReadLine (var f : text; var s : vString);
procedure WriteString (var f : text; var s : vString);
procedure WriteLine (var f : text; var s : vString);
procedure Append (var s1, s2 : vString);
procedure Insert (s1 : vString; var s2 : vString; i : integer);
procedure Delete (var s : vString; i, n : integer);
procedure Substring (var s1 : vString; s2 : vString; i, n : integer);
procedure Assign (var s1 : vString;
                  s2    : packed array [lo..hi : integer] of char);
```

Most of these operations and functions were defined in our previous discussion of variable-length strings. However, our previous discussion assumed a predefined variable-length-string type that was recognized by such built-in operations as the relational operators and the procedures *readln* and *writeln*. Since our do-it-yourself string type is foreign to the underlying Pascal implementation, we will have to provide our own versions of some of the built-in operations and system facilities. Now we'll discuss the additional functions and procedures required.

We have already mentioned the Boolean function *Error*, which returns *true* or *false* depending on whether or not the preceding string operation caused an error condition.

The relational operators $<$, $<=$, $>$, and $>=$ cannot be applied to our representation of variable-length strings; $=$ and $<>$ can be applied, but do not yield the desired results. (Why?) We must therefore define Boolean functions *EqualTo*, *LessThan*, and so on to replace the built-in comparison operators. Only *EqualTo* is actually implemented; the remaining comparison functions are left as exercises.

ReadLine reads an entire line from the textfile *f* and assigns the line read to the string variable *s*.

WriteString writes the value of the string variable *s* to the textfile *f*.

WriteLine is the same as *WriteString* except that *WriteLine* goes to a new line after writing the value of *s*.

In our preceding discussion, we allowed string constants, such as 'computer', to be used as parameters as in

$n := Length('\text{computer}')$

This usage assumes that either (1) string constants represent variable-length strings, or (2) string constants represent fixed-length strings but the system will automatically convert from fixed-length to variable-length strings as required. Unfortunately, neither situation holds in standard Pascal; string constants represent fixed-length strings and, since the system knows nothing of our variable-length-string type, no automatic conversion is possible. Thus for all procedures except *Assign*, only string variables (not string constants) can be used as parameters. Since only string variables can be used as parameters, *vString* parameters have been declared as variable parameters *except* in those cases where we need to make a copy of a parameter value to keep the value from being destroyed before it is used.

To allow the implementation to make use of string constants, the procedure *Assign* converts the fixed-length string constant *s2* to a variable-length string, which is assigned to the string variable *s1*. Thus to find the length of 'computer' with our implementation, we would have to write

Assign (*s*, 'computer');
$n := Length(s)$

The parameter *s2* of *Assign* is a *conformant array parameter*, which will accept arrays of varying sizes. Conformant array parameters are available in ISO Pascal but not in ANSI/IEEE Pascal. When conformant parameters are not available, *Assign* is more cumbersome to write and use, since all fixed-length-string parameters must have the same length, which is determined once and for all when *Assign* is written.

We now turn our attention to the individual functions and procedures that implement *VariableLengthString*.

Error

The Boolean function *Error* returns the value of the *errorFlag* and clears *errorFlag* to *false*.

Skip

The procedure call *Skip* (*s*, *i*, *c*) increments the value of *i* as long as the character of *s* designated by *i* (the value of *s.data*[*i*]) is equal to *c*. The value of *i* is modified as described; the values of *s* and *c* remain unchanged.

If the initial value of *i* is less than 1 or greater than *s.length*, then *errorFlag* is set to *true*. Otherwise, *errorFlag* is set to *false* and the value of *i* is incremented until a character not equal to *c* is encountered or until the scan runs off the end of the string (the value of i is equal to $s.length + 1$). The Boolean variable *skipping* is initially *true* and is set to *false* when a character not equal to the value of c is encountered.

```
errorFlag := false;
skipping := true;
while (i <= s.length) and skipping do
   if s.data[i] = c then
      i := i + 1
   else
      skipping := false
```

StringToInteger

This function converts a string to the integer value that it represents. The function call is invalid if the string does not represent an integer value. The companion procedure *IntegerToString* is left as an exercise. Students may also wish to tackle the much more complex function *StringToReal* and procedure *RealToString*.

The value represented by the string may exceed the largest permissible integer value, *maxint*. In that case, attempting to convert the string to an integer will lead to *integer overflow*—exceeding the value of *maxint*. To prevent integer overflow from occurring unexpectedly during the function's computations, the value represented by the string is computed as a value of type *real*, then converted to type *integer* if it lies in the range allowed for integer values.

The value of the parameter s is the string value to be converted. During conversion, the real variable *value* holds the value of that part of the string that has already been converted. The real variable *limit* holds the real number corresponding to the largest possible integer, *maxint*. An error occurs if the value of *value* exceeds that of *limit*. The integer variable j is used as an index into the string being converted. The integer variable *sign* is set to 1 if a positive number is being converted and to -1 if a negative number is being converted. The character variable c holds the next string character to be processed.

To begin, *limit* is set to the largest value allowed for the result of the conversion, *value* is initialized to 0.0, *sign* is initialized to 1 (a positive number is the default if no sign character is encountered), and j is set to point to the first character of the string to be converted. The procedure *Skip* is called to skip over any leading blanks.

```
limit := maxint;
value := 0.0;
sign := 1;
j := 1;
Skip (s, j, ' ')
```

The variable c is set to the first nonblank character of s. If this character is a plus sign, it is just skipped over (*sign* has already been initialized to 1). If the character is a minus sign, it is skipped and *sign* is set to -1.

```
          if j < = s.length then
            begin
              c := s.data[j];
              if c = '+' then
                j := j + 1
              else if c = '-' then
                begin
                  sign := -1;
                  j := j + 1;
                end
            end
```

The **while** statement scans the string to be converted as long as we have not run off the end of the string and no error has occurred. The variable *c* is set to the next character of the string being converted. If this character is not a digit—if it does not lie in the range '0' through '9'—then *errorFlag* is set to *true*. Otherwise, the digit represented by the value of *c* is incorporated into the converted value.

We use the expression

$$ord(c) - ord('0')$$

to convert the digit *c* to the integer that it represents. For example, if the value of *c* is '5', we have (assuming the ASCII code)

$$ord('5') - ord('0') = 53 - 48 = 5$$

If the value of *c* is '9', we have

$$ord('9') - ord('0') = 57 - 48 = 9$$

and so on.

To incorporate a new digit into the part of the number that has already been converted, we multiply *value* by 10 and add the value of the new digit.

$$value := 10.0 * value + ord(c) - ord('0')$$

To see how this statement works, suppose that the string to be converted is '27534'. Assume that the digits 2, 7, and 5 have already been processed, so that the next digit to be processed is 3. The value of *value* is 275, the part of the number that has already been converted, and the value of *c* is '3', the next digit to be processed. The statement just shown is then executed as follows:

```
value := 10.0 * value + ord(c) - ord('0')
value := 10.0 * 275.0 + ord('3') - ord('0')
value := 2750.0 + 51 - 48
value := 2750.0 + 3
value := 2753.0
```

After each new digit is incorporated in the converted value, that value is checked to see if it exceeds the value of *limit*. If it does, the value being converted is too large to be represented by a value of type *integer*. *Value* is set to the value of the largest permissible integer, and *errorFlag* is set to *true*.

When the repetition terminates, we need only to change the converted value from a real number to an integer, multiply it by the value of *sign*, and return it as the value of *StringToInteger*.

$$StringToInteger := sign * round(value)$$

As long as the maximum number of significant digits for a real number has not been exceeded, our calculations should be exact and the value of *value* should be a whole number. Thus we could, in principle, use either *trunc* or *round* to convert the real number to an integer. In practice, using *round* will help compensate for any small inaccuracies resulting from bugs in the system procedures for real-number arithmetic.

Length

The function call *Length(s)* clears the error flag and returns the length of string *s*. Note that in the statement

$$Length := s.length$$

the field identifier *length* cannot be confused with the function name *Length*, even though Pascal does not distinguish between upper- and lowercase letters. Since *length* is preceded by a period, it must refer to the field identifier; since *Length* is not preceded by a period, it must refer to the function name.

EqualTo

The function call *EqualTo(s1, s2)* returns *true* if strings *s1* and *s2* are equal and *false* otherwise. *EqualTo* plays the same role for variable-length strings as the relational operation = does for fixed-length strings. The = operator cannot be used for variable-length strings, since it would compare all the array components of the string values being compared. But only the array components that are in use need agree in order for two string values to be equal. The unused array components can contain arbitrary values.

The Boolean variable *equal* is set to *false* as soon as it is discovered that the two strings are not equal. When processing is completed, the value of *equal* is returned as the value of *EqualTo*. The function begins by comparing the lengths of strings *s1* and *s2*; if the two strings have different lengths, they cannot possibly be equal, so *equal* is set to *false*.

If the two strings have the same length, *equal* is set to *true*, the index *j* is set to the first character of the two strings, and the two strings are scanned from left to right. The scan continues while there remain more characters to be scanned (the value of $j <= s1.length$ is *true*) and the value of *equal* remains *true*.

At each step of the scan, the values of the *j*th characters in each of the two strings are compared. If the two *j*th characters are not the same, *equal* is set to *false*, terminating the scan and causing the value *false* to be returned as the value of *EqualTo*.

```
j := 1;
while (j <= s1.length) and equal do
   begin
      if s1.data[j] <> s2.data[j] then
         equal := false;
      j := j + 1
   end
```

When processing terminates, the value of *equal* will be *true* only if no discrepancy was found between the two strings—if they have the same length and their corresponding characters are equal. Thus the final value of *equal* is returned as the value of *EqualTo*. Notice that the statements are arranged so as to terminate processing as soon as a discrepancy between the strings is found. This allows unequal strings to be detected quickly. The function does not waste its time completely scanning long strings that have different lengths or that differ in their first few characters.

Another approach to string comparison is to modify the procedures *ReadLine*, *Delete*, *Substring*, and *Assign* to store a given character—say the ASCII null character, *chr*(0)—in all unused positions of the character array. Variable-length strings could then be compared by applying the fixed-length string operators $=, <, >, <=, >=$, and $<>$ to the corresponding data arrays. That is, *s1* would be equal to *s2* only if the value of

$$s1.data = s2.data$$

was *true*.

Index

Starting at position *i* in *s1*, **Index** must search for a substring equal to the value of *s2*. As shown in Figure 11-7, we can think of *s2* as being laid along side *s1* with the first character of *s2* beneath the *i*th character of *s1*. Each character in *s2* is compared with the character immediately above it in *s1*. If all characters agree, the desired substring has been found, and the search terminates. Otherwise, *s2* is slid forward one character and the comparison is repeated. If the desired substring is not found, the search terminates when the last character of *s2* is beneath the last character of *s1*.

The index *j* points to the character in *s1* beneath which the first character in *s2* is placed. The initial value of *j* is *i*, the position in *s1* at which the search is to start. The final value of *j* is *k*, the position of the first character of *s2* when the last character of *s2* coincides with the last character of *s1* (see the fourth diagram in Figure 11-7). The value of *k* is set by

$$k := s1.length - s2.length + 1$$

If the initial value of *j* is less than 1 or greater than the value of *k*, then the requested search cannot be carried out. In that case *errorFlag* is set to *true* and the value 0 is returned by *Index*. Since the value 0 corresponds to "substring not found," it will be possible in some circumstances to rely entirely on the value returned by *Index* and not check the value of *errorFlag*.

If the requested search can be carried out, *errorFlag* is set to *false* and a **repeat** statement is used to slide string *s2* along string *s1*, comparing the characters of *s2* with the corresponding characters of *s1* at each position. The flag *found* is set to *true* if the comparison is successful and to *false* otherwise.

> **repeat**
> "Compare *s2* with the substring of *s1* beginning at
> position *j* and having the same length as *s2*. Set
> *found* to *true* or *false* depending on whether or
> not the comparison is successful."
> $j := j + 1$ { Slide *s2* forward by one position }
> **until** $(j > k)$ **or** *found*

Figure 11-7.

We can think of *Index* as sliding the string *s2* along the string *s1* one character at a time, checking in each position whether every character in *s2* equals the corresponding character in *s1*. Initially, the first character of *s2* coincides with the *i*th character of *s1*. The search terminates unsuccessfully if the last character of *s2* moves beyond the last character of *s1*.

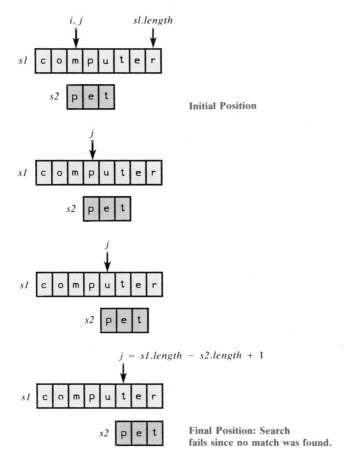

A **while** statement is used to compare *s2* with the corresponding substring of *s1*. Variable *m* is used as an index into *s2*; the character at position *m* in *s2* is compared with the character at position $j + m - 1$ in *s1*.

```
found := true;
m := 1;
while (m <= s2.length) and found do
   begin
      if s1.data[j + m - 1] <> s2.data[m] then
         found := false;
      m := m + 1
   end
```

When the **repeat** statement terminates, the value of *found* is *true* if the sought-after substring was found and *false* otherwise. If the value of *found* is *true*, the index of the substring that was found, the value of $j - 1$, is returned.

(The value of *j* was incremented by 1 after the successful comparison took place.) If the value of *found* is *false*, 0 is returned.

> **if** *found* **then**
>   *Index* := *j* − 1
> **else**
>   *Index* := 0

ReadLine

The procedure call *ReadLine* (*f*, *s*) reads a line from the textfile *f* and assigns it to the string variable *s*. Variable *j* is used as an index into the character array of string variable *s*. Characters are read from file *f* and stored in *s.data* as long as no more than *maxLength* characters have been stored, and the end of the line has not been reached.

> *j* := 1;
> **while** (*j* <= *maxLength*) **and** (**not** *eoln*(*f*)) **do**
>   **begin**
>   *read* (*f*, *c*);
>   *s.data*[*j*] := *c*;
>   *j* := *j* + 1
>   **end**

When the repetition terminates, the length of the newly read string is set to the value of *j* − 1, since the value of *j* was incremented by 1 after the last character was read. Finally, the statement

> *readln* (*f*)

is then executed to move the current position of file *f* to the beginning of the next line. Note that if the line read contains more than *maxLength* characters, the excess characters are discarded.

WriteString and WriteLine

The procedure call *WriteString* (*f*, *s*) writes the characters of string *s* to the textfile *f*. The current line is not terminated after the characters are written. The procedure *WriteLine* calls *WriteString* to write the characters of string *s* to file *f*, then executes

> *writeln* (*f*)

to terminate the current line. The code for the two procedures is straightforward.

Append

The procedure call *Append* (*s1*, *s2*) appends string *s2* to the end of string *s1*. The value of *s1* is modified by the operation; the value of *s2* is not changed.

The length of the string resulting from the append operation is the sum of the lengths of *s1* and *s2*. If this sum exceeds *maxLength*, *errorFlag* is set to *true*. Otherwise, *errorFlag* is set to *false* and the characters of *s2.data* are copied into *s1.data* immediately following the characters of string *s1*.

```
    j := s1.length + 1;
    for k := 1 to s2.length do
      begin
        s1.data[j] := s2.data[k];
        j := j + 1
      end
```

The new length of s1 is set to the old length of s1 plus the length of s2.

$$s1.length := s1.length + s2.length$$

Insert

The procedure call *Insert* (*s1*, *s2*, *i*) inserts string *s1* into string *s2* just before the character designated by *i*. Only the value of *s2* is changed by the operation. The value of *i* can be one greater than the length of *s2*, in which case the value of *s1* is appended to that of *s2*.

Note that the formal parameter *s1* is declared as a value parameter, in contrast to our practice so far of declaring all *vString* parameters as variable parameters. The problem is that the procedure needs the value of *s1* throughout its computations, but it begins immediately to change *s2* as it begins computing the result to be returned. Now suppose that *Insert* is called with the same actual parameter for the formal parameters *s1* and *s2*; that is, suppose we have a call of the form

Insert (s, s, i)

If both *s1* and *s2* were variable parameters, then changes made via *s2* would also change the value being accessed via *s1*, even though the latter value will be needed later in the calculations. What we need to do in this case is save a copy of the original value of *s* before starting to manipulate the value of *s* to produce the result. Making *s1* a value parameter accomplishes this aim; when the procedure is called, a copy of the value of *s* is assigned to *s1*. It is then this copy of the original value of *s*, rather than the current, modified value of *s*, that is referred to via *s1*.

The call to *Insert* is invalid if the value of *i* is less than 1 or greater than *s2.length* + 1, or if the sum of the lengths of *s1* and *s2* is greater than *maxLength*. If the call to *Insert* is invalid, *errorFlag* is set to *true*.

If the call to *Insert* is valid, *errorFlag* is set to *false* and the insertion is carried out. As shown in Figure 11-8, the insertion consists of two steps. First, those characters of *s2* that follow the point of insertion must be moved forward to make room for the characters to be inserted. Second, the characters of *s1* must be copied into the gap thus created in *s2*.

To move a block of values forward in an array, copying must proceed from the end to the beginning of the block of values to be moved. If we started copying at the beginning of the block, some of the moved values might overwrite values of the original block that had not yet been moved. The block of characters to be moved forward in *s2* extends from position *i* to position *s2.length*. After the block has been moved, its end will be at position *s1.length* + *s2.length*, the last position of *s2* after the insertion has been made. Index *j* points to the position from which a character will be moved, and index *k* points to the position to which the character will be moved.

Figure 11-8.

Inserting one string into another involves two steps. First, the characters following the point of insertion must be moved to the right to make room for the string to be inserted. Second, the characters of the string to be inserted must be copied into the gap thus created in the original string.

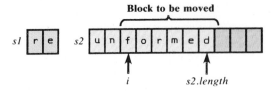

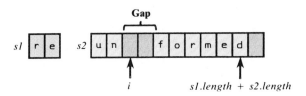

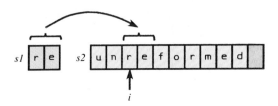

```
j := s2.length;
k := s1.length + s2.length;
while j >= i do
    begin
        s2.data[k] := s2.data[j];
        j := j − 1;
        k := k − 1
    end
```

The characters of *s1* must now be copied into the gap created in *s2*. The gap begins at position *i* and its length is equal to *s1.length*.

```
j := i;
for k := 1 to s1.length do
    begin
        s2.data[j] := s1.data[k];
        j := j + 1
    end
```

Finally, the length of *s2* is increased by the length of *s1*.

```
s2.length := s1.length + s2.length
```

Delete

The procedure call *Delete* (*s*, *i*, *n*) deletes the substring of *s* that begins at position *i* and contains *n* characters; the value of *s* is modified by the deletion; the values of *i* and *n* remain unchanged.

As shown in Figure 11-9, the substring to be deleted extends from position *i* through position $i + n - 1$. If the value of *i* is less than 1, the value of $i + n - 1$ is greater than *s.length*, or the value of *n* is less than zero, *errorFlag* is set to *true*. Otherwise, *errorFlag* is set to *false* and the characters following the substring to be deleted are moved backward in *s* to close the gap left by the deleted substring.

To move a block of values backward in an array, copying must proceed from the beginning to the end of the block of values to be moved. If we started copying at the end of the block, some of the moved values might overwrite values of the original block that have not yet been moved. The block of characters to be moved in *s* extends from position $i + n$ to position *s.length*. This block is to be moved so that it begins at position *i*, the beginning of the gap to be filled.

During copying, we use *j* to designate a position in which a character is to be stored and *k* to designate a position from which a character is to be obtained. Initially, *j* is set to *i*, the first position of the gap to be filled, and *k* is set to $i + n$, the position of the first character in the block to be moved. Copying continues as long as the value of *k* is less than or equal to *s.length*, the position of the last character in the block to be moved.

```
j := i;
k := i + n;
while k <= s.length do
    begin
        s.data[j] := s.data[k];
        j := j + 1;
        k := k + 1
    end
```

Figure 11-9.

To delete a substring, the characters following the deleted substring must be moved to the left to close the gap left by the deletion.

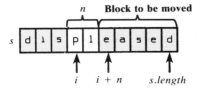

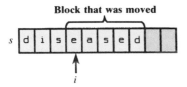

After the copying has been completed, the length of *s* is reduced by *n*, the number of characters that were deleted.

$$s.length := s.length - n$$

Substring

The procedure call *Substring* (*s1*, *s2*, *i*, *n*) assigns to *s1* the substring of *s2* that begins at position *i* and contains *n* characters. The values of *s2*, *i*, and *n* are not changed.

As discussed in connection with *Insert*, we make the formal parameter *s2* a value parameter to assure that calls of the form *Substring* (*s*, *s*, *i*, *n*) will work properly. Actually, a detailed analysis of *Substring* shows that such calls will work properly even if both parameters are variable parameters; none of the characters stored in *s* will overwrite any that will be needed later in the processing. But, when possible, it's often best to make absolutely, positively sure something will work rather than rely on an elaborate analysis to establish this fact.

As with *Delete*, the specified substring extends from position *i* through position $i + n - 1$ of *s2*. If the condition

$$(i < 1) \text{ or } (i + n - 1 > s2.length) \text{ or } (n < 0)$$

is true, the call is invalid and *errorFlag* is set to *true*, Otherwise, *errorFlag* is set to *false* and the specified substring is assigned to *s1*.

The length of *s1* is set to *n*, the number of characters to be copied. Variable *j* points to the next character of *s2* to be copied; initially *j* is set to *i*, the position of the first character of the specified substring. Variable *k* designates the next position of *s1* in which a character is to be placed; the value of *k* varies from 1 to *n*.

```
s1.length := n;
j := i;
for k := 1 to n do
    begin
        s1.data[k] := s2.data[j];
        j := j + 1
    end
```

Assign

The procedure call *Assign* (*s1*, *s2*) converts the fixed-length string *s2* to a variable-length string and assigns the result to *s1*. Only the value of *s1* is changed by the procedure call. *s2* is a value parameter so that string constants as well as variables of Pascal's (fixed-length) string type can be passed. The main purpose of the procedure is to convert Pascal's fixed-length string constants to variable-length strings, thus allowing us the convenience of specifying variable-length-string values by means of string constants.

In order for *Assign* to accept fixed-length strings of different lengths, *s2* must be a special kind of parameter called a *conformant array parameter*. Conformant array parameters, which allow arrays of different sizes to be passed via the same parameter, are a somewhat controversial extension to Pascal that is present in ISO Pascal but not in ANSI/IEEE Pascal. Specifically,

ISO Pascal has two levels: level 0 without conformant array parameters and level 1 with conformant array parameters. ANSI/IEEE Pascal corresponds to level 0 of ISO Pascal and hence does not offer conformant array parameters. Conformant array parameters are not widely implemented; however, readers interested in experimenting with them can find them in recent (Pecan Software Systems) versions of UCSD Pascal.

The conformant array parameter *s2* is declared by the following *conformant array schema*:

$s2$: **packed array** [*lo*..*hi* : *integer*] **of** *char*

Conformant array parameters represent one of only two cases in which the type of a parameter is given by something other than a type identifier. The other case (subprogram parameters) is discussed in Chapter 12. The conformant array schema shown imposes the following restrictions on the actual-parameter array that will be passed via *s2*:

1. The actual parameter must be a packed array because **packed** occurs in the conformant array schema.

2. The component type of the actual parameter must be *char*, the same component type specified in the conformant array schema.

3. The index type of the actual parameter can be any subrange of *integer*, the type specified in the conformant array schema. Thus the size of the actual parameter—the number of components it contains—can vary from one call of the procedure to another. On each call, the identifiers *lo* and *hi* are set to, respectively, the smallest and largest values in the index type of the actual parameter. Thus the procedure can use the values of *lo* and *hi* to determine the proper range of index values to use for accessing the components of *s2*.

Once the declaration of *s2* is understood, the code for the procedure is straightforward. The length of *s1* is set to the number of components in *s2*, and the characters of *s2* are copied to the data array of *s1*. The integer variable *j* is used to designate a component of *s2* and the integer variable *k* is used to designate a component of *s1.data*. Note the values of *lo* and *hi* are used both to compute the length of *s1* (which equals the number of components in *s2*) and to determine the range of values through which *j* will be stepped.

```
errorFlag := false;
s1.length := hi − lo + 1;
k := 1;
for j := lo to hi do
    begin
        s1.data[k] := s2[j];
        k := k + 1
    end
```

Neither the null string nor a one-character string can be represented by a string constant. (There is no such thing as a fixed-length null string, and a single character enclosed in single quotation marks is a character constant rather than a string constant.) To take care of these two cases, we could provide a procedure *AssignNull* (*s*), which would assign the null string to *s*; and a procedure *AssignChar* (*s*, *c*), which would convert the character *c* to a one-character variable-length string and assign the result to *s*.

Substitution for Parameters

One of the most important and widely used applications of string processing is *substitution for parameters*. A piece of text from which copies are to be made contains placeholder symbols called *parameters*. For each copy that is made, given strings—the *parameter values*—are substituted for the parameters. A different set of parameter values can be used for each copy. Thus the original text can be customized for different purposes by substituting different strings for the parameters.

A common application of this technique is personalizing a form letter by inserting personal data pertaining to the individual to whom the letter is addressed. For example, the following master copy of a sales letter contains two parameters, denoted <<1>> and <<2>>:

```
Dear <<1>>,
        As a person who needs to stay well informed,
you <<1>> cannot afford to be without a
subscription to YESTERDAY'S NEWS. If you
subscribe, then as you walk down the main street
of <<2>>, people will say, "There goes <<1>>,
the best informed person in <<2>>." Wouldn't
you like that? Please, <<1>>, send me your
subscription to YESTERDAY'S NEWS right away.

                            J. S. Hardsell
                            Circulation Manager
```

In each copy of the letter, <<1>> is replaced by the name of the person to whom the letter is addressed and <<2>> is replaced by the city in which that person resides. For example, the copy sent to John, who resides in Peoria, looks like this:

```
Dear John,
        As a person who needs to stay well informed,
you John cannot afford to be without a
subscription to YESTERDAY'S NEWS. If you
subscribe, then as you walk down the main street
of Peoria, people will say, "There goes John,
the best informed person in Peoria." Wouldn't
you like that? Please, John, send me your
subscription to YESTERDAY'S NEWS right away.

                            J. S. Hardsell
                            Circulation Manager
```

Parameter substitution also has applications in programming. For example, most assembly languages and some higher-level languages allow programmers to define *macroinstructions*, or *macros*. Each macro is defined as a sequence of instructions. Whenever a macro is invoked, the sequence of instructions given in the macro definition is assembled or compiled. The macro definition can contain parameters, the values for which are provided when the macro is invoked. This allows, for example, each invocation of a macro to refer to different memory locations and use different constant values.

Many operating systems allow macro commands to be defined; a sequence of instructions (possibly containing parameters) is stored in a file and invoked later by typing the name of the file followed by the values to be substituted for the parameters. Such operating system macros are often known as *command files* or *batch files*.

Figure 11-10 shows the program *FormLetter*, which illustrates not only substitution for parameters, but also the use of our abstract data type for variable-length strings. As usual, the code for the abstract data type has not been reprinted in the program; instead, a comment reminds us that the code for *VariableLengthString* must be included in Figure 11-10. We must therefore insert each definition and declaration of Figure 11-6 in the proper definition or declaration section of Figure 11-10.

The program assumes that the master copy of a form letter is contained in the file *letterFile*. The master copy can contain up to 25 parameters, which are denoted <<1>>, <<2>>, <<3>>, and so on. The parameter values are contained in the file *parameterFile*. Each parameter value is on a separate line, and each set of parameters is followed by the sentinel $$END$$. Thus, the parameter file

```
John
Peoria
$$END$$
Sally
Durham
$$END$$
Larry
Austin
$$END$$
```

causes three copies of the form letter to be printed. In the first copy, John is substituted for <<1>> and Peoria is substituted for <<2>>. In the second copy, Sally is substituted for <<1>> and Durham is substituted for <<2>>. The copies are stored in the file *outputFile*.

The program uses the following definitions and declarations, which are in addition to those included from the implementation of the abstract data type.

```
const
    maxLength = 80;
    maxParameter = 25;
var
    letterFile, parameterFile, outputFile : text;
    s, t, sentinel, leftBrackets, rightBrackets : vString;
    pVal : array [1..maxParameter] of vString;
    i, j, k, pEnd : integer;
```

The value of *maxLength* is used by the implementation to set the maximum length of variable-length strings. The constant *maxParameter* is the maximum number of parameters the program can handle. Variables *s, t, sentinel, leftBrackets,* and *rightBrackets* all hold variable-length strings. The array *pVal* is used to hold parameter values; each component of *pVal* holds a variable-length string. The value of the integer variable *pEnd* is the index of the last component of *pVal* that holds a valid parameter value.

The algorithm begins by assigning the string '$$END$$' to *sentinel*, the string '<<' to *leftBrackets*, and the string '>>' to *rightBrackets*.

Figure 11-10.

Program to print copies of a form letter in which parameters
in the original form letter are replaced by strings from a
parameter file.

---

program *FormLetter* (*letterFile*, *parameterFile*, *outputFile*);

{ Print copies of form letter in letter file. For each copy, replace parameters
  by strings from parameter file }

{*** Include *VariableLengthString* *** }

const
   maxLength   = 80;   { maximum length of vString;
                             used by *VariableLengthString* }
   maxParameter = 25;   { maximum number of parameters }
var
   letterFile,   { original form letter }
   parameterFile,   { parameter values }
   outputFile   : *text*;   { copies of form letter }
   s, t,   { misc. vString variables }
   sentinel,   { holds '$$END$$' }
   leftBrackets,   { holds '<<' }
   rightBrackets : *vString*; { holds '>>' }
   pVal   : **array** [1..*maxParameter*] **of** *vString*; { holds values
                                            of parameters }
   i, j, k,   { misc. integer variables }
   pEnd   : *integer*; { index of last parameter in *pVal* }
begin
   Assign (*sentinel*, '$$END$$');
   Assign (*leftBrackets*, '<<');
   Assign (*rightBrackets*, '>>');
   reset (*parameterFile*);
   rewrite (*outputFile*);
   while not *eof*(*parameterFile*) **do**
     begin

{ Read parameter values for next copy }

        i := 1;
        ReadLine (*parameterFile*, *s*);
        while (*i* <= *maxParameter*) **and**
           (**not** *EqualTo*(*s*, *sentinel*)) **do**
         begin
           pVal[*i*] := *s*;
           i := *i* + 1;
           ReadLine (*parameterFile*, *s*)
         end;
        pEnd := *i* − 1;
        while not *EqualTo*(*s*, *sentinel*) **do**
         ReadLine (*parameterFile*, *s*);

Figure 11-10.   *Continued.*

{ Read original form letter line by line, substitute for parameters in each line, and write each line to file holding copies }

```
reset (letterFile);
while not eof(letterFile) do
  begin
    ReadLine (letterFile, s);
    j := Index(s, leftBrackets, 1);
    while j > 0 do
      begin
        k := Index(s, rightBrackets, j);
        if k > 0 then
          begin
            Substring (t, s, j + 2, k − j − 2);
            i := StringToInteger(t);
            if (not Error) and (i >= 1) and
              (i <= pEnd) then
              begin
                Delete (s, j, k − j + 2);
                Insert (pVal[i], s, j)
              end
          end;
        j := Index(s, leftBrackets, j + 1)
      end;
    WriteLine (outputFile, s);
  end;
  page (outputFile)
end
end.
```

```
Assign (sentinel, '$$END$$');
Assign (leftBrackets, '<<');
Assign (rightBrackets, '>>')
```

The main reason for using *two* left brackets and *two* right brackets is that *Assign* can only handle string constants. The single-bracket constants '<' and '>' are character constants, not string constants, and so cannot be assigned with *Assign*.

The parameter file is opened for input and the output file is opened for output.

```
reset (parameterFile);
rewrite (outputFile)
```

Processing continues until the end of the parameter file is reached, that is, while the condition

not *eof(parameterFile)*

is true. Note that the number of sets of parameters in the parameter file determines how many copies of the form letter will be printed.

The first step in producing a copy is to read a set of parameter values from the parameter file. Each parameter value is stored in the corresponding component of *pVal*. Reading continues until the sentinel $$END$$ is encountered or until *maxParameter* parameters have been read.

```
i := 1;
ReadLine (parameterFile, s);
while (i <= maxParameter) and
      (not EqualTo(s, sentinel)) do
  begin
    pVal[i] := s;
    i := i + 1;
    ReadLine (parameterFile, s)
  end
```

Variable *pEnd* is set to the index in *pVal* of the last parameter that was read. (Remember that the value of *i* was increased by 1 after the last parameter value was stored in *pVal*.)

```
pEnd := i - 1
```

If the reading of parameter values was terminated because *maxParameter* values have been read, any additional parameter values in the current parameter set are read and discarded.

```
while not EqualTo(s, sentinel) do
  ReadLine (parameterFile, s)
```

Having read a set of parameter values, the program next reads the master copy line by line, substitutes for parameters in each line, and writes each modified line to the output file. The file containing the master copy is opened for input.

```
reset (letterFile)
```

The contents of *letterFile* are read and processed line by line. Processing continues until the end of *letterFile* is reached.

Each line read from *letterFile* is assigned to the string variable *s*.

```
ReadLine (letterFile, s)
```

Variable *j* is set to the position of the first occurrence of the symbol << in *s*.

```
j := Index(s, leftBrackets, 1)
```

Variable *k* is set to the position of the matching >> symbol.

```
k := Index(s, rightBrackets, j)
```

Note that the search for the >> symbol starts at the position of the << symbol, not at the beginning of the string.

If both *j* and *k* have nonzero values, indicating that a << and a matching >> were found, the << and >> are assumed to enclose a parameter number. The substring containing this number begins at position $j + 2$ in *s* and is $k - j - 2$ characters long. (See Figure 11-11.) This substring is extracted from *s* and assigned to the string variable *t*.

```
Substring (t, s, j + 2, k - j - 2)
```

Variable *i* is set to the integer value represented by the substring *t*.

Figure 11-11.

The situation after a parameter has been located by the form-letter program. Variable j points to the first of the two $<$s preceding the parameter number and k points to the first of the two $>$s following the parameter number. The substring containing the parameter number begins at position $j + 2$ and is $k - j - 2$ characters long.

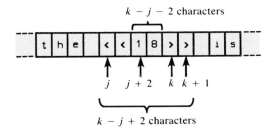

$$i := StringToInteger(t)$$

This integer is the index in $pVal$ of the parameter value that is to be substituted for the parameter being processed. If the string-to-integer conversion did not cause an error, and if the value of i lies in the range 1 to $pEnd$, the parameter being processed is replaced by the parameter value $pVal[i]$.

$$Delete\ (s, j, k - j + 2);$$
$$Insert\ (pVal[i], s, j)$$

Note that the substring to be deleted is four characters longer than the substring containing the parameter number, since the enclosing brackets $<<$ and $>>$ must also be deleted.

Variable j is set to the next occurrence in s of a $<<$ symbol, or to zero if no such occurrence exists.

$$j := Index(s, leftBrackets, j + 1)$$

If the value of j is not zero, the statements for replacing a parameter with the corresponding parameter value are repeated.

When all the parameters on a line have been substituted for, the line is written to the output file.

$$WriteLine\ (outputFile, s)$$

When the entire form letter has been processed (the end of *letterFile* is reached), the output device is sent to the top of a new page.

$$page\ (outputFile)$$

One copy of the form letter is produced for each set of parameter values in the parameter file. Processing terminates when the end of the parameter file is reached.

Review Questions _____

1. Contrast strings, arrays, and files.

2. What is a substring? Describe four common string processing operations involving substrings.

3. Contrast fixed-length-string types and variable-length-string types.

4. Give the rules governing compatibility and assignment compatibility for Pascal string types.

5. What is the type of the constant 'a'? What is the type of the constant 'computer'?

6. What restriction must be satisfied by two fixed-length strings if they are to be compared with $=$, $<$, $>$, $<=$, $>=$, or $<>$?

7. Give the rules for comparing fixed-length strings.

8. What is the null string? Is there such a thing as a fixed-length null string? Why or why not?

9. Why is it often necessary to place an upper limit on the length of the values belonging to a variable-length-string type?

10. Give the rules for comparing variable-length strings.

11. Describe the operation of the procedure *Append* and give an example of its use.

12. Describe the operation of the procedure *Substring* and give an example of its use.

13. Describe the operation of the procedures *Insert* and *Delete* giving an example of the use of each.

14. Describe the operation of the functions *Index* and *Length*. Give statements for finding the first occurrence of the value of *t* in the value of *s* and replacing that occurrence by the value of *u*.

15. Describe the operation of the procedure *Skip* and give an example of its use.

16. Describe and give examples of the operation of the data conversion function *StringToInteger* and procedure *IntegerToString*.

17. Describe three methods of implementing variable-length strings.

18. What is garbage collection? Which method of implementing variable-length strings requires garbage collection? What are the advantages and disadvantages of this method?

19. Describe the string-processing technique of substitution for parameters.

20. Give three applications of parameter substitution.

Exercises

1. Implement Boolean functions *LessThan* and *GreaterThan* that correspond to the operators $<$ and $>$ in the same way that *EqualTo* corresponds to the operator $=$. Each function must scan the strings being compared as long as characters in corresponding positions are equal. When the first pair of unequal characters is encountered, or when the end of one of the strings is reached, the scan should terminate since at this point the value that the function is to return can be determined.

2. The distinction between uppercase and lowercase letters often causes trouble when strings are compared, since humans usually ignore this distinction but computer character codes do not. One solution is to convert all lowercase letters to uppercase (or vice versa) before making a comparison. Write a procedure *Upper(s1, s2)* that assigns to string variable *s1* a copy of string *s2* in which all lowercase letters have been converted to uppercase. Assume the ASCII character code. Note that in ASCII, the ordinal number for a lowercase letter is 32 greater than the ordinal number for the corresponding uppercase letter.

3. Implement the procedure *IntegerToString* that converts an integer into the corresponding string. Note that if *n* is a positive integer, the value of *n* **mod** 10 is the rightmost decimal digit of the integer, and the value of *n* **div** 10 is the integer with the rightmost decimal digit removed. For example, 3245 **mod** 10 equals 5 and 3245 **div** 10 equals 324.

4. Modify the procedure *Substring* so that the user specifies the positions of the first and last character of the substring to be extracted, instead of giving the position of the first character and the length of the substring.

5. Modify the procedure *Delete* so that the user specifies the positions of the first and last character of the substring to be deleted instead of giving the position of the first character and the length of the substring.

6. Modify the procedure *Skip* so that its third argument is a string rather than a character. The modified procedure increments the value of *i* as long as the character at position *i* in *s* is contained in the string given as the third argument.

7. Implement the abstract data type *VariableLengthString* so that strings are stored using the sentinel representation illustrated in Figure 11-2. Use *chr*(0) as the sentinel value.

8. A fundamental operation of string processing is *pattern matching*—locating strings or substrings that match a particular pattern. In fact, pattern matching and substituting one substring for another are the main themes of string processing. The function *Index* does a rudimentary form of pattern matching in which string *s2* is the pattern. More sophisticated pattern matching is obtained by allowing a *wildcard character* in the pattern that can match any character in the substring being sought. For example, if ? is the wildcard character, then the pattern '?ar' matches 'bar', 'car', 'far', 'jar', 'par', 'tar', and 'war'. Likewise, the pattern '?ea?' matches 'beat', 'feat', 'heat', 'heap', 'leap', 'neat', 'peat', 'seat', and 'teat'. Modify *Index* to accept patterns in which ? is used as a wildcard character.

9. In computer adventure games, the player explores a fictional setting such as an eerie castle. The player enters commands such as CLIMB STAIRS, OPEN DOOR, TAKE JEWELS, DRINK POTION, and ATTACK OGRE. After each command, the computer prints what happened when the requested action was attempted. Each command consists of a verb (CLIMB, OPEN, TAKE, . . .) followed by an object (STAIRS, DOOR, JEWELS, . . .). A command can be typed in upper- or lowercase letters, or in a mixture of the two. Write a command interpreter procedure that will accept a command and translate it into two code numbers, one giving the position of the verb in the list of all possible verbs and the other giving the position of the object in the list of all

possible objects. If either verb or object cannot be found on the appropriate list, the procedure should inform the player that it doesn't know the word in question.

10. Write a program to do the following:
    a. Input lines of English text until a sentinel line consisting of a single period is encountered.
    b. Input the maximum number of characters that are to be printed on each line.
    c. Output the text in lines that do not exceed the specified maximum length. Each line will contain as many words as possible, but no word will be broken between lines. *Exception*: A word that is longer than the maximum line length specified will be broken between lines.

11. A *cipher* is a method of sending secret messages that manipulates individual characters rather than entire words or phrases. The original message is the *plaintext*; the secret message is the *ciphertext*. We *encipher* the plaintext when we convert it to ciphertext; we *decipher* the latter when we convert it back to plaintext.

    A *substitution cipher* uses a correspondence between a *plaintext alphabet* and a *cipher alphabet*.

    plaintext alphabet: ABCDEFGHIJKLMNOPQRSTUVWXYZ
    cipher alphabet: VJMQDSBGKYAZPWETXCNLHORFUI

    To encipher, each character in the plaintext alphabet is replaced by the corresponding character in the cipher alphabet. For the alphabets shown, A is replaced by V, B by J, C by M, and so on.

    A substitution cipher is *monoalphabetic* if we use the same cipher alphabet for each character of the plaintext. For example, if we encipher ATTACK AT NOON by monoalphabetic substitution using the alphabets above, we get VLLVMA VL WEEW as the ciphertext. If we assume that the plaintext alphabet is the normal one (A, B, C, and so on), only the cipher alphabet needs to be given.

    Write a program to encipher and decipher messages using monoalphabetic substitution. The program should obey three commands: A (accept a new cipher alphabet), E (encipher the following message), and D (decipher the following message).

12. The program of Exercise 11 leaves spaces in the ciphertext where there were spaces in the plaintext. This provides too many clues for someone trying to break the cipher. Modify the program to print the cipher in groups of five letters. Thus ATTACK AT NOON would be enciphered as VLLVM AVLWE EW.

13. Since cipher alphabets are hard to remember, we would like to be able to generate a cipher alphabet from an easily remembered *key*. One approach is to use a key word or phrase such as SCHOOL ZONE. First, write down the letters of the key, omitting any repetitions.

    SCHOLZNE

    Next, write down the remaining letters of the alphabet in their normal order, but omit any letters already in the key.

    SCHOLZNEABDFGIJKMPQRTUVWXY

This is our cipher alphabet. Modify the program of Exercise 12 to accept a key and generate the cipher alphabet in the manner just explained.

14. A *polyalphabetic substitution* cipher uses more than one cipher alphabet. One type of polyalphabetic substitution uses the following 26 cipher alphabets:

ABCDEFGHIJKLMNOPQRSTUVWXYZ
BCDEFGHIJKLMNOPQRSTUVWXYZA
CDEFGHIJKLMNOPQRSTUVWXYZAB

.

.

.

XYZABCDEFGHIJKLMNOPQRSTUVW
YZABCDEFGHIJKLMNOPQRSTUVWX
ZABCDEFGHIJKLMNOPQRSTUVWXY

To encipher, a key is written repeatedly above the plaintext. If the key is CUB and the plaintext is ATTACK AT NOON, we write

repeated key: CUBCUB CU BCUB
plaintext: ATTACK AT NOON

We encipher each letter of the plaintext using the cipher alphabet that begins with the corresponding letter of the repeated key. With the key CUB, for instance, we encipher the first letter of the plaintext using the cipher alphabet that begins with C, the second letter of the plaintext using the cipher alphabet that begins with U, and so on. The ciphertext for ATTACK AT NOON is CNUCW LCNOQ IO. Write a program to encipher and decipher messages using this technique. Can you think of a way to avoid having to generate and store 26 cipher alphabets? *Hint*: Remember wraparound.

15. In Exercise 14, the sequence in which the different cipher alphabets are used repeats itself throughout the plaintext. This repetition provides a method of breaking the cipher. One way to avoid this problem is to use a pseudorandom number generator to determine which cipher alphabet will be used for each plaintext character. Suppose that the 26 cipher alphabets in Exercise 14 are numbered 1 through 26. If the procedure call *Random* (26, n, *seed*) returns a pseudorandom integer n in the range 1 to 26, we can use the value of n to select the cipher alphabet.

    Write a program to encipher and decipher in this way. Note that the initial value of the seed for the random number generator serves as a key. A message must be deciphered with the same starting value for the seed that was used when the message was enciphered.

12 More About Subprograms

Subprograms were introduced early in this book so that we could begin as soon as possible to use them as basic building blocks for program design and construction. Since we had many other language features to consider in those early chapters, we discussed only the most elementary properties of functions and procedures. More advanced properties were either ignored or discussed in simplified form. In this chapter we remedy these earlier omissions and simplifications by looking at some of the more advanced features of functions and procedures.

Scopes of Identifiers

We recall that a program can have global identifiers, which are accessible throughout the entire program, and local identifiers, which are accessible only from within a given subprogram. The part of the program in which a given identifier is accessible is called the *scope* of that identifier. Thus the scope of a global identifier extends from its point of declaration to the end of the entire program. The scope of a local identifier extends from its point of declaration to the end of the function or procedure in which it is declared.

We also recall that when a local and a global identifier have the same spelling, the local identifier takes precedence over the global identifier. That is, within the subprogram containing the local identifier, any *applied occurrence* of the identifier—any use of it in a statement, in an expression, or in a declaration or definition of another identifier—refers to the local identifier and not the global one. Thus the scope of an identifier can have holes in it, each hole corresponding to a subprogram in which an identically spelled local identifier takes precedence over the global identifier.

To make matters even more interesting, Pascal allows function and procedure declarations to be nested to arbitrary depths. Just as a program can contain function and procedure declarations, a function or procedure declaration can itself contain other function or procedure declarations, which can in turn contain still other function and procedure declarations, and so on. When function and procedure declarations are nested, the scopes of the identifiers declared in the functions and procedures are nested correspondingly. For this reason, Pascal and similar languages are referred to as having *nested scopes*. The first programming language with nested scopes was the trailblazing language Algol 60. For this reason, Pascal is sometimes said to belong to the Algol family of languages.

Current Pascal programming styles generally avoid nested procedure and function declarations, which can make programs hard to read. (The nested subprogram declarations separate the definitions and declarations at the beginning of a function or procedure from the statement part, thus bringing to functions and procedures a separation that is already annoying and confusing for main programs.) Nevertheless, nested scopes do occur in many areas of computer science, so an understanding of them is important. In the remainder of this section, then, we will consider nested function and procedure declarations *without* encouraging the student to adopt them as a programming style. We will approach nested scopes by starting with a simple rule and then amending and extending it to take into account more complex situations.

We will formulate our rules for identifier scopes in terms of *blocks*; a *block* contains the definitions, declarations, and statements of a program, function, or procedure. The formal parameter declarations of a function or procedure belong to the block that contains the function or procedure declaration. This is not true, however, for the name of a function or procedure; it is declared in the block surrounding the one that contains the function or procedure declaration. Thus, we can consider a block as beginning immediately after the function or procedure name, so that the formal parameters are included in the block but the function or procedure name is not. In our illustrations, the program, function, or procedure name will also be used to name the corresponding block. One way to think of a block is as a box with a program or subprogram name painted on the outside but with the rest of the program or subprogram hidden away inside.

We can represent a block in illustrations by enclosing the corresponding part of the program in a box. The program shown in Figure 12-1 has two blocks: an outer block, *PrintFactorials*, for the main program; and an inner block, *FactProc*, for the procedure *FactProc*. Note that the name of the procedure *FactProc* is outside the block *FactProc*, but the declarations for the procedure's formal parameters are inside the block. Diagrams such as that shown in Figure 12-1 are sometimes called *contour diagrams*, because the nested boxes are somewhat reminiscent of the nested contour lines on a map.

The basic rule for identifier scopes is that *the scope of an identifier is the block in which it is declared*. As mentioned, however, this basic rule will require a few extensions and amendments to take into account all the situations that can arise in Pascal programs.

Pascal requires that the definition or declaration of an identifier proceed all uses of it. Thus at any point in a program, applied occurrences can refer only to identifiers that were defined or declared earlier in the program. The first appearance of an identifier in a program must be at the point at which it is defined or declared; this first appearance is called the *defining point* for the identifier. We can take into account the definition-before-use restriction by modifying our basic rules as follows: *The scope of an identifier extends from its defining point to the end of the block, in which the definition or declaration occurs*. Thus in Figure 12-1, the scopes of *n* and *f*, for example, are slightly different, since the scope of each identifier extends from its first appearance in a declaration to the end of the block. In this case the different scopes are of no practical importance, since all applied occurrences lie in the region where the scopes overlap.

The two blocks in Figure 12-1 are nested. We must consider nested blocks in detail because some of the trickiest questions of identifier scopes arise when blocks are nested. For simplicity and clarity, however, we will illustrate our

Figure 12-1.

The program *Printfactorials* has two blocks: an outer block, *PrintFactorials*, for the entire program; and an inner block, *FactProc*, for the procedure *FactProc*.

```
program PrintFactorials   (output);
var
    i      : integer;   { i declared in outer block }
    fact : integer;

    procedure FactProc   (n : integer; var f : integer);
    var
        i : integer;           { i declared in inner block }
    begin
      f := 1;
      for i := 1 to n do
        f := f * i
    end; { FactProc }

begin
    writeln ('Number' :15, 'Factorial' :15);
    writeln;
    for i := 1 to 7 do
      begin
        FactProc (i, fact);
        writeln (i :15, fact :15)
      end
end.
```

discussion with simplified contour diagrams rather than with complete program, function, and procedure declarations. Thus, we will diagram each block as a box. The name of the program, function, or procedure, which we will also use as the name of the block, will appear outside the box. The definitions and declarations of all formal parameters and local identifiers will appear inside the box. To keep the declarations as simple as possible, our examples will usually be *parameterless procedures*—procedures that do not have any formal parameters.

Now look at the contour diagram shown in Figure 12-2, which illustrates four blocks: *P*, *Q1*, *Q2*, and *R*. Each block is represented by a box. The name of each block (which would be the name of the corresponding program, function, or procedure) appears outside the box. The declarations for local variables appear inside the box. The part of the box following the variable declarations and the boxes for nested blocks represents the statement part of the program, function, or procedure.

A simple way to visualize variable scopes is to think of each box as made of one-way glass that allows us to see out of the block but not into it. The name of the block, which we can think of as painted on the outside, is the only identifier associated with the block that is visible from the outside. Because of the one-way glass, none of the identifiers declared within a block is visible from the outside. On the other hand, identifiers declared outside a block are visible from within it.

Figure 12-2.   Contour diagram for nested program and subprogram
declarations. Subprograms *Q1* and *Q2* are declared within *P*,
and subprogram *R* is declared within *Q1*. Variables *a* and *b*
are accessible from within *P*, *Q1*, *Q2*, and *R*; *c* and *d* are
accessible from within *Q1* and *R*; *e* and *f* are accessible from
within *R* only; and *h* and *i* are accessible from within *Q2*
only.

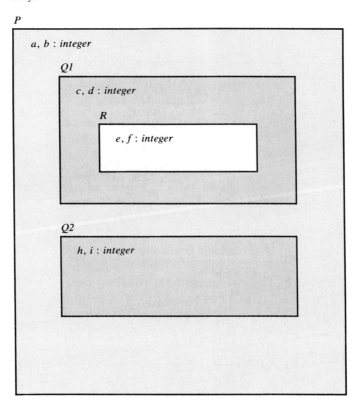

Applying this idea to Figure 12-2, we see that identifiers *P*, *a*, *b*, *Q1*, and
Q2 can be accessed from within any one of the blocks diagrammed; they can
be accessed from within blocks *P*, *Q1*, *Q2*, and *R*. (Note that the block names
P, *Q1*, *Q2*, and *R* are themselves identifiers, each of which has a definite
scope.) Identifiers *c*, *d*, and *R* can be accessed from blocks *Q1* and *R*; they
cannot, however, be accessed from outside block *Q1*. Identifiers *e* and *f* can
only be accessed from inside block *R*. Likewise, identifiers *h* and *i* can only
be accessed from within block *Q2*.

The contour diagram shown in Figure 12-3 illustrates the situation in
which identifiers with identical spellings are declared in different blocks. From
the preceding discussion, it is clear that the identifier *f* declared in block *Q1*
can be accessed only from within block *Q1* and the identifier *f* declared in
block *Q2* can be accessed only within block *Q2*. Since the scopes of the two
*f*s do not overlap, there can never be any confusion as to which *f* is referred
to by a given applied occurrence.

But what about the *a* declared in *P* and the *a* declared in *Q1*? Which *a*
is referred to by an applied occurrence in *Q1*? An analogous question arises
for the *b* declared in *P* and the *b* declared in *Q2*.

Figure 12-3. Contour diagram for nested program and subprogram declarations. The declaration of *a* in *Q1* hides the declaration of *a* in *P*. Therefore, an applied occurrence of *a* in *Q1* refers to the *a* declared in *Q1*, whereas an applied occurrence of *a* in *P* or *Q2* refers to the *a* declared in *P*. Likewise, the declaration of *b* in *Q2* hides the declaration of *b* in *P*, so an applied occurrence of *b* in *Q2* refers to the *b* declared in *Q2*, whereas an applied occurrence of *b* in *P* or *Q1* refers to the *b* declared in *P*.

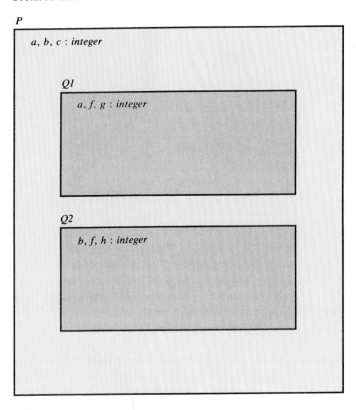

To handle these situations, we need one final amendment to our rule for scopes. *When two identifiers with the same spelling are declared in nested blocks, the inner block is excluded from the scope of the identifier declared in the outer block.* Thus block *Q1* is excluded from the scope of the *a* declared in *P*. Outside of *Q1*, an applied occurrence of *a* designates the *a* declared in *P*; inside *Q1*, an applied occurrence of *a* designates the *a* declared in *Q1*. Likewise, block *Q2* is excluded from the scope of the *b* declared in *P*. An applied occurrence of *b* outside of *Q2* refers to the *b* declared in *P*; an applied occurrence of *b* inside *Q2* refers to the *b* declared in *Q2*.

We can think of a declaration inside a block as hiding the declarations of identically spelled identifiers in surrounding blocks. Thus, the declaration of *a* in *Q1* hides the declaration of *a* in *P*; from inside *Q1* only the declaration of *a* in *Q1* is visible. Likewise, the declaration of *b* in *Q2* hides the declaration of *b* in *P*. From inside *Q2*, only the declaration of *b* in *Q2* is visible.

We can summarize the rules for the scopes of identifiers as follows:

- The scope of an identifier extends from its defining point to the end of the block in which the definition or declaration occurs.

- When two identifiers with the same spelling are declared in nested blocks, the inner block is excluded from the scope of the identifier declared in the outer block.

Finally, let's apply these rules to the program shown in Figure 12-1. The formal parameters *n* and *f* and the local variable *i* are declared in the inner block, *FactProc*. The scope of each extends from the defining point to the end of the procedure declaration for *FactProc*. The variables *i* and *fact* and the procedure identifier *FactProc* are declared in the outer block *Print-Factorials*. (Note that although *FactProc* names the inner block, it is declared in the surrounding block. In fact, if *FactProc* were declared in the inner block, the name would not be visible in the statement part of the main program and so could not be used there to call the procedure *FactProc*.) The scopes of *fact* and *FactProc* each extend from the defining point to the end of the program. (The defining point for *FactProc* is its occurrence in the procedure heading.) The scope of the *i* declared in the main program, however, has a hole in it created by the procedure *FactProc*, which also contains an identifier spelled *i*. Thus applied occurrences of *i* in *FactProc* refer to the *i* declared in *FactProc*; applied occurrences of *i* outside of *FactProc* refer to the *i* declared in *PrintFactorials*.

Activation Records and the Run-Time Stack

Because subprograms play such a fundamental role in program construction, we will find it of interest to look in more detail at how their execution is managed. Whenever a subprogram is invoked, a private memory area called an *activation record* is allocated for the subprogram's use. The activation record remains in existence during the execution of the subprogram and is then *deallocated* (the memory it occupied is made available for other uses) when the subprogram returns. To permit efficient allocation and deallocation, activation records are stored in a stack, a data structure that is of interest in its own right. Because the stack of activation records comes into play when the program is executed or run, it is known as the *execution stack* or the *run-time stack*.

Stacks

A *stack* is a data structure that behaves like a stack of physical objects, such as books or boxes. An object is placed on the stack by placing it on top of the current topmost object. An object is removed from the stack by removing the current topmost object. A little thought will show that objects are removed in just the reverse of the order in which they were placed on the stack. For example, if we stack box A, box B, and box C, in that order, then we must remove box C before we can remove box B and we must remove box B before we can remove Box A. We say that adding and removing objects from a stack follows a *Last-In First-Out*, or *LIFO*, discipline.

Subprograms return in the reverse of the order in which they were called; if subprogram A calls subprogram B, then subprogram B must return its results before subprogram A can complete its calculations. Thus activation records are deallocated in the reverse of the order in which they are allocated; allocation and deallocation of activation records follows a LIFO discipline. This makes a stack the appropriate data structure for storing activation records.

Some of the terminology of stack manipulation derives from an analogy with the spring-loaded device used to hold stacks of plates in cafeterias and buffets. The device maintains the top plate at the level of the countertop. When a new plate is placed on top of the stack, all the plates are pushed down so that the new top plate is at counter level. When a plate is removed, all the plates below it pop up, so that again the new top plate ends up at counter level. With this device in mind, a stack is sometimes called a *push-down stack* or a *push-down list*. We say that an object is *pushed onto* a stack when we place it on top of the stack, and we say that it is *popped off* when we remove it from the stack.

We can define a stack as an abstract data type with the following operations:

NewStack (aStack)	Sets *aStack* to the empty stack, the stack that contains no objects.
Push (aStack, anObject)	Places *anObject* on top of *aStack*.
Pop (aStack)	Removes and discards the topmost object of *aStack*. An error occurs if *aStack* is empty.
Top (aStack)	Returns a copy of the topmost object on *aStack*; *aStack* is not changed, and the topmost object remains on the stack. An error occurs if *aStack* is empty.

Top allows us to inspect the topmost object on the stack. If the definition is followed strictly, only the topmost object is available for inspection. In reality, however, we often ignore *Top* and take the liberty of looking at and even changing any object on the stack. But we still use *Push* and *Pop* for placing objects on the stack and removing objects from the stack. And, most important of all, objects are still popped off in the reverse of the order in which they were pushed on.

We can implement a stack as an array of objects together with an index value indicating which array component holds the topmost object.

```
type
  stack = record
            top  : 0..size;
            data : array [1..size] of objectType
          end;
```

The constant *size* is the maximum number of objects that can be placed on the stack, and *objectType* is the type of the objects.

Figure 12-4 illustrates a stack of integers. The value of *top* designates the top of the stack; we say that the value of *top* points to the top of the stack and we represent that value by an arrow extending from the box representing *top* to the top of the stack. Array components *data*[1] through *data*[*top*] hold the contents of the stack; components *data*[*top* + 1] through *data*[*size*] are unused. For an empty stack the value of *top* is 0, indicating that all the array

Figure 12-4.

A stack can be represented by an array *data* that holds the values on the stack, and an index *top* that points to the array component containing the top value on the stack. Note that when we follow our usual conventions for diagramming arrays, the stack is shown upside down. The bottom of the stack appears at the top of the diagram, and the stack extends downward as new values are pushed onto it.

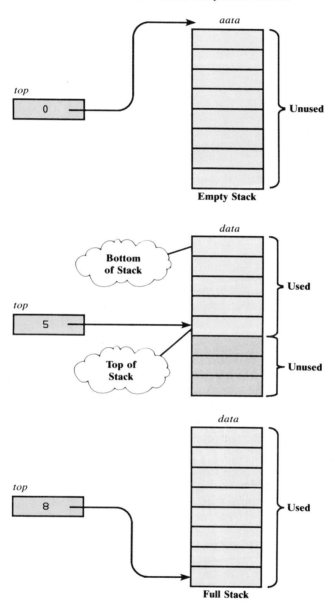

components are unused. As illustrated in Figure 12-4, we push an object on the stack by adding one to the value of *top* and storing the new object in *data*[*top*]; we pop an object from the stack by subtracting one from *top*, so that the topmost object is discarded. The function *Top* returns the value of *data*[*top*]. Note that in Figure 12-4 and similar illustrations, the stack appears

Figure 12-5.

Using a stack to hold the activation records of programs and subprograms. Stacks are shown as in Figure 12-4, with the top of the stack at the bottom of the diagram. The crucial property of subprograms that allows their activation records to be stored in a stack is that subprograms always return in the exact reverse of the order in which they were called.

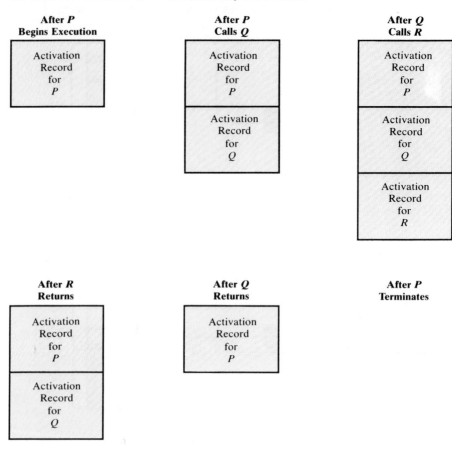

upside down: the top of the stack is at the bottom of the part of the array that is in use, and that part of the array extends downward as additional objects are pushed on the stack.

Managing Subprogram Calls and Returns

Figure 12-5 shows how a stack can be used for managing activation records. The stack is drawn as in our previous diagrams; the top of the stack is nearest the bottom of the page, and vice versa. Suppose that program P calls procedure Q and procedure Q calls procedure R. An activation record for P is created before P begins executing. When P calls Q, the activation record for Q is stacked on top of the activation record for P. (The activation record for Q therefore appears below the activation record for P.) When Q calls R, the activation record for R is stacked on top of the activation record for Q.

Because subprograms return in reverse of the order in which they were called, the activation records can be popped from the stack one by one as

Figure 12-6.

Organization of an activation record. We consider an activation record to begin with the location containing the control link; the locations containing the return address and the actual parameters belong to the activation record for the calling program or subprogram, which is the preceding activation record on the stack (see Figure 12-5). This dividing line between activation records is somewhat arbitrarily drawn, however, because the actual parameters and the return address can be accessed by both the called subprogram and by the calling program or subprogram.

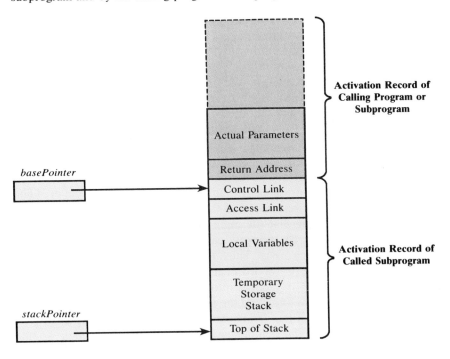

the subprograms return. Thus R returns first, at which time its activation record is popped from the stack to reveal the activation record for Q, which is used to resume the execution of Q. Q returns next, at which time its activation record is popped from the stack to reveal the activation record for P, which is used to resume the execution of P. When the execution of P terminates, its activation record is popped and the stack is empty.

Figure 12-6 shows the details of a typical activation record for a subprogram. (Exact details vary from one language implementation to another.) The memory locations containing the parameters and the return address are referred to by both the calling program and the called subprogram; it is thus problematical whether we should consider these locations as belonging to the activation record of the calling program or to the activation record of the subprogram. For the sake of drawing the line somewhere, we will consider these locations to be part of the activation record of the caller (which is the immediately preceding activation record on the stack). But note that these locations are also accessible to the subprogram.

The parameter area holds the parameters that were passed to the subprogram. This area contains a memory location for each parameter that is to be passed to the subroutine. For each value parameter, the calling program stores the value of the actual parameter in the parameter area; if we think of the location in the parameter area as corresponding to the formal parameter, then the value of the actual parameter is assigned to the formal parameter.

We will defer for now discussing how other kinds of parameters (such as variable parameters) are passed, except to say that every parameter is passed by storing an appropriate value (but not necessarily the value of the actual parameter) in the corresponding location in the parameter area. We can think of each formal parameter as naming a location in the parameter area. But the contents of these locations, and the way in which the subprogram uses the contents, vary with the kind of parameter. Only for value parameters does the location corresponding to the formal parameter contain the value of the actual parameter.

The return address and the control link are used to resume execution of the calling program or subprogram. The return address is the address of the next instruction to be executed in the caller's code. The instruction that calls the subprogram also stores the return address. The control link points to the caller's activation record; specifically, it contains the address of the first memory location in the caller's activation record. The control link is used to locate the beginning of the caller's activation record when the subprogram returns control to the calling program.

The activation record of every subprogram contains, in its control link, the address of the activation record of its caller. (The control link of the activation record of the main program contains a special sentinel value indicating that the main program does not have a caller.) Memory addresses, like array indexes, can be thought of as pointers to memory locations or memory areas. Thus, every program or subprogram contains a pointer to the activation record of its caller. We can think of these pointers as linking the activation records into a chain, as shown in Figure 12-7.

We often use the adjective *static* for properties of a program that depend only on the arrangement of the program text and the adjective *dynamic* for properties that depend on the way the program is executed. Because the chain of activation records just described reflects the order in which the subprograms will return as the program is executed, it is called the *dynamic chain*.

Passing over the access link for the moment, we come to the area containing the local variables of the subprogram. Every local variable names a memory location in this area; each location holds the current value of the corresponding variable.

Following the local variable area is an area used for temporary storage. This area is treated as a small stack within the larger run-time stack. Values are pushed onto this stack when they need to be stored and are popped off when they are no longer needed. In particular, this area is used to store the parameters and return addresses for a subprogram. Before calling the subprogram, the calling program pushes the parameters onto the temporary-storage stack. The instruction that calls the subprogram pushes on the return address. The activation record for the newly called subprogram is constructed following the return address. Thus, by "looking" back into its caller's temporary storage area, a subprogram can access its parameters and return address.

Now let's return to the access link. We have seen that an activation record contains locations corresponding to the subprogram's local variables. Non-local variables—those declared in surrounding blocks but accessible to the subprogram—are stored in the activation records for the blocks in which they

Figure 12-7.   The dynamic and static chains of activation records. Each record except the last contains a *basePointer* value that points to the next activation record on the chain; the last activation record on the chain contains a sentinel value, which is represented in the diagram by a diagonal line. For the dynamic chain, the pointers are control links; for the static chain, the pointers are access links.

Dynamic Chain

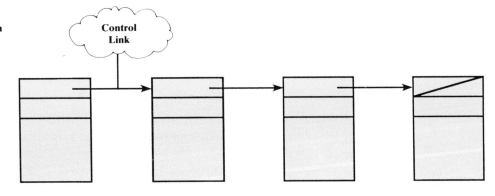

Static Chain

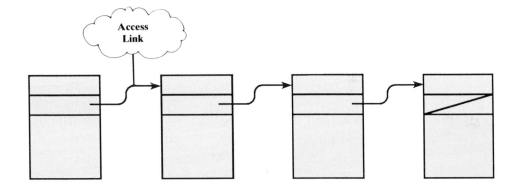

are declared. To access nonlocal variables, then, a subprogram must be able to access activation records other than its own. The access link points to the activation record for the immediately enclosing block, the block in which the subprogram is declared. The activation record of the immediately enclosing block contains, in turn, a pointer to the activation record for the next outermost block in the program text. Thus the access links also serve to link activation records into chains. The chain defined by the access links is called the *static chain*, because it depends only on the way the blocks are nested in the program text, and not on the order in which subprograms are called at run-time. The static and dynamic chains are generally different, because a subprogram need not be called from the block in which it is declared; it can be called from a block nested (however deeply) within the block containing the subprogram declaration. As indicated, the static chain is used to locate activation records containing the values of nonlocal variables.

Let's look in a little more detail at how activation records are created and used. For this purpose we will find it convenient to think of the computer's memory as an array of integers, which we will call *memory*. Pointers into the memory array are stored in two variables, *basePointer* and *stackPointer*, which are usually central processor registers. Thus *memory*[*basePointer*] is the memory location that contains the control link, and *memory*[*stackPointer*] is the top location on the temporary-storage stack, which is also the top memory location on the entire run-time stack. Thus *stackPointer* plays the same role as *top* in our previous discussion of stacks.

Variables and parameters in the activation record are always addressed relative to the value of *basePointer*. That is, every reference to a variable or parameter has the form

$$memory[basePointer + offset]$$

where *offset* is the value that must be added to the address of the control link to get the address of the variable or parameter. The value of *offset* is positive for local variables and negative for parameters.

Values of *basePointer* are always used for pointing to activation records. The control link is the *basePointer* value for the caller's activation record. The access link is the *basePointer* value for the activation record for the block containing the subprogram declaration.

Let's look in detail at how a subprogram is called. As mentioned, the caller begins by pushing the actual parameters onto the temporary storage stack. The caller then executes a Call or Jump-to-Subroutine instruction, which pushes the address of the next instruction in the caller's code onto the temporary stack and transfers control of the computer to the first instruction of the subprogram.

It is the responsibility of the subprogram to construct its own activation record. When the subprogram begins executing, *basePointer* still contains the caller's base pointer, and *stackPointer* points to the return address. The called subprogram's first step is to save the caller's base pointer by pushing it onto the stack.

$$stackPointer := stackPointer + 1;$$
$$memory[stackPointer] := basePointer$$

This saved base pointer becomes the control link for the subprogram's activation record.

Thus, at this point, the top of the stack, which is pointed to by *stackPointer*, contains the control link (the caller's base pointer), which should be pointed to by *basePointer*. Thus *basePointer* is set to point to the current top of the stack.

$$basePointer := stackPointer$$

Next the memory area containing the access link and local variables must be allocated. This is done by moving the stack pointer to the end of the area in question. If *areaSize* is the number of locations in this area, the value of *stackPointer* is modified as follows:

$$stackPointer := stackPointer + areaSize$$

StackPointer now points to the last location of the local variable area; it will move beyond the local variable area as values are pushed onto the temporary-storage stack.

Finally, a pointer to the activation record for the block in which the subprogram was declared must be stored in the access link. We will not go into the details of how this pointer is determined. Suffice it to say that the Pascal compiler knows the static structure of the program—how the blocks are nested—and so can generate the proper machine instructions for determining the access link.

When the subprogram is ready to return, it discards everything beyond the control link by setting the stack pointer to point to the control link (the control link becomes the new top of the stack).

$$stackPointer := basePointer$$

The caller's base pointer—the control link—is popped and stored in *basePointer*.

$$basePointer := memory[stackPointer];$$
$$stackPointer := stackPointer - 1$$

The return address is now on top of the stack. The subprogram executes a Return instruction, which pops the return address and resumes execution of the caller's code at that address.

After the subprogram returns, the caller must pop the parameters from its temporary storage stack, which it does by decreasing the value of *stackPointer* by the number of locations in the parameter area.

$$stackPointer := stackPointer - parameterAreaSize$$

The return is now complete. The values of both *basePointer* and *stackPointer* are now the same as they were before the subprogram call was begun by pushing parameters onto the temporary-storage stack.

A function call differs from a procedure call only in that the value of the function must be returned to the caller. A location in the local variable area is reserved for holding the value to be returned. Every time an assignment to the function name is made, the assigned value is stored in this reserved memory location. Before discarding the local variable area, the function saves the value to be returned in a temporary location, usually a central processor register. After the parameters have been popped from the temporary-storage stack, the return value is pushed onto the temporary stack, where it is stored until needed.

Variable and Subprogram Parameters

In the previous section, we saw how actual value parameters are passed to a subprogram by pushing the parameter values onto the run-time stack before calling the subprogram. We now extend this discussion of parameter passing to two other kinds of parameters: variable parameters, with which we are already quite familiar; and subprogram parameters, which will be introduced in this section.

Variable Parameters

We have previously discussed the passing of variable parameters in terms of substitution: a variable passed to a subprogram via a formal variable parameter is effectively substituted for every occurrence of the formal parameter in the subprogram. Although this method of parameter passing is conceptually correct, it is impractical. Replacing every occurrence of a formal parameter by the corresponding actual parameter is much too slow and cumbersome a process to carry out every time a subprogram is called.

Fortunately, a much simpler method is available. A variable parameter can be handled much like a value parameter, in that a corresponding value can be pushed on the run-time stack before calling the subprogram, and the subprogram can obtain this value by accessing the corresponding memory location in the parameter area. Value and variable parameters differ, however, in that for a variable parameter, the value pushed on the run-time stack is *not* the value of the variable but rather a pointer to the memory location or memory area named by the variable that is being passed. As in the preceding section, a pointer is a memory address, which we represent as an index into the memory array *memory*.

Looking at the matter another way, we recall that a variable is just a named memory location (or, more generally, a named memory area, since an array or record variable, for example, might name a large block of memory containing many memory locations). To pass a variable to a subprogram, therefore, we must provide the subprogram with access to the memory location or memory area corresponding to the variable. We do this by passing a pointer to the memory location or to the first location in a memory area; this pointer can be thought of as the machine-code representation of the corresponding variable name in the source program. We can think of the pointer as a *reference* to corresponding memory area. Thus variables passed via variable parameters are sometimes said to be *passed by reference*, and variable parameters are often called *reference parameters*.

Let's look in a bit more detail at how a memory location can be accessed via a variable parameter. Before the subprogram is called, a pointer to the location will be pushed onto the run-time stack. The location holding this pointer will reside in the parameter area and so can be accessed by indexing into the memory array using the current base pointer and the appropriate negative offset. Let *register1*, *register 2*, and *register3* be storage locations in the central processing unit. To get the value of a variable passed as a variable parameter, the subprogram first executes the following statement:

$$register1 := memory[basePointer + offset]$$

Here, *offset* is the offset of the location in the parameter area that holds the pointer to the desired location. Thus *memory[basePointer + offset]* is the location holding the pointer, and the assignment stores that pointer in *register1*. To access the location designated by the pointer, we must use the pointer as an index into the memory array. Thus, the statement

$$register2 := memory[register1]$$

assigns to *register2* the contents of the location designated by the pointer in *register1*—the pointer that we just finished obtaining from the parameter area.

Now suppose that the subprogram wishes to return a result via a variable parameter. Again, the first step is to obtain from the parameter area the pointer to the memory location that corresponds to the actual parameter.

$$register1 := memory[basePointer + offset]$$

Now suppose that *register3* contains the value that is to be returned via the variable parameter. The contents of *register3* are to be stored in the memory location pointed to by the contents of *register1*. Thus, the subprogram executes the statement

$$memory[register1] := register\ 3$$

We close by reviewing the distinctive properties of variable parameters in light of our discussion. Since the pointer passed to the subprogram can be used both for retrieving values from and storing values in the designated memory location, a variable parameter is a two-way street that can be used both for passing data to a subprogram and for returning results. Because only a pointer to a large memory area (and not the contents of the area) needs to be stored in the parameter area, a subprogram can be given access to large structured values (such as arrays) without the time-consuming process of copying the values themselves into the parameter area. On the other hand, access to a value that can be stored in a single memory location may be less efficient when the value is passed via a variable parameter. If the value were passed as a value parameter, the value itself would be stored in the parameter area, and the subprogram could obtain the value with a single statement.

$$register2 := memory[basePointer + offset]$$

If, however, a variable containing the desired value is passed via a variable parameter, then the subprogram must execute two statements to access the value: one statement to obtain the pointer and another to obtain the value pointed to.

$$register1 := memory[basePointer + offset];$$
$$register2 := memory[register1]$$

Thus when a nonstructured value is to be accessed repeatedly (thousands of times, say), it is more efficient to pass the value via a value parameter.

Subprogram Parameters

Pascal allows a subprogram to be passed to another subprogram as a parameter. The other subprogram can call the subprogram that was passed, or it can pass it on to still another subprogram. We will refer to a parameter via which a subprogram can be passed as a *subprogram parameter*; such a parameter is also frequently referred to as a *functional* or *procedural* parameter according to whether the subprogram to be passed is a function or a procedure.

Subprogram parameters are useful when the task that we wish to give a subprogram is defined by another subprogram, as in the following examples. A subprogram that plots a graph of a function on the display screen needs to be passed the function whose graph is to be plotted. Functions are frequently used to define equations to be solved; a subprogram for solving equations of a particular kind needs to be passed one or more functions describing the particular equations that the user wants solved. Sometimes it is convenient to let a calling program specify the action that a subprogram is to take when an error occurs; the caller can do this by passing to the subprogram a procedure that the subprogram is to call whenever it detects an error.

To illustrate subprogram parameters, let us write a simple procedure to print a table of function values.

```
    procedure Print (low, high : integer;
                        Fnct (parm : integer) : integer);
    var
        index : integer;
    begin
        writeln ('Argument' :10, 'Value' :10);
        writeln;
        for index := low to high do
            writeln (index :10, Fnct(index) :10)
    end;
```

The procedure *Print* has three parameters: the value parameters *high* and *low*, whose values specify the range of argument values over which the value of the function is to be printed; and the functional parameter *Fnct*, which is used to pass the function whose values are to be printed. For example, suppose we wished to print some values of functions named *Factorial* and *Fibonacci*. The procedure call

> *Print* (1, 7, *Factorial*)

prints a table giving the values of the function *Factorial* for arguments in the range 1 through 7. The procedure call

> *Print* (0, 10, *Fibonacci*)

prints a table giving the values of the function *Fibonacci* for argument values in the range 0 through 10.

A subprogram parameter is declared by giving a complete subprogram heading: the functional parameter *Fnct* is declared by the following function heading:

> *Fnct* (*parm* : *integer*) : *integer*

The name of the subprogram (*Fnct*) is the subprogram parameter, the formal parameter whose name will be used to refer to the actual parameter. For example, suppose that *Factorial* has been passed to *Print*. Then the statement

```
    for index := low to high do
        writeln (index :10, Fnct(index) :10)
```

is executed as if *Factorial* were substituted for *Fnct*, that is, as if the statement had been written

```
    for index := low to high do
        writeln (index :10, Factorial(index) :10)
```

If *Fibonacci* were passed instead of *Factorial*, the statement would be executed as if it had been written

```
    for index := low to high do
        writeln (index :10, Fibonacci(index) :10)
```

The subprogram heading that declares a subprogram parameter also specifies for the parameter subprogram the number of parameters, the kinds of parameters (value, variable, or subprogram), the types of the parameters, and (for a functional parameter) the type of the value to be returned. The subprogram passed as an actual parameter must have the same number, kind, and types of parameters and (if a function) the same return type as declared for the formal subprogram parameter. On the other hand, the formal parameter names (such as *parm*) appearing in the declaration of a subprogram parameter are just placeholders. They are never actually referred to, and they do not have to agree with the formal parameter names used in the declaration of the actual subprogram parameter. Thus we are free to use *parm* as the formal parameter in the declaration of *Fnct*, even if the function declarations for *Factorial* and *Fibonacci* use different names for the formal parameter.

Parameter passing for subprogram parameters is similar to that for variable parameters. Conceptually, the subprogram name passed as an actual parameter is substituted for every occurrence of the formal subprogram parameter. In reality, the actual parameter is accessed via pointers to avoid the need for cumbersome substitutions.

A subprogram parameter is passed as two pointers. The first, and most obviously necessary one is a pointer to the code for the subprogram; the value of this pointer is the address of the first machine instruction in the subprogram code. The second, less obviously necessary, pointer is the access link that is to be placed in the activation record when the parameter subprogram is called. We recall that the access link, which is used to access nonlocal variables, depends on where the declaration for a subprogram occurs in the program text. When a subprogram is passed as a parameter, it is essentially uprooted from its context; the subprogram to which it is passed has no way of knowing where the parameter subprogram was declared in the program text. Thus when a subprogram is passed as a parameter, the access link that it is to use in accessing its nonlocal variables must be computed and passed along with the pointer to the program code. When the parameter subprogram is eventually called, this access link will be placed in the activation record for the call.

Recursion

Recursion arises naturally from the fundamental technique of breaking a problem down into subproblems. Sometimes, one or more of the subproblems are simplified versions of the original problem. If a subprogram is general enough to solve both the original and the simplified versions of the problem, we can use the same subprogram to solve both the original problem and the subproblems. Specifically, when we are writing the subprogram to solve the given problem, we can use calls to that subprogram—to the one we are writing—to solve the subproblems. It is this technique of a subprogram calling itself that we refer to as recursion; subprograms that use this technique are said to be *recursive*.

As the name suggests, recursion is related to repetition. Each time a recursive subprogram is called, it simplifies the task it was given to perform, then calls itself to handle the simplified task. Each new call causes the subprogram to simplify the task again, call itself again, and so on. Thus the original problem is repeatedly simplified, with each simplification being performed by a different call to the same subprogram. If the series of recursive calls—calls of the subprogram to itself—is to ever terminate, the original problem eventually must be simplified to the extent that it can be solved without any further recursive calls.

To understand how recursion works, we must look a bit more closely at how subprograms are executed. A particular execution of a subprogram is called an *activation*. An activation begins when a subprogram is called and ends when the subprogram returns control to the program or subprogram that called it. Since one subprogram can be called many times, many activations of a subprogram may take place during a single execution of the main program. As we have seen, the values of the parameters and local variables are stored in the subprogram's activation record. Memory for an activation record is allocated when a subprogram is called and reclaimed when the subprogram returns.

When a recursive call takes place, a new activation of the subprogram is started before the current activation has been completed. If the new activation also makes a recursive call, still another activation is started before the other two have been completed. With recursion, then, many different activations of a subprogram can exist at the same time. All activations use the same function or procedure declaration: the same parameter and variable declarations apply to each activation and the same statements are executed. But the actual parameters and the values of the local variables will generally be different for each activation; thus, each activation must have its own activation record, its own private memory area. Recursion is impossible in languages, such as FORTRAN, that do not create a new activation record each time a subprogram is called.

As with repetition, the programmer has the responsibility to make sure that a recursion terminates—that ultimately, one activation completes its assigned task without making any further recursive calls. Each call to the subprogram must make progress toward reducing the original problem to a trivial form that can be solved without recursive calls. A recursive subprogram must always contain a selection construction to distinguish between the trivial case, which requires no recursive calls, and the more complex cases, which do.

If a recursive subprogram fails to terminate, the activation records created by the repeated subprogram calls will eventually fill all available memory. If the computer system has adequate memory management, it will inform the user that available memory has been exhausted. If memory management is inadequate, as is often the case for microcomputers, the system will crash when the runaway recursion attempts to use memory that is allocated for other purposes.

Because recursion is a form of repetition, or *iteration*, problems that can be solved by recursion can also be solved by repetition, and vice versa. Because of the memory space needed for activation records and the time needed for subprogram calls and returns, a recursive function or procedure is often less efficient than an iterative one. (The adjective *iterative* is frequently applied to a program, subprogram, or problem solution that is based on repetition.) Thus if a simple iterative solution is available, it is usually preferable to a recursive one. But some problems are "naturally" recursive in that a recursive solution is simple and straightforward whereas an iterative solution is complex, inelegant, or at least unobvious. For such problems, recursion is often the preferred technique.

Example 12-1. *Computing Factorials*

The factorial function provides the simplest example of recursion. The factorial of an integer *n* is defined as the product of all the integers from 1 through *n*. For example, *Factorial*(6) is the product of the integers 1 through 6.

$$Factorial(6) = 6 * 5 * 4 * 3 * 2 * 1$$

Because the product

$$5 * 4 * 3 * 2 * 1$$

is just the factorial of 5, the product of all the integers from 1 through 5, we have

$$Factorial(6) = 6 * 5 * 4 * 3 * 2 * 1$$
$$Factorial(6) = 6 * (5 * 4 * 3 * 2 * 1)$$
$$Factorial(6) = 6 * Factorial(5)$$
$$Factorial(6) = 6 * Factorial(6 - 1)$$

Thus we can compute the factorial of 6 by first computing the factorial of 5 and then multiplying the result by 6. We easily convince ourselves that for any value of *n* greater than one,

$$Factorial(n) = n * Factorial(n - 1)$$

We can, in fact, give a *recursive definition* of the factorial function as follows:

$$Factorial(1) = 1$$
$$Factorial(n) = n * Factorial(n - 1) \text{ for } n > 1$$

The second of these equations tells us that for any *n* greater than 1, we can compute the value of *Factorial*(*n*) by multiplying *n* by *Factorial*(*n* − 1). Thus we compute *Factorial*(6) by multiplying 6 by *Factorial*(5); we compute *Factorial*(5) by multiplying 5 by *Factorial*(4); we compute *Factorial*(4) by multiplying 4 by *Factorial*(3), and so on. The first equation, *Factorial*(1) = 1, provides the trivial case that can be computed without any further recursive calls to *Factorial*.

The program in Figure 12-8 defines a recursive version of the factorial function and uses it to compute a short table of factorials. The function *Factorial* is declared as follows:

```
function Factorial (n : integer) : integer;
begin
  if n = 1 then
    Factorial := 1
  else
    Factorial := n * Factorial(n - 1)
end; { Factorial }
```

The **if** statement distinguishes between the trivial case and the one that requires a recursive call to *Factorial*. The trivial case occurs when the value of *n* is 1; since the factorial function should return 1 in this case, the value 1 is assigned to *Factorial*. When the value of *n* is greater than 1, the

Figure 12-8.

Recursive version of the function *Factorial* and a program for testing it.

---

program *ExerciseFactorial* (*input*, *output*);

{ Test *Factorial* by printing a short table of factorials }

var
   number : *integer*;

{ --------------------------------- Function *Factorial* --------------------------------- }

function *Factorial* (*n* : *integer*) : *integer*;

{ Compute factorial of positive, nonzero integer }

begin
  if *n* = 1 **then**
    Factorial : = 1
  else
    Factorial : = *n* * *Factorial*(*n* − 1)
end; { *Factorial* }

{ ----------------------------------- Main Program ----------------------------------- }

begin
  writeln ('Number' :15, 'Factorial' :15);
  writeln;
  for *number* : = 1 **to** 7 **do**
    writeln (*number* :15, *Factorial*(*number*) :15)
end.

---

factorial of *n* is computed by means of a recursive call to *Factorial*. The value of *n* is multiplied by that of *Factorial*(*n* − 1), and the product is returned by assigning it to *Factorial*.

Note that the function name has different meanings when it appears on the left and right sides of an assignment operator, as in

    Factorial : = *n* * *Factorial*(*n* − 1)

When the function name appears to the left of the assignment operator, it represents the memory location designated to hold the value that the function is to return. When the function name appears to the right of the assignment operator, it represents a recursive call to the function.

Figure 12-9 illustrates the original and recursive calls required to compute a factorial. *Factorial* is originally called with an actual parameter of 4. This activation calls *Factorial* with a parameter of 3. The activation with a parameter of 3 calls *Factorial* with a parameter of 2, and the activation with a parameter of 2 calls the function with a parameter of 1. But a parameter value of 1 is the trivial case, so the activation with a parameter of 1 returns the value 1 without any further recursive calls. This

Figure 12-9.

Computation of the factorial of 4 with the recursive function *Factorial*. Each box represents an activation of *Factorial*. The downward arrows represent calls to *Factorial*; the upward arrows represent returns. The label beside each downward (call) arrow gives the parameter value with which *Factorial* was called; the label beside each upward (return) arrow gives the value returned by *Factorial*. The bottom activation, which is called with parameter 1 (the trivial case), completes its computations without any further recursive calls to *Factorial*. The activations return in reverse of the order in which they were called; thus the flow of control is down the call arrows and then up the return arrows. Each activation comes into existence when it is reached via a call arrow and goes out of existence when it is left via a return arrow. When the bottommost activation is being executed, all four activations are in existence simultaneously.

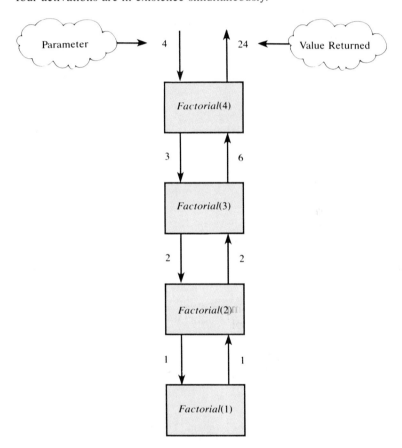

allows the activation with a parameter of 2 to complete its calculations and return the value 2 (= 2 ∗ 1). Now the activation with a parameter of 3 can complete its calculations and return the value 6 (= 3 ∗ 2). Finally, the activation with a parameter of 4 can complete its calculations and return the value 24 (= 4 ∗ 6).

Although computing factorials provides a simple example of recursion, recursion is not the best way to compute factorials. Iterative functions such as the following run faster and require less memory. (Why?)

```
function Factorial (n : integer) : integer;
var
    int, product : integer;
begin
    product := 1;
    for int := 1 to n do
        product := int * product;
    Factorial := product
end; { Factorial }
```

Example 12-2. *The Towers of Hanoi*

We now turn to a problem for which recursion provides the most
straightforward method of solution. Although iterative solutions are known,
they are based on clever insights or tricky reinterpretations that apply to
this problem alone. On the other hand, the recursive techniques we will
use here can be applied to a variety of problems, many of which may not
have simple iterative solutions.

Figure 12-10 illustrates the Towers of Hanoi problem. We have three
pegs labeled A, B, and C. Peg A contains three disks numbered, in order of
increasing size, 1, 2, and 3. The problem is to move the three disks from
peg A to peg C, using peg B as needed during the process. The problem
would be simple except for the following restriction: The disks must be
moved one at a time, and we cannot ever place a larger disk on top of a
smaller one. The problem is easily generalized to any number of disks. No
matter how many disks are used, however, the number of pegs remains
three.

As we have seen, the top-down approach to problem solving advocates
breaking a problem down into simpler subproblems, each of which can be
solved by a subprogram. If one or more of the subproblems are simplified
versions of the original problem, then the use of recursion is indicated: the
subprogram we are writing to solve the original problem can be called
recursively to solve the subproblems.

Because it is so important to break a problem down into simpler
subproblems, a good way to begin work on the solution is to find a
reasonable criterion of simplicity. The Towers of Hanoi problem becomes
simpler as the number of disks is reduced. If we can break the original

Figure 12-10.

The Towers of Hanoi problem. The three disks are to be
moved from peg A to peg C, using peg B as necessary. The
disks must be moved one at a time, and a larger disk may
never be placed on top of a smaller one.

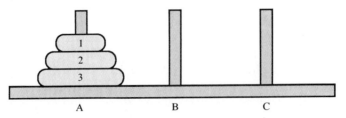

problem down into subproblems involving fewer disks, we will have a basis for a recursive solution. Repeating this simplification will eventually lead us to subproblems involving only one disk. Since a one-disk problem can be solved in a single step (by moving the disk from the peg it is on to the one on which it is desired), the one-disk subproblems can be solved without further recursion.

After some thought about the Towers of Hanoi problem, we get an idea, which is illustrated in Figure 12-11. Suppose we could move all the disks except the bottom one to peg B. Since this uncovers the bottom disk, we can move the bottom disk from peg A to peg C in a single step. If we could now move the rest of the disks from peg B to peg C the problem

Figure 12-11.

A plan for solving the Towers of Hanoi problem. Step 1 moves disks 1 and 2 to peg B. Step 2 moves disk 3 to peg C. Step 3 moves disks 1 and 2 to peg C. Step 2 can be done in a single move and hence requires no further refinement. Steps 1 and 3, however, each involves several moves and so must be broken down into simpler steps.

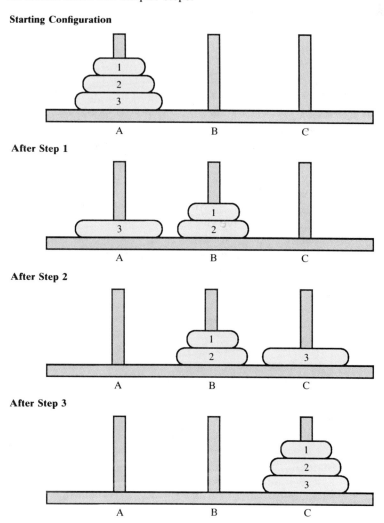

Starting Configuration

After Step 1

After Step 2

After Step 3

would be solved. Of course, we still have the problems of moving the rest of the disks from peg A to peg B and from peg B to peg C. But since those problems involve one fewer disks than the problem we are trying to solve, they make appropriate subproblems to be solved by recursive calls.

Specifically, we outline the solution to the three-disk problem as follows:

1. Move disks 1 and 2 from peg A to peg B
2. Move disk 3 from peg A to peg C
3. Move disks 1 and 2 from peg B to peg C.

This plan is easily generalized to an arbitrary number of disks. If the value of *n* is the number of disks, we have:

1. Move $n - 1$ disks from peg A to peg B
2. Move disk *n* from peg A to peg C
3. Move $n - 1$ disks from peg B to peg C

"Disk *n*" is the disk whose number is equal to the value of *n*. Step 2 is a one-disk problem and can be solved without any further recursive calls. Steps 1 and 3, however, generally involve moving more than one disk and so involve recursive calls.

The program in Figure 12-12 solves the Towers of Hanoi problem by printing instructions for moving the disks. The work of actually solving the problem is done by the recursive procedure *MoveDisks*, which has four value parameters. The integer parameter *n* is the number of disks to be moved. The character parameters *source*, *dest*, and *aux* represent the peg from which the disks are to be moved, the peg to which they are to be moved, and the third peg that is to be used as needed. In the three-disk problem shown in Figure 12-10, the source peg is A, the destination peg is C, and the auxiliary peg is B. The procedure call

MoveDisks (3, 'A', 'C', 'B')

solves this three-disk problem by causing the computer to print the following instructions for moving the disks:

```
Move disk 1 from peg A to peg C
Move disk 2 from peg A to peg B
Move disk 1 from peg C to peg B
Move disk 3 from peg A to peg C
Move disk 1 from peg B to peg A
Move disk 2 from peg B to peg C
Move disk 1 from peg A to peg C
```

Clearly the disks are moved one at a time. You should work through the solution to see that a larger disk is never placed on top of a smaller one, and the disks all end up on peg C in the proper order.

Like all recursive subprograms, *MoveDisks* uses a selection construction to distinguish the trivial case that requires no recursive call from the general case that does require recursive calls. The trivial case occurs when the value of *n* is one. For this case a *writeln* statement instructs the user to move the single disk from the source peg to the destination peg.

Figure 12-12.

This program solves the Towers of Hanoi problem by calling the recursive procedure *MoveDisks*.

```
program Towers (input, output);

{ Solve the Towers of Hanoi problem }

var
    numberOfDisks : integer;

{------------------------------- Procedure MoveDisks ------------------------------- }

procedure MoveDisks (n : integer; source, dest, aux : char);

{ Move n disks from peg source to peg dest using peg aux as the auxiliary
  peg }

begin
  if n = 1 then
      writeln ( 'Move disk 1 from peg ', source,
                ' to peg ', dest)
  else
      begin
        MoveDisks (n − 1, source, aux, dest);
        writeln ('Move disk ', n, ' from peg ', source,
                  ' to peg ', dest);
        MoveDisks (n − 1, aux, dest, source)
      end
end; { MoveDisks }

{--------------------------------- Main Program --------------------------------- }

begin
    write ('How many disks? ');
    readln (numberOfDisks);
    while NumberOfDisks > 0 do
      begin
        MoveDisks (numberOfDisks, 'A', 'C', 'B');
        writeln;
        write ('How many disks? ');
        readln (numberOfDisks)
      end
end.
```

```
writeln ('Move disk 1 from peg ', source,
          ' to peg ', dest)
```

When the value of *n* is greater than one, we must follow the three steps of our outline. Step 1 is to move all but one of the disks to the auxiliary peg. This we accomplish with a recursive call to *MoveDisks*:

```
MoveDisks (n − 1, source, aux, dest)
```

Note that the roles of the auxiliary and destination pegs are reversed for this move. The disks are moved to the auxiliary peg, and the destination peg is used as needed during the move.

In Step 2 we move the remaining disk on the source peg, disk n, from the source peg to the destination peg. Since this is also a one-disk move, we again use a *writeln* statement to instruct the user to make the move.

> *writeln* ('Move disk ', n, ' from peg ', *source*,
>   ' to peg ', *dest*)

Finally, in Step 3 the disks that were moved to the auxiliary peg are now moved from the auxiliary peg to the destination peg. This move is also accomplished with a recursive call to *MoveDisks*.

> *MoveDisks* ($n - 1$, *aux*, *dest*, *source*)

Note that the roles of the source and auxiliary pegs are reversed for this move. The disks are removed from the auxiliary peg, and the source peg is used as needed during the move.

Forward Declarations

The scope of an identifier begins at the point at which the identifier is declared; therefore, declarations of identifiers must always precede their uses. In particular, the declaration of a function or procedure must precede the first point in the program where the function or procedure is called.

There are situations, however, in which this requirement cannot be met. For example, two procedures, say P and Q, may be *mutually recursive*—P calls Q and Q calls P.

```
procedure P (var x, y : integer);
var
  a, b : integer;
begin
  . . .
  Q (a, b);      { invocation of Q }
  . . .
end; { P }

procedure Q (var u, v : integer);
var
  c, d : integer;
begin
  . . .
  P (c, d);      { invocation of P }
  . . .
end; { Q }
```

Regardless of the order in which the two procedure declarations appear, one of the two procedure names is referred to before it is declared.

To avoid this problem, Pascal allows a function or procedure to be declared by means of its heading only. Such a *forward declaration* consists of the function or procedure heading followed by the directive **forward**.

procedure Q (**var** u, v : *integer*); **forward**;

Note the semicolons after the procedure heading and after **forward**. The body of the function or procedure—the part that follows the heading—is declared later in the program at a point where all the identifiers to which it refers have been declared.

```
procedure Q;
var
   c, d : integer;
begin
   . . .
   P (c, d);     { invocation of P }
   . . .
end; { Q }
```

The body is preceded by an abbreviated procedure heading that gives *only* the name of the procedure. The abbreviated heading does not declare formal parameters or a return type for functions, since these have already been declared in the forward declaration.

Now consider the following sequence of declarations:

```
procedure Q (var u, v : integer); forward;

procedure P (var x, y : integer);
var
   a, b : integer;
begin
   . . .
   Q (a, b);     { invocation of Q }
   . . .
end; { P }

procedure Q;
var
   c, d : integer;
begin
   . . .
   P (c, d);     { invocation of P }
   . . .
end; { Q }
```

Procedure Q is declared in the forward declaration, which precedes the reference to Q in the body of procedure P. Since the body of Q is placed after the declaration of P, the reference to P in the body of Q follows the declaration of P, and all is well.

Review Questions

1. What is an applied occurrence of an identifier?

2. What is the defining point of an identifier?

3. What does it mean to say that a language has nested scopes?

4. Why is Pascal said to belong to the Algol family of programming languages?

5. What is a block? How is a block represented in a contour diagram?

6. Of all the identifiers declared in a subprogram, which identifier is considered to be declared outside of the block corresponding to the subprogram declaration? We can think of the corresponding block as beginning at what point in the subprogram declaration?

7. Give the most basic rule governing the scope of an identifier.

8. How must the rule in Question 7 be modified to incorporate the Pascal requirement that an identifier be defined or declared before it is used?

9. Give the rule that applies when an identifier declared in an inner block has the same spelling as an identifier declared in an enclosing, outer block. Which identifier will be referred to by an applied occurrence in
   a. the outer block?
   b. the inner block?
   c. a block nested within the inner block?
   d. an intermediate block that contains the inner block but is contained within the outer block?

10. What is a stack?

11. What characteristic of subprograms assures that the activation records can be stored on a stack?

12. Suppose program P calls subprogram Q; subprogram Q calls subprogram R; and subprogram R calls subprogram S. Diagram the run-time stack before and after each subprogram call and return.

13. In the activation record of a subprogram (including those parts of the caller's activation record that are referred to by the subprogram), describe the use of each of the following locations and areas:
   a. the parameter area.
   b. the return address.
   c. the control link.
   d. the access link.
   e. the local-variable area.
   f. the temporary-storage stack.

14. Describe dynamic and static chains. What is the function of each chain? Why may the two chains differ?

15. What are the functions of the base pointer and the stack pointer? Describe in detail the stack manipulations that take place on subprogram call and return.

16. Describe how variable parameters are passed to a subprogram.

17. Describe subprogram parameters. What names are often used for subprogram parameters when the subprogram is known to be
   a. a function?
   b. a procedure?
   Give several situations in which subprogram parameters are useful.

18. Describe how a formal subprogram parameter is declared. In what respects must the declaration of the actual parameter agree with the declaration of the

formal parameter? What components of the subprogram parameter declaration serve merely as placeholders?

19. Describe recursion. Contrast recursion and repetition. What common obligation do both techniques impose on the programmer?

20. How does the concept of recursion arise naturally out of the top-down approach?

21. What is an activation? An activation record? When is a new activation record created? How long does it remain in existence? What property of activation records is necessary for recursion?

22. If a problem can be solved in a straightforward manner using either repetition or recursion, which technique is likely to yield the most efficient program? Explain.

23. Of the two problems solved by recursion in the text, for which is a recursive solution most appropriate? Which is actually better solved using repetition? Why?

24. What is mutual recursion? Why is the Pascal requirement of declaration before use an obstacle to declaring mutually recursive subprograms?

25. Describe forward declarations. How do forward declarations overcome the obstacle to declaring mutually recursive subprograms?

Exercises

1. Suppose that the program *Craps* in Figure 7-5 (Chapter 7) is rewritten so that subprogram declarations are nested as much as possible. Thus if subprogram Q is called only from the statement part of subprogram P and from subprograms declared within P, then the declaration of Q is nested within the declaration of P. Note that *PlayRemainingRolls* is called only by *PlayOneRound*, *RollDice* is called only by *PlayOneRound* and *PlayRemainingRolls*, and *Random* is called only by *RollDice*. Draw contour diagrams of both the original version of the program and the maximally nested version. For the nested version, write out the declaration for *PlayOneRound*, including, of course, all the nested subprogram declarations. You can abbreviate lengthy parts such as statement parts, but do not omit any essential element of the declarations. Notice how fragmented a subprogram declaration becomes when one or more nested declarations separate the statement part from the subprogram heading and the data-related definitions and declarations.

2. Many calculations call for adding up a series of values returned by a function. Write a function *Sum* to add up values of a function that takes one integer parameter and yields an integer result. If f is such a function, the value of the expression

$$Sum(lo, hi, f)$$

will be the value of

$$f(lo) + f(lo + 1) + \ldots + f(hi - 1) + f(hi)$$

Thus, the value of

$$Sum(1, 7, Factorial)$$

is the sum of the factorials of 1 through 7.

3. The recursive function *Factorial* (Figure 12-8) is deficient in that the recursion fails to terminate for some parameter values. Calling the function with an invalid parameter value will produce an obscure error message or a system crash. Determine the parameter values for which the recursion does not terminate and modify *Factorial* to print an error message and return the value 1 when called with an invalid parameter value.

4. The function *Power*, which raises the real number x to the power n, can be defined recursively as follows:

    $$Power(x, 0) = 1$$
    $$Power(x, n) = x * Power(x, n - 1) \text{ for } n > 0$$

    Use this definition to write a recursive version of *Power*.

5. The greatest common divisor of two nonnegative integers is the largest integer that can be divided evenly into both. For example, the greatest common divisor of 12 and 8 is 4, and the greatest common divisor of 40 and 30 is 10. A function *Gcd(m, n)* that returns the greatest common divisor of m and n can be defined recursively as follows:

    $$Gcd(m, 0) = m$$
    $$Gcd(m, n) = Gcd(n, m \textbf{ mod } n) \text{ for } n > 0$$

    Write *Gcd* as a recursive Pascal function.

6. The sequence of numbers

    $$0, 1, 1, 2, 3, 5, 8, 13, 21, \ldots$$

    is known as *Fibonacci's sequence* and has applications in mathematics and computer science. The first two numbers of the sequence are 0 and 1; each remaining number is the sum of the preceding two. Write a program to print as many terms of the Fibonacci sequence as requested by the user. Formulate an invariant assertion for the repetition construction. *Hints*: (1) It is no accident that Fibonacci's name is given to both the sequence and the rabbit problem (Examples 6-2 and 6-4). (2) It may help to assume that the first term is preceded by two dummy terms, -1 and 1. The dummy terms can be used to initialize variables before starting to compute the terms of the actual sequence. Why are -1 and 1 appropriate dummy terms?

7. Modify the program of Exercise 6 to print all of the terms of the Fibonacci sequence whose values are less than 5000.

8. Suppose that the terms of the Fibonacci sequence (defined in Exercise 6) are numbered as follows:

    Term: 0, 1, 1, 2, 3, 5, 8, 13, . . .
    Number: 0, 1, 2, 3, 4, 5, 6, 7, . . .

    The function *Fibonacci(n)*, which returns the value of the term numbered n, can be defined recursively as follows:

$$Fibonacci(0) = 0$$
$$Fibonacci(1) = 1$$
$$Fibonacci(n) = Fibonacci(n-1) +$$
$$Fibonacci(n-2) \quad \text{for } n > 1$$

Write *Fibonacci* as a recursive Pascal function. Note that there are two trivial cases that are handled without further recursive calls.

9. The recursive function *Fibonacci* defined in Exercise 8 is enormously inefficient. With most small computer systems there will be a very noticeable delay while the computer is calculating the value of, say, *Fibonacci*(18). Explain why this function is so inefficient. To gauge the magnitude of the problem, define a global variable *timesCalled* in the program used to test *Fibonacci*. Modify *Fibonacci* to increment *timesCalled* by one on each call to the function.* Have the program that tests *Fibonacci* initialize *timesCalled* to 1, evaluate *Fibonacci*(18), and print the value of *timesCalled*. Explain why this number is so large. *Hint*: Is the same term of the Fibonacci sequence ever computed more than once?

10. To allow larger factorials to be computed, modify both the iterative and recursive versions of *Factorial* so that the factorial is computed and returned as a real number. The number whose factorial is to be computed should still be supplied as an integer, however.

11. *Mutual recursion* is frequently found in language processors, which often have a separate procedure for each statement that can occur in the programs to be processed. Thus a Pascal language processor might have a procedure *DoIf* to process **if** statements, a procedure *DoFor* to process **for** statements, and a procedure *DoCase* to process **case** statements. Each of these three kinds of statements can contain statements of the same kind or of the other two kinds nested within it. For example, an **if** statement can contain nested **if** statements or it can contain embedded **for** and **case** statements. Thus *DoIf* must be able to call itself to handle nested **if** statements and must be able to call *DoFor* and *DoCase* to handle embedded **for** and **case** statements. Likewise, *DoFor* and *DoCase* must each be able to call not only themselves, but the other two procedures as well. In short, the three procedures are mutually recursive.

There are two approaches to handling this mutual recursion. One approach is to have a procedure *DoStatement* that is called whenever any kind of statement must be processed; *DoStatement* then calls the specific procedure, such as *DoIf*, *DoFor*, or *DoCase*, that applies to the particular statement at hand. With this approach, *DoIf*, *DoFor*, and *DoCase* can all call *DoStatement*; and *DoStatement* can call *DoIf*, *DoFor*, and *DoCase*. The other approach is to let *DoIf*, *DoFor*, and *DoCase* call one another directly, rather than indirectly via *DoStatement*.

For each of the two approaches, outline valid Pascal procedure declarations for *DoIf*, *DoFor*, *DoCase*, and (in the first approach) *DoStatement*. Assume that each procedure has at least one formal parameter.

---

*The global variable *timesCalled* is accessed directly from the statement part of *Fibonacci* rather than being passed as a variable parameter. Direct access to global variables is usually avoided because program structure is clearer when all variables modified by a subprogram are passed as variable parameters. However, such stylistic restrictions are often ignored in "quick and dirty" test programs such as the one contemplated here.

13 Pointers and Linked Lists

A *pointer value* is a value that designates a particular memory location. A *pointer variable* is a variable whose value is used to designate a memory location. As shown in Figure 13-1, a pointer value is usually represented by an arrow extended from the pointer variable to the designated memory location. The term *pointer* is often applied to both pointer values and pointer variables; either may be said to point to the designated location.

We have already seen how array indexes can be used as pointers. In addition, some languages—including Pascal—provide *pointer types* whose values designate memory locations. It is on such pointer types that we will focus in this chapter; however, all the structures we build using values of pointer types could also be built using array indexes as pointers.

The variables we have dealt with so far are said to be *static* because they are named by identifiers in the program text, identifiers that cannot change as the program executes. Although memory for static variables is allocated and deallocated automatically on subprogram call and return, no program can create a static variable other than by calling the subprogram in which the variable is declared, nor can a program dispose of a static variable other than by returning from the subprogram in which the variable is declared. On the other hand, memory locations designated by pointer values can be thought of as *dynamic variables*, because they are not tied to the program identifiers and so can be created or disposed of as needed.

Figure 13-1.

A pointer value is represented by an arrow extending from the pointer variable to the designated memory location. Either the pointer value or the pointer variable may be referred to as a pointer and may be said to point to the designated location.

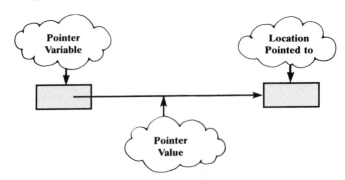

Figure 13-2.

Examples of linked structures or graphs. The dots are called nodes and the lines are called arcs. Part A shows a general graph, with arbitrary connections between the nodes. Part B shows a linked list, in which the nodes and arcs lie on a straight line. Part C shows a tree, in which paths branch out from a common origin called the root.

A.

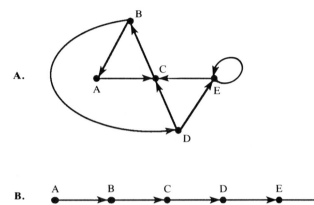

B.

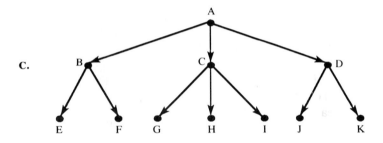

C.

Pointer values can be used to link records to one another. One or more fields of each record contain pointers to locations containing other records. Such linked records represent a mathematical structure known as a *graph* (not to be confused with the graphs used to plot numerical data). Figure 13-2 shows several examples of graphs. The dots, called *nodes*, correspond to the linked records. The connecting lines, called *arcs*, correspond to the pointer values linking the records.

Part A of Figure 13-2 shows a general graph, in which the nodes are linked in an arbitrary manner. Part B shows a *linked list*, in which arcs and nodes form a straight line. (Remember: the static and dynamic chains we discussed in Chapter 12 are both linked lists.) Part C shows a *tree*, in which all paths through the graph start at the same node (called the *root*) and branch out repeatedly without forming closed loops or *cycles*. In this chapter we will focus our attention on linked lists.

Pointer Types

Pointer values are actually memory addresses. Unfortunately, different computers often use quite different schemes for addressing memory. For some computers, a memory address is a single integer value, which can be thought of as an index into a linear memory array, such as the array *memory* discussed in Chapter 12; such computers are said to have *linear address spaces*. Other computers, however, use two integers as a memory address; one designates a particular segment of memory and the other designates a particular location within that segment; such computers are said to have *segmented address spaces*. What's more, computers may impose special restrictions on some integers used as memory addresses, requiring that the integers be even numbers, for example, or multiples of four. These differences present problems for using pointers in portable programs—programs that are to be run on many different computer systems.

To allow programs using pointers to be independent of any particular computer system, Pascal hides all details of pointer representation from the programmer. Pointers can be created only by the system. The programmer can store and retrieve pointer values and can access memory locations designated by pointers but cannot manipulate the internal representations of pointers in any way. Specifically, the programmer cannot assign specific numerical values to the integer or integers constituting a pointer, since the significance of those values would be different for different computer systems. And the programmer cannot carry out arithmetical manipulations on those integers, since again the effect of such manipulations would be different for different computer systems.

When we define a pointer type, we must state the type of values to be stored in the locations designated by the pointers. That is, we must state whether the locations designated by the pointers will hold characters, Boolean values, integers, real numbers, or what. There are several reasons for this. First, most computer systems provide memory locations of different sizes; the size chosen in each instance depends on the type of data to be stored in the location. When we instruct the system to transfer data to or from a memory location, the system must know the size of the location in order to transfer the proper amount of data. Second, when memory locations designated by pointers appear in expressions, the system must know the type of data stored in each location in order to evaluate the expression correctly. Third, specifying the type of data to be stored in each memory location—including locations designated by pointers—allows strong type-checking. The system can guard against programmer errors by insisting that each value be manipulated only by operators, procedures, and functions that are defined for its type.

We define a pointer type in Pascal language with the symbol ↑ followed by the type of values to be stored in the memory locations designated by the pointers. Recall that the upward arrow ↑ appears on most computer terminals as a circumflex or caret (^). For example,

type
    integerPointer = ↑*integer*;

defines a pointer type whose values point to locations containing integers, and

type
    characterPointer = ↑*char*;

defines a pointer type whose values point to locations containing characters. If we declare the pointer variables *p*, *q*, and *r* by

Figure 13-3.

The symbol $p\uparrow$ represents the location pointed to by the pointer variable p.

```
var
    p, q : integerPointer;
    r     : characterPointer;
```

then values of p and q point to locations containing integers, and values of r point to locations containing characters.

The memory location designated by the value of the pointer variable p is denoted by $p\uparrow$. We can think of $p\uparrow$, the memory location designated by the value of p, as analogous to $list[index]$, the array component designated by the value of $index$. Figure 13-3 illustrates the relation between p and $p\uparrow$. The value of p is a pointer, which is represented by an arrow in the figure. The location pointed to by the value of p is designated by $p\uparrow$. Since $p\uparrow$ designates a memory location, it can be used just like any other Pascal variable. We can assign values to $p\uparrow$ and use values of $p\uparrow$ in expressions just as for any other variable. Since values of p point to locations containing integers, $p\uparrow$ is an integer variable; only integers can be assigned to $p\uparrow$ and the value of $p\uparrow$ is always an integer. In Figure 13-3, the value of $p\uparrow$ is 25. After the assignment

$p\uparrow := 1000$

the value of $p\uparrow$ is 1000, and the expression

$3 * p\uparrow + 500$

has the value 3500.

Figure 13-4 further clarifies the relation between p and $p\uparrow$ by contrasting the assignments

$p\uparrow := q\uparrow$

and

$p := q$

The first of these assigns the value of $q\uparrow$ to $p\uparrow$; after the assignment, $p\uparrow$ and $q\uparrow$ have the same value. Nevertheless, $p\uparrow$ and $q\uparrow$ remain distinct memory locations which at the moment just happen to contain the same value. On the other hand, the assignment

$p := q$

causes p and q to point to the same location; thus $p\uparrow$ and $q\uparrow$ designate the same location and so have the same value. Since $p\uparrow$ and $q\uparrow$ designate the same location, assigning a new value to $p\uparrow$ also changes the value of $q\uparrow$, and vice versa.

Pascal provides a predefined pointer value, **nil**, which belongs to all pointer types and, as its name implies, does not designate any memory location. **nil** is often used as a sentinel when processing linked structures. Since **nil** does not point to any memory location, a reference to $p\uparrow$ is illegal if the value of p is **nil**. For example, the second of the following two statements is erroneous:

Figure 13-4.

The assignment $p\uparrow := q\uparrow$ assigns the value of $q\uparrow$ to $p\uparrow$; however, $p\uparrow$ and $q\uparrow$ remain distinct locations that just happen to have the same value (the contents of $p\uparrow$ change but the location itself does not). In contrast, the assignment $p := q$ sets p to point to the same location as q. After this assignment, $p\uparrow$ and $q\uparrow$ represent the same location (the location $p\uparrow$, rather than merely its contents, has changed).

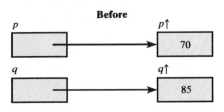

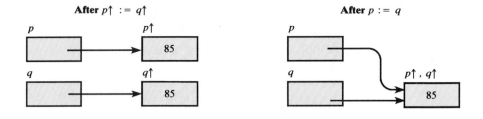

$p := \textbf{nil};$
$p\uparrow := 5$

The second statement instructs the computer to store 5 in the location pointed to by p. But the value of p is **nil**, which does not designate a memory location.

nil is the only pointer constant in Pascal. (For some reason, **nil** is denoted by a reserved word, rather than by an identifier as are other predefined constants such as *true*, *false*, and *maxint*.) As indicated earlier, we cannot represent pointers by numerical constants or obtain them as results of calculations, since the significance of such pointers would depend on a particular computer system. Aside from accessing the location designated by a pointer, the only operation we can carry out on pointers is to compare them with = or <>. The Boolean expression

$p = q$

has the value *true* only if the values of p and q both point to the same memory location or if both values are **nil**.

If pointer values cannot be calculated and cannot be generally represented by constants, then where do they come from? Memory locations designated by pointers are explicitly allocated and deallocated by the programmer. The predefined procedure *new* (p) allocates a new memory location and assigns to p a pointer to the new location. The size of the location allocated depends on the type of the pointer variable. Since the type of p is defined as $\uparrow$*integer,* the procedure call *new* (p) allocates a memory location just large enough to hold an integer.

The procedure *dispose* (p) deallocates the memory location pointed to by p. After the call *dispose* (p), the value of p is meaningless, since the location to which p formerly pointed is no longer available to the program. On most systems, *dispose* recycles memory locations—locations deallocated by *dispose* can be later allocated once again by *new*. *new* and *dispose* provide the programmer with a flexibility in memory management that is not available for memory locations that are automatically allocated and deallocated by the system.

new allocates locations from a memory area called the *heap*. The term *heap* is intended to contrast with *stack*, which describes a memory area in which locations are always deallocated in reverse of the order in which they were allocated. Using calls to *new* and *dispose*, memory locations in a heap can be allocated and deallocated in any order. Thus allocation and deallocation are much less ordered and structured for a heap than they are for a stack. The two names are chosen to reflect this difference.

Figure 13-5 illustrates the operation of *new* and *dispose*. After the pointer variable *p* has been declared by

   p : *integerPointer*;

its contents, represented by a question mark in the figure, are unknown. The contents of *p* could point to any location accessible to the program. Assigning a value to *p*↑ at this point could have disastrous consequences, since the value might be stored in a completely inappropriate location, such as in the user's program code or in that of the operating system.

The procedure call

   new (*p*)

allocates an integer-sized memory location and sets *p* to point to it. When the new location is first allocated, its contents are unknown. The assignment

   p↑ := 100

stores the integer value 100 in the new location.

Figure 13-5.

The contents of a newly declared pointer variable are undefined. The procedure call *new* (*p*) allocates a new memory location and sets *p* to point to it. The contents of the new location are undefined until a value is assigned to *p*↑. After the location pointed to by *p* has been disposed of, the contents of *p* are meaningless.

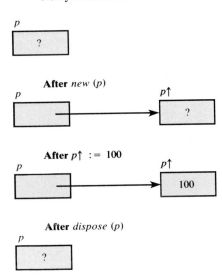

Newly Declared Pointer Variable

p
| ? |

After *new* (*p*)

p   *p*↑
| | ————————————→ | ? |

After *p*↑ := 100

p   *p*↑
| | ————————————→ | 100 |

After *dispose* (*p*)

p
| ? |

The procedure call

> *dispose (p)*

deallocates the memory location pointed to by *p*. The value of *p* is once again meaningless, since it points to a nonexistent memory location. Referring to the value of *p*↑ or assigning a value to it will once again have unpredictable consequences.

We recall that Pascal allows record variants, in which the structure of a record value is determined by the value of one or more tag fields. Record values having different sets of tag-field values may require different amounts of memory, even though they all belong to the same record type. Pascal allows us to specify a particular set of tag-field values when allocating a memory location. The system will allocate only enough memory for a record with the corresponding set of tag-field values. Only records having the given set of tag-field values can be stored in the location, and the tag-field values must be specified when the location is disposed of.

Let *p* be a pointer variable declared by

> *p* : ↑*rt*;

where *rt* is a certain record type. Suppose that *t1*, *t2*, . . . , *tn* are valid tag-field values for records of type *rt*. Then

> *new (p, t1, t2, . . . , tn)*

allocates a location for a record value with tag-field values *t1*, *t2*, . . . , *tn*. Only record values having the given tag-field values can be assigned to *p*↑. When the location pointed to by *p* is deallocated, the tag-field values must again be specified.

> *dispose (p, t1, t2, . . . , tn)*

For example, suppose that type *rt* is defined by

```
type
  rt = record
         case largeSize : Boolean of
           false : (small : array[1..100] of integer);
           true  : (large : array[1..1000] of integer)
       end;
```

The tag field is the Boolean field *largeSize*. The record contains an array of 100 integers when *largeSize* is *false* and an array of 1000 integers when *largeSize* is *true*. Needless to say, a record value occupies much more memory if *largeSize* is *true* than if it is *false*.

If a record of type *rt* is allocated with

> *new (p)*

the system does not know whether the records stored in *p*↑ will contain 100 integers or 1000. The worst case must be assumed, so enough memory must be allocated to hold a record containing an array of 1000 integers. If, however, we use

> *new (p, false)*

we are assuring the system that only records for which *largeSize* is *false* will be stored in *p*↑. Hence, only enough memory for a record with an array of 100 integers must be allocated. In contrast, the procedure call *new* (*p*, *true*)

requests the system to allocate enough memory to hold a record with an array of 1000 integers. A location allocated with *new* (*p*, *false*) must be deallocated with *dispose* (*p*, *false*), and a location allocated with *new* (*p*, *true*) must be deallocated with *dispose* (*p*, *true*).

The use of pointers encourages two kinds of programming errors: *uninitialized pointers* and *dangling pointers*. An uninitialized pointer is a pointer variable to which no pointer value has been assigned, either with *new* or with an assignment statement. As previously discussed, attempting to refer to the location designated by an uninitialized pointer can have unpredictable consequences.

The following pair of statements creates a dangling pointer:

p := *q*;
dispose (*q*)

The assignment statement causes *p* to point to the same location as *q*. The *dispose* statement then deallocates the location pointed to by *q*. Variable *p* is now a dangling pointer, since the location to which it points no longer exists. *dispose* could set *q* to **nil** or to a special error value so that the system could detect an attempt to refer to the disposed location via *q*. But *dispose* has no way of knowing that *p* also contains a pointer to the location being disposed of; hence after *dispose* has been executed, *p* will contain a meaningless pointer. Attempts to refer to *p*↑ will have unpredictable consequences.

Because of these problems, some computer scientists have recommended that pointers themselves be disposed of, and some other means be used to implement graphs. However, since no good substitute for pointers has yet been found, they are still widely used in spite of the dangers of uninitialized and dangling pointers.

Linked Lists

In Chapter 6, we saw how to represent a list of values as an array, the components of which are stored in adjacent memory locations. A list can also be stored in locations scattered throughout memory, provided each location contains a pointer to the location containing the next item on the list. A list stored in this way is called a *linked list* or *chain*. An advantage of linked lists is that insertions and deletions can be made without moving existing items to make room for a new item or to close up the gap left by a deleted item. A disadvantage of linked lists is that only sequential search can be used; faster search techniques, such as binary search, are not available. When faster search techniques are needed and linked structures are still desired, more complex linked structures must be used.

Consider the following definitions:

```
type
  link = ↑cell;
  cell = record
           data : integer;
           next : link
         end
```

Values of type *link* point to memory locations containing values of type *cell*; we will call such memory locations cells. Each cell has two fields: *data*, which contains an integer value; and *next*, which contains a pointer to another cell.

Note that the identifier *cell* is used in the definition of *link* before it is itself defined. This is an exception to Pascal's definition-before-use rule. The definition of a pointer type may precede the definition of the target type—the type of the values pointed to. If this exception were not allowed, the definitions just shown would be impossible. Since *link* is defined in terms of *cell* and *cell* is defined in terms of *link*, no ordering of definitions would satisfy the strict definition-before-use rule.

Figure 13-6 shows the list of integers

        5   9   4   3   2

stored as a linked list of cells. The pointer variable *first* points to the first cell on the list, the one in which the value 5 is stored. The *data* field of each cell contains the list value stored in that cell; the *next* field of each cell contains a pointer to the next cell on the list. The *next* field of the last cell on the list contains **nil**, which is indicated in diagrams by a diagonal line drawn through the field. When processing the list, **nil** serves as a sentinel to indicate the end of the list.

Since *first* points to a cell, it must be of type *link*. Let's declare the variables *first* and *p* as follows:

> **var**
>   *first, p* : *link*;

Assume that *first* points to the first cell of the list shown in Figure 13-6. After the assignment

> *p* := *first*

p will also point to the first cell of the list. The value of *p*↑ is the contents of the first cell. The value of *p*↑.*data* is 5, the contents of the *data* field of the first cell. The contents of *p*↑.*next* is the contents of the *next* field of the first cell, which is a pointer to the second cell.

The assignment statement

> *p* := *p*↑.*next*

Figure 13-6.   Linked list containing the integers 5, 9, 4, 3, and 2.

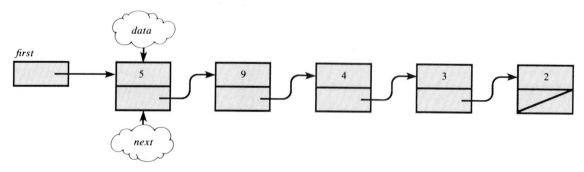

sets p to point to the second cell on the list, the cell pointed to by the *next* field of the first cell. After this assignment statement, the value of $p\uparrow.data$ is 9, the list value stored in the second cell. If

$$p := p\uparrow.next$$

is executed again, p is set to point to the third cell on the list, the one pointed to by the *next* field of the second cell. Subsequent executions of the same assignment statement sets p to point to successive cells on the list. After the assignment statement has been executed four times, p will point to the last cell on the list. Executing the assignment statement again sets p to **nil**, the contents of the *next* field of the last cell. Since $p\uparrow$ is not defined when the value of p is **nil**, no further executions of the assignment statement are possible.

A Linked-List Implementation of *Directory*

We now turn to a linked-list implementation of the abstract data type *Directory*, for which the pseudocode definition and an array implementation were given in Chapter 9. The linked-list implementation (shown in Figure 13-7) uses the following type definitions:

```
type
  link       = ↑entry;
  entry      = record
                  key   : keyType;
                  value : valueType;
                  next  : link
               end;
  directory = link;
```

Keys and values are stored in records of type *entry*. A value of type *link* is a pointer to a record of type *entry*. Entry records are joined into a linked list by their *next* fields, each of which contains either a pointer to the next record on the list or **nil**, which indicates that there are no further records on the list.

A directory is represented by a pointer to the first record of such a linked list; thus a directory is represented by a value of type *link*. To make our terminology here agree with that of the abstract definition and the array implementation, we define type *directory* as being identical to type *link*. Pointers that we regard as designating entire directories will be declared with type *directory*, whereas those we regard as linking together records within a directory will be declared with type *link*. Each procedure of the implementation has a parameter *aDirectory* which is declared with type *directory* and holds a pointer to the first record of the directory on which the procedure is to act.

The first record of a linked list differs from all other records in that it is pointed to by a pointer variable such as *aDirectory*, whereas every other record is pointed to by the *next* field of another record. This sometimes requires that the first record be treated as a special case. One way around this problem is to let the first record be a dummy record that does not contain valid data. Then every record that contains valid data is pointed to by another record, and each can be processed in the same way. The dummy record is created by the procedure *Clear*, which assigns a pointer to the dummy record to the variable passed to the procedure via the variable parameter *aDirectory*.

Figure 13-7.

Linked-list implementation of the abstract data type
Directory.

{ ************* Linked-List Implementation of *Directory* *************}

{ Types *keyType* and *valueType* are defined in the program using *Directory* }

```
type
   link     = ↑entry;                          { pointer to next entry }
   entry    = record                           { directory entry (list cell) }
                 key   : keyType;
                 value : valueType;
                 next  : link
              end;
   directory = link;                           { pointer to directory, that is,
                                                 pointer to first (dummy)
                                                 entry }
```

{----------------------------------- Procedure *Search* ------------------------------------}

```
procedure Search (aDirectory  : directory;
                  searchKey   : keyType;
                  var found   : Boolean;
                  var prev, cur : link);
```

{ Locate entry, if any, with given key; set *found* to reflect outcome of
search, set *cur* to point to entry found, and set *prev* to point to preceding
entry. If search unsuccessful, set *prev* and *cur* to point to entries between
which entry with given key should be inserted }

```
var
   searching : Boolean;
begin
   prev := aDirectory;
   cur := aDirectory↑.next;
   searching := true;
   while (cur <> nil) and searching do
     if cur↑.key >= searchKey then
        searching := false
     else
        begin
          prev := cur;
          cur := cur↑.next
        end;
   if cur = nil then
     found := false
   else if cur↑.key = searchKey then
     found := true
   else
     found := false
end; { Search }
```

Figure 13-7. *Continued.*

{----------------------------------- Procedure *Clear* ------------------------------------}

procedure *Clear* (**var** *aDirectory* : *directory*);

{ Create a new, empty directory. Contrary to what the name implies, this
procedure creates a new directory rather than clearing an existing one }

begin
  new (*aDirectory*);   { create dummy header entry }
  aDirectory↑.*next* : = **nil**
end; { *Clear* }

{----------------------------------- Procedure *Insert* ------------------------------------}

procedure *Insert* (*aDirectory* : *directory*;
                  insertKey : *keyType*;
                  insertValue : *valueType*;
                  var *error* : *Boolean*);

{ Insert a new entry into a directory }

var
  found   : *Boolean*;
  prev, cur, newEntry : *link*;
begin
  Search (*aDirectory, insertKey, found, prev, cur*);
  if *found* **then**
    error : = *true*
  else
    begin
      error : = *false*;
      new (*newEntry*);
      with *newEntry*↑ **do**
        begin
          key : = *insertKey*;
          value : = *insertValue*;
          next : = *cur*
        end;
      prev↑.*next* : = *newEntry*
    end
end; { *Insert* }

{----------------------------------- Procedure *Lookup* ------------------------------------}

procedure *Lookup* (*aDirectory*   : *directory*;
                  searchKey   : *keyType*;
                  var *valueFound* : *valueType*;
                  var *error*   : *Boolean*);

{ Lookup value corresponding to given key and return value found }

Figure 13-7.   *Continued.*

```
var
  found    : Boolean;
  prev, cur : link;
begin
  Search (aDirectory, searchKey, found, prev, cur);
  error := not found;
  if found then
    valueFound := cur↑.value
end; { Lookup }
```

{ ---------------------------------- Procedure *Delete* ----------------------------------}

```
procedure Delete (aDirectory : directory;
                  deleteKey  : keyType;
                  var error  : Boolean);
```

{ Delete entry with given key }

```
var
  found    : Boolean;
  prev, cur : link;
begin
  Search (aDirectory, deleteKey, found, prev, cur);
  error := not found;
  if found then
    begin
      prev↑.next := cur↑.next;
      dispose (cur)
    end
end; { Delete }
```

Only for *Clear* does *aDirectory* have to be a variable parameter, since only *Clear* changes the pointer value stored in *aDirectory*. The other procedures do not change the value of *aDirectory* even though they may change the linked list pointed to by the value of *aDirectory*.

Thus we have another way in which a procedure can return results to its caller. If a pointer to a linked structure is passed to a procedure as a value parameter, then the structure in question can be accessed both by the original pointer in the main program and the copy that was passed to the procedure. The procedure can use its pointer to modify the structure in whatever ways it pleases, and those changes will, of course, show up when the structure is accessed via the original pointer that was retained by the calling program.

The Procedure *Search*

Sequential search is used for locating the record with a given key. The records on the list are maintained in ascending order according to their key values. Keeping the records in order offers no advantage in searching for a record that is on the list. It does, however, allow the search to be terminated sooner if the desired record is not on the list. The search can be terminated as soon as the point is reached where the record would be (according to the order of the keys) if it were present. If the records were not in order, a search for a nonexistent record would always have to go all the way to the end of the list.

Searching is done by a procedure

$$Search \ (aDirectory \quad : directory;$$
$$searchKey \quad : keyType;$$
$$\textbf{var} \ found \quad : Boolean;$$
$$\textbf{var} \ prev, \ cur : link);$$

whose use is illustrated in Figure 13-8. The input parameter *searchKey* is the key being sought. The output parameter *found* is set to *true* if a record with the given key is found and to *false* otherwise. The input/output parameters *prev* (previous) and *cur* (current) are pointers that are set as follows. If the desired record was found, *cur* points to the record that was found and *prev* points to the immediately preceding record. If the desired record was not found, *prev* points to the record that would have preceded the given record, had it been present; and *cur* points to the record that would have followed it.

Note that our description of *Search* assumes that the first record is a dummy record that will never be pointed to by *cur*. If *cur* pointed to the first record, then the value of *prev* would be undefined.

The procedure *Search* scans the list for a record whose key is equal to the value of *searchKey* and sets the values of *found*, *prev*, and *cur* as previously described. The input/output parameters *prev* and *cur* are used as pointers for scanning the list during the search. To begin, *prev* is set to point

Figure 13-8.

The pointers set by the procedure *Search*. If the key being sought was found, *cur* is set to point to the cell with that key, and *prev* is set to point to the preceding cell. Otherwise, *prev* and *cur* are set to point to the adjacent cells between which a cell with the given key should be inserted.

Key 25 Found

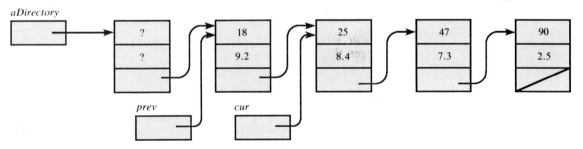

Key 25 Not Found

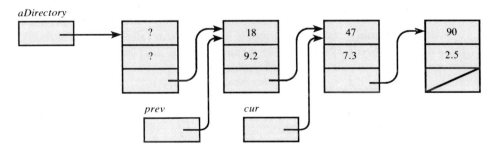

to the first record on the list (the dummy record) and *cur* is set to point to the record following the dummy record (the first record containing a valid data value). The flag *searching* is initialized to *true*.

```
prev := aDirectory;
cur := aDirectory↑.next;
searching := true
```

The search continues until it runs off the end of the list (the value of *cur* becomes **nil**) or until the flag *searching* becomes *false*. At each step of the search, the key field of the record pointed to by *cur* is compared with the value of *searchKey*. If the key field of the record equals *searchKey*, then we have found the desired record. If the key field of the record is greater than *searchKey*, then we have passed the point where the record would be if it were present. In either case, *searching* is set to *false* to terminate the search. If, however, the key field of the current record is less than the value of *searchKey,* the search should continue. Both *prev* and *cur* are moved forward one record in the list: *prev* is set to the value of *cur* and *cur* is set to the value of the *next* field of the record to which it currently points.

```
while (cur <> nil) and searching do
  if cur↑.key >= searchKey then
    searching := false
  else
    begin
      prev := cur;
      cur := cur↑.next
    end
```

When the repetition terminates, we have three cases. If the value of *cur* is **nil**, the desired record was not found. If the value of *cur* is not **nil**, then *cur↑.key* is defined and can be checked. If the value of *cur↑.key* equals the value of *searchKey*, the desired record was found. If the value of *cur↑.key* is not equal to the value of *searchKey*, the desired record was not found. The following multiway selection checks for the three cases and sets the value of *found* accordingly.

```
if cur = nil then
  found := false
else if cur↑.key = searchKey then
  found := true
else
  found := false
```

The Procedure *Clear*

The procedure *Clear* creates a list that contains no valid data records but does contain the dummy record mentioned earlier. *Clear* allocates the dummy record, sets *aDirectory* to point to it, and sets the *next* field of the dummy record to **nil**.

```
new (aDirectory);
aDirectory↑.next := nil
```

The Procedure *Insert*

The procedure *Insert* inserts a new record whose key and value are given by the values of the parameters *insertKey* and *insertValue*. *Insert* begins by calling *Search* to search for a record whose key is equal to *insertKey*. If such a record is found, *error* is set to *true*, since we are not allowed to insert a record with the same key as an existing record. If no such record was found, then *prev* is set to point to the record preceding the point at which the new record should be inserted, and *cur* is set to point to the record following that point. That is, the new record should be inserted between the record pointed to by *prev* and the record pointed to by *cur*. If the new record should be inserted following the last record on the list, *prev* is set to point to the last record and *cur* is set to **nil**.

The record to be inserted is created by *new*.

> *new* (*newEntry*)

The *key* and *value* fields of the new record are set to the values of *insertKey* and *insertValue*.

```
with newEntry↑ do
  begin
    key := insertKey;
    value := insertValue;
    next := cur
  end
```

Also in this **with** statement, the *next* field of the new record is set to point to the record that will follow the new record in the list. The record that is to follow the new record is pointed to by *cur*.

> *next* := *cur*

prev points to the record that is to precede the new record in the list. The *next* field of this record must be set to point to the new record.

> *prev*↑.*next* := *newEntry*

The Procedure *Lookup*

The procedure *Lookup* looks up the value of the parameter *searchKey* and returns the corresponding value via the output parameter *valueFound*. *Lookup* calls *Search* to search the list for a record whose key is equal to *searchKey*. *Search* sets the values of *found*, *prev*, and *cur* as previously described. If the value of *found* is not *true*, the desired key was not found, and *error* is set to *true*. If the value of *found* is *true*, *cur* points to the record having the desired key. *Error* is set to *false*, and the *value* field of the record pointed to by *cur* is returned via the parameter *valueFound*.

```
Search (aDirectory, searchKey, found, prev, cur);
error := not found;
if found then
  valueFound := cur↑.value
```

The Procedure *Delete*

The procedure *Delete* deletes the record whose key field is equal to the parameter *deleteKey*. *Search* is called to find the record with the given key. If no such record is found, *error* is set to *true*. Otherwise, *error* is set to *false* and the record that was found is deleted.

Cur points to the record to be deleted and *prev* points to the preceding record. To delete the record pointed to by *cur*, the link from the preceding record must be routed around the record to be deleted and set to point to the following record. Specifically, the *next* field of the preceding record must be set to point to the record now pointed to by the *next* field of the record to be deleted.

> *prev↑.next* := *cur↑.next*

All that remains to be done is to dispose of the record that was removed from the list.

> *dispose (cur)*

Review and Summary of Pascal Type System

Since we have now taken up all the types offered by Pascal, it is worthwhile to summarize the Pascal type system. Pascal types can be classified as follows:

1. Simple Types
   1.1 Ordinal types
       1.1.1 The predefined types *integer*, *Boolean* and *char*
       1.1.2 Enumerated types
       1.1.3 Subrange types
   1.2 The predefined type *real*
2. Structured Types
   2.1 Array types, including string types
   2.2 File types, including the predefined file type *text*
   2.3 Record types
   2.4 Set types
3. Pointer Types

Pascal designates as *compatible* certain types that are subtypes of some larger type. For example, the subrange types $1..10$ and $50..100$ are compatible, since both are subranges of type *integer*. A related concept is that of *assignment compatibility*. A value is *assignment compatible* with a given type only if the value can be assigned to a variable of the given type. For example, the value 5 is assignment compatible with the subrange type $1..10$ because 5 can be assigned to a variable of type $1..10$.

Before stating the formal requirements for compatibility and assignment compatibility, we need a few definitions.

1. A string type is an array type of the form

    packed array $[1..n]$ **of** *char*

2. Special restrictions are imposed on file types and on structured types whose values contain files as components. Such types cannot serve as component types of file types, and assignment is not allowed for values of such types. These restricted types are defined recursively as follows: *A type is not allowed as a component type of a file type if it is a file type or if it is a structured type with a component type that is not allowed as a component type of a file type.*

3. Two types are considered the same if they are name equivalent; that is, if they are defined by the same occurrence of a type constructor or if their identifiers have been set equal to one another in a type definition such as *directory = link*.

We can now define type compatibility. Types T1 and T2 are compatible if any of the following statements hold:

1. T1 and T2 are the same type.
2. T1 is a subrange of T2, or T2 is a subrange of T1, or both are subranges of the same host type.
3. T1 and T2 are set types with compatible base types. T1 and T2 must be both packed or both unpacked.
4. T1 and T2 are string types with the same number of components.

A value of type T2 is assignment compatible with a type T1 if any of the following statements are true:

1. T1 and T2 are the same type and that type is allowed as a component type of a file type. (Thus assignment is forbidden for values whose types are not allowed as component types of file types.)
2. T1 is type *real* and T2 is type *integer.*
3. T1 and T2 are compatible ordinal types and the value of type T2 belongs to type T1.
4. T1 and T2 are compatible set types and all members of the value of type T2 belong to the base type of type T1.
5. T1 and T2 are compatible string types.

Review Questions

1. What is a pointer value? A pointer variable? What precisely do we mean when we say that a value or a variable points to a certain memory location?

2. What are pointer types? What can serve as pointers in languages that do not provide pointer types?

3. Distinguish between static and dynamic variables.

4. What is a graph? A tree? A linked list? What are nodes? Arcs? Cycles?

5. What does it mean to say that a computer has a linear address space? A segmented address space?

6. Why do many languages hide the details of pointer representations from programmers?

7. Give three reasons why a definition of a pointer type must state the type of values to be stored in the locations pointed to.

8. How is a pointer type declared in Pascal?

9. If p is a pointer variable, how does Pascal designate the location pointed to by the value of p?

10. If p and q are pointer variables, contrast the effects of the assignments

$$p\uparrow := q\uparrow$$

and

$$p := q$$

11. What is **nil**? For what purpose is it often used?

12. Describe the use of the predefined procedure *new*.

13. Describe the use of the predefined procedure *dispose*.

14. What is the heap?

15. Describe the use of *new* and *dispose* with records having variant parts and tag fields.

16. What are uninitialized pointers? Dangling pointers?

17. What is another name for a linked list? What two linked lists have we already encountered (in Chapter 12) under that name?

18. Give and explain a set of type definitions for a linked list.

19. What exception to Pascal's definition-before-use rule is allowed for pointer types?

20. Give and explain the statements needed to move from cell to cell along a linked list.

Exercises

1. In a circular linked list, the last cell contains a pointer to the first cell, so that the list forms a circle or, in graph terminology, a cycle. An advantage of circular linked lists is that a scan through a list can start at any cell.

   Suppose that a circular linked list contains cells of type *entry*. None of the cells is distinguished in any way; there is no special header cell nor does any cell contain a special sentinel value. Write a version of the procedure *Search* that searches a circular linked list for the cell containing a particular key; *found*, *prev*, and *cur* are to be set as described in the text. The pointer passed via *aDirectory* can point to any cell on the list. The tricky part of this exercise is stopping the search after all the cells on the list have been examined without finding the desired key.

2. In a *doubly linked list*, each cell contains two pointer fields: *nextLeft*, which points to the preceding cell on the list; and *nextRight*, which points to the following cell on the list. The value of *nextLeft* is **nil** for the first cell on the list, and the value of *nextRight* is **nil** for the last cell. An advantage of a doubly linked list is that it can be scanned in either direction. Only one pointer into the

list ever need be given, since a pointer to either the preceding or the following cell can always be obtained by following the appropriate link. In some circumstances, an erroneous pointer value can be corrected, since each pointer is represented redundantly by another pointer linking the same cells in the opposite direction. Modify the implementation of *Directory* to use doubly linked lists.

3. Modify the implementation of *Multiset* described in Exercise 9-2 (Chapter 9) so that a multiset is represented by a linked list rather than an array.

4. Modify the linked-list implementation of *Directory* along the lines indicated (for arrays) in Exercise 9-3 in Chapter 9. Keys and values are to be stored in separate parallel linked lists, both of which must be scanned simultaneously to find the value corresponding to a given key. Insertion and deletion operations must also affect both lists.

5. A useful feature of linked lists is that a single record can be on many different lists at the same time; the only requirement is that the record type provide a separate link field for each list to which the record values are to belong. (For doubly linked lists, two link fields are needed for each list.) Suppose that each record contains a salesperson's ID number, the amount the person sold for the current month, and the amount the person has sold since the beginning of the year. We wish to place such records on three linked lists; on the first list the records will be in increasing order according to the record keys; on the second list they will be in decreasing order according to sales for the current month; and on the third list the records will be in decreasing order according to the year-to-date sales. Write a program to build the three lists from sales data entered by the user. Whenever the user enters the data for a salesperson, the program should allocate a new record, assign the user-entered values to the appropriate fields, and insert the record in the proper position in each list. At the request of the user, the program should print any one of the three lists (each list will be printed as a table with columns for the ID number, sales for the current month, and year-to-date sales; each record will be printed on a separate row). That is, the user can request the sales data to be printed with the records in any of the three orders just described.

1

Pascal Reserved Words

and	downto	if	or	then
array	else	in	packed	to
begin	end	label	procedure	type
case	file	mod	program	until
const	for	nil	record	var
div	function	not	repeat	while
do	goto	of	set	with

Pascal Syntax

Programming languages are usually discussed in terms of *syntax* and *semantics*. The syntax—the grammar of the language—identifies the various constructions of interest, such as the **if** statement and the **case** statement, and gives the rules that must be followed in writing each construction. Any violation of those rules results in a syntax error message from the language processor, which refuses to translate or execute a program until the programmer has corrected all errors in syntax. The semantics of a language, on the other hand, give the meanings of the constructions identified by the syntax. For example, many of the constructions in a programming language specify computations, and their meanings are just the computations that they specify.

In this book, the syntax of Pascal has been presented through general statement formats such as

> **if** Boolean-expression **then**
>   statement-1
> **else**
>   statement-2

These general formats were accompanied by discussions of possible variations, such as the fact that the

> **else**
>   statement-2

part of an **if** statement can be omitted.

In the author's opinion, such general formats and accompanying discussions are the most straightforward way of presenting syntax to beginning students of a language. For reference purposes, however, a more concise presentation of the syntax of each construction is desirable. Such a concise presentation is particularly helpful in understanding and correcting syntax errors discovered by a language processor. A traditional method of presenting Pascal syntax is by means of *syntax diagrams* that display graphically the syntactic possibilities and limitations of each construction. This appendix gives syntax diagrams for International Standard Pascal (International Standards Organization—ISO—level 1). Notes on the diagrams indicate one diagram and one option that must be omitted to get the syntax for American standard Pascal (American National Standards Institute/Institute of Electrical and Electronics Engineers—ANSI/IEEE—which is essentially the same as ISO level 0). Both omissions involve conformant array parameters, which are present in ISO level 1 Pascal but not in ISO level 0 or ANSI/IEEE.

In using the diagrams, we must keep in mind that they give only the syntax of Pascal, not its semantics. Thus some of the constructions allowed by the diagrams will not be meaningful; they will be syntactically correct, but they will violate some restriction based on semantics. In particular, the syntax diagrams do not reflect the restrictions imposed by the Pascal type system. For example, the syntax diagrams allow expressions such as

not 25

and

true + false

These expressions are considered syntactically correct, but are meaningless (and hence erroneous) because **not** cannot be applied to integers and + cannot be applied to Boolean values.

The following sections constitute a guided tour of the syntax diagrams. You should read through all this material before using the diagrams for the first time. Study carefully the first few diagrams discussed, which are simple and illustrate clearly how syntax diagrams work. You can skim the remaining, more complex diagrams the first time through. After this overview, you should have no difficulty locating and using the diagrams that apply to any particular construction in which you are interested.

Terminals and Nonterminals

Observe that the diagrams contain two kinds of symbols: *terminal symbols*, which are enclosed in circles or in boxes with rounded sides; and *nonterminal symbols*, which are enclosed in boxes with straight sides.

Terminal symbols (often just called *terminals*) are the symbols that actually appear in Pascal programs. Examples of terminals are reserved words such as **begin**, **end**, **if**, and **for**; operators such as +, −, <=, and ↑; and punctuation marks such as the colon (:) and semicolon (;). There are also three kinds of terminal symbols that are, for convenience, represented by names rather than by listing each possible symbol. The terminal *digit* represents any of the digits 0 through 9; the terminal *letter* represents any uppercase or lowercase letter of the alphabet; and the terminal *character* represents any character allowed in a string constant.

Nonterminal symbols (or just *nonterminals*) are names for language constructions defined by syntax diagrams. Examples of nonterminals are *identifier*, *expression*, *statement*, and *program*, each of which represents the corresponding Pascal construction (for example, the nonterminal *identifier* represents any valid Pascal identifier; the nonterminal *statement* represents any valid Pascal statement; and so on). All nonterminals are defined by diagrams and all diagrams define nonterminals. Each diagram is labeled with the nonterminal it defines.

The nonterminals appearing in any syntax diagram must be defined by other diagrams. The diagrams have been ordered so that, for the most part, nonterminals are defined before they are used in other diagrams. Definition before use is not possible in every case, however, because some diagrams are *recursive*—a nonterminal is defined partially in terms of itself—and some diagrams are *mutually recursive*—several nonterminals are mutually defined in terms of each other. Recursion and mutual recursion always represent the possibility of nested constructions, such as nested statements or nested parentheses in expressions.

As in Pascal programs, reserved words appear in the syntax diagrams in boldface, and operators and punctuation marks appear in lightface Roman (that is, neither boldface nor italics). Names appearing in the diagrams, such as *digit* and *identifier*, are printed in Roman type in the diagrams but are italicized for emphasis in the text of this appendix.

Identifiers, Numbers, Constants, and Variables

Identifiers, numbers, constants, and variables (along with reserved words and operators) are the raw material out of which all Pascal constructions are built. Not only are these basic constructions a logical starting point for discussing Pascal syntax, but the diagrams that represent these constructions are relatively simple and so serve as a good introduction to syntax diagrams.

Using a syntax diagram is something like finding a path through a maze. We enter the diagram along the horizontal line that extends to the left, and we exit the diagram along the horizontal line that extends to the right. The lines in the diagram are all one-way streets: each line can be traversed only in the direction indicated by the arrowhead at the end of the line. In traversing the diagram, we will pass through terminal symbols, which represent such basic program constituents as digits, operators, and reserved words; and through nonterminal symbols, which represent larger constructions defined by other syntax diagrams. Normally, there will be many possible paths through a syntax diagram; each such path represents a valid occurrence of the nonterminal defined by the diagram.

Now let's look at Diagram 1, which defines the nonterminal *identifier*. Starting at the left and moving to the right, we immediately encounter the terminal *letter*. Since there is no way to get around this terminal, we conclude that every identifier must begin with a letter. Passing through the terminal *letter*, we note that the path we are traveling is joined by two other paths; however, we cannot enter those paths at this point because the arrows are pointing in the wrong direction. Instead, we must continue traveling to the right until we reach the junction point on the right-hand side of the diagram.

At the junction point, we have three choices. We can continue traveling to the right until we exit the diagram. If we follow this course, our path through the diagram will represent a single-letter identifier such as *x*, *y*, or *z*. Another alternative is to take the upward path from the junction point, pass through the terminal *letter*, then return to our "main highway," and finally come back to the junction point. If we traverse the upper loop once and then exit from the diagram, our path through the diagram will represent a two-letter identifier such as *id*, *pc*, or *sp*. Our third alternative is to take the downward path from the junction point, the one that passes through the terminal *digit*. If we traverse the lower loop once and then exit, our path through the diagram will represent an identifier having one letter followed by one digit, such as *x1*, *n3*, or *a0*.

After passing through the first occurrence of *letter* we can traverse the letter loop and the digit loop as many times as we wish (including none at all). We can intermix traversals of the two loops in any order; for example, we could traverse the letter loop, then the digit loop, then the letter loop twice, then the digit loop three times, and so on. Thus the entire syntax diagram is equivalent to the statement that an identifier consists of a letter followed by any number of letters and digits in any order. As an exercise, trace the path corresponding to the identifier *r2d2c3po*.

Because identifiers are used for so many different purposes, the diagrams become clearer if we indicate the kind of identifier required at each point. Thus we will often use nonterminals such as *variable-identifier* for an identifier that has been declared in a variable declaration and *function-identifier* for an identifier that has been declared in a function declaration. All of these non-terminals are defined by the diagram for *identifier*, and the syntax would still be correct if each were replaced by just *identifier*. The additional qualification, however, improves the clarity of the syntax diagrams by helping us distinguish the different uses for identifiers.

The diagram for *unsigned-integer* (Diagram 2) tells us that an unsigned integer contains at least one digit, because there is no way we can get through the diagram without passing through the terminal *digit*. Since there is a loop around *digit*, any number of additional digits are allowed. Thus an unsigned integer consists of one or more digits; typical unsigned integers are 1, 25, 352, and 7324.

The diagram for *unsigned-number* (Diagram 3) can represent an integer, a real number in conventional (fixed-point) notation, or a real number in floating-point notation. (Remember that syntax diagrams do not distinguish between data types, so it's not unusual for values of different types, such as integers and real numbers, to be represented by the same diagaram.) Note that two sections of the diagram are optional in that there are lines bypassing them. When approaching either of the two optional sections, we can choose to go through the section, thus generating an instance of the corresponding construction, or we can take the bypass around the section, thus omitting the construction represented by the optional section.

Unsigned-number is our first diagram to contain nonterminals, specifically, two occurrences of the nonterminal *unsigned-integer*. Each occurrence of *unsigned-integer* represents any sequence of characters that can be generated by traversing the diagram for *unsigned-integer*. Since the diagram *unsigned-integer* represents a sequence of one or more digits, each occurrence of the nonterminal *unsigned-integer* likewise represents a sequence of one or more digits.

Thus an unsigned number consists of an unsigned integer followed by either or both of two optional parts. The first optional part (which represents the fractional part of a real number) consists of a decimal point followed by a sequence of digits. The second optional part (which represents the exponent part of a real number in floating-point notation) consists of the letter E followed by an optional plus or minus sign followed by an unsigned integer. Some unsigned numbers are 125, 3.1416, and 3.25E + 20.

To test your understanding at this point, use the syntax diagrams to answer the following questions about unsigned numbers. Must an unsigned number contain a decimal point? Can it begin with a decimal point? Can it end with a decimal point? Must it contain the letter E? Can the decimal point and the letter E be adjacent to one another? Can the letter E precede the decimal point? Must the letter E be followed by a sign? What is the minimum number of digits that can occur to the right of the letter E?

The diagram for *unsigned-constant* (Diagram 4) tells us that an unsigned constant can be an unsigned number, a constant represented by a constant identifier, a character or string constant (a sequence of characters enclosed in single quotation marks), or the pointer constant **nil**. Note the typical ladder-like structure of the diagram, with each rung of the ladder corresponding to a different alternative for an unsigned constant.

The two nonterminals in this diagram are *unsigned-number* and *constant-identifier*. As discussed earlier, *constant-identifier* is just defined by the diagram for *identifier*; the qualifying prefix ''constant-'' clarifies the diagram for *unsigned-constant* by indicating the kind of identifier that can represent an unsigned constant.

The third rung from the top of the ladder represents both character and string constants. Note that a quoted constant must contain at least one character; the null string, which contains no characters, cannot be represented by a string constant in Pascal. This diagram *does not* attempt to describe the convention by which a single quotation mark (or apostrophe) is represented inside a quoted constant by two single quotation marks in succession.

A variable access is any access to a memory location designated by a variable; the access can be for the purpose of storing a new value in the location (as when a variable appears on the left-hand side of an assignment statement) or for retrieving the value stored in the location (as when a variable appears in an expression).

The simplest variable access is just a variable identifier such as x. If x is an array variable, then we can use indexing to refer to component variables, giving variable accesses such as $x[5]$ or $x[3, 2]$. If x is a record variable, then field designators such as $x.date$ and $x.date.year$ are also variable accesses. Finally, if x is a file variable then $x\uparrow$ is the corresponding buffer variable, and if x is a pointer variable then $x\uparrow$ refers to the location pointed to; in either case $x\uparrow$ is a variable access. Thus a variable access consists of a variable identifier optionally followed by one or more constructions for indexing an array, for designating a component of a record, for designating a buffer variable, or for designating the variable referred to by a pointer.

Traversing the diagram for *variable-access* (Diagram 5), we first encounter the variable identifier that is the basis for every variable access. A field identifier is allowed in place of the variable identifier; however, the field-identifier option can only be used inside a **with** statement that designates a record value to which the field identifier can refer. The ladder part of the diagram represents the optional qualifying constructions. The top rung corresponds to indexing, the middle rung to accessing a component of a record, and the bottom rung to accessing a buffer variable or a memory location designated by a pointer. Note two things. First, the qualifying constructions are optional, since there is a path that bypasses the entire ladder part of the diagram. Second, the ladder part is enclosed in a loop, so we can use as many qualifying constructions as needed for a particular access. For example, the variable access

$x\uparrow[3]\uparrow[5].date.year$

is syntactically correct; whether it makes sense or not depends, of course, on how x is declared.

Expressions

We recall that our main difficulty with expressions was specifying the order in which the operations called for by an expression would be carried out. We solved this problem with the concept of operator precedence along with additional rules such as the rule for handling parentheses.

The manner in which a computation is carried out lies in the domain of semantics. But we can formulate a purely syntactic version of the same problem by asking how an expression is to be broken down into subexpressions. For example, given the expression

$$3 + 4 * 5$$

the elements of the expression can conceivably be grouped as

$$(3 + 4) * 5$$

or as

$$3 + (4 * 5)$$

With the first possible grouping, we have an operator * with two operands, one represented by the subexpression $3 + 4$ and the other by the constant 5. With the second grouping, we have an operator + with two operands, one represented by the constant 3 and the other by the subexpression $4 * 5$. We can interpret the rules for operator precedence as saying that, in forming such subexpressions, we should first try to form subexpressions with * and / before forming subexpressions with + and $-$. This interpretation of operator precedence singles out the second grouping as the correct one. Given the semantic rule that the operands of an operator must be evaluated before the operator can be applied, the second grouping will result in the multiplication being carried out before the addition.

With syntax diagrams, we can describe not only expressions but the various kinds of subexpressions into which an expression can be broken down. A set of syntax diagrams for expressions and subexpressions constitutes a prescription for decomposing an expression into subexpressions. Thus syntax diagrams can take the place of the rules for operator precedence.

The diagrams for *factor*, *term*, *simple-expression*, and *expression* (Diagrams 6–9) define a four-level hierarchy of different kinds of expressions and subexpressions. At the bottom of this hierarchy are factors, which are the most basic constructions for representing values; at the top of the hierarchy are expressions, which, as their name implies, represent the most general possible expressions. Factors are used to define terms, terms are used to define simple expressions, and simple expressions are used to define expressions. Thus, to decompose an expression into subexpressions, we must first combine the basic elements of the expression to form factors, then combine the factors to form terms, then combine the terms to form simple expressions, and finally combine the simple expressions to form an expression. Consequently, operators that occur in factors take precedence over operators that occur in terms; operators that occur in terms take precedence over those that occur in simple expressions, and operators that occur in simple expressions take precedence over those that occur in expressions.

The diagram for *factor* (Diagram 6) is a ladder, the top four rungs of which correspond to basic ways of representing values. Specifically, the top rung corresponds to obtaining the value of a variable, the second rung to an unsigned constant, the third rung to a function invocation, and the fourth rung to a set constructor. Note that the third rung contains a miniladder giving the four kinds of actual parameters allowed in a function invocation. From top to bottom, these are value parameters, variable parameters, functional parameters, and procedural parameters.

The next-to-bottom rung of the *factor* diagram represents the rule that parentheses override operator precedence. Any part of an expression that is enclosed in parentheses is just treated as a factor—a basic way of representing a value. In evaluating the surrounding expression, all the details of the parenthesized expression, including the precedences of its operators, are ignored. The bottom rung of the ladder tells us that **not** has a higher precedence than any other operator.

The remaining subexpression and expression diagrams are much simpler than the diagram for *factor*. The diagram for *term* (Diagram 7) tells us that terms are built by combining factors with the so-called multiplying operators *, /, **div**, **mod**, and **and**; the precedence of the multiplying operators, then, is one level below that of **not**. The diagram for *simple-expression* (Diagram 8) tells us that simple expressions are built by combining terms with the so-called adding operators + , − , and **or**; the precedence of the adding operators, then, is one level below that of the multiplying operators. Finally, the diagram for *expression* (Diagram 9) tells us that expressions are built by combining simple expressions with the relational operators = , < , > , < = , > = , <> , and **in**; the precedence of the relational operators, then, is one level below that of the adding operators.

Our diagrams for expressions and subexpressions provide our first examples of recursion and mutual recursion, which correspond to nesting in Pascal. The simplest case of recursion occurs in the bottom rung of the diagram for *factor* (Diagram 6), which says that a factor can be prefixed with the operator **not** to get a new factor. (The semantics, but not the syntax, require that the factor so prefixed represent a value of type *Boolean*.) Thus since *true* is a factor, so is **not** *true*; since **not** *true* is a factor, so is **not not** *true*; since **not not** *true* is a factor, so is **not not not** *true*; and so on. Therefore, any expression of the form

> **not** factor

can contain a nested expression of the same form.

Mutual recursion is represented by the occurrences of *expression* in the diagram for *factor*; that diagram tells us that expressions can be used as value parameters, in set constructors, and as parenthesized subexpressions. Since the expressions are at the top of our expression-subexpression hierarchy, it follows that any of the four kinds of expression and subexpression can be embedded in a factor. But since factors are at the bottom of the hierarchy, any of the four kinds of expression and subexpression can contain an embedded factor. Consequently, each of the four kinds of expression and subexpression can, courtesy of *factor*, contain subexpressions of any of the four kinds. As a result, our four expression-subexpression diagrams are mutually recursive—each is defined partially in terms of the others.

Statements

The diagram for *statement* (Diagram 10) is a giant ladder diagram, each rung of which describes a different Pascal statement. Most of the statement descriptions are straightforward and require no further discussion. Note that many of the statement descriptions contain the nonterminal *statement*. Thus the diagram for *statement* is recursive, and this recursion corresponds to the familiar property of Pascal that many kinds of statements can contain other statements nested within them.

The top rung of the ladder describes the assignment statement. To the left of the assignment operator we can have either a variable access (for assignment to a variable) or a function identifier (for specifying the result to be returned by a function).

The second rung from the top describes the procedure statement. Like a function, a procedure can have four kinds of actual parameter: value parameters represented by expressions, variable parameters represented by variable accesses, functional parameters represented by function identifiers, and procedural parameters represented by procedure identifiers.

According to the syntax diagram, each value parameter can be followed by up to two optional value parameters, with each optional parameter preceded by a colon. The syntax diagram does not place any restriction on the use of these optional parameters. The semantics of Pascal, however, restrict the use of the optional parameters to the procedures *write* and *writeln*, where the optional parameters are just the familiar field-width parameters.

The bottom rung of the ladder is the null statement, which contains no text and (according to the only reasonable semantics) causes no action to be taken. Students often introduce null statements into their programs accidentally. For example, if you place a semicolon after the last statement in a compound statement (a common error), the language processor will not give an error message but will just consider there to be a null statement between the final semicolon and the **end** that closes the compound statement. A reasonable use for the null statement is in a **case** statement. If the colon that terminates a list of constants is immediately followed by a semicolon, then the statement for that case is the null statement, and no action is taken when that case occurs.

Finally, something needs to be said about the **goto** statement, which is not otherwise discussed in this book. A **goto** statement causes the computer to jump to a label somewhere else in the program and continue execution with the statement following the label. A label consists of a sequence of digits and is separated from the following statement by a semicolon. For example, consider the following program fragment:

> 25: *DisplayPrompt*;
>   *GetCommand (command)*;
>   *DoCommand (command)*;
>   **goto** 25

When the computer executes the **goto** statement, it will jump to the statement following the label 25. Thus, the three procedure calls will be repeated indefinitely.

A **goto** statement cannot be used to jump into the middle of a structure such as an **if** statement, a **while** statement, or a procedure declaration, although a **goto** statement *can* be used to jump out of such a structure. The **goto** statement is avoided in contemporary programming styles because it encourages the programmer to build complex, hard-to-understand control structures instead of using the simpler, clearer structures embodied in such Pascal statements as **if**, **case**, **while**, and **repeat**. The **goto** statement is discussed here only the formal parameter list of a function or procedure, contains a ladder diagram with three rungs. The top rung represents a declaration of one or more variable parameters, value parameters, or (in Level 1 ISO Pascal only) conformant-array parameters; the middle rung represents a declaration of a functional parameter; and the bottom rung represents a declaration of a procedural parameter.

The definition and declaration parts of a block are represented by the diagrams for *label-decls*, *constant-defs*, *type-defs*, *variable-decls*, and *func-and-proc-decls* (Diagrams 17–21). The rarely used label declaration part declares digit sequences that are to be used as statement labels. The types used to define type identifiers and declare variables are represented by type denoters. Since functions and procedures are considered major program structures, the details of their declarations are considered in the next section.

Blocks, Subprogram Declarations, and Programs

Our final set of syntax diagrams defines the major structural units of a Pascal program: blocks, function declarations, procedure declarations, and complete programs.

The definition of a block that we use with syntax diagrams differs slightly from the definition in Chapter 12. In Chapter 12, we considered a block to begin immediately after a program, function, or procedure identifier, so that the formal parameter declarations were included in the block. For syntax diagrams, it is simpler to keep the parameter declarations separate and let the block begin immediately after the program or subprogram heading. Thus a block consists of a series of optional definition and declaration parts followed by a compound statement. Referring to the diagram for *block* (Diagram 22), we see that each of the definition and declaration parts is optional, but those that are present must appear in the same order as in the diagram. A label declaration part precedes all other definition and declaration parts.

From the diagram for *function-decl* (Diagram 23), we see that a function declaration consists of a function heading (which is described in detail in the diagram) followed by either a block (for a complete declaration) or the reserved word **forward** (for a forward declaration). There is also an option that omits not only the formal parameter list but also the declaration of a return type; this option can be used only for supplying the body of a function that was previously declared in a **forward** declaration.

The diagram for *procedure-decl* (Diagram 24) is similar to that for *function-decl* except that no return type is declared; since there is no return type, we do not require a special option for supplying the body of a procedure previously declared in a forward declaration.

The semicolon that follows a function or procedure declaration appears in the diagram *func-and-proc-decls* (Diagram 21) not in the diagram for *function-decl* or *procedure-decl*.

The diagram for *program* (Diagram 25) is similar to that for *procedure-decl* with the following exceptions:

1. The parameter list is just a list of identifiers, not a list of formal-parameter declarations.

2. The program heading must be followed by a block; there is no such thing as a forward declaration for programs.

because constructions associated with it appear in several places in the syntax diagram.

In the diagram for *statement*, we find the **goto** statement just below the procedure statement. At the very top of the diagram is the construction for a statement label; any statement can be optionally preceded by a label, which consists of a sequence of digits and is separated from the statement by a colon. A label must be declared in the block in which it is used to label a statement; thus label declarations will appear in the syntax diagrams that deal with definitions and declarations.

Definitions and Declarations

We begin by considering the constructions used to represent constants and types in definitions and declarations. The nonterminal *constant* (Diagram 11) which is used to represent constant values in definitions and declarations, differs from *unsigned-constant* in two ways.

1. A numeric constant can be preceded by a plus or minus sign.

2. The pointer constant **nil** is not allowed. (Thus **nil** cannot occur in a definition or declaration and, in particular, cannot be the value of a constant identifier.)

The diagrams for *variant-part*, *field-list*, and *type-denoter* (Diagrams 12–14) are mutually recursive and so much be considered together. A variant part is the **case** construction that defines the variant part of a record. For each case the variant part provides a field list, which defines zero or more field identifiers.

A field list is used to declare the field identifiers in the fixed or variant part of a record. A field list can be a variant part, or it can consist of a series of field-identifier declarations optionally followed by a variant part.

Note that in a field-identifier declaration, the identifier being declared is represented by *identifier* rather than *field-identifier*. Qualifications such as "*field-*" refer to restrictions imposed by a previous definition or declaration. No such restrictions yet apply to an identifier that is in the process of being defined or declared, hence the identifier that is the subject of a definition or declaration will always be represented by just plain *identifier*.

The type declared for a field identifier is given by a type denoter. The diagram for *type-denoter* (Diagram 14) is a ladder diagram with a rung for each possible way of designating a type. The top rung corresponds to a type represented by a type identifier. Each of the remaining rungs corresponds to what we have called a type constructor—a construction that defines a new type in terms of previously defined types. Starting with the second rung and working down, the type constructors define, respectively, enumerated types, subrange types, array types, record types, set types, file types, and pointer types. Note that rungs for the structured types all share the optional reserved word **packed**. Note also the use of *field-list* in the constructor for a record type.

The diagram *conf-array-schema* (Diagram 15) represents a conformant array schema, which is used to declare conformant array parameters in Level 1 ISO Pascal. Conformant array parameters are treated only briefly in this book and we will not explore conformant array schemas in detail.

Declarations occur in formal parameter lists as well as in the declaration parts of a block. The diagram *parameter-list* (Diagram 16), which represents

3. The block is followed by a period, which indicates the end of the program.

Note that the same nonterminal *block* defines the bodies of programs, functions, and procedures. Thus, as emphasized in the text, these three structures differ only in their headings.

Syntax Diagrams

Diagram 1

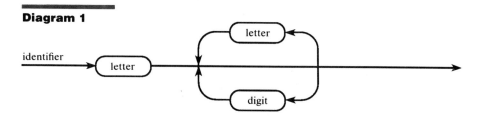

Diagram 2

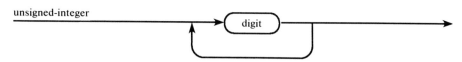

Diagram 3

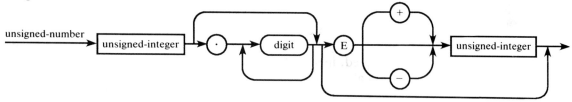

Diagram 4

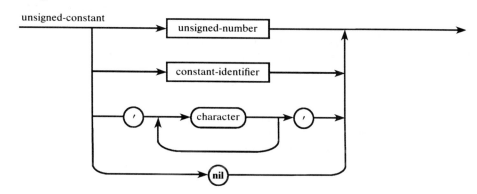

Diagram 5

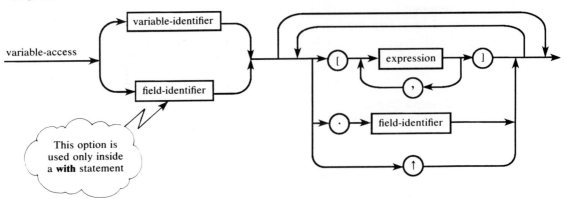

Diagram 6

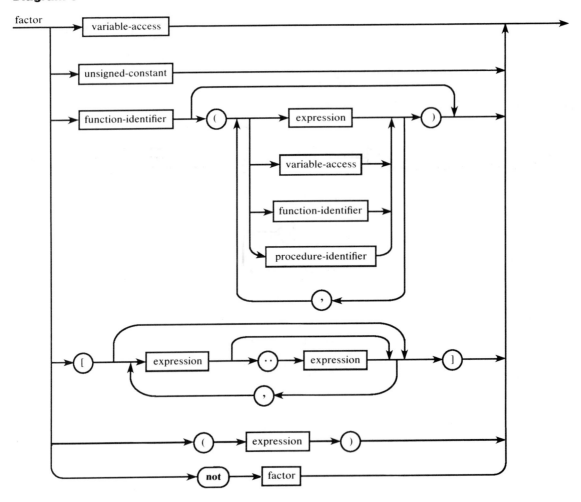

Diagram 7

term

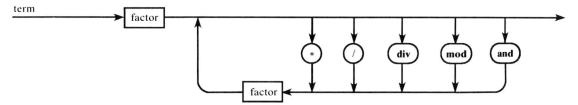

Diagram 8

simple-expression

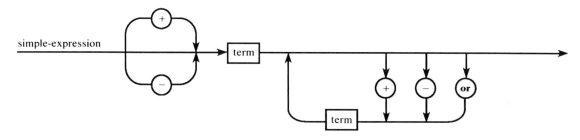

Diagram 9

expression

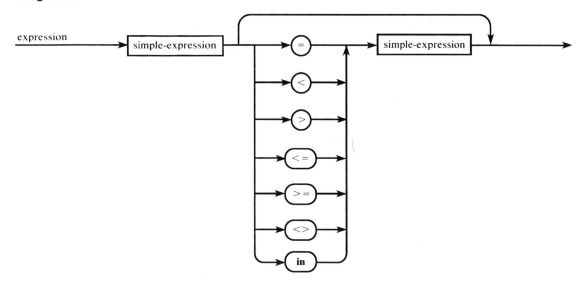

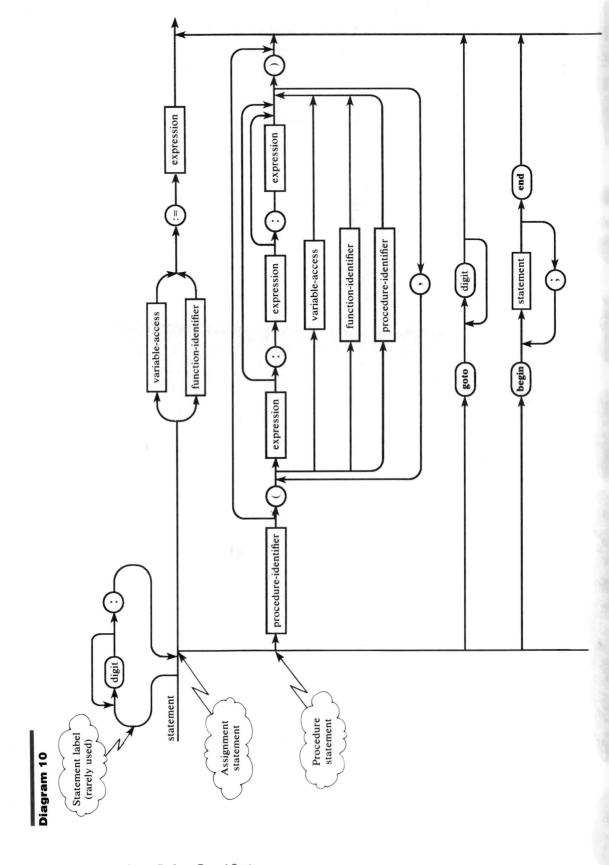

Diagram 10

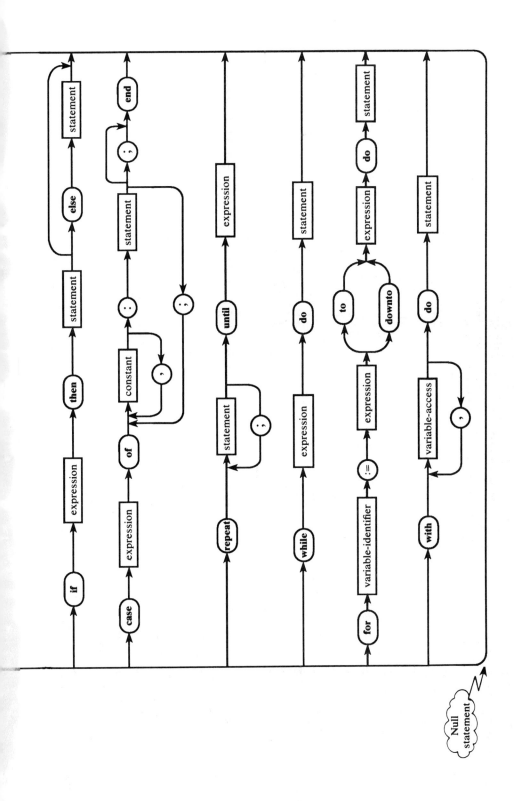

Null
statement

Diagram 11

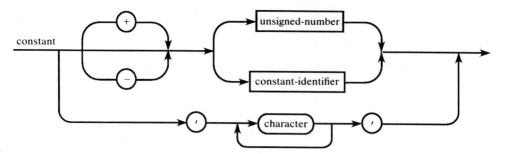

Diagram 12

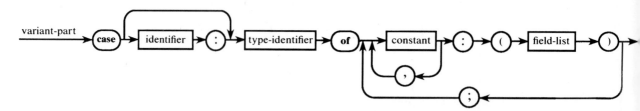

Diagram 13

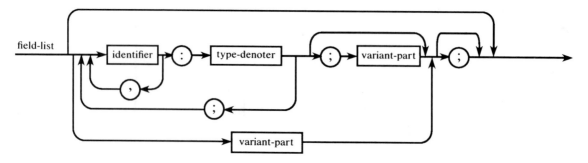

Diagram 14

type-denoter

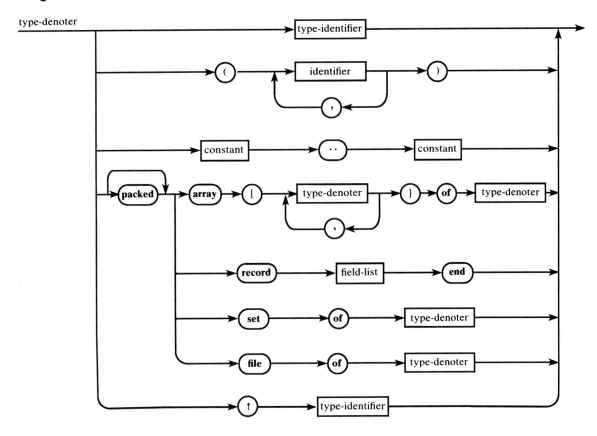

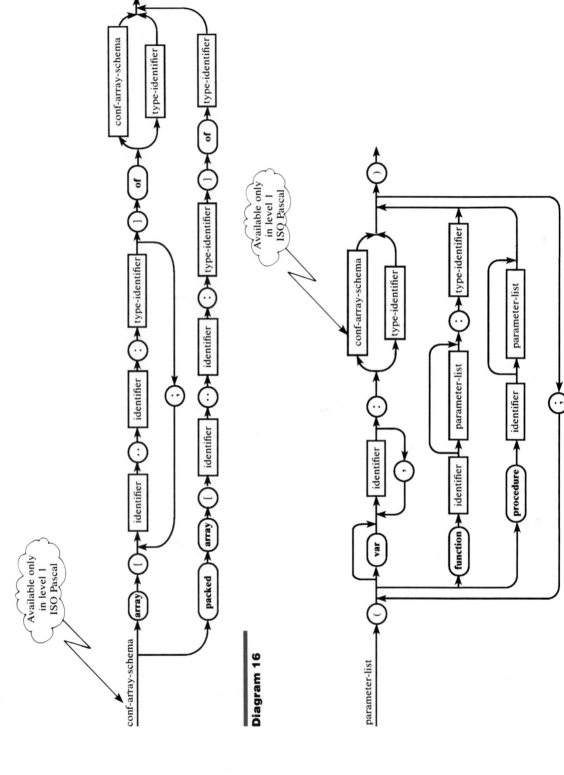

Diagram 15

Diagram 16

Diagram 17

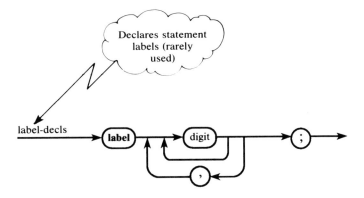

Diagram 18

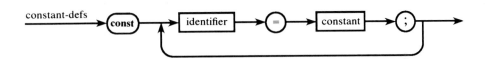

Diagram 19

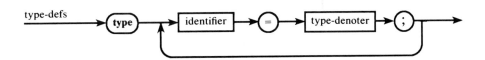

Diagram 20

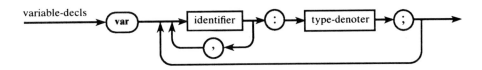

Diagram 21

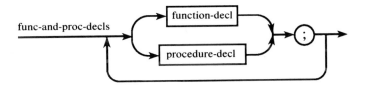

Diagram 22

block
label-decls
constant-defs
type-defs
variable-decls
func-and-proc-decls
begin
statement
;
end

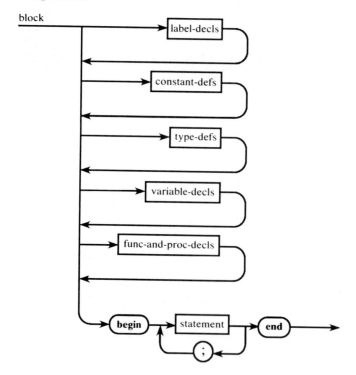

Diagram 23

function-decl
function
identifier
parameter-list
:
type-identifier
;
block
forward
This option allowed only if function previously declared in forward declaration.
;
block

Diagram 24

procedure-decl
procedure
identifier
parameter-list
;
block
forward

Diagram 25

program
program
identifier
(
identifier
,
)
;
block
.

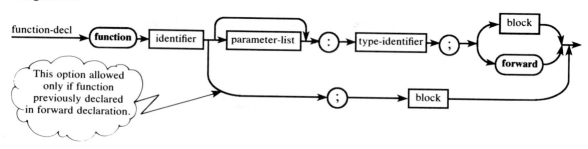

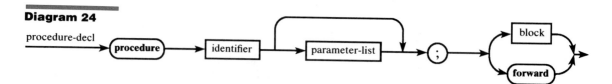

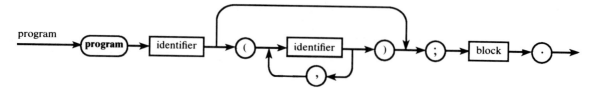

Turbo Pascal 3

This appendix briefly describes the most important differences between Turbo and ANSI/IEEE Pascal. Emphasis is on the differences with which the reader must be familiar to adapt the discussions in the text to Turbo Pascal. We do not attempt to provide extensive coverage of Turbo Pascal extensions to standard Pascal. The most important extensions, such as variable-length strings, are introduced briefly, but the reader is referred to the Turbo Pascal reference manual for further details.

This appendix is based on Version 3.0 of Turbo Pascal for PC-DOS and MS-DOS. The section on I/O redirection is specific to PC-DOS and MS-DOS; most of the remaining material should also apply to other versions of Turbo Pascal.

Additional Reserved Words

Besides the words set forth in Appendix 1, the following additional words are reserved in Turbo Pascal:

absolute	**external**	**inline**	**overlay**
shl	**shr**	**string**	**xor**

As with the standard reserved words, these words cannot be used as identifiers.

Identifiers

An identifier can be up to 127 characters long; since no one would ever use an identifier that long, the length of identifiers is, for all practical purposes, unlimited. All the characters of an identifier are significant. Turbo Pascal allows the underscore character in identifiers, so identifiers such as *year_to_date_total* are allowed.

Like standard Pascal, Turbo Pascal ignores the distinction between upper- and lowercase letters. Readers will note that the Turbo Pascal reference manual uses different capitalization conventions than the ones used in this book. (The reference manual capitalizes the first letter of all identifiers, including predefined identifiers such as *Readln* and *Integer*.) Such patterns of capitalization are purely matters of style, and readers are free to use whatever capitalization conventions they prefer.

Program Parameters and File Variables

Turbo Pascal does not require file variables (such as *input* and *output*) to be listed as parameters in the program heading. Doing so is allowed, however, for purposes of documentation and for compatibility with standard Pascal; any file variables that are so listed are ignored by the compiler. Thus the program heading

> **program** *Conversation (input, output)*;

could be written in Turbo Pascal as just given or in the abbreviated form:

> **program** *Conversation*;

Which form is used has no effect on the compilation and execution of the program.

The standard identifiers *input* and *output* are known to the compiler, so no further description of the standard input and output files is required. For other files, see the section on file processing.

Compiler Directives

A compiler directive provides the Pascal compiler with instructions as to how a program is to be compiled. It is a Pascal convention (which Turbo Pascal follows) for a compiler directive to be given as a *pseudocomment*—a sequence of characters enclosed by {$ and } or by (*$ and *). For example, the compiler directive R+ (the use of which is described in the section or range checking) can be included in the program in either of the following two equivalent forms:

```
{$R +}
(*$R + *)
```

No spaces may appear before or after the dollar sign; if any do, the directive will be treated as an ordinary comment and ignored. Several compiler directives can be included in the same pseudocomment. For example, the pseudocomment

```
{$R + ,G256,P256}
```

includes the compiler directives R+ , G256, and P256. (The use of G256 and P256 is described in the section on I/O redirection.) The same effect could be achieved with

```
{$R +}
{$G256,P256}
```

or with

```
{$R +}
{$G256}
{$P256}
```

A compiler directive can occur anywhere a comment is allowed; directives are placed at the point in the program at which they are intended to take effect. Directives that apply to the entire program should be placed before the program heading, as in

{$R + }
{$G256,P256}
program *TableLookup*;

Enabling Range Checking

When a program attempts to use a value as an array index or assign it to a variable of a subrange type, Pascal should check that the value lies in the specified subrange and give a run-time error message if it does not. Such error messages greatly simplify program debugging; if out-of-range values were allowed to go undetected, they could cause a system crash or produce hard-to-diagnose program malfunctions. In Turbo Pascal, such range checking must be enabled explicitly by the compiler directive R+. (In general, a compiler directive ending in + enables a feature and one ending in − disables a feature; thus the directive R− disables range checking.) Students should routinely enable range checking for all programs that use arrays or subrange types. Such programs should include the pseudocomment

{$R + }

before the program heading.

Enabling I/O Redirection (PC-DOS and MS-DOS Only)

PC-DOS and MS-DOS allow I/O redirection (also known as file redirection). The user can specify the standard input and output files that, in Pascal, are represented by the predefined identifiers *input* and *output*. For example, the PC-DOS or MS-DOS command line

```
myprog <olddata.txt >newdata.txt
```

calls the program `myprog` with the disk file `olddata.txt` as the standard input file and the disk file `newdata.txt` as the standard output file. Note that the name of the input file is preceded by < and the name of the output file is preceded by > .

Turbo Pascal allows I/O redirection only if it is enabled by compiler directives. The directive G256 enables redirection for the standard input file and P256 enables redirection for the standard output file. (The 256 gives the size in bytes of a buffer area in main memory that will be used for temporary storage of data being read from or written to a file.) Thus, the pseudocomment

{$G256,P256}

enables I/O redirection for the standard input and output files. This pseudocomment should be placed before the program heading.

Improved *case* Statement

The **case** statement in Turbo Pascal provides two needed improvements over the **case** statement in standard Pascal.

First, subranges are allowed in case lists. For example, a case list that contains all the upper- and lowercase letters of the alphabet can be written like this:

'A'..'Z', 'a'..'z'

In standard Pascal, all 52 upper- and lowercase letters would have to be listed individually.

Second, a **case** statement can contain an optional **else** part:

```
case expression of
    case-list-1: controlled-statement-1;
    case-list-2: controlled-statement-2;
    case-list-3: controlled-statement-3;
          .
          .
          .
    case-list-n: controlled-statement-n
else
    controlled-statement-(n + 1)
end
```

If the value of the selector expression does not occur on any of the case lists, then the statement in the **else** part is executed. If the **else** part is omitted, then no action is taken when the value of the selector expression is not on any of the case lists. Note that even with the **else** part omitted, the Turbo Pascal **case** statement behaves differently from the corresponding statement in standard Pascal. In standard Pascal, a run-time error occurs if the value of the selector expression is not on any of the case lists.

Both of these improvements are illustrated by the following **case** statement, which classifies the value of the character variable *ch* as a letter, a digit, or neither:

```
case ch of
    'A'..'Z', 'a'..'z':
        writeln (ch, ' is a letter');
    '0'..'9':
        writeln (ch, ' is a digit')
else
    writeln (ch, ' is neither a letter nor a digit')
end
```

File Processing in Turbo Pascal

File processing is the area in which the most differences between standard and Turbo Pascal occur. We discuss the differences individually and then give an example that illustrates them all.

The *assign* Statement

In standard Pascal, it is left to the operating system to establish a correspondence between Pascal file variables (which serve as internal file names) and the external file names known to the operating system. In Turbo Pascal, this correspondence is set up automatically for the standard files *input* and *output*. For other files, the programmer must set up the correspondence explicitly by a call to the procedure *assign*. The procedure call has the following form:

assign (file-variable, external-file-name)

The file variable is a Pascal identifier that has been declared as a file variable; the external file name is a Turbo Pascal string expression (which can be a string constant). For example, the statement

assign (*inFile*, 'rollbook.dat')

causes the file variable *inFile* to refer to the disk file `rollbook.dat`.

The *close* Statement

A file is opened when a connection is established between the program and the file; the file is closed when that connection is broken. In standard Pascal, files are opened with *reset* and *rewrite* but are closed automatically. In Turbo Pascal, the programmer must close files explicitly with the procedure *close*. A call to *close* has the form

close (file-variable)

where the file variable is the internal name of the file to be closed.

The standard files *input* and *output* are opened and closed automatically and must not be explicitly opened or closed by the programmer. Other files should be closed. Files used for output *must* be closed, or some of the data written to the file may be lost. Closing files used for input is also desirable, since most operating systems allow only a certain number of files to be open at the same time; leaving a file open reduces the number of other files that can be open at one time.

No *get, put,* or Buffer Variables

Turbo Pascal does not provide the standard procedures *get* and *put* nor does it allow access to the buffer variable associated with a file variable. Programs that use *get* and *put* must be modified to use *read* and *write* instead before they can be run under Turbo Pascal.

No *page*

The procedure *page*, which causes a printer to go to the top of a new page, is not implemented in Turbo Pascal. In place of

page (*outFile*)

you can use

write (*outFile*, *chr*(12))

The *write* statement sends an ASCII form-feed character, *chr*(12), to *outFile*. Most printers respond to a form-feed character by going to the top of a new page.

File Processing Example

As an example of file processing in Turbo Pascal, we will write code to copy records from one file to another. The input file is represented by the file variable *inFile* and has the external file name `oldrecs.dat`. The output file is represented by the file variable *outFile* and has the external file name `newrecs.dat`. We need the following definitions and declarations:

```
type
   accntRec = record
                  idNum  : integer;
                  balance : real
              end;
var
   inFile, outFile : file of accntRec;
   curntRec        : accntRec;
```

Each record will be read from the input file into the variable *curntRec* and then written from *curntRec* to the output file. The following code does the job:

```
assign (inFile, 'oldrecs.dat');
assign (outFile, 'newrecs.dat');
reset (inFile);
rewrite (outFile);
while not eof(inFile) do
   begin
      read (inFile, curntRec);
      write (outFile, curntRec)
   end;
close (inFile);
close (outFile)
```

Reserved Word *packed* Is Ignored

In Turbo Pascal the reserved word **packed** is ignored. It thus makes absolutely no difference whether or not a structured type is declared to be packed.

No Subprogram Parameters

Turbo Pascal does not allow functions and procedures to be passed to subprograms as parameters (as described in Chaper 12).

No Variant Record Specifications in *new*

When allocating memory for a record with *new*, we cannot provide tag-value parameters to designate a particular record variant (as described in Chapter

13). Referring to the example in Chapter 13, we cannot use the calls *new* (*p*, *true*) and *new* (*p*, *false*) to allocate different size records for different values of the tag field *largeSize*. Only the call *new* (*p*) would be valid in Turbo Pascal.

Extensions to Standard Pascal

Turbo Pascal provides many extensions to standard Pascal. Some of these, such as the ability to include assembly language in Turbo Pascal programs, are of little interest to computer science students, regardless of how convenient they may occasionally be for practicing programmers. This section surveys three popular Turbo Pascal extensions; in each case the reader is referred to the Turbo Pascal reference manual for further details.

Relaxed Declaration Order and the Include Directive

Turbo Pascal allows the various definition and declaration sections to occur in any order, and there may be more than one section of a given kind—more than one variable declaration section, for example. As illustrated in Chapter 8, this extension greatly aids the use of abstract data types, because it allows all the definitions and declarations for an abstract-data-type implementation to be grouped together in the program. If a program uses several different implementations, the definitions and declaration for each implementation can be grouped together, and comments can be used to indicate the beginning and end of the text of each implementation.

The Turbo Pascal compiler directive I (for include) can be used to include an abstract-data-type implementation in a program when the program is compiled. For example, suppose that the file `directry.inc` contains the Pascal code for an implementation of the abstract data type *Directory*. In writing a program that uses *Directory*, we place the following pseudocomment at the point at which we wish the code for *Directory* to appear:

{$I directry.inc}

When the compiler reaches this pseudocomment, it will read and compile the contents of the file `directry.inc` before continuing to compile the program containing the pseudocomment. Thus the contents of the file `directry.inc` are effectively included in the program containing the pseudocomment, even though only the pseudocomment actually appears in the program text.

Direct or Random Access

Standard Pascal provides only sequential access to files. On input, records must be read in the order that they are stored in the file; on output, records must be written in the order that they are to be stored.

The ability to read records in arbitrary order is known as direct or random access. Turbo Pascal provides direct access with the procedure *seek*. The records in a file are considered to be numbered, starting with zero for the first record. A call to *seek* specifies which file record will be affected by the next call to *read* or *write*. For example, we can read record 10 of the file *dataFile* into the variable *curntRec* with the following statements:

```
        seek (dataFile, 10);
        read (dataFile, curntRec)
```

To store the value of *curntRec* as record 45 of the file, we would use the following statements:

```
        seek (dataFile, 45);
        write (dataFile, curntRec)
```

Variable-Length Strings

Turbo Pascal provides variable-length string types similar to those discussed in Chapter 11. The following examples illustrate how string variables are declared:

```
    var
        userName : string[20];
        fileName  : string[16];
        textLine  : string[80];
```

The number in brackets gives the maximum length of the strings that can be stored. Thus, *userName* can hold strings with lengths of 0 to 20 characters, *fileName* can hold strings with lengths of 0 to 16 characters and *textLine* can hold strings with lengths of 0 to 80 characters. The greatest maximum length that can be specified is 255. There is no default maximum length; a maximum length must always be specified when a string variable is declared.

Variable-length strings can be read with *read* and *readln*, and they can be written with *write* and *writeln*. String constants can be used to represent variable-length strings including the null string. For example, the following assignments are valid:

```
    userName := 'Johnny';
    fileName  := 'c:oldMastr.dat';
    textLine  := ''        { null string }
```

Turbo Pascal provides procedures, functions, and one operator for manipulating variable-length strings. The manipulations that can be carried out are similar to those discussed in Chapter 11.

UCSD Pascal

4

This appendix briefly describes the most important differences between UCSD and ANSI/IEEE Pascal. Emphasis is on the differences with which the reader must be familiar to adapt the discussions in the text to UCSD Pascal. We do not attempt to provide extensive coverage of UCSD Pascal extensions to standard Pascal. The most important extensions, such as variable-length strings and units, are introduced briefly, but the reader is referred to the UCSD Pascal user manual for further details.

Additional Reserved Words

In addition to the words set forth in Appendix 1, the following words are reserved in UCSD Pascal:

implementation	**interface**	**process**	**segment**
separate	**unit**	**uses**	

As with the standard reserved words, these words cannot be used as identifiers.

Identifiers

An identifier can be of any length as long as it is not broken between lines. However, only the first eight characters of an identifier are significant; the compiler cannot distinguish between two identifiers that have the same first eight characters. Thus the compiler considers *inputRecA* and *inputRecB* to be the same identifier, because both have *inputRec* as their first eight characters. Likewise, the compiler would confuse *Interest* (which might be the name of a program or subprogram) with *interestRate* (which might be a variable in that program or subprogram). (Like standard Pascal, UCSD Pascal does not distinguish between upper- and lowercase letters.)

UCSD Pascal allows the underscore character in identifiers, so identifiers such as *year_to_date_total* are allowed. The availabililty of the underscore character encourages long, descriptive variable names, the use of which is good programming style. Don't forget, however, that names of distinct variables *must* differ in their first eight characters.

Program Parameters and File Variables

UCSD Pascal does not require file variables (such as *input* and *output*) to be listed as parameters in the program heading. Doing so is allowed, however, for purposes of documentation and for compatibility with standard Pascal; any file variables that are so listed are ignored by the compiler. Thus the program heading

      program *Conversation* (*input*, *output*);

could be written in UCSD Pascal as just given or in the abbreviated form:

      program *Conversation*;

Which form is used has no effect on the compilation and execution of the program.

    The standard identifiers *input* and *output* are known to the compiler, so no further description of the standard input and output files is required. For other files, see the section on file processing.

No Boolean Values in *write* and *writeln*

UCSD Pascal does not allow Boolean values to be written to textfiles with *write* and *writeln*. Thus if *flag* is a Boolean variable, the statement

      write (*flag*)

is invalid. We can use the following instead:

      if *flag* **then**
        write ('true')
      else
        write ('false')

No I/O Redirection

UCSD Pascal does not provide I/O redirection, (also called file redirection), which is suggested in the text as a simple approach to processing disk files. Techniques for processing disk files in UCSD Pascal are illustrated in the section on file processing.

No Run-time Error for *case* Statement

In UCSD Pascal, a **case** statement takes no action if the value of the selector expression does not occur on any of the case lists; the case statement is skipped over and execution continues with the next statement in the program. In the same circumstances, standard Pascal terminates the program with a run-time error message. This property of the UCSD Pascal **case** statement can simplify a program when there are values of the selector expression that should be ignored. On the other hand, it can increase the difficulty of finding bugs that result from inadvertently failing to provide statements to handle some values of the selector expression.

File Processing in UCSD Pascal

Aside from major extensions, file processing is the area in which UCSD Pascal deviates most from standard Pascal. We discuss the deviations individually and then illustrate them with two examples.

The *close* Statement

A file is opened when a connection is established between the program and the file; the file is closed when that connection is broken. In standard Pascal, files are opened with *reset* and *rewrite* but are closed automatically. UCSD Pascal also closes files automatically, but in such a way that any data written to a disk file is lost. To save data written to disk files, the programmer must close the files in question explicitly with a call to the procedure *close*. A call to *close* has one of the following forms:

> *close* (file-variable)
> *close* (file-variable, option)

where the file variable is the internal name of the file to be closed. The option, if present, is one of the words NORMAL, LOCK, PURGE, and CRUNCH. When the option is omitted, the option NORMAL is assumed. The options determine what the contents of a disk file will be after it is closed.

Option	Effect
NORMAL or option omitted	The file retains the contents it had before it was opened; Any changes made to the file while it was open are lost.
LOCK	Any changes made to the file while it was open are retained. This option *must* be used to save data written to a disk file.
PURGE	The file is deleted from the disk.
CRUNCH	Any records following the last one that was accessed while the file was open are deleted.

When a UCSD Pascal program finishes its execution normally, all open files are automatically closed with the option NORMAL. If any of these are disk files, then any data that was written to them is lost. To save data written to a disk file, the programmer must close the file explicitly by calling *close* with the option LOCK.

External File Names in *reset* and *rewrite*

In standard Pascal, it is left to the operating system to establish a correspondence between Pascal file variables (which serve as internal file names) and the external file names known to the operating system. In UCSD Pascal, this correspondence is set up automatically for the standard files *input* and *output*. For other files, the programmer must set up the correspondence explicitly by including the external file name in the call to *reset* or *rewrite* that opens the file. Calls to these procedures have the following form in UCSD Pascal:

> *reset* (file-variable, external-file-name)
> *rewrite* (file-variable, external-file-name)

The file variable is a Pascal identifier that has been declared as a file variable; the external file name is a UCSD Pascal string expression (which can be a string constant). For example, the statement

> *reset* (*inFile*, 'rollbook.data')

associates *inFile* with the disk file `rollbook.data` and opens the file for input. The statement

> *rewrite* (*outFile*, 'report.text')

associates *outFile* with the disk file `report.text` and opens the file for output.

No *read* and *write* for Binary Files

The procedures *read* and *write* are allowed only for textfiles. For binary (nontext) files, we must use *get*, *put*, and access to buffer variables.

File Processing Example: Textfiles

As an example of processing textfiles in UCSD Pascal, we will write code to read records (that is, lines containing data values) from an input textfile. Each record contains an account number (an integer) and a balance (a real number). Those records for which the balance is greater than 1000.0 will be written to an output textfile. The input file is represented by the file variable *inFile* and has the external name `oldfile.text`. The output file is represented by the file variable *outFile* and has the external name `newfile.text`. We must declare the file variables as well as variables to hold the account number and the balance.

> **var**
>   *inFile*, *outFile* : *text*;
>   *acctNo*   : *integer*;
>   *balance*   : *real*;

The following code carries out the desired processing:

> *reset* (*inFile*, 'oldfile.text');
> *rewrite* (*outFile*, 'newfile.text');
> **while not** *eof*(*inFile*) **do**
>   **begin**
>   *readln* (*inFile*, *acctNo*, *balance*);
>   **if** *balance* > 1000.0 **then**
>   *writeln* (*outFile*, *acctNo* :8, *balance* :8:2)
>   **end**;
> *close* (*outFile*, LOCK)

File Processing Example: Binary Files

As an example of processing binary files in UCSD Pascal, we will write code to copy records from one file to another. The input file is represented by the file variable *inFile* and has the external file name `oldrecs.data`. The output file is represented by the file variable *outFile* and has the external file name `newrecs.data`. We need the following definitions and declarations:

```
type
    accntRec = record
                    idNum   : integer;
                    balance : real
               end;
var
    inFile, outFile : file of accntRec;
```

The following code does the desired processing:

```
reset (inFile, 'oldrecs.data');
rewrite (outFile, 'newrecs.data');
while not eof(inFile) do
  begin
    outFile↑ := inFile↑;
    put (outFile);
    get (inFile)
  end;
close (outFile, LOCK)
```

Extensions to Standard Pascal

UCSD Pascal provides many extensions to standard Pascal. This section surveys three popular UCSD Pascal extensions; in each case the reader is referred to the UCSD Pascal user manual for further details.

Direct or Random Access

Standard Pascal provides only sequential access to files. On input, records must be read in the order that they are stored in the file; on output, records must be written in the order that they are to be stored.

The ability to read records in arbitrary order is known as direct or random access. UCSD Pascal provides direct access with the procedure *seek*, which can only be used with binary files. The records in a file are considered to be numbered, starting with zero for the first record. A call to *seek* specifies which file record will be affected by the next call to *get* or *put*. For example, we can assign record 10 of the file *dataFile* to the variable *curntRec* with the following statements:

```
seek (dataFile, 10);
get (dataFile);
curntRec := dataFile↑
```

To store the value of *curntRec* as record 45 of the file, we would use the following statements:

```
        dataFile↑ := curntRec;
        seek (dataFile, 45);
        put (dataFile)
```

Variable-Length Strings

UCSD Pascal provides variable-length string types similar to those discussed
in Chapter 11. The following examples illustrate how string variables are
declared:

```
    var
        userName : string[20];
        fileName  : string[16];
        textLine  : string;
```

The number in brackets gives the maximum length of the strings that can be
stored. Thus *userName* can hold strings with lengths of 0 to 20 characters,
and *fileName* can hold strings with lengths of 0 to 16 characters. If no maximum length is provided, a default maximum length of 80 is assumed. Thus
textLine can hold strings with lengths of 0 to 80 characters. The greatest
maximum length that can be specified is 255.

Variable-length strings can be read with *read* and *readln*, and they can
be written with *write* and *writeln*. String constants can be used to represent
variable-length strings including the null string. For example, the following
assignments are valid:

```
        userName := 'Johnny';
        fileName  := 'oldMastr.data';
        textLine  := ''      { null string }
```

UCSD Pascal provides procedures and functions for manipulating variable-length strings. The manipulations that can be carried out are similar to
those discussed in Chapter 11.

Units

Units are one of the most desirable UCSD Pascal extensions, because they
provide precisely the kind of encapsulation construction that we wished for
in Chapter 8. A module, such as an implementation of an abstract data type,
can be written as a unit, which can then be compiled independently of any
program that uses it. The compiled unit can be stored in a program library;
any program that needs to use the unit can do so by listing the name of the
unit in a **uses** clause.

A unit has two major sections: the interface section (which is introduced
by the reserved word **interface**) and the implementation section (which is
introduced by the reserved word **implementation**). Identifiers that are to be
exported—made available to programs that use the unit—are defined or declared in the interface section. Identifiers that are not to be exported—that
are to be used only within the unit—are declared in the implementation section. The implementation section also contains the code for all subprograms.

A unit can declare two kinds of subprogram. A private subprogram is
for use only within the unit; it is not made available to programs using the
unit. A private subprogram is declared entirely within the implementation
section. A public subprogram is made available to programs using the unit.

The declaration for a public subprogram is split. The full subprogram heading goes in the interface section. The body of the subprogram, preceded by an abbreviated heading that gives only the subprogram name, goes in the implementation section.

For example, consider the procedure that would normally be declared as follows:

```
procedure ResetCounter (var aCounter : counter);
begin
  aCounter.overflowFlag := false;
  aCounter.curCount := 0
end; { ResetCounter }
```

To make this a public procedure of a unit, we place the procedure heading

```
procedure ResetCounter (var aCounter : counter);
```

in the interface section. In the implementation section, we place the remainder of the procedure, preceded by an abbreviated heading that gives only the procedure name.

```
procedure ResetCounter;
begin
  aCounter.overflowFlag := false;
  aCounter.curCount := 0
end; { ResetCounter }
```

Figure A4-1 shows a unit *CounterType*, which implements the abstract data type *Counter* defined in Chapter 8. The interface section defines the type *counter* and (by means of subprogram headings) declares the public subprograms *ResetCounter*, *Increment*, *Count*, and *OverflowQ*. The bodies of the subprograms are contained in the implementation section.

All the identifiers defined or declared in the interface section are exported. (**Exception:** The subprogram formal parameters are, as usual, local to the

---

Figure A4-1.

Unit *CounterType*, which encapsulates an implementation of the abstract data type *Counter*. The unit can be compiled independently and stored in a program library. Programs can make use of the compiled unit by listing its name in a **uses** clause.

```
unit CounterType;

interface { Interface section begins here }

const
  maxCount = 999; { largest possible counter reading }
type
  counterReading = 0..maxCount;
  counter        = record
                     overflowFlag : Boolean;
                     curCount     : counterReading;
                   end;
```

```
procedure ResetCounter (var aCounter : counter);
{ Clear count to zero and reset overflow indicator }

procedure Increment (var aCounter : counter);
{ Increase count by one. If overflow, set count to zero and overflow flag to
  false }

function Count (aCounter : counter) : integer;
{ Return current count }

function OverflowQ (aCounter : counter) : Boolean;
{ Return true if overflow has occurred and false otherwise }

implementation { Implementation section begins here }

procedure ResetCounter;
begin
  aCounter.overflowFlag := false;
  aCounter.curCount := 0
end; { ResetCounter }

procedure Increment;
begin
  if aCounter.curCount = maxCount then
    begin
      aCounter.overflowFlag := true;
      aCounter.curCount := 0
    end
  else
    aCounter.curCount := aCounter.curCount + 1
end; { Increment }

function Count;
begin
  Count := aCounter.curCount
end; { Count }

function OverflowQ;
begin
  OverflowQ := aCounter.overflowFlag
end; { OverflowQ }

end. { End of unit CounterType }
```

subprogram declarations and so are not exported, even though the formal parameter declarations appear in the interface section.) Thus the identifiers that we wish to make available—*counter*, *ResetCounter*, *Increment*, *Count*, and *OverflowQ*—are all exported. The field identifiers *overflowFlag* and *curCount* are exported along with *counter*; they can be used outside the unit to refer to components of variables of type *counter*. The auxiliary identifiers *maxCount* and *counterReading*, used to define *counter*, are also exported. Some extended versions of Pascal allow us to designate which identifiers will be exported from an interface section, thus letting us avoid exporting purely auxiliary identifiers such as *maxCount* and *counterReading*. In UCSD Pascal, however, all identifiers declared in the interface section (except for formal parameters) are exported.

A program that uses the unit *CounterType* would contain the **uses** clause

uses *CounterType*

immediately following the program heading. The program could then use any of the exported identifiers. Thus it could use *counter* to declare counter variables

var
    cntr1, *cntr2* : *counter*;

and use *ResetCounter*, *Increment*, *Count*, and *OverflowQ* to manipulate and access the values of the variables so declared, as in

ResetCounter (*cntr1*);
ResetCounter (*cntr2*)

Data Representation

Inside a computer, all data values must be represented by bit patterns—patterns of zeros and ones. A scheme for representing information in this way is called a *binary code*. In this section we will examine the internal representations for values of the simple standard types *Boolean, char, integer,* and *real.* Before focusing on the individual types, however, we will first look at some general principles governing the representation of information by binary codes.

Binary Codes

Representing information is a matter of representing alternatives. For example, the post office uses two-letter codes for the states—FL for Florida, GA for Georgia, WV for West Virginia, and so on. Because there are 26 letters in the alphabet, there are 26 × 26 or 676 possible two-letter combinations. (The order in which the letters are written is, of course, significant. For example, MN and NM represent different states, as do AL and LA.) Thus there are far more two-letter codes than we now need. We can rest assured that if any reasonable number of new states join the Union in the future, the post office will be able to find two-letter codes for them.

Now let's look at the number of alternatives that can be represented using a binary code with a given number of bits. With a single bit, which can be either 0 or 1, we can represent two alternatives. A single bit can be used to record the response to any question that has only two possible answers. The simplest question of this kind is one whose answer is either "yes" or "no."

Suppose you are asked, "Did you go to the beach last weekend?" Unless you change the subject to avoid answering, you have only two possible responses, "yes" or "no." By letting 0 stand for "no" and 1 stand for "yes," we can represent your answer in a computer by a single bit. If the bit is 0, it means your answer was "no"; if the bit is 1, it means your answer was "yes."

But what about questions with more than two possible answers? For instance, suppose a robot waiter asks you what flavor of ice cream you want? The four flavors on the menu are vanilla, chocolate, strawberry, and peach. How many bits are required to record your choice?

Two bits will do the job. With two bits, there are four possible codes—00, 01, 10, and 11. For example, the four flavors of ice cream could be represented as follows:

Flavor	Code
Vanilla	00
Chocolate	01
Strawberry	10
Peach	11

Any other correspondence between flavors and two-bit codes would work just as well. The only requirement is consistency; once we decide on a correspondence, we must stick to it.

Thus, with one bit we can represent two alternatives, and with two bits we can represent 2×2 or four alternatives. We won't be surprised to find that with three bits we can represent $2 \times 2 \times 2$ or eight alternatives. The eight possible three-bit codes follow:

000	100
001	101
010	110
011	111

We should now be able to see the pattern that is forming. We expect that there will be $2 \times 2 \times 2 \times 2$ or 16 four-bit codes, $2 \times 2 \times 2 \times 2 \times 2$ or 32 five-bit codes, and so on. Why does the number of alternatives double every time another bit is added to the code?

Mathematicians have a shorthand notation, called *exponential notation,* for repeated products such as 2×2 and $2 \times 2 \times 2$. They write 2 as 2^1, 2×2 as 2^2, $2 \times 2 \times 2$ as 2^3, and so on. By convention, 2^0 is taken to be 1. The numbers 2^0, 2^1, 2^2, 2^3, and so on, are called *powers of two.* We calculate each power of two by starting with 1 and multiplying by the specified number of twos. This is easy to do with a calculator, but to save you the trouble, the first nine powers of two follow:

Power of Two	Value
2^0	1
2^1	2
2^2	4
2^3	8
2^4	16
2^5	32
2^6	64
2^7	128
2^8	256

We can use powers of two to determine how many bits are need to represent a particular number of alternatives. For instance, if we want to represent the digits 0 through 9 (ten alternatives), we need four bits since three bits give only eight alternatives, which are not enough. Because four bits provide sixteen alternatives, and we only need ten, six combinations of bits will not be used. In fact, the decimal digits 0 through 9 are often represented as follows:

Digit	Binary Code	Digit	Binary Code
0	0000	5	0101
1	0001	6	0110
2	0010	7	0111
3	0011	8	1000
4	0100	9	1001

This representation, called *binary-coded decimal (BCD)*, is frequently used to represent decimal digits inside a computer. Note that the six codes 1010, 1011, 1100, 1101, 1110, and 1111 are not used.

Common sizes for locations in main memory are one byte (8 bits), two bytes (16 bits), four bytes (32 bits) and eight bytes (64 bits). The number of alternatives that can be represented by one-, two-, four-, and eight-byte codes follows:

Bytes	Bits	Number of Alternatives	
1	8	2^8 =	256
2	16	2^{16} =	65,536
4	32	2^{32} =	4,294,967,296
8	64	2^{64} =	18,446,744,073,709,551,616

Clearly, the amount of information that can be stored in one or even two bytes is strongly limited by the number of alternatives that can be represented. With eight bytes, however, we can feel reasonably confident of being able to represent the values of any simple type. Of course, structured values such as lists and tables, each consisting of many simple values, will require larger amounts of memory.

Binary Notation

The system for representing numbers that we use in everyday life makes use of the ten digits 0 through 9. We call it the *base-10* or *decimal system*, and we say that a number represented in this system is in *decimal notation*.

One way to represent numbers in binary form is to express them in decimal notation and represent each decimal digit by a four-bit binary code using the binary-coded decimal (BCD) representation mentioned earlier. The number 8274 would be represented in BCD as follows:

Decimal digits:	8	2	7	4
Binary codes:	1000	0010	0111	0100

The BCD representation is, in fact, often used for business arithmetic, which (because of our decimal system of currency) is strongly oriented toward decimal notation. For most purposes, however, the most natural way to represent numbers in binary form is to take as our digits the 0s and 1s from which all binary codes are constructed. The number system that uses only the two digits 0 and 1 is called the *base-2* or *binary number system*. Numbers represented in the binary system are said to be in *binary notation*.

The easiest way to understand the binary system is to compare it with the already-familiar decimal system. Let's begin, then, by reviewing some properties of decimal notation. The number 10 enters the base-10 system in two ways:

1. Every number is represented by a combination of the ten digits 0, 1, 2, 3, 4, 5, 6, 7, 8, and 9.

2. The digits of a decimal number, taken from right to left, represent ones, tens, hundreds, thousands, and so on. The numbers 1, 10, 100, and 1000 are just the powers of 10—10^0, 10^1, 10^2, and 10^3 in exponential notation—that we get by starting with 1 and multiplying repeatedly by 10.

For example, the decimal number 8274 can be analyzed as

Thousands	Hundreds	Tens	Ones
8	2	7	4

That is, 8274 represents eight thousands, two hundreds, seven tens, and four ones. Arithmetically, we can express this as

$$8274 = 8 \times 1000 + 2 \times 100 + 7 \times 10 + 4 \times 1$$

or, using exponential notation for the powers of 10, as

$$8274 = 8 \times 10^3 + 2 \times 10^2 + 7 \times 10^1 + 4 \times 10^0$$

The number 2 plays exactly the same role in the binary system that 10 does in the decimal system. Thus, 2 enters the base-2 system in the following two ways:

1. Every number is represented by a combination of the two digits 0 and 1.

2. The digits of a binary number, taken from right to left, represent ones, twos, fours, eights, and so on. The numbers 1, 2, 4, 8, and so on are the powers of two—2^0, 2^1, 2^2, 2^3, in exponential notation—that we get by starting with 1 and multiplying repeatedly by 2.

For example, the binary number 1101 can be analyzed as

Eights	Fours	Twos	Ones
1	1	0	1

That is, 1101 represents one eight, one four, zero twos, and one one. Arithmetically, we can express this as

$$1101 = 1 \times 8 + 1 \times 4 + 0 \times 2 + 1 \times 1 = 13$$

or, using exponential notation for the powers of 2, as

$$1101 = 1 \times 2^3 + 1 \times 2^2 + 0 \times 2^1 + 1 \times 2^0 = 13$$

These equations could be confusing, since we might not realize that 1101 is in the binary system and wonder how one thousand, one hundred, and one can equal 13. When the possibility of confusion exists, we can write the equations more clearly as

$$1101_2 = 1 \times 8 + 1 \times 4 + 0 \times 2 + 1 \times 1 = 13$$

and

$$1101_2 = 1 \times 2^3 + 1 \times 2^2 + 0 \times 2^1 + 1 \times 2^0 = 13$$

We can see how to count in binary notation by imagining a counter, such as the mileage indicator on a car. Suppose, however, that each dial of the counter has only two digits, 0 and 1, instead of the usual 0 through 9. What's more, whenever a dial turns from 1 back to 0, it causes the dial to the left to advance one place, just as happens with an ordinary counter when a dial turns from 9 back to 0.

Suppose the counter has four dials. Its initial reading is 0000, and the first count causes it to advance to 0001. The next count causes the rightmost dial to turn from 1 back to 0. This, in turn, causes the next dial to the left to advance one position. So after two counts the counter reads 0010, after three counts it reads 0011, after four counts it reads 0100 (Why?), after five counts it reads 0101, and so on.

Type *Boolean*

Since type *Boolean* has only two values, each can be represented by a single bit. Normally, *false* is represented by 0 and *true* is represented by 1.

Most computers can manipulate bytes and words more efficiently than individual bits. To take advantage of this characteristic, a bit representing a Boolean value is often embedded in a larger unit of data. For example, we might represent *false* by a byte whose rightmost bit is 0 and *true* by a byte whose rightmost bit is 1. Thus *false* and *true* would be represented by bytes as follows:

Value	Representation
false	00000000
true	00000001

Data values are said to be *packed* when as many values as possible are stored in each memory location. Packing allows Boolean values to be stored eight per byte, with each of the eight values represented by a separate bit. Thus the eight truth values

    true *false* *true* *true* *false* *false* *true* *true*

can be represented by the following byte:

    10110011

The leftmost bit represents the leftmost truth value, the next bit to the right represents the next truth value, and so on.

For manipulating Boolean values, the arithmetic/logic unit provides the logical operations AND, OR, and NOT, which correspond to the Pascal Boolean operators **and**, **or**, or **not**. The logical operator AND yields 1 only if both its operands are 1.

Expression	Value
0 AND 0	0
0 AND 1	0
1 AND 0	0
1 AND 1	1

The logical operator OR gives a result of 1 if either or both of the operands are 1.

Expression	Value
0 OR 0	0
0 OR 1	1
1 OR 0	1
1 OR 1	1

The logical operator NOT changes 0 to 1 and vice versa.

Expression	Value
NOT 0	1
NOT 1	0

The logical operators apply to all the bits of a byte or word. For example, we can use OR with two bytes as follows:

```
     10010010
OR   11000111
     11010111
```

This property of the logical operators allows them to be applied to a bit regardless of where it is situated in a byte or word. It is also convenient for manipulating packed bits when all are to be subjected to the same logical operation.

Besides implementing the Boolean operations, the logical operators are generally useful for manipulating individual bits within bytes and words. For example, suppose we wish to clear—set to 0—the leftmost four bits of the byte 11011001. We can accomplish this by ANDing the byte in question with the byte 00001111:

```
      11011001
AND   00001111
      00001001
```

The byte 00001111 is called a *mask* since it allows only selected bits (the four rightmost) to "show through" and it "hides" the rest.

The binary code representing a data value can always be interpreted as a binary number, and this interpretation often turns out to be useful. For values of ordinal types (*Boolean, char,* and *integer* but not *real*), the number obtained in this way is called the *ordinal number* of the data value. Since *false* and *true* are represented by 0 and 1, respectively, the ordinal number of *false* is zero and that of *true* is one.

The arithmetic/logic unit provides operations for determining whether one binary number is less than, equal to, or greater than another. These operations are also used for ordering other binary codes that do not represent numbers. Values of the ordinal types are arranged in numerical order according to their ordinal numbers. For the Boolean values, *false* with ordinal number zero precedes *true* with ordinal number one.

Type *char*

Characters are typically represented by seven- or eight-bit codes. The size of a byte was specifically chosen so that a one-byte memory location could conveniently store a single character code. Thus on byte-oriented machines, character codes are stored one per byte and packing is not needed. For non-byte-oriented machines, however, packing may be required. For example, if the smallest available memory location holds 32 bits, then considerable memory space will be wasted if eight-bit character codes are stored one per memory location; more likely the codes will have to be packed four per memory location.

The two most widely used coding schemes are the ASCII and EBCDIC codes mentioned earlier in this chapter. ASCII is a seven-bit code, so it can represent 2^7 or 128 alternatives. Sometimes the additional bit available in a byte is used to extend ASCII to eight bits, thus providing another 128 alternatives, for a total of 256. The additional alternatives are usually used to represent special-purpose characters such as foreign-language characters, mathematical signs, and characters to aid in producing simple drawings. EBCDIC is an eight-bit code, so it can represent 2^8 or 256 alternatives, many of which are not used.

Figure A5-1 gives the ASCII code and Figure A5-2 gives the EBCDIC code. To use these figures, find the row and column containing the character of interest. To find the binary code for the character, write down the bits at the top of the column (three for ASCII, four for EBCDIC) followed by the four bits at the left of the row. To find the ordinal number for the character, add the decimal number at the top of the column to the decimal number at the left of the row.

The ordinal number of a character is the value obtained when its code is interpreted as a binary number. This number depends, of course, on the particular coding scheme being used. In Figures A5-1 and A5-2, the decimal numbers at the left of the rows are just the decimal values of the corresponding binary codes. Because the codes at the top of the columns are to be shifted four places to the left, their decimal values must be multiplied by 16. (Shifting a binary number one place to the left multiplies it by 2; shifting it left by four places multiplies it by $2 \times 2 \times 2 \times 2$ or 2^4, which equals 16.) Thus each decimal number at the top of a column is 16 times the decimal value of the corresponding binary code.

Comparing the collating sequences in Figure 3-2 with the character-code tables in Figures A5-1 and A5-2, we see that characters are ordered according to ascending values of their ordinal numbers. This allows the arithmetic/logic unit to determine whether one character precedes or follows another by com-

Figure A5-1.

The ASCII representation for type *char*. The two- and three-letter abbreviations represent control characters; the square block represents the blank space. To use the table, first locate the row and column containing the character of interest. The binary code for the character consists of the three bits at the top of the column followed by the four bits to the left of the row. The ordinal number of the character is the sum of the decimal number at the top of the column and the decimal number to the left of the row.

		0 000	16 001	32 010	48 011	64 100	80 101	96 110	112 111
						Leftmost Three Bits			
	0 0000	NUL	DLE	□	0	@	P	`	p
	1 0001	SOH	DC1	!	1	A	Q	a	q
	2 0010	STX	DC2	"	2	B	R	b	r
	3 0011	ETX	DC3	#	3	C	S	c	s
	4 0100	EOT	DC4	$	4	D	T	d	t
	5 0101	ENQ	NAK	%	5	E	U	e	u
Rightmost	6 0110	ACK	SYN	&	6	F	V	f	v
Four	7 0111	BEL	ETB	'	7	G	W	g	w
Bits	8 1000	BS	CAN	(	8	H	X	h	x
	9 1001	HT	EM	)	9	I	Y	i	y
	10 1010	LF	SUB	*	:	J	Z	j	z
	11 1011	VT	ESC	+	;	K	[	k	{
	12 1100	FF	FS	,	<	L	\	l	¦
	13 1101	CR	GS	–	=	M	]	m	}
	14 1110	SO	RS	.	>	N	^	n	~
	15 1111	SI	US	/	?	O	_	o	DEL

paring the numerical values of their codes. Unfortunately, it means that the collating sequence is representation dependent. It is no problem for a computer to convert codes from ASCII to EBCDIC and vice versa; a more serious problem, however, is that data items sorted in lexicographical order using one code may not be in lexicographical order after conversion to the other code.

The two- and three-letter abbreviations in the ASCII table (Figure A5-1) represent control characters. We won't go through all of them since many are used for specialized technical purposes. The following three are commonly used: CR, *carriage return,* returns the typing mechanism to the left margin; LF, *line feed,* advances the paper by one line; BEL, *bell,* causes a bell or other alarm device to sound.

Most computer keyboards intended for use with ASCII have a *Ctrl* key for typing control characters. To type a control character, you hold down the Ctrl key and type the corresponding key in the 100 or 101 column of Figure A5-1. Thus, we can type the control character NUL by holding down the Ctrl key and typing @; this key combination is usually written Ctrl–@. Likewise,

Figure A5-2. The EBCDIC representation for type *char*. Only printable characters are shown; four columns that contain only control characters are omitted. The square block represents the blank space. To use the table, first locate the row and column containing the character of interest. The binary code for the character consists of the four bits at the top of the column followed by the four bits to the left of the row. The ordinal number of the character is the sum of the decimal number at the top of the column and the decimal number to the left of the row.

Rightmost Four Bits	Leftmost Four Bits											
	64 0100	80 0101	96 0110	112 0111	128 1000	144 1001	160 1010	176 1011	192 1100	208 1101	224 1110	240 1111
0 0000	□	&	–									0
1 0001				/	a	j		\	A	J		1
2 0010					b	k	s	{	B	K	S	2
3 0011					c	l	t	}	C	L	T	3
4 0100					d	m	u	[	D	M	U	4
5 0101					e	n	v	]	E	N	V	5
6 0110					f	o	w		F	O	W	6
7 0111					g	p	x		G	P	X	7
8 1000					h	q	y		H	Q	Y	8
9 1001					i	r	z		I	R	Z	9
10 1010	¢	!	^	:								
11 1011	.	$	,	#								
12 1100	<	*	%	@								
13 1101	(	)	_	'								
14 1110	+	;	>	=								
15 1111	|	¬	?	"								

SOH is Ctrl–A, STX is Ctrl–B, DC1 is Ctrl–Q, and so on. CR is Ctrl–M, LF is Ctrl–J, and BEL is Ctrl–G.

For simplicity, the EBCDIC table (Figure A5-2) shows only printing characters; four columns that contain only control characters are omitted, so the table starts with column 0100 rather than column 0000. The mainframes on which EBCDIC is used often employ means other than character codes to accomplish control functions. When control characters are used, they are usually handled by low-level system routines and hence are rarely encountered by users and applications programmers.

Type *integer*

Integers are normally stored as either 16-bit or 32-bit words. A 16-bit word can represent 2^{16} or 65536 alternatives; these are sufficient to represent integers in the range -32767 through 32767 (thus giving *maxint* the value 32767). A 32-bit word can represent 2^{32} or 4,294,967,296 alternatives; these are sufficient to represent integers in the range $-2,147,483,647$ through $2,147,483,647$ (thus giving *maxint* the value $2,147,483,647$). In each case one alternative is unused; this can be an annoyance, as we will see presently, because an arithmetical operation may yield the unused alternative.

Since the binary codes for integers represent signed numbers, ordinal numbers of integers are just the integer values themselves, considered as signed numbers. For example, the ordinal number of 25 is 25 and the ordinal number of -10 is -10. Thus the order for the integers is just ordinary numerical order for signed numbers.

Arithmetical Operations on Unsigned Numbers.   Although integers are signed numbers, we will find it simplest to begin our study of arithmetical operations with the unsigned binary numbers with which we are already familiar. In our arithmetical examples we will always use four- and eight-bit binary numbers, because the eyes tend to glaze over at the sight of 16 or 32 zeros and ones.

Let's start with addition. The addition table for binary numbers is as follows:

$$0 + 0 = 0$$
$$0 + 1 = 1$$
$$1 + 0 = 1$$
$$1 + 1 = 10_2 \text{ (That is, 0 with 1 to carry.)}$$

Notice how simple this is compared to the addition table for the decimal system that we all had to learn as schoolchildren. The simplicity of the addition table leads to a corresponding simplicity in the electrical circuits that perform the addition in a computer.

With the help of the addition table, we can easily work out a binary addition. To help you follow the examples, the decimal value of each binary number will be written in parentheses beside the binary value.

```
   1001      (9)
 + 0101      (5)
   1110     (14)
```

Note that the addition in the rightmost column produces a carry.

As in decimal notation, the addition table also provides us with the information we need to do subtractions.

```
   1001      (9)
 - 0101      (5)
   0100      (4)
```

Note that the subtraction in the second column from the left requires a borrow.

The binary system uses the following multiplication table:

$$0 \times 0 = 0$$
$$0 \times 1 = 0$$
$$1 \times 0 = 0$$
$$1 \times 1 = 1$$

This is even simpler than the addition table, since no carries are involved. We arrange our work for a binary multiplication much as we do in the decimal system.

```
    1010        (10)
×   1101        (13)
    1010
    0000
    1010
    1010
-----------
 10000010       (130)
```

Of course, we usually don't bother to write out a row of zeros when doing a multiplication. We've just written them out here to make the overall pattern of the multiplication as clear as possible.

Like multiplication, division is done much as in the decimal system, but using the binary addition and multiplication tables.

```
                          1101        (13)
(11)            1011 )10010110        (150)
                     1011
                     ----
                     1111
                     1011
                     ----
                      1001
                      0000
                      ----
                      10010
                       1011
                       ----
                        111        (7)
```

Signed Numbers.   The two most popular methods of representing signed numbers are the *sign-magnitude representation* and the *twos-complement representation*. The latter is the representation most commonly used for binary-coded integers. We will also consider the sign-magnitude representation, however, since it is often used for other kinds of numbers, such as real numbers and numbers stored in the binary-coded decimal representation.

The Sign-Magnitude Representation.   In the sign-magnitude representation, the leftmost bit of a binary code represents the sign of the value (0 for positive, 1 for negative); the remaining bits represent the magnitude (the value with the sign ignored) in ordinary binary notation.

Let's use four-bit binary codes as examples. In 0011, the leftmost 0 is the sign bit and tells us that the number is positive. The remaining three bits, 011, represent the magnitude of the number in ordinary binary notation. Since 011 represents 3, 0011 represents +3 in the sign-magnitude representation. Likewise, 1011 represents −3; the magnitude is the same, but the sign bit of 1 tells us that the number is negative. Here are all the numbers that can be represented with four bits using the sign-magnitude representation:

Sign-Magnitude Representation			
Value	Representation	Value	Representation
+0	0000	−0	1000
+1	0001	−1	1001
+2	0010	−2	1010
+3	0011	−3	1011
+4	0100	−4	1100
+5	0101	−5	1101
+6	0110	−6	1110
+7	0111	−7	1111

The sign-magnitude representation is easy for humans to understand and use. Unfortunately, it has some drawbacks for computers. Before adding two sign-magnitude numbers, the computer must examine their signs. If the two have the same sign, their magnitudes are to be added; if they have opposite signs, however, the smaller magnitude is to be subtracted from the larger. If the two numbers had the same sign, that sign will also be the sign of the result. If the two had opposite signs; the sign of the result will be the sign of the number with the larger magnitude. All this comparing of signs, deciding what operation to perform, and determining the sign of the result slows the computer down. We would prefer a method whereby the computer could perform a simple binary addition without having to take into account the signs of the numbers being added.

Another drawback to the sign-magnitude representation is that +0 and −0 are represented by different codes. In arithmetic, +0 and −0 are equal, so the computer must not make any distinction between +0 and −0. One way to accomplish this is to change −0 to +0 whenever the former occurs as the result of an arithmetical operation—which gives the computer one more thing that must be checked for on each operation. The code for −0 is the unused alternative mentioned earlier.

The Twos-Complement Representation. The following table shows the values that can be represented by four-bit binary codes using the twos-complement representation:

Twos-Complement Representation			
Value	Representation	Value	Representation
+0	0000	−1	1111
+1	0001	−2	1110
+2	0010	−3	1101
+3	0011	−4	1100
+4	0100	−5	1011
+5	0101	−6	1010
+6	0110	−7	1001
+7	0111	−8	1000

As in the sign-magnitude representation, the leftmost bit serves as a sign bit: codes with the leftmost bit equal to 0 represent positive numbers; those with the leftmost bit equal to 1 represent negative numbers. The two columns on the left, which give the representations for positive numbers, are the same for the twos-complement and the sign-magnitude representations; positive numbers are represented the same way in each representation. The two columns on the right, however, which give the representations for negative numbers, are not the same. The -0 is missing (good riddance) and an additional negative number, -8, is present. The representation column has simply been turned upside down, so that now 1000 is at the bottom (representing -8 instead of -0) and 1111 is at the top (representing -1 instead of -7).

To change the sign of a number, we subtract its twos-complement representation—considered as an unsigned number—from 2^n, when n is the number of bits in the binary codes. For four-bit codes, we change the sign of a number by subtracting it from 2^4, which equals 16 or 10000. For example, to change $+5$ to -5, we subtract the code for $+5$, 0101, from 10000.

$$
\begin{array}{rl}
10000 & \\
-\ \underline{0101} & (+5) \\
1011 & (-5)
\end{array}
$$

The result, 1011, is the code for -5, as we confirm from our table. Likewise, to change -2 to $+2$, we subtract the code for -2, 1110, from 10000.

$$
\begin{array}{rl}
10000 & \\
-\ \underline{1110} & (-2) \\
0010 & (+2)
\end{array}
$$

The result, 0010, is the code for $+2$. The operation of subtracting from 2^n is referred to as taking the *twos complement* of a number. The twos-complement system is so named because each negative number is represented by the twos complement of the code for the corresponding positive number.

The most important characteristic of the twos-complement system is that the binary codes can be added and subtracted as if they were unsigned binary numbers, without regard to the signs of the numbers they actually represent. Any carry from or borrow by the leftmost column is ignored. For example, to add $+4$ and -3, we simply add the corresponding binary codes, 0100 and 1101

$$
\begin{array}{rl}
0100 & (+4) \\
+\ \underline{1101} & (-3) \\
0001 & (+1)
\end{array}
$$

A carry from the leftmost column has been ignored. The result, 0001, is the code for $+1$, the sum of $+4$ and -3. Likewise, to subtract $+7$ from $+3$, we subtract the code for $+7$, 0111 from that for $+3$, 0011.

$$
\begin{array}{rl}
0011 & (+3) \\
-\ \underline{0111} & (+7) \\
1100 & (-4)
\end{array}
$$

A borrow by the leftmost column has been ignored. The result, 1100, is the code for -4, the result of subtracting $+7$ from $+3$.

Not only are addition and subtraction simplified in the twos-complement system, the bothersome -0 is eliminated. In its place we get -8, a negative number for which there is no corresponding positive number. Since values of type *integer* range from –*maxint* through *maxint,* the extra negative number is not a permissible value of type *integer.* Some Pascal implementations allow it anyway; others treat it as an error.

The twos-complement system offers no particular advantages for multiplication and division; in fact, many computers convert twos-complement numbers to the sign-magnitude representation before multiplying or dividing them, then convert the results back to the twos-complement representation. Addition and subtraction, however, are by far the most frequent operations performed on binary integers, so any system that speeds up addition and subtraction is worthwhile even if it makes multiplication and division slightly more complicated.

Type *real*

So far, we have seen how to represent only whole numbers. To represent fractional values, we can follow the method familiar to us from the decimal system. The integer and fractional parts of a number are separated by a "decimal point," hereafter called a *radix point,* since its use is not limited to the decimal number system.

Again we find it helpful to review the familiar decimal system before tackling the unfamiliar binary system. In the decimal system, the digits to the right of the radix point, read from left to right, represent tenths, hundredths, thousandths, and so on. For example, we can analyze 27.45 as

Tens	Ones	Tenths	Hundredths
2	7	4	5

Thus, 27.45 represents two tens, seven ones, four tenths, and five hundredths. Arithmetically, we can express this as

$$27.45 = 2 \times 10 + 7 \times 1 + 4 \times \frac{1}{10} + 5 \times \frac{1}{100}$$

We can represent the powers of ten in exponential notation by using the convention that a number with a negative exponent is one over the number with the corresponding positive exponent—in symbols, $a^{-n} = 1/a^n$. Thus we can write 1/10 as 10^{-1} and 1/100 as 10^{-2}.

$$27.45 = 2 \times 10^1 + 7 \times 10^0 + 4 \times 10^{-1} + 5 \times 10^{-2}$$

In binary notation, the digits to the right of the radix point, taken from left to right, represent halves, quarters, eighths, and so on. For example, we can analyze 10.11_2 as

Twos	Ones	Halves	Quarters
1	0	1	1

Thus, 10.11_2 represents one two, zero ones, one half, and one quarter. Arithmetically, we can express this as

$$10.11_2 = 1 \times 2 + 0 \times 1 + 1 \times \frac{1}{2} + 1 \times \frac{1}{4}$$
$$= 2 + 0 + .5 + .25$$
$$= 2.75$$

Using exponential notation for the powers of two gives us:

$$10.11_2 = 1 \times 2^1 + 0 \times 2^0 + 1 \times 2^{-1} + 1 \times 2^{-2}$$

In the decimal system, we often write numbers in scientific or floating-point notation. The significant digits of a number are always written with the radix point between the first and second digits; this part of the number is called the *significand*. The significand is multiplied by a power of ten to move the radix point to the desired position. For example, 1,250,000 is written

$$1.25 \times 10^6$$

The significand is 1.25. Since multiplying a number by 10 moves the radix point one place to the right, multiplying by 10^6—multiplying by 10 six times—moves the radix point six places to the right, giving 1,250,000. Note that the floating-point notation introduced earlier is a variant of notation used here; 1.25E6 is another way of writing 1.25×10^6.

In the same way, 0.0000352 can be written in floating-point notation as

$$3.52 \times 10^{-5}$$

The significand is 3.52. Since multiplying a number by 1/10 moves the radix-point one place to the left, multiplying by 10^{-5}—multiplying by 1/10 five times—moves the radix point five places to the left, giving 0.0000352.

The advantage of floating-point notation is that nonsignificant zeros—zeros that serve only to show the position of the radix point—do not have to be written out. This is particularly important in computing, for we usually have only a fixed number of digits with which to represent a number inside a computer. If some of those digits are wasted on nonsignificant zeros, fewer digits are available to represent the significant part of the number, and the accuracy with which the number can be represented is reduced.

Binary numbers can also be written in floating-point notation in much the same way as decimal numbers, except that powers of two rather than powers of ten are used to shift the radix point. For example, 11010000 can be written as

$$1.101_2 \times 2^7$$

and 0.0000111 can be written as

$$1.11_2 \times 2^{-5}$$

For ease of reading, the exponents (7 and -5) are written in decimal notation, although they must, of course, be coded in binary notation before being stored in the computer.

Let's look at one way of representing floating-point numbers by binary codes. A floating-point number has three parts, or *fields,* that must be coded and stored: the *sign,* the *exponent,* and the *significand.* The sign-magnitude representation is often used for floating-point numbers; floating-point arithmetic involves so much processing that any additional work occasioned by the sign-magnitude representation is negligible. Also, some frequently performed manipulations, such as rounding off to a given number of digits, are easier to perform in the sign-magnitude representation. Thus, the first field of our floating-point representation will be the sign bit, which will be 0 for a positive number and 1 for a negative number.

The second field of a floating-point number is its exponent. We must be able to represent both positive and negative exponents. Rather than using the sign-magnitude or the twos-complement representation for the exponent, it turns out to be most convenient to add a constant value, or *bias,* to the exponent, so that negative numbers are converted into positive ones. For example, suppose we choose a bias of 127; we add 127 to the value of each exponent before storing it, so an exponent of 5 is stored as 127 + 5 or 132 and an exponent of -5 is stored as $127 + (-5)$ or 122. If the actual exponent ranges from -127 through 128, the *biased exponent*—the value actually stored, will range from 0 through 255. This is the range of values that can be represented by 8-bit, unsigned binary numbers. Thus we will store biased exponents as unsigned binary numbers in an 8-bit field.

The significand is said to be *normalized* when the digit to the left of the radix point is 1. Every significand, *except the one corresponding to the number zero,* can be normalized by choosing the exponent so that the radix point falls to the right of the leftmost 1 bit. Ignoring zero for the moment, we will assume that every significand is normalized. Since the digit to the left of the radix point is 1, we don't actually have to store it; only the bits to the right of the radix point need be stored. The significand is often stored in a 23-bit field, and we will use this size field for our representation. Thus, the significand field will consist of the 23-bits to the right of the radix point in the significand.

Now let's see how

$$1.101_2 \times 2^7$$

is stored. The sign bit is 0, and the biased exponent is $7 + 127 = 134 = 10000110_2$. The bits to the right of the radix point in the significand are 101 followed by enough zeros to fill out the 23-bit significand field.

Sign	Biased Exponent	Significand
0	10000110	10100000000000000000000

Likewise,

$$-1.11_2 \times 2^{-5}$$

is represented as

Sign	Biased Exponent	Significand
1	01111010	11000000000000000000000

The biased exponent is $-5 + 127 = 122 = 1111010_2$. The entire floating-point number takes up 32 bits or four bytes, a convenient size for a byte-oriented machine.

We still have to find a way to represent zero, which cannot be normalized and so does not fit into the representation just given. The simplest method is to specify that, as a special case, a floating-point number consisting of all zeros represents zero. Thus

Sign	Biased Exponent	Significand
0	00000000	00000000000000000000000

represents 0 instead of 2^{-127}, which it would represent if we had not made it a special case.

A slightly more general approach is to treat a biased exponent of zero as a special case. When the biased exponent is zero, then (1) the bit to the left of the radix point is assumed to be 0, and (2) the exponent is assumed to be -126. Put another way, when the biased exponent is zero, the significand is assumed to be an *unnormalized* binary fraction, which is to be multiplied by 2^{-126}. For example,

Sign	Biased Exponent	Significand
0	00000000	00000110000000000000000

represents

$$0.0000011_2 \times 2^{-126}$$

which equals

$$1.1_2 \times 2^{-132}$$

a value that could not be represented in our system without the provision for unnormalized significands. With this method, too, zero is represented by

Sign	Biased Exponent	Significand
0	00000000	00000000000000000000000

since

$$0.0 \times 2^{-126} \text{ equals } 0.0$$

Note that unnormalized significands provide fewer significant digits than normalized ones because some of the bits are taken up by nonsignificant leading zeros. However, significance is lost gradually as the unnormalized values get smaller rather than being lost completely when a value becomes less than the smallest value that can be represented in normalized form.

Figure A5-3 illustrates four-byte and eight-byte floating-point numbers. The four-byte numbers use the representation just discussed; 1 bit is used for the sign, 8 for the exponent, and 23 for the significand. Digits can be stored with the equivalent of seven significant decimal digits, although the least significant digit is often erroneous due to roundoff error. Thus many systems that use this representation consider the accuracy to be six significant digits. The largest value that can be represented is approximately 1.0E38, and the smallest nonzero positive value that can be represented without loss of significance (that is, in normalized form) is approximately 1.0E−38.

The eight-byte numbers use 1 bit for the sign, 11 bits for the biased exponent (bias is 1023), and 52 bits for the significand. Accuracy is the equivalent of sixteen significant decimal digits; roundoff error in the least significant

Typical representations for four- and eight-byte floating-point numbers. A four-byte number has a sign bit, an 8-bit biased exponent (bias = 127), and a 23-bit significand. An eight-byte number has a sign bit, an 11-bit biased exponent (bias = 1023), and a 52-bit significand. Each normalized value has an additional hidden significand bit that is always 1 and so does not have to be stored. Thus the four-byte representation gives a precision of 24 bits or about 7 decimal digits (each decimal digit of precision requires about 3.3 bits). The eight-byte representation gives a precision of 53 bits or about 16 decimal digits.

Sign	Exponent 8 bits	Significand 23 bits plus one hidden bit	Four Bytes (32 bits)

Sign	Exponent 11 bits	Significand 52 bits plus one hidden bit	Eight Bytes (64 bits)

digit is not so much a concern because so many significant digits are available. The largest value that can be represented is approximately 1.0E308; the smallest value that can be represented without loss of significance is approximately 1.0E−308.

For Further Reading

Chapter 1

History

Augarten, Stan. *Bit by Bit: An Illustrated History of Computers*. New York: Ticknor & Fields, 1984.

Freiberger, Paul, and Michael Swaine. *Fire in the Valley: The Making of the Personal Computer*. Berkeley, Calif.: Osborne/McGraw-Hill, 1984.

Goldstine, Herman H. *The Computer from Pascal to von Neumann*. Princeton, N.J.: Princeton University Press, 1972.

Hodges, Andrew. *Alan Turing: The Enigma*. New York: Simon and Schuster, 1983.

Augarten provides good overall coverage of the history of computing and many photographs of early computing equipment. Freiberger and Swaine describe the rise of personal computing in California's Silicon Valley. Goldstine focuses on the construction of the early electronic computers in the 1940s. Hodges's biography of British mathematician and computer pioneer Alan Turing describes some of the early work on computing in Great Britian.

Computers and Computing

Curran, Susan, and Ray Curnow. *Overcoming Computer Illiteracy*. Hammondsworth, Middlesex, England: Penguin Books. 1983.

Deitel, Harvey M., and Barbara Deitel. *Computers and Data Processing*. Orlando, Fla.: Academic Press, 1985.

Ditlea, Steve, ed. *Digital Deli*. New York: Workman Publishing, 1984.

Dologite, D. G. *Using Small Business Computers*. Englewood Cliffs, N.J.: Prentice-Hall, 1984.

Graham, Neill. *The Mind Tool*, 4th ed. St. Paul. Minn.: West Publishing Co., 1986.

Walter, Russ. *The Secret Guide to Computers*. Boston: Birkhäuser Boston, 1984.

These books provide general coverage of computers and their applications.

Computer Periodicals

BYTE: The Small Systems Journal, McGraw-Hill.

InfoWorld, CW Communications.

Macworld, PCW Communications.

PC Magazine, Ziff-Davis Publishing Co.

Keeping up with the rapidly changing computer field requires reading the computer periodicals; four of the most well known are listed here. BYTE often addresses technical issues in greater depth than many other computer magazines. The newspaper InfoWorld *focuses on events of interest to corporate computer uses and managers.* PC Magazine *covers IBM Personal Computers and compatibles;* Macworld *is devoted to the Apple Macintosh line.*

Chapters 2–7

Pascal Standards

IEEE Pascal Standards Committee and ANSI/X3J9 of American National Standards Committee X3. *An American National Standard / IEEE Standard Pascal Computer Programming Language.* New York: Institute of Electrical and Electronics Engineers, 1983.

Jensen, Kathleen, and Niklaus Wirth. *Pascal User Manual and Report.* Berlin: Springer-Verlag, 1974.

Zenrowski, Kenneth M. "Differences betwen ANS and ISO Standards for Pascal." *Sigplan Notices* (August 1984): 119–126.

The report by Jensen and Wirth provided the first standard for Pascal; older Pascal implementations generally follow the Jensen and Wirth standard. The IEEE document defines the ANSI/IEEE standard followed in this book; Zenrowski describes the differences between the American ANSI/IEEE standard and the international ISO standard.

Pascal Texts

Cooper, Doug, and Michael Clancy. *Oh! Pascal!*, 2nd ed. New York: W. W. Norton, 1985.

Koffman, Elliot B. *Problem Solving and Structured Programming in Pascal*, 2nd ed. Reading, Mass.: Addison-Wesley Publishing Co., 1985.

Schneider, G.M., and S.C. Bruell. *Advanced Programming and Problem Solving with Pascal.* New York: John Wiley & Sons, 1981.

Because of the popularity of Pascal, textbooks on the language abound, and most libraries and bookstores will yield a representative selection. The textbooks listed here emphasaize good problem solving and program development practices.

Problem Solving

Polya, G. *How to Solve It.* Princeton, N.J.: Princeton University Press, 1945.

Wickelgren, Wayne A. *How to Solve Problems.* San Francisco: W.H. Freeman, 1974.

The general principles of problem solving that were discussed in Chapter 2 were first enunciated by Polya, whose classic book, How to Solve It, *should be read by every computer science student. Wickelgren also provides excellent coverage of this subject.*

Learning to Program

Meyer, Richard E. "The Psychology of How Novices Learn Computer Programming." *Computing Surveys* (March 1981): 121–141.

———, et al. "Learning to Program and Learning to Think: What's the Connection?" *Communications of the ACM* (July 1986): 605–610.

Soloway, Elliot. "Learning to Program = Learning to Construct Mechanisms and Explanations." *Communications of the ACM* (September 1986): 850–858.

Spohrer, James C., and Elliot Soloway. "Novice Mistakes: Are the Folk Wisdoms Correct?" *Communications of the ACM* (July 1986): 624–632.

These papers investigate the skills needed for proficiency in programming. Although the papers are primarily directed at teachers, students may also find them helpful.

Structured Programming

Dijkstra, Edsger W. "Notes on Structured Programming." In O.-J. Dahl, et al. *Structured Programming*. New York: Academic Press, 1972.

Wirth, Niklaus. "Program Development by Stepwise Refinement." *Communications of the ACM* (April 1971): 221–227.

———. "On the Composition of Well-Structured Programs." *Computing Surveys* (December 1974): 247–259.

Yourdon, Edward J. *Techniques of Program Structure and Design*. Englewood Cliffs, N.J.: Prentice-Hall, 1975.

The papers by Dijkstra and Wirth established structured programming as a discipline emphasizing the use of well understood control structures, stepwise refinement, and top-down design. Yourdon's book describes the application of these techniques to practical programming problems.

Testing and Debugging

Adrion, W. Richards, et al. "Validation, Verification, and Testing of Computer Software." *Computing Surveys* (June 1982): 159–192.

Dunn, Robert. *Software Defect Removal*. New York: McGraw-Hill, 1984.

Howden, William E. "Validation of Scientific Programs." *Computing Surveys* (June 1982): 193–227.

Huang, J. C. "An Approach to Program Testing." *Computing Surveys* (September 1975): 113–128.

These works address the difficult problem of finding and correcting program errors.

Software Engineering

Brooks, Jr., Fredrick P. *The Mythical Man-Month*. Reading, Mass.: Addison-Wesley Publishing Co., 1975.

Brown, P. J. "Programming and Documenting Software Projects." *Computing Surveys* (December 1974): 213–220.

Charette, Robert N. *Software Engineering Environments*. New York: Intertext Publications (McGraw-Hill), 1986.

Vick, C. R., and C. V. Ramamoorthy. *Handbook of Software Engineering*. New York: Van Nostrand Reinhold Co., 1984.

Yohe, J. M. "An Overview of Programming Practices." *Computing Surveys* (December 1974): 221–245.

Zelkowitz, Marvin V. "Perspectives on Software Engineering." *Computing Surveys* (June 1978): 197–216.

These works are concerned with the engineering and management techniques needed to produce reliable software at predictable cost and with predictable development time. Brooks's work is a classic treatment of the ways in which software projects can go wrong.

Chapters 8–9

Theory of Data Types

Cardelli, Luca, and Peter Wegner. "On Understanding Types, Data Asbtraction, and Polymorphism." *Computing Surveys* (December 1985): 471–522.

Although this survey may prove to be too technical for the average student, those with a strong interest in the principles of computer science and with some background in discrete mathematics will find it interesting and challenging.

Data Abstraction and Information Hiding

Guttag, John V., et al. "Abstract Data Types and Software Verification." *Communications of the ACM* (December 1978): 1048–1064.

Parnas, D. L. "A Technique for Software Module Specification with Examples." *Communications of the ACM* (May 1972): 330–336.

———. "On the Criteria to Be Used in Decomposing Systems into Modules." *Communications of the ACM* (December 1972): 1053–1058.

The classic papers by Parnas were the first to advocate specifying the behavior of a module completely in terms of the external effects of the module's operations. The paper of Guttag, et al, is a good introduction to the modern concept of an abstract data type and to the use of algebraic axioms (as opposed to the pseudocode used in this book) for specifying the operations.

Chapter 10

File-Update Problem

Dijkstra, Edsger W. *A Discipline of Programming.* Englewood Cliffs, N.J.: Prentice-Hall, 1976, Chapter 15.

Dwyer, B. "One More Time—How to Update a Master File." *Communications of the ACM* (January 1981): 3–8.

Levy, Michael R. "Modularity and the Sequential File Update Problem." *Communications of the ACM* (June 1982): 362–367.

Updating a master file from a transaction file is a traditional problem in data processing. However, many of the early programs used by the data processing community were insufficiently general or even erroneous. For example, the program might not handle properly the case of a master record that is created, updated, and then deleted, all during the same program run. The general treatment of file updating in Dijkstra's book was later elaborated by Dwyer and Levy. Our discussion in Chapter 10 follows Levy's approach.

Chapter 11

String Extensions

Turbo Pascal Reference Manual. Scotts Valley, Calif.: Borland International, 1985.

UCSD Pascal User Manual. Brooklyn, New York: Pecan Software Systems, 1985.

Many Pascal implementations provide variable-length strings as an extension to the Pascal standard. Two of the most popular such implementations are Turbo Pascal and UCSD Pascal. Details of their (similar) implementations of variable-length strings can be found in the corresponding reference manuals.

Chapter 12 Pascal Contrasted with Other Programming Languages

Cailliau, R. "How to Avoid Getting Schlonked by Pascal." *Sigplan Notices* (December 1982): 31–40.

Clarke, L. A., et al. "Nesting in Ada Programs Is for the Birds." *Sigplan Notices* (November 1980): 139–145.

Tucker, Jr., Allen B. *Programming Languages*, 2nd ed. New York: McGraw-Hill, 1986.

Nested scopes and recursion are major characteristics that relate Pascal to some programming languages and distinguish it from others. Tucker's survey of popular programming languages will help the reader contrast Pascal with other languages. Cailliau's critique of Pascal contains interesting material on the history of the language and the pros and cons of various language features. Clarke, writing about the Ada language, was one of the first to enunciate the advantages of avoiding deeply nested subprogram declarations.

Recursion

Hofstadter, Douglas R. *Gödel, Escher, Bach*: An Eternal Golden Braid. New York: Basic Books, 1979.

Recursion is a form of self reference—a recursive subprogram is defined partially in terms of itself. Self reference in mathematics, art, music, and computer science is the theme of Hofstadter's Pulitzer prize winning book.

Chapter 13 Data Structures

Gotlieb, C. C., and Leo R. Gotlieb. *Data Types and Structures*. Englewood Cliffs, N.J.: Prentice-Hall, 1978.

Horowitz, Ellis, and Sartaj Sahni. *Fundamentals of Data Structures in Pascal*. Rockville, Md.: Computer Science Press, 1984.

Wirth, Niklaus. *Algorithms + Data Structures = Programs*. Englewood Cliffs, N.J.: Prentice-Hall, 1976.

Further discussion of pointers and their uses can be found in these and other textbooks on data structures.

LISP

Winston, Patrick Henry, and Berthold Klaus Paul Horn. *LISP*, 2nd ed. Reading, Mass.: Addison-Wesley Publishing Co., 1984.

Wilensky, Robert. *LISPCraft*. New York: W. W. Norton, 1984.

LISP (LISt Processor) is a programming language based on linked lists. The linked-list concept is sufficiently general that all data structures (and not just lists) can be represented in LISP. The two books cited here are recommended to students interested in exploring LISP.

Appendix 2   Syntax Diagrams

Aretz, F. E. J. Kruseman. "Syntax Diagrams for ISO Pascal Standard." *Sigplan Notices* (October 1982): 73–78.

Jensen, Kathleen, and Niklaus Wirth. *Pascal User Manual and Report.* Berlin: Springer-Verlag, 1974.

Syntax diagrams for Pascal first appeared in the Jensen and Wirth report. The ANSI/IEEE and ISO Pascal standards do not provide syntax diagrams. This deficiency is remedied by Artez, who provides syntax diagrams for ISO Pascal. The syntax diagrams in this book follow those of Aretz in content but those of Jensen and Wirth in style and presentation.

Appendix 3   Reference Manual

Turbo Pascal Reference Manual. Scotts Valley, Calif.: Borland International, 1985.

The edition of the reference manual should correspond to the version of Turbo Pascal that you are using.

Appendix 4   Reference Manual

UCSD Pascal User Manual. Brooklyn, New York: Pecan Software Systems, 1985.

The edition of the reference manual should correspond to the version of UCSD Pascal that you are using.

Appendix 5   Data Representation

Standards Committee of the IEEE Computer Society. "An American National Standard / IEEE Standard for Binary Floating-Point Arithmetic." *Sigplan Notices* (February 1987): 9–25.

Tanenbaum, Andrew S. *Structured Computer Organization.* Englewood Cliffs, N.J.: Prentice-Hall, 1976.

Further information on data representation and the internal workings of computers can be found in Tanenbaum's text. Details of floating-point representations can be found in the ANSI/IEEE standard for binary floating-point arithmetic.

Index